D0786867

THE
OPEN-AIR CHURCHES
OF
SIXTEENTH-CENTURY
MEXICO

By order of the Catholic Kings, the happy discovery of the first lands of the Indies was celebrated
all over Spain with festival illuminations and peal-
ing of bells in all churches, and Te Deums were
sung in thanksgiving. As soon as the King sent him
news of the discovery of the new peoples, Pope
Alexander the Sixth ordered the same to be done
in Rome.

Fray Juan José de la Cruz y Moya (1756)

John McAndrew

THE

OPEN-AIR CHURCHES

OF

SIXTEENTH-CENTURY

MEXICO

Atrios, Posas, Open Chapels,
and other studies

Cambridge, Massachusetts
HARVARD UNIVERSITY PRESS

© COPYRIGHT 1965 BY THE PRESIDENT AND
FELLOWS OF HARVARD COLLEGE
ALL RIGHTS RESERVED
SECOND PRINTING, 1969

DISTRIBUTED IN GREAT BRITAIN BY OXFORD
UNIVERSITY PRESS, LONDON

PUBLICATION OF THIS BOOK HAS BEEN AIDED
BY A GRANT FROM THE FORD FOUNDATION

LIBRARY OF CONGRESS CATALOG CARD
NUMBER 63–17205

PRINTED IN THE UNITED STATES OF AMERICA

For

MANUEL TOUSSAINT (1890-1955)
and
SALVADOR TOSCANO (1912-1949)
unforgettable friends, with whom I first saw
many of the monuments shown in this book.

This is a much treasured book in my library
which shall go to a much-treasured friend
who will use it with much more frequency —

For Marjorie Jackson —

con todo cariño

Mama (Kennet)

Marjorie left Mexico & returned
this book — noviembre 1996 DK.

PREFACE

This book is concerned with what may be the most dramatic American architectural innovation before the skyscraper: the outdoor church of the Indians of Mexico. Called into being in the sixteenth century by the urgencies of a vast campaign of religious conversion, the outdoor church can be properly understood today only as a product of that conversion, and of some of the peculiar local conditions, for, as Frank Lloyd Wright long insisted, "A building grows out of conditions as a plant grows out of the soil." In other words, this book has to begin with some history, but as I am not legitimately a writer of history, I must beg indulgence for trespassing into that field, though trespass I must since no other route leads so clearly to the field of architecture and my particular goals in it.

Some may see it as a shortcoming that so many conclusions have been drawn from incomplete evidence. Yet conclusions about the architecture — if any were to be drawn — had to depend on the random samples time has left standing, and on the equally random but more elusive references in old chronicles. Conclusions about history have been drawn also from limited evidence, but here mainly because I have not exhausted the printed documents. Unable to boast of having read every preserved text, I have, nonetheless, read enough to be reasonably sure of the main facts, or as sure as one can be in this unmowed field where so many writers, both old and new, are arrantly partisan, and slipshod with evidence. Consequently I have gone to some pains to try to make clear the differences between conjecture, the assumption of strong probability, and good hard facts. Were it not in English, much of the text would demand verbs in the subjunctive. As it is, almost all figures are to be understood as if prefixed by an invisible *circa*.

This is particularly true of dates. Until the Gregorian Calendar was adopted in 1582 (and even after that out in the country or among the very old) either of two calendars might be used. Those who followed the Old Style began their new year on the Feast of the Annunciation, March 25, and others began it on the Feast of the Circumcision, January 1. Inasmuch as writers would not record in their texts which calendar they were following, it is often not possible to tell whether an event recorded as having happened on a date such as February 15, 1561, really happened then according to our reckoning, or in 1562. Furthermore, many Spanish chroniclers were sometimes offhand with their dates and reckonings of time. Native annalists did

not always transpose accurately from their own efficient calendar into the
Julian or Gregorian. Consequently, dates in sixteenth-century affairs in
Mexico cannot unquestioningly be accepted as hard facts, but must be con-
sidered a little elastic until proved firm.

Because it does not pretend to proffer dramatically new ideas, but tries
rather to reinforce, reorganize, and elucidate what is already known to a few
scholars, and occasionally to add some hitherto unnoticed written evidence,
some hitherto unnoticed monuments, and a few new deductions from old
material, this book is offered not only to the small band of specialists in early
Mexican architecture, but hopefully also to a larger and more mixed audience: to any literate reader interested in architecture in general, or in Mexico
in general, or even to one interested in some special effects of the conversion
of millions of Indians. It does not presume to compete with George Kubler's
monumental *Mexican Architecture of the Sixteenth Century,* which has already won its place as the most authoritative work in a larger field.

Most of the quotations found all through the text are from men who were
contemporary with the buildings and happenings concerned, or who wrote
within a few generations of them, often with the aid of earlier accounts now
lost. Despite the bias and carelessness of some of these writers, I have quoted
them copiously, in the hope that their old words may evoke more vividly than
any new ones the circumstances which so strongly affected the buildings
which are the chief concern of this book. Most of the translations are my own,
and they are fairly literal, respecting the inconsistencies and occasional ob-
scurities of the originals, though not *all* of their grammatical meanderings,
caprices of punctuation, or sentences as miscellaneously packed as Noah's
Ark. Where printed translations by others were available, I have given reference to them in the notes, occasionally making minor adjustments for the
sake of consistency. The language of vintage translations, such as the 1604
version of Acosta, has been transcribed intact for the sake of the bouquet.

Also essential — not more nor less than the written sources but, simply,
essential — are the buildings which still are standing, whole or in ruin. For
an architectural historian there can be no satisfactory substitute for direct
visual experience. I have, therefore, made particular efforts to see these survivors, over many years on many trips to Mexico, and have visited almost
every one of the sites considered in the text (as well as many others, only to
find that not even ruins are left), and have examined at some length all the
extant monuments discussed in more than a few phrases. It was the first
sight of some of the handsomest, and the aesthetic satisfaction and historical
curiosity which that aroused, that made me undertake to write this book.

Its chronological limits run from 1521, the climactic year of the Conquest, to about 1600, when the Conversion was largely over, and the special
architecture it had engendered was entering another phase. Historically, eco-

nomically, and ecclesiastically, the sixteenth century in Mexico may for convenience be divided into three periods: 1521–35 for the establishing of the Spanish state, 1535–75 for the prosperous age of the best early viceroys and, after the terrible plague of 1575–76, a sort of *détente* lasting until 1600 or later.

These simplified historical divisions are not, however, coincident with the phases of architectural development. There are almost no intact monuments or big fragments from the first period (1521–35), although we know that some of the most influential ideas then took shape. There are plenty of monuments from the second period (1535–75), but there are more striking differences between those of its first ten years and those of its last thirty than between all of them and the monuments of the last quarter of the century which belong more to a lively Indian summer than to a *détente*.

As for geographical limits, in the sixteenth century Mexico was usually included in "The Indies" — geographic terms designating parts of the New World were disconcertingly elastic — and what we now call Mexico and Central America at first lay within "New Spain." Despite its statutory definition as all the mainland and islands north of the Isthmus of Panama, "New Spain" came more and more to be understood as only its major constituent, the Viceregency of Mexico. This book is limited to New Spain in this last sense, and more specifically to those parts of it which in the sixteenth century were sufficiently incorporated into its church, state, and culture to have produced architecture of at least average quality. This means, roughly, the southern half of the modern Republic of Mexico, excluding mountaintops, jungles, swamps, deserts, and other wasteland.

Guatemala, soon after being detached and given entity as a Captaincy General, was usually designated separately; the same was soon true of the rest of Central America. Adjoining both Mexico and Guatemala, Chiapas and Yucatan were variously assigned to each, civilly and ecclesiastically, and as a result were sometimes understood as in New Spain, and sometimes not. They are included here because architecturally they were dependent parts of Mexico during most of the sixteenth century. It would seem improper to exclude Yucatan, as has sometimes been done, when its most important group of buildings were its Franciscan monasteries, modeled directly on those of central Mexico. Chiapas' architecture, like its coasts and mountains, was then clearly a continuation of Mexican Oaxaca. During the seventeenth century, however, it came architecturally to depend more on Guatemala, which was for the first time developing its own curious provincial style. Chiapas is a sort of New World Alsace, and just as old Alsace has to be considered in the artistic history of both Germany and France, so does Chiapas demand inclusion with both Mexico and Guatemala.

Nueva Galicia (western Mexico, including Jalisco and the mining regions in Zacatecas and Durango) was usually understood as part of New Spain, though because of its remoteness it was early given its own Audiencia and bishop. Its most important sixteenth-century architecture was built by the Franciscans, who had an autonomous Province there, but the poor and impermanent buildings they put up count as no more than a minor episode of the architecture of New Spain.

Somewhat arbitrarily, the book is both selective and inclusive. Much more space is accorded some buildings and architectural ideas than others perhaps equally worthy but, alas, less interesting. Some monuments are therefore allotted a dozen pages while others must do with a dozen lines or words if extended discussion would add only more data but no new ideas. Texts are sometimes longer when an important building has disappeared, or is in unphotographable condition, and shorter when illustrations are clearer, more informative, and more eloquent than words. The text is inclusive in the sense that it mentions and classifies all the known surviving monuments, but also, in another sense, because it is self-indulgent in including related but peripheral matters which seemed rewarding enough in themselves to deserve discussion (such as the extraordinary successes of European music, or Saint Joseph). Here my policy was less like that of my own packing for a trip, when I ask "can I possibly do without this?" (and leave it out) than like that of my wife who asks "could I ever have any use for this?" (and puts it in).

A NOTE ON NOMENCLATURE AND TERMINOLOGY

Place names are given in their current Mexican official spelling: that used by the Post Office, Census Bureau, and the Church. This is by now almost uniform, though often quite different from the uninhibited variants improvised by sixteenth-century writers and scribes. Many of the Indian names may dismay foreigners by their seemingly outlandish sequences of syllables but, since modern Mexican spelling is intelligently and intelligibly phonetic (with the exception only of sibilants and the strangely variable letter "x"), and the accentuation invariable, pronunciation ought not to be difficult to the attentive — no more than with the names encountered in reading Dostoievsky. Those who know no Spanish may still relish pronouncing some of these mouth-filling exotics if they consult the simple guide printed with the glossary at the back of the book. Many of the older names — Spanish and Mexican — have been given modern spelling (including accents even where they are not mandatory but where they may help the pronunciation of these who know no Spanish or Náhuatl).

Perhaps because most of the work was done in Spanish-speaking lands and with Spanish texts, I have Anglicized very few words: among the proper names only Mexico, Yucatan, and Panama (by omitting the accents). Current Mexican forms have been kept for some terms for which there are half-accepted but unnecessary Anglicizations: hence *Maya, Tarasco, Zapoteca, Tlaxcalteca,* and not *Mayan, Tarascan,* and so forth. Inaccurate and illegitimate as it is, the word *Aztec* is too well established to repudiate now. It derives from Aztlán, the legendary place of the Aztecs' origin. At the time of the Conquest, however, they were usually known as the *Mexica,* a term which — like *México* — derives from Mexitli, their war god, better known to the Spaniards as Huitzilopochtli or some rough approximation such as Huichilobos. In the sixteenth century, *México* designated only the capital city, though that was more commonly called Tenochtitlán, "city in the middle of the lake of the moon." *México* today can mean the capital city, its state, or the whole country; and *Tlaxcala, Puebla,* or *Oaxaca* can mean either the state or its chief city (just as does *New York*). Although *Mexico City* has become standard in English, no equivalent title has been extended to the others, and although clear, it would be an awkward affectation to say *Tlaxcala City* or *Puebla City;* the context will, I hope, each time indicate the proper meaning.

What we now call the Valley of Mexico, the mountain-fenced plateau on which the modern city is so melodramatically set, was then called *Anáhuac,* meaning "near water," for around the settlement at its center were two large lakes, one fresh, one salt. The language of Anáhuac and the surrounding country was called *Náhua, Náhuatl,* or later, *Mexicano;* after the wide conquests of the Aztecs, it became a general *lingua franca,* understood and used for trading, religion, and governing from one end of the Aztec "Empire" to the other. It is still quite widely spoken.

The so-called "Emperor" Motecuhzoma II, Moteuhcçomatzin, Moctecuzoma, Moctheozoma, or Moteçuçoma, as the early Spaniards struggled to transcribe it, will hereafter be called simply the Emperor *Moctezuma,* in accord with current Spanish-American usage, though he was not quite an Emperor and his name was not quite Moctezuma. The "Empire" was largely a federation of city-states, some powerful, some tribute-paying, dominated by Tenochtitlán (whose rulers came from one family but not necessarily in primogenitary sequence). Although its conqueror, Cortés, signed himself *Fernando,* and was regularly called *Fernando* in contemporary documents, I have bowed to modern practice in calling him *Hernán.*

For a few terms which have no English equivalent but are the names of things which have to be discussed — such as *atrio* or *posa* — I have adopted and naturalized the Spanish words. Inasmuch as the English for some Spanish church terms might be misleading to some readers, I have kept the Spanish: *Custodia* rather than Custody, for example. It has seemed sensible also to naturalize a few useful Náhuatl terms, such as *teocalli* and *tequitqui.*

The figures given for the populations of towns have been drawn mainly from the 1580 census *relaciones,* and from Cook and Simpson's *Population of Central Mexico in the Sixteenth Century,* although its figures, which are among the highest proposed by any respectable authority, have not yet been entirely accepted by everyone (nor have they, incidentally, been disproved by anyone). For other population figures, based on the number of tribute-payers, it has been assumed that families averaged three children, one husband, one wife.

The measure of one league, given in so many old texts, has been converted roughly to three miles. In the sixteenth century it seems to have stretched and shrunk from around two and a half to three and a half, or more, an elasticity still so often preserved that when told by a native, "Señor, it is not at all far, only four long leagues or five little ones," I have improvised my own conversion table.

SOME ACKNOWLEDGMENTS

It could never be possible for a scholar who has worked in Mexico to thank everyone who had given him help for, since Mexicans are so kind to visitors and so extraordinarily polite, the list would have to include a large fraction of those he had met and stretch to a very large fraction of the length of his text. I have reluctantly had to exert gringo ruthlessness in cutting my roster.

Above all, my gratitude goes to the late Manuel Toussaint and the late Salvador Toscano, leading scholars of Mexico's colonial art, who went with me on countless instructive and enjoyable trips, who lent me books and gave me photographs, and who always welcomed talk of the art of their country, past or present. The late Rafael García Granados, Raúl Flores Guerrero, and Mauricio Campos were always most kind and helpful with information. I owe countless debts to Elizabeth Wilder Weismann for her unending generosity with the products of her camera, her learning, her perceptiveness, and her very sharp eyes. Heinrich Berlin, Charles Gibson, Isabel Kelly, George Kubler, Francisco de la Maza, Jorge Olvera, and the late George Conway and George Vaillant have at one time or another been most generous with information, often still unpublished. Elisa Vargas de Bosch has called recent discoveries to my attention, and has traveled many leagues to take photographs of obscure monuments, and Efraín Gasque has done the same to measure some of them. Edgar Kaufmann, Jr., has been helpful in countless ways, and has made possible the acquisition of many photographs and drawings.

A number of people have been kind and patient enough to read parts of the manuscript at various stages, and I am indebted for their helpful criticisms to John Phelan, Father H. A. Reinhold, Eleanor Barton, Bernard Heyl, Isabel Pope Conant, and again Manuel Toussaint and Salvador Toscano. Especially am I grateful to Ann Ferry and to my wife for smoothing roughnesses and spotting cracks, and to Alfred and Margaret Barr for particularly welcome encouragement.

PREFACE

Since many of the books about colonial Mexico are collector's treasures, for their kindness in making volumes available from their own enviable libraries, I am indebted to the late Luis Cabrera, and Federico Gómez de Orozco, and also to Philip Hofer and Eleanor Garvey for facilitating the use of the Houghton, Peabody, and Widener libraries at Harvard.

The study of Mexican colonial art cannot be done entirely in books: much of it has been for me an active hunt for buildings, since astonishingly few people know what is still standing or even where the old towns are or how they can be reached. For their company and their helpful observations on many long monument hunts — in car or jeep, on horse, burro, or foot — I wish to record deep-felt thanks to many of the preceding again, and also to Harry and María Luisa Cabrera de Block, Max and Catherine Cetto, Henry Clifford, Lorenzo Gamio, Stephen Greene, Robert and Emanuela Amor de Hill, Ricardo Martínez de Hoyos, Diego de Mesa, Harold Emery Moore, Grace McCann Morley, Maud Oakes, Josefina Ortiz Rubio, Inés Amor de Pérez Espinosa, Jorge Rubio, Aline Saarinen, Juan Soriano, and my pupils at the Instituto Nacional de Antropología e Historia.

Work was begun on a grant from the Coordinator for Latin-American Affairs, and publication has been facilitated by grants from the Trustees of Wellesley College and the Kaufmann Foundation, to whom I wish here to express my thanks and enduring gratitude.

John McAndrew

Venice 1964

CONTENTS

CONTENTS

xvi

CONTENTS

CONTENTS

CONTENTS

ILLUSTRATIONS

Special thanks for many kinds of help in connection with the illustrations are very gratefully extended

to the Dirección de Monumentos Coloniales of the Instituto Nacional de Antropología e Historia of Mexico City for many photographs (here indicated M C);

to Señora Elisa Vargas Lugo de Bosch for many more (here E V L), and to Max Cetto, Henry Clifford, Donald Cordry, and Elizabeth Wilder Weismann for several others; (unaccredited photographs are by the author);

to Doctor Justino Fernández, Director of the Instituto de Investigaciones Estéticas of the Universidad Nacional Autónoma of Mexico for permission to reproduce drawings from a number of official Mexican publications, several of them edited by him, and for illustration 228, which he drew;

to Kenneth J. Conant for his reconstruction of the *Capilla Real* at Cholula;

to the Bibliothèque Nationale in Paris for permission to reproduce parts of the *Códice Azcatítlan* and the *Codex Mexicanus 23–24;*

to the Department of Printing and Graphic Arts of Harvard University for permission to reproduce plates from several rare books in the Houghton Library, and to the Peabody Museum of Harvard for the use of their copy of Diego de Valadés' *Rhetorica Christiana* (here H C L and Peabody);

to John P. Bennett of Frederick A. Stahl Associates of Cambridge for making many of the special drawings and supervising the making of others.

ILLUSTRATIONS

ILLUSTRATIONS

ILLUSTRATIONS

Chapter IX. THE OPEN CHAPEL

Chapter X. THE FIRST OPEN CHAPELS: I

ILLUSTRATIONS

ILLUSTRATIONS

ILLUSTRATIONS

ILLUSTRATIONS

THE

OPEN-AIR CHURCHES

OF

SIXTEENTH-CENTURY

MEXICO

1 SPANIARDS APPROACHING MEXICO (Durán, *Atlas*)

I

THE SPANISH MASTERS

Strongly polarized in the self and in the universe, at the two ends of the gamut of man's interests, the Spanish character neglects the middle stretches, where grow the political, social, and municipal virtues. It follows that the Spaniard is apt to be more genuine when serving his own self and mankind in the widest sense than when applying his energy to any intermediate activity between these two extremes. — *Salvador de Madariaga* [1]

IN 1519 when Cortés and his band of adventurers had just landed on the coast of the Gulf of Mexico, in the land of the Totonacas, they were determined, according to Bernal Díaz del Castillo, the most vivid eyewitness chronicler of the Conquest, "at once to found the Villa Rica de la Vera Cruz. We laid out plans of a church, market place, and arsenals, and all the things needed for a town, and we built a fort . . . Cortés himself was the first to set to work and carry the earth and stone on his back and dig foundations, and all his captains and soldiers followed his example; we kept on laboring without pause so as to finish the work quickly, some of us digging foundations and others building walls, working in the lime-kilns, or making bricks and tiles. . . . Others worked at the timber, and the blacksmiths — for we had two blacksmiths with us — made nails." [2] Thus began town-founding and church-building in sixteenth-century Mexico, soon to become a campaign more vast and energetic than any Christian Europe had ever seen.

In the summer of 1521 the Conquest came to its dread climax in Cortés' 75-day storming and razing of Moctezuma's glittering capital. Despite the objections of almost everyone to its defendable but unhealthy and inconvenient site in the middle of a large lake, "Captain Cortés ordered that the Spaniards should remain in the capital, where he soon began to build a very beautiful and big city" (according to Francisco de Aguilar, who was there). [3] Wrecked Tenochtitlán slowly rose again in a new form and with a new name, México-Tenochtitlán, which within a generation was shortened simply to México. The architectural needs of the Spaniards must still have been much the same as at Veracruz: houses, fortifications, churches. Now it was the Indians and not the Spaniards who were digging the foundations, building the walls, and making the bricks and tiles. So many worked so hard that after only five months Cortés could write the King-Emperor Charles that the city was "already very beautiful," and after three years that "so well and so quickly does the work go . . . that many of the houses are already finished, and others are well on their way. There is such a plenty of stone, lime, wood, and bricks which the natives make that the houses are mostly large and comely, and Your Sacred Majesty may believe that within five years this will be the noblest and most populous city in the world, as well as one of the best built." [4] Very soon it was the largest city in all of Charles' vast empire.

The earliest and one of the most reliable of the religious chroniclers, Father Motolinía, described the fevered rebuilding he had witnessed in terms of one of the ten plagues of Egypt: "The seventh plague was the building of the great city of Mexico. During the first years, more people were busy in the work than in the building of the Temple of Jerusalem in the time of Solomon. So many were working on the buildings . . . that a man could hardly pick his way through the streets. . . . Many were killed by falling beams or by

2 THE MARCH ON TENOCHTITLÁN, 1519

Bearded Cortés (carrying his hat) and doña Marina (wearing a long and wide huipil), *accompanied by a Negro groom and a white horse, lead the armored Spanish soldiers and bare-skinned Indian bearers. Over all floats Cortés' banner emblazoned with the Dove of the Holy Trinity.* (Códice Azcatítlan, c1572)

falling from a height; others lost their life under buildings they were taking down in one place to put up in another, especially when they dismantled the chief temples of the Devil. Many Indians died in this work, and many years passed before these temples were completely destroyed. . . .

"It is the custom of this land — not the best in the world — that the Indians do the work and search for the materials at their own expense, and pay the stonecutters and the carpenters. If they do not bring their own food, they must go without. They carry everything on their backs; they drag the beams and heavy stones along the ground with ropes; and since their numbers had to make up for their lack of ingenuity, the stone or beam that called for a hundred men was moved by four hundred.

"As they are accustomed to go about singing and shouting, their songs and shouts scarcely ceased either by night or day because of the great zeal they showed in the building of the city during the first days."[5]

To understand the peculiar forms of much of the architecture of sixteenth-century New Spain, particularly that with which this book is concerned, one must examine some of the peculiarities of the society which called the buildings into being.

3 AN EPISODE IN THE SIEGE OF TENOCHTITLÁN
Pedro de Alvarado (in steel armor) fights a native knight, near six Spaniards in the water, beside one of the brigantines Cortés had had made in Tlaxcala, and assembled, blessed, and launched in Texcoco for the final amphibious assaults.
(Códice Azcatítlan, c1572)

3

SPANISH MASTERS

THE GOVERNMENT

Cortés had to take charge of governing from the first. He envisioned Mexico not as a colony, but as a land to be politically incorporated with Spain itself, and that was why he chose to call it "New Spain of the Ocean Sea." Hoping to administer the country as though he had made a peaceful palace revolution rather than a bloody conquest, he called the surviving native lords to his house in Coyoacán, and explained how the traditional tributes formerly paid to the divinely sanctioned Emperor Moctezuma were now to go to the divinely sanctioned Emperor Charles. If the tributes could be smoothly transferred, then much of the local civil administration could continue smoothly in the old way. New Spanish masters would take the place of the old Indian masters, and Spanish clergy would take the place of the Indian priests. The old political base could support the new political superstructure much as the bases of the pyramids of the old religion would support the superposed structures of the new.

Cortés became the official head of the improvised government when the King named him Governor and Captain General, 14 months after the fall of Tenochtitlán; but soon afterward, while he was away on his catastrophic campaign in Honduras, his enemies and their plots and slanders succeeded in deposing him. Hoping to exonerate himself and exact the recognition and recompense due him, he sailed for Spain, taking along an eye-opening assortment of native novelties to amaze the King: gold-, jewel-, and fancy feather-work; strange birds and beasts; albinos and dwarfs; a team of players with rubber balls (a much admired surprise); four acrobats dressed as birds who dove off a high pole and spiraled around it on unwinding ropes (a *volador*); a group of dancers who introduced the pavane to Europe; and a retinue of forty young Indian nobles in splendid native attire. Charles V, who was known to be particularly charmed by animals, birds, and jesters, was so delighted that he sent the best of the troupe on to the Pope, rich and artistically fastidious Clement VII de' Medici. To the noble boys he gave Spanish capes and doublets of velvet, and fine hose, hats, and shirts. The Emperor's delight did not benefit Cortés, however, for instead of being named Viceroy, as he had hoped, he was made only a Knight of Santiago and a marquess, though with vast lands and revenues.

4 A *VOLADOR* OR FLYING GAME

(*after* Códice Azcatítlan)

4

To replace the corrupt interim administration which, having announced that Cortés had died in Honduras, had held a fraudulent funeral for him and then helped itself to his properties, the Crown despatched an Audiencia of four to the troubled new land. It soon became the cruelest government in all the tortured history of Mexico, perhaps the cruelest in the history of the Americas, unless that superlative was better earned by the bloody Pizarros of Peru. It robbed the Indians; it murdered them; it worked them literally to death; it sold over 15,000 as slaves to Santo Domingo, so many that the once-flourishing Huaxteca region became virtually deserted. One hundred Indians were traded for one horse; one boy for one cheese. The Audiencia forced up the traditional tributes which Cortés had maintained: at Chimalhuacán Chalco, for example, from 1500 bushels of corn to 5000. Courageous Bishop Zumárraga excommunicated the governors, put the capital under the interdict, and withdrew to the country with all the clergy. Meanwhile the ordinary Indians, denied any status above day-laborer and abused even on that level, began to desert the cities and towns for the hills. They were frightened of all Spaniards, especially the officials. About half a million died or were done to death between 1524 and '27.

The Second Audiencia sent over in the winter of 1530–31 was a welcome change. Its organization had been modeled on the Audiencias which had been evolved as instruments of discipline on lands won from infidel Moslems, because of which they seemed suitable models for lands won from infidel Indians. Since Cortés' policy of conciliating and assimilating the native ruling classes seemed to work, it was resumed. But after what had already happened to them, the ordinary Indians could not imagine that they would be allowed any status in the new society other than victims.

*

At the apex of the new intercontinental regime was the King-Emperor, supported by his Council of the Indies, the chief legislative body for the New World. Spain in the second quarter of the sixteenth century was at the peak of her power, and her ruler, Charles I, had been crowned Charles V of the Holy Roman Empire two months after the fall of the Aztec Empire to his men. Soon the military and spiritual conquests of Mexico and Central America were marching ahead in a crescendo of successes, the conquest of Peru was advancing, and Charles' banners were flying in triumph over an empire larger than Alexander's, Caesar's, or Charlemagne's. At the end of his life, the conditions in some parts of this empire troubled his conscience. Preparing for death in the monastery at Yuste, broken in bodily health but inspirited by religious exaltation, he asked himself whether he ought not to go to America to try "to undo and rectify the hurts and harms his Spanish vassals had done," [6] and to assume unto himself the protection and salvation of the natives.

5

SPANISH MASTERS

The tributes paid him from the New World had been indispensable for his major activities. The chief source of his income, he found them nonetheless inadequate, and kept trying to increase them. More than half came from the "royal fifth" of all the gold and silver mined. Next came the taxes from the agricultural estates, from foodstuffs, silk, cotton, indigo, and soon also from cattle and cochineal. The total royal take doubled after the first decade and again after the second. Still, it was not enough.

By 1535, when the Second Audiencia had handed its highest authority over to the first Viceroy, don Antonio de Mendoza, the new Kingdom of New Spain was more stable than ever during the preceding 14 years of shifting rule. A friend to the Indians and to the Church, Mendoza found his worst problems in settling the settlers and organizing a workable government for the strangely compounded society. When his reign ended (1550), New Spain was a durably organized state.

Beginning in the middle of the century, with the reign of the second Viceroy, don Luis de Velasco (1550–64), the running of the now still bigger country was still better organized. Under Philip II, who had taken charge of the Indies for his father in 1546, there were many more regulations and many more agents to carry them out. Less humane, less intelligent, less imaginative than his father, a fanatic for orthodoxy, disliking and distrusting almost everything not Spanish (except the painting of Titian and Bosch), Philip managed to preserve the Catholic unity of his lands, but at the cost of depressing their intellectual level below that of the rest of western Europe. His reign was one long Lent.

He had inherited little money and many debts, and the income from the New World was inadequate for his projects in the Old. This income, however, continued to increase. Almost everyone in New Spain had to send him money in one way or another. The Spanish settlers, ever more numerous, were taxed directly, and they also had to pay the Crown part of whatever tribute they collected from the Indians. Since virtually all of the money was produced by native labor of some kind, the labor of men being brought into the Catholic fold in one hemisphere was contributing importantly to the campaign to keep men from leaving it in the other. Bonanzas at Zacatecas and Guanajuato sextupled Mexican metal production in the third quarter of the century, and the output was tripled again in the fourth, despite terrible depopulation by the plague of 1576. Just how vast the total revenue was in modern terms it is impossible to figure, but it was enough to dislocate much of the major economy of western Europe. Still, Philip felt he had to institute a sales tax and to sell offices (a procedure again increased to help finance his Invincible Armada, built in part of timbers from New Spain). No matter how much money the Americas sent, Philip led Spain to bankruptcy every twenty years: in 1557, 1575, and 1596.

CIVILIANS

Meanwhile, in Mexico, affairs were not going well. The third Viceroy, don Gastón de Peralta, Marqués de Falces, who arrived after an interregnum of a year and a half, accomplished so little in his reign of another year and a half (1566–67) that he was suspended for incompetence. Chaos and corruption again seemed immanent until, after yet another year and a half, the fourth Viceroy arrived. Don Martín Enríquez (1568–80), was an able statesman and administrator, almost of the caliber of Mendoza and Velasco. After his, a series of short and relatively uneventful terms ran until the end of the century.

*

The most difficult chapters in the conversion and pacification which had followed the Conquest were over by the 1570's, but new problems kept appearing. Efforts to organize and justify colonialism and exploitation finally produced a humanitarian legal code, but the repeated complaints, readjustments, and corrections which swell the files of later sixteenth-century documents show that stability was not to be won by edicts, no matter how many, and that the regime, though it was able to find a momentary *modus operandi,* was not able to find a lasting solution to its chief problem: the relation of the Indians to Spanish rule, Spanish economy, and Spanish religion. The wants of the administration, of the civilians, and of the Church were on too many counts too antagonistic to the wants of the inarticulate but impressively numerous Indians who were, moreover, economically so valuable. Not until the seventeenth century, when the character of the administration, the civilians, the Church, and the Indians had changed, could there be a really peaceful regime.

THE SPANISH CIVILIANS

> *On account of the black and inordinate greed for gold in this land, how many, oh! how many are burning in Hell!*
> — *Father Motolinía* (c1540) [7]

Recognizing that economic attractions would have to be proffered to the conquistadores to make them settle down as permanent residents, Cortés gave them not only land, but also the right to collect tribute from the Indians on the land, much as the Crown had already done in the Antilles. Such grants were called *encomiendas* (from *encomendar,* "to entrust"). At first each *encomendero* was to have no more than three hundred Indians subject to him, but this was soon raised to five hundred or more. Whereas the first encomiendas had been granted to conquistadores in payment for having bought the land with their sweat and blood, later they were granted to Spanish settlers just because they were Spanish and had promised to be settlers. Toward the

7

end of the century the place of the encomienda was taken by the *reparti-miento,* a milder but essentially similar system of labor-drafting.

Appropriation of lands by the Crown and grants of land to Spaniards — the encomienda was a grant of tribute, not of land — did not disrupt the daily life of the natives as much as might be supposed. Since the tribute system was largely a continuation of that imposed by the Aztecs, to the ordinary Indian the encomendero was just another tax collector, new but not very different unless more rapacious and harder to understand.

A supplementary reason for granting encomiendas was that it would deploy authorized, effective, and loyal Spaniards about the country where they might not only bring in new revenue, but in addition keep the revenue-producing Indians under control, for New Spain had no standing army nor any equivalent organized protection. The encomenderos were under obligation to bear firearms for the King and to keep horses, and as the Indians for a long time were allowed neither and were terrified of both, the encomenderos came to constitute a sort of mounted police. Even the Franciscans — usually their sternest critics — acknowledged their usefulness in keeping the land secure, secure for its new owners from its old owners.

*

To gentlemen brought up in the tradition that all manual work was for Moorish underlings, or to ambitious men of inferior station envious of the inheritors of that superior tradition, the sight of so many Indians who could be made underlings had an effect like catnip. Conquistadores, encomenderos, and other settlers who in Spain had been artisans or tradesmen came in New Spain to regard any manual labor, even farming, with a revulsion approaching neurosis. They became rabid fortune-hunters who won less by sharp swords than by sharp deals.

Since their legal tenure was repeatedly being altered or threatened, the encomenderos often felt insecure, and hence anxious to get as much as they could out of their grants while the getting was good and still recognized as legal. As time went by, the privileges extended to the conquistadores by the Crown were gradually curtailed, suspended, or withdrawn, and the encomenderos, too, lost more and more of their independence. Their fate was that of any group which seemed to the distrustful Spanish Crown to have power of its own. Despite the troubles and doubts it raised on both sides of the ocean, however, the encomienda and the repartimiento were the foundation of the Mexican economy throughout the sixteenth century.

*

Each settler in New Spain had to be screened for purity of blood and faith. All descendants of Moslems and Jews were barred, as they had been from the Antilles, and all gypsies, Negroes (except slaves), reformed heretics, and children and grandchildren of heretics. When the first Bishop, Juan de

Zumárraga, asked for some married Moriscos (Christianized Moors) to instruct the natives in the professional secrets of silk raising, a profitable occupation which might relieve the natives' economic plight, he was refused. From the middle of the century on, Philip took endless pains that none but irreproachably orthodox and thoroughbred Spaniards should be admitted, and had the licensing system tightened to keep out all but demonstrably pure Castillians. Nevertheless, quite a few "undesirables" managed to come in.

Though diverse and often highly individual, the settlers did have some important traits in common. Most were from provincial towns rather than from the larger and more progressive cities, and this is probably the chief reason that they clung so long to mediaeval notions. Though not without conspicuous courage and loyalty which could sometimes reach grandeur, the conquistadores and first settlers had been a hard-bitten and unruly lot. Since they had won a rich new land by their own hard work and often at the risk of their necks, they felt that they should be given its fruits to enjoy. Except for Cortés, most of them were not what one would call "thinking" men, yet their particular character affected the whole crucial relation between Europeans and natives, and consequently qualified the future.

The next generations of colonists were a little less aggressive. From the permits to emigrate we learn that one in ten was married, one was a cleric or government official, and one a tradesman. The level of their culture and education cannot have been high, and any knowledge of the arts or even any interest in them must have been rare outside the clergy. Only one settler in fifty had a university degree, and most of those were churchmen. The great nobles of Spain had not participated, but had watched the winning of the New World with caution, yet one settler in ten claimed noble blood. There are so many references to nobility in the contemporary listings of settlers, that many of lower birth must have been trying to pass themselves off as noble. (In Spain, in the middle of the sixteenth century, only one out of eighty taxpayers was an hidalgo.) We are told, for example, that there were no less than fifty nobles among those who founded Valladolid (now Morelia) in Michoacán, when it was no more than a flimsy village of adobe huts (1540–41). The Franciscan chronicler Mendieta found that "once across the sea, the pettiest Spaniard thinks himself the greatest gentleman and . . . there is not a man among them, no matter how lowly, who will touch a hoe or plow." [8]

One of the strongest compulsions of the colonists was to gratify their egos, and the best way was realized by displays of valor, of "honor," and of material gains. The glorification of the warrior during the centuries of struggle against the Moors, and the much-read adventure tales such as *Amadís of Gaul* seem to have made the Spaniard vaunt bravery and "honor" more than anyone in Europe. Fighting, jousting, and elaborate chivalric codes of manners, as well as genealogical pretensions, fed that hunger, and the maximum exploitation of native labor could produce the conspicuous waste that fed the accompanying hunger for the display of wealth. While the capital city was still barely habitable, in 1526, the conquistadores' longing for elegance — or that of their wives — led to the opening of a dancing academy.

Although glory best was won by bold deeds, handsome accouterments could serve as a substitute. "Since everyone becomes swollen with the desire to spend and possess, by the end of a year and a half he who is a miner, a farmer, or a swineherd no longer wishes to be . . . and he tries to spend everything he has on ornaments and silks, and the same holds for his wife. . . . The wives of mechanics and public women wear more silks than does the wife of a gentleman in Castile" (1525).[9] In the capital, over forty looms were making silk velvet in 1543, and more were making satin and taffeta. In Spain, the Spaniards had liked to dress so showily that even the Ambassador from ostentatious Venice was amazed: New Spain was as showy if not showier. The competitive exhibitionism of the *nouveaux riches* soared so dizzily that the King several times issued sumptuary decrees against the wearing of silks and cloth of gold, and ordered the local gold- and silversmiths to stop making and selling jewelry. There was also such extravagant gaming that both Cortés and Viceroy Mendoza tried to prohibit card-playing. One settler had become so rich by the 1570's that he not only underwrote the newly arrived Jesuits' church and college, but also sent silver from his mines in Pachuca and Ixmiquilpan to Rome to help pay for Michelangelo's Saint Peter's.[10]

One gratifying way of making a show was building. Except for Cortés, who kept trying to have more and more churches built, few of the new capitalists in the new boom-capital cared about building anything but houses for themselves, big houses which they could call palaces, with pretentious escutcheons over the portals and proud towers at the corners. Many of these were so quickly put up that they quickly fell down; most were of easily worked materials such as wood or adobe; and all have of course now disappeared. Cortés' palace was the largest and grandest; he had the siege-battered walls of one of Moctezuma's vast palaces remodeled and hispanized, with four battlemented towers at the corners. The symbolic message of such an architectural occupation could hardly be missed. Even when they left the city and began to live in the country as lords of the surrounding lands and the Indians on them, the Spaniards never, as might have been expected, built castles in New Spain.

*

The encomenderos did not often build churches in the country. Each encomendero was charged with various duties to his Indians; above all he was to see that they were converted; and unless there were friars nearby he was supposed to have a church built and a priest put in it. He was also to keep the natives from lapsing into their old habits of idolatry, "vices," "laziness," and any other non-European kinds of behavior distasteful to the European masters. But, since many encomenderos were absentee masters, less interested in their laborers than in the fruits of their labor, the Indians' morals and religious life did not bother them much, no more than whether their Indians had proper churches.

Although racked by fear and greed, the encomenderos and other palace-building Spaniards were the backbone of the Spanish colony, and one of the three groups which determined the tenor of the regime. The other two were the local government and the Church. Below these three strong groups was a weak and ineffective middle class: a few artisans and farmers sent from Spain, together with some prosperous *criollos* (born in New Spain of Spanish stock), and a few prosperous *mestizos* (born of mixed Spanish and Indian stock), though most mestizos were as poor as most Indians, and in the same class. Although the middle class grew throughout the century, particularly in the larger cities, it was always small. At the bottom, below the three ruling groups and below the middle class, was the largest and weakest group: the nine or ten million subject Indians, the poor downtrodden majority.

INDIANS SUBJECT TO CIVILIAN MASTERS

The Christianized Indians were not all affected by the Spanish colonists and their government to the same degree. A few Indian nobles entered almost fully into the new ways of the Spaniards, either by intermarriage — the conquistadores liked to marry heiresses—or by interpolation to some upper level of Spanish colonial society. A somewhat larger group in the cities became semi-hispanized at a lower social and cultural level by working for the Spaniards, and voluntarily or unwittingly assimilating some foreign customs while rejecting or slowly disremembering some of their old ways and their old speech. The third, largest, and lowest group, the Indian laborers in the encomiendas and monastery towns, was tempted to far less acculturation, and kept itself far more Indian. Such Indians were scorned by the superior Spaniards as inferior to any Spaniard, or even to any Moslem or Jew.

Only in the sierras or beyond the ever-retreating frontier did any Indians remain as Indian as their forefathers. Unassimilated and unconverted, the uncivilized tribes of the northern half of the country — many of them Otomí nomads — were commonly lumped together under the name of *Chichimecas*. Highly skilled as bowmen, they were skilled at little else. Although intermittently they had an effect on the security and economy of New Spain, except as it drove them bit by bit back to poorer and poorer land, for a long time New Spain had little effect on them.

The converted Indians kept on working much as they had worked before — the work changed more in quantity than in kind — but now it was to enrich Spanish instead of Indian masters. Inasmuch as the principal sources of gold — placer mining and loot from tomb and temple — began to give out in the 1540's, the Spaniards had to exploit something else for profit, and during the interim before the 1560's when the big silver bonanzas came in, they increasingly worked a rich source right at hand: the labor of the Indians of the bottom group. Slow to realize that it was to their economic interest to keep this group large, they always knew that it was to their advantage to keep it inarticulate, unorganized, and impotent. The natives' harmless old agrarian way of life could continue with little change, save through the introduction of the plow and of cattle, and the need to meet steeply increased quotas. Meanwhile, their urban and ceremonial lives were being drastically transformed.

The ethical and economic problems entailed by a respectable yet effective exploitation of the Indians were unending. Not only the prosperity but the whole economic existence of the country depended on their labor, yet the Spaniards' "right" to them was predicated on making them Christians: hence the local government was faced with the dilemma of how to save their souls while making money from their bodies. The civilians concentrated on their bodies, and left their souls to the Church. The government usually stood uncertainly somewhere between.

Having been charged "to extend the knowledge, cult, and splendor of religion," Viceroy Mendoza foresaw the clash inevitable between the two aims of the Spanish regime: more cash *and* more converts. This conflict may have been aggravated by another: the "cultural shock" of the clash between Indian and European ways of life, a shock which may have driven deeper the trauma already there from the shame of defeat in the Conquest. The conquerors imposed not only their religion, but also many "masculine" cultural elements, including monumental architecture — 90 percent of the immigrants were men — and the conquered Indians could keep little more than their "feminine" or domestic cultural habits.

The regulations sent from Spain were not uniformly helpful: some, inspired by laymen, were practical but not ethical, while others, inspired by churchmen, were ethical but not practical. A decent minimum standard of living and working conditions was assured — or supposed to be — but the regulations which assured it had to be repeated and repeated, for laws made in Spain and behavior in New Spain were not automatically connected as cause and effect. Royal edicts were sometimes received by local officers by being kissed, held on the crown of the head "in token of great obedience," and then courteously killed with the words *obedezco pero no cumplo,* "I obey but I do not carry out."

Over and over again sixteenth-century documents deplored the lot of the Indians and decreed that it must be bettered. Queen Isabella had ordered that the Indians of the Antilles were to be made Christians and not slaves at a time when it would have been natural to treat them like Africans. While there can be no doubt that Charles V, too, was truly concerned, there can also be no doubt that his concern was ineffective. He made laws to protect his Indian subjects from being murderously overworked, or made slaves and branded, but he had to repeat them again and again. Even after most of the natives laboring for the Spaniards were already baptized, Viceroy Mendoza twice had to ask the Emperor to forbid their Christian masters from working them Sundays and keeping them from Mass, and there were still more complaints about this later. Viceroy Velasco said that it would be better to lose the profit from the mines than the souls of the miners, and Charles V prohibited pearl fishing, which was killing many, "because we value the saving of their lives more than whatever might come to us from the pearls." Mining and pearl fishing, nevertheless, were not interrupted.[11]

*

In the second half of the century the plight of the Indians became such that a storm of complaints was showered on the Spanish authorities, principally by the conscientious clergy. Fray Pedro de Gante, one of the first and most important of the Franciscans in Mexico, told of laborers sent away from their wives and children who then had no way of supporting themselves, of families required to pay tribute in produce they did not have, of families so poor that they were eating roots and grasses. (Conditions must have shocked him, used to fat Flanders, more than they would someone reared in arid Spain, or someone who had lived under Aztec rule.) He pointed to the drop in population and warned that the whole land might become worthless or even lost within another generation if the Indians were not treated decently enough to keep them from dying off.[12] In 1588 it was pointed out that since "the wealth of this land until now has been in the infinite multitude of Indians in it more than in the silver taken out of it, and since they are being destroyed, these provinces will become as poor and desolate as the great islands of Jamaica, Cuba, and Hispaniola" (where the Spaniards had destroyed *all* the natives).[13]

Throughout the century more documents piled up, hundreds filled with further complaints, and hundreds with hopeful regulations for the humane control of human labor. Finding conditions still "unspeakable" in 1595, the new Viceroy ordered a change, and another flood of benevolent but ineffectual regulations issued from the King and Council of the Indies. But all these individual orders did not produce general order. Their ineffectualness

13

appears almost as comic as tragic when one finds Philip III in 1609 still ordering a curb to the abuses of the Indians on the big estates, for it parrots hundreds and hundreds ordered by his father and grandfather. No other evidence is needed to show that the Indians were not allowed even nominal human rights in the new society. While in theory they constituted a state within a state, a *república de los indios* with its own laws and judges, it was Spanish officials who determined the major policies which the lesser Indian officials were to carry out locally. When the wishes of the Spanish masters were in conflict with those of the Indian subjects, then regardless of humanitarian edicts from the Crown and Council of the Indies, the Spaniards on the spot almost always won.

*

Not only overwork was killing the Indians, but also the transplanting to labor camps in different climates and at different altitudes which their lungs could not stand. The Spaniards came to recognize that the seemingly strong natives, who used to work harder and live longer, now were "of all people those who most easily die of an illness," [14] without realizing that they were dying mainly from sicknesses already minor to the immunized Spaniards but major to the Indians who had not yet built up resistances. They had been healthy for generations and had not known epidemics until smallpox became a grim ally of Cortés a year before he took Tenochtitlán; it may have killed a quarter of the Indians within its reach. It was particularly severe in the capital, where it killed Moctezuma's brief successor, Cuitláhuac. In 1531 there was a deadly epidemic of measles. In the plague of 1544–46, which had been heralded by a comet, a fountain of blood, a giant rainbow, and a volcanic eruption, 800,000 to 1,000,000 may have died, more than in the Conquest, more than in any disaster in Europe since the Black Death two centuries before. Conditions were so grave that the King, told that all would be dead within forty years, temporarily remitted tribute. A lesser epidemic hit the region of Tlaxcala in 1566, and in 1575 came the most murderous of all, of the same terrifying *cocolixtle* or *matlazáhuatl,* which killed Indians and spared Spaniards. This rose to its horrible climax in 1576, and did not abate until 1579. Some said it had killed 2,000,000 in one year, a not impossible figure accepted by contemporary and later chroniclers. The Indians died so fast that they had to be buried, eighty to a hundred at a time, in ditches cut through the churchyards. Some thought that half of the Christian Indians had died; other said two-thirds. Some towns were half depopulated, some two-thirds, some nine-tenths. There were no longer enough hands to till the fields, and the plague was followed by a famine so cruel that the Indians again ate roots and weeds. Another epidemic came in 1588, and the corn crop failed again. In southern Mexico the once rich Mixteca was so devastated by a pestilence in 1591–92 that whole cities were deserted. Yet another came in 1595–96. By 1600 there had been seven major plagues.

Not only did the white man's work and the white man's diseases kill the Indians: they killed each other, and they killed themselves. Tributes had not been proportionately reduced after the population was reduced by the plagues, and to pay their quotas nearly everywhere the survivors would have to work doubly, or triply, or quadruply. Pressed for tribute they could not pay, they would sell their captives as slaves to the Spaniards, sell their relatives, and finally sell their own children — legally or illegally — and occasionally there would flare a contagious frenzy of infanticide or mass suicide.

*

Depopulation came not only from plagues, crop failures, and self-destruction. Between 1550 and 1570 when there were no major disasters of this sort in central Mexico, endemic disease, social dislocation, and over-work kept shrinking the Indian population by 2 to 4 percent every year. By 1550 it had already dropped to about half of the 10,000,000 we assume it had been at the time of the Conquest. (The population of Spain was then about 7,000,000.) The closer the Indians lived to Spaniards, the faster they died. Some of the big agricultural estates had to be converted to cattle raising because there were not enough hands to plant and reap. By 1565, after the last native slaves had been freed, the population had already dropped to two-fifths. No wonder Father Mendieta repeatedly sounded the alarm: "Without being entirely finished off, how can the Indians, being so few and every day fewer, keep on serving and supporting the Spaniards, every day more?" [15] His warning was not exaggerated, for before the end of the century, four-fifths were gone. The Franciscans grimly pointed out that, even with no pestilences or wars, from 1587 to '94 some 1,500,000 In-dians had disappeared. At the end of the century there were perhaps only 1,500,000 left, probably not more than 2,000,000. It took the country an entire century to work out of the depression which inexorably followed the Great Plague. Some wondered why Mexico was being savagely punished. Others accepted the raids by Drake and Hawkins and the devastating earth-quake of 1591 as evidence of divine displeasure at the Spanish settlers' inhumanity.

It is, however, impossible to know exactly how many Indians died or were killed, or to know just how badly they were treated, since most of our evidence is from interested and biased parties. As most of the Spaniards were pleased to believe that Providence had put the Indians there expressly for them to use, it may have seemed natural to treat them as slaves. Con-ditions must have seemed less shocking to sixteenth-century consciences, used to a harder world and familiar with no society without slaves or serfs, than they do to modern men. Some of the Spaniards tried lulling their con-

15

sciences by maintaining that the Indians were not men but another species between monkey and man, created to serve man, to domesticate or kill whom was no worse than to domesticate or kill other animals. (No Spaniard would concede the corollary that Indian women must then be animals too, and that many Spaniards were liable to the death penalty for the sin of bestiality.) In 1537 Pope Paul III settled finally, favorably, and forcefully the question of whether the natives were members of the human race, and sons of Adam: his magnificent Bulls, *Veritas Ipsa, Sublimis Deus,* and *Altitudo Divini Consilii* (1537), were declarations no Catholic could ignore.

No matter what happened to them, until the end of the sixteenth century, there were always enough Indians available for building monasteries, and more every year were being trained in European procedures which enabled fewer workmen to put up more buildings. Meanwhile the Spanish local population was increasing. By the middle of the century it must have reached about 7,000, and more Spaniards arrived with each annual fleet. They were both prosperous and healthy: the plagues did not kill them; there were no major wars to kill them; their higher standard of living insured that far fewer Spanish than Indian babies died.

*

The encomenderos, mine-owners, and other masters slowly came to realize that they could get more work out of their workers if they took good care of them, just as they took good care of their plows, smelters, or other instruments of production. If the masters should not be aware of this, there were now more workable laws and more effective means of enforcement to remind them. Paradoxically, this improvement had been largely brought about by the most unworkable and least enforced laws of the century: the famous New Laws of 1542, inspired by Bishop Bartolomé de las Casas. These would have all but abolished the encomiendas. Viceroy Mendoza contrived, however, to have the carrying-out of the most drastic clauses delayed long enough so that most of them could be repealed before they were put into effect. The repeal helped the Indians as much as enforcement, if not more, for if the encomenderos did not feel they owned their Indians, they might have less interest in preserving them than when they counted them their own private property. They would not want to see their Indians die off any more than they would want to see their cattle die off. A moderate income that came in was preferable to a higher one that did not and — what is more — a higher one that seemed to be killing the golden geese.

Because conditions at the end of the sixteenth century were in some respects less bad does not mean that they could be called good. The Indians continued to live under acute strain, economic, social, and psychological. The standards of the first two viceregal regimes were not maintained after Velasco left in 1566, and the standards of government in Spain were not maintained after 1546, when Charles V gave the responsibilities for the New World to Prince Philip.

Although they preserved many of the outer forms in order to insure effective collection of tribute, the Spaniards disrupted something deep and vital in the old communities, and so destroyed the Indians' old ethical discipline, inseparable from their religion. Harsh as much of it was, the old society had had high standards of behavior, and had worked well insofar as everyone knew his place, his duties, and the punishment that civil or religious infractions would bring. Under the Spaniards' rule, the Indians tended to become lax, if not morally bankrupt. In the full meaning of the word, they were "de-moralized." The Spaniards made countless complaints about their laziness and petty thieving, though rarely about anything more criminal. Defeated, humbled, and treated like slaves or children, gradually they came more and more to have the mentality of slaves or maltreated children. The governing Spaniards were either too far away physically or — even if physically near — too far away psychologically to understand the Indians' social and spiritual needs. The church was converting them to a new religion, and converting them fast, but it did not and could not provide an effective code of behavior for all their nonreligious activities nor discipline all of their actions. The Spanish laymen did not set them consistent examples of good behavior: in fact there were as many complaints about how the Indians learned the Spaniards' vices as there were about their native vices which, of course, increased when their old codes of behavior lapsed. Father Sahagún, who came to know them as well as any non-Indian ever did, thought that the Indians had deteriorated because the Spaniards had deteriorated.

*

Doctor Zorita (in Mexico 1554–64) once asked an Indian lord what the basic trouble was. The answer: "Because neither do you understand us nor do we understand you nor what you want. You took away our good order and way of governing ourselves, and we do not understand what you have put in its place; hence everything is very confused, and without order or harmony." [16] Father Mendieta said that the Indians felt that the trouble was that while they were still infidels "no one did his own will, but did what he was ordered; and now too much liberty is harming us" (1562).[17] Whereas the Spaniards were generally strong individualists, intolerant of most discipline unless it was religious or military, the Indians were generally the opposite, strong conformists with a natural bias toward discipline.

While it is dangerous to make many assumptions about the temper of an inarticulate people of four centuries ago, there is abundant documentary evidence to show some components of their temper. Undoubtedly they loved order and to follow orders; when groups were waiting for anything, they would naturally arrange themselves in queues without being told. Chroniclers very often spoke with astonishment of their great docility, patience, and politeness. Furthermore, once they surrendered their arms, the material implements of resistance, they seem to have given up their inner resistance too; they fully accepted defeat and, tamed or not, they were obedient. Valiant in war, they seemed to become spiritless in peacetime. Father Mendieta observed that with respect to Spaniards they were "like sardines in respect to young whales," and that one Indian in front of a Spaniard was "like a puppy in front of a big lion, and he knows very well that the Spaniard has bad intentions, and the mettle to make short work of all the Indians in New Spain if he is let to lay hands on them; the Indian is so phlegmatic and meek that he would not harm a fly, and takes it for granted that the Spaniard is the one who will offend and the Indian the one who will suffer." [18] Instead of making things happen, they let things happen to them; they were not so much the subjects as the objects of the verbs of history.

The new regime left little hope to any Indian that he might better his lot. They rarely got more land; more often they lost some of what they had. Most of the country Indians were indentured in encomiedas. The city Indian could be only a laborer, servant, small trader, or artisan. There was no way of improving his position in the first two, and little in the last two. The guild system which became effective in the third quarter of the century, was strict, and natives were not allowed to take the examinations to become masters. Though they did nearly all the work, they could not profit from it. Not many Spanish craftsmen emigrated now, for ever since the expulsion of the Jews, Moslems, and Moriscos, craftsmen were in demand in Spain. Those who came to Mexico usually became entrepreneurs with Indians working for them, or bettered their positions by some other means so that they might rise from trade into fashionable idleness. The Indians could not do the same.

Another cause of trouble may have been that the tributes, once a well-adjusted integer in a balanced society, became a fresh threat to the equilibrium every time they were upped by the goldsick Spaniards. Only when tributes were not paid because they were so high that they could not be, did the Crown arrange more reasonable rates.

One might think that a third cause of the friction between Spaniards and Indians lay in the unassimilability of the late neolithic Indians into a society reflecting late mediaeval and renaissance Europe. But the Indians were far from uncivilized, and their culture was so maturely developed that it was perhaps verging as near decadence in central Mexico as it surely was in Yucatan. The extraordinary aptitude of Indian craftsmen for learning new techniques and turning their old techniques to new uses must have compensated a great deal for the differences in cultural level between them and their conquerors. Furthermore, their culture was not always inferior. To realize something of the quality of native achievement it is necessary only to recall their art — above all their wonderful sculpture — or their occasional advances in science (when it escaped from magic), particularly in medicine, astronomy, and the measurement of time.

Another reason that there was no more of a problem may have been that except in religion no major effort was made to transfer the great majority of the Indians into a European or would-be European society. The lay Spaniards wanted little of the Indians but their labor; only the Church wanted to touch more of their lives.

THE CHURCH

The one group that tried persistently to alleviate the Indians' burdens was the clergy. No others understood them half so well. Furthermore, as Cortés had foreseen, the clergy came to constitute the most steadying force in sixteenth-century Mexico, little swayed by the local economic and political upheavals. They could claim truthfully that had it not been for them conditions in New Spain might have been like those in Santo Domingo or Peru: out-and-out catastrophic. The Indians were more often aware of their spiritual than of their civil masters, for the Church was every day in some sort of active contact with millions of natives, while the Government touched them only intermittently — hardest when tributes were due.

A long series of eloquent letters from prelates and friars gradually revealed to the King and his Council of the Indies a picture of conditions in the country often unlike that given by the civil officials. These letters also made it clear that the country could not be run successfully on any theory or experience gained only in Europe, because the country was peopled by Indians, and these Indians — as the churchmen early had learned — were not like any of the other subjects of the Crown.

The differences between layman and churchman were even more marked than they were in Spain, mainly — perhaps — because of the greater opportunities offered to fulfill their diametrically divergent desires: hopes which had remained inert in Spain could be activated in New Spain on a grand scale. The civilians were usually materialistic, and constantly tempted by chances for quick gains, while the clergy were spurred by the immeasurable opportunities for converting the Indians, saving their souls, establishing ideal Christian communities, and for strengthening a Church already menaced in Europe by spreading Lutheranism. Nowhere did the theocentric idealism of the Middle Ages keep so alive as in the Church of the New World.

The Church was the chief patron of the arts in Spanish America, not only of architecture, and the painting and sculpture auxiliary to it in churches, but also of music and literature. Churchmen were the first scholars of the language, history, medicine, and extraordinary chronometry of the natives. Printing was brought by the Church, and the Church supplied the whole educational system, and dominated the University. The Church had a monopoly of education in two senses: it had nearly all of the educated men (except a few officials), and it did all of the educating.

THE SECULAR CLERGY

Although organized like the European Church in both its branches, *secular* (parish priests, bishops, archbishops), and *regular* (friars or monks, priors or abbots or guardians, provincials, generals), the Mexican Church did not operate in exactly the same way. All through the sixteenth century one major difference was that the regulars in Mexico bore the daily burden of pastoral duties carried by the seculars in Europe. Further divergence came from the fact that the Mexican Church was isolated, not merely by the intervening ocean, but also by its unending preoccupation with its own problems, peculiar problems unknown to Europe and so pressing that the Mexican clergy sometimes showed what looked like indifference to ecclesiastical affairs which seemed pressing to Europeans. For example, the Mexican bishops asked to be permanently relieved of the requisite episcopal visit to Rome. All but one of those bidden to the Council of Trent said that they were too busy to leave Mexico. Truly too busy, they must have been busier than any bishops in Europe. Yet an important part of the business of the Council was to discuss, regulate, and validate certain irregular practices in the administration of the Sacraments in the New World. The one bishop who accepted never got to Trent; the Mexican Church was represented only by an Augustinian friar, and he was there only for a few sessions.

*

Another way in which the Mexican Church was different was in the nature of its highest authority. Since this was half merged with the civil government, the Mexican bishops often seemed to be civil servants as well as prelates. (This was occasionally true in Europe: remember Cardinals Wolsey and Cisneros and such prince-bishops as those of Salzburg, Cologne, or Liège.) The Spanish kings had gained the right to name all church officers in Spain, and this *patronato real* was extended to Spanish America. Run by recent emigrants, the Mexican Church was a national Church, less in the orbit of the Roman Tiara than of the Spanish Crown. Rome could do nothing in the New World without the cooperation and consent of the Spanish monarch, a situation unprecedented in ecclesiastical tradition. No direct emissary of a pope set foot in Mexico until 1851.

Spanish Alexander VI had presented the New World "for the honor and glory of Almighty God, the propagation of the Christian Empire, and the Exaltation of the Holy Catholic Faith to . . . the King of Castile and

León . . . with free, full, and absolute power, authority, and jurisdiction."
Such papal "donations" of heathen lands to Christian sovereigns were a long
accepted practice. (Sardinia and the Canaries had already been "donated"
to suitable temporal rulers.) The Pope was much too far away to undertake
the conversion of the "islands and remote lands until now unknown," or
whatever it might be that Columbus had discovered. The Church almost *had*
to surrender this new land (and its new Church) to some king who could
provide a fleet and occupation force. Partly in compensation for the cost of
the Conquest, but mainly in recognition of the guarantee to Christianize the
natives, the Crown was awarded further privileges of unparalleled independence by Alexander VI and Julius II. Of course these popes did not have
any idea how large, rich, and populous America was when they gave its
Church away.

The authority of the king was pontifical in all but the most exclusively
spiritual matters, and even there any papal decision had to come through the
king and his Council of the Indies, and then in Mexico be submitted to the
viceroy and his Audiencia, who could either put it into effect or suspend it.
Even Papal Bulls were not binding in the New World until endorsed by the
king in a special *ejecutorial*. All revenues which elsewhere would automatically have accrued to the Church went instead to the Crown; the king then
defrayed Church expenses out of his royal treasury. If the local income was
inadequate, he would make up the balance, though he did not have to do
this often. Only because the kings were devout and sympathetic to most of
the wishes of the popes could the extraordinary arrangement work.

*

As soon as the existence of the vast, well-peopled, and potentially profitable mainland began to emerge, Charles V began to plan the organization of
its church. A whole year before the real exploration and Conquest was undertaken, the Emperor and the Pope, in anticipation, announced the creation of
the Diocese of Cozumel, "Island of the Sea of India" (1518). The next year
Leo X formally erected the Diocese, but no bishop was ever established there.
In 1525, when more was known about the ever-expanding realm being won
for him, the Emperor and Pope Clement VII transferred this bishopric to the
big Indian city of Tlaxcala, and in 1539 it was officially shifted to the new,
small, but Spanish city of Puebla de los Angeles, though the actual transfer
was delayed a few years. In 1528, the See of Mexico was created, and its first
bishop, Fray Juan de Zumárraga, arrived there without having yet been consecrated because Charles could not obtain the requisite Bulls from the Pope,
with whom he happened to be at war. This irregularity was remedied in a
few years, and by the middle of the century Zumárraga was Archbishop with
four bishops under him, at Puebla, Oaxaca, Guatemala, and Michoacán. As
titular head of its Church, he became the most powerful man in New Spain

after the viceroy. He had some jurisdiction over the friars — bishops had traditionally had this since Charlemagne — and although not always clearly nor consistently defined this power grew as the century unrolled.

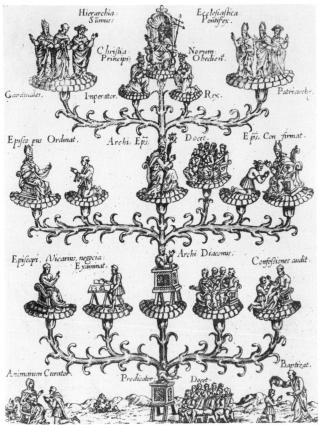

5 THE TREE OF THE ECCLESIASTICAL HIER–ARCHY *crowned by the Pope above two kings, flanked by cardinals and patriarchs above bishops ordaining, teaching, and confirming: below them the regulating of trade, preaching, hearing confession, and baptizing.*
(Valadés, Rhetorica, 1579)

The earliest bishops were able and effective men, and at least three were of heroic mold. Fray Juan de Zumárraga, first Bishop and Archbishop of Mexico, a humanist responsible for the first university, Indian college, and printing press, was not only a figure of moral grandeur but also a practical and daring man of action. Don Vasco de Quiroga, a jurisconsulist who had served eminently in the Second Audiencia, as first Bishop of Michoacán won glory by his grand-scale charity and by his imaginative understanding of the

22

problems of his Indians. To these two there should be added the name of that still controversial figure, that tempestuous, indignant, courageous, inaccurate, humanitarian crank and pamphleteer, Fray Bartolomé de las Casas, briefly the first Bishop of Chiapas. Each left his mark on the century as indelibly as any of the civil governors whom, indeed, they complimented or rivaled.

The bishops of the second half of the century were somewhat less well chosen. One archbishop, Francisco Alonso de Montúfar, seems at times to have become a quarrelsome paranoiac. Spain was by now deep-dyed in the contentious orthodoxy of the Counter-Reform. Historical chance had thrown her into close contact with Flanders, Germany, and Italy, and hence with the chief centers of advanced humanistic thought. As a result, her shocked Church chose to retrocede to a mediaeval point of view which lacked, alas, those positive values of the Middle Ages that had illumined the first generation of churchmen in New Spain. The withdrawal coincided, significantly, with the succession of Philip II to Charles V. In Mexico, the new orthodoxy was stiffened when Doctor Moya de Contreras, who had been sent over as Inquisitor, was elevated to Archbishop (1572).

In the beginning Charles V had categorically banned seculars from all of New Spain. Their first parishes outside the major cities were not set up until 1541, chiefly for Spaniards. Outside the cities there were very few seculars during the first forty years. By 1575, however, there were already 158 in the Archdiocese of Mexico, and by 1600 there were enough to serve between four and five hundred parishes in the whole country. Encomenderos were under obligation to have priests in their towns unless there happened to be a monastery nearby. These would not have been ordinary parishes with fixed congregations, fixed limits, and a predictable income from benefices, but *doctrinas,* with no stated congregation, boundaries, or income, but with only a priest paid by the encomendero to preach to whomever came. Few encomenderos fulfilled this obligation, however, and until the end of the century secular priests (curates, *curas, clérigos,* or pastors) did not minister to a fraction as many Indians as the friars, nor achieve anything like their importance.

Even though the friars were usually older — some, indeed, very old men — the seculars lacked both their stamina and moral caliber. Complaints were unending, second only to complaints against the encomenderos. From the beginning, Bishop Zumárraga objected to the quality of the curates he was sent; he sent some back in 1538. They did not "lead decent lives" and had "Indian women living in their houses." (Later, suitably aged female domestics were permitted.) To insure better quality, it was asked that only "university men or scholars" or "honest clerics of good life and example" be sent over. Viceroy Mendoza warned his successor that "the pastors who come to these parts are all mean, base, and self-seeking," and that "the Indians would be better off without them." Viceroy Velasco agreed that friars were more successful than

23

seculars, and "could be supported for less." Father Mendieta found a few years later that the seculars "have done more damage than service, for they have preached and indoctrinated very little, and have disturbed and obstructed the friars very much." Himself a friar, he felt so strongly about the seculars' shortcomings that he used language of such violence that it had to be expunged from his letters.[19]

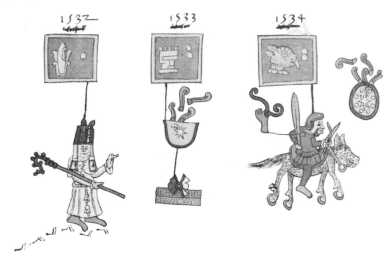

6 A LEAF OF THE CODEX TELLERIANO–REMENSIS, c1570
"*1532, the year of the flint blade, there came the first Bishop of Mexico, don Fray Juan de Zumárraga.*" (He arrived in December 1528, and left in 1532 to be consecrated in Spain.)
"*1533, the year of two houses, the earth shook once.*"
"*1534, the year of three rabbits, there arrived don Antonio de Mendoza, Viceroy of New Spain.*" (He arrived in 1535.)
(The correcting of the dates at the top was done in the sixteenth century.)

It was repeatedly charged that the curates were ignorant, worldly, covetous, and licentious, and that they were squeezing labor and money out of the Indians while giving little in return. Often they did not bother to learn the language of their congregations, and thought they were carrying out their full duties merely by reciting Masses. They were so "dissolute and do such dishonest things . . . that the Indians, seeing and understanding their bad example, dare do the same or worse, saying 'the *padre* does thus and so, so why shouldn't I?' "[20] The King had to order them not to linger in native villages. Special regulations had to be made to keep them from sporting silks, elegant colored clothes and hats, or perfumed gloves, to keep them from bowling, going to bullfights, gambling, acting in comedies, or from going out at night in civilian dress and with musical instruments.

24

The quality must have improved by the end of the century when the seculars took over the greater part of the religious administration of the natives from the friars.

All during the sixteenth century, except for the splendid large cathedrals which we still may admire in Mexico City, Puebla, Guadalajara, and Mérida — transplanted European schemes for transplanted European congregations — the architectural undertakings of the seculars were less important than those of the friars. This was partly because the seculars were less energetic and effective, and partly because they had fewer and smaller congregations and smaller funds. As it is doubtful that they could ever have obtained anything like such quantities of Indian labor or gifts as the friars regularly enjoyed, it is equally doubtful that they were ever responsible for building any notable churches except those few built for their prosperous Spanish congregations in the cities. Although the Crown repeatedly ordered new parish churches put in towns where there was no church already, and offered to pay a third of their cost, such orders were more often ignored than obeyed. As the encomenderos until the later part of the century had lacked confidence that their tenure of the towns was enduring, they seem not to have had much interest in seeing to it that enduring (and expensive) masonry church buildings were constructed.

There are too few well preserved remains of sixteenth-century secular parish churches to give any clear idea of their appearance as a type, yet there must have been between four and five hundred standing at the end of the century. They cannot have been so well built as the typical churches of the friars, which have endured so much better, and most must have been of cheap, easily worked materials, presumably not very durable. By the seventeenth century, however, they could compete with the monasteries.

THE REGULAR CLERGY

The friars are the ones who accomplish the most, and where they do not go, there is no Christianity.

— *Bishop Zumárraga* (1540) [21]

In her will, Queen Isabella had charged her successors with the conversion of the American natives. The principal instrument for this was to be not the secular but the regular clergy: Mendicants sent across the sea expressly for this mission. The Indians were made the charges of the friars, and the viceroys were instructed to see that the friars converted them. Because it had been given the major task, during the sixteenth century the major branch of the American Church was the regular. As a corollary, one finds that since the friars came first, they built first and fastest, and soon established the local church types.

SPANISH MASTERS

Three Mendicant Orders — Franciscan, Dominican, and Augustinian — were the only ones licensed to work in New Spain during the first fifty years. Together they made a highly organized sub-state within the viceregency, politically and economically semi-independent. Only at the top was this Mendicant organization subject to the civil government: it was fully responsible only to the king and his Council of the Indies, and less fully and less clearly to the local bishops, archbishop, and viceroy, to whom submission was no more than occasional. Although they did in effect form a solid unit in the fundamental structure, the Orders did not always agree with each other on immediate matters nor always act in unison.

The Mendicants had a hierarchic organization parallel to that of the seculars. At the top, subordinate only to the pope, were the three Generals who presided over the affairs of their Orders from Rome. In Spain there was a resident *Comisario General,* the delegate from the headquarters of each Order in Rome. In Mexico there was another *Comisario,* subject to the one in Spain. He appointed the *Provinciales* who headed each Province of the Order.

Within the Provinces there might be subordinate *Custodias* (under the direction of *Custodios*) which might in time become independent Provinces. In each Province and *Custodia* there were monasteries administered by Priors or Guardians, superior to the resident friars. The narrowly correct name in English for these establishments — then called either *monasterios* or *conventos* — is "friary" or "convent," but as "friary" sometimes sounds awkward in modern speech, and "convent" is more often understood as an establishment of nuns, "monastery" will be most often used here. (The word can correctly apply to any community residence or group of religious who recite Divine Offices together.)

The monasteries in Mexico were houses of Mendicant friars engaged in active missionary work, and not retreats for monks, like most of the monasteries in Europe. Since the thirteenth century, "friar," a term of fraternal address among early Christians, had been used specifically to designate a member of one of the Mendicant Orders, whereas "monk," originally applied to hermits, came to apply to members of most of the other Orders (such as Benedictines, or Cistercians). Like monks, friars recited many canonical offices daily — Matins, Lauds, Compline, Vespers, and so on — and lived according to rule (*regula,* hence regular clergy). Unlike monks, they were not in retreat from the world but constantly out preaching in it, teaching, or caring for its poor and sick. Almost from the time of their founding, the Franciscans had been concerned with missionary work — Saint Francis himself had spent a year trying to convert Turks — and one of the main considerations in the founding of the Dominican Order had been the organization of a campaign of preaching against heretics. While monks in their monasteries in Spain were vowed to the contemplative life, and regarded almost everything other than the recitation of offices and chanting of Masses as extracurricular, the friars in Mexico, less like Mary and more like Martha, were specifically committed to works in the world outside.

Not only were the friars in Mexico more active than monks in Spain; they were more active than friars there. Fray Martín de Valencia once said that he had rendered more service to God in two busy years in Mexico than in thirty in Spain; others said forty. Nearly all of the friars in Mexico were also ordained priests, though a few were only lay brothers who could not say Mass or administer other Sacraments. Most of the ritual and much of the routine was, of course, the same on both sides of the water: the great difference lay in the special work with Indians. The friars in New Spain made expeditions into the country to convert the Indians, sometimes after "order" had already been brought there by the sword, sometimes before. After preaching and teaching, they baptized the Indians and then continued to preach and teach. They supervised the construction of monasteries by Indian laborers, and directed other related undertakings, such as the building of aqueducts, hospitals, and schools. Their missions were of two kinds: of occupation, or of penetration. The more numerous, and architecturally the more important, were those of occupation, whether planted in old Indian centers or in specially created new towns. Those of penetration were often smaller and of unassuming temporary construction, at least during their first decades.

In the hamlets and villages of the countryside around each monastery, the friars would establish *visitas,* perhaps two, perhaps ten, twenty, or thirty. These were little churches or chapels, usually equipped with a lockable sacristy or storeroom, and perhaps a cell or two for the friars who would visit periodically in order to minister to the Indian villagers; until the end of the century no friar was permanently resident. This was an adaptation of a mediaeval practice: a Norman "minster church," for example, had a body of clergy under special discipline who would travel out to serve country churches where no parochial arrangements had yet been made. Something similar was current practice in Spain, where pairs of religious would visit in rotation the churchless villages on the periphery of a big parish. Similar systems continue today in some places such as the great Austrian abbeys of Sankt Florian, Altenburg, or Melk. In Mexico there were also occasionally *vicarías,* particularly later in the century when there were more friars. Little is known about them now except that like visitas they were small and dependent on monasteries, but unlike visitas they had resident friars. Their organization and architectural arrangements were more like a little monastery than like a big visita.

The Orders began also to establish nunneries in some cities, but these were too few and too small to have much importance in the sixteenth century. Their main function was to teach girls, and also to provide a suitable haven for unmarried ladies of quality. The nuns were not engaged in con-

2 7

verting Indians and consequently did not have to face the problems that posed for the friars. Architecturally the nunneries did not find their particular character until the next century. Also negligible in the sixteenth century was the architecture of the Orders who arrived later: the Carmelites, Dieguinos, Mercedarians, and the Jesuits.

7 A MONASTERY AND ITS VISITAS, *as shown on* AN INDIAN MAP OF THE TOWN OF COXCATLÁN, *c1580*

Probably at first a visita of Teotitlán del Camino to the south (right), on the highway to Oaxaca, Coxcatlán was transferred to Tehuacán to the north (left) soon after 1568. Lesser visitas are shown with the roads that led to them, and the streams that watered the different parts of this fertile valley in the rainy season. Coxcatlán had a municipal fountain on one side of the church, and municipal gallows on the other. The town still exists, as does Santa María Calipa, to the left.

28

Friars were supposed to know how to sew, cook, barber, garden, and nurse, and to possess themselves of other desirable practical skills. The ideal age for a friar coming to Mexico was held to be between thirty and forty. Conscientiously chosen, the first Mendicants proved to be energetic and resourceful as well as pious men, more able than the average conquistador, and far more able and honest than the average encomendero or mine-owner. They hardly ever showed the greed and cruelty of the Spanish civilians, and rarely accumulated much arrogance or vanity. When they did, it usually showed itself in a special way: it took the form of churchly splendor. Capable, often saintly, rarely unkind, they have become the heroes of this book.

*

Cortés had asked the Emperor for particularly exemplary clergy so that they might not suffer damaging comparison with the Aztec priests, who had been fanatically chaste and strict in their observances. This must have been one of the reasons why Mendicants were chosen in preference to seculars in the first place. (Spain was at the time very much aware of recent Mendicant reforms.) On the whole they were well educated; many had been at the great universities — especially Salamanca and Alcalá — and many of those who had traveled had been at the Sorbonne. A surprising number were of noble birth, which then presumably assured a literate upbringing plus some modicum of secondary education and culture.

*

They were not Spaniards only. Charles V was in Flanders when he received Pope Hadrian's letter confirming the rights of the Franciscans in the New World, and the first three friars he sent out were Flemings: the lay brother Pedro de Gante (Ghent) was one of the great formative influences in the early Mexican Church. He asked for more Flemings to be sent, and with them came all kinds of Spaniards, and others whose names reveal Portuguese, French, or Italian origins. Still others, though Spanish, had been in monasteries in France or Italy, or at foreign universities. One was of royal Danish blood; one a royal Scot.

*

In its beginnings, then, the Spiritual Conquest of Mexico was as international as had been the Reconquest of Spain. Such cosmopolitanism in the clergy was not to last, however, for xenophobe Philip proclaimed that Spaniards were not to leave Spain to study, teach, or learn, nor to reside in seats of learning outside Spain (1559). Soon he ordered all Franciscans not of Spanish origin to leave Mexico. (Fortunately, they did not.) One consequence was that the quality of the clergy began to decline. Another was that connections with the monumental architecture of any country other than Spain all but disappeared.

29

and the Indians then imitated the Spaniards, more deeply impressed than they had been by anything since the first appearance of mounted strangers shooting guns. Seeing how deferential mighty Cortés had been to them — Cortés whom many had thought a god or the divine emissary of a god — the Indians realized that the twelve friars must be very, very important, and henceforth spoke to them as they had spoken to their own divine rulers, with hats off and eyes lowered. The whole scene was so dramatic and touching, above all in the contrast between the powerful, proud Spaniards and the mild, barefoot Franciscans before whom they humbled themselves, that it soon became a well-liked subject for mural decorations (as can still be seen in the monasteries at Ozumba and Tlalmanalco). Perhaps the scene also echoed part of the legend of Saint Francis (as told by Saint Bonaventura) for he, too, walked on a cloak thrown down in homage when he entered Assisi.

Together with the few handfuls of friars sent to join them, the Twelve carried out a conquest as thoroughgoing and drastic in its effects, though not in its means, as that so bloodily carried out by Cortés, his few hundred Spaniards, his gunpowder and horses, and his 100,000 to 150,000 Indian warrior allies. Furthermore, the friars' conversion covered a larger territory.

The Franciscans' clashes with the interim government while Cortés was in Honduras and with the dreadful First Audiencia which replaced it both ended in victory. The friars never came into such violent conflict with the civil authorities again: they did not have to. Under Viceroys Mendoza and Velasco they were encouraged and upheld. Almost everyone knew that the land Cortés had conquered could not have remained conquered had it not been for the Franciscans, and nearly everyone came to realize that the little band of meek-seeming friars could be more useful than soldiers. Monasteries of penetration were therefore deployed along the dangerous Chichimeca frontier and along the road to the mines of Zacatecas.

Tireless and almost obsessed evangelizers, the friars would let nothing stand in their way. They were not timid in reminding the awesome King-Emperor that he had been entrusted with the New World to bring its inhabitants into the Church, and that they, the Mendicants, were the chosen instrument for this, authorized not only by him but also by his one superior, the Pope, or rather by an impressive series of popes. The friars could be sharp in reminding Philip of the humane policies of his father.

Even though they grew in numbers, there were always surprisingly few of them. Cortés wrote a special short letter and stressed in his fourth long letter, written soon after the Twelve had arrived, the great need for sending friars. A few more came almost every year, and a score in 1529. Clement VII gave a permit for 120 in 1532, but that quota was not filled. By 1536 there were only 60 all together, right at the time of the greatest need, when the Conversion was at last successfully under way; but there never seemed enough to keep it steadily advancing. Soon ten monasteries serving some 100,000 Indians had to be abandoned for lack of staff. Charles V begged the Pope to send 120 brothers at once, but only 25 came by the next fleet. In 1541, 150 more were allotted to Mexico as a result of appeals to the Council of Mantua, but in 1542 there were probably not very many more than 100 there all together. By the middle of the century there were perhaps 200, but still there never seemed to be enough. Many were old; many died. In towns where 10 or 12 were said to be needed there were only 2. In 1554, 36 more came, and the total was said to have reached 380 in 1559. After seeing the annual fleet come in without any new friars in 1566 and '67, the Franciscans again had to pull back. They talked of giving up a score of houses, and in 1567 they felt themselves forced actually to abandon eleven because there was no one to man them. Even the Indian lesser rulers, or political bosses, the *caciques,* were alarmed; ten of them wrote a joint protest to the King. By the 1580's there were perhaps as many as 500 or 600 friars. Each of the Orders wanted to be able to count on 4 friars in every monastery, but there were too few friars and too many monasteries to allow that often.

In 1524 the Franciscans set up their first four houses with four friars each, quartered in borrowed buildings at México-Tenochtitlán, Texcoco, Tlaxcala, and Huejotzingo. The houses were placed near together, in case one might need quick aid from the others. Cuernavaca was founded next, in 1525, after another boat from Spain had brought a few more friars. All this was done before the tide of religious capitulation had turned. As soon as converts did begin to flood in, and as the number of friars fitfully increased, the evangelical campaign was successfully spread farther and farther afield. Houses were founded at Tepeaca, Cuautitlán, Toluca, and Tlalmanalco, all reassuringly close to the center, none more than 40 miles away. In 1529 there were a dozen; by 1531, a score. In that year the friars dared push much farther out, as far to the west as Ajijic, Colima, and Zapotlán (now Ciudad Guzmán), 400 miles from the capital.

By 1535, when the Second Audiencia turned the government over to Viceroy Mendoza, it was generally felt that the country had been pacified, and it was recognized that the Franciscans had been the chief instrument of pacification. They were now raised from the minor status of *Custodia* to an independent Province. The friars continued to plant their houses — about 40 by 1540 — in an ever-widening field: 50 by 1554; 80 by 1559; 90 by 1571; 155 by 1588. In the main Province, where there had been only 30 in 1570, Father Mendieta counted 66 in 1590, plus 24 in the new Province to the north, 54 in the new Province of Michoacán, and 22 in Yucatan: 166 Franciscan establishments in all. By the end of the century the monasteries were so thickly strewn through the central Province that one could travel its length without ever having to sleep in anything but a Franciscan house.[23]

33

8 A MURAL PAINTING
IN THE FRANCISCAN CLOISTER AT HUEJOTZINGO

The "Virgin of the Magnificat," shown here, was so called from the Canticle she had sung during her Visitation with Saint Elizabeth (Luke 1:39) and which was repeated every day by friars at Vespers.

Surrounding her are metaphorical attributes, many from the Song of Solomon: City of God, Fountain of Gardens, Tower of David, Star of the Sea (from a mis-reading of Isaiah), Gate of Heaven, Well of Living Water, Enclosed Garden, lily, rose, wild olive, and so on. She is "clear as the sun" and "fair as the moon."

On one side Thomas Aquinas announces "Mary was exempt from detestable Original Sin and free from personal sin." On the other, Duns Scotus asks "Deem me worthy to praise thee, O Blessed Virgin!"

Dominican Saint Thomas, the Doctor Angelicus (standing above a crown indicative of his royal blood), had been opposed by Franciscan Duns Scotus, the Doctor Subtilis (wearing a biretta indicative of his professorship at Oxford), in defense of the doctrine of the Immaculate Conception, to which the central picture here may also refer, for above Mary's head is written "Thou art fair, my love: there is no spot in thee" (Song of Songs 4:7). The dispute between the two great scholastics as to whether Mary was born free of Original Sin or was later freed of it by the special miracle of the Immaculate Conception developed into a polemic between the two Orders. Duns Scotus' writings, including his affirmation of the Immaculate Conception, which had not yet been accepted as Dogma, became one of the doctrinal bases of Franciscan thought.

More widely professed in Spain than in any other European country — as a wealth of later painting and sculpture attests — the doctrine was not proclaimed as Dogma until the nineteenth century.

34

In what is pertinent to their building, the story of the other Orders is so like that of the Franciscans that it need not be detailed. All figures are, of course, smaller, for the Dominicans and Augustinians together rarely equaled the Franciscan totals.

*

Although in Europe the Franciscans were traditionally the chief missionary Order and the more learned and intellectual Dominicans the teaching and preaching Order, in the New World these differences diminished. The Dominicans probably stressed writing, printing, and theory more, and after 1571 were particularly involved in the management of the Inquisition, of little concern to the other Orders.

Having supported Columbus at the Spanish Court, and in consequence having gained priority in Santo Domingo, the Dominicans felt they should share in the conversion of New Spain. Accordingly, they hastened to send a mission of twelve in 1526. They were plagued by misfortunes: five died within a year, and four, ill, had to go back to Spain; as a result the Dominicans were slower than the Franciscans in making their mission effective. Although occasionally divergent in their basic attitude toward the Indians — they were less paternalistic — the Dominicans asked the Franciscans for advice and help, and followed most of the successful procedures for conversion and the founding of monasteries that the Franciscans had worked out from experience.

In 1528 two dozen more Dominican friars arrived, and within two years they were well established with their own temporary church in the capital, and with work starting on a permanent one. The Pope gave a license for some 70 more friars to come in 1532, but the quota was not filled. In 1534 they were separated from the Province of Santo Domingo and became an independent Province, dedicated to Santiago and under the particular patronage of Clement VII, who all through his pontificate had favored their Order. Now able to go ahead more vigorously, they determined in 1535 to found a dozen more monasteries and staff them with 30 friars "who would go forth, two by two, to preach the Gospel . . . in imitation of Christ's Disciples." By 1538 there were about 70 friars, and 30 more arrived in that year's fleet. Nine establishments had been set up: Mexico City, Oaxtepec, Coyoacán, Chimalhuacán Chalco, Tepetlaóztoc, Oaxaca, Yanhuitlán (soon relinquished), Puebla, and one in Guatemala. They were noticeably slower than the Franciscans in establishing themselves in Indian towns: they preferred the Spanish cities of Mexico, Oaxaca, and Puebla. After repeated proddings, they were forced into widespread permanent monastery-building only after 1549, when the Emperor and Prince Philip both sent orders for them to stop wandering, and to settle down and build. Perhaps the skirmishes with the Zapotecas from 1547 onwards made the Crown think it would be politic just then to send pacifying friars into the region of Oaxaca, and it was here that the Dominicans made a major effort. By 1551 there were enough Dominican friars (about 200) in enough houses spread over so much territory that the southeastern regions of Chiapas and Guatemala were detached to become a separate Province. In 1559 there were about forty Dominican monasteries in the Province of Mexico alone, and in 1578 there were fifty, with about 300 friars. By 1596, when Oaxaca was separated as a Province, there were between seventy and eighty houses, about a third of which were large and architecturally noteworthy. The chain stretched 120 leagues from Mexico City to Tehuantepec, and usually one could journey along it from one house to the next between mid-day dinner and nightfall; only a few were a whole day's trip apart. There were 4, 5, or 6 friars in the smaller houses now, and about 25 in Oaxaca, 30 in Puebla, and 80 or more in the head house in the capital.

By 1533 the Franciscans and Dominicans were joined by the Augustinians, with substantially the same program and privileges. This entailed some change in their status, for they had not been equated with their brother Mendicant Orders in Europe. The Augustinian Order had long been more like an association of hermits, and had in 1256 been officially constituted as such. It was not formally congregated with the other Mendicant Orders until 1567, after it had been working closely parallel to them for a generation in New Spain. Its activities there redounded so to its credit that learned Fray Alonso de la Vera Cruz was asked back to Spain to report them. He had studied at Alcalá and at Salamanca under Victoria; he had written works on dialectic, and was professor of theology at the new University of Mexico. Covered with honors, he returned from Spain in 1573, with sixty boxes of books for Augustinian libraries. The Augustinians were on the whole the most learned of the friars in New Spain, and the most concerned with doctrinal and theological problems. They contributed importantly to the faculty of the new University, in contrast to the Franciscans who traditionally had been suspicious of higher learning. In numbers of friars and establishments, the Augustinians were roughly equivalent to the Dominicans. Separated as a Province in 1543, by 1559 they had over 200 friars in forty monasteries; forty-five by 1572; and toward the end of the century some seventy or eighty, with over 400 friars. Moctezuma's much-married daughter, pious doña Isabel, had given them their first house in the capital, and she continued to be their generous patroness with each of her successive husbands.

Distribution of the Orders

The territory of the Viceregency was partitioned for the concerted campaigns of the Mendicants. Large regions were allotted exclusively to one Order: Tlaxcala, Jalisco, and Yucatan, for example, were Franciscan monopolies. The Franciscans also extended their work farther and farther west, to the Pacific coast and then up northwest along it; at the same time they intensified work in the heart of the country by building more monasteries in what are now the states of Mexico, Morelos, and Puebla.

The Augustinians, not very active outside the capital until the middle of the century, began with a false start in the wilderness of Guerrero (which they did not like) and a sort of poaching between the Franciscan houses in the benevolent Valley of Morelos (which they liked very much). Their major activity began with a drive to the north and west of the Valley of Mexico, gradually pushing back the heathen frontier through what are now the states of Hidalgo and Michoacán. For a long time their main house was at Tiripetío in Michoacán, founded in 1537 and expanded into an important seminary in 1540.

Delayed in starting, the Dominicans began their long and splendid chain only in the middle of the century, and slowly extended it from Puebla down through the bleak, moonlike mountains of the Mixteca Alta to the fertile Valley of Oaxaca, on to the Isthmus of Tehuantepec, and then on still farther through the jungles and highlands of Chiapas to end in Guatemala. Chiapas and Guatemala were made a Dominican Province in 1551; Oaxaca in 1595.

*

As the best of the country had been apportioned among these three, there was nothing suitable left for the Mercedarians when they wanted to set up missions a generation later; they were therefore shunted to Guatemala. Tabasco, Veracruz, the Huaxteca, and Guerrero, though well-populated in parts, were either ignored or halfheartedly approached and then quickly repudiated. Many of the Indians were moved to more accessible centers. Bishop Montúfar, ever eager to complain about the friars, said that they deliberately stayed out of the rough mountains and hot lowlands. (Anyone who has hunted out provincial sixteenth-century monastery buildings today has often wished that his complaint were truer!)

*

A long series of royal edicts encouraged, requested, or ordered the building of more monasteries. Regulations were made to keep the friars from favoring the pleasanter valleys, from settling too near one another, and from invading other Orders' territories; but these orders were often ignored, particularly when they were closely followed by others urging that more monasteries be built at once wherever there seemed to be a need. There were so many so close together in the valleys of Mexico and Morelos that Philip II had to ban the erection of any new monastery within 15 miles of one already built. By 1550 there were 75 or 80 monasteries of all the Orders spread through the country, about a quarter of which survive in good shape today.

37

Toward the end of the sixteenth century Father Mendieta calculated that there were already

400 monasteries in
400 monastery towns (and also
400 parish churches administered by seculars).[24]

There were said to be over 1500 friars. (The Second Audiencia had said in 1531 that 2000 would not suffice.) Although of suspicious roundness and symmetry, these figures of Father Mendieta's cannot be far from the truth. Since they include Guatemala and Nicaragua, they should be reduced by about 5 or 10 percent for Mexico alone. In addition to almost 400 monasteries, there were thousands of supplementary visitas where traveling friars celebrated Mass only periodically; the Franciscans claimed to have 10,000 of these by 1585. Spain, with half to two-thirds the population of Mexico, had twenty-five times as many monasteries, many of them signally rich and filled with scores of monks.

Maintenance and Mendicant Poverty

Although tithes had been largely outlawed for European churches, Cortés proposed to the Emperor that the Mexican Church be financed partly by them. This was tried, however, only by the seculars. When tithes were offered to the Mendicants, they agreed to reject them because the Indians, already heavily burdened with other tributes, could pay no more, and also because if the Indians did pay tithes they might then think that they were *buying* the Sacraments. The seculars, subsisting by necessity largely on tithes, resented that the regulars were supported by gifts and gifts alone: gifts from the king, from the encomenderos, and even from the Indians.

Although Mendicants were constitutionally directed to subsist by alms, in the early years their monasteries in New Spain were in large part supported by grants from the Throne. In addition, the king paid for the maintenance and transportation of each friar, portal to portal, from the moment he left his monastery in Spain until he was settled in a new one in New Spain. The encomenderos also had to contribute to the support of any neighboring monasteries, and the Indians contributed labor — at first free, then modestly paid — and sometimes voluntarily offered tribute of goods or of part of their meager savings or material possessions. The huge monastery of San Francisco in the capital, for example, was built entirely by the Indians, with no royal gifts of money; the Franciscans announced that they did not want any because they got along perfectly well on what the Indians gave them. Towards the end of the century, however, the friars did partially depend on royal charity because they did not want to become a weight on the Indians, now fewer and poorer. The arrangements varied widely from time to time and place to place.

The Franciscans felt bound by their vows of poverty more than the other Mendicants, and probably managed their big establishments on smaller budgets. There are many more notices of their frugality and abstinence from display than there are for the other Orders. The first Franciscans were so committed to poverty that Fray Toribio de Benavente changed his name to the Náhuatl word for "poor," *motolinía,* when he heard the Indians in the Tlaxcala market place say it over and over in wonderment at the ragged friars walking barefoot to the capital. It was the first word he learned. (Perhaps he remembered that Saint Francis had liked to be called *poverello.*) The Indians told the Second Audiencia that they loved the Franciscans "because like us they go about poorly clad and barefoot, partake of the same food we eat, abide in our midst, and deal meekly with us." [25]

The Franciscans did allow themselves "precious things in the Sacristies, if they be not redundant and superfluous," in accordance with a special Bull of Sixtus IV.[26] The other Orders, except for occasional indulgence in ostentatious building and equipment, cannot often have been what could be called extravagant. Viceroy Velasco, a relatively unpartisan judge for the time, paid them this tribute: "It cannot fairly be said that the friars seek worldly goods, for I do not know that they have until now had any private property, and their clothing consists of habits of sackcloth and frieze, and their meals are so modest that they sustain themselves only with great effort, and if on some day of the year they have something extra, they give it to the poor." [27]

To save money and to make their frugality dramatically clear, the Franciscans often had Indians ravel old robes too worn to wear, and then weave new ones with the salvaged threads. Because indigo was the cheapest and commonest fast local dye, they took to blue robes as soon as those they had worn over from Europe fell irretrievably apart. (Although the ordinary Spanish Franciscans and the reformed friars commonly wore gray at this time, color was not held significant since Saint Francis had specified no color for habits, only that they be "vile.")

Whereas the Mendicants were allowed to solicit alms from the encomenderos, though not from the Indians, they could accept gifts or bequests from both. Thus, despite their statutory poverty, they began to acquire property, and edicts were issued by both King and Pope enabling them to keep it. The Council of Trent released them still more from the strictures of their original vows, and sanctioned corporate ownership of revenue- or produce-bearing lands for all but the Franciscans. Although the Dominicans had voted in 1535 not to own income-producing properties but to live entirely on alms, they changed their minds in 1541. They held some towns in encomienda very early, and they came into so much property during the middle decades of the century that there were complaints loud enough to evoke royal orders to sell. In time, more and more property accrued to all the

Orders, until they were such major landowners in New Spain that the King forbade them to acquire any more land. Half the good land in Spain already belonged to the Church, and the Crown was anxious not to lose so much of it in New Spain. Nevertheless, by the late sixteenth century the Church already owned half the good land. In 1578, the Cabildo of Mexico City complained that the Augustinians and Dominicans together owned the better part of metropolitan real estate, and asked — unsuccessfully — that additional accessions be prohibited. The friars in the country sometimes had as many Indians working under them as did the big landowners. The Dominicans of Puebla ran a large and successful sugar mill. Profits, however, were always turned back into the main missionary enterprise, often to produce useful equipment, such as chalices and altars, or churches, monastery buildings, asylums, schools, hospitals, or entire new towns. Despite occasional restraints, the Orders kept accumulating properties, not only by bequest, but sometimes by being officially assigned villages or encomiendas to add to their income for a hospital, school, orphanage, or some other worthy undertaking.

Native Friars?

In the beginning, some Spaniards hoped that Indians might successfully be trained for the priesthood. As early as 1525 the Royal Accountant pointed out that one Indian priest would be more effective in winning Indian converts than fifty Europeans; but the majority of Spaniards, apprehensive of giving authority to Indians, did not wish to risk this. Some monasteries may have allowed one or two Indians to start out as novices, but they were not advanced farther, and were soon dropped. Some feared that the Indians would not be able to grasp the essentials of Catholicism securely enough to keep from wandering innocently into dangerous heretical byways. Some feared that once they could read the Old Testament freely they would find out about plural wives and other distracting items which might suggest subversive parallels to their old pagan ways and lead to immoral unchristian behavior. Others said that Indians were congenital drunkards, unable to remain chaste, or that they lacked aptitude for the intellectual application required. Such objections were obstinately maintained right in the face of the Royal College of the Holy Cross of Santiago Tlatelolco, which since 1536 had been training native Latinists and young humanists whom even the students of the University, founded 15 years later, could not surpass. The pupils at Tlatelolco were so bright and apparently so clearly suited to clerical careers that in 1555 the institution was deliberately downgraded to a school for interpreters by those who did not want to see Indians in the clergy or benefited in any other way. (Cruel contrast with the lot of the converted Moslems, for whom Charles V was having a luxurious college built at Tortosa in these same years. Moslem Granada had already been given a university.) Although some Franciscans continued to hope for native friar-priests, in 1538 the Dominicans ruled against accepting them. At a meeting in 1539 the bishops decided to give Indians and mestizos who were bright in their schools the four minor orders — not demanding celibacy — so that they could serve as porters, readers, exorcists, and acolytes, but nothing more. There were always plenty of altar boys.

Though a few benevolent Spaniards, like Viceroy Mendoza, thought that in time they could be, by the middle of the century nearly everyone was agreed that Indians should not be ordained. The First Mexican Church Council made this official in 1555. The *Constituciones* of the Franciscans of 1570 not only forbade the ordination of Indians, but also barred mestizos and even *criollos* except by special ruling. The Dominicans followed suit in 1576. Occasionally an important voice was raised to protest their exclusion: Fray Jacobo Daciano, a Dane of royal blood who had walked all the way to Madrid when heresies threatened Copenhagen, maintained that the Church of New Spain was falsely established because it had no native priests. He was refuted in public debate by the still more learned Fray Juan de Gaona. Bishop Vasco de Quiroga of Michoacán, accused perhaps falsely of tonsuring and ordaining mestizo youths, was ordered to desist in 1556. Surprisingly, Archbishop Montúfar, who often complained about the Indians (as well as about everything else), agreed that it would be proper to ordain them. When Philip II heard that he had ordained "mestizos and other people born in the land," he summarily ordered him to stop. The Bishop received the order, kissed it, held it over his head, and denied that he had been guilty. Despite the fact that Gregory XIII had clearly sanctioned the ordination of mestizos in 1576, the King repeated his ban in 1578 — he must have heard that it had been disobeyed — and in 1582 explained that by "mestizo" he meant those with one full-blooded Indian parent, not the son of a mestizo and a Spaniard. Henceforth, it was legally permissible to ordain a man who was one quarter Indian, or less. The Council of 1585 reaffirmed the exclusive clauses of the Council of 1555, denying this leniency of Philip's, and went on to make many new restrictions, but they did leave the door open a crack.

Although the friars soon won the Indians' confidence, for a century the Indians did not win enough confidence from the friars to be accepted into their ranks. The basic objection to ordaining them was partly a genuine apprehensiveness on the part of the friars who, after all, knew them best and who, on the whole, became less anxious to ordain them as they had more experience with them. It was partly also the result of the anti-Indian feeling of many Spaniards, an attitude immeasurably stiffened by the early activities of the encomenderos, mine-owners, and men like Nuño de Guzmán who so bloodily widened the psychological gap between the races. After him it took several generations before either could trust the other. Although still barred by the Orders, mestizos and *criollos* began to be admitted to the ranks of the secular clergy in the last third of the century, and the practice was officially sanctioned in 1588.

In some monasteries pious Indians were allowed to live, somewhat like lay brothers. The friars found them useful and often admirable; they were allowed to wear a sort of habit; and they were called *donados,* because they "gave" their services and lives. The friars also used native boys, not only as acolytes but, in cases of linguistic need, for preaching and catechizing as well, particularly in the early years. Neither these boys, called *doctrineros,* nor the *donados* could administer any of the Sacraments. When, because of them, it was not anomalous to see men with dark skins wearing monastic habits, a few exceptions began to be made. The first mestizo friar of whom there is record was Diego de Valadés, grandson of a fighter of Moors, son of a conquistador father and probably a Tlaxcalteca mother. Fray Diego, an Observant, was the first Mexican to have a book published in Europe, where he spent many years in important ecclesiastical positions. His book, *Rhetorica Christiana* (Perugia, 1579), contains the first printed firsthand account of the evangelization of Mexico, for that of Gómara (1552) was not firsthand, and those of the other great chroniclers were not printed until later even though some, such as Motolinía's (1538–42), were written considerably earlier. Once a pupil and then presumably some sort of secretary of Fray Pedro de Gante, Fray Diego may likely have owed his ordination (*c*1549) to his patron's special influence. The first full-blooded Indian admitted to the priesthood was probably don Pablo Caltzontzín, son of the last King of the Tarascos (*c*1570 — he died in 1576). Fray Francisco Tenorio, also an Indian, was adopted as a child by Spaniards who took him back to Spain, where, despite contrary regulations, he somehow became a Franciscan; later he returned to Mexico to work in Michoacán until he died. Juan de Tovar of the royal house of Texcoco was admitted to the Jesuit Order in 1573, and ordained a priest at the age of twenty-two. In Guatemala, probably because there was such a desperate shortage of imported white friars and so little hope of getting more, the Franciscans decided to accept natives as soon as they were separated from Mexico as an autonomous Province in 1567. But even they did not accept very many. A native in the Church was everywhere exceptional until into the seventeenth century.

INDIANS SUBJECT TO THE FRIARS

The lay Spaniards had crossed the ocean in order to better their lot — surely none gave up better in Spain for worse in New Spain — whereas the friars had crossed the same ocean in order to better the lot of the natives. Although the friars' means may sometimes have been similar to the laymen's, their aims were not: the laymen were there to turn the Indians into profit-producing workers, whereas the friars were there to turn them into Christians. Just as the Mendicants in Europe had been pro-peasant and anti-baron, so now in America they were pro-native and anti-colonist, clearly and consistently.

The friars' first and greatest task was to change the natives' religion, and this they accomplished with spectacular success. Once they had made converts, the chief task was to serve them as priests and teachers, and also to serve as political and economic administrators of the monastery towns, and to organize their community life so that it could operate within the new Spanish regime. In order to protect them, the friars tried not only to keep their Indians insulated in their own villages (which meant that they would remain Indian), but also to keep them productive there, for as long as they produced enough they were fairly safe from officials molestation no matter how Indian their nonreligious life might be. The friars repeatedly announced that they could run their new Christian communities very well as long as no Spaniards were allowed to live in them.

The mission towns were the materializations of a practical ideal of communal life which was in part an echo of both Spanish and Indian town organization. Paternalistically in charge of virtually everything, the friars administered the communal funds and the communal lands. (As under the Aztecs, there was little private property.) They dispensed justice, administered the schools, regulated trade and inheritances, and cared for widows, orphans, the sick and the poor. Minor authority was delegated to selected Indians equivalent to those who had been in authority before the Spaniards came. The economy was primarily agrarian: as well as their own small plots the Indians cultivated mission lands on a schedule worked out by the friars, who kept the tools and seed, distributed the produce, and sold the surplus. Many of the towns prospered, for the friars' administration was not only altruistic but also often efficient. They introduced European crops with success — wheat, fruits, olives, silk — and also European cattle, a great novelty to the Indians, who had not had domestic animals before. The friars also developed a few native novelties for the European trade, such as cochineal and indigo. (The churches and palaces of Europe display miles of brocades and damasks still splendidly carmine or purple from Mexican *coccus cacti* gathered by the Indians of monastery towns in the sixteenth and seventeenth centuries; many of the reds in European painting of the same time came from the same source.)

In organizing full-time routines for the natives' worship, work, and leisure, the brothers took over the leadership once exercised by the pagan priests. The Franciscans hoped that the Indians would be able to slip naturally into the regular round of work and ceremonial, despite the change in religion and in masters. The Augustinians soon devised an even more elaborate program of worship, community praying, singing, processions, and penance; it must have been fully as time-consuming as that of the old religion. The new regimens, however, did not wholly succeed in replacing or preserving the Indians' old way of life, and when their old patterns were destroyed, the Indians "began to lose the harmony and discipline and severe judgment which they formerly had." While they were becoming more Christian outwardly, they were often deteriorating inwardly. During the second half of the century, complaints increased about their laxness, lying, and drunkenness. Being subject to Spaniards was not the same as being subject to other Indians. (No one in the sixteenth century considered the possibility of their not being subject at all.) The deterioration was not the aftermath of neglect, for not only did the friars supervise their charges' main activities painstakingly, but they also gave more sympathetic attention than anyone else to the minor matters of their daily lives. Father Vázquez saw that "the ministers who have made the greatest harvest among the Indians are those who have been most human with them, mastering their customs (those which are not sinful) in order to win their souls." [28]

*

There can be no doubt that nearly all the friars came to love their Indians: sometimes they loved them because they could be saved, sometimes they loved them as fellow men, but more often they loved them as parents love children. They often referred to them as children, ordered them about and punished them, and like some parents, did not encourage them to grow up and become self-sufficient. "Like little birds in their nests, whose wings were not yet grown and never would grow big enough for them to fly alone, they would always need their attentive parents to tend and feed them in their nests. . . . The clergy are their fathers and mothers." [29] Father Grijalva thought that "as a father may whip his child, or a tutor his pupil, so may a friar, like a father, chastise his Indians; because of their limitations, they never withdraw from the power of their tutors." [30] The friars foresaw no native society where there would not always be missionaries in charge. Protected by the friars, and treated like children, the natives seem to have become weaker and more child-like, needing and depending on the benevolent protection the friars gave.

At the same time that they loved, bossed, and punished them, the friars generally recognized the Indians' particular accomplishments and abilities. As early as 1533 a group of Franciscans had written the Emperor: "How can anyone call them irrational or beasts? . . . How can they be held incapable, with such sumptuousness in their buildings, such subtle exquisiteness in their handiwork? and when they are such notable silversmiths and painters, and also such merchants and assessors of tribute? when they are skilled in administering and allocating labor? . . . when they have elective offices, punishment of crime and excess? . . . and finally when they are capable of accepting discipline in their ethical, political, and economic life?" No one but the friars knew them well enough to see all this, and no one but the friars cared enough to point it out.[31]

Although it was far from their intention, the lay Spaniards were driving the Indians into the friars' arms by treating them as badly as had their own preconquest lords, or worse. They had always been treated cruelly but, whereas the pagan Indians had sacrificed humans and eaten parts of them, this was only on compelling religious occasions, while the Christian lay Spaniards gave them to be eaten alive by dogs, dragged behind horses, burned, stoned, tortured by water or the rack — to get gold and women. If we can believe the evidence (which is copious), this was done again and again. Small wonder the natives turned to the kindly and sometimes valiant friars who protected them.

According to nearly all the friar-chroniclers, who knew them best but were probably the most partial, the Indians loved their friars. The genuineness of their affection can occasionally be corroborated from impartial sources such as the young English sailor who, after having been captured at the rout of John Hawkins' boats at San Juan de Ulúa in 1568, served a sentence as an indentured servant in Mexico for a few years. He said that the Indians truly did love the friars and knew that the friars protected them and had won them their freedom from slavery.[32] The Tarascos of Uruapan, coaxed by Fray Juan de San Miguel back from the hills where the butcheries of Nuño de Guzmán had driven them, made a life-size commemorative statue of their beloved Fray Juan — the first portrait sculpture in American art — and set it in a niche over the doorway of the chapel of the hospital he had built them. (When it was later walled up, the hospital was struck by lightning, killing thirty-three. The niche was opened immediately, and the hospital had no more such trouble.)[33] Father Mendieta may not have been exaggerating when he wrote: "No one who did not see it could believe or understand the devotion which the Indians paid Saint Francis and his friars from the beginning of their conversion."[34] They even revered the Franciscan habit, and when they could not have friars, because there were never enough, they begged to have a friar's old habit which they could raise up on a pole. Devout Indians dedicated children to the Saint and dressed them in little Franciscan robes. In the diary account of Father Ponce's travels through New Spain (1585–88), there are countless descriptions of how he was welcomed with enthusiasm by town after town, with flowery arbors, dances, sham-battles, plays, and an astonishing amount of trumpet music.

45

The Indians preferred their friars to the seculars, and they made trouble if the civil government tried to replace any of them with seculars. For example, the young Indians of Cuautitlán caught their friars stealing away to the capital by a back road after having been ordered to surrender their church to seculars and, as respectfully as they could, the youths carried the brothers back to Cuautitlán on their shoulders to reinstall them in the church. At Zinacantepec, when the Bishop tried to install a curate, the Indians drove him out and drove out each of his luckless successors until the Franciscans were reinstated (in 1563, which is probably when they began to build the trim monastery still there). At Tehuacán Viejo the Indians walled up their beloved Franciscan for three months in the monastery from which he was about to be transferred. He escaped, but they soon caught another Franciscan who was passing through on the highway from Oaxaca. When the mayor of Tepeaca approached with soldiers to remove him by Viceregal authority, the Tehuacanos kidnapped this already captive friar and hid him and themselves in the mountains. These were not wild Chichimecas but, quite the contrary, men "more docile and sincere" than the Indians of the Valley of Mexico. After three months the authorities caught up, but the natives swore they would prefer hanging to turning him in for a secular, and the authorities had to acquiesce. The town moved to its present site and the Indians promptly built a church for the Franciscans. They may have been particularly fond of their friars because they had been particularly abused by their encomenderos here.

The Indians sometimes became so attached to their friars that they would not let them be replaced by friars of another Order. When Dominicans were substituted for the Franciscans at Tlaquiltenango, the whole town put on mourning. When the Franciscan visita of Cuautinchán was transferred to the Dominicans — the Dominicans wanted a monastery in an Indian town to help support their handsome establishment in nearby Puebla — the natives struck, locked the little Franciscan establishment, and hid its keys and all its equipment for saying Mass. The Dominicans marched into an apparently deserted town — the Indians all stayed indoors — and, unable to rouse anyone, burned the door of the visita in desperation, entered, and took possession. The Indians refused to have anything to do with the Dominicans, to give them anything to eat or even water to drink. A native delegation walked to Puebla to try to settle the matter with the Bishop who, after pretending to be angry and throwing them all in jail, finally — confronted with their steadfast and touching partisanship — had to give in. The Franciscans returned in triumph, and began to build the handsome monastery and church still dominating flowery Cuautinchán. Similar jurisdictional strikes occurred in other towns, as at San Juan Teotihuacán where everyone stole away one night and stayed away a whole year until they got

46

their favorite Franciscans back. (They had so resented the Augustinians assigned to them that they scratched out the faces of all the Augustinian saints painted in the vestibule of the monastery.)

Although the surviving written evidence is almost all from the friars' side, it is copious and seems factual enough in the most reliable chroniclers, such as Fathers Motolinía, Torquemada, Remesal, or Mendieta, to show that the friars' relationship with the Indians was unlike that of any other group of Spaniards. It shows that they were the only group of Europeans who won the confidence and affection of the natives and not just their fear or grudging respect. Their stabilizing effect on the whole Spanish occupation of the New World can hardly be exaggerated. Sometimes friars were sent into troubled regions to calm the Indians who had repulsed conquest by arms: Dominicans were said to have turned the "Land of War" in Guatemala into the "Land of True Peace" (still called *La Verapaz*). The Emperor chose to have friars rather than military garrisons hold most of his frontier. As late as the end of the sixteenth century the Franciscan establishments along the border and along the roads to the mines at Zacatecas were considered as important as any military stations, in fact an effective and economical substitute for them.

II

THE GREAT CONVERSION

Once the country had been subdued by Spanish arms, a work was begun which was far more difficult than the Conquest: the transformation of the conquered into a new people who would receive gradually the Christian civilization brought by the conquerors.
— *Joaquín García Icazbalceta* [1]

THE belligerent religious nationalism kindled during the Reconquest of Spain fired both the military and religious conquests of New Spain. While the first goal of the Spaniards was conquest, which led naturally to colonization, the Crown insisted on conversion as equally essential. There was, therefore, an unending dilemma, for conversion could never be fully reconciled with colonization: the tension between Christian humanitarianism and economic exploitation — that is the tension between the Church on the one hand and the Government and colonists on the other — could not be lessened without surrendering too much of what each side wanted. The Crown was committed to both sides. Whereas the Conquest represented the beginning of a tradition of imperialist colonization on a grand scale, the Conversion represented the end of a tradition of militant religious idealism (which was preserved through the sixteenth century by being slowly frozen into the reactionary forms of the Counter Reformation).

For this book, the Conversion is more important than the Conquest, for during the Great Conversion, as it may be called, the friars worked out not only their methods of proselytizing, but also their particular architectural ideas, ideas which they kept on using throughout the century. Although its last quarter was almost as productive of architecture, it was not as creative as the half century between 1525 and '75, and although it added a few stylistic novelties, it did not constitute in itself a separate stylistic phase.

EXTENT AND NATURE

To understand this architecture of the Great Conversion, it is necessary to know what it was built for: in other words, to know how the Conversion was carried out. Still surprising today are the speed, the numbers converted, the extent of the territory covered, and the ingenious means worked out by

48

the handful of inexperienced and unarmed friars. These achievements were recognized as astonishing at the time, even by lay Spaniards; some said that never before had so many been converted so quickly, not even by Saint Peter or Saint James.

The first friars, worthy contemporaries of Saint Ignatius, Saint Teresa, and Saint John of the Cross, must have been extraordinarily hard-working men, for the Conversion was brought about mainly by their labors and their labors alone. The larger conversions of earlier history were said often to have been led by a saint and aided by miracles and martyrdoms, but no generally accepted miracles were reported during the Mexican Conversion. (The apparition of the Virgin of Guadalupe came to be considered of major importance only during the next century.) No friars were martyred until 1541, after the most difficult years of the Conversion were over, and altogether only a very few friars were killed by the violence of the Indians, not nearly so many as were killed in the same years by the violence of the climate, diet, asperity of mountain trails, and by the violence of their own exertions.

SCOPE AND SPEED

Fray Pedro de Gante, the most important of the first three Franciscans, wrote his kinsman Charles V that for the first three years (1523–26) the natives had been "unreasonable and untamable," and unwilling to be shepherded to church. They had fled from all Spaniards "like animals" — even from the friars on the infrequent occasions when they ventured out among the natives during the first dangerous seasons. (It was only from 1526 onwards that the friars went out regularly to preach to crowds.)[2] Father Motolinía found that the Indians were "very apathetic and . . . showed little interest. After five years many of them became active, and built churches, so that now many Indians attend Mass every day" (1536). For a while, however, there were occasional "sacrifices and drunken rites, though not as a general rule" (1531). After the big pagan underground led by the Lord of Texcoco was discovered and stamped out, one might have agreed with the Indian annalist Chimalpahín that in the heart of the country success was already assured. Cortés believed that it was; by 1532 he could write the Emperor that success had really been won, and he wrote the same again three years later. Father Motolinía found that by 1540 the Christian Indians hardly remembered their pagan past and, though this may sound like blind wishfulness, he was one of the least blind and most observant of contemporary writers. By 1546 less accurate Doctor Cervantes de Salazar could blandly say that "the whole land is as Catholic as ours," and though surely exaggerated, that is still evidence of substantial success. He had seen more crowds at more Masses in more of central Mexico than Father Motolinía had ten years before.[3] But although the tide had turned and success *was* assured, there still lay a vast task ahead.

Fray Martín de Valencia claimed that each of the original Twelve had baptized over 100,000 natives, thus amassing a total of over 1,000,000 converts during their first five years. Bishop Zumárraga believed that they had reached 1,500,000 by 1531. The Franciscans optimistically claimed 4,000,000 more for their second five years, and a total of 6,000,000 by 1541, and 9,000,000 by 1543. Father Franco estimated 8,000,000. During Lent in 1536, 600,000 were said said to have been baptized in Tepeaca alone. On one memorable day, 15,000 Aztecs were baptized at Xochimilco, and the two friars who had been taking turns at it said that they would have gone on to baptize many more that same day had they still been able to muster the muscular force to lift their arms. (They must have been baptizing a dozen men a minute.) Fray Pedro de Gante, who boasted of often baptizing 8,000 or 10,000 in a day, claimed to have converted 6,000 men by one sermon, and to have made them all leave their concubines that morning, and then that same afternoon all get married. Not to be outdone by the Franciscans, the Augustinians claimed that two of their friars had evangelized the whole long coast of Michoacán in two years, christening millions, and building 500 churches.[4]

These amazing figures must be viewed with chilling suspicion, but even cut to conservative probabilities, they are still informative and impressive. Recent studies on the whole accept the estimates of men such as Motolinía and his friend Bishop Zumárraga for, though long held preposterous by scholars who said that the friars claimed to have converted more Indians than there were in the whole country, their figures do withstand modern systematic scrutiny. A few Indian texts not written by friars — who might exaggerate — seem to corroborate them.

By the 1550's, most of the Indians in the towns in the heart of New Spain must have lived all or most of their adult life as Christians, sometimes perhaps of a peculiar kind, but still Christians. The most vigorous men — all but those over 45 or 50 — can have had but faint if any habits or memories of the old pagan worship for, while they were still children or infants, it had been well suppressed in the most important centers, though less in the villages and very little in the remote sierras, as the Church Council of 1555 sharply pointed out. By 1560 or '70 the same was true in the south, and all the regions which had had a high civilization when the Spaniards came were already predominantly Christian by habit. Although Charles V and Philip II saw more and more of their enemies and even some of their own European subjects desert the Catholic Church for heresies, Father Mendieta could comfortingly point out that Cortés (whom he erroneously believed born the same year as Luther) had gained as many souls for the Church as Luther had lost.[5] This was an understatement — rare for Mendieta — for the American converts far outnumbered the European apostates.

Before the plague of 1576, not only nearly all the civilized Indians but also many of the sedentary semi-barbarians had been converted, and conversion had become routine. There were pockets of obdurate heathens in the hills — even near places as central as Quecholac — but these were scattered, small, and ineffective. The campaign of conversion was still being carried forward importantly only along the frontiers and among unsettled mountain tribes where, partly to help settle them, missions of penetration were being systematically planted. By the 1580's Father Mendieta found all Indians under Spanish rule free from any traces of idolatry, another exaggeration but not an outrageous one.[6] (This is not to say that superstitions did not continue, for of course they did. However, an Indian could bury *amate* bark-paper dolls in his field to make the corn grow, and still be more a Christian than a votary of the Aztec cult.) The nomadic Chichimecas were not subdued until 1591, when they were virtually bought off, and they were brought into the Christian fold more slowly, more spottily, and less securely than had been the more civilized Indians of central and southern Mexico.

Nowhere else in the world has so widespread a conversion been accomplished with so little bloodshed. Had there ever been anything like it before in the history of Christendom? Perhaps only the mass conversions of the Teutonic tribes in the fifth and sixth centuries. Yet, while those entailed comparable historical consequences, the totals were lower, to be counted in the hundreds of thousands rather than in the millions. In character, the Conversion of Mexico was perhaps more like that of Ireland in the fifth century. There, as in Mexico, a monk-bishop, Saint Patrick, organized a whole country by monastic missions, a country which, like Mexico but unlike the rest of Europe, had never been subject to Roman civilization. While not forgetting that nearly all our evidence is from one side, we must acknowledge that, after the first few years, resistance to the friars was surprisingly weak. It was unorganized politically and lacked massive popular emotional support.

Conversion had come most easily where the lord of a town chose it, for the majority of Indians would follow their lord in almost anything. Even before the first Franciscans arrived, Charles V had suggested that the native nobles be converted first since that would speed the conversion of a people so obedient. The Lord of Izúcar had asked to be converted while the Conquest was still being fought; he was followed soon by the lords of Oaxtepec, Tláhuac, Toluca, Xochimilco, and many other towns. Caltzontzín, the monarch of Michoacán, journeyed twice to México-Tenochtitlán to submit himself voluntarily to the Spanish Emperor and Church, and to beg for friars to convert his subjects. (The momentum this gave the Conversion was arrested

5 1

when Nuño de Guzmán burned him alive to get his treasure — which turned out to be imaginary.) Non-Aztec towns which had recently been forced to submit to the Aztecs were found to submit to the Spaniards and the Spanish religion more easily than towns with no memory of recent subjugation.

DEPTH

Although we know how broad the Conversion was, we do not know how deep. Indians are so much more masked than most people that it is peculiarly difficult to know what they think or what they feel. Almost everyone agreed that they were converted easily and that they soon became devout in outward observances. Many Spaniards in daily association with Indians believed in their inner devoutness as well, and few shared the doubts of Father Sahagún and Father Durán about its genuineness. Almost all the friars of the first half century believed that they had been successful in making acceptable Christians out of infidels. Although most of these friars put quantity before quality (in their preserved writings), they wanted to believe in the validity of their work. It must have been hard to distinguish between belief and acquiescence based on expediency or obedience, and particularly hard in view of the Indians' extraordinary docility and uncommunicativeness. One of the reasons that the efficacy of the Conversion is sometimes doubted today, and called only a glaze over a resistant pagan core — a glaze reflecting the ideas of an observer outside without revealing the ideas inside the observed — is the very fact that it was accomplished on such a big scale in such a short time. The truth is that we do not know the truth, for we have no way of finding out what was believed then, or how it was believed in the depths of the Indian soul. (What would historians not give to have the lost account of the Conquest and Conversion written by doña María Barbola, an Indian lady of Ixtapalapa!)

While many wrote of the touching piety of the newly won natives, others were alarmed lest they slip into their old ways the minute they were not supervised by friars backed with punitive authority. It took as much work to keep them Christians as to make them Christians in the first place. When the Audiencia defined the punishments for idolatry in 1546, it was thinking not of the unconverted but of backsliders who might be Christian in public but pagan in private. Viceroy Velasco believed that the Indians were not yet securely enough grounded in Catholicism nor so forgetful of their old religion to be trusted without Spaniards ever present to keep them on the narrow path. Most religious would probably have agreed.

Many saw that the natives would accept the new religion more easily than they would abandon the old. Although heathen beliefs were hidden beneath outward conformity in some cases, the important fact is that after about only twenty years, any heathen feelings almost always *were* kept hidden. Idols were still worshipped and animals offered up in place of humans (harder to do in secret, though children occasionally were sacrificed), but every year it was done in a more minor and covert way. The remote and uncivilized mountain people held longest — and are said in remote regions still somewhat to hold — to their pagan customs. Outward conformity to Christianity was general: anything else exceptional. The persistence of minor pagan practices was often the result of habit, conservatism, or confusion, rather than persistence of any tenacious belief in the old religion.

Who can surely distinguish persistence of paganism from ignorance of orthodoxy? When natives of Cholula called a Madonna "Tonantzín," were they worshipping the Aztec mother-goddess with a new statue, or Mary with a new name? Was it faith, obedience, or expediency which made the Indians of the armies of penetration along the frontiers *always* remain loyal to their fellow-Christian Spaniards — whom they outnumbered 25 or even 100 to one — and *never* shift their allegiance to their fellow-Indian heathens? Whatever its reason, this is an impressive fact.

Since the discovery of America, Spanish theologians had questioned how Christian its natives must become to be acceptable to the Church, and had disagreed not only on this but on whether they even *could* become acceptable. The Dominicans, with their traditions of theological scholarship and their responsibilities as directors of the Inquisition, were most active in pursuing these problems. They led a particularly important debate at Salamanca: should the Indians, invincibly ignorant of the full meaning of Christianity, be accepted as Christians if they believed simply in the Christian God and followed Christian moral laws without more explicit knowledge of the tenets of the Christian Faith? or must they have "implicit" Faith, and learn as much dogma as their limited natural reason allowed? How far would "implicit" Faith need an explicit knowledge of Mysteries such as the Trinity or the Incarnation? Echoes of these polemics were heard in America, but the friars here were too busy converting to have time for scholastic refinements.

Sensing the limitations of their converts, the friars at first did not try to expound the more difficult concepts of Catholicism. The endless catechizing, as time-consuming as any of the friars' activities, was not designed to bring the heathens around intellectually or emotionally: it was simply to impress the fundamental tenets on neophytes by rote drilling. Emphasis was on basic beliefs and ethics. The first friars may have been more like the Early Christians than they knew, for they postponed and minimized many of the accretions which had grown around the original Christian core of beliefs. They brought the essence of the new religion to the new converts unencumbered by much of what might have made that essence more difficult to accept. This is the more surprising in view of the fact that the Conquest and Conversion took place in a time of militantly reactionary orthodoxy in Spain, so militantly reactionary that it might perhaps have been opposed to the Early Christians themselves. But the sternest qualities of this Spanish orthodoxy were surprisingly little felt in New Spain, despite directives from abroad, until Inquisitor-Archbishop Moya de Contreras' first big *auto de fe* (1574), and that *auto* was primarily concerned with captured English sailors and other unfortunates suspected of Lutheranism, heresies, blasphemies, or bigamy. If the simplifications and emphases of the early friars seem liberal now, they were indeed bold then. The return to first principles could have been Erasmian, for Erasmus was much read and admired by the Observants, and Bishop Zumárraga paraphrased Erasmus in his *Doctrina Breve* (1544) so extensively that Bishop Montúfar later suppressed it. Had Mexico been conquered half a century sooner, the Conversion might have been carried out in a yet more liberal manner, reflecting an age of greater toleration in pre-Habsburg Spain.

The most successful large-scale triumphs in the Conversion were with the civilized Indians of the nations of the fertile center and south. The nomadic Chichimecas of the north and northwest borders, with no developed religion of their own and no central government, were not won to Christianity so easily. Hostile and elusive as they were to Spanish civilians and soldiers during the century of Conversion, they rarely molested the friars, for they seemed to recognize that the friars were different from all the others.

PERSUASION OR PERSECUTION?

The Great Conversion was unlike any other in the history of Christianity not only because of its scale and speed but also because of the relatively gentle and bloodless way it was carried out. How different from the forced conversion and massacres of the more comfortable minorities of Spanish Jews, or Moslems of Granada! The unconverted Indians, outnumbering the Christian Spaniards many thousands to one, could hardly have been coerced in the same violent and provocative way. Persuasion, in the Mexican circumstances, was preferable to persecution. Mexican historians do not now agree in the interpretation of this evidence, for religious or nationalistic partisanship makes disinterested appraisal of anything directly connected with the Conquest or Conversion extraordinarily rare. (See for example the willful and doctrinaire prejudice in Diego Rivera's painted histories. In 1930 the Secretary of Education tried to have Quetzalcóatl substituted for Saint Nicholas and the Three Kings as the source of little Mexican boys' surprise gifts in the Christmas season.) Even after four centuries, the issues are still warm.

Flexible in many of their relations with the Indians, the friars were firm where conversion was concerned. Their firmness rarely hardened into persecution, except against the pagan priests and those leaders with big potential followings and therefore great political consequence. Even these influential men were not actually persecuted by the friars, but investigated, and then sometimes indicted — more often by seculars than by regulars — and passed on to the civil authorities for punishment. Other persecutions were inflicted not so much on those the Church wished to convert as on those it suspected of apostasy, such as the Zapotecas burned at Tehuantepec by the Bishop of Oaxaca, or the Mayas of Maní flogged and tortured by the civil arm on charges brought by Fray Diego de Landa (1562), who had been told of a cave of idolaters accidentally discovered by the porter of Izamal on a rabbit hunt. Such *autos de fe* were not activities of the friars but of the bishops. Though a friar when he made the *auto* at Maní, Landa was acting in place of the Bishop, who had not yet arrived in Yucatan. The extent of Landa's responsibility in this ugly event is not clear. Thanks to powerful and talkative enemies he was sent to Spain for trial, and condemned, but then he was exculpated of charges of abuse of power and abuse of the Indians. They gave him a great welcome when Philip II sent him back to Yucatan, not only exonerated but made Bishop in place of his enemy. Not Bishop Landa but the chief civil officer was punished for the *auto*. When Landa died in Mérida (1579) he was mourned, apparently, by all.

There is no reason to believe that the Indians associated the aggressive *autos* with the friars, or even that they were apprehensive of the Inquisition, which was put in charge of *autos* in 1571, for according to royal and ecclesiastical legislation the Indians as "new Christians" were not juridically subject to the Inquisition. Only one case in ten brought before it was against an Indian.

Had any been attempted, there would have been nobody to enforce a big campaign of compulsory conversion. While the Aztecs had had compulsory military service, the Spaniards did not. There was no standing army; the few soldiers were mostly irregulars engaged in conquest and border warfare far from the civilized centers where the first big conversions had taken place. There was no police force outside the few cities that had a large fraction of Spanish citizens. The encomenderos, who might be thought a substitute disciplinary force, were not much concerned with forcing Christianity on any natives, though they had been repeatedly enjoined to do so in their land and labor grants. In fact they hampered the Conversion more often than they helped. There was, then, no one to press conversion except a few unarmed and inexperienced but skillful and convinced friars.

Only after the Indians had been persuaded to become Christian and to belong to one of the brothers' Christian communities could pressure safely be used to make them behave with a modicum of conformity to what the friars considered seemly Christian ways. Bishop Zumárraga explained this clearly in a letter to the Council of the Indies (1536): "the natives need to be attracted to our Faith by kindness and love; then after they are members of the Church, some pious chastisement is often needed because of their natural temper, which is less neglectful of material than of spiritual matters; and they need a spur, since they do not often want to come to church unless they are compelled." [7] For the "pious chastisement" the monasteries had whips and sometimes stocks, but lashing was rejected as a punishment for those who had missed their Catechism lessons. A few monasteries had little jails, or something very like jails. Informed of these — inaccurately perhaps — by enemies of the friars, Philip II categorically prohibited monastery jails (1562) and forbade lashing; but again, *se obedece pero no se cumple.*

The Indians seem soon to have realized that the friars who preached to them did not torment them nor try to grind money or its equivalent in labor out of them — or at any rate not so much as the lay Spaniards. This may have predisposed them to listen more sympathetically to the friars' proselytizing talks. Father Sahagún reported that right from the beginning the Twelve explained the new religion in a "friendly and reasonable" manner to native nobles, many of whom voluntarily chose to be converted after such colloquies.

FAVORABLE CONDITIONS

The reason for the astonishing size and speed of the Conversion — whatever its depth — cannot be deduced without making use of opinions as well as facts, but as neither the fairness of the opinions nor the authenticity of some of the "facts" can be conceded, one must proceed warily with both, and state conclusions only in the subjunctive.

If persuasion was more usual and more effective than persecution, was persuasion made easier by particular circumstances which favored conversion? Study shows that the most effectively favorable conditions seem to have been a result: first, of some local political or social conditions; second, of the powerful backing given to conversion by the Spanish Throne and its representatives in Mexico; third, of the special character of those who were doing the converting; fourth, of the special character of those who were being converted; fifth, of some adventitious resemblances between the old and new religions; and sixth, in a quite different and negative way, of the nature of the old religion itself.

*

When the Spaniards destroyed the Aztec Empire, it was already in danger of destroying itself by its own tensions and lack of coherence. The state religion made the government dangerously top-heavy. (There were 5000 priests in the capital who served only Huitzilopochtli, "left-handed hummingbird," god of the sun and of war.) Moctezuma II had not been as strong a ruler as the trying times demanded. He had not been able to absorb or even subdue the big inland islands of Metztitlán or Tlaxcala, less than a day's journey from his capital; in fact only 15 years before Cortés landed, he had been beaten by the Tlaxcaltecas in a pitched battle. No more had he been able to conquer the Tarasca Kingdom of Michoacán to the west. His so-called Empire, grown from a few small islands in a swamp two centuries before, was not really so much an empire as an amorphous, ingenious, but unstable coalition, including more or less independent kingdoms or seigneuries, at Tacuba or Texcoco nearby, or at Huejotzingo, Cholula, or Tehuantepec, farther away. There can have been little sense of permanence or security felt by the widely scattered citizens of different racial and linguistic strains, living in worlds different both geographically and botanically. Many of his subjects had been defeated, and had to pay him heavy tribute. When Cortés and his Indian allies destroyed this overextended congeries, the endemic insecurity sometimes became panic. Since the old ways had failed, the Indians seem to have been inclined to accept the efficacy of the new ways which had destroyed the old, and since both the old and the new ways were inextricable from the religions which were part of them, the endemic insecurity and then the defeat of the old religion may have cleared the approach to the new.

Many Indians may have been impelled to accede quickly and frictionlessly to the Spaniards and their religion because they believed Cortés to be either one of their own gods or his awesome emissary. An all-but-incredible set of coincidences made Cortés, the time and manner of his arriving, and even his beard, his monotheism, and opposition to human sacrifice all fit into the conditions expected at the return of the once-banished benevolent god, Quetzalcóatl. Moctezuma, who had been warned by the oracular King of Texcoco that a divine invasion was immanent and had had this confirmed by the appearance of a comet, probably believed something of this kind until the end of his life. The possibility that such beliefs were widespread and affected native policy cannot be dismissed. They may have made Moctezuma submit to Cortés (why else?); they may have made many important Indians accept Cortés' religion. Strong when Cortés first appeared, these fantasies may have been effective for quite a few years.

9 MOCTEZUMA OBSERVES AN OMINOUS COMET FROM THE *AZOTEA* OF HIS PALACE.
(*Durán*, Atlas, c1580)

THE GREAT CONVERSION

The Spanish Crown gave powerful backing to the Conversion. Charles V was a sincerely religious monarch, and to bring his multitudinous new subjects into the Church was for him a genuine and urgent concern. He rejoiced that Cortés had found the Indians of New Spain more intelligent than those of the Antilles, because they could therefore become better Christians. His solicitude may have been intensified by the new threats and the actual losses of other subjects to the heresies of Luther. Philip was even more anxious to preserve and extend the uncontaminated Catholic Faith, and if either monarch should momentarily forget his religious duties to the New World, there were plenty of determined Counter-Reformation churchmen at hand to remind him; and also, plenty of worldly laymen were aware of the correlative political and economic advantages of tying the natives to the Spanish Church.

The Mendicants had, thus, not only the most powerful backing in Spain, but in the early critical years they had equally powerful backing in New Spain. Cortés' religious sincerity must be accepted as a historical fact, like his personal courage, his military cunning, and his obsessive maneuverings for power. He heard Mass every morning, and traveled with a Book of Hours. Father Motolinía and others who saw him often observed his occasional cruelty, his pride, love of money, and irregular marital habits — all common sixteenth-century traits — and yet they attested over and over again to his true devoutness. On his banner was Constantine's legend: AMICI SEQUAMUR CRUCEM, SI ENIM FIDEM HABUERIMUS, IN HOC SIGNO VINCE–MUS (Friends, let us follow the Cross, and if we have faith, under this sign we shall conquer). He had been instructed that his "principal motive is and must be to spread the Holy Catholic Faith," and he took this charge more to heart than any other conquistador or civil official. During the Conquest, according to accurate uninventive Bernal Díaz, he often exhorted the natives about Christianity through an interpreter, using some sort of set speech for the purpose. The two priests with him acted only as chaplains, and did not try to effect any change in the religion of the Indians, as he did; on occasion, Father Olmedo had to restrain him. Cortés' religious impetuosity — often inopportune — was apparently his only irrational and impractical public trait. From the beginning he made Conversion a corollary of Conquest, and during the years of his power tried to make that conjunction clear to the other Spaniards. The fact that the friars could carry their campaign so steadily forward, even in the trying years between his fall and the arrival of the Second Audiencia, was in large part thanks to the early support of Cortés as well as to the backing of the Crown. Under the first two viceroys, Mendoza and Velasco, his policy of support for the friars was vigorously continued.[8]

*

Favorable also was the extraordinary character of the first friars. Not only could they woo and win an astonishing number of Indians with astonishing speed, they could also fight back against uncooperative Spaniards. For example, they excommunicated those members of the First Audiencia who in 1530 had kidnapped two Indians who had sought asylum in the main Franciscan monastery. No group picked at random could have accomplished half of what was done by the carefully chosen first generation of zealous and resolute friars. While the subsequent generations — those active after 1550 — were not as idealistically devoted to the betterment of the Indians, their efforts did not damage the effect made by their predecessors, but added to it.

Unlike the conquistadores, the friars had never fought any Indians, and during the Conversion the Indians do not seem to have associated the friars closely with the soldiers who had beaten them nor with the encomenderos who were mistreating them. The compassionate friars did not form a liason group between the Indians and their Spanish masters: they joined the despised Indian group and became its advocates. This rejection and division, which had been forced to a traumatic crisis by the First Audiencia and the rapacious encomenderos, persisted throughout the century, and affected not only the social and economic life of the century, but also the forms of its architecture.

*

The rush for baptism may have been a protective reaction to the brutalities and extortion to which the natives were so quickly subjected. Something in their past may also have made the way to conversion shorter. The masses of Indians were so used to being roughly bossed by their native lords that they automatically obeyed their authoritarian new masters, including the friars. If one were to suppose that they had not been very badly treated because they never revolted from their old lords, one should remember that hundreds of thousands of them were revolting when they sided with Cortés against Moctezuma and the Aztecs. Hatred of the Aztecs was perhaps the strongest of Cortés' weapons, and the Conquest ought probably to be seen in large part as a revolution. The Indian population had never constituted anything like a unified nation — their dozens of different languages show how fragmented and dispersed they were — and although most were subject to the Aztecs they did not rally to their support after Tenochtitlán had fallen. If anything could have united them, one would have thought it would have been a common enemy. Instead they united with one branch of the enemy: the Church.

*

The nature of the Indians was another vital determinant of the Conversion. Over and over early writers remarked their "docility" or "submissiveness." Father Torquemada found: "It is certain that God did not create nor are there on earth people who are poorer or more content with their poverty than the Indians, or freer from greed." He saw them as "peaceful and mild,"

59

and rich in the monkish virtues of humility, obedience, and patience, incredible patience. Father Ojea found them less virtuous *and* less vicious than Spaniards, and "merciful, charitable, religious, and very much inclined to the holy cult." [9] Others repeatedly noted how in their natural uncorrupted state they were free of the specially Spanish sins of greed and pride, and found, therefore, that because of their meekness, obedience, and disintrest in the things of this world they were particularly suited to become good Christians, perhaps even better Christians than the Spaniards.

Fray Pedro de Gante, who had arrived before much change had been forced on the natives, made observations which are perhaps unbiased (he was well educated and not a Spaniard) and are surely drawn from his own fresh experience. He wrote his brother Franciscans in Flanders (1529) that the natives had the weakness of being abject or servile "because they do nothing unless forced, and nothing for love or good will." Father Mendieta, though long their fiery defender, considered that "when subject to the Spaniards . . . they stay like boys nine or ten years old, needing to be ruled by tutors . . . it is plain that a Spanish or mestizo boy under ten can take what he wants from any Indian, however big. . . . The Indians are usually weak and lazy, and their nature is timid and pusillanimous." [10] There are so many more notices of their submissiveness, gentleness, and patience (which persist today) than of their wildness when aroused (which also persists) that one understands why persuasion was more effective than coercion, as well as easier and safer.

After the cruel casualties they suffered in the Conquest, the natives began to lose heart. The Spaniards had been aided in the Conquest by a terrifying ally, smallpox, which killed so many Indians in 1520–21 that there were not enough left to raise enough food, and the pestilence then brought in another ally, famine. The Conversion, too, may have been aided by these unprecedented, incomprehensible, Apocalyptic disasters, compounded by the disheartening effects of defeat. The second gruesome epidemic, in 1531, may have been a sort of *coup de grâce*.

THE OLD RELIGION AND THE NEW

Both the Indians and the Spaniards were preoccupied with religion — seldom have two more truculently religious peoples been joined — and this coincidence was another asset to the Conversion. The Indians were already accustomed to a cult which exacted daily observances and provided a repetitive pattern of time-consuming ritual. Catholicism did the same, and thus, on the level of social habit, the shock in the shift from one religion to another was reduced in much the same way that the shock in the shift from one empire to another had been reduced.

The importance of similarities between some preconquest religious beliefs and activities and some in Christianity must not be overestimated as an element in facilitating conversion. The friars played such similarities down more often than up, from fear they might confuse the Indians or, worse, make it possible for them to accept the outer forms of the new religion while concealing inner allegiances to the old. None of the similarities was more than superficial, vague, or coincidental: stories of a flood and a sort of Eve, presentation of newborn in the temple for baptism with water, a form of confession and penance, belief in life after death, acceptance of a hierarchy of priests and monasteries. Writers who knew the baptism and confession in the old cult did not connect them with Christian baptism or confession unless, occasionally, to say that the old ways were the work of clever devils, an evil travesty of Christian ways liable to mislead the Indians. Nevertheless, though not exploited by the friars, the similarities must have facilitated acceptance if not understanding of the Christian ideas of after-life, damnation, heaven, and penance, despite the dangers of confusion and heresy which might follow.

10 INDIANS DANCING TO THE RHYTHMS OF THE *TEPONAXTLE* AND *HUEHUETL* (*Durán*, Atlas, c1580)

61

THE GREAT CONVERSION

It was only in safely secondary matters that the friars would allow no great break with past customs: in dancing, parading, wearing costumes, making offerings of flowers, or decorating shrines. Here what was done could be similar to the old ways with propriety so long as it was made clear that the reason for doing it had changed. General jubilations, if without symbolic meaning, were not held dangerous even when they continued familiar pre-conquest customs. The friars felt they must change a few Indian habits which had nothing to do with religion, however. They made men wear more clothes — the Emperor devoted a whole letter to the need for wearing trousers — and they stopped Indian officials from wearing extravagant ear- and lip-plugs.

A dangerous relation might be found when the Indians became markedly receptive to those ritual elements and usages which were closest in character to the magic in their old religion. They showed a predisposition for images, for being blessed, for reciting prayers and parts of the Catechism as though they were incantations; they showed an alarming avidity for Holy Water, taking it from the churches by the jugful, and giving it to their babies like medicine. Certain kinds of painful physical penance in the new religion could come too close to customs in the old: Indians who had lashed themselves with knouts for Tezcatlipoca could continue to lash themselves during Lent, but who could be sure for what god they were lashing? Penitential blood-letting continues in Mexico to this day with an intensity found in no country without Mexico's long pagan background of self-torture. Pilgrims to Chalma, San Juan de los Lagos, or Atotonilco still often walk with heavy spiny crosses on their bare backs, or with pads of spiny cactus strapped to their bodies; for the big December festivals Indians still go all the way from the heart of Mexico City to the Shrine of the Virgin of Guadalupe on their bleeding knees.

Many of the Indian social and civic usages had been incorporated into the new regime, and many elements, close to religion yet not in themselves religious, could survive the shift unchanged. Indian ethics, for example, were stern and surprisingly close to Christian ethics, and the shift from one to the other cannot have been upsetting. (The later ethical breakdown came from other causes.) The sense of relying on a priesthood for the organization of community life and providing a routine of ceremonial in it could continue, too, although the priests and the ceremonial were different. The friars replaced — which was not the same as continuing — some of the heathen festivals with Christian ones, much as earlier priests had replaced the pagan festivals of fourth- and fifth-century Rome or Near Eastern cities with coincident Christian ones. Except in religion, the friars let the Indians remain Indian, and did not try to turn them into second-class Spaniards. The friars were deliberate in this policy, and did not try to make any but the leaders of the Indians learn to speak Spanish, though they did urge hispanified garments on the rank and file. Perhaps the change of religions was easier for the Indians because it involved so little change in anything except the fundamentals of religion. Once the Conquest was over, the routine of day-to-day life was not violently disrupted. Except for the terrible new slavery in the mines, work was much the same, though there was increasingly more of it; so also was the tribute, changed more in quantity than in kind. Life was worse, but perhaps not fundamentally different.

DEVALUATION AND RESISTANCE

Conversion to Christianity demanded vitiation of the old religion. In the beginning many of the Indians, from Moctezuma downward, were willing to accept the new God, but not to renounce their old gods for exclusive devotion to Him. Soon, however, the old gods became generally discredited, and the sons of important pagan priests did not hesitate to testify against their fathers' pagan activities. In every important way the old religion was stopped, and the traces of it which have cropped up on the edges of civilized parts of Mexico since about 1575 are exceptional, peripheral, and curtailed; their importance has been very much exaggerated, though they have some folkloristic and anthropological interest. They seem to be at least as much the result of inertia as of persisting conviction. Far more surprising than the stunted and corrupt bits which survive is the unarguable fact that the enormous and elaborate religious structure of the Indians was so quickly, easily, and effectively toppled. The friars were passionately committed to its annihilation, and in this, as in little else, they were wholeheartedly seconded by the Spanish civilians.

One reason for its devaluation may have been that it had been defeated. Indian warriors must have resented the impotence of gods who had been unable to save them from conquest by white strangers. The brave Chamulas of Chiapas, for example, were dismayed at the gods who did nothing to avenge themselves when their idols were destroyed and temples defiled. When natives everywhere saw that sun, rain, and crops were not lessened when sacrifices were stopped, they may well have lessened or stopped their old allegiances.

Whether or not the friars boosted their figures of temples and idols destroyed, old texts show beyond question that the native cult and its physical apparatus were soon destroyed, largely by the Indians themselves. Once Tenochtitlán had been wrecked, they did not seem to care very much about fighting for its crippled religion. Although they felt a need for religion, they do not seem to have felt that it had to be their own. There is no evidence of mass resistence to the Conversion anything like as determined as that offered to the Conquest. With a few exceptions — such as Moctezuma and Cuauhté-moc — the Indians do not seem to have clung tenaciously to their gods the way believers have done elsewhere, and little is heard of martyrs, perhaps because the friars' methods of conversion did not lead easily to martyrdom. (Executions by the Inquisition and events like the *auto* of Maní were rare.) Many chose to abandon the old and take up the new faith by their own more-or-less free will, a choice often affected no doubt by seeing on which side their bread was buttered. Shiftings known to have been made for other reasons show religious feelings to have been secondary: for example, the Xiu lords of Maní, living handsomely on the fruits of slavery, began to object to the Christianity of the Franciscans who had converted them only when the Franciscans began to preach against slavery.

✷

In addition, there seems to have been something negative, unsatisfying, or even burdensome in the essential nature of the old religion which contributed to its devaluation. Fray Pedro de Gante, after seeing the first six critical years of the Conversion, wrote that "all their sacrifices, which were to kill their own children or to mutilate them, they did from fear and not from love of their gods." Fear seems to have been widespread and strong. Father Acosta surmised that "the Indians were so wearied with the heavy and unsupportable yoke of Sathan's lawes, his sacrifices and ceremonies . . . that they consulted among themselves to seek out a new law and another God to serve. And therefore, the law of Christ seemed [good] unto them" (1589).[11]

This could be wishful thinking after the fact, but there is contemporary and near-contemporary evidence to validate it. Father Mendieta reported that the old Indians of Tula had accepted the preaching of the first Franciscans there "because the law of God and His divine words were preached and propounded publicly to everyone . . . which had not been done by the priests of their idols, who never gave any reason to the people for the acts of their religion, and had wanted everything to be concealed except what they chose to say and order for the rites and worship of devils, and for their own benefit . . . and they begrimed their faces and put on ugly masks for their diabolical rites, and they used infernal songs and music and other frightening tricks." Father Acosta also reported that a friar had asked "of an auntient Indian, a man of qualitie" how it had come about that the Indians had rejected their own and accepted the Christian religion with so little question, and had been answered: "Beleeve not, Father, that we have embraced the Law of Christ so rashly as they say, for I will tell you that we were already weary and discontented with such things as the idolls commaunded us, and were determined to leave it and take another Law. But whenas we found that the religion that you preached had no crueties in it, and that it was fit for us, and both just and good, we understood and beleeved that it was the true Law, and so we received it willingly." The mass of Indians, who had pitifully little to lose, accepted it most easily though often apathetically. The chiefs, who would lose most of their power and most of their wives, accepted it less readily. What real resistance there was came mainly from the pagan priests, who would lose everything.[12]

THE NATURE OF THE OLD RELIGION

Although there is no valid way of measuring its effect, the peculiar nature of the native religions was probably one of the chief impulsions to the natives' susceptibility to conversion. More is known about the Aztec than any of the other religions, and presumably they were like enough for it to stand here for all.

The religion of the Aztecs was a military theocracy. It regulated something of almost all the activities of Aztec life, public and private, with greater demands on a citizen's time than the heavy ritual worship of Egypt or China. Perhaps the pomp and unending ritual were important in establishing its hold, for these are usually more seductive to the "primitive" mind than a spiritual creed or ethical code. Ordinary people cannot have understood the basic tenets and structure of the religion, for most of these were dizzily complex if not contradictory: they were known only to the priestly-noble hierarchy. Like the ancient Romans, the Aztecs had welcomed the gods of whomever they had conquered into their roomy pantheon (after the new idols had been kept on probation in a sacred house of detention). By the time the Spaniards came, the idea of deity had been fragmented into some 13 principal gods and between 200 and 2000 capricious demigods of natural forces, with unaccountable jurisdictions. Without his religion the individual Indian could do very little for himself. He had to sacrifice regularly to make the rain fall and corn grow, and again and again to insure other benefits from the seasonal functionings of nature. To make his corn grow, *when* he placated the gods was more important than how or when he planted the corn. The behavior of the gods could be affected by powerful magic. Taught that the world had already come to an end three times, the Aztec was filled with anxiety to be sure he made the proper propitiations at the proper time lest it fail once more. This seems to have reached a stage of mass hysteria after several years of famine and two rare, disastrous, and frightening snowstorms in the middle of the fifteenth century. This obsession with keeping natural forces to a regularly recurrent timetable led to extraordinary accuracy in the measurement of time. (It was a retrogression when the Julian calendar was substituted for the more accurate Mexican *tonalámatl* in 1521, not remedied until 1583, when the Gregorian was adopted.) The Indian priests were so obsessed with the passing and measurement of time that they made longer and fuller chronicles — painstakingly stuffed with dates — than any culture except the Chinese. When the priestly hierarchy was broken up, and novices could not be given the full and incredibly complex indoctrination — too time-consuming

65

to be done in secret — there was no one to keep up the essential schedules of ritual, and without them the religion could not be kept going.

The failure of the solar system could not be prevented unless the major gods (who were themselves the solar system, among other things) were kept from destroying the world and themselves by being fed fresh human blood. None of the gods demanded love or good behavior — just blood. Thus, for their continued existence, they were as dependent on man as he was on them. Self-torture to obtain blood and constant wars to take live captives who could be bloodily sacrificed were never-ending necessities. Tens of thousands of men were said to have been sacrificed on great feasts (no more than on the Eve of Saint Bartholomew, but it happened oftener; the numbers killed — 20,000 to 50,000 year after year — were not surpassed until Hitler).

Objection to blood came only from the Spaniards, and they objected to the ritual cannibalism far more than to the sacrificial slaughter. (After all, during the Conquest, when they ran short of grease, they would kill and render a fat Indian.) Some non-Aztec religions had been less bloody, but the Aztec cult with its insistence on many victims had been superposed on these with little difficulty. When the vassals of the Aztec Empire broke into revolt on the side of Cortés, it was not from any objection to the bloodthirstiness of the religion imposed by the Aztecs, but as much from the burden of tributes demanded in chocolate, cloth, and feathers as from the burden of supplying victims for sacrifice.

No matter how many sacrifices were offered them, the gods never guaranteed security; but the functioning of natural forces could be kept going only by keeping them fed: there was no idea of gaining security or merit by pleasing them. Although the Aztecs were energetic in their everyday life, at bottom they were pessimistic and defeatist, for part of the central myth of their religion was that the world was doomed to destruction by earthquake and that the sun, lord of everything, would vanish. All sorts of other disasters were threatened, and there was little hope for any pleasant future for the ordinary man. The best part of the Aztec heaven was reserved for those who had met a violent death: for warriors killed in combat or in sacrificial rites (they became hummingbirds), and for women who had died in childbirth. If not so fortunate as to have come to one of these painful but exalted ends, the ordinary Aztec could not hope to reach any of the better paradises, but only the nether world of Mictlantecuhtli, where he would either go on leading a dronelike afterlife much like the life he had just left, or else he would simply disappear into black nothingness. Ethical and moral values were a part of social custom, not of religion. The equivalents of Heaven and Hell were not a reward or punishment: one went to one or to the other not as a result of how one had lived but of how one had died. One could hope for nothing from the only benevolent Mexican god, Quetzalcóatl (who had sought to stay the sacrificial blood-bath by offering up snakes and butterflies, but had also invented such personal penances as pulling a string of thorns through the ear-lobes or tongue), for Quetzalcóatl had been expelled by evil Tezcatlipoca.

We know the outward conduct and the mythology of the native cults, but cannot sense their spiritual core. We know the rites, code of behavior, and murky theogony, but not the doctrine. Did they have one? Or was the religion, based on a pessimistic view of a doomed world, just magic machinery for temporary survival, for temporary propitiation of maleficent gods? It was a religion haunted by insecurity, small comfort to men living in an insecure "empire" threatened with collapse. Recognizing and fearing harmful natural forces, it tried to repel them and attract benevolent forces. The whole religion was based on struggle: everything good was threatened by an equivalent bad: even the stars were seen as battling armies, the stars of the east arrayed against the stars of the west. The sun had to battle and best his aunt and uncles, the moon and stars, every morning before he was borne on a litter (by warriors killed in battle and after midday by women killed in childbirth) to reach the place of his daily death at sunset. Evil in a world created by gods — something difficult to justify in many religions — was explained by the existence of many powerful evil gods who struggled with the good. There was duality and struggle in everything and they were almost always accompanied by slaughter.

One can sense something of the death-haunted spirit of the Aztec religion from its cruel (but magnificent!) sculpture, concerned not with physical suffering for spiritual triumph like so much Spanish Christian art, but with brutal menace and propitiation. Closer to Leviticus than to the Beatitudes, and insistent on a strict code of social behavior without rewards, the religion was nevertheless at bottom primitive. Like most such religions, as Bergson long ago pointed out, it was essentially a political agency for preserving the community, not involved with personal destiny and individual salvation. Hope and the idea of rewards for good conduct and good works must have appeared as attractive novelties proffered by the friars.

If there were elements in the crucler aspects of the old religion which satisfied something masochistic deep in the native psyche — as may be supposed but not proved — the new religion had something to offer even for that: the fear of Hell, the flagellant processions of some of the religious brotherhoods, the bloody penances, and the self-inflicted "disciplines" worn under the clothes, of hair-shirts or little pieces of hooked mail which dug into the flesh. In the nineteenth century the Chamulas in Chiapas still crucified a young Indian every Easter. Within memory, women of Tzintzuntzan spent Holy Week fasting while they sat in the cloister with crowns of sharp thorns on their heads and scourged themselves with nettles. May these not be Christian substitutions for something similar in the old religion?

67

THE GREAT CONVERSION

Of all the peoples of Europe in the 1520's and '30's, the Spaniards were by temperament probably the least unlike the Aztecs: remember the cruelties in the Spanish religion, the severe ethics, the strictness with children, the pride, and the reliance on elaborate ritual. What other European people was so obsessively aware of death, and with such intense fatalism? What other Christians, then, could more understandingly convert these heathens to their own faith?

MEANS AND PROCEDURES

The first friars were allowed exceptional latitude in working out the means which would be effective for converting hordes of Indians, thanks to a series of dispensations granted by a succession of popes and confirmed by a succession of kings. For their previous missionary expeditions, the Franciscans had already accumulated a number of papal privileges, and for their work in the Crusades and Reconquest, Spaniards had been granted extra privileges and indulgences: all these were automatically extended to the New World. When Cortés wrote Charles V asking for friars, the Emperor notified Leo X de' Medici who — characteristically — gave the matter no new thought but issued a Bull again awarding the Spanish Franciscans the rights and privileges they already had for foreign missions. In 1522 Hadrian VI gave them apostolic authority in whatever they might deem necessary for the conversion of Indians who lived more than two days' journey from the nearest bishop. (As there was not yet any bishop in New Spain, this included all the Indians there.) Hadrian's principal Bull, known as the *Omnimoda,* reconfirmed all the earlier privileges, and became the cornerstone of the whole structure of Mendicant privileges in New Spain.

In addition to converting, the friars (except the few lay brothers) were thus empowered to perform all of the usual functions of parish priests: saying Masses for their flocks, preaching to them, baptizing them, hearing their confessions, marrying them, and burying them. All monastery churches had also the status of parish churches, and the friars had the important right, usually reserved to bishops, of consecrating their own churches and altars.

Paul III Farnese not only reconfirmed these privileges in 1535, but went further and eliminated the restrictions on activities near bishops (of whom there were now four) in any case where the friars might find independent action necessary. This made clear what was to be the relation of the regular friars to the secular bishops for half a century: although the bishops had jurisdiction in theory, in fact it was feeble. Never had friars had such autonomous power; never had their power been so explicitly legislated; never had they had so many souls on whom to exercise it.

MEANS AND PROCEDURES

Backed as they were by privileges from popes and kings, the first friars still had to find effective immediate means to accomplish their enormous task. None had had any practical experience in missions, not even the Observants. Often improvising, they ingeniously adapted preaching and teaching to the temperament, aptitudes, and numbers of the Indians, without slipping beyond the borders of orthodoxy. Two special practices were critically important: learning to preach in native languages, and making use of specially taught native children.

Unlike the first friars sent to the Antilles, the three Flemings and the Twelve quickly saw the futility of expounding the Creed and other beginners' texts to Indians who could understand neither the Latin of the text nor the Spanish of the exegesis. Therefore they set out at once to learn Náhuatl, which was — and to some extent still is — the language of the peoples of the central part of the country. Náhuatl was also used elsewhere officially by those who used other tongues domestically, and it had even been proposed as the official language of Mexico because most of the natives understood it. Its more-than-local value could be seen, for example, when Franciscans who had learned Náhuatl found that they could convert the Matlatzinca-speaking tribes of the Valley of Toluca who also knew Náhuatl years before they could convert those who did not. (It was some time before any friars mastered jaw-cracking Matlatzinca.) Far from the most formidable of the Indian languages, Náhuatl is nonetheless thorny with astonishingly extended words, with glottal stops and other non-Spanish sounds, and with shifts of meaning resulting from shifts of accent. Notwithstanding, all but two of the first fifteen friars mastered it in a reasonable time. Some could converse after six months; others were able to teach and preach after two years. Yet so many found it so intractable that they felt the need of heavenly help, and accordingly named Saint Michael "Patron of Tongues," and offered him special prayers at Compline. (Neither the early bishops, Garcés, Zumárraga, Quiroga, nor the first leader of the Dominicans, Fray Domingo de Betanzos, were able to learn a native language, yet all were passionately active to defend and better the lot of the Indians.)

When asked by the newly arrived Twelve what he and his Flemish companions had been able to accomplish in their first year, Fray Juan de Tecto answered that they had mastered "a *theology* Saint Augustine never knew," and went on to explain that for Mexico, Náhuatl was as vital as much conventional theology. He may have remembered that Saint Augustine had declared language one of man's greatest works, and had said that it was easier for two animals of different species to live together than two men of different languages.[13]

Father Acosta recognized this when he wrote: "as the Lordes of Cuzco and Mexico conquered new landes, so they brought in their owne language, for although there was . . . great diversitie of tongues, yet the courtlie speech of Cuzco did . . . runne above a thousand leagues, and that of Mexico did not extend farre less, which hath not beene of small importance, but hath profited in making the preaching easie at such a time, when as the preachers had not the gift of many tongues . . . He that would knowe what a helpe it hath been for the conversion of the people in these two great Empyres, and the greate difficultie they have founde to reduce those Indians to Christ, which acknowledge no Soveraigne Lord, let him goe to Florida, Brazil . . . and other places where they have not prevailed so much by their preaching in fiftie years as they have done in Peru and Newe Spaine in lesse than five." [14]

After Náhuatl, the most widespread language was the difficult monosyllabic Otomí. In addition, about twenty major and well over a hundred minor languages and dialects were spoken in the regions being evangelized. Linguistically, New Spain was as varied as Europe. The six Franciscans who began the conversion of Yucatan stayed in Campeche for eight months, until all were able to preach in Maya. Erudite Fray Alonso de la Vera Cruz took advantage of the "fulness, culture, elegance, and energy" of the Tarasca spoken in Michoacán to write several treatises, including one on meteors which would have been difficult even in Spanish.[15] Others found Tarasca "clear and easy, in some ways like Latin." [16] Some dialects were so primitive that it was difficult to convey any ideas in them: they lent themselves only to the barest statements of fact. Progress was slowed where the native languages were the most difficult: Popoloca, for example, or the curious tongue spoken only in Ocuilan. Notwithstanding, by the middle of the century friars were somehow preaching in all of the important languages. They felt they must keep preaching and preaching and instructing in the Catechism without pause so that their new converts would not wander into unorthodoxy or blasphemy, dangers which the Council of Toledo had so forcefully exposed after experience with not-quite-converted Moslems.

An additional reason for mastering Indian speech was that the friars could then communicate without the natives' having to learn Spanish, which would not only have been discouragingly slow and difficult — it had been suggested by the King — but would also have led the natives into more contact with the lay Spaniards and their vices, which the friars anxiously wished to avoid. An additional and attractive impetus came when Pope Pius V gave a two-day indulgence for each sermon preached in a native tongue. Furthermore, one of the reasons the Indians liked the friars was because the friars did learn their speech, and one of the incidental reasons why they did not like the other Spaniards was because they did not. Even the parish priests were not compelled to learn until near the end of the century. The friars found that the Indians were impressed with their seemingly marvelous skill in learning Indian languages — marvelous because so few Indians could learn Spanish — and that therefore the Indians revered them more, a great help in converting. Father Mendieta's fluency was thought to be a supernatural gift.

So many friars became linguists that it had to be made explicit that those who did not — a few truly could not — were not thereby committing a sin. By 1580 Philip II could reasonably ask that henceforth no one be ordained who was not already multilingual. Mastery of languages made some forget Saint Francis' urging of brief sermons ("because the Lord, when on earth, spoke briefly"). Many became virtuosos: a friar at Coixtlahuaca used to preach for half an hour in Mixteco and then for half an hour in Chochona; others would deliver the same sermon successively in several languages — three, four, sometimes even six — in regions where the mixed Indians in the congregations knew only their own and not each others' tongues. (In the Sierra de Puebla and Chiapas, the divisions in the markets are still determined by what the Indians speak rather than by what they sell.) The University of Mexico set up chairs for Náhuatl and Otomí, and there was one of Tarasca at Valladolid (Morelia). Seminaries gave still more varied linguistic instruction. As late as the middle of the eighteenth century the native languages were regularly used in the country churches of some regions, although the seculars were no longer pressed to learn them. Outside the cities, sermons in Yucatan are today delivered in Maya because nothing else would be understood, and local speech still prevails in country pulpits in Michoacán, Oaxaca, Chiapas, and other scattered backwaters.

Friars who had not mastered languages sometimes adopted an ingenious device for teaching and preaching: "On one cloth they had the Articles of the Faith painted; on another, the Ten Commandments; and on another, the Seven Sacraments or whatever else of the Christian Doctrine was needed. When the priest wanted to preach on the Commandments, they hung that cloth near him. He could point out whatever part he wanted with a staff, and thus he could expound the whole Doctrine clearly." [17] Heaven would be depicted full of happy angels and saints and happy Indians who had led a correct Christian life, and on the same picture, Hell, with devils tormenting the unconverted and backsliding. "It is a most apt and beneficial thing for these people, because we have seen from experience that in those towns where the Doctrine has been taught by pictures, the Indians are well grounded in the essentials of our Catholic Faith, and understand them well." [18] Since they had no writing, but had developed an efficient means of communication by pictures, the Indians were prepared for pictures made expressly to convey ideas. (Unfortunately none of these teaching pictures has been preserved: the altar frontals in relief at Amecameca may give an idea of their character.) A

Ad sensus aptat coelestia dona magister,
Aridaq́ eloquij pectora fonte rigat.

11 PREACHING ON THE PASSION WITH PICTURES
(*Valadés, Rhetorica, 1579*)

series of pictures on a canvas ruled off into squares, which could be unrolled like a windowshade and hung on a pole, used to be displayed by singers at fairs in Spain, so that they could point to appropriate illustrations of episodes in their long narrative ballads. The religious pictures of similar format in Mexico may be adaptations of some such humble form of popular art.

Other visual aids were sometimes tried. For example, one friar, unable to master any native language, yet managed to preach with interpreters and dramatic spectacles. "To show what the infernal punishments would be, in the patio of a church in Jalisco he made a deep pit like a furnace with a wide-spreading mouth, and he had dogs, cats, and other animals thrown into it; and when a fire was lit they howled fearfully, and the Indians were terrified by the horrible spectacle, and thereafter avoided offending God." [19]

We may find these devices quaint, and smile at them as suitable for primitive and child-like people living in a remote place; the remoteness, however, is less than we may think. Similar spectacles had been common in quattrocento Florence; and in Rome, at this time the most civilized and sophisticated city in the Christian world, a big statue of the Madonna was levitated on a platform of artificial clouds during the celebrations in the Pantheon on Assumption Day — up, up, and out through the hole in the top of the dome. Ever since the fourteenth century, in Santa María at Elche in southeastern Spain, every year on Assumption Day four boys dressed as angels descend from the dome in a golden "pomegranate," and then ascend with a statue of the soul of the Virgin, up 150 feet to an artificial cloud suspended in the dome. The religious play of which this is a part is not in Spanish but, as in Mexico, it is all spoken in the local tongue. Such performances were banned by the Council of Trent, and most of them came to an end in Europe. These particular strictures of Trent seem to have had little effect in Mexico.

12 WOODCUT FROM THE *DOCTRINA* OF FRAY JUAN DE LA CRUZ, 1571

Friars administer Communion to Indians. The accompanying text is in Huaxteco with Spanish words for the religious terms Sancta Yglesia, domingo, *and* missa.

73

Knowledge of languages was requisite not alone for preaching but for everything the friars wanted to teach or tell the Indians that was not part of the Latin liturgy. The Catechism was translated into Náhuatl by Fray Pedro de Gante and Fray Juan de Tecto and by four of the Twelve, and other useful texts were soon prepared. To facilitate and expedite evangelization, a printing press was set up in Mexico City by 1539. The first book, a Catechism in Náhuatl and Spanish, was printed less than a century after the first book in Europe and more than a century before the first book in the British American colonies. The primary function of the press was to produce catechisms, missals, pietistic literature, dictionaries, and grammars, many of them in local languages never before fixed in print. (Books in Spanish could be imported from Spain.) The texts by Fray Pedro de Gante, Bishop Zumárraga, and Father Motolinía were so much in demand that they had to be reprinted in several new editions, and were so very much used that very few copies have survived. (Those that have are now among the most prized American incunabula.) Gothic letters were used until after the middle of the century. By 1580 over 100 texts had been printed in nine different languages.

The Provincial Council of 1565, called to discuss the latest decrees of the Council of Trent and fearful lest free translations lead to questionable religious ideas, forbade letting literate Indians have anything in their hands but specifically approved catechisms, such as that just issued at Trent but not yet translated. The Inquisition felt it had to suppress several doubtful translations, including even Archbishop Zumárraga's, which had borrowed ideas and whole paragraphs from Erasmus. Although Náhuatl is rich and can be eloquent, it presented peculiar difficulties in the strict translating of doctrinal texts. Cautious translators did not risk paraphrasing the specifically Christian terms for any important Christian tenet for fear of accidental unorthodoxy or heresy; instead they took over the Spanish or Latin words into otherwise Náhuatl sentences. As a supplemental aid to the printed books, some friars composed little grammars and word lists, which were copied by hand and circulated from monastery to monastery. Others wrote sermons in different tongues in order to lighten the work of later friars, and left copies in the main centers where each was spoken. So that their votaries might understand them, the stories of the lives of the patron saints of various towns were also put into the vernacular. Father Sahagún, for example, translated a life of Saint Bernardino into Náhuatl at the request of the Indians of Xochimilco. Some hundred books written by friars had been printed by 1570: more than half in Náhuatl, and the rest in Tarasca, Otomí, Mixteco, Huaxteco, Totonaco, Zapoteco, and even the rare and difficult Pirinda. The friars had to deform these unwritten languages in reducing them to European orthography, and also, presumably, in reducing them to a practical grammatical system grounded on Latin or Romance.

Following Catholic policy in Europe, the standard prayers were taught in Latin, even though the friars knew that the Indians could not understand the words. While the Protestants were translating everything into the local European languages, the Catholics held to prayers in Latin as a sign of orthodoxy.

CHILDREN — TAUGHT AND TEACHING

Even in poorer parishes where there are no boys who know how to read, at prime and vesper time other poor boys come to teach them how to say the Pater Noster and Ave Maria, and in this way they have learned not only the Psalms, but also antiphonal chants; and it is something to make one praise God to see them in the churches and oratories of the Stations of the Cross . . . and it fills us with admiration and devotion, for it seems that already throughout this land, omnis spiritus et omnia lingua laudat Dominum.

— *Father Motolinía* (c1537/41) [20]

While the first friars were still struggling with Náhuatl, a wonderful aid was found in children. King Ferdinand the Catholic had ordered that the young sons of the chiefs of the Indies should be given to the Franciscans for four years to learn the Catechism and to read and write Spanish. Transplanted to Mexico at the suggestion of Cortés, this system scored success. It cannot have seemed unnatural to the Indians since before the Conquest their own priests had conducted similar schools. At first some Aztec and Maya nobles were too mistrustful of the friars to surrender their own children — no people makes more of children than the Mexicans — and they would substitute the children of their servants. These lowborn but lucky boys, after having been educated by the friars, grew up into a sort of élite, and became the magistrates, mayors, governors, or other officers which the noble boys might have become. Some Indians were found to be brighter than Spanish boys of the same age, and it was regretted that they seemed to lose some of their ability as they grew up. Both Charles V and Paul III wanted to have a group of noble Indian children sent to Spain for their higher education, and then sent back to spread what they had learned in the Old World among their fellows in the New. This was not done, and only a few Indians were ever seen in Spain, such as the forty nobles who accompanied Cortés, or other nobles who came to the King with requests. A few mestizo sons of noble Indian heiresses also appeared in Spain. (In El Greco's *Burial of the Count of Orgaz,* painted in 1586, might the eighth noble from the left, above Saint Augustine's miter, be such a well-born young mestizo?)

The friars' schools thus not only put them in charge of the education of those who would soon be leaders, easier to convert and control than the actual mature leaders, but also put them in a uniquely advantageous position to get surreptitious education *from* these same children. Many adult Indians soon held the friars in such reverence that they would not speak in their presence or even raise their eyes. After at first despairing of finding anyone bold enough and willing to teach them Náhuatl, with or without the loss of face they would have suffered had they had to submit to the inferior position of becoming the pupils of Indians, the brothers began to take time to play games with their young charges, after which they would all write down the Indian words they had learned — in some Spanish phonetic equivalent — and then compare notes. The next day they would try out these words, and so, little by little, accumulate a vocabulary and a syntax to stick it together. (One wonders how such a children's vocabulary served to expound the principles of Christianity; it must, however, have been better than pictures.) Soon they found a small bilingual Spanish child, borrowed him from his pious widowed mother, and had him teach them. Little Alonso de Molina grew up to be a friar "with the best Mexican tongue among all the Spaniards in New Spain." He made the most important Náhuatl translation of the Catechism (printed in 1555 and again in '71). Eventually he became Guardian of the important monastery at Texcoco, a city where the purest Náhuatl of all was current.

By 1531, groups of 500 children were being taught at several monasteries. Fray Pedro de Gante claimed he had had 300 or 400 in 1532, and 1000 in his school by 1558. At first he locked in the sons of the most important Indian lords from 40 leagues around, so that they could not see their powerful but still possibly heathen parents and be exposed to infection from their unchristian ways. After a couple of decades his boys no longer had to be kept under guard. Although some put on airs and had to be restrained from wearing gloves and other fripperies, after four years in the school, most were considered indoctrinated enough to be safely returned to their families. The danger of infection was now the other way around, for the children were a great help in leading their powerful but cowed parents to orthodoxy, and also sometimes a great help through their informing on any relatives who might be planning secret celebrations of the forbidden rites. The same system worked equally well in Yucatan where there was another school of 1000 boys. It was claimed that there were schools for reading, writing, and singing in every town where there were friars.

Bishop Zumárraga, pleased with his ten schools of 300 or 400 boys and his Indian College of Santiago Tlatelolco, saw that while there was little hope for the older Indians, long and deep-rooted in their pagan ways, "among the young reared in the monasteries it now seems that the Christian Faith is shining" (1537). He soon asked to have a new Catechism printed in Náhuatl "because there are so many who can read." [21] (It was published in 1546.) Pairs of the brightest boys were trained to go out from Fray Pedro's school to preach the primary elements of Christianity in the market places of the lesser towns in the surrounding valley (as early as 1531). Tepotzotlán and "the great and beautiful city" of Cuautitlán were chosen first not only because they were near but also because among the noble child-preachers were two of the royal house of Moctezuma who, as the heirs apparent of these towns, were guaranteed respectful attention.

The Franciscan boys were so effective that they were recommended to the Dominicans planning their first campaigns. If a friar was not fluent in Náhuatl, he would outline a sermon in Spanish to a bright boy who, standing by his mentor's side, would then do the actual preaching. Recognizing that these teams were under the protection of the government, the Indians rarely molested them despite the verbal attacks they made on the listeners' religion and the material attacks on its images. The people were sometimes terrified of the preaching squads, and rightly so, for fifteen boys could and did break up drunken pagan rites involving two hundred or more grown men and bring the ringleaders back to the monasteries for punishment (whipping interspersed with lessons in Christian Doctrine). The schools were thus not only educational institutions but also effective centers of religious propaganda.[22] Some of Fray Pedro de Gante's children were allowed to recite Canonical Hours to groups which had made some advancement, and might even prepare them for the proper Masses to come by reciting Dry Masses.

SPECIAL PROBLEMS IN ADMINISTERING THE SACRAMENTS

> *In Spain we know it for a common thing that when priests have to preach a sermon they are so tired and in such a sweat that they have to change their clothes . . . And if after he had preached, a priest were told to sing a Mass or comfort a sick man or bury a dead one, he would think it the same as digging his own grave. But in this land it happened every day that one lone friar would count the people in the morning, then preach to them and sing Mass, and after that baptize both children and adults, confess the sick no matter how many, and then bury any dead there might be. And so it was for thirty or forty years, and in some places so it is still. There were some (and I knew them) who preached three sermons in different languages, one after the other, and then sang Mass, and did everything else that had to be done, all before having anything to eat.* — *Father Mendieta* (c1585) [23]

Obviously, to cope with the fantastically abnormal conditions which had come to seem normal in New Spain, friars would have to be allowed to curtail certain standard procedures. Without some official exemption their gi-

77

gantic undertaking could never have been accomplished. We must take it as a laconic understatement, for example, when told that Fray Marcos Palé, in order to carry out his "million" baptisms in Chiapas and Guatemala, had to be "careless in catechizing." [24]

Bishop Zumárraga called a meeting of the Orders in 1537 to discuss how so few could minister to so many, and to find some workable conformity for the administration of the Sacraments. Although the three Orders soon signed an accord, conformity was not achieved until the great urgency was past and there was time to tidy up details. Philip II interested himself in these details, particularly in the validity of marriages. Before their regimentation by the Council of Trent, practices had not been standardized even in Europe. After it, the Mexican Church had also come to want strict orderliness; its Second Council in 1565 tried again to coordinate the administration of the Sacraments and, by another generation, Mexican practices were nearly concordant with practices elsewhere in the Catholic world. There were always, however, some special regulations. For example, Indians were excused from keeping two out of three of the feast days of the Spaniards, ostensibly because of their poverty, but more probably to keep them working longer.

Some modifications were made for reasons other than time- and labor-saving. While the standard liturgies were unassailably suitable for Spaniards, who called themselves *gente de razón* (people of reason), some parts seemed unsuitable for Indians, who were not considered to possess sufficient "reason"; these parts might be simplified as long as they did not become schismatical or heretical. The status of American natives as rational human beings possessed of souls, first announced by a group of theologians in Salamanca in 1517, was reaffirmed in 1532 by a conclave of Mexican bishops, priors, and magistrates. Thanks to a moving and beautiful Latin letter sent by old Bishop Garcés of Puebla-Tlaxcala, it was definitely assured in 1537 by Paul III in *Sublimis Deus* and *Veritas Ipsa:* Indians were sons of Adam, human, and rational. (Despite his age and the number of his activities in Rome, Paul III gave more time and thought to American problems than any other sixteenth-century pontiff.) *Sublimis Deus* was emphatically endorsed by a conclave of Mexican bishops and provincials in 1546. Although the theologians at Salamanca had officially decided that those who held the Indians incapable of receiving the Faith were themselves guilty of heresy, the suitability of accepting them as practicing Catholics was still debated, even after the Bulls of Paul III had unequivocally declared them capable of receiving the Christian Faith with all Sacraments. Nevertheless, many Spaniards arrogantly used the term *cristiano* to mean a Spaniard as distinguished from an Indian.

*

There were many bothersome minor problems in working out the mechanics of a transplanted religious regime. Almost no wine was made in the

New World and, as pure grape wine is requisite for every Mass, every Ordination, and the consecration of every altar, considerable quantities had to be brought with every fleet. It was usually a gift from the King, as was oil. Candles too are requisite for Masses — as symbols of joy — and the Indians loved processions in which they could march with lighted candles. Church candles must be at least half pure beeswax, and there were not enough bees in Mexico to make enough wax. Soon, however, production was increased in Yucatan (which badly needed some profitable export), and wax was shipped to the capital. In 1574 special ordinances were issued to the candlemakers to assure a good standard product. When there were no candles and no wine, as must quite often have been the case, Dry Masses must have been said. By permission these had been substituted quite commonly in the later Middle Ages for the full Mass on pilgrimages, military campaigns, hunting trips, or on ships when the sea was rough. (Columbus had had Dry Masses said every morning on shipboard, and so probably did Cortés.) In the early days they must have been the regular thing in Mexico outside the big cities, and later must have continued commonly on the frontiers and at visitas. Lay brothers could say them, or so could any properly authorized persons (for example, Fray Pedro de Gante's boys).

BAPTISM

In a land peopled with converts, Baptism took on special importance. The first of the Sacraments instituted by Christ, Baptism was held essential for Salvation, and no other Sacrament could be given to converts until they were baptized and thus made "Children of God." After the Council of Trent it was made explicit that this also conferred Grace, and purged them of the stain of Original Sin. At first the Indians were not baptized with the usual European rites, which were for children, because all the converts were adults, and as such had to profess the Faith and know the Creed.

The Indians seem to have been particularly eager for Baptism: some genuinely wished to be saved; some allowed themselves to be baptized because they calculated it would help them get along better under their Spanish masters; some may have valued it as an equivalent to something similar in their old religion although, even after memories of any such rite would have evaporated, they were still enthusiastic for Baptism, particularly for their children. More children and fewer adults were baptized as the second half of the century progressed.

The punctilious Augustinians charged that the Franciscans often cut their baptisms so drastically that they were worthless and would have to be repeated. They criticized the simultaneous baptism of crowds with hyssop (though irreproachable Cardinal Cisneros' priests had thus mass-sprinkled the Moors); the Franciscans denied that they had ever done this. The Augustinians also objected to baptism without candles, which the Franciscans said they omitted only because in the open air the wind blew them out. Some questioned the propriety of baptism in water only, which the friars justified by analogy with Early Christian simple immersion and the rites used in the conversions of Germany and England, and also by the simplifications recently practised in the forcible baptisms of Moslems. The Franciscans maintained that water alone was acceptable if it had been properly exorcised and blessed, and provided also that each Indian had individually been exorcised and catechised, and that salt, saliva, book, and candle had been applied to a token two or three symbolically for the group. Inasmuch as a shortened baptism is held as valid as a long one, provided water is poured, it is not now clear just what objections were raised to what curtailment. The Pope made it explicit that the friars who had been curtailing the rites had not thereby committed mortal sin, as their critics in other Orders had harshly insisted, provided that the need at the time had been great. Nowhere in the Catholic World was it greater.

13 A FRIAR BAPTIZING AN INDIAN *who for the occasion has shed his new European shirt, but wears his new European trousers. In front is a stone font; in back, an ideograph of a church.*
(*after* Códice Azcatítlan, c1572)

The Franciscans said they applied oil and chrism whenever they could. Oils had to be imported, and ordinarily were still acceptable only for one year after having been blessed, but a sensible dispensation soon extended this to three in New Spain. Chrism, properly consecrated only by a Bishop, was made of olive oil and balsam from Jerusalem, and was hard to obtain in Europe and yet harder in America. The Mexican bishops asked the Emperor and the Emperor asked the Pope for authorization to use local balsam — it had been allowed as an emergency measure — and finally after naturalists had assured him that it was safely similar, the Pope, Paul III, permitted fragrant balsam from Peru and Brazil. (American balsam is now commonly used in Europe.) Oil and chrism were kept in special metal containers which could be put into a "pretty painted wooden box" for traveling, along with vestments, and everything else needed for administering Baptism. Each monastery was equipped with such a kit, and it could be taken out to visitas, or to the houses of the sick or dying.

Giving different individual names to each child or adult at the huge mass baptisms could be complicated and time-consuming: consequently the understaffed Franciscans sometimes gave all the males baptized on one day the same name, say Juan, and all the females another, say María, and the next time all another name, Pedro or Ana, and so on. Lest he forget it, each neophyte was given a little seal with his new name on it.

Baptism made the Indians very happy. They would trim the font with garlands, and trim themselves with bright crowns of flowers and new white clothes, as the Early Christians had done, and have many musicians for joyous accompaniment to the ceremony. Their enthusiasm did not make matters any easier for the friars, for some liked being baptized so well that they would come back to have it done again, saying that they had not quite understood everything properly the first time. Charles V had to make a special rule against such repetition, pointing out that it was a grave sin.

Perhaps the importance of this rite in a vast conversion and the Indians' enthusiasm for it account for the extraordinary size and richness of the sixteenth-century fonts still preserved in Mexican churches. Big blocks of hard stone were carved with symbolic emblems and floral decorations in great variety (as at Acatzingo, Jalatcingo, or at Chimalhuacán Chalco, inscribed with the name of the reigning pontiff, Paul III). Occasionally they were of elaborately modeled terra cotta (Tepepan, Zinacantepec). Hardly ever in sixteenth-century Europe were fonts such a major piece of church equipment. For a parallel, as so often in sixteenth-century Mexico, we must go back to the earlier Middle Ages or to Early Christian times. Then too, Baptism was given only a few times a year, and to groups of adults; then too, fonts were usually large. After the Council of 1555 in Mexico, it was allowed to administer Baptism twice a week, and the crowds henceforth could be reduced by division.

SIXTEENTH–CENTURY BAPTISMAL FONTS

14 ACATZINGO   15 TECALI

THE GREAT CONVERSION

MARRIAGE

Baptism and Marriage were the only Sacraments regularly given to the natives. The first marriages were those of a few prominent noble converts: the lords of Texcoco were married at an impressive public ceremony where a thousand young Indian warriors performed jubilant dances in towering feather headdresses (and little else). Soon many marriages were solemnized for the young alumni of the monastery schools, properly trained as Christians and not, like so many of their elders, encumbered with problematically plural wives, near-wives, or non-wives. Marriage of their elders could be a vexing problem because a decision had to be made as to whether their pre-Christian unions could be held valid. Cortés called a special conference to debate this, but with no effective result as no one yet knew enough Náhuatl to handle the delicate questioning necessary. After consulting qualified cardinals, Paul III had specifically validated pre-Christian marriages, but the dubious Viceroy called in the bishops and heads of the three Orders to re-examine the problem, and three times sent to Spain for further advice on certain difficult points. Finally it was decided that preconquest marriages were to be accepted if not plural; when they were, the polygamous husband was to put aside the extra wives and concubines and remarry the first wife in a Christian ceremony. If he could not remember which had been his first, he might select and remarry any one wife from his group. Special tribunals were set up in México-Tenochtitlán and Texcoco to weed the supplementary wives and subsidiary concubines from those monogamously acceptable. It was usually the Indians with the most money and importance who had the most wives, for the poor were by economic necessity monogamous, and so consistently so that the friars found their marriages enough like Christian ones not to have to be repeated.

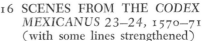

16 SCENES FROM THE CODEX MEXICANUS 23–24, 1570–71 (with some lines strengthened)

Above the glyph for 1529 (right), the year in which marriage was instituted for converted natives, a cowled barefoot friar marries an Indian boy wearing a tilma *(cloak) knotted over his shoulder to a girl wearing a* huipil *(blouse). He joins their hands with his left hand, and blesses them with his right. The oblong she wears around her neck may be the tag with the new name she has just been given at baptism.*

Above the glyph for 1528 (marked 1531, at the left) is a miter surmounted by a cross, symbolizing the arrival of Bishop Zumárraga.

Marriages were performed in numbers second only to baptisms. Father Mendieta wrote of the efficient combination of the two when three thousand had to be dealt with in one morning: "The Indian men were lined up in rows, each paired with his woman . . . a priest administered oil . . . and then without getting out of order, they marched with lighted candles up to the font where another priest baptized them . . . Once baptized, they went out in the order in which they had come in, following the cross carried by the other religious singing litanies with the Indian singers of the church . . . and then the priest who had given them oil began to give them chrism. The priest who had just baptized them . . . took their hands and administered the Sacrament of Marriage." Then they all heard Mass.[25]

PENANCE

Most authorities agreed that the Indians should also be confessed with the recognized procedures. This was done for the first time in Texcoco in 1526, and it became more common as the century unrolled. In 1552 the Council of Lund ruled that all Indians should receive three Sacraments: Baptism, Marriage, and Penance (Confession). The thousands baptized in big lots did not have individually to confess their past sins because these were all absolved by Baptism. Individual confession for everyone was still fairly new, and even in Europe confessionals were a novelty in church furniture less than a century old. Although they had occasionally been used in monastery churches such as Totimehuacán and Huejotzingo, only in 1585 were they made mandatory for Mexican churches in order that priests might more discreetly hear the confessions of women. Confessors were supposed to be more than thirty years old and masters of the local speech, though confession through an interpreter was accepted when unavoidable.

In the early years there was some sort of general confession by groups, and it was also handled according to an Early Christian precedent by having the penitent check his transgressions against a list of the Ten Commandments which the priest would read or, when there were linguistic obstacles, against a set of ten pictures which the priest would display. The Indians had little sense of arithmetic, and often disturbed the friars by blandly saying that they had committed each of the sins the same number of times. Following ordinary late mediaeval usage, as set forth by the Fourth Lateran Council in 1215, the Mexican Council of 1555 decided that healthy Indians were to confess once a year, preferably during Lent; the chronically ill, twice; boys and girls were to confess before they were married.

*

In time the natives came to have almost as much enthusiasm for confessing as they did for being baptized. As the old Aztec form of confession to their priests had automatically given absolution, some Indians could not

83

at first understand why they should be punished by civil authorities for wrongdoings already confessed to clergy. Still, they loved to confess. When the friars went out from the capital in boats, a little fleet of native canoes would sometimes sail after them; the Indians would throw themselves into the lake and swim up to the friars and start breathlessly to confess while treading water. (One sometimes wonders less at the friars' lack of conformity than at how they managed to be as correct as they did.) By the end of the century, when memory of their old kind of confession had evaporated, the natives still had such confidence in confession that they would ask for it when bothered by no more than a headache.

After confession, various kinds of penance could be prescribed. As has already been said, the natives showed an alarming enthusiasm for physical penance. Father Motolinía wrote that Indians disciplined themselves three times a week during Lent, often drawing blood. Even at the end of the century, when almost none can have remembered their masochistic pre-Christian rites, natives still had orgies in the churchyards at night, by turns scourging one another and praying. Father Torquemada even noticed what medical science verified only 350 years later: Indians are less sensitive than Caucasians to physical pain.[26]

CONFIRMATION

Only a few natives were confirmed during the first decades because, it was said, of the scarcity of the requisite oils. Whereas Baptism was essential for Salvation, Confirmation — theologically its supplement — was not, and therefore, until the goal of baptizing the uncountable Indians was reached, confirming them might be considered a postponable spiritual luxury. Herein Father Motolinía and Bishop Zumárraga disagreed, and with his characteristic Christian truculence, Zumárraga took matters into his own hands and — oil or no oil — began a bold campaign of confirming in 1548. He was said to have confirmed 400,000: 14,500 of them in only four days at the tiny Dominican monastery of Tepetlaóztoc across the lake from the capital, exerting himself so much at the age of 72 that it brought on his death. His insistence on Confirmation seems the more remarkable when we remember that it was then not fully standardized and not even officially assured of the rank of a Sacrament until so voted by the Council of Trent. After that, the Franciscans decided that everyone should be confirmed, but preferred to leave the actual ceremony to a bishop whenever there was one in the vicinity.

COMMUNION

For the first 15 years or so, the Indians were not given Communion, and after that there was little agreement as to when or whether they should receive it. Since it was not held necessary for Salvation, Communion was not then regularly offered even to Spaniards oftener than once a year, as had been ordered by the Fourth Lateran Council. Saint Cajetan (1480–1547) had advised it four times a year, and at the end of his life even oftener, but his views did not become influential until after the Council of Trent. The fact that the Mexican clergy in 1546 had to reaffirm Paul III's Bull of 1537, which proclaimed unequivocally that Indians *could* be given the Eucharist, shows that the practice was still far from general in the New World. Some were still maintaining that the Indians were so far from ready for it that they should not receive it at all. Fray Cristóbal de Agurto devoted a book of 91 pages (1573) to arguing that they should. In 1578 the King ordered that Communion *was* to be given to the natives, and that they should be suitably prepared forthwith. The Council of 1585 restated this explicitly. The friars began to examine all candidates, and anyone "approved for the Holy Sacrament" was called a *Comuniotlácatl* (in a typical example of the grafting into Náhuatl of an untranslatable European religious term). In general one might say that the Indians who had been confessing for four or five years received the Sacrament once a year, a few days after their most recent Confession. Those about to die were given Communion with less argument than anyone else. This followed European minimal practice, but clearly there was a great deal of variation. In neither Europe nor America was wine given — only the wafer. Communion was prized as a great privilege, and for the enviable occasion the Indians would put on clean white clothes or wedding costumes with towering crowns of flowers, and go down the nave on their knees.

EXTREME UNCTION

In the first years there were too many deaths for the too few friars to give Extreme Unction to everyone; consequently Indians were rarely shriven and buried with the usual European rites. *Donados* or other dependable Indian servitors in the monasteries usually did the actual burying: in holy ground, and with prayers, but without any Mass or formal services. In Michoacán and Jalisco the Indians used to come to the monastery hospitals to die, knowing that there they might be given the Viaticum and fuller last rites than they could hope to have at home. By the time there were substantially more friars and curates, and substantially fewer Indians, this Sacrament was more usual. Even then it was not common, although the Third Mexican Council of 1585 had ordered that Extreme Unction must be administered in the homes of the dying.

ORDINATION

Ordination proceeded much as in Spain. The principal local problem — whether it would be suitable to ordain qualified Indians — has already been discussed.

THE GREAT CONVERSION

THE DECLINE OF THE MENDICANT DOMINION

For half a century the friars were as important as the civil government: each was indispensable. Inasmuch as during most of that time the seculars were banned by royal decree from regions administered by the regulars on pain of excommunication, and were everywhere outnumbered by them, the friars enjoyed an almost autonomous near-monopoly outside the chief cities. The attitude of the local civil government and even of the higher clergy reflected the royal favoring of the friars. Viceroy Mendoza was particularly partial to them, and informed his successor that without them nothing could be done (1550). He felt certain that he had been right to favor them, and advised Velasco to do the same. Should it ever become necessary to reprove them, it had best be done in secret. Viceroy Velasco continued this pro-Mendicant policy, but friction began to develop. The sour new Archbishop, Alonso de Montúfar, soon came to view the opportune position of the regulars with a jealous eye, though he himself was a Dominican. He began complaining to the King every few months, and his jealousy rose close to persecution mania. His carping cannot have been without effect on Philip, by nature and habit now suspicious, particularly of any power not his own.

The real conflict began when the Mexican bishops, led by Montúfar, decided at their first Council (1555) that the Mendicants should be curbed and the parish priests favored. Friars were henceforth not to be in charge of Indian marriages, and were not to catechize in new towns because the papal privileges for these two major activities had been granted only for the emergency of the Conversion, and that was now past. The King did not agree, however, and not only reaffirmed the friars' old rights, but also told the Viceroy to encourage them to build *more* monasteries, with the reservation only that these be located more with regard to the salvation of the Indians than to the "contentment and consolation of the friars." After he had refused to ordain any more friars of any kind (1560) a series of orders was sent to Montúfar, telling him to behave better and to fulfill his obligations.[27]

The Bishop may have been jealous not only of the backing which the friars had from the King but also of the backing from the Pope and of their status as a sort of apostolic succession of evangelizers. The Mexican bishops had their authority not from the Pope but from the King, by virtue of the *patronato real*. They continued to attack the favored Mendicants, and the Mendicants parried the attacks with outspoken letters to the King. The seculars seemed to win a decisive triumph when the Council of the Indies, following a decision of the Council of Trent affirmed by the Pope, voted that no cleric not subject to a bishop should have jurisdiction over laymen. This meant that the friars in most of their Indian towns would have to be supplemented or replaced by seculars, or that the friars would have to become parish pastors and submit to the bishops. The entire Mendicant seigneury would fall. Philip instructed Viceroy Enríquez to prevent secular-regular friction, and now had to admit that the friars were more effective and more reliable than the seculars. After the new Pope, Gregory XIII, changed papal policy yet again, Philip wavered the other way, and issued new ordinances which attacked the Mendicant privileges. The Franciscans countered with a sort of strike, threatening to shut their missions rather than submit to such curtailment. Philip backed down again — temporarily. But soon his anti-Mendicant ordinances were put into effect, without fanfare, bit by bit, so gradually that there was no counteraction from the friars.

Even so, in 1580 the friars were still doing most of the work which secular curates did in Europe, and Viceroy Enríquez confidentially told his successor that they still ran many *parts* of the country, though by now they had less voice in the general running of the *whole* country. The bulk of their most active work was in rural regions, and impressive though this was in total volume, it was so fragmented that it had much less political force. The friars became involved in many disputes with the seculars, with civilians, and with the government, and the opposition was every year more powerful. Philip renewed his anti-Mendicant efforts, spurred by the jealous bishops and backed by a new Bull; he again ordered the friars to give up their work as parish priests (1583) wherever there were any seculars to take over. The Mendicants protested again, saying that he had not been shown the actual facts, and again the decision was suspended (1585); but the Mendicants again lost ground. By this time the seculars had a new ally in the Jesuits, who had arrived in 1571. As the friars' problems with the Indians diminished, thanks to the friars' own efforts, they themselves seem to have become less stimulated, less forceful, often less confident, and more vulnerable. Now those resentful of the Mendicants' power could really damage it.

From 1583 onward there was enough effective royal preference for the seculars to shift the wavering balance. Philip was completing the change from a policy of conquest-and-crusade to one of colonial imperialism, although presumably he did not intend or even know that such a change would be the result of his firmer Counter-Reformation policies. At the Third Mexican Council (1585) Archbishop Moya de Contreras carried to victory the anti-Mendicant campaign begun by Archbishop Montúfar thirty years earlier. The regulars, aware also of the dangers to them of the growing absolutism of the King, tried to defend their own sovereign rights against it — but too late. In 1607 the Viceroy was still asking for more seculars, and more came.

Friction between the two branches of the Church flared into open jurisdictional warfare when seculars began to be put in towns which had been visitas of monasteries. All monastery churches had the status of parish churches by papal decree, a privilege understood by the friars to be permanent. The regulars' monopoly began to weaken when more seculars than friars arrived from Spain, and more were ordained by the Mexican bishops. Concurrently, the character of the bishops underwent a change, perhaps because the majority, hitherto drawn from the ranks of the friars, now came from the seculars. The third archbishop, Pedro Moya de Contreras, had been a secular, and the shift in the relative importance of the regular and secular hierarchies was made very evident when he was named acting viceroy in 1584.

At the same time, another conflict began to flare up among the friars: a debate as to whether those who had taken their vows in Spain or in New Spain should be favored and given control of the local Mendicant Provinces. In the 1580's, pro-Spanish Father Ponce, deep in this polemic, was disaccredited as Franciscan *Comisario General* by the pro-Mexican friars, excommunicated by them, and banished by the Viceroy. Commissioner Ponce sat out the struggle doggedly, and won; but this violent rift left the once-dominant Order weakened when it could ill-afford to be. Meanwhile there was another clash over the matter of tithes and general income.

It may be that one cause of these several sorts of conflict was that the friars, particularly the Franciscans, were profoundly affected by a daring dream, so daring that it was not expressed in public and perhaps not even frankly acknowledged in private. They seem to have envisioned an ideal theocratic state where they would shepherd ideally Christian Indians without any interference from Spanish colonists, civil officials, or secular clergy. Except the friars, there would be no Spaniards in New Spain. In some of their writings, especially those of Father Mendieta, there can be sensed a strong undertone of yearning for such a heaven on New World earth, not as a remote vision like Saint Augustine's City of God, but as something real and poignantly near at hand.[28] Such a quietly subversive ideal may have made the friars seem intractable to the Spanish civil authorities, and as a result it may have contributed to their gradual disestablishment.

Toward the end of the century the character of the brothers themselves would appear to have changed, and some Mendicant writers had to admit that the high standards of earlier times had been relaxed. They must have become weaker — brother for brother — for even though they still outnumbered the seculars two to one the seculars had, by the first years of the next century, twice their political power. A comparison of the writings of Father Franco and his contemporaries with those of Father Motolinía makes the changes that had come about in a hundred years all too plain. The later chroniclers dwelt more and more on routine penance and humility, and on near-miracles, and less and less on the essential business of saving souls. Many more friars fasted, refused wine more obsessively, and wore hair shirts.

Some went much further. Insistence on mortification of the flesh sometimes grew so extravagant that it seemed to recall or rival Aztec excesses. Father Grijalva could admiringly write of Fray Antonio de Roa: "When he said Mass his tears were so abundant that his sacristans had to give him three successive handkerchiefs." When Fray Antonio traveled to mountain visitas, he had two Indians lead him by a halter, and whenever they came to a wayside cross — there were many in the region of Molango where this occurred — he had an Indian give him fifty lashes. After preaching, he had himself stripped to the waist and led into the churchyard, where he walked barefoot over live coals and through bonfires specially lighted in each corner. Then, suffering very visibly, he would preach to the Indians, warning them that the fires of Hell were much worse. He had little *ermitas* built at Molango, where he would have himself bound to a column and whipped, after which he would enact parts of the Via Crucis while carrying a big cross. At one *ermita* where there was a picture of the Magdalen anointing the feet of Christ, he would kiss the feet of an Indian judge, and then have himself stripped and bound and lashed until he bled profusely; then pitch would be poured on him and lighted.[29] Whether this is entirely accurate or not is less important than that Father Grijalva, writing fifty years after the event, found it admirable.

There was another change in the later sixteenth-century friars: compassion and persuasion seem sometimes to have given way to authoritarianism. Francisco Gonzaga, General of the Franciscans, issued an exhortation to the whole Order (1579): "the lash is the master of religion. Where there are youths who have been corrected and punished, then they are fortified and disciplined." This sounds more like a follower of Saint Ignatius than of Saint Francis. General Gonzaga found that too many men of inferior caliber had been admitted to the Church, and that they had brought it low. Henceforth there was to be much more scrupulous selection, and everyone was to pay particular attention to the rulings of the Council of Trent. When the ideals of the mediaeval founders of the Mendicant Orders and the ideals of the Counter Reformation conflicted, the latter won.[30]

Toward the end of the century, the patriarchal role of the monasteries also began to decline, as the Indians began to be more involved in the life of mixed communities, and as there began to be fewer Indians, more Spaniards, and more mestizos and mulattoes. In many places friars had become like benevolent encomenderos running big enterprises in a business-like way, with interest in their success rather than in the winning of souls. Within the frontiers there were now not many heathen souls to win; except for some pockets in the mountains, all the Indians were at least nominally converted, and the Christian Indian communities were well established, pacified, and running smoothly.

This decline in power and prestige had less effect on the friars' building than one might expect and, although the most inventive architectural period was past, no important decline in the quality of Mendicant building appeared in the sixteenth century. Architecture assumed such a different character and style in the seventeenth century that comparisons with the sixteenth are of limited usefulness. The change in kind hampers any gauging of change in quality. The decline in quantity after the plague of 1575–79 was not reversed until well into the next century. In comparison to what happened to the Indians, this decline was slight.

En la lengua Guasteca.

17 ANGELS WITH A CHALICE AND HOST

A woodcut used in Mexico several times by the printer Pedro Ocharte, here before a brief Catechism for those about to take Communion, in the Doctrina Christiana en la lengua Guasteca *by Fray Juan de la Cruz, prior of the Augustinian monastery at Huejutla* (1571).

III

NEW TOWNS

Let the Indians be persuaded — or compelled by the Royal Author-
ities if necessary, but with the least possible vexation — to congre-
gate in convenient locations and in reasonable towns where they
may live in a politic and Christian manner, and where they can be
given the Holy Sacraments and be instructed in matters necessary
for their Salvation, and be succored in their sicknesses and be
helped, when the time comes, to die in a proper Christian way.
                    — First Mexican Church Council (1555) [1]

THE Conquest had been at once the last big mediaeval crusade and the first big modern war of imperialist expansion. Both these efforts called for new towns: the first so that the Indians could be congregated for Christian indoctrination, and the second so that they could be congregated for labor pools to increase production and its profits. For once, the government, the bishops, and the friars were agreed: the natives must be gathered into towns.

Although repeatedly ordered into new towns by their Spanish masters, the natives repeatedly resisted, sometimes even more than they resisted the new religion. They did not want to leave their fields, and they did not want to build themselves new houses — particularly when already tired from putting up palaces, churches, and monasteries for the Spaniards. Since their new masters did not want them grouped on defendable hills, even though their old fortifications there had been made to repel no missiles more forceful than arrows, the masters urged or drove them down to flat sites which could facilitate better control, as well as offer more water and easier communications.

*

Since many towns were dislocated and relocated once or twice, it is by no means assured that a town with a preconquest name today still stands on its preconquest site. Though there had been many villages, there had not been many large native cities except such major religious and administrative centers as Tenochtitlán, Tlaxcala, Texcoco, Tzintzuntzan, Coixtlahuaca, or

Cholula. Preconquest agriculture could only with exceptional effort sustain a big city. Where the native population, though uncoagulated, was already fairly dense, *congregaciones* could be created quickly, provided that the Indians were willing or easily coercible. For one example among hundreds: the Franciscans transformed Calimaya in a year from a bleak and blank wilderness in the Valley of Toluca (a mile and a half above sea level) into an orderly prospering town of some 15,000 inhabitants in 3,000 Indian households.[2]

*

The most important of the first new towns were those conjunct to the monasteries or to their neighboring visitas. All monasteries and visitas were in towns either instituted expressly for them or adapted from preconquest predecessors. Here the missionary friars gathered the Indians not only to indoctrinate them, but also to teach them agriculture and crafts, thus recovering or improving their old standards of living while making them productive in the new society. Sometimes when the Indians valued the advantages offered by the friars, they moved into their new towns voluntarily; more often they had to be pushed. While organized town-building began as a corollary of the Conversion, after the main activities of the Conversion were past, it continued through the century with little change in an uninterrupted program, now diminuendo, now crescendo, with a special climax at the end. The Augustinians were the most masterly of all in the rapid, systematic, and efficient organization of towns. Their place in the general history of town-planning has only rarely been recognized.

In some ways more like the Arabs than like more northerly Europeans, ordinary late-mediaeval Spaniards showed an antipathy to living anywhere other than in huddled towns or cities. In view of this and of their understandable anxieties, the government thought it prudent to plant a few strategic "cities" of Spaniards among the Indian settlements. Mexico, Puebla, Oaxaca, and Guadalajara were soon founded — mainly to keep the country in order, and at the same time to protect the Spaniards from the Indians. (The friars' towns were intended to protect the Indians from the Spaniards.)

Prelates and magistrates early agreed that it would be better if no Spaniards were allowed to live in Indian towns. While usually it was Negroes, mulattoes, and mestizos who were denounced as corrupters, the paternalistic Mendicants insisted that the Indians lost not only their natural "respectfulness" but also the necessary orderliness in their devotions if any Spaniard came to live among them. Accordingly, in 1550, the King barred all Spaniards from living in Indians towns. As late as the middle of the last century, whites were not permitted to live in many Indian villages (for example, in Morelos), and there are still many towns which are known as *pueblos de indios* where today it would be unprecedented and anomalous for any non-Indian to live.

In order to put the great zeal he had for converting the Indians to its fullest effect [Fray Juan de San Miguel, in the 1520's and '30's] persuaded them to leave the wild mountainous regions where they were living, and come down to the land which was more level, fertile, and cool. Here he founded orderly towns, and thus made their inhabitants worthy to be called men, which they had not been where they had been living before, all scattered far from one another.

— *Father Espinosa* (c1740) [3]

From the beginning the Spaniards showed a preference for a well systematized plan for their new towns. Cortés, for example, gave the following directions (1525): "After felling the trees you must begin to clear the site, and then, following the plan I have made, you must mark out the public places just as they are shown: the plaza, church, town hall and jail, market and slaughterhouse, hospital . . . Then you will indicate to each citizen his particular lot, as shown on the plan, and do the same for those who come later. You will make sure that the streets are very straight, and accordingly will find people who know how to lay them out." [4]

Although Spanish-dominated life in New Spain was in many ways an extension of the late Middle Ages into a new continent and a new century, certain ideal projects which were in advance of mediaeval attitudes took material form there earlier than in Europe. The plan used for many of the new settlements, for example, shows an intrusion of renaissance idealistic thought into what had been a neolithic culture only a few years before.

In the planning and building of new towns, Mexico was ahead not only of her sister colonies in the Antilles but a whole cultural age ahead of the mediaeval alleys and planless cowpaths which later were to determine the configuration of the Portuguese settlements in Brazil, of British Boston, or Dutch Nieuw Amsterdam, at an equivalent time in their development. Of the six countries that founded towns in the New World, Spain alone laid them out on an organized and standardized plan. Enjoined by royal edicts, the Spaniards in Mexico abandoned the haphazard way in which they had let all their towns in the Antilles save Santo Domingo come into being for the previous thirty years. A standardized scheme was possible only in towns built under a strong centralized authority — the Mendicant hierarchy, the secular Church, or the State — and desirable where an equable division and distribution of land was a major consideration.

After the middle of the century, when the plan-type had already been well established, building ordinances were often sent over from Spain. These were directed more to settlements for Spaniards or to Crown towns than to monastery towns. Supererogatory, like so many other ordinances, they pains-takingly instructed people to do what they were already doing. Not all were practical for, like so much of what Spain pontificated for New Spain, many were academic idealizations. There were copious specifications how to arrange towns on rivers and seacoast, superfluous advice for a land where an ever-present problem was the scarcity of rivers and harbors. What was useful in the ordinances was applied; what was not was quietly ignored.

*

For settlements of Spanish civilians there are more texts than towns, but for monastery settlements for Indians, far more towns than texts. Since the two kinds of towns were generally so much alike in basic plan, and since that changed so little during the century, the very full Ordinances of 1573 can be quoted to exemplify the whole long miscellany of directives. These Royal Ordinances show little change from those which had been sent earlier and which consequently had had more direct — though no different — effect on early monastery towns:

"On arriving at the locality where the new settlement is to be founded (which according to our will must be one which is vacant, and can be occu-pied without doing harm to the Indians, or with their consent) the plan with its squares, streets, and building lots is to be laid out by means of cords and rods, beginning with the main square from which the streets are to run to the gates and principal roads, and leaving sufficient open space so that even if the town grows it can always be extended in a similar manner . . .

"The main plaza should be in the center of the town, oblong in shape, with its length at least one and a half times its width, for this proportion is the best for festivals where horses are used and for other celebrations which are to be held. [This did not apply particularly to early monastery towns where there were few, if any, horses] . . .

"The size of the plaza shall be in proportion to the number of residents, heed being given to the fact that the towns of Indians, being new, are bound to grow; and it is intended that they shall. Therefore the plaza is to be planned with reference to the possible growth of the town. It shall not be less than 200 feet wide and 300 feet long, nor more than 800 feet long and 300 feet wide. A well-proportioned plaza of medium size is one 600 feet long and 400 wide.

"The four principal streets lead out from the plaza, one from the middle of each of its sides, and two from each of its corners. The four corners of the plaza are to be toward the four points of the compass, because thus the streets leading from the plaza will not be directly exposed to the four principal winds, which would cause much inconvenience. [The winds of Mexico are not now and cannot then have been so standardized.]

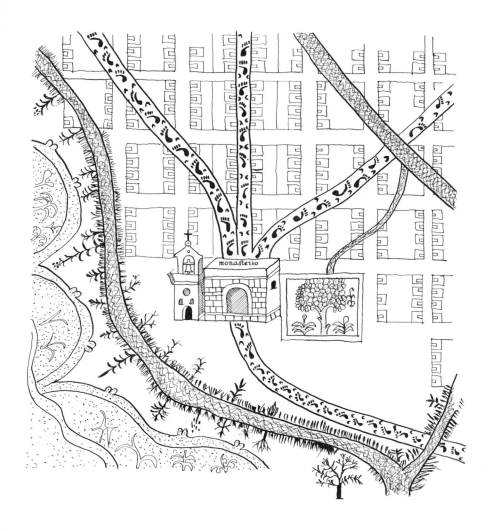

18 INDIAN MAP OF THE TOWN OF TEJUPAN, 1579 (redrawn)

Uniform blocks and houses, a monastery, and its church, with a bell in an espadaña are on one side and a tree-planted churchyard on the other. Footprints mark the direction of the highways (which would not have cut the blocks in the way shown). The lower road comes from the capital; the branch to the left leads to Coixtlahuaca; the one to the right to Oaxaca.

At the lower left are hills, and between them and the town runs a stream lined with reeds and trees; a branch stream runs off to the right, and then comes back across the upper corner of the town.

19 PORTALES OF THE MAIN PLAZA OF CHOLULA

"The whole plaza and the four main streets diverging from it shall have arcades [*portales*], for these are a great convenience to those who resort there for trade . . .

"The streets in cold regions shall be wide; in hot, narrow; but for purposes of defense, where there are horses, let them be wide . . .

"In inland towns the church is not to be right on the plaza, but at a distance where it can stand free, separated from other buildings so that it can be seen from all around; thus it will be more beautiful and authoritative. It should be raised somewhat above the ground so that people will have to go up a flight of steps to reach its entrance . . . The hospital of the poor who are ill with diseases which are not contagious shall be built facing the north, so as to have a southern exposure . . .

"No building lots around the main plaza are to be given to private individuals, but are to be reserved for the church, *casas reales,* and municipal buildings, and for the shops and dwellings of the merchants, which are the first to be built . . .

"The remaining building plots shall be distributed by lot to those of the settlers who are entitled to build around the main plaza . . .

"The plots and the buildings built on them are to be disposed so that in the living quarters one may enjoy air from the south and from the north, since they are the best. All the town houses [of Spaniards] are to be planned so that they can serve as a defense against those who might attempt to create disturbances or occupy the town . . .

"All buildings, so far as possible, are to be uniform, for the sake of the beauty of the town . . . [not usually done].

"If the natives should wish to oppose the establishment of a settlement, they are to be told that the settlers want to build a town there not in order

96

to deprive them of their property but to be friendly with them, to teach them to live in a civilized way, and to teach them to know God and His Law by means of which they shall be saved. This the friars and the clergy and persons delegated by the governor shall explain to them through good interpreters. [Nearly all this was done by the friars.]

"While the settlers are building a new town, as far as possible they shall try to avoid communication and intercourse with Indians, and must not go to their villages . . . Nor are the Indians to enter the circuit of the settlement until it is complete and defendable, with the houses all built, so that when the Indians see them they will be filled with admiration and will realize that the Spaniards are settling there permanently and not temporarily. They will consequently fear the Spaniards so much that they will not dare to offend them, and will respect them and desire their friendship . . ." (This is most unrealistic: of course the Indians saw the towns before completion because they were there building them. Also, it is doubtful that many Spaniards extended "friendship" once they thought the Indians sufficiently frightened.) [5]

There are many examples of the typical scheme. At the right-angled intersection of the two main streets lies a rectangular plaza, similar to that of a number of non-Islamic Mediterranean towns where it had been developed mainly for markets and military drills. It was not an enlargement of a crossroads as it had been in ancient towns and military settlements but, quite the contrary, the plaza was an obstacle to traffic clearly considered as important if not more important than arteries for circulation. The Indians at once moved their *tianguis* or markets into the new plazas, where once a week they became the main activity of the town. (Even today market day is known as *día de plaza*.) Faced on the east by the church and its big yard, on the other side it was faced by the town hall, granary, jail, and other public buildings. If the town was sunny and hot, *portales* might be built around the perimeter of the plaza so that, as several ordinances suggested, pedestrians could stroll comfortably in the shade.

The plaza was often the object of considerable municipal pride. At Puebla, for example, the gibbet was early banished from the plaza to the outskirts as something indecorous of the "honor of the town" (1535); plots were so allotted that the plaza would always remain at the center (1536); soon a fountain was set up (cf. ill. 7) [6] perhaps similar to the very mediaeval survivors still offering their cool waters to the Indians of Chiapa de Corzo or Tuxtla Chico in Chiapas, of Tochimilco in Puebla (or the handsome but now dry basins at Atlixco, Epazoyucan, Etzatlán, Izúcar, Ocuituco, Tepeaca, or — biggest of all — Ciudad Hidalgo). Such municipal fountains were not only a practical necessity but also a civic landmark and an important hub of community life.

20 CIUDAD HIDALGO (once Tajimaroa)

The basin of the font (once the municipal fountain),
in the parish church (once the Franciscan monastery church).

Around the rim of the basin runs a half-illegible inscription
which repeats the alphabet twice, perhaps for the use of the
friars in teaching.

Legislation regulated, or was hopefully intended to regulate, the size and shape of the plaza toward an ideal norm of about 240,000 square feet. There is, of course, a great variety in sizes, down to about 20,000 square feet. Acatzingo, with 300,000, seems spacious but not exceptional. Beyond the orderly rectangular nucleus, additional streets would form a fairly regular gridiron pattern. The usual block was about 350 feet square, bounded by 35-foot streets, and divided into eight plots. Ex-conquistadores with horses were awarded lots twice as big as those of former foot soldiers. The same grid was used not only on flat sites, but also rather arbitrarily on a few hilly ones (such as Uruapan, Pátzcuaro, Metztitlán, or Huejutla), with results almost as Procrustean as modern Seattle or San Francisco. By exception, a few of the larger mining settlements in the mountains evolved more suitable irregular plans, and some of the middle-sized ones grew up planless and even streetless, no more than loose clusters of huts probably similar to the loose clusters of huts still forming some towns (such as Chamula, in Chiapas). The great majority, however, approximated freehand checkerboards; and naturally these seem now the most important.

*

The following description of Tepeaca, written in 1580, could be used for many: "the streets of this city are well laid out, and very even. . . . On the east side of the plaza is a monastery of the Franciscan Order, with its vaulted church . . . its kitchen garden, and a yard in front of the entrance to the church, all walled with masonry. To the west there are stoutly built

98

administration buildings with many rooms above and below; here lives the chief magistrate who governs the city and province, and in his house is the jail." [7] The plaza had been made extra large to accommodate Tepeaca's famous bird market — 8,000 fowl, domestic and European, were sold every market day — and in its center there still stands the exotic brick *rollo* built in 1559, a Moorish-looking tower from which justice was administered. Until recently there were also the remains of a large circular paved platform and of a handsome big fountain whose eight jets spouted good water led in from the hills through a 15-mile aqueduct (constructed in 1543, the year the town was moved and neatly laid out on its present site. By 1590 it was in sad decline, and by 1950, much sadder.) [8]

21 THE *ROLLO* AT TEPEACA, 1559
The rectangular element containing the clock is a nineteenth-century addition. While the general form comes from Moorish towers in Spain, all the details here are gothic or renaissance.

99

NEW TOWNS

For administrative and religious purposes, the larger towns were divided into wards or *barrios* — four usually, though sometimes more. Uruapan, laid out by Fray Juan de San Miguel (probably in 1532), had and still has nine barrios, each with its own chapel at the end of a street.[9] Effort was usually made to resettle Indians from the same preconquest hamlet together in the same new barrio. As in the older Indian towns the head of each family owned their house and adjoining small plot, and the community as a whole owned larger areas of fields outside the main nucleus, and sometimes also pastures.

22 AMECAMECA, at the foot of cloud-covered Ixtaccíhuatl

In front of the Dominican monastery is the churchyard; opposite the church the triple gateway leads out to the extensive market plaza. Except for the long low buildings, which are comparatively modern, the aspect of the town, including the general plan, the church, and the monastery block, is normal for the sixteenth century.

One of the most rewarding ways to see the design of old towns is to fly over them, for from above some still show themselves essentially unchanged despite the later filling of open areas within the town, accretions around the edges, and the metamorphoses of individual buildings. From the many plans made in the 1570's and now filed in the Archive of the Indies in Seville, we can half-see with sixteenth-century eyes how some old towns looked in their original state; and with twentieth-century eyes we can visit scores of six-teenth-century towns off the main highways which have not become too swollen with later buildings to keep us from enjoying many of their original qualities.

*

Skirting the snow-capped peaks of the Valley of Mexico, for random sam-ples, one can visit pretty Chimalhuacán Chalco among its avocado and *zapote* trees and brooklets at the foot of Ixtaccíhuatl; then Ocuituco among its peach orchards on the slope of Popocatépetl; Totolapan and Tlayacapan in the opulent Valley of Morelos; or Cuautinchán and Tochimilco among the cam-phor trees on the other side of the mountains — all of them still green and open. Their simple small houses still have plots of garden or orchard set be-hind the long, straight, stone walls which line the village streets. Much of their twentieth-century daily life must be like that of the sixteenth.

*

Off the highways, Hidalgo and Oaxaca have preserved many more such communities, and Yucatan, above all, still has hundreds of agreeable villages neatly laid out in checkerboards, with walled streets along which almost identical oval one-room cottages stand opposite each other every few hundred feet — closer in the middle of town — each with a little wedge of front yard between flaring walls setting the house back from the street, and gen-erous space for trees and plants and animals behind. Here the tradition re-mains so strong that one cannot tell whether one is looking at a sixteenth-cen-tury town or a nineteenth-century one. (Yucatan is poor now: there are no twentieth-century towns.) It is unlikely, however, that many sixteenth-cen-tury houses remain, for the 1579 *Relación* of Mérida tells that "the houses are all of wood and roofed with straw; they appear but a group of cabins . . . Although they often burn, they are nonetheless good dwellings. There are no stone houses because the Indians fall sick in them and die, and for their way of living . . . straw ones are better." (The Mayas have since learned to survive in stone houses.) [10]

Some town plazas have kept many of their sixteenth-century virtues. It is not hard, for example, to evoke the original intentions at Huaquechula, de-spite the chronological dissonance of its charmingly wayward cast-iron band-stand. At the plaza of Metztitlán, there can have been little visual change effected by the successive metempsychoses of the silver-white buildings with silver-gray roofs, or of the four voluminous *madroños* which shade the square with their glossy dark leaves, brilliant above deep red trunks and pale red soil. Raised on a dramatic promontory above the town, the lordly Augustinian monastery must look now much as it did when new. Backed by a tall cliff and fronted by a river, the ensemble makes one of the handsomest townscapes surviving from the century of the Great Conversion.

*

The visitor may be astonished at the grand scale of some sixteenth-century plans. At Uruapan, although the long original plaza has been fractioned by two rows of houses built across it, each of the resulting three new squares is of generous size. When it was a century old and little altered, Father la Rea wrote that Uruapan was so well planned "that it could not have been bettered by the aristocracy of Rome," thinking no doubt — since he had seen neither — of an ideal ancient Rome rather than the largely irregular Rome of his own time. The plaza was probably made so large because Uruapan was an important trading town at a junction between prolific temperate and subtropical agricultural zones; there was a market every day and it was exceptionally large.[11]

Occasionally a Mexican plaza would be traced in a novel shape, compounded of two or more rectangles, as in the diagonally overlapping squares at Tlatlauquitepec in the Sierra de Puebla (before 1567?), or the two squares and former forecourt of Cortés' Palace set diagonally point-to-point at Cuernavaca, where the monastery is several blocks removed, probably because the standard plan had had to be modified when Cuernavaca was fitted to its ridge atop the ruins of Cuauhnáhuac (in the 1520's and '30's).

*

It is usually more difficult to evoke the original appearance of a city than of a village. One would expect the buildings which make the plan material, and thus more apprehensible to the eye, to be architecturally more mature than they are, but when they were built they were less advanced and coherent than the plan, and subsequently more vulnerable to alterations. At Puebla, for example, though we can still sense the grand plan of the 1530's and '40's, it is only by a willed effort, since we now see almost no sixteenth-century buildings. We know, however, that they were so neatly arranged that one unfortunate citizen whose housefront was out of line had to pull it down and set it up again true to the others.

In some other old cities the space, the trees, and the scale of the later surrounding buildings are still able to present the essence of a sixteenth-century plaza, as at Oaxaca, where the surrounding streets still look "all alike and laid out straight with cords." [12] The big square at Mérida, with its incomparable dark Indian laurel trees, is still flanked by the sixteenth-century Cathedral on one side, the sixteenth-century palace of conquistador Montejo authoritatively on the center axis of another, and a town hall and other buildings which, while not contemporary, still can recall the scale of their predecessors in height and in the scansion of their arcades and windows. The ensemble cannot be far from the intentions of Montejo when he drew the first plan on a big parchment and proudly signed his name.[13]

The shabby, sleepy plaza at Tlaxcala, too, still holds to its original size, and still has its showy *casas reales* (c1550) and other buildings of little-changed size and scale, though the so-called *capilla real* — actually a government building — was pulled down a century ago, and most of its display of heraldic sculpture and its stone colossus of Philip II destroyed. The eight-spouted fountain, too, has gone. The old *rollo* has been replaced by a fancy bandstand, but in imagination we can substitute the *rollo* of Tepeaca since it may have been built by the same man.[14]

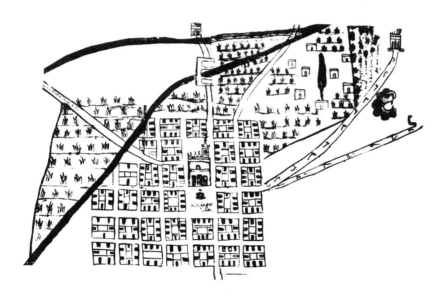

23 INDIAN MAP OF TECAMACHALCO, 1605
The Franciscan monastery church is at the back of the town plaza (with its fountain in the middle), and round about, 34 blocks of houses set between straight streets. At the edge of town are cultivated fields, isolated houses, and three arches of the monastery aqueduct. The road running off from the upper left leads north to Quecholac, and that from the upper right, south to Tehuacán, both towns with Franciscan monasteries.

THE SOURCES OF THE TOWN PLAN

It is difficult to identify and separate the likely European and native forerunners of the standard Mexican plan because, for once, there are too many clues, though few lead to clear facts. Nevertheless, since no single source explains the standard plan, it is necessary to consider a miscellany of practice and theory in Europe — antique, mediaeval, and renaissance — and of preconquest practice in Mexico.

One might expect to find the most pertinent antique precedents in Spain: none, however, is discoverable there, not even in the wreckage of the Roman regularity which had disciplined some sections of Tarragona and Mérida. While Braga in Portugal may preserve parts of its Roman plan, there seems to be no valid reason to relate it to Mexico, nor would there seem to be any connection with the antique gridiron plans which were still visible, admired, and used in remoter cities such as Turin or Zadar (Zara), like though they may look.

No more does anything seem to have been inherited from the mediaeval Spanish Moslems, except the term *barrio* (from *rabad*). Despite their builders' extensive knowledge of antique culture, the Moors' cities and towns had been so huddled within walls that the streets were as narrow and irregular as anywhere in Europe. The broad courtyards of the mosques took the social function of the town plaza, while the commercial function, the market, was kept outside the walls. The focus of the Moslem town plan — if it can be said to have had one — was not an open space but one busy main street (as it still is on the *Sierpes* in Seville).

Broad straight streets and gridiron plans have been laid out at many different times in many parts of the world. They had occasionally occurred in Europe in the twelfth, thirteenth, and fourteenth centuries, perhaps partly inspired by Saint Thomas Aquinas' contention (backed by *Revelations* and Saint Augustine) that a perfected ideal city would be the best community for devout Christian life. It is not easy to concede that any of these European regular towns, whether mediaeval Dalmatian ports or post-Albigensian "new towns" in southern France, would have had any direct effect on those in Mexico, similar though a first glance may make them seem. There was little tradition and no body of theory to transmit their forms across three thousand miles and three hundred years, and there are no examples with which we can reasonably imagine any kind of effective connection except perhaps for a few in northern Spain. While these last may be related to the French "new towns," that is not certain, since some were built in the twelfth and thirteenth centuries — as early as any in Europe — under conditions during the Reconquest similar to those which were engendering the "new towns" in France. Whether or not they were related to anything French may not matter here, for despite their fumbling approximations of rectangularity and irresolute suggestions of reticulated planning, these small Spanish examples seem too removed in form, date, and place to be able to claim a convincing parentage to the far more developed Mexican plans. It would be surprising to find that Mexico had been conquered, settled, or controlled by any influential men from such towns. While a connection cannot be ruled out, influence seems improbable.[15] If there is any effective Spanish prototype, it would more likely be in *later* plans, plans more likely known to early settlers in Mexico, such as Fray Alonso de Borja, for example, who came from Gandía before 1531. Like Alicante, not far along the east coast, Gandía had a fairly regular grid plan with straight narrow streets which, even in their present form, presumably antedate any Mexican examples. (Both towns lack, however, the plaza essential to the Mexican scheme.)

✳

In the New World, the city of Santo Domingo is said to have been laid out on a gridiron plan in 1502, possibly following the formal fortified camp where Ferdinand and Isabella held court and received Columbus (which developed into the town of Santa Fe de Granada), or perhaps their similar Puerto Real on the Bay of Cádiz. While these may have been based on earlier Reconquest towns of somewhat regularized plan, and while they could have affected Mexican planning, contemporary Mexican writers did not so far as we know once refer to Santo Domingo, Santa Fe, Puerto Real, or any Reconquest towns, or to any regularly planned towns in Spain or anywhere else in Europe, antique, mediaeval, or renaissance. It would seem that none was well known to these writers, and perhaps no more to the actual planners of the standardized Mexican towns.[16]

The closest European equivalent might seem to be Valletta, the new capital of Malta, planned in 1562, and begun in 1566 by the Knights of Saint John of Jerusalem. They had recently left Rhodes, site of the most famous grid-plan of antiquity; but probably this is a meaningless coincidence since the antique disposition was mutilated, buried, and invisible. Valletta must have been only a coincident parallel, perhaps dependent on similar antecedents. If it is any sort of younger cousin, Santo Domingo is an older sister. Any similarity is probably the result of the then exceptional fact that all three were new cities, planned fresh, and not adapted, enlarged, evolved, or in any way derived from older work on the sites. When new land is divided into lots and streets, unless there is some topographical difficulty, rectangular regularity seems to be the easiest and most natural form for the layout to take.[17] When the Sung emperors laid out the Hang-Chow which so amazed Marco Polo, on a pleasant flat site, they naturally had the streets made straight and the blocks uniform rectangles.

NEW TOWNS

The Mexican gridiron plan shows two main differences from nearly all the regular European towns. First is the systematic incorporation of a big plaza as the heart of the town, on a scale and of an orderly form unmatched in Europe. In mediaeval and renaissance Spain any but small plazas had been rare because nearly all towns were compressed within circuit walls and, except in the north, which had not long been under Moslem domination, any activities calling for open space, such as markets, were generally held outside the town. No regular rectangular Spanish plazas are known to be earlier than those in Mexico, save possibly that at Santiago de Compostela. Although Lérida had had a municipal plaza from the fourteenth century, this was not of regular or monumental form; nor was that of Valladolid, which was at least as old as the plazas in Mexico. Las Palmas in the Canaries was given its plaza in the sixteenth century, no earlier than those in Mexico and, though "colonial" like them and little hampered by tradition, it was less developed in form. The second major difference from early European examples is that in Mexican monastery or important visita towns, a large churchyard and a church were coordinated with the plaza. Although the Franciscan church at Seville had a big churchyard or plaza of its own, which might make the arrangement there seem similar, this space was not related to any monumental municipal plaza. As there are no really valid precedents in Europe, it may be supposed that the typical Mexican arrangement must either have been found or worked out locally in Mexico.[18]

To well-educated European eyes, the Mexican plans may not have appeared to follow any existing European models. Instead they may have recalled the rational *ideal* of a renaissance town scheme, recognized as desirable but not yet materialized in Europe, thanks to the surfeit of traditions and old buildings and the lack of any equivalent campaign of town-founding. The European ideal town, however, often had its streets arranged radially from a central plaza rather than in an all-over unfocused crisscross. (The uncommon renaissance gridiron schemes in Europe — at towns such as Nancy, Vitry-le-François, Ferrara, Sabbioneta, Mannheim, Leghorn, or Valletta, but none in Spain — were carried out only after the Mexican type was established; and like it they were probably based on new theory more than on any old towns or long-standing traditions.) Theory prescribed regularity not only for the lines of the streets but also for the lines of the buildings. The clear order of the flat plan was to be made visually manifest and aesthetically significant by the harmonious similarity of the solid buildings rising from it. Such theory presupposed a society with equable distribution of wealth among the builders, but as such was far from the case in Mexico, the buildings were in general not so well organized as the plan despite the surprising fact that uniformity for the sake of aesthetic values was urged in some of the royal ordinances.

106

Though no one seems to have seen any *built* precedents in Europe, some men in Mexico were familiar with *written* ones. The ideas of several Greek theorists were still accessible, incapsulated within the texts of later writers: ancient, such as Vitruvius, or modern, such as Alberti. The Italian Filarete, too, after half-absorbing some ideas of Vitruvius, had written (between 1451–64) of an ideal city in terms many of which could almost as well be used for Mexico a century later: "At the eastern end of the piazza is the principal church. Opposite, on the west, is the princely palace. On the north, the square of the merchants . . . on the south, the great market . . . At the west of this I will erect the palace of the captain of the police . . . The principal streets will lead into the piazza." But, although there was a copy of Filarete's manuscript in Spain, it had not been published, and any direct connection with New Spain is unlikely. The relation, again, is of cousin rather than parent, for probably his text shows a theoretical parallel to what was evolved more pragmatically in Mexico.[19]

A substantial body of ideal planning theory was, nevertheless, available in Mexico early enough to be effective. The Latin texts of Vitruvius and Alberti existed in Italian and French editions, and a Spanish treatise by Diego de Sagredo, *Medidas del Romano,* was published in 1526 and again in 1539, 1542, 1549, and 1563. Humanistic Viceroy Mendoza was reminded by the Valladolid he founded in Michoacán of the seven conditions Plato had formulated for an ideal city. Doctor Cervantes de Salazar cited Vitruvius only 33 years after the fall of Tenochtitlán, while describing the up-to-date wonders of its successor. (Thanks to his training at the University of Salamanca, he was more concerned with ancient Rome than modern Spain — but then he was so obsessed by antiquity that he could not write down the rules of a ball game without mentioning Pollux, Lycurgus, Solon, Numa Pompilius and his nymph.) The town Ordinances of the 1570's show knowledge of Vitruvius, and it is known that copies of Vitruvius, Alberti, and Serlio had been imported by booksellers. (Translations of Serlio and Vitruvius had become available in Spain in 1563 and '65.) There may well have been architectural texts in the sixty boxes of books which Fray Alonso de la Vera Cruz brought back in 1573. In his will, Doctor Cervantes specified that a book of *cosas romanas* be returned to the lawyer from whom he had borrowed it; might it have been an architectural treatise? [20]

There is one undeniable difference, however, between the European theories and the Mexican facts: whereas the ideal schemes took their forms as much from aesthetic considerations as from practical, the usual Mexican scheme was primarily utilitarian, and whatever aesthetic qualities are discernible today are mainly either by-products, fortunate accidents, or the pleasing transformations wrought by time. Despite the uniformity "for the sake of the beauty of the town" advocated by the Ordinances of 1573, the Mexican scheme is less akin to aesthetic renaissance ideals than to more practical antique precepts, and cognate to the hard-headedly utilitarian scheme of Dürer, unpublished and hence unknown in Spain or America. (There is a fascinating possibility that Dürer had seen a regularized synoptic plan of México-Tenochtitlán in a woodcut perhaps based on a sketch by Cortés.) [21]

*

There is a relation not only to European theory but occasionally also to Mexican practice, for some of the Indian cities — above all Tenochtitlán — had had long and straight main streets leading out at more or less right angles from a plaza fronted by the main religious buildings. The *Conquistador Anónimo,* who claimed to have seen them intact — he may have been lying — found that many of them rivaled or surpassed cities he knew in Spain. Father Torquemada (writing about 1610 but relying on many earlier sources) imagined that "to see Cholula was a great delight . . . In width and length the streets were and still are among the best of any city in the world; they are not crooked, but begin straight and end the same way they began; and even now . . . without the beauty of those great temples and towers, nor any memory of them, it looks so pretty and so trim that it is a pleasure to look at any part of it you wish." [22] Some of the less important parts of a city might also be regular, as we are shown on the extraordinary plan of Tlatelolco on *amate* paper, probably in part preconquest, preserved in the Museo Nacional of Mexico. Here about four hundred households with gardens (*chinampas*) are plotted with the neatest regularity. This may have been unusual for the domestic part of an Indian settlement, sometimes no more than planless huddles of huts as we can see in a large part of Tehuacán Viejo, an Indian town taken over by the Franciscans in the 1530's and abandoned within a generation — because of malaria, rattlesnakes, and ants — before it can have been much rebuilt.[23]

The Indian cities, particularly in their grander parts with temples and palaces, had aroused the astonishment and approbation of the European writers who saw them whole, and over and over they praised the straightness of the streets and orderliness of the plazas, both novelties to men reared in Spain. Cortés, Aguilar, Bernal Díaz, and the *Conquistador Anónimo* compared the Mexican cities favorably with Granada, Salamanca, Segovia, Seville, or Burgos, the proudest cities of Spain. From a Spaniard, there could be *no* higher praise. Those who had not seen it might question whether flat Tenochtitlán could be handsomer than Spanish hilltop cities, but they could concede that it might rival flat Ghent, Milan, or even Seville. The mestizo historian Muñoz Camargo boasted that Cortés had had Tenochtitlán rebuilt "in our way," and that the fine quality of the plan and houses there in his time (1576) came from this Indian heritage.[24]

24 *"TEMIXTITAN" based on a sketch made for or possibly by Cortés and sent by him to Charles V with the Third Letter, known now only through this "translation" into woodcut, used to illustrate the Second Letter in the Latin version by Pietro Savorgnano published at Nürnberg in 1524.*

NEW TOWNS

The relative effect of preconquest planning and European theory on post-conquest towns cannot be measured. While the gridiron could have come as an importation from Europe, more likely it was derived from native practice, and merely disciplined by imported ideals, and perhaps affected also as much from the convenience of laying it out with cords, rods, and stakes. The central plaza, the adjoining courtyard, and the dominant location of the church at the back of the courtyard all have more and closer counterparts in earlier America than in earlier Europe, but their integration with the grid was probably affected by the discipline of European theory. There is, however, no proof. All that is certain is that there was a successful fusion, and that its result was more "advanced" than what was being carried out currently in Europe. This must have been strikingly evident in the new capital.

25 THE TWIN–TEMPLED TEOCALLI OF HUITZILOPOCHTLI AND TLALOC *in the walled precinct at the center of Tenochtitlán.*
(Códice Florentino, c1564–65)

> Mexico Tenochtitlan yn atlihtic, atlixicco, yn tultzallan, yn acatza-
> llan, in cuauhtli ynequetzayan, yn cuauhtli ypatlanian, yn cuauhtli
> ypipitzcayan, yn cuauhtli yçomocan, yn michi ypatlanian . . .
> *México-Tenochtitlán, in the lagoon, amid the many waters, the*
> *reeds, and the rushes, where rise the eagles and fly and cry, where*
> *hiss the serpents, where swim the fish.*
> — Domingo Francisco de San Antón Muñón Chimalpahín
> (c1612) [25]

The first to realize a reticulated plan was México-Tenochtitlán, and closest there to the European ideal of ordered buildings on an ordered plan were
three ensembles salvaged in part from the Aztec city: the main square, the
main street of palaces, and the market plaza of Tlatelolco. These must have
been laid out in the hard-pressed campaign of rebuilding which Cortés began
early in 1522, with legions of native laborers recruited largely from the
armies with which he had destroyed the city. Thousands of loyal hands from
Texcoco helped, led by Prince Ixtlilxóchitl, carrying his load of building
stones in a tiger skin.

For a few months Cortés had considered making his capital elsewhere,
but finally, despite the objections of most of his old companions in arms, he
decided to rebuild it on the island site. Knowing that the Indians could remember and revere the grand Tenochtitlán he had destroyed, he determined
to match it: as a durable affirmation of durable victory and also, perhaps, as
a gratification of his own vanity. Many Indians soon moved into the city,
though the Spaniards held back until it should be more comfortably rebuilt.
After only a few months, Cortés found it "already very beautiful" — perhaps
because of spared old buildings and the spectacular site. In 1524, after some
30,000 Indians had come back, he proudly wrote the Emperor: "Your Sacred
Majesty may be certain that within five years it will be the noblest and most
populous city in the world, and one of the best built." [26] Who else during
the Renaissance had such an opportunity to plan and build so large, so rich,
and so important a city? Alberti's, Filarete's, or Serlio's projects seem modest
dreams beside it, impractical as well as unbuilt. No European builder since
Justinian had had so much money and so many workmen.

Cortés commissioned Alonso García Bravo, "a very good geometer" (surveyor), to work on a plan for rebuilding the main part of the city. A soldier-
conquistador who had come to Mexico during the Conquest, García Bravo
would not likely have known either Vitruvius or renaissance theories, but he
had had some practice in making the fortified settlement at Veracruz and a
stockade in the Pánuco. (Later he laid out Oaxaca.) It is possible that he

111

took important suggestions for México-Tenochtitlán from Cortés, or that he or some associate knew the schematic plans of some military settlement of the last days of the Reconquest in Spain, or perhaps the early plan of Santo Domingo. Not much is clear about Alonso García Bravo. (Another Alonso García, a mason, also came to Mexico before the fall of Tenochtitlán, and yet another Alonso García Bravo appeared soon after.) Cortés' man presumably began work late in 1523 or in 1524, as soon as the Aztec wreckage had been enough cleared away. He traced the streets, plazas, and building lots, and indicated something for Cortés' palace, as big as any castle in Spain. The complete city plan included a reticulated residential zone for Spaniards (the *traza*), a reconstruction or revision of the Tlatelolco market place, and a civic-religious center. The Audiencia reported in 1531: "We know no city which has so many good houses, and all are on a *traza* save a very few." The principal old plaza was remodeled for the main new plaza, and the old avenues leading from it to the causeways across the lake became the main directive lines of the new checkerboard plan. Formerly they had led out from the great pyramid-temple, but after that was flattened, they crossed where once it had risen, purposely perhaps for the psychological impact. The houses of the Indians, and their *chinampas* (polder-like, but *not* floating gardens) were not coordinated into the Spanish checkerboard and were left, probably, much as in the preconquest city which — as shown on the *amate*-paper plan — was fairly regular.[27]

Something of the character of the dozen-year-old new city can be learned from Father Motolinía (1537): "In a material way, México-Tenochtitlán is well planned, and even better built, with good large strong houses and very handsome streets. It is well supplied with all the necessities, both native and Spanish . . . They spend more than in two or three cities of the same size in Spain; this is because all the houses are full of people who spend heavily." [28] When he wrote there cannot have been more than a few hundred Spanish heads of families or bachelors, but most had not only big houses but big households. Thanks to the influx of Indians (already perhaps 100,000), there were no cities of comparable size in Spain, though few in Spain were aware of this. Viceroy Mendoza saw his capital triple in size in the 15 years of his term (1535–50). By 1552 it was said by Gómara that there were "a hundred thousand houses" (implying about 500,000 people!) in what was now beyond any question "one of the greatest cities in the world," where each of the 2,000 Europeans had a horse and a stable. Gómara, an unusually well-informed historian, had never seen the city, however. More reasonable modern estimates reduce the population to something between 100,000 and 300,000, more probably nearer the latter.[29]

Every year the new capital grew not only more populous and prosperous but also, as its new formal order became clearer, more handsome. The tons of wreckage and the many little canals still presented problems, and the soil of the city was often so soggy or even flooded that some of its heavy new buildings began to list or sink almost as soon as they were built. Conditions had become such by 1552 that there was another debate about moving to a healthier site, possibly Texcoco.

Despite these disadvantages, the capital became a model for other cities for Spaniards; first for Puebla, and then for smaller settlements. Admiring appraisals continued through the second half of the century. Still "the most beautiful city in the world," it was now acknowledged by all to be bigger than Toledo or Seville, bigger than any in the Spanish Empire, bigger in fact than any Spanish city had been since the decline of Moslem Córdoba five centuries before. An Englishman, one of the few foreigners who managed to see it (1560), was very much struck that he could see "down the streetes made very broad and right," for an unimpeded mile, something he had never been able to do at home. "The Citie goeth wonderfully forwards in building of Frieries and Nunneries and Chappels, and is like in time to come to be the most populous city in the world." There were some three thousand Spanish houses by about 1580. Father Ponce (there for the first time in 1585) found that it was "the most populous, noble, and sightly in all New Spain, or even Peru . . . with very good houses and handsome streets, broad and long, which appear all to have been made from the same mold since they are so equal and alike." It must have been not only nobler than most of the European cities he knew, but also cleaner, for the streets were regularly swept and flushed by a crew of twenty-four.[30]

Samuel de Champlain, who had seen many parts of the world by the time he began to write an account of his travels, visited Mexico in 1599. He was stirred to rhapsody by the countryside between Veracruz and the capital: "Il ne se peult veoir ny desirer ung plus beau païs que ce royaulme de la Nove Espaigne." Later: "but all the contentment I felt at the sight of things so pleasing was but little in regard to what I experienced when I beheld the beautiful city of Mexico, which I had not supposed to be so superbly constructed, of splendid churches, palaces, and fine houses, and the streets so extremely well laid out." A decade later, Father Ojea found that it had "the best plan one could wish in the world." Father Vázquez de Espinosa (who left in 1622) saw it as "one of the best and biggest in the world, with an excellent climate and a marvellous sky . . . The streets are very straight, broad, and unencumbered." Such straight streets were still an amazing innovation to Europeans. A Neapolitan globetrotter, Giovanni Francesco Gemelli Carreri, was particularly struck by the checkerboard pattern which made the whole city one huge square (1697). It rivaled his Italian cities "not only in the beauty of its buildings, but surpassed them in the beauty of its women." Father de la Cruz y Moya, writing in the eighteenth century but on the basis of early accounts, said: "The plan of the new City of Mexico was arranged with such fine symmetry and handsomeness that, like the City of the Apocalypse, it makes a perfect square. Its streets are alike and straight, facing the four winds . . . They are 40 feet wide, and thus four carriages [some said five] can be driven down them abreast without jostling." [31] Each block, old or new, was still 600 to 700 feet long and 300 to 400 wide, the dimensions established by the original plan of Alonso García Bravo. No one thought the city commonplace, apparently, for every writer who commented on its aspect praised not only its regularity but also its exceptional beauty. Its beauty, then, may be accepted as a hard historical fact.

*

The longest, straightest street was built over the Aztec street which had led from the main temple square out across a causeway to the venerable city of Tacuba. It is one of the few streets which not only survives but also retains its old name: the *Calle de Tacuba*. In one of his Latin *Dialogues* (1554), Doctor Cervantes de Salazar, Professor of Rhetoric and future Rector of the new University, wrote of it with characteristic effusiveness:

"How the view of the street exhilarates the mind and refreshes the eyes! How long it is! how wide! How straight it is! how level! and the entire street is paved with stones to prevent its becoming muddy and filthy in the rainy season . . .

"What do you think of the houses on both sides, built so regularly and evenly that none varies a finger's breadth from another?

"They are all magnificent and elaborate, and appropriate to the wealthiest and noblest citizens . . .

". . . the houses do not exceed a proper height. This was done, if I am not mistaken, so that they might not fall of their own height when shaken by earthquakes which, I hear, are frequent in these regions, and also so that all might equally admit the sun, with none shading the others.

"For the same reason it was proper not only for the streets to be made wide and spacious, as you see, but also for the houses to be not too tall, as you well remarked, so that the city would be more healthful, with no very high buildings preventing the winds from blowing back and forth; for those along with the sun disperse and drive off the pestilential vapors which the neighboring swamp emits." [32]

Doctor Cervantes may have looked at his Vitruvius as much as at the Calle de Tacuba when he was writing this, for much of what he chose to see and how he chose to judge it seems dictated by Vitruvius. (This way of seeing is not unusual: we have nearly all seen sightseers who looked at buildings only to confirm what Baedecker has said.) Here there is no specific reference to Vitruvius — as there is on one other occasion in Cervantes de

Salazar — but since we know he read Vitruvius and was not much of an observer of his surroundings, we may assume that his way of thinking of civic criteria was borrowed.

Spaniards were prohibited from building on any streets outside the main grid or *traza* except on this Calle de Tacuba which, thanks to their houses on it, constituted a shielded avenue of escape. These houses and those around the perimeter of the gridiron were at first (1528) built contiguously, in order to form a long defensive wall, a *casa-muro*. The *Conquistador Anónimo* assumed (c1535?) that there were already over four hundred masonry mansions for the Spaniards, all the same height except for their towers; he believed that the impressive effect was unmatched in Europe. Towers, valued for their defensive potentialities, were not supposed to be built except by nobles who had obtained a license, but the parvenu conquistadores and encomenderos were not denied desired towers, because their individual lack of secure quarterings was more than matched by the common gain in security of quarters.[33]

Observant, but not always accurate, Father Pablo de la Purísima Concepción Beaumont also believed that the houses were uniformly low — because of earthquakes. The houses in Mexico City were not, however, lower than houses in Spain, though perhaps they were lower than in eighteenth-century France where he had been reared. He, too, found (1777) that Mexico still was more beautiful than European cities because of the regularity of its blocks, a feature determined early in the sixteenth century when it was specified that facades must be of stone, built straight and flush with adjacent facades, all toeing the property line. (Some, however, were only of stuccoed brick.)[34]

*

From the beginning, the hard-headed conquistadores had been particularly interested by the Indian market, or *tianguis,* of Tlatelolco. Bernal Díaz said that "some soldiers among us who had been in many parts of the world, in Constantinople and all over Italy, and in Rome, said that they had never before seen so large a market place, so full of people, and so well regulated and arranged."[35] This is a curious observation, for orderly market squares (like that at Padua) were not at all common in Italy, and one wonders how many of Cortés' soldiers could have known Constantinople, then in the hands of the very Turks Charles V was fighting. Market squares were not so much a Mediterranean as a northern specialty, but neither Flanders nor Germany had anything to compare with the *tianguis* of Tlatelolco in area or clarity of shape. After the old city of Tlatelolco had been incorporated into the new capital as an Indian quarter, its already regular market place had been rebuilt and re-regularized with long new colonnades such as Alberti had recommended for market places in specific directions not yet so fully realized anywhere in Europe. Cortés, Bernal Díaz, and the *Conquistador Anónimo* were especially struck by the size and impressive orderliness of both the Aztec *tianguis* and the Spanish reconstruction and remodeling, and calculated it to be two or three times larger than the plaza of Salamanca, which at this time, though irregular in shape, was famous for its size. The market plaza of Tlatelolco and the main civic-religious plaza of México-Tenochtitlán were said to be able to hold crowds of 50,000 to 60,000 each — some said 100,000.[36]

The civic plaza in the heart of the new-old city must have been its climax. In his *Dialogues*, Doctor Cervantes wrote:

"Now here is the plaza. Look carefully please, and note whether you have seen another which could equal it in size and grandeur."

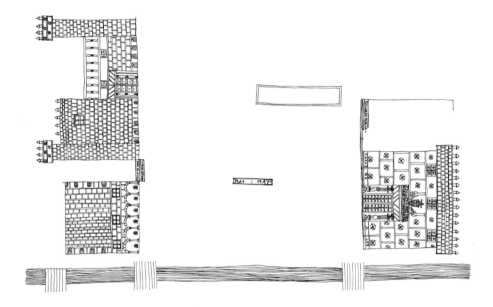

26 THE SOUTH PART OF THE PLAZA MAYOR OF MEXICO CITY IN THE MID–1560's (redrawn from a map in the Archive of the Indies)

At the right, above a canal with bridges, is the Palace of the Viceroy, made of a palace which Cortés had made of the "New" Palace of Moctezuma; the summary drawing emphasizes its monumental doorway (ornamented with the name of Philip II and his royal arms), as well as its fancy rustication and battlemented top.

At the left are the portalés of the merchants, and beyond them the huge palace Cortés had made of the "Old" Palace of Moctezuma (or Axayácatl); it had shops below what appears to be a balustraded azotea above the doorway, and battlemented towers at the corners. Beside the far tower, the Calle de Tacuba runs straight west out of the plaza.

"None that I can remember. Nor do I believe that its equal can be found in either hemisphere. Good heavens! how level it is! and how spacious! How gay! How greatly embellished by the superb and magnificent buildings that surround it on all sides! What order! What beauty! What a situation and location!" [37]

What fulsomeness! Still, Doctor Cervantes had not seen the equal of this thirty-year-old square anywhere in the Old World, and he had traveled not only in Spain but as far as Flanders.

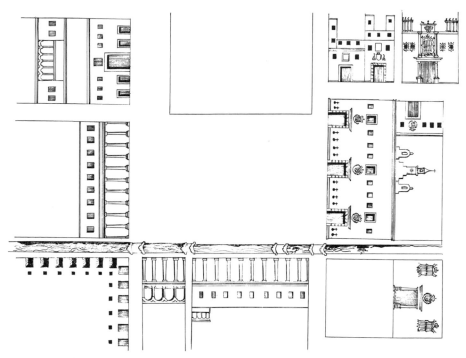

27 THE SOUTH PART OF THE PLAZA MAYOR IN 1596 (redrawn from another map in the Archive of the Indies)

The Palace of the Viceroy has been lengthened to fill the entire block from the canal to the Calle de Moneda, and a clock and bells have been added to the top in place of the battements.

The lower part of the drawing shows the portales *of the* Ayuntamiento *on the south side of the canal. At the left are the* portales *of the merchants, perhaps remodeled since the 1560's, and beyond them the palace of the Cortés family with a new loggia at the top.*

Neither of these two pictures is to be taken as a realistic description, and the differences shown in the same building in one plan and the other may have been less than appears here.

It may well have merited the praise in the early descriptions not only from its size but also from the homogeneity of its new arcades and the new buildings behind them. While not exactly matched, these were all of the same stone and about the same height except for their towers. Most had been built at more or less the same time, largely by the same crews of Indian masons, and were therefore presumably all in more or less the same style — or similar lack of style?

Although nothing solid survives at the Plaza Mayor (now called the *Zócalo*), the space, somewhat altered, is still there, one of the largest though not, in its present condition, one of the most impressive major civic areas in the world, except as illuminated at night. Lionello Venturi compared it justly to the dull main square of Milan. The Cathedral fronting it is magnificent, and the National Palace, on the site of the "New" Palace of Moctezuma which Cortés had remodeled, has an authoritative individuality rare in official building, but the square they face and partially define is no longer either magnificent, authoritative, or individual. The main open area of the central Aztec plaza, excluding the periphery of lesser shrines and courts within the sacred enclosure, had been something like 500 by 600 feet, which has now become about 750 by 1000, plus a third as much again if the adjacent open space on either side of the Cathedral is included (which would bring it close to the 1300 by 1300 of the whole Aztec sacred enclosure). It conforms to the tradition of the Mexican plaza (which it helped to form), with church and its forecourt at one end, government buildings along one side, and — until recently — arcades and shops along the other sides, and a tree-shaded garden in the middle. It differs from other plazas mainly because of its grander scale. The appearance in the sixteenth century is not easy to imagine now that all the early buildings are gone, with the first Cathedral removed from the middle to make way for the existing mixed-style masterpiece set to one side and faced another way. Furthermore, the plaza no longer has the same shape, having spread somewhat to the south. The National Palace replaced Cortés' big palace on the east side in the seventeenth century, and lost much of its majesty and strangeness in 1927 when a fussy little top story was added to its eighth-of-a-mile facade, longer even than the cliff-like front of the Bourbon Palace at Caserta which then held the European record.[38]

*

If the boasts of eyewitnesses are to be believed, the new renaissance ideal of a monumental plaza flanked by uniform or intentionally related buildings — quite different from the smaller, irregular, and far less formal mediaeval town square — had not yet dominated any important European city space as it dominated these two huge plazas in México-Tenochtitlán. In Europe there were a few important squares which were fairly regular but not fully renaissance in design, such as the Piazza San Marco in Venice, the setting of the Cathedral of Siena, or a few big, trim market squares in the north, such as those at Bruges or Ypres. Although some well-developed renaissance designs existed as projects, they had not yet been built; fine idealistic schemes were shown only in drawings and a few paintings or, like Michelangelo's Campidoglio, they awaited building. Bernardo Rossellino's tiny trapezoidal Pienza was more the result of adapting an existing site and neatly completing its buildings than of the ideal willed symmetry sometimes willed on it by art historians; Antonio da San Gallo's Piazza della Santissima Annunziata in Florence was still fragmentary; and the arcaded piazza built for Lodovico il Moro at Vigevano, while remarkably regular, was remote and little known.

In all Spain, possibly only the big plazas at Medina del Campo and Santiago de Compostela could be thought to rival these two Mexican squares in size, but Medina seems to have had only an irregular and unorganized space for annual fairs, and the handsome plaza at Santiago, while made with some conception of a unified architectural whole, half renaissance and half mediaeval, was still less homogeneous than the Plaza Mayor of México-Tenochtitlán. Salamanca had a big plaza by 1548, but it was of uncertain form, probably not regular. That at Valladolid was rebuilt and probably regularized only in 1561. Philip II's Madrid, almost as much a new city as Cortés' Mexico, would have to wait until the seventeenth century to have its orderly Plaza Mayor, long after Mexico, Puebla, and Oaxaca. Small wonder Doctor Cervantes was impressed! [39]

＊

While the new capital displayed these advanced and disciplined European ideas, it was still almost as bright with flowering trees and gardens as the fantastic archipelagian metropolis of Moctezuma. Although the Spaniards began to replace its skein of canals with streets, there were still so many gleaming little waterways threading the city, here and there alternating with the streets, that many travelers were reminded of Venice; some called it "Great Venice," for México-Tenochtitlán was much larger. It was also far more regular, and opened up with more large squares. Celebrated for its flowers, the preconquest city had not grown its own food, which instead was brought across the lake by little flotillas of canoes from the score of surrounding garden villages. The Spaniards interspersed the native flowers with lilies, carnations, and roses, and they planted European fruit trees. In 1636 the renegade English friar, Thomas Gage, found that: "There is nothing in Mexico wanting which may make a city happy; and certainly had those who have so much extolled with their pens the parts of Granada in Spain, Lombardy and Florence in Italy, making them the earthly paradise, had they been acquainted with the New World and with Mexico, they would have recanted their untruths." [40] If one has lived there, one has no will to argue with him.

NEW TOWNS

With about 700,000 people, Mexico in the eighteenth century was still the largest city in the Spanish Empire. A fastidious Mexican Jesuit, unhappy in exile in Bologna, could say that almost everything he had seen in eighteenth-century European cities was inferior: the streets, the palaces, the plazas. Above all, the European climate could not match that of the Mexican Elysium where it was possible to have Indians deliver flowers from their boats every day in the year.[41] Deforestation and drainage of the lakes have reduced these last delights in recent times: fewer flowers, harsher climate.

Even three centuries after Cortés, it had kept enough of the virtues of both cities — the orderly new plan of the Spaniards, and the flowers and waterways of the Indians — to make cosmopolitan Baron von Humboldt count it among the handsomest cities in the world, "for its level site, for the regularity and breadth of its streets, and the grandeur of its public squares," [42] fundamentally still a heritage from the days of Cortés and Mendoza, when they were already in part a heritage from Aztec times. It is tragic to see how much of this has been vitiated, not by the usual scapegoat nineteenth century so much as by the far less pardonable heedlessness of what should have been the better informed last thirty years of our "enlightened" twentieth, which has seen the city expand fourfold. It is still larger than any city in Spain, but no longer do many travelers call it one of the most beautiful in the world.

IV

NEW MONASTERIES

The first thing they do on the land they are settling is to lay out the monastery, with a great expanse of gardens and patios, and this is the right thing to do . . . and when it is all done, they begin the church and monastery buildings, which they put up very quickly and very well. — Doctor Vasco de Puga (1564) [1]

IN the monastery towns, the most important buildings were naturally the monasteries. The bold program of the Franciscans, Dominicans, and Augustinians made them the busiest of all the sixteenth-century builders. Although everything was made with mediaeval or even neolithic tools, and virtually without the help of draft animals, once it was well under way the building campaign was carried on at a speed and scale not surpassed anywhere until after the Industrial Revolution had transformed the means of production.

Whereas the civilians, never quite sure they could keep their lands and laborers, sometimes hoped to retire to Spain with their money, the friars knew that *they* would likely live out the rest of their days, and die and be buried in their new monasteries. Small wonder that they built so enduringly when they could. This difference in lay and clerical attitudes was perhaps most marked in the time of Viceroy Mendoza, when the encomenderos were most insecure and when the friars were confidently trying out the types and forms their friaries would repeat through the century. In the earlier decades, the need and wish for permanent buildings were qualified by two conditions which tended to keep them modest: first, they had to be built by Indians inexperienced in European ways; second, the friars were teaching their religion in a manner so modest that its buildings often took on some of that modest character. Both conditions were considerably modified after the middle of the century.

The conquistadores were soldiers, and the first friars were missionaries: neither were architects. Although a random few had had some experience as carpenters or masons, so far as we now know, with one possible exception, no friar had been trained as an architect. Consequently, the buildings of the first dozen years were largely improvised in both plan and structure, so much so that many soon had to be rebuilt. The hundred "churches" Fray Pedro de Gante claimed to have put up by 1529 cannot have been either well designed or well constructed, nor can many of the "many churches" Cortés claimed were in use a few years later have been more than sheds or huts. The first Franciscan church at Tetlán, near Guadalajara, for example, was a small, hastily built adobe box (1532). In some cases no more than the general layout can have been recognizably European, as at Maní in Yucatan, where two thousand Indians built an entire church and monastery for the newly arrived Franciscans in one day, all of light wood without a single nail. This was an unusually speedy performance, and to European eyes the result must have been an unusual architectural ensemble. Father Motolinía marveled at how they were often able to "put no spike or nail in their buildings, which do not lack strength because of that." [2]

THE EARLIEST MONASTERIES

The Audiencia said that there were "almost 20" monasteries in Mexico in 1531. Viceroy Mendoza arrived in 1535 with instructions to see that more were founded, particularly in regions where there were not yet any. On the floor and slopes of the Valley of Mexico, the Franciscans had organized more than 40 Christian towns by 1537, 12 with monasteries and the rest with visita chapels. In three or four years Father Motolinía calculated that besides the monasteries, in all New Spain there were already more than 500 active churches or chapels of one sort or another — mostly another — and he believed that had the Indians had their way there would have been 1000, since each barrio and even each head of an important family now wanted a separate church. It was claimed that every church had a bell.[3]

By 1540 there must have been about 45 monasteries, over twice as many as a decade before. With more collaboration from more converts an energetic building drive was well under way, and many of the earlier borrowed or makeshift constructions were being replaced by durable masonry. Already ahead in quantity, New Spain now surpassed Santo Domingo in quality. A few substantial survivors from the period can still be seen:

One nearly complete monastic establishment at Franciscan Tlaquiltenango near Cuernavaca, once inscribed "finished in 1540"; [4]

Another at Augustinian Epazoyucan, among the pulque haciendas on the plains of Hidalgo, noted by Basalenque and Grijalva as having been built in seven months in 1540–41; [5]

One ruined church without its monastery block at Franciscan Tehuacán Viejo; [6]

One monastery block without its church at Augustinian Ocuituco; [7]

Several simple cloisters — at Acatlán near Epazoyucan, the smaller cloister at Acolman, La Comunidad at Metztitlán, Huaquechula, Ocuituco, Totolapan, and Yecapixtla; [8]

Probably the fine open chapel at Cuernavaca and the strange small one at Tlaxcala.[9]

Except perhaps for the simple crude cloisters, none of these survivors from before 1541 relates closely enough to any others to form the nucleus of a definite stylistic group; their relation is chronological, not morphological; they are samples in one series, not one species. Furthermore, what time happens to have left may not be what was typical and may not represent more than one class of work, for the survivors are of stone and owe their survival to it. Before 1541 stone buildings must have been exceptions, far outnumbered by buildings of wood, adobe, or rammed earth, all now disintegrated. From the two big stone monasteries fortunately still upright at Tlaquiltenango and Epazoyucan, however, and from bits of others, it is clear that a standard scheme was beginning to take shape around 1540, although it had not yet quite coalesced into its final form.

*

From the later years of Viceroy Mendoza's reign and the first decade of Velasco's — that is, from the late 1540's to around 1560 — there remains in fair condition a large group of monasteries, similar in plan, general design, and style (mainly late gothic, renaissance plateresque, or a mixture). The controlling authority of an official scheme is clear: there are few important deviations. The following are major examples:

Acolman (Mex.)	Malinalco (Mex.)
Actopan (Hgo.)	Maní (Yuc.)
Amecameca (Mex.)	Metztitlán (Hgo.)
Atlixco (Pue.)	Molango (Hgo.)
Atotonilco el Grande (Hgo.)	Oaxtepec (Mor.)
Calpan (Pue.)	Otumba (Mex.)
Campeche (Camp.)	Puebla (Pue.)
Chimalhuacán Chalco (Mex.)	Quecholac (Pue.)
Cholula (Pue.)	Tecali (Pue.)
Cuernavaca (Mor.)	Tecamachalco (Pue.)
Cuilapan (Oax.)	Tehuantepec (Oax.)
Cuitzeo (Mich.)	Tepeaca (Pue.)
Etzatlán (Jal.)	Tlatlauquitepec (Pue.)
Huaquechula (Pue.)	Tlaxiaco (Oax.)
Huejotzingo (Pue.)	Tlayacapan (Mor.)
Huejutla (Hgo.)	Tula (Hgo.)
Ixmiquilpan (Hgo.)	Valladolid (Yuc.)
Izamal (Yuc.)	Yecapixtla (Mor.)
Izúcar de Matamoros (Pue.)	Yuriria (Gto.)

There are additional examples, mostly more fragmentary.

NEW MONASTERIES

The earliest monasteries in some other parts of the country were probably similar, though built later. In Yucatan, conquered 20 years after Tenochtitlán, those the Franciscans built in the '50's seem to correspond to those of central Mexico 15 or 20 years before. The monasteries built still later as the grand campaign worked north into the regions of Zacatecas and Durango perhaps also were similar. The establishments at Nombre de Díos, Sombrerete, or the cities of Zacatecas or Durango retain nothing of their early construction (save perhaps some characterless walls at Nombre de Díos), but they were presumably equivalent, as were also the simple adobe establishments of Jalisco and Colima.

28 TLAQUILTENANGO
   Section and interior of the Franciscan church of 1540.
   Beyond the barrel-vaulted nave is the chancel arch, carried on rounded jambs which are reeded like giant columns. The apse has been altered or rebuilt. The vaults have been patched, and buttresses have been added outside after damage from quakes.

THE STANDARD PLAN, FRIAR ARCHITECTS, AND INDIAN WORKMEN

While the general scheme began to emerge in the 1530's, and take definite shape in the '40's, it was not yet mandatory. In the late 1540's and early '50's, Philip II issued several edicts ordering more monasteries to be built, and in 1548 he ordered them to conform to a standard scheme. This must have been formulated on the basis of successful Franciscan and perhaps Augustinian examples built during Viceroy Mendoza's term. In 1550 he urged his successor to see that a "moderate plan" which he had approved should continue to be used (presumably the same plan promulgated in 1548) in order to avoid the "great errors" already made in work built without proper architects. As one able to curb such errors he particularly recommended an experienced architect and building inspector, Hernando Toribio de Alcaraz. The Franciscans and Augustinians were now conforming easily to official wishes (which were chiefly a codification of their own practice), but the Dominicans were undertaking enormous monasteries in the Mixteca (Teposcolula, Coixtlahuaca, Yanhuitlán) which would soon be found too discrepant.[10]

During the 1550's and '60's the standard scheme was again promulgated several times as a norm from which there was to be no variation. The Franciscans chose their house at San Juan Teotihuacán as a model for small monasteries, and that at Cholula for larger ones with seminaries. The Dominicans chose Atzcapotzalco as their archetype. The Franciscan Chapter of 1569 decided that a plan should be sent to all those of the Order about to build, to be "carried out without any excess whatsoever" in buildings which should be "plain, strong, and without any novelty." After a decade more orders were sent to circumvent anyone's building anything out of the ordinary. That the builders had so often to be told what not to do shows that they were not always conforming to what they had been told to do. Architectural disobedience and deviation, engaging as they sometimes can be, have far less importance here than the fact that there *was* an official norm: another example of the way Spain regulated — or tried to regulate — almost every phase of life in New Spain.[11] Such uniformity may seem surprising decades before the formulation of the academic classicizing canons in the treatises which were printed later in the sixteenth century. The closest earlier analogy may be in the standard plan for churches and monasteries which had controlled the buildings of the Cistercians until about 1200. Though there can be no direct connection with the Mexican friars' program, the Cistercians, too, had insisted that their monasteries be plain, strong, and without any novelty.

*

The basic scheme for the monasteries, which provided suitable spaces for their many varied activities, was probably the creation of the friars — amateurs or semi-amateurs — whose pooled experience was already determining its form before the first professional architects arrived. There cannot have been any trained architects among the "many artificers" brought over by Viceroy Mendoza before the middle of the century, for he himself soon complained that it was the lack of them that was causing "many errors" and "grave defects." No one was found fit to undertake the building of a new Cathedral. Consequently, other kinds of craftsmen or bold tyros had to substitute for architects: willing non-professionals such as Alonso García Bravo, Martín de Sepúlveda, Diego Díaz, and several shadowy others about whom nothing very informative is known, for though their names have been preserved their identifiable works have not. Moreover, these men were active in the capital and are not known to have had anything to do with the construction of typical monasteries or the evolution of their plan. That must have been done mainly in the country. It can only have been the work of the friars themselves, and they must have evolved their satisfactory type of monastery not only before the arrival of any professionals or the establishment of any professional guild of building workers, but also in independence of those practicing non-professionals in the capital — at a time when all building, whether for or by friars or civilians, was at least half improvised. Only later in the century did the guilds set up professional standards for craftsmanship and materials, standards which may or may not have been generally respected in monastery building. Certainly they were matched in the best work.[12]

Although Saint Francis had said that each brother was to learn to do something useful with his hands, very few of those who came to Mexico can have had even amateur building experience in Spain. Father Focher said that "more than once friars with no knowledge of architecture have built . . . so well that one would think they had been trained since childhood." To the general inexperience there may be one documented elusive exception: Fray Martín de Valencia who, according to Father Motolinía — and to Torquemada and Vetancurt following him — had built a monastery at Belvís in central Spain for an Observant community founded in 1509. Inasmuch as several friars from Belvís came early to Mexico, and as the Twelve spent some time there before embarking, Belvís could have been influential. Unfortunately its buildings have lain in uninformative ruin for two centuries. Unfortunately also, though Father Motolinía who knew him well said that Fray Martín had done some work at Tlaxcala while Guardian there, he cannot be connected with any surviving building there or anywhere in Mexico. Busy with administration and missionary work during his decade in Mexico (1523–34), he cannot have had many hours free to give to architecture. It is not even sure that he was an architect or amateur architect, for when a chronicler wrote that the Guardian of a monastery "built" something it may mean only that he ordered something built — "built" it in the sense that Philip II "built" the Escorial. Viceroy Mendoza cannot have considered Fray Martín an architect because he complained that there were none in the country. Neither Father Vetancurt nor any later chronicler associated him with any specific building in Mexico, which means either that nothing he built was still standing, or that he built nothing. When accurate Father Grijalva wrote that there were no experienced architects in the early days, either he forgot Fray Martín, knew no work by him, or did not consider him an experienced architect. While Fray Martín may have been effective in the genesis of the monastery type — there is no one with a better claim — the threads of evidence are not strong enough to sustain more than a conjecture.[13]

Knowledge of other friar builders is no more satisfactory, for not only is their relation to the formulation of the standard plan unclear, but so is their relation to the practice of architecture, professional or amateur. For example, Father Basalenque called Fray Juan de Utrera, who had built much of the monastery at Ucareo, "a very great architect," but probably not so much for his designs as for his speeded-up methods of construction, ingeniously derived from the Biblical account of the building of Solomon's Temple. Although Fray Juan de San Román was said to have worked as a mason to ready himself for building monasteries and churches in Mexico, as well as to mortify his body, nothing is known of his work, not even whether there ever was any. Fray Juan de Gracia "helped" build monasteries in the west (Sayula, Zacoalco, Guadalajara), but one may question how architectural was his help when told that his regular job was gardening. There are equally uninformative hints of other amateurs, even of one quite untrained but extolled as a "natural" or "born" architect. Father Basalenque may have given a clue — though a questionable one — when he wrote that there had been an "abundance of good Spanish craftsmen" at Tiripetío, working for the friars and training Indians to work for them in good Spanish ways. But what sort of work? Crafts such as weaving and pottery-making? or building? Knowledge of the friar builders is not only scant, but thin in quality.[14]

Despite the complaints that there were no acceptable architects or builders in the 1540's or '50's, evidence to the contrary is proclaimed by a few dozen competent buildings, and proclaimed *fortissimo* by two or three which are far more than merely competent. To produce these, some friars must have become respectable autodidact architects, and they must have learned not in Spain but in New Spain.

Some friars, while they may not qualify as true architects, were active builders or important architectural entrepreneurs, and mixed among them are probably some of the admirable autodidacts: the Augustinians Diego de Chávez (Tiripetío, Tacámbaro, Yuriria), Andrés de Mata (Actopan, Ixmiquilpan), and Juan de Utrera (Ucareo); the Dominicans Lorenzo de la Asunción (Atzcapotzalco, Tacubaya, Yautepec), Ambrosio de Santa María (Coyoacán); the Franciscans Juan de Mérida (Mérida, Maní, Izamal, Valladolid), or the puzzling Juan de Alameda (Huejotzingo, Atlixco, Huaquechula, and perhaps parts of Tula). Some, like the historian Gerónimo de Mendieta, were surely no more than administrators who did not design the churches they caused to be built. How much, if at all, the others took part in designing remains uncertain, but important though this may be, it is not pertinent here, for those about whom anything is known crossed the sea too late to have affected the standard scheme. The first known professional, Toribio de Alcaraz, was endorsed as an architect by Viceroy Mendoza specifically in connection with monasteries, but he did not arrive in Mexico until 1544:[15] he may well have been instrumental in codifying or clarifying the standard scheme, but not in creating it.

NEW MONASTERIES

The paucity of traces of architects with training may not, after all, be impeditive here, for the building of the early monasteries could have been directed successfully by intelligent men without specialized skill: because they are mechanically so simple and stylistically so neutral or undeveloped save for superficial decorative details. (These — whether doorways, windows, cornices, or capitals — presumably could have been left to the varying skills of subordinate craftsmen, not architects or near-architects.) Although not surely typical, an episode in the building of the College of Santa María de Todos Santos in the capital (1565) may be revealing: only *after* the materials had been brought to the site and the building had already been begun was it decided to ask for the assistance of an architect. As there were "no Indian architects in those rude days of beginning," help was sought from the Spanish architect of the new Cathedral, Claudio de Arciniega (who only very doubtfully would have had time to spare for the project).[16]

There is little likelihood that the monastery scheme was based on plans prepared in Spain, for few plans of any kind were sent over before 1550, and presumably none before 1540 when the standard scheme was already taking shape. The plans which were sent later arrived too late to affect its formation; some 210 drawings came in 1572, but it is not known of what.[17] Furthermore, though its parts are almost entirely derived from Spanish models, the whole does not look convincingly like official Spanish work of the time.

The standard plan *must* have been a Mexican creation or a synthesis made in Mexico. It could have been worked out for some of the first Franciscan houses, entirely or in part, by Fray Martín de Valencia before he died in 1534; it could have evolved entirely from anonymous collective experience during the same years; it could have been systematized by Toribio de Alcaraz: without more facts it is not possible to know.

*

One must remember the quantity and quality of the workmen available: quantity perhaps unequaled since Imperial Rome or Byzantium, and quality often high. The Indian workmen were the products of a long and distinguished architectural culture, and so adept that they learned European forms and procedures with a speed and facility that delighted and sometimes alarmed their European masters. The European "designers" contributed less than their opposite numbers in Europe, and the adaptability and inbred skill of the native craftsmen sometimes counterbalanced or concealed their masters' imperfect mastery.

Outnumbering the scores of skilled craftsmen were thousands of ordinary laborers. Father Motolinía said that "all the Indians work: they carry the stone; they make the lime, adobe, and bricks; they make the walls, square the beams, and carry the boards." The Franciscans thought church-building a particularly salutary activity for their ordinary Indians, and wrote that "this is why those who ruled them in the time of their unbelief kept them busy most of the time in building temples" (1569).[18] The other Orders concurred. The Indians' way of working for the friars must have been much like their old way of working before the Spaniards came when the emphasis was on big communal undertakings, with everyone doing his share. The procedure was gradually systematized by the Spaniards into the usual late mediaeval hierarchy, with masters, apprentices, and armies of common workmen below them; the highest ranks, barred to Indians, must have been proportionally smaller than in Europe.

Doctor Zorita (in Mexico 1554–64) noticed that "in this way they have made the churches and monasteries in their towns, with much contentment and rejoicing, and not too much work." At about the same time Father Mendieta found that "A wonderful thing was the fervor and diligence with which the Indians . . . managed to build churches in all their towns, with even the women and children attending to the carrying of the building materials, one group trying to get ahead of the other by making their church bigger and better, and ornamenting it as much as possible." Father Torquemada, who arrived a decade later, wrote: "Although it is too well known to ask, who built the many churches and monasteries which the friars have here in New Spain? who but the Indians? With their own hands and sweat, of their own will, and with great joy . . . And when they knew that the friars were coming . . . the Indians went out to meet them, the streets swept and full of flowers, with music (of the kind they have) and dances of great rejoicing. If the monastery is not already built, they do not delay in building it, and just as they have been instructed. It was a wonderful thing how quickly they finished building them, all in good stone masonry, in half a year or at most a whole year. When there was foreknowledge, some were all built and finished when the friars arrived." [19]

Until late in the century, the Indians who built for the friars were not usually paid, but the natives of a town were nonetheless expected to be responsible for building its church. They seem to have taken this for granted, and sometimes even volunteered. Again the evidence is from one side, but again it is so copious that proof must come from those who would refute it. Sometimes the Indians would offer their services before they were asked (as when in 1543 they offered to build a house for the two friars who were somehow living on top of the church of Santiago Tlatelolco).[20] When, later in the century, native carpenters and masons were paid, they were paid well, but these must have been the most skilled workmen. Conditions were not always happy, as the existence of stocks and whipping posts attests. Discipline sometimes had to be administered — the Indians were used to that and even expected to be whipped — but the friars seem to have been moderate except when carried away by un-Mendicant enthusiasm for building some grand new monastery.

There were not many complaints about the labor the Indians gave the friars, nor were many made about the secular parish churches, but there are thousands of complaints preserved against the lay Spaniards. When they were building the elaborate church and monastery for the Augustinians at Acolman the Indians did not complain about the work, so far as is known, but they did complain bitterly about the exorbitant services being demanded by the local encomenderos (1550's). Clarence Haring once observed that while the missionaries were sometimes accused by civilians of exploiting the Indians, this was "a privilege the civilian population would have preferred to reserve exclusively for itself." [21]

Often jealous of the friars' privileged position, the civilian authorities and the secular clergy did not always concur with the friars' estimates of their own disinterestedness, and would point out that the monasteries had been built by unpaid native labor. Of course they pointed at the biggest and most luxurious establishments and, while correct in saying that these had been built *by* the Indians, they could not get around the fact that they had been built also *for* the Indians. Although some churches were rich-looking, the quarters of the friars were not. The Indians saw the lack of creature comforts and (usually) the scorn of money; they knew that the friars had refused to collect the tithes the Crown had proposed; they knew also the cupidity, hedonism, and cruelty of many Spanish civilians; and these contrasts must have helped convince them of the spirituality, disinterestedness, and benevolence of the friars.

While few of the monasteries owed much to any Spanish civilian, beyond occasional gifts from pious ladies and frightened men near death, all owed a great deal to the local Indians. The Indians also owed a great deal to the friars for whom they not unwillingly built: they owed them what well-being they had, and sometimes they owed them their lives.

*

Surprisingly independent of Spain in their campaign of conversion, the Mexican friars were equally independent in their architecture. Their buildings are never replicas of buildings in Spain, nor often clear provincial echoes, any more than renaissance churches in Spain are replicas or echoes of renaissance churches in Italy. In addition to the divergences brought about by different needs, the Mexican buildings show several other dissimilarities: first, from the independence of the Mexican regulars; second, from their remoteness from Spain; third, from their nearness to old local building traditions; fourth, from the unfamiliarity with Spanish architectural traditions on the part of the amateur friar builders and their native workmen.

Although it presented a few idiosyncrasies, the real importance of the monastery scheme did not depend on its novelty any more than did the town plan but — quite the contrary — on the knowing combination of familiar elements into a scheme so satisfactory from any pertinent point of view that it could remain in active use with only minor modifications for the next three centuries. The style of the doorways or windows or decorative details changed again and again, from late gothic to renaissance plateresque to mudéjar or purist and then on to the many phases of the local baroque, but the underlying scheme did not change. It was not subject to changing styles because it depended on uses that did not change.

Its three major components were largely determined by local needs and must have been tried out together early. All three were clear by 1540 at Tlaquiltenango and Epazoyucan, and had become standardized in the monasteries built around 1550. All three are regularly present in the yet larger group from the next three decades and — after the lull following the plague of 1576 — in works from the last decades of the century.

The three parts were

> the *church,*
>
> the *monastery building* adjoining it, and
>
> the forecourt, patio, or *atrio* in front of it.

THE MONASTERY CHURCH

> *Inside, the churches are beautiful, cleanly, and devotional; and outside, they are handsome, and battlemented; and in the country, which is gay and florid in itself . . . the churches look very fine, and give a pretty aspect to Mexico.*
>
> — *Father Motolinía* (1537) [22]

The most important of the architectural elements making up the monastery was quite properly the church. As a group, the sixteenth-century churches of Mexico have become known only during the last thirty years; almost none had appeared in a publication before 1927. Manuel Revilla all but ignored them in his pleasant but slight essays of 1893, with one glancing comment on the Franciscan church at Tlaxcala, which is almost all of the seventeenth century. In 1910 Sylvester Baxter published ten handsome volumes on Mexican colonial architecture innocent of the character or extent of sixteenth-century work. (He limited himself to what he could see from a private railway car.) In 1915 Federico Mariscal and Max Leopold Wagner, the first of the modern Mexican and the first of the modern European historians of viceregal architecture, both thought that the sixteenth century was exemplified by the church of Santiago Tlatelolco. They knew only the exterior, which they believed to have been built in 1524, a century before its true date. In 1918 a young Franciscan, Fray Luis del Refugio de Palacio, wrote serious notices of the early Franciscan monasteries at Huejotzingo and Cholula, and appraised several others. His precocious investigations were more antiquarian than scholarly, perhaps more limited than thorough, and furthermore, they were not published until 1937. Manuel Romero de Terreros wrote perceptively on the Augustinian monastery at Acolman in 1921, and could name a dozen other monasteries — reachable by railway — which he recognized rightly as typical of the sixteenth century. Without denying their due to these intelligent amateurs, the real honor of discovering the extraordinary wealth of sixteenth-century architecture in Mexico must be accorded to Manuel Toussaint who, after locating and photographing most of the major monuments and scouring records for their histories, in 1927 published *La arquitectura religiosa en la Nueva España en el siglo XVI*. He continued to seek, study, and sift, and during the next thirty years published a series of scholarly, perceptive, and beautifully written studies of many phases of colonial art. They remain unsurpassed. Following him, the last generation has made its contributions: the researches of Toussaint's most important pupil, Francisco de la Maza, and of the American George Kubler, have extended knowledge of the colonial architecture of Mexico in many rewarding directions. The later work of Manuel Romero de Terreros has made a series of welcome scholarly additions. Justino Fernández has edited important compendiums of all the churches in Hidalgo and Yucatan.

Still standing unstudied in remote sites there may be a score or more of sixteenth-century churches awaiting a "discoverer." Prospectors, archaeologists, and folklorists have penetrated considerable *terra* otherwise *incognita*, but who with a knowledge of colonial art knows what, if anything, would repay a trip to Alcozauca, Atlixtac, or Pungarabato in the State of Guerrero, or if anything of the early Augustinian monasteries is visible at quake-racked Tlapa and Chilapa? What is at Poncitlán, Tolimán, and many other old towns in Jalisco? Jalatlaco or Texcatepec in the State of Mexico? Sirosto or Tancítaro in Michoacán, or Tingambato, once the richest in that rich province, supported by the friars' big sugar mill nearby? Has any historian of art visited Hueyapan in Morelos? Acaponeta or Ahuacatlán in Nayarit? Villa Alta de San Ildefonso, Teotitlán del Camino, or Tilantongo in Oaxaca? Chietla, Chiautla, Huehuetlán, Hueytlalpan, Tepexi de Rodríguez (once "Tepexi of Silk"), Tepeoxuma, or Santo Tomás Hueyotlipan (or de Acatzingo) in the State of Puebla? In 1924 Bishop Vera y Zuria admired a magnificent mudéjar wood ceiling at Ixtacamaxtitlán in Puebla,[23] but it has since burned, and who has been there to see what, if anything, is left? Who has been able to reach Xilitla in San Luis Potosí, near the Pan-American Highway but across a river where the primitive ferry is almost always broken down? While it is doubtful that much remains at many of these, until they are visited and examined by practiced scholars, who can be sure?

Thanks to the photographic files of the Department of Colonial Monuments in Mexico City and of the Instituto de Investigaciones Estéticas of the University, visual information has been made available about many other monasteries of the period, but by necessity it is often only fragmentary. The extensive but incomplete files of plans at Bienes Nacionales do not distinguish between work forty and four hundred years old. These comments are not complaints — all scholars are deeply grateful to Manuel Toussaint and the others who have so assiduously gathered the graphic documentation — but merely indications that there are more discoveries to be made. There are now almost no professional scholars, and few architects, laymen, or clergy who are concerned or even interested. The collapse and unprotested destruction of a few monuments of Mexico's great architectural past every year continues: shockingly few people know of it, or care.

*

The friars regularly observed the current European proprieties in building their churches. First: the church must be consecrated (or sometimes merely blessed), and contain at least one consecrated altar. Second: it must be built to be a church, and never be used for any other purpose, for that would constitute a sacrilege. Third: it should be a permanent structure if possible (clearly not possible in the first missions in new lands). Fourth: it must be arranged with a sanctuary for the altar and celebrants (at the east end if possible), a nave for the congregation, a choir for the singers, a baptismal font with a suitable space around it, and a porch or portal or some suitable space outside the church for use at the beginning of the Baptismal Rite.

These imperatives were standard, and applicable to Catholic churches anywhere. Monastery churches had two more: there must be a large choir where the friars could recite or chant their daily offices (commonly but not necessarily the same as the choir for the singers at public Masses); and there must be a direct entrance from the monastery building (usually from its cloister).

Mexican monastery churches were made primarily for the friars' conventual Masses and the reciting and chanting of their prescribed offices. The necessities were consequently the same as those for small monastery churches in Spain or anywhere else. Such Mexican monastery churches had not been built to house the local congregations of Indians, for their needs were ordinarily satisfied by other architectural elements; nor were these churches primarily for the Spanish or mestizo townspeople although they did make up most of the congregations at the public Masses in the church on Sundays and feast days. Because they were used principally for the friars' own offices, the churches of the monasteries were only incidentally a part of the architecture

133

of the Great Conversion and, interesting and handsome as they often are, they need be only incidentally considered here.

❧

The standard type of monastery church was set principally by the Franciscans because they started building first. The Augustinians began to build importantly only after the standard type had been developed, and the Dominicans also began their major architectural campaign later. There had been no significant differences between Franciscan and Dominican churches in Spain, for both were derived mainly from a combination of local Spanish traditions with the simple tradition of Mendicant building in Italy, where the churches were large, plain preaching halls which could hold an entire town. The Mexican churches may be related as well to lesser southern Spanish churches with flat roofs, thick walls, few and small windows, though of course similar climatic conditions in Mexico may be as important for these features as any memory of simple Spanish models. Inasmuch as there are surprisingly few churches in sixteenth-century Spain that clearly belong to the same species as the standard Mexican monastery church, it is probable that the pooled experience of the earliest friars determined the plain, economical, and easily constructed standard type locally, far more than any memories of European models, necessarily blurred and diluted in the pooling.

Architecturally, nearly all the surviving sixteenth-century churches of Mexico belong to one family. A few, however, particularly among the earliest, belonged to a separate group, with a nave flanked by aisles, an arrangement which, when the construction was of wood, made it easier to roof a large space. Although this scheme later recurred occasionally, most often in the large cities, the great majority of monastery churches had one broad aisleless nave. Mendicant churches in Europe had also often been aisleless, though usually on a larger scale. While the Franciscan church at Xochimilco was one of the roomiest — about 70 feet wide and 200 long — most were but half that size.[24]

Unlike the grander Spanish churches but like many modest provincial ones, the great majority of Mexican churches had no transepts. (Rare exceptions are at Yuriria and Copanabastla.) Only a few in the sixteenth century had side chapels, probably because there was rarely any religious activity that would call for them. Some of the friars were chary of separate images such as subordinate chapels might house, lest the new religion seem as polytheistic as the old, or lest some special image come to be considered divine in itself, as the lovely picture of the Virgin of Guadalupe soon would be. This may be a local equivalent of the reformist attitude of Saint John of the Cross who, in direct opposition to the general Spanish attitude, was insisting that truly devout men need few images. The Dominicans occasionally began to want separate chapels sometime after their organization of confraternities for

the Rosary in 1538, and the demand increased with the intensified veneration of the Rosary after the great semi-Spanish victory at Lepanto in 1571 on
the day of the Feast of the Rosary. A booklet about the uses, occasions, festivals, and singing clubs of the Rosary was published by a Dominican in
Puebla in 1559, and had to be reprinted several times before 1600. According to chroniclers, the Indians became very enthusiastic about confraternities,
and those of the Rosary spread from the capital, Puebla, and Oaxaca to all
the Dominican houses, though only late in the century did they begin to have
their own special chapels. The Dominicans had weighed the question of separate chapels for private families, which they encouraged in Spain, and decided against them for New Spain. While not so rare as side chapels, side
altars must also have been uncommon until the end of the century. Altogether the Dominicans departed more often from the standard plan than the
other two Orders.

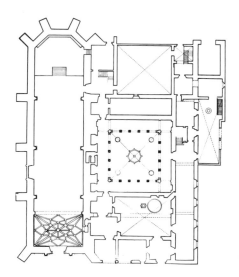

29 THE FRANCISCAN MONAS–
TERY AT HUEJOTZINGO *laid
out in the early 1540's and largely
completed in the next twenty or thirty
years.*

*The heavy-walled and deep-but-
tressed church, with a choir-balcony
and a raised chancel, is typical. The
opening under the choir-balcony at
the right leads to a confessional which*
*a friar-priest could enter unseen from
the monastery side; another is accessible from the cloister: these are unusual features. The doorway by the
chancel leads to the sacristy. The
once-important north side door of the
church has been walled up. In the
monastery block, the long room east
of the cloister was the* Sala de Profundis, *and the longer room in the southwest corner was the refectory.*

135

30 SAN AGUSTÍN ACOLMAN

Most of the monastery church was built c1558. The white sanctuary walls were painted a generation later, with monumentally enthroned ecclesiastics, in red, ocher, and black. The retable and other fittings were added in subsequent centuries.

136

THEIR CHURCHES

The nave was long, high, and plain. Ordinarily its walls were uninterruptedly flat. Only rarely was it divided into bays, as by the arcades on the walls at Oaxtepec, or by the archways of the flanking chapels which are opened to each other as well to form a sort of side aisle in a few Dominican churches. Generally the walls were cut only by the small accents of the windows at their top, or by a door to the sacristy or occasionally a baptistery, or sometimes by small doors to confessionals sunk in the thick walls.

Often the surfaces were enlivened with didactic black-and-white paintings in imitation of European models, more often woodcuts from the northern countries than murals in Spain. Although there were doubtless more frescoes to be seen in Spanish monasteries then than now, there never were many, and the murals uncovered in about seventy-five Mexican monasteries during the last half century constitute the largest corpus of sixteenth-century "frescoes" anywhere in the Hispanic world. None surviving is likely older than 1550.[25] The handsomest were conceived as monumental architectural decoration, but somewhat nearsightedly. Uncoordinated with their architectural context, others seem not so much to have been designed for their walls as merely to have happened to be painted there. At Tepeaca there are small painted retables on the side walls, presumably as substitutes for costlier carving.

The Spaniards had been impressed by the elaborately painted walls of Indian temples and palaces, and the murals in churches and monastery buildings may reflect that admiration. Because of the glossiness of the surface, at first glance the technique may appear more Indian than European, but closer examination shows the reverse to be true. There are no close antecedents in preconquest painting, and the technique is often identifiably Spanish: not "true" fresco which was rare in Spain before Philip II imported Italian artists to decorate his Escorial, but a variation of the commoner *fresco secco* in some locally adapted recipe. The black of the outlines and shading (often hatched as in a woodcut or copperplate) appears to have been made of iron sulphate and charcoal, like much contemporary ink. This was usually applied to dry plaster made of lime and volcanic sand with a smooth surface film of sifted slaked lime. The black did not sink into this hard dry plaster any more than ink sank into good paper. Occasionally something more like tempera paint was used, particularly for color. The Painters' Guild of Mexico City issued regulations fixing procedures for technique and for perspective and shading (1557). Though so simplified as to look vaguely Indian, the anatomy of the figures and the spatial relation to their settings came as surely from European traditions as did the Christian subject matter. The iconographical models were probably portable imports: small paintings, pictures in books, or religious prints. Reflections and copies of ornaments in books have been identified, and also figure compositions in prints from Flanders, Italy, France, and Germany, even of engravings by Dürer and Schongauer. Sometimes old woodblocks were imported for re-use on local presses. The friars had ample supplies of popular religious prints which they gave to deserving Indians. A box with 210 drawings came over in 1572. There were plenty of European models, and only a negligible relation to preconquest wall- or manuscript-painting traditions. A new tradition was started, which like the architecture of the monasteries was based on imperfect memories of an accidental miscellany of European works. Mural painting did not pass beyond the limits of minor provincial art, for the diluted European manner, though spiced with a few Indian mannerisms, was never entirely able to keep itself above insipidity. It was, nevertheless, the beginning of an intermittent tradition which produced mural paintings of international renown four centuries later.[26]

31 "FRESCOES" ON THE STAIRWAY AT ACTOPAN *representing Augustinian theologians: Fray Gerónimo of Naples, Archbishop Alonso de Toledo of Seville, Bishop Guillermo de Vecchio of Florence, sitting on throne-like chairs and working at their desks. Between confronted beasts, the frieze below the figures displays the Augustinian emblem of the pierced Heart of Jesus, and the birds and stars of Saint Nicholas of Tolentino. The painting is mainly in black on a white ground, with small touches of vivid color. There has been considerable discreet restoration.*

Small arched and splayed windows were cut inaccessibly high in the thick walls of the nave without weakening them. Possibly the Spanish supervisors did not trust their Indian workmen's walls well enough to strain them as big openings might in a country rocked by earthquakes. Sometimes the apertures were left entirely open to the outdoors, and sometimes the sunny glare might be filtered by waxed cloth or translucent sheets of alabaster-like *tecali*. In the dim and characteristically mediaeval light inside, the congregation watched and listened; to participate in the service in such an age of faith it was not necessary to read, as it might be in a later age of reason. Moreover, the few who could read had few books. Individual prayerbooks were a luxurious rarity, as they still were in Europe, and still are in Mexico outside the cities.

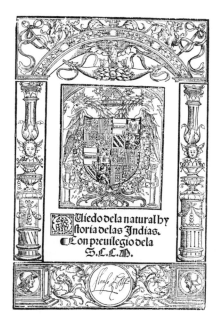

32 FRONTISPIECE OF FER–
NÁNDEZ DE OVIEDO'S
HISTORIA, 1535
The plateresque enframement of segmental arches on candelabra columns dividing the wall at Acto-pan is like the ornament in many sixteenth-century Spanish books.

33 THE NAVE OF THE FRANCISCAN MONASTERY CHURCH AT TE–
PEACA *begun in the mid-1540's. The general scale and the square domical
ribbed vaults are typical of the best work of the time. The arcades forming
shallow niches for side altars (with carved retables or imitations painted on
the wall) are exceptional. So also is the lower row of windows and the terra
cotta balls in their reveals, an ornament repeated in the upper windows, which
are otherwise normal, one under the wall arch of each of the five vaults. The
big wooden columns and baldacchino over the altar are nineteenth-century
additions.*

140

34 HUAQUECHULA
Carved stone pulpit, painted and gilded, in the monastery church, attached to the right-hand wall at the beginning of the chancel. Two panels display angels in abrupt relief, wearing diadems with jeweled crosses, and an embroidered tunic with long oversleeves. At the left a censer swings from the girdle. Their wings grow more from their collarbones than shoulder blades. The rippling hem and floating feet show that they are flying.

Near the east end of the nave there was always a pulpit. Its form not fixed by decree or custom, it must often have been a massive but movable cabinet-maker's or carpenter's construction, as it was in most Mendicant churches in Europe; but the few dozen pulpits surviving in Mexico (Cuilapan, Huaquechula, Huejotzingo, Huexotla, Molango, Tlaxcala, Tochimilco, Totimehuacán, Yecapixtla, or Zinacantepec) are of carved stone fixed to the wall. This probably reflects a custom also earlier introduced in Europe by the preaching Mendicants of Spain, possibly modified from Moslem models. In Mexico there sometimes were twin stone lecterns for the reading of the Gospel and Epistle (as at Tlalmanalco or at Izúcar where they are now so drastically "freshened up" with paint and gold leaf as to look more like fake antiques than the genuine articles they surely are).

THE SANCTUARY

Following millenary European custom, the nave was the space for the congregation. At either end there were special spaces for the clergy: at the west, the balcony for the choir, and at the east, the sanctuary or chancel for the celebrants officiating at the altar. The sanctuary was an extension of the long nave space, either of the same width or differentiated by being a little narrower. It was almost always set back and enframed by a special arch which marked the frontier between the laymen's nave and the clergy's chancel. The distinction was usually indicated also by a communion rail running across the church where the chancel began. (No women were meant to go beyond this, nor are they still in Mexico today.) The sanctuary was often further marked

141

by being raised a few steps above the level of the nave floor — three, five, or seven — by custom an odd number. Occasionally there was as well a lockable grille between the nave and sanctuary.

Strictly, the sanctuary was made up of the apse and chancel, terms not always precise though the latter is usually understood as the space in back of the communion rail and in front of the altar and apse. The apse itself was sometimes square, more often polygonal, rarely semicircular. At its back stood the main altar, simple and table-like, immovable, and by tradition made of stone. Against the back wall in the churches that could afford it, there often rose a many-storied and many-compartmented reredos or retable, gilded and made colorful with panel paintings and polychrome sculpture. Statutarily committed to poverty, the Franciscans were not allowed to make retables without special license from the Father Provincial. Notwithstanding, the handsomest sixteenth-century retables surviving (at Huejotzingo, Xochimilco, and Cuautinchán) were commissioned for Franciscan friaries. There were so many retable painters and gilders by 1557 that they formed a guild and made regulations to insure good workmanship and good pay. Although Indians were no more admitted to this guild than to any other, even as apprentices, many commissions were carried out by Indians. All painters, Spanish or Indian, were subject to examination by the Church before being permitted to paint for churches. There was a vogue for imported Flemish pictures, some of which were worked into retables, such as those by Martin de Vos still preserved at Cuautitlán. A few Flemish painters were attracted enough by the Mexican market to migrate, for example, Simon Pereyns, author of the big retable at Huejotzingo.

Even richer than the retable were the appointments of the altar, commonly of silver, occasionally of gold, and sometimes set with gems or turquoise mosaic. The *custodia* of San Francisco in Puebla was of gilded silver, and stood over a yard high; and in the main church of the Dominicans in the capital there was a Virgin of gold and silver studded with jewels and pearls. The frontals, vestments, miters, and banners might be embroidered in multicolored silks and gold thread, or elaborated in the preconquest tapestry technique of shimmering hummingbird feathers. The Indians made sets of feather chasubles and dalmatics for San Francisco in México-Tenochtitlán. When Clement VII, a Medici familiar with Raphael and Michelangelo, was presented with fine featherwork from Mexico (1532), he welcomed it as worthy of his greatest admiration; and when a feather picture of Saint Francis was given to Sixtus V, after touching it to make sure it was not painted, he pronounced it indeed marvellous. (These offerings perhaps resembled the feathered miter now shown in the Ethnological Museum at Vienna, and the shield of Philip II in the Armory at Madrid.) [27]

35 THE RETABLE OF THE HIGH ALTAR OF THE FRANCISCAN MON–
ASTERY CHURCH AT HUEJOTZINGO *by the painter Simon Pereyns and
the sculptor Pedro de Requena, 1584–. Four tiers of life-size polychrome
figures are set between gilded columns, which also frame paintings (in the
wings) and relief pictures (in the center section.)*

NEW MONASTERIES

Since the items requisite for the Mass were at first so hard to obtain in the New World, the King made it a practice to present some of them to new monasteries. To his regular gifts of oil, wheat flour, and wine, he would sometimes add a silver chalice, a lamp, and a bell. The clergy received many similar offerings from pious local Spaniards, local Indian lords, and poorer Indians who worked for years and saved up their pittances to make at least one handsome gift to their church before they died. By the end of the century, the amount of gold and silver in the altar services of the Dominicans and Augustinians — by now mostly made in Mexico — had accumulated to an impressive treasure. The processional cross at Augustinian Yuriria was so big that it took four men to carry it, and the monstrance was as high as a man. The Franciscans were not supposed to amass such treasures, and they were not even allowed to accept gifts of new altar services under the pretext that more and larger fittings were needed for the special problems of serving more and more Indians. No gold was permitted them, not even in the embroidery of vestments or frontals, and no silver for censers or candlesticks. Precious metal was prescribed only for the chalice and monstrance, and supposedly proscribed for everything else. Surviving pieces show, however, that these orders were handsomely disobeyed.[28]

The decorations were not limited to these durable pieces. "The Indians celebrate the Feasts of Easter and Christmas, and those of Our Lady and the Patron Saints of the towns with great rejoicing and impressive show; they adorn the churches very prettily with whatever hangings there are, and what they lack in tapestries they make up with many boughs, leaves, and flowers of the many kinds this land produces in such abundance (quite different from those of our Spain), and also with those flowers we have brought over." [29] This custom, happily, has not been given up.

THE CHOIR-BALCONY

The west end of the nave was spanned by a balcony for the choir, used not only during Masses but off and on during the day and night for the many canonical offices the friars recited or chanted — Matins, Lauds, Prime, Terce, Sext, None, Vespers, and Compline. Sometimes the balcony was so big that it covered a third of the nave below (as at Cholula, Puebla, Cuernavaca, or Izúcar). A similar sort of balcony had recently been arranged in a number of prominent Mendicant churches built by Ferdinand and Isabella where, as a result of a special devotion to the altar service and a wish to make it easily visible, the choir with its many singers and obstructive furniture was moved from in front of the altar to the other end of the church. (Striking examples are at Avila, León, Salamanca, and in lesser late fifteenth-century churches in Andalusia.)

36 A TYPICAL CHOIR–BALCONY, ACATZINGO
The location of the font·on axis with the doorway is a modern innovation.

The balcony was lighted from a window in the facade, and was usually brighter than the nave because the members of the choir had to be able to read and the congregation did not. The window was also a feature of the design of the facade, where occasionally it took the traditional gothic form of a traceried rose (at Yecapixtla, Molango, Atotonilco el Grande, or Tapalapa in Chiapas).

The choir-balcony was supported sometimes by beams and sometimes by a shallow vault, usually in accord with the covering of the rest of the church. Under the balcony were the holy water stoups, on either side of the front door. (One can still see a particularly handsome pair with little stone hoods in the "basilica" at Cuilapan.) The baptismal font also usually stood close by the front door, almost necessarily, since so many had to be baptized at once and some of the rites were by custom held outside the entrance to the church. Sometimes the font was screened within a lockable grille of wood or iron. In a few major establishments it had its own separate baptistery room, still handy to the front doorway (Cuilapan, or Actopan). As holy water was so prized and so profusely used, stoups were sometimes made so large and elaborate that they can be mistaken for fonts.

145

37 WINDOW AT MOLANGO
A late-gothic rose with fine-scale stone tracery, giving light to the friars and musicians in the choir-balcony.

38 STOUP AT CUILAPAN
The rim of the basin is broken.

TIMBER CEILINGS

Many churches, particularly the earlier ones, were originally covered with two-pitched roofs laid on heavy close-set timbers (as still shown by the rafter slots left in the top of the chancel walls at Tehuacán Viejo, before 1540). Many of the early aisled churches must have had their roofs supported in part also by intermediate columns of wood, like many churches in rural Andalusia. Underneath the roofs sometimes there were elaborate wooden ceilings: *artesonados* sunk deep with many coffers, or *alfarjes* compounded of many short pieces ingeniously fitted together in patterns full of interlaces and stars. Trusses supporting the roof were either hidden, as in Moslem work which favored decoration over revealed structure (much as Moslem culture, despite its skills in mathematics, had often favored imagination over reason) or, if trusses were revealed, the most prominent structural members, such as paired cross beams, would be made more decorative and less structural-looking by interlaced openwork traceries of wood. The grandest ceilings (such as those once admired at Tiripetío, Tláhuac, or Xochimilco) are now gone, but something of their character may be seen in the surviving bits of smaller ceilings as in the cloisters at Tlaxcala, Tzintzuntzan,

Zinacantepec, or Atzcapotzalco). Elaborate orientalizing wood ceilings were particularly popular in Chiapas, and several simple later ones still extant show persistence of the tradition there.

An important specimen of sixteenth-century woodwork on more than a small or now fragmentary scale is the massive choir-balcony at Epazoyucan, a unique construction of close-set beams, heavily braced to shorten the effective span, like a nineteenth-century wood railway trestle, or the shoring of a mine. A more normal arrangement still in a good state has recently been rediscovered at Huatlatláuca in Puebla, where the choir is carried on a large cypress beam, carved and painted in the same style as the splendid and well preserved church ceiling.

39 THE RUINED CHURCH OF THE DOMINICANS AT TECBATÁN, *c1575. The diaphragm arches over the nave carried a wooden ceiling and roof. The low arch at the far end supported a choir-balcony.*

147

NEW MONASTERIES

Sometimes exposed wooden ceilings were divided into separate bays by a sequence of masonry arches spanning the nave, an arrangement long common on the Spanish coast from Andalusia to Catalonia and also in Galicia and Extremadura. Such diaphragm arches strengthened the whole building, required no large timbers, and hindered the spread of fire. (A clear example from 1607–25, considerably restored, survives at San Juan de Díos in Mérida; another is in a chapel beside the monastery church at Izamal; and fragments of others are at Molango, Tecbatán, Zacatlán, and San Pedro Atocpa, and also in Mexico City in the parish church of San Sebastián if the work there is part of the extensive repairs of 1558–61 as it appears to be.) [30]

For such ceilings there had been plenty of timber available nearby. Father Motolinía praised the stands of cedar, cypress, and pine near the capital, and in the middle of the century Gómara took note of the abundance of good cedar trees — some were 120 feet high — and of the 7000 cedar beams in the house of Pánfilo de Narváez. The destruction of the forests of the Valley of Mexico, begun for the rebuilding of Tenochtitlán, was already signaled by 1550. Other forests near gold and silver mines were quickly devoured as fuel for smelting. Choice wood was sent to Spain — for Philip's Escorial and later for his Invincible Armada. Topsoil soon began to wash down into the valleys, filling up the lakes around the capital with silt and leaving the hills barren *tepetate,* as one sees them still today. As the lake bottoms rose, the run-off increased, and floods became more frequent and more serious, even though the total rainfall had become less. By the end of the sixteenth century, big trees for building timbers had all but disappeared. Since 1570 the remaining timber had been protected — on paper — by legislation: no tree was to be cut without a license, but of course many were. Deforestation became so drastic as to affect not only the forms of architecture but also the

40 ACATZINGO, CHANCEL

41 CUAUTINCHÁN, NAVE

42 TLAXIACO, CHOIR–BALCONY   43 HUAQUECHULA, CHANCEL

looks of the landscape, the wetness of the weather, and the productivity of the soil. As they did also in Sicily and southern Italy, the Spaniards made parts of once-green Mexico visually and climatically into another Spain.[31]

VAULTS

Many of the best churches were vaulted. Preconquest Indian architects had been able to use big wooden beams to advantage, but they had not known how to construct masonry vaults. The so-called "vaults" of the Mayas were not of true vault construction, but usually an assemblage of irregular stones drowned in clayey mud behind a corbeled cut-stone facing. Their possible span was much too limited for the large interior spaces the Spaniards needed. Furthermore they were not known in central Mexico at this time, either by the Indians or the Spaniards. No more, as has been suggested by some writers, can the gable-like tunnels of the Zapotecas, awkwardly roofed by two stone slabs leaning diagonally on one another at the apex, have had any relation to the vaulting of big, broad churches.

True vaults, built of wedge-shaped voussoirs laid up on the principle of the arch, were a novelty introduced by the Spaniards. Father Motolinía, who had probably seen it being built, described the raising of the first one: "In 1525 the church of San Francisco was built in Mexico City. It is a small church. The chancel has a vault made by a mason from Castile. The Indians were greatly astonished to see something vaulted, and could only suppose that when the supporting scaffold was taken away, everything would surely fall down." [32] They were afraid to walk under the vault, certain that the stones (re-used from the steps of the Pyramid of Huitzilopochtli and Tláloc) would not long stay up in the air by themselves.[33]

149

NEW MONASTERIES

The Indians' fear was dispelled by experience. Nuño de Guzmán soon built a big arch, and more and more churches were vaulted, until by the middle of the century, vaulting was commonly accepted. Sometimes it was only over the sanctuary, but many stone churches were soon vaulted throughout. The simplest scheme was to run a barrel vault over both chancel and nave, making an interior like a tall tunnel (as at Tlaquiltenango, 1540, ill. 28). Cut stone, which took special skill, money, and time, was kept to a minimum. Instead, most vaults were formed of roughly shaped stones sunk in mortar, making a sort of rubble which, when dry and hardened, was almost a continuous solid of unreinforced concrete, and consequently had little thrust. This amalgam was as much like some kinds of massive preconquest rubble masonry as like anything Spanish — in substance, that is, not in form. It was not combined with corbeling, as in Maya work, but often supplemented true vaulting of cut stone or brick.

*

Although there were several pronouncements about the virtues of architectural poverty which would preclude the use of vaults in Mexico, they were repeatedly ignored, sometimes flauntingly. (Similar strictures had proved similarly ineffectual among Mendicant communities in Europe.) Stressing their poverty as a virtue, and citing the Constitutions of Saint Bonaventura, the Franciscans of Guatemala went so far as to forbid any vaults on their churches except over the sanctuary (1567); these directives were broken within a decade, even in Guatemala where monumental building and knowledge of vaulting were far less developed than in Mexico.[34] Not only civil servants but also friars could say *obedezco pero no cumplo*.

The grander churches might have ribbed vaults over the sanctuary, in late-gothic flower-, star-, or crystal-patterns. Some were rib-vaulted over the length of the nave as well. There is no more handsome or dramatic display of the successful transplanting of mediaeval artistic forms to the New World than these thoroughly gothic interiors. In contrast to equivalent European vaults — thin-shelled, light, mechanically complicated, and expertly constructed — the Mexican vaults are usually thick, heavy, mechanically simple, and coarsely built. Since the under surface was covered with plaster, as commonly then also in gothic Europe, the quality of the stonecutting was not important for appearance's sake; and fortunately so, for a smooth surface and a neat net-pattern of joints would not have been obtainable from native workmen without the long tradition of European skills behind them. The stereotomy was more slapdash than systematic, and often the whole "vault" was little more than a heavy shell of rubble a foot or more thick, ornamented perhaps by cut-stone ribs attached like moldings to its under surface. Visually the vaults might be made lighter by the play of ribs below them; physically they might be made lighter by being constructed of brick or of a porous light-weight stone such as pumice.

Although Indian workmen overcame their distrust enough to vault more than a hundred churches in the sixteenth century, many of their Spanish supervisors must have remained mistrustful, for not only are the vaults over-cautiously thick, but they are often given support and buttressing far in excess of their need. Some of the walls at Totimehuacán are 14 feet thick, at Tepoztlán 12, and at otherwise modest Acatlán, over 10; these are not rare cases.

44 VAULT CARRYING THE CHOIR–BALCONY AT TECAMACHALCO *painted by Juan Gerson or Jerson in 1562. The ribs are white, crisscrossed with turquoise leaves. The oval scenes from the Apocalypse and Old Testament are bright with a wide range of colors.*

EXTERIOR

Outside, the typical monastery church was blocky, and most of it was bare. Whatever carving the friars allowed themselves was usually deployed around the front door and the window above it, treated frankly as an en-framement, and little correlated with the rest of the building. Trimming, with no function other than to look pretty, it did not emphasize the basic structure, or measure off the building into rhythmical units or proportioned areas, or organize any sort of total composition, as ornament often did in Italy at this time. In Spain, similar uncoordinated handling of major decoration was a striking characteristic in most of the sixteenth-century styles.

151

45 TLAXIACO, 1550's   46 TULA, 1550's

The ornamented doorway and window were not generally combined in a coherent design, though once in a while there might be some effort to conjoin them (Malinalco or Tecamachalco). The disciplines of late gothic had been lost in crossing the ocean, and plateresque license was far more frequent than plateresque organization. In a very few cases (Coixtlahuaca, Atotonilco el Grande, or Copanabastla and Copainalà, if of the sixteenth century), there seems to have been a wish to work the whole area of the church front into one composition, disciplined by some rhythmic recurrence of columns, pilasters, or niches in somewhat the same way as in the more organized of the plateresque facades in Spain or as in retables. (Retables, once influenced by facade design, had for some years been influencing Spanish facades.) Dis-

47 CUILAPAN, 1560's   48 ZACATLÁN, 1560's

cipline by pilasters or any other element able to subsume several ornamental items was not yet common in Mexico. Lack of such discipline was far more typical, and it was often an advertisement of the amateur status of the designers.

A carved facade might be enlivened with color, and sometimes even with gilding (Acolman).[35] Facades and flanks of churches might be painted or coated with a skin of stucco *sgraffito,* often patterned in imitation of masonry, as still shows in considerable patches on many church walls (Quecholac, Zinacantepec, Zinapécuaro, or half a dozen monasteries in Morelos). Renaissance plateresque in Spain had often used rustication freely to make a textural allover pattern so divorced from any tectonic reality as to be independent of the actual courses of stones. It was easier, of course, to execute such patterns superficially with thin paint than deeply with thick masonry. The

49 MALINALCO, *c*1565   50 ZACAPU, *c*1585

tradition went back to the Moors. Although the designs in Mexico are always European — some are Moorish and some may come from woodcuts in Serlio — the idea of covering the outside of a building with painted patterning may as well be Indian; several Spaniards recorded their admiration for preconquest examples of similar surface decoration.

*

Although towers had been outlawed for Franciscans by the Constitutions of Barcelona, a few important Franciscan churches in New Spain had them nonetheless, and one small group had twin bell-towers terminating the sides of the facade. Bells were considered a necessary item in municipal equipment from the beginning: most of the towns on the route from Veracruz to the capital were already able to greet the Twelve with their own bells in 1524

153

51 THE AUGUSTINIAN CHURCH AT METZTITLÁN,
crowned with its original espadaña.

(according to Bernal Díaz), though just what kind of bells it is hard to guess. Within a year or two bells were being regularly cast in México-Tenochtitlán. When not hung in church towers, they were often hung in *espadañas* (arch-pierced gables, or bell-screens, which might crown either the facade or sometimes the churchyard wall, as at Molango or Tepeyanco).[36]

*

The church usually had a supplementary doorway on its north side. Since the south flank abutted the monastery block in most cases the north was the only flank where a side doorway could be cut. North doors might have been reserved for Spaniards when crowds of Indians were trooping in the front door, or perhaps, conversely, Indians came in the side while the more important front access was reserved for the more important Spaniards; as it is doubtful that large numbers of Spaniards and Indians would have been using the church simultaneously, neither alternative has much force.

At Franciscan Huejotzingo the north door is called *Porciúncula*, the name of the hut where Saint Francis lived and of the chapel where the hut is enshrined in the church of Santa Maria degli Angeli near Assisi. This chapel is ordinarily entered through a door in the north flank of the church. The church, on the site of the first vision of his calling and the site of his death, is deeply venerated by Franciscans, and Mexican Franciscans were aware of its great prestige. There is one local reference to it as early as 1544.[37] A "Porciúncula Indulgence" may be granted to those who on August 2nd visit a church which has been specially endowed with that privilege. Although there are no references to it in Mexico in the sixteenth century — it has only recently become plenary — festivals for this indulgence were held there in the seventeenth century. While there might thus be some reason to call Franciscan north doors *Porciúnculas*, it would not explain the equal richness of Dominican or Augustinian north doors.[38]

These doors are sometimes ornamented so emphatically that they seem to claim some specific significance. It could come from the symbolism long associated with the north side of churches. The reading of the Gospel from the north end of the altar or from a lectern on the north side of the chancel had long symbolized the desire of the Church to convert barbarians. In the sixteenth century that tradition might have meant more in Mexico than in Spain, and more in Spain than anywhere else in western Europe.

*

In the city, churches were sometimes roofed with lead, but the commonest roofing materials must always have been tiles or split shingles. The vaulted churches did not need roofs over their vaults because these were well enough put together and coated with enough fine stucco to be proof against the rare and brief rains of the central plateau. The top of the vaults did not show from the ground because the heavy side walls were carried up beyond

52 UNROOFED VAULTS AT ACOLMAN
with the espadaña *which crowns the facade.*

the springing of the vaults, perhaps in order that the added mass might aid in buttressing. Thus the walls made a decisive straight termination around the top of the building, an edge often enlivened with the staccato verticals of sharp merlons and the more widely spaced horizontals of waterspouts.

The walls had to be thick not only because of the weight of the vaults or the timber roof they had to carry but also because of the weight of their own substance, usually rubble. It is unwise to try to make a thin rubble wall, and it would be rash in a region racked by earthquakes. Allover cut-stone ashlar masonry (as at Huejotzingo, Cholula, Tula, or Yanhuitlán) even if used only on the surfaces would be stronger than rubble, but it cost much more and took much longer to build; consequently it was rare for churches, and was pointed out at the time as something remarkable in the few handsome cases where it was used. A more economical and practical way of making walls, suited to common materials and labor conditions, can be seen in the now-ruined church at Tehuacán Viejo (probably finished by 1540, surely by '57).[39] Here carefully cut stone, demanding still hard-to-find skilled laborers, was used only at exterior corners, and at door- and window-openings, which must be vertically true and resistant to chipping. The remainder of the walls, about 4 feet thick, were faced with stones only roughly squared, small enough for one man to lift into place unaided. Between the two stone facings, which could be built up independently a few feet at a time, smaller irregular stones and chips were laid, and a wet mixture of mortar and mud was dumped over them until the interstices were filled. (As old as Rome or Teoti-huacán, this way of building a wall is still current in central Mexico.) Where

156

53 BARREL VAULT OF THE NAVE AT YURIRIA
with the domical vaults of the crossing and transepts.

the mud was clayey enough, whole walls could be built of rubble with very little stone, the mud mixture having been dumped and tamped between wooden forms which would hold it in place until it had hardened. Such primitive concrete or *pisé* construction was locally called *tapia*. There were other variations of rubble wall construction, but only few and fragmentary examples survive.

In many cases the church walls were stiffened by plain pier buttresses, strategically reinforcing not only the front corners from which they often projected diagonally, but also the beginning of the apse, and perhaps one or two additional points along the flanks. These buttresses could project with extraordinary boldness (16 feet at Epazoyucan and Tiripetío), invigorating and dramatizing the whole inert blocky mass of the church. In a few cases (Oaxtepec, for instance), they were set along the nave inside the church, and were joined together by arches just below the vault, forming shallow recesses like side chapels, an arrangement favored by the Dominicans.

*

The character of the sixteenth-century monastery churches was practical and vigorous, even in buildings as lavishly ornamented as the Augustinians' Yuriria or the Dominicans' Yanhuitlán. Even two centuries later the aesthetic authoritativeness of a church like Tepeaca could impress a worldly official like Villaseñor y Sánchez or a sophisticated Jesuit like Father Clavijero as "renowned and beautiful," "one of the best in the country," rare tribute to a church in the mediaeval style which eighteenth-century Latins usually considered barbarous.[40]

54 BUTTRESSED FLANK AND APSE OF THE FRANCISCAN CHURCH
AT CHOLULA *built in the 1550's except for the top of the tower.*

55 FLANK OF THE FRANCISCAN CHURCH AT TEPEACA, 1550's
The reservoir is probably also a work of the sixteenth century.

56 ATOTONILCO EL GRANDE   57 HUEXOTLA

Mid-sixteenth-century CLOISTERS; *that at Atotonilco c1550; that at Yuriria c1560, with ribbed vaults and piers with engaged fluted columns making it as elaborate as any in Mexico; Huexotla, c1570, is one of the smallest, and has an upper story of wood above stone columns.*

58 YURIRIA

159

59 ATLATLÁUHCAN
*painted pattern on this vault
used also at*
60 METZTITLÁN

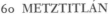

THE MONASTERY BUILDING

As in southern Europe, the church was usually flanked on its protected and sunny south side by the main monastery building, and this was wrapped around a still more sheltered small square cloister. In the warm regions of Oaxaca or Chiapas the monastery block might be more comfortably disposed along the shadier north wall of the church, and in Yucatan the cloister was often set directly behind the church for reasons — if there were any — now unrecognized. The cloister was usually in two stories, an arrangement as uncommon in Spain (outside Catalonia, Levante, and scattered Moslem-inspired work, unlikely as a source here) as it was common in Mexico where, conversely, the one-story cloister was as rare (outside Yucatan) as it was common in Spain. The Mexican cloister had a small garden plot in the center, perhaps planted around a fountain with nostalgically familiar European flowers — carnations, lilies, roses — and a few prized medicinal herbs.

On the side of the cloister across from the church stood the refectory, where the brothers ate in silence while someone read them suitable texts. Adjoining it at one corner was the kitchen. Somewhere along the other two

61 THE REFECTORY AT ACTOPAN

The barrel vault has deeply sunk octagonal coffers and is painted with renaissance patterns in black and bright orange on a white ground. Beyond the two windows facing south to the garden is the pulpit for readings during meals.

161

sides were the additional rooms needed for the friars' simple regimen. The chapter hall, or *sala de profundis* (thus called from the first words of Psalm 130 read at the close of meetings held there), was a simple room, smaller than was customary in Spain. It was not opened to the cloister by an arcade, as so often there, but by a simple door.

A broad stone stairway led from the lower cloister walk to an upper one, and to the entrance to the choir-balcony at the west end of the church. The quarters of the prior and the library were on this floor, and also the cells, usually with beds but without mattresses. Each had a single window, and often a little stone seat for meditation and reading tucked in the thickness of the wall at one side of the window embrasure. All the rooms on each of the floors were simple rectangles, undifferentiated except in size. Their form was scarcely affected by their varied functions; except for the kitchens, today it is difficult to identify particular rooms by anything more than their location; it is usually safe, for example, to call a large long room next to a kitchen a refectory.

62 THE MAIN
STAIRWAY
AT YURIRIA
*with stair rail and
door restored on
the basis of old
fragments.*

63 SIXTEENTH–CENTURY
CARVED WOOD DOOR IN THE
MONASTERY BLOCK AT CUL–
HUACÁN, *with*
the monogram of Christ,
the Instruments of the Passion,
the Augustinian pierced Heart,
the monogram of Mary,
and a chalice.

The cells overlooked the big garden of carefully nurtured plants and fruit trees, some native — such as avocados, guavas, papayas, *tejocotes,* and *zapotes* — and some imported from the mother country — such as peaches, pears, plums, pomegranates, quinces, figs, oranges, and lemons. Exotics — such as bananas and *mameyes* — were successfully transplanted from Santo Domingo to monasteries in suitably warm regions. The coconut was brought from Africa to Santo Domingo, and thence to New Spain. Often there was an herb garden here as well as in the cloister, for the friars quickly adopted many of the well-developed herbal remedies of the Aztecs, and passed them into European medical practice. The vegetable gardens — with their imported lettuce, onions, and garlic, and native tomatoes, peppers, squashes, corn, and sweet potatoes — were close to the kitchen but still well removed from the church building. Many friars were gardeners: all Dominicans had to be. What food the friars did not raise, the Indians gave to them and, after Spain, the fare seemed abundant.

Sometimes water was brought in through a special aqueduct (as at Tochimilco, Tecamachalco, Etla, or Otumba). There had been important precedents for this not only in Spain but also in preconquest Mexico. Huge stone-lined rectangular cisterns might also be built next to the monastery (still visible at Cuitzeo, Tehuacán Viejo, Tepeapulco, Tepeaca, Tecali, and

Ucareo). The barns were located at a suitable distance, and in the beginning were of exceptional importance because of the rarity of cattle. The first cows, traditionally those kept by the Franciscans at Huejotzingo, were quite literally rarer than gold.

*

The outside of the two-story monastery block had few or no major architectural features. The most prominent was usually the main entrance, near or next to the facade of the church. Called the *portería,* or sometimes the *portico del racionero* or *portal de peregrinos,* it took the form either of a recessed vestibule or of a projecting porch, occasionally both. This would be opened out to the courtyard in front by a broad arch, or sometimes two or three; in the grander establishments there could be as many as six or seven, making an impressive introduction to the monastery behind. Occasionally there was another arcade above it, accessible from the second story of the monastery building. Decoration — if there was any — was generally simpler than on the church: a few moldings around the windows, a projecting cornice, or perhaps a flat parapet-band. In Morelos there were often extensive surface patterns of *sgraffito* or a terminating frieze of the emblems of the Order. (Particularly handsome examples outside Morelos are at Tláhuac and Zinapécuaro.)

The large porterías served not only as entryways but also as waiting rooms for groups having business with the friars or for the poor waiting for the distribution of food. During epidemics a portería might become a half-

64 CALPAN
The double window of the church facade has been made higher and a new arcade has been added above the old portería.

65 MIXCOAC   66 TEJUPAN

outdoor dispensary. Sick Indians would be brought there to be confirmed so
that they might die in better spiritual circumstances. So many sick died on
their way to confess or be confirmed in the portería that the friars were ordered to visit the houses of the very sick in order to forestall them. Otherwise, friars were not supposed to penetrate into the profane world beyond
the portería except in pairs.

*

The portería might serve also as the entrance to the schools which the
friars administered for the children of Indian nobles and other influential
townspeople. Sometimes the classrooms were in the front of the monastery
building, sometimes in a separate wing, sometimes in a separate building
nearby. Architecturally they were indistinguishable from the rest of the conventual complex, and as a result cannot be surely identified today. There
had to be easy access for the students to the big yard in front of the church
— some of their instruction was given there — and for the friars, easy
access to the monastery. The portería was the busy junction for both lines
of traffic and also the communicating link to the other classes for the children of the poor which were held entirely in the churchyard. In or near the
monastery building there was often another room, or rooms, for Indians:
a jail for the disobedient, usually apostates.

*

Arts-and-crafts schools for adult Indians were sometimes in the monastery block, but probably more often located nearby in a separate building, also facing the churchyard but not necessarily connected to it by way
of the portería. Instruction was given in useful and profitable crafts, such
as carpentry, masonry, metal-working, and weaving. Every Franciscan and
nearly every other monastery ran such a school. The Augustinians set up a

particularly important one at Tiripetío, their first major house, and here the Tarasco Indians learned Spanish techniques from Spanish craftsmen so quickly and so well that the school soon became the training center for all Michoacán, and was famous all over New Spain. The nimble-fingered Tarasco boys became tailors, dyers, carpenters, and cabinet-makers, painters, carvers, lacquerers, and featherworkers, potters, masons, and smiths. Unfortunately nothing identifiable of their early work survives physically today, although traces of their influence may persist in the lively popular arts of Michoacán. Spanish writers did not know what to admire most, the aptitude of the Indians for learning European techniques and imitating the European forms taught them in the schools, or the native skills which the friars encouraged their Indians to apply to the manufacture of fittings for the churches — work in feather mosaic, lacquered wood, or cane pith. All who mentioned their craftsmanship admired it.

67 ZOOMORPHIC STONE WATERSPOUTS *on the monastery block at* ZINACANTEPEC

Like the church, the typical cloister, refectory, and cells show no significant local innovations. The brothers wanted not only their churches but all their buildings in the uneasy and unfamiliar new land to look as reassuringly as possible like their former quarters in a safe and familiar homeland. It seems more surprising, then, to find so few direct references to particular Spanish buildings, yet, except for the big churchyard and its small auxiliary buildings, the arrangement showed nothing that was novel, nothing that would not have been easy even for amateurs to remember from city and country work in Europe — if they did not remember too clearly. It came as an almost inevitable combination, brought about by the half-unconscious application of what must have seemed the natural way of solving a thousand-year-old problem: how to build a practical and comfortable monastery. It was even less specifically Spanish than the church, and probably more a simplification of general European practice, synthesized from uneven memories of friars from many parts of Charles' patchwork of a European Empire. On the whole it was a little old-fashioned, and less particularized in style than contemporary work in Spain which might be expected to be more-or-less equivalent; no one could have mistaken a Mexican monastery building for one in Spain.

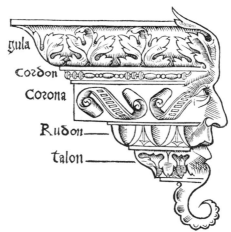

ℳ Edidas del Romano:

engravings from the architectural treatise of Diego de Sagredo, first published in Toledo in 1526.

68 *A Corinthian capital*

69 *A richly carved cornice with ideal physiognomical proportions.*

V

THE NEW ARCHITECTURE
AND THE OLD

BEFORE turning to the atrio and its auxiliary buildings, it is necessary to consider the peculiarities of the architectural style of the monasteries as distinct from their plan, and something of their range from rich to meager. Their individual style does not reveal any relation so simple as a direct transplanting of developed ideas from Spain any more than did their general type. The roots of style were transplanted, but what soon grew from them often developed discrepantly in the new soil and new climate, and under the attention no longer of Spanish but of Indian hands. The result was different not only from the ancestral forms in Spain but also from the forms native to earlier Mexico.

IMPORTED SPANISH STYLES

For three centuries, memories of Spain conditioned the appearance of all but the humblest buildings. Such memories were at first weak and uncertain, diminished by distance, diluted by the amateur builders' lack of professional knowledge, and sometimes distorted by the adjustments demanded by local conditions. This kind of reduction could lead to forms which might at first appear to be new, but on serious second scrutiny show themselves to be distortions more than inventions.

While the general scheme of the monastery as a whole was not distinctively Spanish, the style of its individual passages of ornamentation usually was, or was intended to be. Although homesick friars might have been expected to try to recreate or represent a familiar portal from here or a cloister from there, such specific derivation can be traced only rarely and even then never surely, for the amateurs were not masters enough of architectural vocabulary and syntax to memorize and quote accurately. Nostalgia was never lettered enough to lead to pedantry.

The monastery-building program was part of a highly organized enterprise, and each semi-standardized monastery in a semi-standardized town was a cog in that system; the formation and disposition of its main parts was semi-standardized too, but their ornamental detail was not. Parts of the outer dress might change, but not the body beneath. In the sixteenth century, the style of most of the major architecture in Spain was a matter of fashion, in somewhat the same manner as furniture or costume, though not to the same degree. Gothic and renaissance had come as fashionable importations into Spain, and had already been modified and mixed there with more freedom than was liked in the lands where they had originated. While some of the handsomest buildings in Spain were in the latest imported renaissance mode, many more were in its homemade and handsome but impure dilution, the late plateresque.

Most of the renaissance commissions reflected the taste of the Court, where new modes were adopted quickly and enthusiastically. Many "important" buildings in Spain, obedient to the fluctuations of fashion, can now be dated quite accurately by the stage of their stylistic evolution. This is not true in Mexico, where there was less changing of style to be *in* style. Stylistic elements did not necessarily reappear in the same sequence they had followed in Spain, because different friars would build less from any well-informed partiality for current modes than from ill-informed memories. Thus gothic and renaissance are contemporaneous rather than successive in Mexico, and appear side by side on one facade as blurred reflections of Spanish buildings hundreds of miles and hundreds of years apart. Furthermore, both mediaeval and renaissance, often already modulated by Moorish traditions in Spain, were liable to additional and yet more peculiar metmorphoses in New Spain, from the traditions of the brown hands which were giving tangible form to the uncertain European memories.

70 *A sample plate from Sagredo's* Medidas del Romano. *Columns, with normal shafts* (P), *bases* (V), *and Composite capitals* (A), *carry a full entablature with a pediment* (S *and* R) *topped by pedestals* (I) *for acroterial figures (the outer ones shown up to the waist). All this frames a niche, which is covered by a coffered barrel vault.*

169

The terms properly used for European styles do not always apply accurately in the New World. This is partly because of the chronological and genealogical disparities just mentioned, and partly because so many European general terms fail to fit work in Spain itself. The name for the clear style of Alberti and Bramante, for example, must be stretched to tenuous unsubstantiability if it is also to cover the many Spanish "renaissance" buildings whose mannerist dress has been slipped over half-mediaeval or nondescript bodies. The most familiar plateresque, although it used a vocabulary of decorative renaissance forms, did not arrange them in discreet renaissance combinations or quantities, but in crowded patterns still sympathetic to the crowded patterns of the preceding late-gothic plateresque (Isabelino) or mudéjar.

71

CHANCEL VAULT   AT HUEJOTZINGO

The most precise nomenclature in Spain is not to be found in the terms used for the foreign styles imported and denatured, but rather in the terms coined for homegrown styles such as the plateresque or the Moslem-derived but Christian-built mudéjar. Even these cannot be applied properly in Mexico without trimming them down or stretching them out. As a consequence, many stylistic terms used hereafter for Mexican work are to be understood only in a loose way, as though qualified by quotation marks. Furthermore, they will generally apply only to decorative surface features. "Style" will have little to do with construction, quality of space, or big-scale planning, much as it had little to do with them in the plateresque and mudéjar of Spain, where both were styles chiefly of decoration for decoration's sake, with no more than negative relation to construction or planning. (Construction or quality of space remained subordinate, meager, or wanting throughout the Mexican baroque, and are still secondary in most Mexican architecture, save in the bold new concrete shells of the Spaniard Candela.)

Gothic in Mexico was conceived mainly in a decorative, antistructural, gothic-plateresque taste. Elements of gothic ornamentation are most often found in work earlier than 1570. They occur not only in the patterns of the ribbed vaults but also in portals, traceried windows, pointed arches (of windows, but rarely of doorways), zoomorphic waterspouts, and in miscellaneous decorative details of bases, capitals, or moldings. The suavity of the best Spanish late gothic is not there, but sometimes there may be found an unsuave energy or a somewhat coarse magnificence. In Dominican work there are curiously few gothic elements, perhaps because the most ambitious Dominican monasteries — those in Oaxaca — were finished late in the century. An exotic surprise is the occasional rank flowering of *manoelino,* the late gothic of Portugal strangely colored from its contacts with Africa and perhaps Asia.

72 MOLANGO
Below the late-gothic rose window, the arch of the romanesque-looking main portal is enclosed in a mudéjar alfiz *compounded of renaissance baluster-columns and a modified classical cornice. The carving everywhere betrays strong Indian aesthetic preferences, though the details are everywhere European.*

While a few scattered episodes may appear to be clumsy apings of romanesque (the main portal of Molango or parts of the "basilica" at Cuilapan), scrutiny will usually show them to come more from some correspondingly primitive handling of carved forms than from any specific recollections of romanesque style. Mexican architecture of the sixteenth century includes many other atavisms which point somewhat unsurely toward more primitive modes already extinct in Spain.

The renaissance style, still an aristocratic mode and not yet "popular" in Spain, most often appeared in Mexico in richly carved late plateresque decorations. These would be confined to a single feature, such as a portal (ills. 45–51), and would not often dominate a whole facade (as at Acolman, Cuitzeo, or Copándaro). Indoors, the style might control the decorated architectural framework of the many-tiered gold retables (Huejotzingo, ill. 35,

73 THE PORTAL OF THE FRANCISCAN CHURCH AT TECALI, *possibly affected by designs in Serlio's treatise.*

THREE PLATES IN SERLIO
74 his own design (above)
75 the Arch of the Gavii, Verona (lower left)
76 the Arch of Trajan, Ancona (lower right)

or Xochimilco). Plateresque in Spain was usually characterized by an un-structural system of decoration, with architectural elements and free orna-ment often hung on the walls without pretending to be even mimetically self-supporting or tectonic in any way, often also without coherence of scale between juxtaposed parts, or even without axial continuity.

For reasons not clear, the Augustinians chose renaissance plateresque more often than the other Orders. It may have been because they had little mediaeval past in Spain; it may have corresponded to the humanistic learning many Augustinian friars had acquired at the universities of Alcalá or Sala-manca; or it may have resulted from their memories of handsome plateresque buildings there.

Another school of purer, more academic, and more tectonic renaissance design, the *purista* — strictly a Court style in Spain and perhaps correspond-ing to contemporary classicizing and Italianate poetry — came to Mexico in the next generation. It dominated one small group of classicizing basilican churches (Tecali, Quecholac, Zacatlán), and occasional doorways and de-tails elsewhere. By 1589 the carpenters' and masons' guilds required masters to pass an examination in drawing the five Roman Orders. Much must have been based on the volumes of Vitruvius, Serlio, and Alberti which were be-ing imported, and building in New Spain may have depended on the plates in these books more than did many purist buildings in Spain, where purist style had appeared before the illustrated treatises were published. Of all these, Serlio's was the most influential in Mexico, perhaps because it offered the most pictures with the least theory.[1]

Although less showily than in Colombia, mudéjar appeared in Mexico, per-haps most richly in the now vanished *alfarje* or *artesonado* wooden ceilings. Mudéjar never dominated the whole scheme (except in one major case which will be discussed in Chapter X) but it asserted itself in decoration. Mudéjar features appear in pyramid-topped battlements, doorways enclosed in rectan-gular *alfiz* moldings, and in a few lobed or scalloped arches. Painted decora-tions on walls, ceilings, and vaults were often made up of mudéjar patterns, and a mudéjar love of mesmeric repetition sometimes imprinted most of a facade with a rug-like relief of multiplied renaissance or gothic motifs.

As Mexico City was the cultural capital, the latest imported styles must have been known there first. The grandest palaces were there, exemplars for those in lesser cities. Monasteries, however, were less affected by the styles of viceregal court circles. Though the metropolitan churches were large and elaborate and often more up-to-date, they were apparently not often models for the design of country establishments.

In general, while the monasteries showed no major novelties in style, nothing unknown in their Spanish forebears, local flavor might spice some of the details, either through imperfect understanding of Spanish models, or through persistence of Indian taste in the carving of ornament. The workmen and craftsmen were regularly Indian, most of them trained in the monastery schools. Spanish craftsmen had the upper hand only in the main city churches and a very few other major establishments (at Acolman?), and even here they must have been outnumbered by their native assistants. Monasteries far from the capital can rarely have been touched by European workmen, and they often display this independence in erratic details. All the earliest and perhaps most subsequent sixteenth-century work was to some degree stylistically provincial, and like much provincial building all over the world, showed little resistance to the provincial voracity for decoration, gratified at the expense of structural and functional logic or even of visual coherence.

It would be a mistake to search for originality of style. The freshness and aesthetic novelty — and because they are not measurable is no reason to assume that they do not exist — come from new combinations of old elements rather than from any invention of new ones. Although there is no new language, there are striking new statements compounded of old words. There were no significant novelties in construction or in new forms evolved for new functions. One new function did produce the outdoor church, but this materialized far more from a creative synthesis of old forms than from the invention of any new ones (as will be shown in Chapter IX).

This is not to belittle the quality of Mexican architecture of the sixteenth century: synthesis can be artistically as valid as invention. How original is the work of such sixteenth-century masters as Palladio, Lescot, Holl, or Herrera if judged chiefly for invention of forms? Whether the Spaniards or the Indians were able to invent is beside the point. What is pertinent is that while they did not, they managed to do so well with the old forms at hand.

In the work of both Spaniards and natives, the role of tradition was dominant, for originality was not fostered by the authoritarian conditions of patronage of either people. In one respect the two traditions were curiously attuned: Spaniards and Indians alike exploited exuberant richness and bare simplicity, often in purposeful contrast. Spanish, precolombian, and Mexican colonial art can not often be satisfactorily discussed without dwelling on these sovereign poles of extravagance and asceticism; and here, asceticism is one kind of extravagance.

AUSTERITY AND LAVISHNESS

> Well I know that in those early days, the Golden Age of our Province, those magnificent churches and sumptuous monasteries seemed to the early fathers of the Thebaid of Michoacán to be contrary to the strict poverty of our Order . . . Our venerable Father

Chávez said that God had been the prime mover in the making of the Tabernacle, on which many millions in gold and silver and precious stones had been spent, while Solomon, wisest of men, inspired by the same God, created the magnificent temple on which so many talents were spent. All this, Tabernacle and Temple, were merely to house the Ark of the Covenant in which the Manna was kept. "And therefore, if for the Manna, precursor and prefigurer of the Sacrament," said Chávez, "God countenanced expenditures and sumptuous buildings, how much greater should be those which are made to guard the true Manna, Cristo Sacramentado?"

— *Father Escobar* (1729)[2]

The poverty preached by Saint Francis and Saint Dominic had at first been accepted architecturally by their followers as a denial of ornament: in theory, carving was banned, and even moldings were frowned on. By the end of the Reconquest, such artistic asceticism was being repudiated in Spain. Although the Aztec Empire was as rich, and potentially richer, than the Moorish Empire, the buildings the Christians placed there after the Conquest were poorer and plainer than those they built after the Reconquest in Spain, and were shaped more by practical needs and less by the pride of victory. (The typical churches of the Reconquest had not been built by Mendicant friars.) The lavish church is as rare in sixteenth-century Mexico as the simple one of comparable scale in Spain.

Stringent simplicity was official, and was prescribed often. Into their local statutes the Franciscans wrote in 1541: "Item: the buildings erected for the residence of the friars shall be very, very poor [*paupérrimo*], in accordance with the wishes of our father Saint Francis; and the monasteries shall be so planned as to have no more than six cells in the dormitory, eight by nine feet, and the dormitory corridor shall be no more than five feet wide; and the cloister shall not have two stories and shall be but seven feet wide." [3] These regulations are so similar to those written by Saint Peter of Alcántara for his new Observant Province in Spain (1555–59) that it is possible both had the same antecedent, which is hardly surprising since so many of the early friars in Mexico had been Observants in Spain. It is barely possible that the Mexican regulations affected the Spanish. These Mexican specifications were sent for endorsement to the General of the Order in Rome; he showed them to Pope Paul III who not only "approved and confirmed" them but singled out the clauses about poverty "to be kept inviolably by all the friars of the Province, present and future." [4] (Paul III, while thus commending architectural asceticism for Mexico, was busy with his own Farnese Palace in Rome, making it the largest and grandest urban dwelling built there since the palaces of the pagan Emperors.)

ARCHITECTURE NEW AND OLD

The standard monastery approved by the Pope was too minimal even for the Franciscans, and few such were ever built (Huexotla, where Father Mendieta wrote, was one); of those which were, most were later expanded and enriched. Outside Yucatan few cloisters were kept to one story. Although these particular limitations were not often fully observed, many severely simple monasteries were built all through the sixteenth century. Certain parts of the country, such as Franciscan Yucatan and Jalisco, hardly ever saw anything else. Churches along frontiers made difficult by hostile heathens were also generally kept plain; some were doubtless as impoverished as the shelters used by Saint Francis himself.

Every decade the Franciscans would reaffirm allegiance to architectural asceticism as a suitable expression of their essential humility, following Observant practice. As soon as they made handsome buildings — which they repeatedly did, ordinances or no ordinances — there were complaints; and the brothers' lapses from meagerness were either denied, or justified because "it was necessary to ornament and make a show of the churches in order to elevate the Indians' souls and to move them towards things of God, because their very nature, which is remiss and forgetful of inner things, needs to be helped by the outward aspect." [5] Viceroy Velasco agreed, and recognized that "ornaments, easy to obtain here, attract the Indians into the churches." Some of the exaggerated complaints were prompted by jealousy or rivalry for the friars' Indians and land. The Franciscan monastery at Guadalajara, for example, was invidiously compared to Santo Tomás at Avila and to extravagant San Pablo at Valladolid although it was but a sad affair of adobe, unplaned wood, and thatch.[6] Since the most ambitious churches are usually the most striking, handsome, and interesting, they have always attracted the most attention despite the fact that they were an atypical minority.

*

While the poverty-wed Franciscans were for the most part free from architectural self-indulgence, the Dominicans and Augustinians could less often resist the opportunities for eye-filling splendor offered by free supplies of skilled and semi-skilled labor. Though also committed to poverty in their charter — buildings must be "humble and mediocre" — the Dominicans began their first church elaborately enough to earn a letter of reproof from the Queen when it was hardly above ground, because Franciscan Bishop Zumárraga had warned that it was "more beautiful than monasteries in Spain, and . . . useless." They recommitted themselves to poverty in 1540, but immediately got into new trouble. They tried to exonerate themselves by explaining to the King that if some of their houses were sumptuous it was because the Indians building them wished in that way to honor their villages. At first the Provincial was to see that they avoided "curiosities and paintings," but in a few years painting, sculpture, and ornaments "useful for the service of God" were declared acceptable. The Dominicans were able to acquire these because they kept most of the tithes they were ordered to collect, though they had at first protested along with the other Orders against any tithing. The Dominicans were fortunate in having taken for their particular province the old Zapoteca and Mixteca kingdoms, which were populous, agriculturally and mineralogically rich, and rich also in traditions of fine craftsmanship. Only the combination of local wealth, skill, and plentiful labor can explain the scale and splendor of such monasteries as Coixtlahuaca, Yanhuitlán, or Santo Domingo in Oaxaca. (Dominican frontier houses such as Nejapa or Jalapa del Marqués were, naturally, smaller and barer.) In their daily life the friars remained poor, and often looked poor. Their many-times-mended woolen habits and undergarments were so coarse and rough that they aroused comment in Rome. The friars laboring on Santo Domingo in Oaxaca made poignant contrast to their own lavish handiwork.[7]

Although not statutorily committed to poverty, the Augustinians were able to forget that their patron, Saint Augustine, had maintained that beauty did not inhabit corporeal things. They were the most often ostentatious, not only in easy plains (as at Acolman or Yuriria) but even in difficult sierras (as at Metztitlán). They provoked more complaints than the Dominicans, and many more than the Franciscans, because of their "impertinent buildings for sixty where only four friars need be maintained,"[8] or their buildings said to be of a size "like the Escorial." Their monastery at Ucareo was begun on a scale so outrageous that orders were issued to limit it. Fray Juan de Utrera was building it "not according to the requirements of the place, but to those of his art." They laid foundations at Huango (now Villa Morelos, Michoacán) for a church so immoderate that it soon had to be abandoned in favor of its sacristy, itself roomy enough to serve as an adequate church (which it still does). The King had to write more than once to remind the Augustinians and Dominicans that they must not accumulate so much valuable property.[9]

Bishop Zumárraga wrote to the Emperor (1537) of the Augustinians' presumptuousness at Ocuituco, high on the slope of Popocatépetl, with the result that they were twice ordered to stop all work on their vaulted residential wing — "more sumptuous than the village could suffer" — and to finish the church without further elaboration. This church was ruined by fire a century ago, but the vaulted monastery block still stands, and looks surprisingly modest now. It is hard to know why it seemed so excessive, unless at this early date vaulting in itself was held a luxury. The Augustinians were compelled to pull down the two jails they had just put up in Ocuituco to hold those Indians who had not been working hard enough to suit them. After more criticism they abandoned the entire project in a huff (1541) for another monastery they had only two leagues away in the lovely leafy valley of Totolapan. They took along their bells, church ornaments, and anything valuable which was movable — even the locks — and some items which might not ordinarily be classified as movable, such as their recently planted orange trees.[10]

The Augustinians vindicated their luxuriousness by saying that it was a necessary means of stimulating the uncertain Indians: the earthly splendor achieved by a conspicuous show was to dim rival memories of heathen shrines and at the same time give an elevating foretaste of the glories of the Christian hereafter. (The disputes evoke resonant echoes of Abbot Suger and Saint Bernard.) It was a common saying that the Indians' faith came through the eyes, and that they were like Doubting Thomas in having to experience directly before believing. The Augustinians disagreed with Saint John of the Cross who, at the same time in Spain, was preaching that churches where the senses are the least likely to be entertained were the most suitable for true devotions. They agreed more with the recently published Pseudo-Dionysius that the steps of spiritual enlightenment rose from sensuous to intellectual to spiritual knowledge, and that images and material richnesses were helpful in making the first step. Sumptuousness was soon persuasively urged by Saint Charles Borromeo in his *Instructiones fabricae et supellectilis ecclesiasticae,* which followed the decrees of the Council of Trent in extolling ancient traditions of churchly splendor, and exhorted priests and architects to keep it up, though never in a worldly way. (His writing took more effect in Mexico, however, in the baroque seventeenth century. Father Grijalva cited him as justification for Augustinian pomp in 1623.) [11] When the character of the Mexican Church was no longer stringently missionary, but richly and comfortably colonial, the character of the churches changed too. By the seventeenth century some rivaled Spain in sumptuousness, and by the eighteenth some could compete with any in Europe.

Despite contemporary complaints, it is doubtful that any establishment in sixteenth-century Mexico, early or late, would have looked luxurious in the contemporary Spain of the *Siglo de Oro.* Compared to their neighbors in New Spain, a few now do look luxurious, and must have seemed even more so since they provoked such hyperbolic praise and condemnation. Even among clerics the standards of veracity were not always high, and were liable to be lowered by jealousy. Perhaps the luxury which tempted some of the early friars was their pious equivalent of the gold-lust which so racked the conquistadores and other lay Spaniards; perhaps it was only a natural continuation of Spanish traditions, a nostalgic echo of the splendors of some Mendicant country seat in Spain; and perhaps as well it was consciously intended to rival and replace the unforgettable sanctuaries that the first converts knew from their pagan past or the later converts heard glorified at second- or third-hand. When the friars spoke of such a competitive incentive as this last, they may have been giving a valid reason as well as an excuse.

When the Aztec state was broken forever, its civilization was broken too, and when the Aztec religion died, so nearly did its arts, for they were too closely bound to its service to survive alone. There were no new clients who would want and could pay for Aztec painting or sculpture so long as it remained Aztec. Although the Spaniards sometimes admired them as skillfully made curiosities, they did not really want carved jades, feather headdresses, or gold lip-plugs. They cared so much more for the cash value of the gold than the artistic value of its form or workmanship that they quickly melted down every piece they could get.

Their attitude toward the local architecture was not so very different. The conquistadores had been astonished by the trim and shining white Indian towns they passed on their march to the central plateau, particularly by the size and splendor of the strange religious monuments. Small wonder! Cholula and Tenochtitlán must have been among the most spectacular cities in the world. As tough a soldier as Diego de Ordaz, who while reconnoitering for Cortés had been the first European to see Tenochtitlán, had said that it filled him "with terror." The temple-towers of Cholula so impressed Cortés and several others that they paused to count them (with disparate results ranging from one to four hundred). Bernal Díaz, no optical gourmandizer, was overwhelmed by. the delicious beauty of Oaxtepec and its gardens. Before seeing these cities, the Spaniards had seen no comparable native monuments — they knew only the Antilles — no buildings of such size, nor so well made (of cut stone), nor so elegantly surfaced (with painted stucco or with ornamental carving).

Today we reverently visit the wreckage of the ancient holy cities — Teotihuacán, Tula, Xochicalco, Calixtlahuaca, or Malinalco (Tenochtitlán and Cholula being forever lost) — and consider ourselves well rewarded, although we have seen only pitiful bits of the original design, and that little ravaged by time and weather. We see pyramids now without their temples, like torsos without heads.

The first Spaniards looked with understandable revulsion on the monuments of the bloody religion they were stamping out; but when they saw them in their full splendor, with the burnished stucco glistening so brightly that they mistook it for silver, they succumbed to admiration. Pedro Martír de Anglería, a conscientious collector of eyewitness accounts, dared declare that no buildings in Spain were handsomer or better built than the temples of Tenochtitlán. Even tough Bernal Díaz could be kindled to poetic wonderment — to his one lyric flight — by the sight of the unravaged Valley of Mexico: "and when we saw so many cities and villages built in the water, and other great towns on dry land . . . we were amazed, and said it was like

179

the enchantments they tell of in the book of Amadís, because of the great towers and *cúes* and other buildings rising out of the water, and all built of stone. And some of our soldiers even asked whether the things we saw were not a dream. It is not to be wondered that I here write it down in this manner, for there is so much to think over that I do not know how to describe it, seeing things as we did that had never been seen or heard before, nor even dreamed about." [12]

We know Tenochtitlán now chiefly from descriptions written by men who wanted to make it seem impressive so that they, its conquerors, would seem impressive, but the accumulation of eulogies is too extensive to be dismissed as no more than propaganda. The old city was systematically razed by Cortés during the siege. He regretfully wrote Charles V that he did not know how to avoid destroying the city, which was "the noblest and greatest," as well as "the most beautiful city in the world." The tension between Christian and aesthetic values was exposed again when he urged Charles to oblige the *señores cristianos* to destroy the heathen temples (1526), but at the same time urged that one or two be saved "to remember by." [13] There cannot have been many masonry buildings in the Aztec city, or surely more fragments of them would survive in the buildings which have taken their place. Furthermore, Cortés would not have been able to flatten in three months anything as solidly built as Avila or Santiago or any such stony Spanish city. Probably only the royal palaces and chief temples of Tenochtitlán were of stone. The houses were more likely of adobe, and the best ones would have been stuccoed.

The amazement and admiration of the Spaniards did not save any Indian monuments — no matter how stony — nor did they affect appreciably what was put in their place. There are very few exceptions. Although aesthetically the destruction was a tragedy, one must accept it as an inevitable corollary of the military and religious conquests. It was by no means an exceptional one: remember what other soldiers of Charles V did to Rome in the same decade, and what his uncle Henry VIII did to the abbeys of England, and then what was done by Edward VI and by Elizabeth.

In the very first years, while the temples were still standing, the friars felt that their gains were not yet secure enough, even among the Indians who came to their Masses, for those same Indians could so easily slip back afterwards to the celebrations of their old cults, some of which were still being held half-openly at the old shrines. Accordingly, on New Year's Day of 1525, the friars began an active campaign of destruction, first at friendly Texcoco, with its "beautiful turreted temples," and then at México-Tenochtitlán, Tlaxcala, and Huejotzingo, the towns where they were about to plant their first monasteries. They saw to it that within a decade of its fall, not one pagan religious building still stood in Tenochtitlán. Reporting progress in his diocese, Bishop Zumárraga wrote that by 1531, 20,000 "figures of devils" and over 500 "houses of the devil" had already been destroyed. Father Vetancurt said that Fray Martín de Valencia "reduced over 160,000 idols to dust." [14] Some Spaniards wanted to hold the friars back, fearful they might provoke revolt, but the friars were not to be stopped. They did not fear martyrdom and, already understanding typical Indian reactions, saw that their fearlessness might speed conversion, while pusillanimity would not. They saw the temples as rivals which had to be invalidated, preferably by the most forceful visible demonstration: destruction. They wrecked most of the major ones in the early 1530's, helped not only by their trained boys but also by groups of townspeople who wanted to demonstrate their adherence to the new religion or their solidarity with the winning side. Most of the idol-smashing was done by the friars' own hands; most of the collecting of idols was done by the boys, some of whom, because of their zeal, became the first Christian martyrs on the continent. The destruction of the massive temples called for more foot-pounds than the few aging friars could have exerted alone; the lack was met by hundreds of able Indians who believed enough in their new religion to be willing to destroy the shrines of the old.

After this first decade of mediaeval crusading fervor — a strong echo of the Reconquest — the wrecking began to be less violent and less rapid. As for almost any other activity, permission to demolish had to be obtained from the Crown. Since some Indians were found still to be celebrating the old rites, in the mid-1530's the bishops wrote Charles V to ask authority to pull down what had not already been pulled down. They were authorized to proceed (1538), but without any more disturbance or "scandal" than necessary, and they were told to save and use again the conveniently cut stones for building churches and monasteries. The Crown sometimes encouraged the occupation of the old religious centers by transferring to the new priests the same lands the pagan priests had held in fief, and along with them transferring their revenues. It had been noticed that the Indians instinctively returned with gifts to the new shrines in the places where they used to make offerings to the old.[15]

When a generation had passed, and the danger of native religious relapse seemed sufficiently abated, a few scholarly friars began to gather information about preconquest culture — about history, government, religion, and medicine — and to write the texts which are now the most important sources of knowledge of what other friars had destroyed. As early as 1533, the leader of the Franciscans and the President of the Second Audiencia commissioned Fray Andrés de Olmos to write a book on Indian antiquities (now, alas, lost). Fray Bernardino de Sahagún began his monumental *Historia general de las cosas de Nueva España* in 1557, writing first in Náhuatl and then in Spanish. One of the masterworks of the sixteenth century, and the first systematic and scientific study of a whole people, their culture, and religion, it was not only unprecedented, but anticipated much of what was later to be developed in anthropological method. It must not be forgotten what good humanists some of the Spaniards were: in the second half of the century many university-trained friars could read not only Latin, but Greek and Hebrew; many officials had law degrees from Salamanca; Doctor Zorita in his *History of New Spain* referred familiarly to Apuleius, Herodotus, Hesiod, and Plato, to Horace, Juvenal, Ovid, Pliny, Plutarch, Seneca, Tacitus, and Vergil, to many of the Church Fathers, and to modern Erasmus and Petrarch. Yet Zorita was by no means the most cultured. The bibliographical reference lists of Father Valadés and Father Torquemada run into the hundreds. Humanistic antiquarianism and missionary activity were not, however, usually compatible. The desire to save preconquest monuments came only after all the major ones had been defaced or destroyed by the first zealous missionaries. About 1540 Father Motolinía felt that he must describe the temples clearly because so few people still remembered them, and Bishop las Casas wrote of them as something past. Father Mendieta, only a generation later, found that "it would be good to mention here the infinite numbers of very large temples which there used to be in this land . . . for now nearly all are flat on the ground." By 1600 Father Torquemada found that the Indians often no longer recognized their old idols nor knew or cared what they had once meant.[16]

There was a material as well as a strategic spiritual gain in destroying the pyramid-temples: since they were so massively piled up, they made convenient quarries for rubble or ready-squared stones, or sometimes lumber-yards for ready-cut beams. Much of Catholic Mexico City was built of the stones of pagan Tenochtitlán in the same years and in the same way that much of Catholic Counter-Reformation Rome was being built of the stones of pagan Rome. The pyramid of Tláloc and Huitzilopochtli, major shrine of Tenochtitlán, was so mountainously big that it took generations to pull it all down and use it all up: the walls of the first Cathedral were built of its blocks; the broad Plaza Mayor was paved with smooth stones from its patio; the Franciscan church was made of other materials pilfered from it, even to the flagging of the huge forecourt; Father Torquemada still saw "hills" of its masonry being buried for the foundations of the present Cathedral.[17]

There was so much stone in the Maya sanctuary of T'Ho that what the Franciscans did not need for the big monastery they began on its ruins (1547) they gave to the Spanish settlers, who used it to surround the monastery with a new city, which they called Mérida because its quantities of Maya masonry reminded conquistador Montejo of Roman Mérida in Spain. Four of the five hill-like pyramids in its center were flattened, and the fifth was made into a base for the monastery group. After forty years there was still a generous supply of stone not yet used, and eighty years later still enough to make a big fort around the monastery.[18]

When large establishments (Tula or Cholula) are built of neatly squared stones even to their churchyard walls, one suspects that there too the material was appropriated from preconquest monuments, and is not surprised to find that there were once important temples nearby. Since many of the carefully shaped stones of the monastery church at Huejotzingo appear not to have been cut with metal tools, as the stones of such regular ashlar presumably would have been by the time this important church was built, they may come from some preconquest monument, perhaps from nearby Cholula. Telltale fragments often reveal the dereliction of an old sanctuary for the sake of a new one; it is possible to identify re-used preconquest stones with carving spotted in the walls at Tultitlán or Mixquic, or in the flanks of the Franciscan churches at Huaquechula and Tepeapulco.

It is curious that the Spaniards who so insistently avoided taking over heathen religious buildings for their own use in Mexico, unless they could remodel them enough to devalue them symbolically and render them unrecognizable, had felt so few scruples about taking them over earlier in Spain. There many captured mosques had been promptly and easily turned into churches, with minimal alterations. This practice had not stopped, for when Charles V took Tunis (1535) the old mosques became churches almost overnight. Perhaps the Moslems here, and in Tarifa, Oran, and Tripoli, were beaten badly enough not to be in any position to take back their old religion, whereas in Mexico there were too many Indians who had not been beaten (not all had been on the losing side). The military Conquest had been part of an important Indian revolution against the Aztec tyrants, a revolution which a small group of Spaniards promoted and then subverted.

Only if the hundreds of Spaniards destroyed the Indian temples could they be sure that the millions of Indians would not use them again. If they did not destroy the temples, the friars would not be in any position for quite a few decades to keep all of them idle. Furthermore, the Spaniards' revulsion to the brutal Aztec rites seems to have been stronger than to the mild Moslem rites, and this too may have hastened destruction. The early chroniclers described human sacrifice many times, and often repeated the sum of 20,000 sacrificed at the dedication of the Great Temple of Tenochitilán. Even the toughest Spanish soldiers were really shocked by human sacrifice and ritual cannibalism. (It is not unlikely that the accounts of both are exaggerated.)

Therefore it is hardly surprising that so little native architecture in active use when the Spaniards came has survived in any but broken bits. Nearly all of the most spectacular archaeological sites of today (Teotihuacán, Tula, Xochicalco, Monte Albán, Palenque, or Chichén) had already been abandoned when the Spaniards arrived, and hence were not systematically wrecked by them. No major religious site which the Spaniards saw in use remains major today.

This hostility was not, however, extended to civil building: Indian dwellings could be occupied without much remodeling, and there was nothing spiritually objectionable about such a practice. Cortés took over two royal palaces in Tenochtitlán, probably for reasons of symbolic prestige as well as for convenience and the saving of time and money. He had good precedent: Ferdinand and Isabella, still ruling when he left Spain, had similarly appropriated the *alcázares* of the Moslems in several cities (and unlike Cortés, never got around to building a real palace for themselves).

THE APPROPRIATION OF PRECONQUEST SITES

While occasionally part of an existing wall or some rooms in an old non-religious building could be pressed into temporary service until a proper monastery was built, only in Yucatan (at Izamal and Mérida) did the friars move into the religious buildings of an old cult and stay there. Unlike anything in Mexico proper, the Maya monuments contained large rooms "vaulted" in stone-faced rubble concrete. Because the Maya religion had been found somewhat less repugnant, because these rooms had not been used for heathen ritual but merely to house priests and other dignitaries, and because their form was usable, they could prudently be taken over as economical ready-made substitutes for the equivalent quarters in monasteries. At Izamal the Maya work was gradually replaced by new building; at Mérida it was kept in use for 270 years, until the War of Liberation (1820) and, although ruins were still visible in 1838 and 1841, and mounds of rubble in 1845, nothing is left now to show how the adaptation was managed.[19]

77 SECTION THROUGH A TYPI-CAL MAYA "VAULT," *showing irregular corbeling sunk in rubble.*

In the very earliest days, old buildings had to be used for a while by the friars wherever they went, but in central Mexico these were apparently parts of palaces or civic buildings, and they were quickly abandoned. Actual temple buildings were repudiated everywhere, here and in Yucatan. Usually made of masses of earth or rubble contained between sloping walls of stone, their general form was either that of a truncated pyramid stepped back two or three times (as at Tenayuca or Tenochtitlán), or of a lower platform with inclined sides (as at Zempoala in Veracruz, or Teopanzalco and Xochicalco in Morelos, or as shown often in manuscript painting). In either case

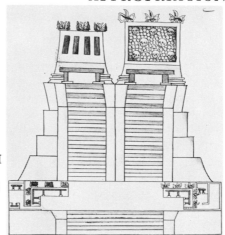

78 THE DOUBLE TEOCALLI
OF TENOCHTITLÁN
(*Durán,* Atlas, c1580)

the top was a flat area, 20 or 30 feet square or often larger; here stood one or sometimes two ornate little shrines of stone or wood. They had to be raised on lofty bases because they were for the gods, who lived in the sky above the level of man's mundane affairs. Shrine and base together constituted a *teocalli,* and this was the typical native temple. So many were made so mountainously big that the Indians called a pyramid-base a *tlachioaltépetl,* or "mountain made by hand."

Although the first Mass in what was to be New Spain was celebrated on top of a teocalli at Cozumel, in 1519, and Cortés had had Mass melodramatically sung on the foremost teocalli of Tenochtitlán, monasteries were not built on the tops of pyramids, as sometimes claimed by guides and guidebooks. The flat area on top would have been inadequate, and access up the steep-stepped sides would have been grotesquely awkward. Furthermore, the site of fresh human sacrifices was unthinkable for the symbolic sacrifice of the Mass. As a sort of spiritual prophylaxis, the friars did place crosses on the spots where the idols or altars had stood, or sometimes they placed little Calvary chapels prominently there in order to show that the old religion had been supplanted by the new. The most famous example is at Cholula, where a whole church was set atop a pyramid so immense that some had compared it to Babylon and some to Babel. Smaller pyramid-borne Calvary shrines may still be seen at Culhuacán near the capital and at Xiutetelco in the Sierra de Puebla; and Father Ponce saw several in Yucatan at Ichmul, Izamal, and Motul.[20] Nowhere in Mexico are there such startling superpositions as at the Dominican church of Cuzco in Peru, where a Christian apse was dramatically, deliberately, and very visibly imposed on the magnificent walls of the Inca Temple of the Sun. An exception (perhaps post-sixteenth-century) may be at Mitla in Oaxaca, where a Dominican apse rests on three monumental doorways once the entrance to an important Zapoteca courtyard; the Christian altar may be directly above its extinguished pagan altar, or something equally revered.

A much more typical re-use of preconquest work was that of remodeled platforms or cut-down pyramids. A convenient way of raising the church dominatingly above the level of the rest of the town, as royal building ordinances suggested, was to set it on an old platform, or a new platform made of the rubble of old wreckage. It may be that since the pyramid or platform was but a *base* and not, like the shrine on top, a religious *building,* the former could be appropriated for Christian religious use without impropriety, while the latter could not. Just as a raised site had been considered the "place of honor" for a temple, so was it often thought fitting for a church.[21]

Once in a while, other preconquest fragments were used to demonstrate the defeat of the old religion by being made to serve the new. For instance, the stone cross in the monastery patio at Cuernavaca stands — in what is surely a premeditated symbolic triumph — on a *cuaxicalli,* a stone box once used for freshly sacrificed human hearts. Lying beside the present Cathedral of Mexico City, are still the stumps of the columns of the earlier Cathedral, their bases patterned with the sacred scales of a humbled and denatured serpent which once had proudly crowned the long *coatepantli* or circuit wall of the temple precinct there.

With very few exceptions recognizable pre-Christian religious monuments in New Spain were either destroyed or drastically defaced before Christian buildings were put on their sites. Inasmuch as it was feared that the sites themselves might retain magic prestige with the Indians, even after the idols had been thrown down and smashed or burned in public and their temples obliterated, the friars often took over the same areas, exorcised, and then occupied them with clean new Christian buildings. Thus they were able not only to disorganize the pagan religious life by destroying its physical frame, but also to offer a dramatic, instructive, and admonitory replacement. The brothers may not have recalled that a thousand years before, the Christians had done the same thing in Europe, to the buildings of different heathen gods, and that then there was less fastidiousness about using the old temples over again. It was not a new but a very old custom, as the architectural palimpsests in almost any venerable European city can show.

THE PERSISTENCE OF NATIVE TRADITIONS

Although the monuments of the preconquest religions supplied part of the physical *substance* of their postconquest successors, the latter showed little or nothing of the architectural *forms* of the native repertory. Native religious building had much less influence on new building than has commonly but carelessly or chauvinistically been assumed. This is particularly surprising in view of one age-old peculiarity of Spanish architecture: although the Spaniards have never invented a complete architectural style of their own, but instead have borrowed styles from outside, they have so assimilated and hispanized these that within a generation they became as thoroughly Spanish as they had ever been French, Flemish, or Italian. Why, then, did the Spanish conquerors not borrow from the splendid preconquest architecture which they so ambivalently admired? Their rejection of it, both in its main forms and in its details, is so complete as to seem the result of a deliberate policy, if not of a compulsive phobia.

SURVIVAL OF PRECONQUEST FORMS

What had been most impressive in native architecture — the religious building — was almost useless to the Spaniards; what was most useful — the domestic building — was not often impressive, and it offered no practical conveniences the Spaniards did not already know. Though some of the functional requirements for religious buildings were little different for the Spanish Christians and the Mexican heathens, and though the materials, climate, and kinds of labor were identical, the nonfunctional, aesthetic, or expressive demands were not at all alike. Preconquest architecture had been made specifically for the ritual of one religion, and postconquest architecture for the very different ritual of a religion of a very different character. Their architectural forms were therefore necessarily different. This is not to say that the spirit of the Conversion was eloquently incarnated in its buildings, for it never fully was, and often it was scarcely expressed at all; but had the new religion chosen to house itself in forms borrowed from the old, only confusion and conflict could have resulted. While the great number and great richness of the preconquest temples made the friars anxious not to have their churches seem inferior, such stimulus led only to emulation of effects, not to imitation of forms.

Let us not be dazzled by the size, magnificence, and romantic strangeness of the preconquest monuments; or if we are dazzled aesthetically — and it is hard not to be — let us not be dazzled historically too. Beautiful and wonderful as it often was, this architecture was narrowly limited. It was a sort of grandly monumental abstract sculpture, plain and simple of form but rich and complex of surface. Even more than the Egyptian, Chinese, or Greek, it seems to have been predominantly an architecture of exterior design, often monumental and oppressively massive. Shapes and details were repeated over and over; the reiterated ornamental stereotypes were perhaps related to the reiterated ritual that went on in front of them.

Although it provided simple shelter and splendid ceremonial scenery for Indian religious life, Indian architecture could not be made to serve the more specifically defined and varied demands of the more complex Spanish ways. Constructions as solid as the platforms or pyramidal bases did not lend themselves to remodeling into anything but other solid bases. In the buildings above these solids there was remarkably little interior space. Only in the big Indian palaces were there any usable large rooms. Cortés, Bernal Díaz, Aguilar, and Sahagún mentioned a few great halls, and Pomar boasted of rooms in Texcoco in the palace of his kinsman, Prince Netzahualcóyotl, which would hold a hundred men; [22] but all such spaces were either pinched tightly between walls or pierced by wood posts. For the greater interior needs of the Spaniards, such Indian halls could not have been satisfactory.

Except for the platforms, almost no postconquest work shows a large architectural form which is recognizably of native origin. Aside from them, one finds only a few small decorative items of Indian character, relegated to subordinate positions where they could awake no dangerous ideas in insecure converts. Sometimes it is hard to tell whether a characteristic form comes from European or local traditions or from both, since the two can on occasion be so similar. For example, there are equally strong family resemblances to either mudéjar or Aztec forebears in the parapets made of a flat frieze between two flat bands or two fat torus moldings, so often used by friar-builders in place of a crowning cornice. In the same way, the sloping base of the gate of the churchyard at Tepeaca or of the Doendó Cross at Jilotepec could continue the batter either of typical preconquest or typical European military bases. Are the fancy merlons of the churchyard wall at Tepeji del Río enough like those in preconquest manuscripts to be counted as a survival? Should the base of the stone cross at Natívitas Zacapa be called preconquest

79 GATEWAY TO CHURCHYARD AT TEPEACA

80 THE DOENDÓ CROSS OUTSIDE JILOTEPEC

in style because it gives the date in native glyphs? One must search a long time to find such minor but certain persistences as the eagle-knights on the doorway of a house in Cholula or the heads emitting speech-scroll-symbols on the doorway of the church at Coixtlahuaca. Such odd episodes, though surely of Indian descent, are no more than very minor items in the postconquest decorative vocabulary.

*

In buildings other than churches, where there need not have been the same strictures against them, surprisingly few survivals can be found. The best Indian domestic building had little to offer the Spaniards: except for a few palaces, houses had no more than one story, and had no windows at all; and many practical elements — such as central patios, wood-beamed ceilings, wood columns, stuccoed stone, brick, or adobe walls — matched familiar Spanish elements. Since Doctor Cervantes de Salazar singled it out for comment, the flat roof might appear to have been a novelty, but his notice showed that he knew few in Spain rather than that few were there. On the contrary, flat roofs were a common survival from Moorish and Roman building habits in those parts where there was little rainfall, as Cortés — less learned but sharper-eyed than Doctor Cervantes — recalled as soon as he landed and saw local flat roofs. Other writers took them for granted, and Aguilar went out of his way to praise the many native roof-terraces, though not as any novelty.[23]

In humbler buildings the survival of preconquest forms was far greater. The minimal one-room house of the poorest Aztecs continued to be reproduced in the monastery towns but, though it may sometimes have folkloristic charm, it lacks genuine architectural interest, and its occasional aesthetic appeal is accidental. The type has persisted in folk-building, so that in the older villages of the Valley of Mexico (Mixquic, Tepepan, Milpa Alta, or Huexotla) it is now all but impossible to say whether a little stone house is five, fifty, or five hundred years old. Had they survived, the same would doubtless be true of adobe or wattle-and-daub houses, for the windowless modern examples appear in every way the counterparts of their ancestors, even more than do the Indians who live in them. A number of survivals of other preconquest building types can be seen in rural building in many parts of Mexico, above all in Michoacán, Oaxaca, and Yucatan, in *temascales* (sweat baths) or *coscomates* (round corncribs), types for which there was no Spanish equivalent; but these are folk-architecture, apart from monumental architecture and with no influence on it. Some of the now vanished visitas or humble parish churches might properly have been classified as folk-architecture, as well as some of the earliest provisional monasteries and some of the poorest later ones, such as those of adobe in Jalisco, Michoacán, and the Huaxteca.

ARCHITECTURE NEW AND OLD

Although it produced many handsome monuments, native architecture was so restricted in its material means that it made no major technical changes in the architecture the Spaniards built or, rather, had the natives build for them. The only effects were minor, and came more from the manual performance of the common laborers than from any intellectual or aesthetic decisions by designers or foremen. Though the upper ranks in the organization of the building trades had been disrupted by the Conquest, there was considerable continuity on the lower levels. The crews of ordinary workmen were called to the capital from the same towns that had traditionally supplied them, and they could keep on working much as they had worked before, so long as their old ways were not too different from Spanish ways.

Several examples of this sort of technical continuity are found in the ways walls were made. One of the commonest is still to pile up stones which have been flattened only on the side that will show, and which have not been squared to make a regular pattern but, left roughly polygonal, exhibit joints which are irregular in direction, width, and depth. Inside, much of the wall is rubble, drowned in a mortar made with volcanic sand, carbonate of lime, and clayey mud, or a mixture of such mortar with still more mud. Since this mortar is often not strong in large amounts by itself and becomes weaker through contact with wet weather, whenever an exposed joint is big and wide, the surface of the mortar is reduced by inserting small stones, somewhat as in Roman *opus incertum,* though much less uniformly. The mortar is made more durable because it presents less surface to the weather, and because it has more surfaces to stick to than it would if left uninterrupted in larger amounts. The resulting pattern of masonry, called *rejoneado,* can be pleasing, with its varied areas of the building stone separated by meandering paths of light-colored mortar and dotted lines of inserted dark red or purple-black lava, or perhaps chips of pink brick. This simple, practical, and pretty

81 REJONEADO

technique affected the physical composition of the buildings where it was used, but not the architectural design, since for an important wall or facade in the best preconquest and colonial work, *rejoneado* was normally surfaced with stucco. (It was not allowed to show itself in important architectural contexts until modern architects happily decided to make it respectable in the 1940's.)

82 WINDOWLESS ADOBE HOUSES AT SAN HIPÓLITO,
PUEBLA

Another practice probably carried over directly from pre- to postconquest building was the use of thick rubble walls reinforced by cut stone at exterior corners, door jambs, and other places vulnerable to chipping or gouging. There might be areas of cut-stone facing also at special zones with carved decoration, perhaps on the wall around a doorway. Many sixteenth-century church facades were arranged this way, with a trim cut-stone frontispiece of carved European-style detail set against a cheaper and simpler building shell with cut-stone edging (at Tlaquiltenango and Cuernavaca, for example, where fields of ashlar made smooth backgrounds for the ornamental side portals). There are, however, equivalent occurrences in Spain and in the rest of Europe, particularly when masonry tradition or the supply of skilled masons was wanting or weak. Inasmuch as in Mexico, Indian workmen were quickly drafted without much specific training in European ways, such rubble-and-cut-stone walls there were probably less European than Indian. This is another example of the many coincidences in European and native building habits — similar conditions having produced similar practices — where the native, in no conflict with the European, was allowed to continue. Sometimes economical native procedures were hidden behind more costly Spanish ones where they would not show: at the exceptionally well-finished establishments at Huejotzingo and Yanhuitlán, the core of the cut-stone walls in many places is rubble and rammed earth.[24]

191

83 *South side door of the Franciscan monastery church at* TLAQUILTE—NANGO, *added after 1552, a smooth ashlar frontispiece set on a rough rubble wall. The buttresses have finished cut stone only at their corners.*

The use of adobe construction, common in preconquest building, was a novelty to some Spaniards, though similar sun-dried brick had long been used for unassuming work in southern Spain. Some Spaniards knew how to use it, and some Indians, surprisingly, did not.[25] Perhaps the novelty was not so much in the material itself as in its use for monumental buildings, such as the palaces of Moctezuma or the mammoth pyramid at Cholula. For some of their large undertakings, the friars sensibly made use of native adobe in the beginning, and also all through the century in regions such as the western provinces where nothing more durable was at hand. Though there are very few old texts or surviving examples for corroboration, it is also probable that construction in earth, clay, and straw, rammed into wood frames to make a sort of monolithic adobe concrete or *tapia,* was a native novelty early adopted by the Spaniards. The workmen knew how to produce it; all the Spaniards had to do was approve and use it.

*

A native technique particularly admired by the Spaniards was that of finishing buildings and pavements with stucco burnished by rubbing with smooth pebbles. The early chroniclers often spoke of entire cities "shining," "like silver," or "made of jewels," and the surviving fragments of glossy preconquest walls justify their enthusiasm. The painted stucco surfaces of many monasteries appear to continue this attractive practice, which seems natural enough since the work was done by Indian painters. The decorative patterns, however, are not Indian but European; and the glossiness, moreover, does not always come from burnishing but often from an accidental chemical change brought about merely by the passage of time: one cannot always tell which. Nevertheless, the idea of surfacing important buildings with sleek painted stucco may come as much from striking preconquest examples as memories of mudéjar precedents in Spain.

For paving large areas, a particularly hard shiny stucco was often adopted by the friars. At Cholula the Franciscans had their Indian laborers cover the whole churchyard with dark red stucco, a handsome surface they must have seen and admired underfoot in many of the sanctuaries of the widely extended holy city they were helping to destroy or overlay. Local folklore has this pavement made with an admixture of mortar and egg, but direct study shows it to be the same as local preconquest paving: volcanic sand and good clay, pounded down to a hard even surface, and then coated with a wash of lime and powdered red lava. Patches of preconquest pavement turn up all over Cholula today, and are indistinguishable from what the friars used around their church; some of the latter may still be part of the paving of the pagan courtyard which the monastery courtyard replaces. At Otumba and Tlalmanalco also, and several other sites, it is not possible to say whether areas of shiny red were made for the pre-Christian or Christian shrines. As also with wall construction, it is not certain that the models for such pavements were exclusively preconquest, for there had been some Spanish antecedents in Moorish work in the thirteenth and fourteenth centuries (said to be dyed red with bulls' blood), and even earlier in Roman and Hellenistic work; but, much as some antique forecourts resemble those of the Mexican monasteries, common sense insists on sources nearer home. What seems most probable is that, having seen old paved courts, when they needed new courts, the friars had the Indians make them in their familiar old way; possibly the friars' decision was reinforced by memories of handsome Moorish pavements, possibly not: it does not matter, for again the traditions coincide.[26]

Preconquest architects would take extreme pains for aesthetic appearance, and even neglect integrity of structure for effectiveness of surface.[27] Although it has not been commonly said, it is not surprising to find that from the 1540's on, the Christian religious buildings were usually better built than their pagan predecessors. That vault over the choir of San Francisco was not only a new form: it was presumably also the proclamation of a new attitude toward structural integrity and, in a very simple way, of a new attitude toward the frank relating of construction and artistic form.

ARCHITECTURE NEW AND OLD

SURVIVAL OF PRECONQUEST STYLE: TEQUITQUI

Almost all the good and notable handiwork here in the Indies (at least in New Spain) is done by the Indians, because the Spaniards, masters of many crafts, rarely do more than give the work to the Indians, and tell them how they want it done. And they do it so well, no one could do it better.   — Father Mendieta (c1580)

It is not meet that the Indians should know Latin, rhetoric, philosophy, or any other science, but rather they should learn handicrafts, to which they are naturally and enthusiastically inclined.
— Archbishop Moya de Contreras (1585) [28]

Sixteenth-century texts so often praise the skill of native craftsmen that it could be accepted as a documented fact even if the eloquent material evidence was no longer here to enjoy. One surprising testimonial came from Albrecht Dürer, who saw in Antwerp some of the treasure which Moctezuma had sent Cortés and Cortés had sent Charles V (1520). With his usual high coefficient of egocentricity, Dürer wrote in his journal: "All the days of my life I have seen nothing that gladdened my heart as much as these things, for I saw among them wonderful works of art, and I marvelled at the subtle *ingenua* of men in foreign lands. Indeed I cannot express all that I thought thereby." When Fray Pedro Martír de Anglería saw these same exotica in Spain, he wrote: "I do not really admire the gold and precious stones: what astounds me is the skill and cleverness wherewith the workmanship surpasses the material." [29] A walk through the wonderful but confusingly arranged collections of the National Museum of Mexico will still confirm contemporary praise. Because their evaluations were conditioned by their European religious and aesthetic *Gestalt,* the early Spanish writers found the Indians' idols ill-proportioned, ugly, and even monstrous. Just as regularly they found the technical skills surprising, admirable, and even enviable.

Sixteenth-century chroniclers told many stories of the Indian artists' quick aptitudes, and of their quick adaptability after the Conquest. Bishop Zumárraga wrote that the thirteen master-craftsmen working for him had learned in two years to carve Spanish saints good enough for his Cathedral. Father Torquemada found that they learned "like monkeys." [30]

Since European cutting tools of metal were rare and expensive, most of the earliest work was carved with traditional neolithic tools. While such a change in implements might have entailed some change in style, none is apparent, for by the time the new tools had become generally available the Indian craftsmen had already established their own acceptable versions of European styles. Although they had had some implements of copper before the Conquest, these were neither very common nor very hard, and had not in any way affected the style of carving. The change in tools cannot have affected forms so much as it affected the time needed to produce them.

Native artists became quickly adept also at painting in European ways. Father Motolinía boasted that by 1540 "great painters have arisen . . . since the samples and images have been brought by the Spaniards from Flanders and Italy, there is no image nor retable, no matter how excellent, which they do not imitate well." Father la Rea, easily stimulated to wonder and thence to hyperbole, thought the European-style pictures with which the Tarasco artists were brightening the churches of Michoacán a century later were as satisfactory as anything from Rome, the topmost pinnacle of praise from this Italophile. Native artists were able to make large paintings and statues on the basis of small European engravings, mostly mannerist and mostly from Antwerp, the chief printing center of Europe at the time. They learned all sorts of European techniques speedily when taught, and sometimes just as speedily when not taught — by spying on Spanish craftsmen at work. Doctor Zorita told how some Indians mastered ceramic secrets by peeking at Spanish potters through a hole they had poked in the roof. Skilled Spaniards soon began to hide their professional secrets for fear of a flood of cheap competition.[31]

*

The Indians who had had the most advanced cultures before the Conquest were the first to be conquered and converted, and were therefore the most subject to new Spanish ways. In other words, those with most to lose lost soonest and lost most, but they also learned most; whereas those with less to lose kept that less longer, but they learned less.

In the cities of the most advanced cultures there had been large workshops devoted to making sculpture. Inasmuch as their repertory was entirely religious, and the Spaniards looked on the native sculptors as heathen idol-makers, the sculptors' shops must have suffered even worse disruption after the Conquest than those of the masons or carpenters. It is not surprising, then, that everyone who has studied them both finds preconquest sculpture artistically superior to postconquest. Preconquest architecture, though it may have been richer, was far less varied than postconquest. Painting seems to have been the weakest of the Indian arts and the one most invigorated by Spanish transfusions but, even thus stimulated, it was weaker and later in developing than its sister arts in colonial times.

*

What was most admirable in preconquest art did not automatically pass over into postconquest art, for as the best shops were probably the worst disrupted, little could survive at the higher levels of artistic production. Something could persist at lower levels, something not only of the manual skills but also of old aesthetic preferences which now and then could assert themselves half-automatically and almost secretly within the new European forms demanded by the Spaniards.

Consequently, any important relation with preconquest architecture is to be sought not so much in the basic architectural ideas of the new building as in matters of taste and ornamental style. With only a few minor exceptions and one major one (discussed in the next chapter), native architecture had no significant effect on the basic design of the architecture that took its place. The new architecture was, of course, regularly built by Indian workmen — when possible by the best — and although their brown hands were guided by white ones, they were still Indian hands. Rather than memories of specific old forms, this now seems more probably the explanation of the Indian character of the sloping bases of the cross at Jilotepec and gate at Tepeaca. They look Indian because they were made by Indians, but the forms are probably not so much Indian as part of the currency of contemporary or earlier European military building which had been described to the Indians by the friars, and then matched by the Indians to forms they already knew. Moreover, these are fairly rare examples. Any genuinely native character in the new building is most often found in the handmade details of the execution, above all in the carved ornament. Manually deft and clever at imitation, the Indians who had been directed to work in some gothic, mudéjar, plateresque, or mixed vocabulary, could often carry out their Spanish masters' wishes satisfactorily and apparently quite literally; but more often the finished products show the result — perhaps conscious but more likely not — of a quiet resistance, of another *se obedece pero no se cumple.* This is one of the conditions which makes these works unique.

Although the big workshops and grand-scale patronage of preconquest art were destroyed, traces of its aesthetic vitality reappeared in the smaller shops under the smaller-scale patronage of the friars. It was more or less concealed in some European fancy dress, for to whatever of their own craft skills the Indians retained there was necessarily added a knowledge of European decorative vocabularies as well as of European techniques. Spanish aesthetic preferences were imposed on native preferences: sometimes one was stronger; sometimes the other; sometimes they all but canceled one another; and sometimes they intermingled compatibly. When the last occurred, the resulting hybrid was so often stylistically consistent that it may be classified as a separate style or sub-style. Recently it has been given a name of its own (by the late José Moreno Villa): *tequitqui.*[32]

Tequitqui is the American cousin of mudéjar. The word is the Náhuatl term for "one who pays tribute," or a "subject person," while *mudéjar* is a hispanization of the Arab *mudayyan,* which means more or less the same. Each term has been extended to the art that the conquered made for their

84 SANTA MARÍA TULPETLAC

conquerors, or to the conquerors' assumption of the style of the conquered. The relation, however, is not identical: the peculiarly individual character of tequitqui comes from its metamorphosis of European ornamental forms by a non-European temperament, whereas mudéjar resulted not so much from the use of European forms by non-Europeans as from the extensive use of non-European forms. Perhaps tequitqui is in a cousinly way also equivalent to the florid late gothic of the reign of Isabella, the *Isabelino* or *gothic plateresque,* where a wealth of Burgundian or Flemish gothic detail would be assembled in zones of dense and carpet-like patterns which were essentially an inherited trait of late Moorish taste, even though none of the detail in them need be Moorish.

Although the most and the best examples are found in regions where preconquest sculpture in stone had flourished most distinctively, stylistic differences between the native arts of different regions, cities, or ateliers are scarcely to be traced in the tequitqui of the sixteenth century. Such distinctive local touches as make it possible to separate the manuscript painting of Tenochtitlán from that of Texcoco are not found in tequitqui carving.[33] It was only some of the qualities fundamental to preconquest art in general which gave tequitqui its essential character.

85 Visita church at
MIXQUIAHUALA,
c1570

The stylistic qualities of tequitqui are inherent, and do not lie in the occasional persistence of preconquest motifs of design, such as date or place glyphs, speech symbols, or stylized squash blossoms. The essential Indian nature is less tangible and more fundamental. It resides in an underlying conception of form and decoration which can be discerned to a considerable extent in both preconquest and Indian-executed postconquest work. In preconquest art, this was expressed with a native vocabulary; in postconquest, with a European one. Even when preconquest items do appear in decoration — most frequently in the earliest work when continuity with native tradition was strongest — it is not this but the stylistic transformation of European motifs which is more original, widespread, and important. In other words, there must be a European vocabulary *and* a strong Indian accent.

A great deal of pre- and postconquest work was linear. The lines in tequitqui do not act like the weightless conductors of movement in so much European linear ornament; instead, visibly thickened in substance, they coil and shove their very corporeal forms with a restless serpentine force much as they had done in preconquest carving. Never the massless, darting transmitters of volts which often enliven European linear ornament, the Indian lines seem to have embodied the mass and pushing energy of foot-pounds. The curved elements do not ripple rhythmically on a regular wavelength, as so often in Europe; they curve and straighten out in a slow, tense sequence

198

from which they seem to want to break free. The many stressed episodes do not add up to an expression of continuous movement, but remain separate shoves and swirls. They act on one another more by repulsion than attraction.

The movement is repetitive, and occasionally spasmodic, rather than flowing, more like a staccato tom-tom beat than a sequence which accumulates into a melodic phrase. Such all-over, metronomic, never-ending repetition, as opposed to metrical scansion with phrased grouping of accents, is one of the fundamental differences between the typical Indian and European expressions in ornament. As a result, in the most successful examples of tequitqui, the whole holds together chiefly by an all-over surface tension, and not by the subordinating power of a few dominant forms or currents of movement. Coherence comes not from any organic or sequential interrelation of parts, but from their insistent repetition in tight and seemingly endless patterns, and from the incessant interaction of their outlines. Almost everything seems equally important because almost nothing submits to subordination. As in so much preconquest art and many other kinds of primitive and folk art, there is usually more success in details than ensembles (with exceptions made, of course, for a few masterpieces).

Perhaps the second most animating element in the design is the abrupt pattern of sharp edges and abrupt light-and-shade pattern which accompanies it, a step behind, like the second voice in a musical canon. More often in tequitqui than in preconquest work, zones of flattened relief stand

86 Hospital chapel at
ACÁMBARO

87 Visita church at SAN
PEDRO ATARÁCUARO

out in front of a neutral flat ground which has been cut back to an even depth behind them, so that everything lies as strictly on the two levels as if the ornament had been neatly punched out with a cookie-cutter and laid on a flat surface. There is little or no modeling, and the whole is more in two-and-a-fraction than in three dimensions. One might say that it looked sometimes like a stiffened exaggeration of the two-level patterns of cut velvet. Everywhere in tequitqui one sees European forms pressed out flat and presented in this kind of sharp silhouette, raised evenly above a half-seen neutral ground. No other kind of ornament is so sparkling in the bright Mexican sun, where the shadows are always transparent and the fresh, vivid light is not blurred by haze or smoke.[34]

The individual shapes, flattened and juxtaposed in jostling movement, lose their European suavity, but often gain a new kind of vigor. Smooth continuity of curvature and sinuous inflection give way to lines now briefly straight and now forcibly bent into short curves, like the lines in much preconquest carving. The closest European parallel is not to be sought — as one might expect — in the elegant Spanish sixteenth-century works which were the tequitqui artist's unseen models, but rather in the remoter works produced by an equivalent earlier union of disparate tastes: when Roman forms, for example, were coarsened but invigorated by the carvers of the newly Christian Teutonic kingdoms of the Dark Ages.

Although some of the constituent items of tequitqui carving may come from representational models, they are not presented realistically. In much the same way, preconquest ornament had avoided showing identifiable plants, flowers, or leaves, so common in European ornament, for stylization was always preferred to description. The half-abstracted individual forms of tequitqui — originally gothic, renaissance, or mudéjar — are repeated and multiplied by *horror vacui,* until they make the typically dense, never-ending, unaccented patterns antagonistic to the phrased spacing with which Europeans had habitually deployed these forms.

In western Europe, only in Spain was this kind of difference in rhythm familiarly understood in the sixteenth century, because only in Spain was an important non-European heritage still alive: a heritage from the exotic art of Islam active in mudéjar and some plateresque. Consequently, in Spanish-Indian Mexico, it is sometimes not possible to determine whether a typical transformation of gothic or renaissance repertory is basically Spanish plateresque or Mexican tequitqui, since both worked their borrowed forms into equivalently dense patterns, flat patterns which often made strange tensions by contrast with the inert bulk whose surface they enlivened. Also, plateresque and tequitqui both rearranged forms which once had had tectonic meaning into entirely decorative and even anti-tectonic contexts. Here is another case where European and American traditions are too close always to be distinguishable. To isolate true tequitqui from provincial plateresque, one must look for three characteristics: unmodeled relief silhouetted on two levels, a peculiar Indian quality of line, and the vigorous abrupt shapes inherited from preconquest art, quite different from the languid late Moorish or mudéjar.

*

Except for the adoption of the Aztec religious courtyard, to be considered in the next chapter, only three significant Indian contributions are discernible in Mexican sixteenth-century architecture, nationalistic Mexicans and romantic foreigners to the contrary. They are

> the tequitqui carving of ornament,
> a very few decorative motifs, and
> the occasional persistence of minor preconquest building techniques.

It is not so surprising how *much* Indian survives — as it has been culturally fashionable to maintain since the Mexican Renaissance of the 1920's, and the happy rediscovery of Mexico by Mexican intellectuals — but rather, how *little*. But what is not Indian is not necessarily therefore Spanish, and what is not Spanish is not necessarily Indian: the forced association of the two cultures produced validly original work which, neither truly Indian nor Spanish, nor yet half-Indian and half-Spanish, is something closely and legitimately related to both while distinct from either: it is a sort of strong artistic mestizo, and may best be called, simply, "Mexican." One of its earliest and liveliest expressions is in the tequitqui.

88 Jamb of posa chapel at CALPAN,
c1555

201

VI

THE ATRIO

*All the monasteries here in New Spain have a large walled patio in
front of the church . . . The old men keep these patios swept
and clean, and usually they are adorned with trees set in orderly
rows. In the hot country there are alternate rows of cypresses and
orange trees, and in the temperate and cold regions there are cypresses and pepper trees from Peru which stay green all year. To
walk into these patios is something to make one praise God.*
        — Father Mendieta (between 1574–96) [1]

DURING the formative years and on through the century, both the church
and monastery building were wistfully intended to look like their European
forebears. Never the image of one identifiable ancestor, and sometimes oddly
disguised or distorted by native taste, they were nonetheless legitimate
country cousins of their sophisticated Spanish contemporaries. Unlike the
church and monastery block, the third component of the friary scheme, the
forecourt with its auxiliary architecture, was not an immigrant European
form: it was a new element, synthesized locally from older models in order
to satisfy new demands. Thus it was the most striking novelty in the ensemble, without true parallels in Spain or anywhere else in Europe.

This most Mexican component likewise consisted of three parts:
> the forecourt proper, called the *patio* or *atrio,*
> the *open chapel* facing it,
> the four *posas,* small chapel-like buildings in its corners.

*

The first permanent church on the American mainland, the original
San Francisco in México-Tenochtitlán, was granted ten building lots in 1527
for dependencies and "patio," and it was probably this early example which
established the precedent for thousands of church forecourts laid out during
the next four centuries. This parent court soon must have been given some
substantial demarcation, for in 1530 two *oidores* of the First Audiencia

kidnapped two Indians from the "corral" of the church, and in 1534, when preaching in Spain on their right of asylum, Bishop Zumárraga spoke of the "circuit and walls of the corral." There was probably no more than a high, plain, masonry barrier around the court, pierced by two gateways. Such courts, or *atrios* as they are now called, remain one of the most characteristic and attractive features of many Mexican towns. Every sixteenth-century monastery must originally have had one, even in the larger cities, and they were regularly given to secular parish churches. There is nothing in Europe to compare with them in scale and number.[2]

A typical sixteenth-century example — to choose one at random — is at Santa Ana Chiautempan: a walled area in front of the monastery church and roughly on axis with it, with a gateway at the head of broad steps leading down a few feet to the town plaza, comparable in size to the atrio and axially symmetrical with it. Magnificent ash trees, now towering some 120 feet, fill the atrio with neat regularity, as though set out on the coordinates of giant squared paper. The plaza is agreeably shaded too, with slightly smaller trees set out on another militaristic planting plan.

There are hundreds and hundreds of similar arrangements in Mexico. On a grander scale, one can still see the same main features at Quecholac or Huejotzingo, Huaquechula or Tzintzuntzan, or on a smaller scale at Chimalhuacán Atenco, Alfajayucan, and scores of other villages. In Oaxaca, Michoacán, and Jalisco, such churchyards were often planted with scores of orange or other fruit trees set in orderly rows — occasionally with olives, and in Yucatan with avocados — not just for ornament or fruit but also for welcome shade during the long, sunny, dry season; without them the atrios in low-lying towns might have been considered unhospitably hot for recent converts. Many paved atrios were punctuated with a rhythmical pattern of special holes for trees, in the Andalusian manner inherited from the sybaritic Moslems. Often there were shrubs and neat garden plots for smaller plants. Father Torquemada noted with pleasure the flowers that bloomed in some patios all year round, something he had never seen in Spain.[3]

THE USES OF THE ATRIO

> *The monasteries have a large walled patio in front of the church . . . made to be used mainly on holy days, so that when all the townspeople are gathered together, they can hear Mass, and be preached to in the patio, for they will not fit inside the body of the church, which they use only when, through piety, they come to hear Mass on weekdays.*
>
> — *Father Mendieta (between 1574–96)* [4]

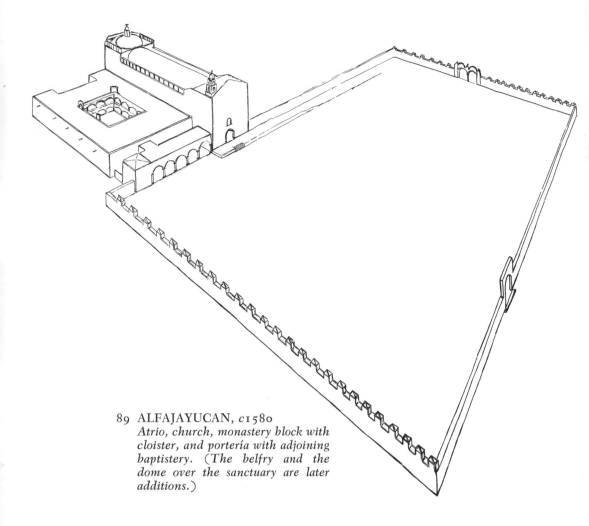

89 ALFAJAYUCAN, *c*1580
*Atrio, church, monastery block with
cloister, and portería with adjoining
baptistery. (The belfry and the
dome over the sanctuary are later
additions.)*

MASS

During the first half of the sixteenth century, ordinary church ritual
was not as uniform in Europe as it was to be after the Council of Trent
fixed theory and practice so firmly that there were not even any ecumenical
councils for over three centuries. Following its decisions, Pius V standardized Catholic liturgy (1570), but until the new regulations should be fully
published New Spain decided to keep on with its own fairly free "Mexican
Rite." The sixteenth-century Spanish Church and Court, however, were already so unbendingly conservative that modifications of any kind — at home
or across the sea — were eyed as disturbing and unnatural: experiments
would be even worse.

In spite of this, its geographical isolation from the family of European Churches allowed both arms of the Mexican Church a modicum of freedom in a few practices not yet rigidified by established Church Doctrine (a freedom stemming from earlier liberalism in Spain, but unthinkable there in the middle of the sixteenth century). Some practical modifications had to be countenanced, even in matters as central as the administering of the Sacraments. Most of the local variations were established in the difficult days near the beginning of the Conversion: the most arresting of them was the use of the atrio as an outdoor church.

The special needs of the millions of Indian converts and potential converts were the cause of this amazing divarication from European practice. The use of a courtyard to contain the congregation during services — virtually as the nave of a church — was probably accepted for the regulars because it solved a difficult procedural problem for which there were no usable European precedents. Contemporary chroniclers described this use often, knowing that to European readers it would be so unfamiliar as to need explaining. The seculars avoided it — they were always closer to the hierarchy in Spain — and were eventually forbidden (1555 and '85) to make such use of their courtyards.[5]

Having had no congregational demands for several centuries that could not be met with the ordinary repertory of church-building forms, Europe had had no need for anything like atrios. The Mendicants had long preached sermons to crowds outdoors, but this was not equivalent to the Mexican use of the atrio because they merely preached to their outdoor crowds whereas the Mexican Mendicants said Masses for theirs. In Europe the Mendicants preached in the open air only irregularly, whenever there seemed to be sufficient special reason and wherever there was a handy big space. They would improvise a space in city squares, at markets or fairs, in fields outside of town, with the preacher sometimes perched in a tree in order to make himself visible and audible above the heads of his flock. The Mexican atrios, on the other hand, were special places which had been particularly and permanently arranged — often with considerable labor — for many religious uses of which the most important was as an outdoor church.

From its beginning the Christian religion had been one where worship took place *inside* a building. The essential rite was the Mass, and its symbolism and traditions demanded that it take place indoors. The Early Christians, who set the precedents, always worshiped indoors, whether in borrowed halls or in their own buildings. As a consequence, Christian architecture had from the first emphasized the interior of its churches rather than the exterior: where Mass was to be celebrated, a fine setting ought to be provided, and the setting had to be indoors. Soon there was agreement also that the church must be a permanent structure, permanent in the two senses that it be durably built and that it be intended always to remain a church. Consecrated, usually by a bishop, the building itself became a holy object, like the altar or font or the liturgical equipment it enshrined.

The Mexican atrio, though used as a church, could never be a church in this traditional sense. It cannot have been formally consecrated or dedicated; instead it probably was merely blessed, as chapels or private oratories were, though possibly it was not formally sanctified at all, any more than would be the space where an outdoor Mass for an army or hunting party might be said. Even today Canon Law makes no provision for temporary churches, and when the first atrio began to serve for Masses it may well have been viewed as a temporary makeshift. Its unconsecrated status could have persisted after the atrio had become virtually a permanent church.

As a standard element, the Mexican atrio-church must fairly soon have been found disturbing to many of the authorities in Spain. Anything so unprecedented in such close connection with the celebration of Christian ritual might have raised suspicions of unorthodoxy bordering on heresy. It is astonishing that Spaniards were able to accept and even encourage its use. Either they were not fully aware of what was being done in the atrios of New Spain until it had long been done with no heretical or schismatic consequences, or else they came to understand that without the atrio-church the Conversion might have been both slower and smaller. It must have been fully accepted before fussy Inquisitor Moya de Contreras was elevated to Archbishop in 1572. Before that, formal religious discipline in Mexico had been relatively mild, partly through default, since the pursuit of Indian gold and the conversion of Indian souls had seemed more imperative to those in power. Had the Mexican Church not been more liberal than the Spanish during its first fifty years, there would have been no Masses for Indians in the atrios, and without them, perhaps the Conversion would not have had such success.

*

For their Masses the natives could not be conveniently subdivided into more manageable groups which could be fitted into the monastery church, for there would not have been enough friars to go around. As it was, there were surprisingly few in most of the monasteries. Large groups were found only in the head houses of the Orders, houses in cathedral cities, houses with novitiates, or a few others with special conditions of some sort. The irreducible minimum was two — friars must lead a communal life — and all through the sixteenth century many Franciscan houses can never have had more. Four or five quite often lived in Augustinian establishments, which were often physically larger. From the beginning the Dominicans had had to waive their European rule of at least seven friars to a house, and in Mexico usually they had no more than the Augustinians. Even at the end of the century there were not many more in the ordinary monasteries, for although there were now more friars there were also more friaries. Like a European priest a Mexican secular was supposed to say only one Mass daily (except on Christmas). Unless there was specific dispensation, bination, or the saying of two Masses on one day by one priest, was forbidden. It had been banned centuries before when too many scandalous priests began to say too many Masses to gain more money. No matter what special exemptions were granted the Mexican friars, with all the services to be celebrated in the churches, atrios, and visitas, it would have been impossible for them to manage with anything as restricted as one, two, or even three services per friar. There is some evidence that a single friar would conduct services at more than one place on the same day, but it is not clear just how this was managed or to what extent.

The Latin-American ratio of pastor to flock must have been the lowest in the Catholic world. Pairs of brothers had to indoctrinate, catechize, and teach thousands of Indians in their dozens of difficult tongues, and then baptize them, celebrate Mass for them every Sunday and feast day, marry them, periodically confess them, and sometimes bury them. During the first decades most of this was carried on in the atrios, for the crowds who came to be baptized, married, or just to attend Mass, were far too big for the churches.

The brothers could not have carried out such a program if they had been restricted to congregations small enough to be crammed into even a large church. Many churches held no more than two or three hundred, and few could hold two thousand. Furthermore, the building of a large church might be costly in money and in time, whereas the atrio could be made much more cheaply and quickly, and could easily be as capacious as needed for the biggest congregation which could be gathered to see and hear one priest celebrating Mass.

The natives had not been converted gradually — conveniently one by one — but torrentially, tidally, in inordinate hordes. A church building that had been big enough *last* month might not be big enough *next* month to hold the extra thousands someone might be baptizing *this* month. A big atrio could accommodate thousands or tens of thousands, and a few thousand fresh converts brought in by some fortunate friar after a particularly fruitful excursion would present no problem at all, and the same limited number of friars could serve them.

*

Having seen Masses held there, sixteenth-century chroniclers sometimes referred to the atrio as an *iglesia*. In addition, it was the principal and particular place of assembly for the religious life of the Indians living in and near the monastery towns. It was the Sunday School and weekday classroom, the theater for religious plays, and sometimes the cemetery (in which case part of it was surely consecrated ground). It became also a sort of community center, where the natives came to feel so much at home that they began to use it for some of their favorite fiestas which were not Christian at all, provided they were not close enough to the old religion to be judged unsafe by the friars. The Indians made themselves so very much at home that orders had to be issued (1555) to stop them from sleeping in the atrios. They had to be forbidden to play cards, or ball, or other games they had learned from the Spaniards — even bull-baiting (1585).[6]

The atrio was the Indians' own church, recognized as theirs and theirs alone. In the beginning, natives had been put out of the first small Cathedral to make room for Spaniards, and this was symptomatic of their position then and in the future. During the first century of their conversion they were not accepted as equal or regular members of the same congregations as the Europeans, and were kept in separate religious as well as separate social groups. They themselves felt that they were a separate religious group. For example, when the Bishop thought of making two parish churches in the capital interracial (so that the Indians might keep them in repair at their own expense, redecorate them, and serve and maintain the curates), the Indians chose instead to go to their own outdoor church in the atrio of San Francisco (1568). When the parish church of San Pablo was transferred to the Augustinians the Bishop objected not only because the Augustinians already had one monastery in the capital but also, since the Spaniards might boycott an interracial church, because the transfer might take a church from the local Spaniards and give it to the Indians (1576).[7] If Spaniards did use the same church building as Indians — as they often must have at monasteries in the country — and if there were enough friars to divide, the Indians were not usually served at the same Masses or by the same friars. The early chroniclers repeatedly differentiated between "preacher to Spaniards" and "preacher to Indians" or "confessor to Spaniards" and "confessor to Indians," as separate activities performed by different individuals.

The ordinary Indians were not asked to try to become Spaniards — no one, Indian or Spaniard, would have wanted that — and for several generations, except for the native aristocracy, domestics, and laborers in the big cities, they were not encouraged to learn Spanish. They had been cut off from their old religious ideas, but in their villages, where Europeans were not supposed to live or even spend the night, they were still allowed many of the forms of their old society. Along with this sense of social entity they seem to have had some sense of a religion that was meant for them, even though it was not their old religion, because they had been formed into their own congregations which had their own services, conducted by their own friars, with sermons in their own languages, celebrated in their own atrios. In other words they had their own church, their outdoor church. (One suspects that they sometimes had such a curious understanding of Christianity that they also had what amounted to their own religion in their own church.)

They had their own religious brotherhoods, which cared for the atrios and took charge of the big fiestas there; each confraternity had its particular fiesta on a particular day when all other activities were suspended.

When they did attend unsegregated churches, the Spaniards sometimes sat apart in the chancel, screened from the natives in the nave by a wooden grille. No matter what the arrangements, the Spaniards somehow showed their conviction of racial superiority, and the Indians were consequently made to feel a separate and inferior group. Only toward the end of the century were they generally allowed to attend the same Masses as the Spaniards. As a result, some of the activities in the atrios must then have been reduced but, as there were still enough secondary activities held there to justify them, atrios were still regularly laid out at all churches save a few on cramped city lots.

It is curious how few concrete facts are recorded as to when the Indians used the regular covered churches, or when they stopped having their ordinary Masses in their atrios. In some few cases, they were served in the monastery churches from the beginning, but presumably this was rare. Since Father Mendieta, who referred to Indian Masses both indoors and outdoors, was first in Mexico from 1554 to '71, and then again writing his *Historia ecclesiastica indiana* from 1574 to '96, perhaps most of his references to Masses in atrios were written from his experience during those first 17 years, and the references to Indians at Masses in churches from experience during his second stay. Father Juan Focher wrote a long *Itinerario* for the actively evangelizing Franciscans in 1570, describing and explaining local religious practices and problems, which was edited by Fray Diego de Valadés and published in Seville in 1574: atrio Masses were never mentioned, and it is difficult to venture why. They must still have been usual in many places. It is probable that the shift did not come everywhere at the same time or in the same way, but that most of it took place after the great plague of 1576, during the '80's and '90's. This assumption is based necessarily on inference, for the evidence is sparse.

*

Father Mendieta wrote of another use of the atrio: "After Matins, at two or three o'clock in the morning, the friars go through the barrios, one calling loudly to the people to gather in the designated places, where he will be able to find out whether they are all present. Assembled by four o'clock at the latest, they start out for the church, all in order as though in a procession, the men in one row and the women in another. They are guided by an Indian who goes in front with the standard of each barrio, made of red silk with the insignia of whatever Saint the barrio has taken for patron . . . When they come to the patios they pray to the Most Holy Sacrament, kneeling in front of the church door . . . They seat themselves in rows, the men squatting on their

209

heels in their customary way (on the Evangel side) and the women apart by themselves (on the Epistle side). Then they are counted by means of special tallies, and whoever is absent is listed for special penance, which is half a dozen lashes on the back." [8]

Separation of the sexes in church goes back to early Roman and Eastern rituals which because they included the Kiss of Peace between members of the congregation — Saint Paul had said *Salutate invicem in osculo sancto* — customarily separated the men and women. The Gallican Rite, preserving both early Roman and Eastern forms, had been used in Spain by the Visigoths, and many of its practices persisted here and there through the fourteenth and fifteenth centuries as the Mozarabic Rite, which still included the congregational Kiss of Peace. (Mozarabic here is a misnomer since this rite had nothing to do with the Mozarabic Christians.) Suppressed in 1500, except at Toledo and for occasional special Masses elsewhere, the Mozarabic Rite was preserved, nevertheless, in a miscellaneous residuum of old usages which were eliminated only after the Standard Revised Missal was introduced in Spain in 1570. (The Missal reached Mexico within three years.) [9] Earlier, because of Spain's peculiar heritage and independence from Rome, Mexico too may have preserved some of Spain's antiquated variations. Separation of the sexes, already obsolete or obsolescent elsewhere in the Catholic world, may have been, then, a persistence from the earliest church practices; or it may, instead, have been a Franciscan tradition, for the men and women of the crowds who came to hear the Franciscan outdoor preachers in public places in Italy had been divided by a cord; on the other hand, separation in Mexico need not claim any of these impressive ancestries, for it may have been merely a precaution or a convenience in taking attendance. One still sees it in country churches and in Indian-frequented pilgrimage shrines, where families divide at the door, the men going together to the left and the women to the right. In Morelos there are sometimes imperative little signs to remind them. (Perhaps a parallel persistence of pre-Tridentine usage accounts for the segregation of men and women in some village churches in the Pyrenees and in once-Spanish Sicily and Apulia and even in non-Spanish Catholic Dalmatia.)

*

Men and women often prayed with their arms outstretched to form a cross or *psi,* the attitude of an Early Christian *orans;* today one quite often sees this in Mexican pilgrimage or village churches, and sometimes still in Spain, though rarely in other countries. It was common in Europe during the Middle Ages. Fray Martín de Valencia, Observant leader of the Twelve, taught it to the Indians at the beginning of the Conversion, and they would keep their arms extended through seven Pater Nosters and seven Ave Marias.[10]

INSTRUCTION

> *Every day at sunrise, in the patios of the churches, they gather to-gether the children of the common people . . . and after Mass (which on weekdays is always said early because the friars have so much to do) they divide them and have them sit in various groups, according to what they have to learn. To some, who are just begin-ning, they teach the* Per Signum; *to others, the* Pater Noster; *and to others, the Commandments . . . and they are examined in or-der to be advanced from grade to grade. When they know the entire Catechism, and give a good account of themselves in it, they are dismissed and sent home. (1569)* [11]

A cardinal activity which affected the architecture of conversion was the readying of the natives for acceptance into the community of the Church. This took place entirely in the atrio, and was one of the main reasons for its existence. Here the converts were taught the rudiments of Christian Doctrine while they were still catechumens (those who, having asked for acceptance by the Church, were being prepared for Baptism). Inasmuch as their teach-ing was continued and intensified after they had been baptized, they were permanent catechumens *de facto* even after they became full church mem-bers *de jure*. Although oral lessons preceding what is now called the Mass had been an integral part of the liturgy of the Early Christians, such lessons had already been detached from normal Masses in the Roman Rite. The same oral instruction of unbaptized children and adults was what came to be known in the sixteenth century as Catechism. In Mexico these lessons atavistically reattached themselves to the Sunday Masses for Indians, usually at the be-ginning but sometimes at the end. Very large groups might be involved — even an entire town. At Zapotlán in Jalisco (now Ciudad Guzmán), "in order to teach the Doctrine to the Indians in their large patio more effectively, Fray Juan de Padilla built six high steps like benches all around it, so that everyone could find a place and hear comfortably all that was taught and preached." The Augustinians at Cuitzeo and Tiripetío arranged three tiers of steps for their children to sit on during lessons, under trees specially planted to shade them. A cross with similar steps is shown at Tacuba on the "Santa Cruz" plan of the Valley of Mexico, in front of the church of the Sanctorum (then known as Santa María de la Victoria).[12]

During the most active phase of the Conversion, basic Christian elements, such as the Creed, the idea of Salvation, and simple Christian ethics were particularly stressed in these outdoor lessons. Only later when the urgency of converting was over and the new spiritual climate had been chilled by the

90 THE SEVEN DEADLY SINS *made systematically easy for Indians to memo-*
rize by counting them off on the two joints of the thumb and five tips of the
fingers.

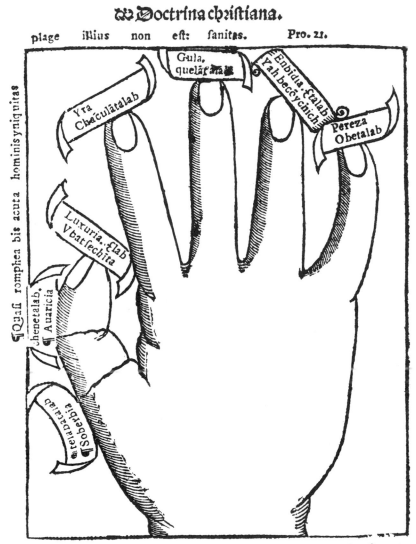

₡Doctrina chꝛiſtiana.

plage   illius   non   eſt: ſanitas.   Pro. 21.

¶No te oluides de pelear contra los ſiete pecados mortales que ſon ſierpes
matadoras que enponzoñan las almas y las lleuan al infierno que el angel
de Dios: tu guardador te ayuda y ſi tu quieres no te venceran ten quenta ꝺ
tu mano te los eſcriuo como veras en eſta mano.

91 THE FOURTEEN ARTICLES OF THE FAITH *to be counted off on the fourteen joints of all five fingers.*

(*both from* Doctrina Christiana en la Lengua Guasteca, *1571*)

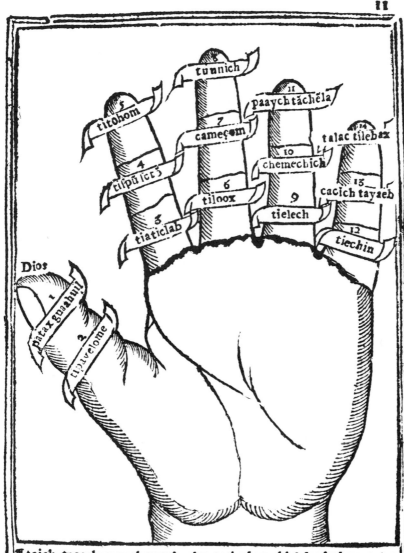

Inquisition and the Council of Trent, was more emphasis put on the punctilios of formal theology, hierarchies, rituals, repetition of prayers, and so forth. Consequently, the early sixteenth century seems closer to the Early Church Fathers and Erasmus, and late sixteenth century to the Counter Reformation. The Franciscans of the Province of Nueva Galicia were about half way between when they taught their Indians (1569) "the Catechism in Latin *and* in the Mexican language, the Pater Noster, Ave Maria, Salve Regina, Credo, the Articles of Faith, Commandments of God, and the Commandments and Sacraments of the Church, and the Mortal Sins and Works of Mercy, and the Theological and Cardinal Virtues — half one day and half the next" — which they learned to recite "better than many Spaniards." The Franciscans of the Province of Mexico taught them also the Seven Deadly Sins and Seven complementary Virtues, the Seven Gifts of the Holy Spirit, the Seven Beatitudes, and other memorizable sets of sevens. The Augustinians added the fourteen Works of Mercy, seven corporal and seven spiritual. [13]

On weekdays the teaching in the atrio was different. "Every day . . . children (who are the cleverer ones, chosen also for their treble voices) go to school in the patio of the church to learn to read and write so that they may serve the town or the church as scribes or singers." [14] The children of the most important Indians were taught indoors, and were full-time boarders; the poor children were instructed in the patios, mainly in crafts and husbandry, and were day pupils, with school only during the mornings, leaving afternoons free so they could help their parents. In much the same way, before the Conquest, boys had been sent to different schools according to their rank; the young élite had been taught to recite historical and religious epics by heart, and for this they had been taken from their families for years, and kept in strict boarding schools under the direction of specially chosen old men. The friars appear to have taken over much of this traditional system with a major change only in the subjects taught. Weekday classes were not for boys only. Father Mendieta wrote: "While Guardian of a monastery in some country town, I have had more than three hundred marriageable maidens gathered in the patio, having some teach others. In this way many of them are kept busy in the patio, teaching, until they are married, or just before." [15]

One of Cardinal Cisneros' reforms of the Spanish Church had come from his insistence on an important and forceful sermon or explanation of the Gospel at every celebration of the Mass, and his ideals were still effective among the Mendicants in New Spain. Preaching was given particular importance, and the lessons in the atrio were often preceded or followed by a sermon. Since the sermons were preached in the local language, they were often the most accessible part of the service for the Indians, but the most dif-

ficult part for the friars, who could not often count on ready-made translations to help them, as they could for the Catechism. If a friar had not yet
mastered the particular local language, he might "preach" with one of those
sets of pictures (ill. 12), or he might have the sermon acted out. The chronicler Vetancurt described how the Passion was preached with the aid of *exem-
plos historiales:* when Longinus pierced Christ's side with his lance, a
sack of colored water hidden in the image seemed to make it bleed; for the
Ascension the image was pulled by ropes into a heaven of artificial clouds.
Others favored a kind of play called a *neixcuitilli* in which the entire sermon
was acted in a pantomime synchronized with the text, perhaps because they
were familiar with Franciscan precedents for this in Europe. Other vivid and
ingenious didactic devices were tried without the sanction of European antecedents.[16]

Sometimes a special pulpit was raised above the heads of the crowd in
the atrio so that the preacher could make himself effectively seen and heard
by a congregation of thousands. Temporary or portable pulpits had sometimes been used for the outdoor preaching of the Mendicants in Europe, particularly the Franciscans, who used and developed the form more than any
other group. In Spain there was a particularly rich tradition of pulpits, perhaps because of the prominent Moslem *mimbars,* high canopied affairs approached by steps, which were standard equipment for mosques. It is not certain what the preaching arrangements were in the ordinary atrios of New
Spain, for the only concrete evidence preserved is slight: the elevated outdoor stone pulpits in a very few atrios (Cuernavaca, Tlalmanalco, Tochimilco, and Atotonilco de Tula).

BAPTISM

> *All the neighboring towns were called to the town where the solemn
> Baptism was to be; they trimmed the churches, patios, streets, and
> houses with so many boughs that there was not a green branch left
> in the woods, nor a single pretty flower in the fields . . . All the
> adults who were to be baptized formed a procession . . . holding
> little chains and big garlands of flowers . . . dressed in their fin-
> est white cotton which, while not rich, is still very sightly.*
>
> — Father Grijalva (c1620) [17]

Baptism was another of the important activities in the atrio. Because of
the procedural problems which resulted from so many natives to be baptized
and so few friars to do it, the rites, though of the greatest symbolic significance in a campaign of conversion, had had to be curtailed. Without the
functionally efficient atrio, even the condensed baptisms could not have been

administered, and many Indians would have had to go unbaptized. How, for instance, could a single friar baptize 3,000 or 4,000 with water, oil, and chrism in one day if he had to work in cramped quarters inside a church?

In the earliest days all baptisms were outdoors in the atrio, and the friars would tell their catechumens how Saint John had performed the first baptisms outdoors also. Many adults would be baptized at once, and there would be a big celebration. "In all the monasteries we have a baptismal font . . . sometimes outside the church . . . which is a good place, because then at any time the blessing can be done with solemn impressiveness, and without disturbing those who are saying Mass or celebrating divine offices inside the church" (1544).[18] By the end of the century, when the peak of the load had been passed, baptisms took place more often within the churches, where the big stone font was usually installed just inside the front door. Individuals or small groups, but no large crowds, were baptized together, and their average age grew lower and lower. It must have been more like Europe.

PROCESSIONS AND PLAYS

Accustomed to it in their old religion, the Indians were greatly attracted by pomp, and of all the peoples of Europe the Spaniards were by temperament and experience the most fitted to supply it. On feast days, wonderful processions would wind through the monastery towns and reach their climax in the atrio, where their arrival would have been heralded by men on the top of the church blowing trumpets and waving long banners between the battlements. The Indians would have brightened the atrio with fanciful constructions of flowers and feathers, and the many marchers — almost everyone marched — would carry more. Doctor Zorita thought that there were more Indians in the processions on Holy Thursday and Easter morning in Mexico City than in the combined congregations marching in any four cities in Spain, while others believed the number of floats, crosses, and candles greater than that of any other city in Christendom. In the patio of San Francisco, 20,000 Indians would parade, carrying crucifixes, banners, and floral ornaments. Despite the Spaniards' pride in their processions, the Indians outdid them.[19]

The processions not only marched into and around the atrio, they often developed into dances there. Though at first expressly forbidden to use the atrios for their old *mitotes* — the Church feared that the excitement might lead to drink, apostasy, killing, and even animal or human sacrifices — the Indians did not really have to stop: they soon transformed and Christianized them, changing the patron from Huitzilopochtli to the Virgin or some suitable Saint. Thus denatured, or successfully disguised, the dances seemed to be acceptable as harmless concomitants of Christian ritual. The natives might not wear their old costumes or secret emblems, sing their old songs, or dance at night or in the church itself; but they were allowed to dance in the patio after Christian feasts if the proposed performance had first been approved by one of the friars. When Father Burgoa admired five hundred youths prancing in green plumes in the atrio of Yanhuitlán, he was admiring a denatured pagan intermezzo in a Christian celebration. (We can sometimes see a dozen old men shuffle around there now.) If the friars did not connect them with the old religious rites, old routines as recognizable as the spectacular *volador* spiral flying dance (ill. 4) could reappear in atrios in Veracruz and Hidalgo (still to be seen on Corpus Christi). The Indians were allowed to use their old instruments, such as the *teponaxtle* and the *huéhuetl* (drums). The depaganized extravaganzas could be so notable that Viceroy Velasco thought it suitable to send a troupe of native *danzantes* to Charles V, who spent an interesting afternoon watching them from a balcony in Valladolid. Still, there persistently remained doubt as to how disinfected of paganism the dances were, and new orders against *mitotes* were issued in 1585. These were accepted more as a warning than a ban, however, and dances remained — and remain today — a lively feature of the Indians' religious life.[20]

There was a great deal of singing, most commonly of *alabados,* hymns in praise of the Sacrament and the Immaculate Conception popularized by the Franciscans, or devotional *romances, Pasiones,* or *Calvarios,* taught by the Augustinians. Some performances were elaborately staged. Father Motolinía wrote: "A group of singers marched in the procession, like a choir with the organ playing, their singing in harmony with the musical instruments — flutes, trumpets, drums, large and small bells. Entering and leaving the church, the choir and band performed together, and it was as if the music came from heaven." Father Ponce wrote that the Indians of Acámbaro had "many dances. Especially notable was one of the blacksmiths; they brought some big bellows to the patio of the monastery where they had set up an ornamental forge, and there they were hammering and working iron to the sound of a little drum. The masons likewise were dancing and working stone to the sound of another drum." Before the Conquest there had been special dances representing different trades, and the friars must have considered them a harmless enough entertainment to accept into the atrio.[21]

Sometimes there were religious dramas in the atrio, called *autos sacramentales.* The Indians liked these particularly, and gave many performances which were all-Indian, in language, actors, and audience. More like morality plays of the late Middle Ages than Spanish dramas of the *Siglo de Oro,* some were adapted from century-old successes still current in provincial Spain, while others were invented locally to meet local needs. Both gained vitality from the gusto and color contributed by the Indian performers. Although they had not evolved any complete dramatic forms before the Conquest, the Indians had been constant spectators or participants in semi-theatrical rituals.

2 1 7

THE ATRIO

The Christian plays were so much enjoyed by the Indians, and found not only instructive but so very interesting in themselves, that some clerics feared it impossible to keep the performances within the proper bounds of religious edification, and tried to have them prohibited — but without success. The later strictures of the Council of Trent did not hamper them at all, and the Franciscans continued to promote them as effective teaching devices particularly useful since books were so often lacking. Special plays during Lent were said to move their native audiences so much that they quickly repented their sins and doubled their devotions.

Descendants of such plays are still sometimes seen in village atrios, though the forms are diluted or degenerated, and the mediaeval "mansions" no longer used for scenery. Fortunately, eyewitnesses have left accounts of a number of noteworthy sixteenth-century performances.

More than anywhere else in Europe, Corpus Christi had been celebrated with particular pomp in Spain: as an assertion of Christian Faith in the face of heathen Moslems. Perhaps its early importance in Mexico came from equivalent conditions in regard to the heathen Indians. Toward the end of the century it was given new prominence by the Council of Trent as an assertion of Catholic Faith in the face of heretic Protestants.

Epiphany, too, was thought particularly appropriate for Christian-Indian festivals because it was then that the first Gentiles were converted (and because one of the Kings was not white?). A Twelfth-Night play in Jalisco so impressed Father Ponce that he devoted several pages to it: "For a long time the Indians of Tlajomulco have had the custom every year of acting out the Epiphany just as our Holy Mother Church teaches us it happened . . . From the top of a hill near the town the Magi came down on horseback, very slowly, not only so that they would be dignified but also because the hill was high and the road rough; it took them nearly two hours to reach the patio . . . Meanwhile a band of angels came out and danced before the gate, singing verses in Náhuatl and making many reverences and genuflections to the Child. Then came a band of shepherds . . . While they were all together in the middle of the patio, an angel came out of a little wooden tower and sang *Gloria in Excelsis Deo,* at the sound of which the shepherds fell to the ground as though struck senseless. But the angel comforted them in their language and told them the news of the birth of the Child, and so they got up and ran to the gate with great rejoicing . . . and offered the Child what they had: one a kid, another a lamb, another some bread, another a mantle, and others, other things. All this they did with such reverence that they inspired great piety among the spectators . . . The Kings came to the gate of the patio, guided by a star the Indians had made of tinsel; it ran on two cords from the top of the hill to the tower of the church. At intervals, tall wooden towers had been built, from which they pushed the star along on the cords . . . When the Kings left Herod's presence, the star came out of the tower and moved on to the church, where the gate of Bethlehem was. There they prostrated themselves before the Child and offered him their gifts, which were several silver vases, and each one knelt down and said a short prayer in Náhuatl." [22]

Father Motolinía gave a long description of a play done in Tlaxcala (which he may have composed himself, 1539): "They had a place prepared for a mystery play, representing the Fall of our First Parents. In the opinion of those who saw it, it was one of the most notable things yet achieved in New Spain. The abode of Adam and Eve was ornamented to look as much as possible like the earthly paradise. There were various fruit trees with flowers made of feathers and gold . . . On a single tree I counted forty parrots, large and small. There were also beautiful birds made of gold and feathers . . . and also two ocelots, tied up because they were so fierce . . . Once during the play Eve was careless and went near one of them and, as if trained, the beast went away. This was before the sin; had it happened after the sin, she might not have been so lucky . . . There were other feigned animals with boys inside . . . The tree of life was in the center of paradise, and near it stood the tree of knowledge of good and evil, with many beautiful fruits contrived of gold and feathers . . .

"As soon as the procession arrived, the stage play began. It lasted a long time because, before Eve ate and Adam consented, Eve went from the serpent to her husband three or four times . . . then taking him on her lap, she pleaded with him so that at last he went with her to the forbidden tree. Here in the presence of Adam, she ate of its fruit and gave him to eat. While eating, they at once knew the evil they had done. Although they hid themselves as well as they could, they were not able to keep God from seeing them. God entered in great majesty, accompanied by many angels. . . . Then angels brought two garments . . . and clothed Adam and Eve. What made the greatest impression was to see the two depart, banished and in tears . . . This play was presented by the Indians in their own language. Many of them were deeply moved and shed tears, especially when Adam was banished from paradise and put in the world." [23]

THE FORM OF THE ATRIO

SHAPE AND SIZE

Normally the atrio was a simple rectangle spread out more or less symmetrically in front of the church (as early as 1540 at Santiago Tlatelolco in the capital, or at Ocuituco or Epazoyucan). Occasionally it was L-shaped, with one arm in front of the church and the other along its side (probably before 1540 at Cuernavaca or Xochimilco). The side arm would be used to provide space in front of a chapel set next to the church, or else to give access to one of those important north doors (as at San Francisco in Mexico City or at Yecapixtla, both probably before 1540). A few other early atrios show variations, perhaps experimental, with main areas off center or on different levels.

Atrios vary in size but are almost always large and not far from square, with the average something like 250 feet on a side — as big as twenty tennis courts. Even remote houses had this scale (Hocabá in Yucatan, 200 by 240, and Tlanchinol in the sierras of Hidalgo, 200 by 300). Those of 100 feet (Chimalhuacán Atenco) or 150 (Mitla) or even 200 (Copándaro) seem small, while those about 315 feet square (Epazoyucan, Santiago Tlatelolco) or 270 by 370 (Atlatláuhcan) seem ample but not exceptional. An atrio 150 by 300 fronted by a plaza 300 by 350 does not seem extravagant (Tacámbaro). A few atrios are truly enormous: that at Totimehuacán stretches to over 500 feet on a side; that at Tzintzuntzan, 600 feet; the monastery at Jalapa was on a plot 550 by 850 feet of which more than half must have been atrio; Toluca had 850 by 600; Actopan stood on a plot 950 by 600. It was claimed that some of these could take crowds of 40,000 or 50,000.[24]

92 (left)
THE FRANCISCAN ESTAB–LISHMENT AT CHOLULA *looking northward across the paved atrio*

(right) 93
THE FRANCISCAN ESTAB–LISHMENT AT XOCHIMILCO *monastery, atrio, and plaza*

The monastery at Xochimilco still has a handsome example: about 380 feet deep and 520 wide, and originally augmented by a 200-foot-square arm north of the church. Now a cornfield, this last has unfortunately been walled off, and the south half of the atrio has been invaded (1941) by a big school building. By the end of the seventeenth century, the atrio covered about 240,000 square feet — equivalent to a hundred tennis courts — in addition to which the monastery had two gardens and two orchards. On axis, in front of the atrio, there was a still larger town plaza. Only a few cities in the world can boast such a large organized open space, and most of those were planned for capitals. Traditionally the first settlement on the lake, Xochimilco had not

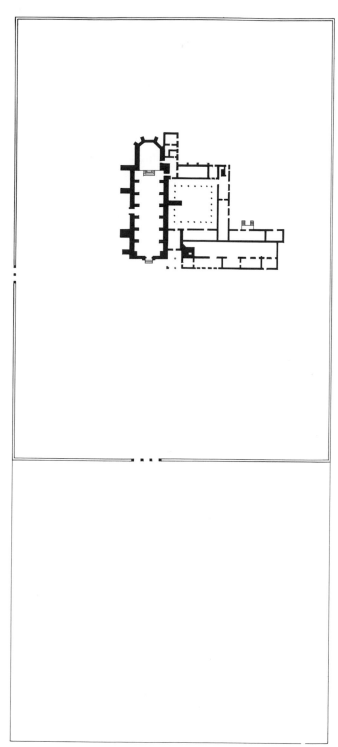

0'   50'   100'   150'

been a capital, but only an agricultural, mercantile, and minor religious center, with many smaller settlements clustered about it, famous for gardeners, reed-mat makers, and carpenters. Cortés had found it "a great city" and, unable to coax it to his side, had burned it, "truly a sorrowful sight to see." Only a dozen miles across the lake from the capital, it had been one of the first chosen to be converted and given a monastery (1525). A big conventual complex had been set in the ruins of the old town by 1535, presumably with an atrio, and a major building or rebuilding campaign was completed about 1551. Despite minor changes and another building campaign in 1583, the present ensemble may well be basically what was planned between 1525 and '51. By the end of the century the church was reputed to be the "largest in the Indies." The large population needed large spaces for its gatherings. We know that on Corpus Christi natives from all thirteen visitas would swarm into the plaza to watch agile young men dressed as lions and eagles dance to the *teponaxtle*. It was still considered an Indian city and famous for its carpenters in the middle of the eighteenth century, and today remains dominantly Indian. Since preconquest times it has been a garden city supplying the capital with flowers, fruit, and vegetables, though never from any "floating gardens" as we are repeatedly misinformed by guides and guidebooks.[25]

Obviously the atrio must have been considered an important component of the monastery scheme; otherwise it would not have been so prevalent, so big, or so prodigal of the time and labor demanded by so much leveling or terracing and the building of so many long stretches of wall. The size was not always equated with the size of the local population, for monasteries in small settlements were given some of the largest atrios (for example, at Tecámac in the State of Mexico). Perhaps the size depended more on the energy and ambition of the friars and the available amount of Indian labor and materials than it did on the size of the congregation that would use it. Sometimes it was determined by some open space surviving from a preconquest layout.

In a town where there was not a large native population, or in the native dormitory suburb of a predominantly Spanish city, the atrio could be smaller. Such may have been the case at Atlixco (less than 20,000 square feet — seven tennis courts), a new Spanish town drawing for its labor pool on a long-established native settlement (Acapetlahuaca). The Indian barrio was administered as a separate community by the friars of the small Franciscan monastery which stood at the edge of the Spanish town (where the Spaniards had their own parish church administered by a secular). Not very many Indians lived close by (500 in 1569) because half had fled to avoid maltreatment by the Spaniards. The monastery, then, had few Indians in its immediate flock — most were in visitas — and therefore no need for a big atrio. It was suggested in 1581 that the monastery could become a house for religious retreat because there were so few Indians to occupy the friars' time; by then there can have been little need for any atrio at all.[26]

The atrio of the Franciscans in Puebla was also small although, unlike Atlixco which is on a steep hillside, there was plenty of level space. As at Atlixco, there were few Indians (about 1000 around 1570). The atrios of the Franciscans and Augustinians in Valladolid (Morelia) were small since the city had been planned for Spaniards and long had had only a small Indian population. (Both atrios are now markets.) The Dominicans in the city of Oaxaca, building the most grandiose of all sixteenth-century monasteries, laid out an atrio which was surprisingly mean in comparison with everything else. There was no reason to make a large atrio, as the establishment was not intended to be a mission for Indians but a training-center for novices. Now fenced in iron, with Victorian cast-iron angels from Ohio, this atrio originally had a typical battlemented stone wall.[27]

LOCATION

The atrio was normally located just east of the town plaza, with which it made one big rectangular pool of space and greenery. All four sides of the plaza were bounded by streets, one of which separated it from the atrio; and the sides of the atrio were similarly bounded, except on the east, where the church and monastery building stood, flanked by walled gardens or fields. This pattern of a big, tree-planted, twofold space in the center of town was repeated all over the country, and persisted as the regular scheme for parish churches long after monastery-building had become less important. (Typical sixteenth-century examples of green atrio-and-plaza centers can be seen — to name a random few — at Acatzingo, Amecameca, Atlatláuhcan, Chimalhuacán Atenco, Metepec, Tecali, or Totimehuacán.)

Only exceptionally was the atrio not in front of the church and an axial complement of the plaza. (At Oaxtepec the Dominicans set their monastery 20 feet above the level of the much-admired preconquest town: the terrain was too steep, spongy, and full of mineral springs for a normal atrio in front; instead it was spread out comfortably to the north.) Monasteries inserted in old Indian towns which already had their plazas often had to accept adjustments in the ideal arrangement, and the old plaza, though still in front, might be off axis with the new monastery (as at Izúcar, where the Dominicans took over a busy trading city of 3000 houses [28]). It might be at one side (as at Ixmiquilpan where the Augustinians emplanted their new house in the old capital of the Otomíes, or at Totolapan where they interpolated themselves into a Tlahuica town, or at Copándaro into a Tarasco town; at Tlacolula and Coixtlahuaca the Dominicans fitted themselves into well-established Zapoteca towns). In the Mixteca region, the plaza was sometimes set directly behind the monastery (at Teposcolula, Yanhuitlán, or Tejupan). Sometimes, instead of making a new flat space for the atrio, the friars would take over an old space, in the same way they more often did for a plaza; we learn, for example, that when the Franciscan church at Tepeaca was consecrated (1535), the old "market which was held within its enclosure was suppressed."[29] Only rarely are the atrio and plaza not somehow contiguous (as at Cuernavaca, where the terrain and the old buildings of the preconquest town may have presented too many obstructions to the usual layout).

94 COATEPEC CHALCO *Stairway leading to the raised atrio*

Sometimes on sites of irregular profile, the ground for the atrio would have to be specially built up. At Huejutla and Metztitlán, both in the steep sierras of Hidalgo, earth was piled up at the bottom to make an atrio-terrace level with the top of the slope — level, that is, with the solid ground on which the church stood. The town plazas here are in front of the churches and atrios, as usual, but well below them. It was an audacious undertaking at Metztitlán to pile up over a million cubic feet of earth against the vertiginous cliffs of the Sierra Madre in order to gain a level space of 120,000 square feet for the atrio. At Molango, in what without exaggeration must be called one of the most beautiful sites in the world, the front of the atrio looms 50 feet above the village reared on thousands of tons of earth and stone, including the wreckage of the sanctuary of a local god named Mola, all laboriously carried there in order to make an atrio level with the spur of the sierra on which the church and monastery stand. An easy lower site (chosen in 1536 or '38) had been abandoned for this more difficult and dominating one (where work was begun probably in 1545). The atrio can afford to be modest in size, and it covers only 35,000 square feet.[30]

224

At Jalapa the Franciscans were faced with a similar problem, but in reverse: the atrio was level with the highway at its entrance, and extended out on a steep spur, half natural and half man-made; this built-up area (550 by 850 feet) carried church and monastery at the far end which, as at Delphi, looked melodramatically *down* several thousand feet onto the backs of the eagles flying over the forest below. The monastery and its vaulted and battlemented church (begun 1541, damaged by a quake in '46, finished in '55) stood fairly intact until 1886, when half slid down into the valley. The remainder was promptly pulled down. Nothing is left now but bits of walls and most of the built-up atrio, metamorphosed into the Parque Benito Juárez by flower beds garish with salvia, cannas, and scorched roses.[31]

The opposite situation was faced at various other establishments (Calpan, Tecamachalco, Tepoztlán, Tepeji del Río, Tepeyanco) where the buildings are at the lower end of sloping land and where to make a level forecourt many yards of earth had to be cut out of the hillside and carried away. One enters these atrios by walking *down* into them from the village. The plazas, though adjacent, are at a higher level, and cannot easily be associated with the atrios in a spatial sense, for the two spaces are not experienced simultaneously but sequentially.

Under other conditions (at Yanhuitlán or Coatepec Chalco) a platform would be built because the natural condition of the soil was inhospitable, and stable foundations had to be assured for the heavy buildings of church and monastery. This rational cause is surprisingly slight in proportion to the extravagant effect of the far-larger-than-needed platforms. Sometimes (again as at Yanhuitlán) special circumstances made it easier to build a big earth platform than not, because something had to be done with all the earth left over after shearing down the huge pyramids the friars wanted to subtract from the site.[32]

To achieve a fine spatial setting for their monasteries the friars might take as much advantage of their vast free labor supply as they did for any of their buildings. Big platforms were something the Indians had been making for their religious centers for centuries, and it must have been easier to keep them making big platforms than it would have been to get workmen to undertake similar enterprises in Europe. Gigantic piles of earth, 10 or 20 feet high, and 300, 400, or even 500 feet on a side were nothing uncommon (as one can still see at Huejotzingo, Oaxtepec, Otumba, Tlayacapan, Tula, or Tultitlán). It seems to have been felt that the church was "honored" properly if it was set above the rest of the town, and if it was set back in a courtyard. Even the modest houses in Franciscan Yucatan might, therefore, painstakingly be raised a yard or two above the rest of the town (Hocabá). Impressive arrangements of this kind were particularly fancied by the Dominicans (with notable results at Izúcar, Yanhuitlán, or Coixtlahuaca).[33]

THE ATRIO

Nowhere else in the Christian world was such attention regularly accorded the settings of religious buildings. This was not vainglorious extravagance to obtain something uselessly handsome. Although the effect of the atrio reared above the roofs of the town is so grand at Metztitlán or Molango that one must wonder whether the friars may not have been stimulated largely by aesthetic bravura, it must be remembered that the atrio was not just a pretty park, but that it had a religious function as important as that of any of the buildings of the friars, as important as that of the monastery church. Extravagant effects might be legitimatized by the same reasoning by which the friars wished to justify their occasional extravagances in churches: architectural beauty or impressiveness might facilitate or reinforce conversion, not only by its own power but also by matching the impressiveness of pagan predecessors. Such impressiveness demanded only two expenditures — imagination and time — since labor and materials were free.

WALLS AND GATEWAYS

The church and monastery building stood at the east side of their atrio, often flanked right and left by parts of their gardens, fields, or orchards. In front of these and all along the three other sides the atrio was bounded by masonry walls. Although said to be needed to keep animals out, the height of these walls and their finish show that something more than practical needs stimulated their growth. They bespeak another huge investment of labor, materials, and time, which was made for the same reasons, presumably, as other big expenditures on the atrio.

The combination of grand scale and elementary form often makes the walls one of the most notable architectural features of the townscape. At Xochimilco, for example, there were some 1500 feet of stone-capped rubble wall, 12 feet high. Occasionally they might become even more impressive than the church or monastery building, as at Tultitlán (in construction

1570, wall inscribed with date 1571, complete by 1580).[34] Such walls can achieve a sort of Egyptian monumentality, uncompromisingly simple and aggressively massive. From the inside their uninterrupted sweep bounds the plain rectangle of the atrio space with such clear finality that it too becomes an architectural entity, as essential to the ensemble as the solids of the

95 TULTITLÁN
Masonry wall bounding south side of atrio

church or monastery blocks. The decorative battlements which so often enliven the top of the walls also emphasize the scale of the atrio, for our eye skips from merlon to merlon, measuring out the total length by adding up the interstices, much as our glance apprehends more energetically a vista which is measured off by a row of telephone poles or pickets than it does an unmetered space in the middle of a meadow.

Occasionally a short length of wall might be built up higher than the rest, and pierced with a few small arches in which bells could be hung, thus forming an *espadaña* or arcaded belfry such as were often found in Spanish rural churches, and in the gables of Augustinian churches in Mexico. (Atrio walls with *espadañas* survive at Tlanchinol, Tepeyanco, Tumbalá in Chiapas [35] and, until recently, also at Molango). ⚜

96 MOLANGO
the espadaña *on the atrio wall (recently destroyed after damage by earthquake)*

The Augustinians were planning something special for the atrio wall of their house in the capital according to Doctor Cervantes de Salazar (1554): "The great space that you see in front of the church is to be an open square, to which an ascent consisting of several steps will be made. From the square to the entrance of the church there will be a level space of equal extent, framed on all sides by marble columns, separated from one another by an appropriate distance. On top of the columns will be placed stone lions, joined by a large iron chain, to serve — as it were — as guardians." [36] This, if it was ever built, must have been an exception, and its space more like a garth beside a Spanish cathedral than an atrio of a Mexican monastery.

*

Opposite the church a gateway pierced the atrio wall, often at the top of wide steps which led up a few feet from the town plaza. Such steps could add greatly to the monumentality of the simple ensemble as, for example, at Epazoyucan, where they surely were part of the early scheme.[37] Monumental stairs in context with a plaza and church were still rare in Europe; at Santiago de Compostela in Galicia or Trani in Apulia, though venerable, they were out of the ordinary.

227

97 ATRIO GATE AT HUEJOTZINGO

The atrio gateway was often a monumental frontispiece and a landmark
in the town. Even quite small establishments might be given big gateways (as
at San Andrés Chiautla, a visita, then vicaría of Texcoco, or at tiny San Bartolomé de los Tepetates near Tepeapulco, where the gateway is far more imposing than the church to which it leads). The Augustinians at Actopan put
up such an ample seven-arched propylaeum that it dominated everything
else in the broad town square, and fittingly announced the scale and grandeur
of the monastery behind.

The main atrio gate was usually composed of three round arches resting
on columns. Occasionally, instead of columns, slender square piers would
carry the arches (Tepeyanco, or Otumba), piers hardly greater in bulk than
the cylindrical shafts of the columns. Uniquely, the north gate at Tlaxcala
has fluted engaged columns resting on fluted consoles, carrying arches which
carry an attic with a secret passage inside, leading from the monastery to the
bell-tower. This odd arrangement may be descended from Spanish city gates.
It seems to be a patchwork made of elements of varying dates, not all of them
early. The simpler west gate at Tlaxcala also has fluted columns, arranged in

98 ATRIO GATE  AT ACATZINGO

99 ATRIO GATE AT COYOACÁN

a more normal immediate context, though the total context and many details at Tlaxcala are far from normal.

With few exceptions (Acatzingo and Tlayacapan) which have pointed arches, the design of atrio gateways was less mediaeval than renaissance, though perhaps more often not truly characterized as of any namable style. The typical European monastery gate, which might have been thought the likely model, had been something built to keep people out, and only very exceptionally was it a sort of welcoming triple triumphal arch (as it was at Cluny where it also led into a monastery forecourt capacious enough for thousands). The Mexican atrio gateways made a link between the protected religious precinct and the more open everyday world outside, between the well-bounded space of the atrio and the less enclosed space of the plaza. The walls and the archways of the atrio together manage to indicate a place which, while symbolically set apart from the nonreligious daily life of the people and physically set apart from the busy market place of the plaza, does not seem unapproachable. Even the gateways with heavy piers (Tepeaca and its echoes at Tecali and Totimehuacán) do not seem to shut the monastery in, cutting it off from the profane world outside but, like the others, seem to open out and to welcome people into the atrio. No gates were there to close the apertures.

Gateways with only two openings were not often chosen for the main access, perhaps because they could never seem either so monumental or so inviting with their single central support obstructing the symbolically significant axis of open space running from the plaza to the door of the church. Out of favor in the Renaissance, the occasional double gateways are probably

229

THE ATRIO

100 ATRIO GATE AT ZINACANTEPEC

a mediaeval survival, though contradictorily the handsomest Mexican examples (Cholula and Coyoacán) are carried out with renaissance detail. That at Coyoacán, now amputated from its walls and standing free in the pretty park which was once the atrio of the Dominican monastery, is carried out with a greater wealth of renaissance detail than any other Mexican atrio entrance. At Izúcar too, the main gateway is double, here not axially in front of the church, but set near one corner to give easier access to the plaza which is yet farther off axis presumably because fitted into the preconquest town. Malinalco, exceptionally, has a double gateway on axis with the church without any visible extenuating conditions.

For large establishments, gateways with a single opening were not common and usually there is some special limiting circumstance justifying the choice. At Zinapécuaro, for example, the main gate tops a long narrow stairway constricted on either side by the packed houses of the town. This had been a preconquest settlement, an outpost of the Tarascos against the Chichimecas, and as the Indians' houses may already have been just as densely crowded when the monastery was first set on the hilltop as they are now, it would have been no easier then than now to plow out a wide approach. Smaller monasteries (such as Xochítepec, near Cuernavaca) could suitably have a single-arched entrance, and might trim it with merlons, a pediment, or other such enrichment. Visitas, with smaller congregations than monasteries, and smaller atrio space, could be content with simple single gateways.

Often there were additional gateways on the sides of the atrio. These would not have to be set in the center — as there is no meaningful cross-axis to an atrio, there would be no reason — but were often put back con-

230

veniently near the church, particularly to be handy to its north doorway. Sometimes they would be in line with side streets leading to different wards of the town. The archways are most often single, though there was no objection to double ones for side entrances (as at Huejotzingo, Ozumba, Xochimilco, or Zinacantepec). They might even be triple, particularly if the terrain of the town made a side entrance the one most frequently used (Tepeyanco or Cuernavaca).

101
ATRIO GATE
AT
XOCHÍTEPEC

THE ANTECEDENTS OF THE ATRIO
CHRISTIAN

Broad open spaces were already spread at the front or side of many churches in Spain. Often they were very like those in Mexico (as at Carmona or at San Isidoro del Campo just outside Seville), but while these garth areas in Spain were by no means as consistent in their shape, location, or presence as the Mexican atrios, they may have suggested and strengthened the idea of the Mexican atrio by giving it the sanction of Spanish precedent. Nonetheless, the characteristic size and shape as well as the regular use of the atrio for important functions unknown in Spanish churchyards — whatever their form — make it necessary to search the genealogy of the atrio and to search outside Spain. (Although serious study of Mexican church and monastery buildings also demands scanning of their family trees, all their most important branches could almost surely be found in Spain, and the connections would be clear and probably without important surprises.)

2 3 1

THE ATRIO

The open forecourt used as an essential of a Christian ensemble recalls the atrium in front of the major Early Christian basilicas of Rome (and a few other Mediterranean cities) where it served as a receptacle for the pilgrims pouring in to the shrines of the Holy City during the first centuries of church-building. At certain times such an atrium might be filled with penitents or catechumens, who were to attend the first part of the service in the church but were dismissed — supposedly to the adjacent narthex — before the last half of the Mass was celebrated. The Indians, though like the catechumens in that they were a special group being indoctrinated, were not sent out of the church in this way for any doctrinal reason: they were kept out for a physical reason — available floor space — and kept out only on Sundays when there were too many of them to be contained inside. Indoors for Spaniards or outdoors for Indians, there was presumably no significant difference in the Masses except for the language of the sermon.

Despite the parallels — some apparently deliberate — between the way the first Christians in New Spain met some of their problems of conversion and the way the first Christians in Rome had met theirs, it is unlikely that the Early Christian atrium was the immediate model for the Mexican atrio: there are too many intrinsic differences. First, the Early Christian atriums were regularly enclosed by colonnades as one of their standard components, whereas the early Mexican atrios were never colonnaded. Second, in the center of the atrium stood a *labrum* or *cantharus,* a fountain for ritual ablutions, whereas in the center of the atrio there was a large cross. Third, the atrium was a forecourt used only for preliminaries to more important rites inside the church or for general gatherings without liturgical character, whereas the atrio was not only a court to be used with a church, but more importantly a court to be used *as* a church. Early Christian Masses, so far as anyone in Spain or Mexico knew, were said only in a church consecrated as the House of God, and therefore holy in itself. The atrium was not holy in itself, and neither was the atrio, though during Masses it was associated with a holy altar.

Furthermore, the Early Christian atrium was already obsolete, removed from the atrio-building Mendicants not only by considerable space but by considerable time as well. Its function had atrophied during the Dark Ages when there were fewer penitents and catechumens in Rome, when there were fewer people there altogether and more churches for them to go to. What atriums in Rome might have been seen by the few friars who were to go to Mexico early enough to contribute to the development of the atrio there (friars who had first been in Rome, such as Pedro de Gante and Martín de Valencia)? The biggest, oldest, and most prestigious, at Old Saint Peter's and Saint Paul's, were then used only to accommodate crowds of pilgrims and, far from having the character of a church, they were more like waiting rooms surrounded by stalls selling trinkets and food. The atriums of other important pilgrimage churches, San Sebastiano, San Lorenzo, Santa Croce in Gerusalemme, were much the same. Such smaller, later, and less important atriums still visible then, such as those of San Clemente, Santa Cecilia, or Sant'Agnese, had been built more from habit than from need, and may be dismissed because their resemblance, physical or functional, to early Mexican atrios in negligible. It is also unlikely that any more modern arcaded atriums (such as those at the Santissima Annunziata in Florence, or at Montecassino) could have left any effective imprint on the memories of Spanish friars later to go to America. Few Spanish Mendicants would have seen them, and even if some had, these atriums had no pertinent meanings or associations which would make them be remembered in connection with Mexican problems. Although by the middle of the century a score of friars had been to Rome on business or pious excursion, such trips were made after the atrio had appeared in New Spain in its typical form; hence it is irrelevant whether these friars happened to notice any atriums in Italy or not. No more do there seem to have been any Early Christian or later atriums in Spain where some early friar might have picked up the idea nearer home.

Even those friars who consciously identified themselves with their Early Christian forebears were not likely to have known about the conscious revival of Early Christian forms in renaissance Italy. (The humanist revival at the Papal Court counted Constantine's churches as works of classical antiquity, and was thus enabled to be antiquarian without being pagan.) One must remember that Rome was remote from Mexico not only in a physical sense: the church hierarchies were not at all close. In the early sixteenth century the Mendicant Orders were far less bound to Rome than they had been during the Middle Ages. Consequently, it seems far less probable that the friars in Mexico reproduced a form already obsolete in Rome than that they reinvented a similar form from a similar need.[38]

Occasionally religious chroniclers in Mexico would refer to groups of Indians as *catecúmenos,* perhaps revealing again their wish to emphasize the identity of their work with that of the Early Christian proselytizers. This conscious parallelism was only linguistic, however, based on literary associations deduced from early texts and not on visual knowledge of early buildings. Literate friars were familiar with what had happened, what was thought, and what was believed in Early Christian Rome — Torquemada cited over fifty Patristic authors — but they had faint idea what it looked like. When he compared it to a quite dissimilar arrangement at Tlaxcala, Father Mendieta did not visualize the "splendid double stairway" of the Roman Aracoeli very well: that was not a double but a single stairway with a ramp near it. This reference — inaccurate as it is — seems to be unique in sixteenth-century writing in Mexico.[39]

233

THE ATRIO

No more does the fact that the atrium and atrio are called by the same name indicate parental relation, for the sixteenth-century Mexican atrios were never called atrios by sixteenth-century writers, but *patios*. It is likely that to them *atrio* or *atrium* would still have the mediaeval Latin meaning: cemetery. The word *atrio* did not appear in the sixteenth-century friars' dictionaries of native tongues which, being written for other friars, listed useful current words referring to the church. Only in the next century were monastery *patios* first called *atrios,* by a more learned few who, now recognizing perhaps the resemblance to the atriums of Rome, wished to exhibit their fashionable knowledge of antiquity. Father Ojea, just back from Europe, used the novel word *atrio* once (1604), in describing the elegant and somewhat atypical establishment of the Dominicans in the capital. Learned Father Remesal (writing in 1613–19), also used the word only once, though he used *patio* many times. Father Grijalva (who completed his chronicle in 1623) always wrote *patio*.

It may be that the term *atrio* — if considered at all — had been avoided at first because in sixteenth-century Spain it could refer not only to a cemetery but also to a different auxiliary area: a smaller, paved, and raised garth, adjacent to a church, though often at one side. (In Rome, *atrio* was regularly used for church atriums, and also for other spaces: for example, the Cortile del Belvedere of the Vatican was known as the *Atrio del Piacere*.) Since in Spanish the word *patio* was also commonly and correctly used to denote several other kinds of enclosed but unroofed spaces not necessarily associated with a church, *atrio* came in time to be the special word to denote a large walled church forecourt. In Mexico, where a special word was needed, this came to be its normal meaning. By the eighteenth century it was a standard term (as used for example by Villaseñor y Sánchez, Juarros, or la Cruz y Moya). Smaller unwalled forecourts built not for Indians but for monumental effect were not called either *patios* or *atrios* but *plazas* (for example that of the Jesuits in Puebla, 1588).[40]

There seems to be no more connection with mediaeval atriums than with Early Christian. The church at Santiago de Compostela and several other major mediaeval pilgrimage centers such as Cluny or Tours had large open areas in front to contain the throngs of pilgrims who waited and even slept there between attendance at Masses and visits to the relics and images. Some of these churches may have been more familiar than Rome to the few friars in Mexico who had traveled outside Spain or to Santiago. Such open squares, however, were never functionally a part of the church as the Mexican atrios always were, and architecturally they had no standard shape. Only in Italy were they given monumental form, at Montecassino, for example, or Bari. (The bishop of Bari was Patriarch of the Indies from 1533–46, but the title was honorary and it is improbable that he could have affected building forms in Mexico where atrios already existed before he became Patriarch.) Such forecourts were — and the plaza at Santiago still is — primarily for the storage of surplus pilgrims at the time of peak load, a function unlike that of the outdoor churches of New Spain. Despite some apparent similarities, it is unlikely that these open areas can have been the immediate source of the Mexican atrio, although their impressive size and the overwhelming prestige of the churches they fronted may have haunted the memories of a few influential friars.

MOSLEM ANTECEDENTS

There is another possible European source: the patios of the mosques abandoned by the Moslems in their retreat through Spain. Some of these had become associated with churches when the victorious Christians took over mosques to use as handsome but ungainly houses of worship. When mosques were pulled down and replaced, the old patio might remain, adjoining the new church as it had adjoined its old mosque. So little is known about major mosques serving as churches in the early sixteenth century — only that at Córdoba survives in anything more than bits — that it is impossible to define any clear architectural relation with Mexico for them or for their patios. One exceptional connection did exist in one exceptional building in Mexico, San José de los Naturales, and this will be taken up in a later chapter.

The mosque patios were planted with rows of trees. In the sixteenth century the Patio de los Naranjos, beside the Cathedral which had replaced the mosque at Seville, was planted with palms, lemons, oranges, and cedars in straight rows; it also had a gate in the middle of each of its walls; this seems enough like a Mexican atrio perhaps to show that memories of mosque patios already conjoined to Spanish churches might have suggested the pleasant files of shade trees in some Mexican atrios. The Twelve had spent some months in Andalusia before sailing, and may have seen attractive ex-Moslem patios there. Two of the Twelve were natives of Andalusia: Fray Andrés de Córdoba and Fray Juan de Palos. On the other hand, it is possible that a friar, seeing the need for shade in an atrio newly laid out in New Spain, would decide to have trees planted, and naturally would have them set in straight rows. He would not need memories of Seville or Granada to make that decision. (All the formal similarities in past art are not causal. That the Indians in the atrios squatted on their heels in the same way as had the Moors establishes no connection. Why would a friar want to teach his Indians to squat like infidel Moslems? Both Indians and Moors had been so squatting for generations: it seems to be more comfortable for their slim legs than for ours with their heavier bones and calves.)

THE ATRIO

The mosque patios were bounded by arcaded walks like their forebears, the Early Christian atriums of the East, and their contemporaries and cousins, the cloisters. Arcaded walks were not built around the Mexican atrios in the sixteenth century. (The striking arcades at Izamal are an afterthought added for shelter from the fierce sun of Yucatan.) Though the relation of the Mexican atrio to the mosques of Spain is not clear, it probably was not strong enough to have had importance save in the exceptional case of San José de los Naturales.

*

Another type of Moslem building in Spain bore some resemblance to the atrio: the *muṣallàs* or *sărīa's* of Andalusia.[41] These were built on the edge of cities (Almería, Córdoba, Granada, Málaga, Tortosa, and Valencia) for the occasions when crowds prayed together — as when imploring for rain — groups so large that there was not room for them all in a mosque. The form was regularly a plain walled court, usually with a *mihrâb* or niche toward the east, as in a mosque, and sometimes with a *mimbar* or pulpit. The entrance was a monumental gate. Although the *muṣallàs* were the answer to a problem of what to do with too many faithful gathered at one devotion, and hence comparable to the similar answer to the similar problem in Mexico, there is little likelihood of a causal connection. There were not many *muṣallàs* in Spain and they were confined to a small region. Not many — if any — were standing in the sixteenth century in recognizable form. (A number still exist in North Africa.)

It is not so much their form as their use which seems close to the Mexican atrio; but by the time any friars later to go to Mexico could have seen any *muṣallàs* in Spain, their form had been destroyed or their use had been changed. Still, one must recall again that two of the Twelve were Andalusians, that all had spent some months in Andalusia, and that the second *Comisario General* of the Franciscan Order in New Spain (1533–41) was Fray Juan de Granada, who could have known not only the mosque but the *muṣallà* there. Some relation is possible, but not at all probable. (Fray Martín de Valencia, leader of the Twelve, need not have known the *musallà* at Valencia, newly named *La Exedrea,* because he was not a native of that Valencia but of Valencia de Don Juan, in León. One of the first missionaries sent out from México-Tenochtitlán to Michoacán was Fray ·Angel de Valencia, who did, however, come from the right Valencia.)

NATIVE ANTECEDENTS

To sum up: the essential of an atrio is that there be a religious celebration with a priest in a special chapel open toward a congregation in an unroofed court. The monastery atrio was made for Mass, and had no true equivalent in the functionings of the Early Christian atriums, mediaeval pilgrimage forecourts, or Moslem patios in Spain, for nothing of religious significance took place in these. No services were held in the open in Europe except for extraordinary occasions, such as when armies were about to go into battle, or gentry about to go on a hunt; there was no architectural form for such occasions.

In the search for models, why travel so far in space or time as to Rome, Santiago, or the mosques and *muṣallàs?* While trying to solve an awkward local problem, the friars may have found their answer in a local solution; right at hand they could all too often see crowds of Indians standing in walled enclosures, passively participating in a ritual performed by a priest in a special sanctuary facing the court, a sanctuary which served as an architectural setting to dignify and emphasize the ritual. All of the developed preconquest cultures had made positive use of large empty spaces at the dramatic center of their religious groups. Circumstantial evidence thus points to the teocalli court as the true parent of the atrio, and the resemblance seems far too close to be no more than coincidental.

The early chroniclers were well aware of such native arrangements; some of those who had seen the Indian ceremonials at first hand, when describing them showed almost as much admiration for the architectural arrangements as revulsion at the rites. Father Motolinía, who had arrived early enough to see many, wrote: "The kind of temples found in this land of Anáhuac or New Spain had never before been seen or heard of. In size, design, and every other feature, they are unique . . . The temples are called *teocallis* . . . [The Indians] leveled a large square patio in the best part of the town. In the larger towns the patio measured a crossbow-shot on a side, and in the smaller towns, less. The square was surrounded by a wall . . . The gates fronted the principal streets and roads, which all led to the patio. On the highest part of this patio was a large building whose base was square." He goes on to describe the low pyramid, with its altar and shrine on top, the teocalli proper. "The demon was not satisfied with the teocallis just described. In every town and district . . . they had other small patios with three or four teocallis . . . and along the road and in the cornfields there were many more . . . It seemed as if the land was filled with patios of the demon, and it was a very beautiful sight." [42] Bernal Díaz remembered the huge square before the great pyramid of Tlatelolco, "with two walls of masonry surrounding it, and the court itself all paved with very smooth great white flagstones. And where there were not these stones, it was stuccoed and burnished, and all very clean, so that one could not find any dust or a straw in the whole place." The patio of the chief pyramid of Tenochtitlán was similar, and paved with those "very large flagstones . . . so slippery that the horses fell." [43]

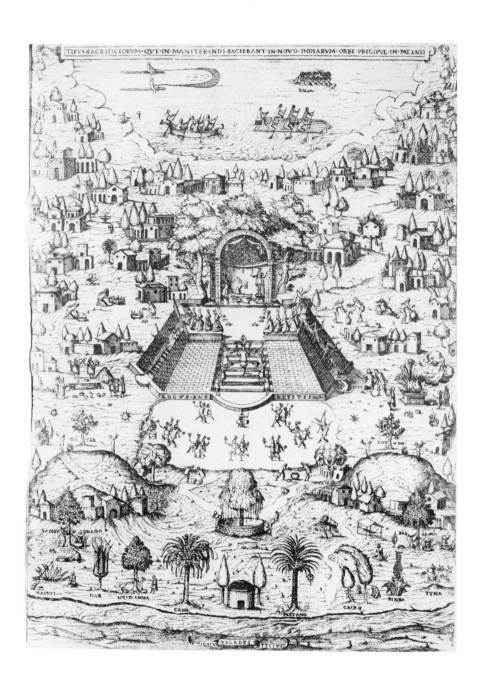

238

These patios contained not only the teocalli but sometimes other cult buildings and a dwelling-place for the priests not dissimilar in function to the frairs' monastery buildings (ill. 25). There was always a big clear area for ritual dances — some involved 10,000 celebrants — screened from the surrounding town by walls crested with something like battlements, and pierced by a gate on each side. Sometimes there were trees and gardens.

In explaining heathen shrines to Spanish readers, friars often used the terms they used for atrios. They said that the little shrines atop the pyramids were "just like chapels," and they called the courtyards "patios"; Indian writers in the sixteenth century called the chapels fronting Christian atrios by the old Aztec term "teocalli." The adoption of the pagan court must have taken place early, for in 1540 Father Motolinía said that the memory of them was already fading. When Father Valadés made an engraving of a teocalli which looked more like a Christian chapel than an Aztec shrine, it was because, born in 1533, he probably could not clearly remember how teocallis looked. (Furthermore, he made his engraving in Rome in 1579, after eight years in Europe. He wrote — one might say drew — in Latin.) Similarly, when Archbishop Dávila Padilla described teocalli courts in terms interchangeable with those for monastery atrios as late as the 1590's, it was because he was familiar with atrios from experience, and Aztec courts only from hearsay: "In front of these temples they made large patios which were always well swept, and in them they planted rows of trees which they call *ahuehuetl* [Náhuatl for 'old man,' a kind of giant cypress]; these are green all year, and give healthy shade, and for this they are much esteemed by the Indians." This sounds too much like Father Mendieta's description of a church atrio quoted at the beginning of this chapter not to have been borrowed from it (or from its source), and shows that while the atrio had originally been borrowed from the preconquest patio, within two generations it had so completely replaced its model that a description of an atrio would be borrowed to explain its own parent.[44]

*

102 A TEOCALLI *drawn in Rome in* 1579 *by Fray Diego de Valadés for this* engraving in his Rhetorica Christiana.

While the temple, the pyramid, and many of the other buildings are not Indian at all and resemble nothing yet seen in New Spain, the surrounding genre scenes are thoroughly Mexican.

In the lake at the top are native rafts, boats, and nets.

At the middle left, women grind corn on a metate *and roast tortillas on a* comal.

Across the bottom are native flora or acclimated exotics still unfamiliar to Europe: maguey, maize, sweet gum (liquidambar), *cassia, banana, chocolate* (cacao), *pineapple, and* nopal *cactus with its* tunas *(fruit).*

239

In the first year or two, before they could build anything of their own, the Twelve must have made use of Indian patios. Father Mendieta wrote that they began teaching men and women "in large patios which they had next to the houses where they were lodged." [45] Such patios can only have been old ones, more likely adjuncts of palaces than of teocallis. When first lodged in Texcoco, the Franciscans occupied part of the huge rambling palace of Prince Netzahualcóyotl or Prince Netzahualpilli, and naturally they would have used one of the many courtyards, particularly in those first years when it was thought imprudent to venture outside. If the old ones had served their new purpose well it would have been natural later on to make new courtyards like the old. From the first steps in catechistic instruction it would be natural in such patios to proceed to the celebration of Mass, once there were enough well-catechized Indians to form a congregation. Only the presence of an altar would make a courtyard, old or new, into any sort of "church" where Mass could be said.

In the beginning, the old courts must have made the handiest temporary churches, peculiar on many counts, but most peculiar to Europeans because they had no roof. The Indian congregations cannot have found this peculiar: they cannot have minded worshipping in the open air because they had never worshipped anywhere else. The friars must soon have realized that the benign Mexican climate — even more benign then, before deforestation and the draining of Lake Texcoco — called for no roof over a congregation. It must have seemed suitable, then, to accommodate them in roofless "churches" not only in the desperate beginning but for quite a few generations afterwards.

*

An important exception to the Spaniards' rejection of Indian forms is presumably to be found here in the teocalli court. Preconquest forms could be adopted with practicality and propriety — as nowhere else in the monastery complex — because, once these fairly neutral courtyards and platforms were cleansed of every sign of the cult that built them, then with little alteration they could quickly and cheaply be pressed into use as courtyards and platforms for monasteries. Since the friars needed to efface or disguise the work of their predecessors, they might make a few more alterations than were demanded by strictly physical functionalism. At first some friars may have preferred old pagan courts to building new courts, not so much for economy as for propaganda: to show which religion had triumphed over which.

Whether built as platforms, or made from the lower stages of pyramids, the larger preconquest raised areas were big enough to serve as a base for an entire monastery and its atrio, to lift the whole establishment authoritatively above the town plaza spread out at its feet. Smaller and lower flat-topped preconquest bases — some were only two feet high — could be used as a sort of pedestal for the church and monastery block only, to raise them above the atrio in front (which might or might not be an adaptation of an old forecourt).

Without excavating it is not possible to identify securely all borrowed and denatured bases. They are reasonably sure, however, at Santiago Tlatelolco, Acolman, Churubusco, Culhuacán, Huexotla, Mixquic, and Tacuba in the Valley of Mexico; at Tepeapulco and Otumba on the pulque plains of Apam; at Tzintzuntzan and Zinapécuaro in Michoacán; at Totimehuacán in Puebla; at Etla and Tejupan in Oaxaca; at Calkiní in Campeche; and at Izamal in Yucatan. Although preconquest platforms were somehow adapted here, it cannot be determined precisely how, or how much, since both time and the friars have effected changes. All that is certain is that a good part of the bulk of these platforms was once part of the bulk of other platforms or pyramids. It is equally certain that many more Indian substructures are still to be revealed under other colonial work, particularly in the State of Oaxaca.

103 HUEXOTLA *Stairway between the two atrios*

The results of the expropriations can still be impressive. The little Franciscan monastery at Huexotla, for example, in the wooded hills overlooking the meadows and lake of Texcoco, is commandingly imposed on the highest of three terraces of a preconquest sanctuary (each about 230 feet square). The double atrio occupies the two lower terraces, now planted with rows of towering cypresses, and the church stands imperiously on the top one, on the spot where the teocalli must once have stood.

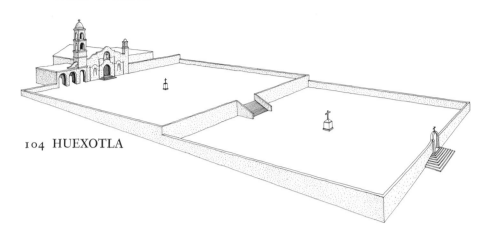

104 HUEXOTLA

Most imposing of all is the Franciscan monastery at Izamal in Yucatan (1553–61) which Fray Diego de Landa and his presumed architect, Fray Juan de Mérida, built on the heart of what had been one of the most important Maya religious centers, dedicated to the god Itzamná, "Dew from Heaven," legendary progenitor of the Itzáes. The entire monastery, with its large church and huge atrio, was set on a Maya platform, a *mul* or *cu* called *P'pa p'phol chac* ("built of stones of astounding size"). Part was pulled down along with the temples which had stood on its top, but there remained a

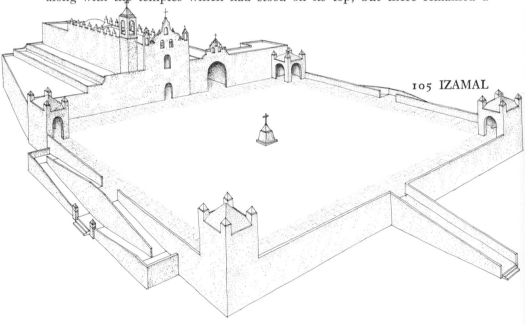

105 IZAMAL

vast mass which still rivals, despite subsequent alterations, the most megalo-
maniac temple emplacement of Imperial Rome, that at Baalbek in Lebanon.
(Baalbek: main court about 410 by 380 feet. Izamal: platform about 520 by
430 feet at the widest parts.) Three years after it was finished, Bishop
Francisco del Toral wrote: "It is a fine thing to see it, and a scandal to permit
it, for surely Saint Francis condemns it in his rule." Something equally grandiose was done when Maya T'Ho became Christian Mérida, and conquistador
Montejo, after considering whether to turn the cluster of giant *cúes* into forts
and a castle for himself, gave it instead to the Franciscans (1542). They set
monastery and atrio on one platform, and razed the others.

106 SOUTH APPROACH TO THE ATRIO PLATFORM AT IZAMAL
*The arcades were added in the seventeenth century, and the cresting over the
main arch in the eighteenth or nineteenth.*

At Izamal the organization of the open space of both town and monastery
is uncommonly handsome, with civic plazas on three sides of the monastery
platform. A long ramp leads from the main plaza up to the west end of the
atrio, axially opposite the church, and converging pairs of stairways, now
somewhat altered, lead from the side plazas up to the sides of the atrio. These
long approaches took on a special function, for Indians would ascend them
on their knees when making pilgrimages to the miraculous image of *Nuestra
Señora de Izamal* which had been brought by Bishop Landa on donkeyback
from Guatemala in 1558, and was soon venerated as Patroness of Yucatan.
(The cult continues today, though diminished since the substitution of a
copy after the burning of the original polychrome image in 1829.) [46]

There is a similar arrangement of plazas, one in front and one on each
side, around the still much-visited pilgrimage church of Saint Nicholas at
Bari in the heel of Italy, which possibly could have suggested the trio of
plazas at Izamal to any friars who had been there before coming to Mexico.

243

There is, however, no evidence for this, nor can any connection be established through that Bishop of Bari who was "Patriarch of the Indies," because he died seven years before Izamal was begun. Otherwise the layout at Izamal is unique and it is tempting to imagine that it owes much to the layout of its famous Maya predecessor. (Part of the platform collapsed in 1943, making a landslide which buried half of one of the side plazas during a Sunday bullfight and killed 43 people.)

*

The evidence is often puzzling. For example, the population of Huejotzingo was said to have been moved from a chasm in the slopes of Ixtaccíhuatl to the plain, where Fray Juan de Alameda laid out a new town (1529) and began a monastery, yet the big platform at Huejotzingo is full of potsherds and other preconquest litter, while the surrounding fields are not. Perhaps Fray Juan went out of his way to use archaeological wreckage on his new site in order to show how the new religion had quashed the old, or perhaps he sensibly made good use of local building material otherwise useless, cumbersome, and potentially subversive. He may have done the same at Tula, where the atrio, although again several miles from the old religious center, also contains many preconquest fragments. There were several pyramids next to the primitive church at Yanhuitlán in Oaxaca, which was demolished before the present church was begun (1550), and before deforestation had shriveled that once-great city to a village; their combined bulk must have contributed to the extraordinary bulk of the platform built to receive the new monastery, for it spreads 350 by 500 feet, and is 20 feet high.[47] The hundreds of tons of earth piled under the atrios at Quecholac or Tlayacapan could be explained most easily in this same way.

It is clear, then, that preconquest monuments were sometimes cut down and remodeled, and sometimes demolished, with the resulting rubble and earth piled in a new way to make a new platform, perhaps on the old site, perhaps nearby. Such was presumably the case at Epazoyucan, where the atrio and church platforms are full of bits of pots but not bits of old construction; it is not possible to say whether from an unrecorded preconquest shrine on the same spot or merely one in the same general neighborhood. There must have been a temple somewhere, either in or closely accessible to the town. The town was built on a low hill named, significantly, *Tláloc,* for the rain god. The atrio rises about 12 feet above the town, and the church and monastery block, approached by the broadest flight of steps in sixteenth-century Mexico, stand on a terrace 12 feet above the level of the atrio. The grading (1540) was early recognized as "very beautiful and expensive." [48]

At Tepeapulco, after the Franciscans had converted the population and made them destroy their many teocallis, including a particularly mountainous

one of the war god Huitzilopochtli (1527),[49] they made them raise a 400-
by-500 foot platform 25 feet above the town in front. The atrio was then, as
it still is, higher than the tops of the houses. No doubt the Tepeapulqueños
piled up the combined earth and rubble of several teocallis to make this one
huge substitute. A grand stairway leads from the level of the town up to the
atrio, on axis with the church which, with its monastery, is raised another 15
feet at the back, most likely on or near the spot where its pagan predecessor
rose above its court. The church (after 1557) handsomely dominates the
atrio, plaza, and town in a composition which can rival the setting of many a
Roman temple at the end of a forum or sacred precinct. Only an imperial
state religion such as the Roman or Aztec could have afforded to undertake
settings which called for so much space, raw material, and man-hours of
work. The religion of the friars who took over such preconquest settings or
imitated them on just as grand a scale was also backed by a powerful imperial
state.

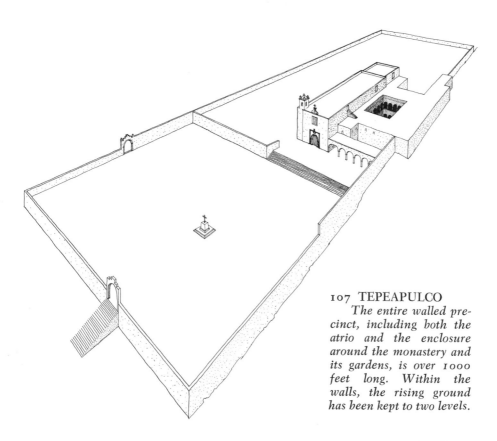

107 TEPEAPULCO
   *The entire walled pre-
cinct, including both the
atrio and the enclosure
around the monastery and
its gardens, is over 1000
feet long. Within the
walls, the rising ground
has been kept to two levels.*

245

THE ATRIO

Often when there is no evidence of preconquest remains, the new platforms of atrios and churches look the same as those which are known to be
adaptations. The Augustinian establishment at Ocuituco, for example, crowns
an ascending triad of terraces, all apparently new in the 1530's, with an impressiveness rivaling the pre-Spanish layout at Huexotla. Often the emphasis
of the new arrangements, like the old, is concentrated at the east end, where
the church and monastery will be raised above the rest, as at Atlixco, or
Charo, or obscure Copainalá in Chiapas. While not unknown, such expressive lifting of churches was rare in post-Roman pre-baroque Europe, but it
was common in postconquest Mexico, and something almost identical had
been common in preconquest Mexico too.

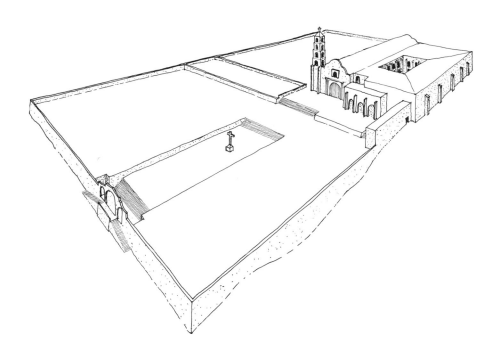

108 THE AUGUSTINIAN ESTABLISHMENT AT OCUITUCO
*First laid out presumably in the 1530's and, except for the church and the
atrio gateway, still much as it must have been in the middle of the sixteenth
century.*

*The split stairway in front of the gateway, and the arrangement of two broad
flights of steps in the lowered area in back of it are unusual, perhaps unique.*

246

THE ATRIO CROSS

> *Everywhere in this land the emblem of the Cross is raised aloft . . .*
> *It is said that in no part of the Christian world is the Cross found*
> *so often, esteemed so highly, adorned so richly, and made so large.*
> *Those in the patios of the churches are especially stately, and every*
> *Sunday and feast day the Indians adorn them with many roses,*
> *other flowers, and garlands.* — *Father Motolinía* (c1540) [50]

Cortés had begun setting up big wood crosses as soon as he landed, and he continued to set them up in every important town on his way up to the central plateau. When new towns were founded, the first public act was the raising of a cross. One of the first visible assertions the friars made of their mission, once any local temples had been pulled down and cleared away, was to raise a prominent cross in the center of the future atrio. Every atrio had to have a cross, for it was a symbol demanded by the special uses for which the atrio had been built. Because of its striking shape, size, and height, and its location in the place of honor in the center of a large, flat, and otherwise un-ornamented area, the cross was made visually emphatic. It could even be visually eloquent, and give meaning to the empty atrio space it pierced: it seemed to be its very heart.

When properly blessed a cross is sacramental (as are all processional crosses and the crosses which stand on altars) but, no matter how venerated, it is doubtful that atrio crosses, unprotected against mutilation or desecration, could have been so considered.

The particular and wide devotion to the Cross in sixteenth-century Mexico is attested by the number and richness of the stone crosses surviving. Nowhere else can one see such a vivid continuation of the power of preconquest sculpture, perhaps because a cross, like the idols it replaced, could be regarded as a magic object. "In many places they have erected the refulgent staff of the sacred wood of the Cross, which the Indians have adored and do adore with great affection" (1532).[51] Sometimes it stands triumphantly on pagan fragments (Cuernavaca) or is inlaid at the intersection of the arms with a disc of obsidian, like the disc symbolizing the spirit in an idol (in Michoacán at Atarácuaro, Ciudad Hidalgo, San Felipe de los Alzati). The Indians of Tlaxcala called the Cross *Tonacaquáhuitl,* "the tree that sustains our life," a term they had applied to some sort of preconquest crosses they revered, and which represented perhaps the four cardinal directions.[52]

The *ahuehuete*-wood cross, nearly 200 feet high, which stood in the atrio of San Francisco, was made from the tallest of the giant cypresses of Moctezuma's gardens of Chapultepec, and it towered over everything else in México-Tenochtitlán. The top could be seen from the stone causeways lead-

247

ing in to the island city, and even from towns across the lake. Some said that the Indians had raised it one Christmas Eve as a surprise for the friars; others said that the friars had commissioned it from specially expert Chalca carpenters before the church was built. The Indian nobles supposedly found it so heavy to raise that they concluded that the Devil must be sitting on it, but he was quickly routed by the exorcism of a friar. By the end of the century it was considered *too* tall — it had begun to lean over the church — and it was pulled down. The Indians saved chips from it like relics. A smaller cross was made from the arm, and this endured another hundred years. The cross at Jalapa was said to have been made from the masts of one of the ships in which Cortés had landed. These, too, must have been notable timbers, for the cross was a landmark for miles around. Such giants were soon found to be lightning hazards, and the Church sent out word that henceforth crosses were to be lower "because the Cross of Christ our Redeemer was not tall," and that they were to be made of stone when possible because wood exposed to the weather was liable to rot and fall (1539). The cross at Jalapa was replaced at the end of the century with another one of wood, but with a stone base. Sometimes the Indians themselves voluntarily replaced wood crosses with stone ones, as at Querétaro in 1555 when they substituted for their 35-foot wood cross a plain stone one, and then one of superior pink and white stone, so that it might "remain forever." The Indians of Huejotzingo set up a towering wood cross by their miraculous well of San Diego, and used to dance around it in cross formations. When it became weakened by the wind, they replaced it with a lower stone cross which continued, miraculously, the swaying movements of its more flexible predecessor.[53]

Fortunately, many stone crosses survive on their original bases still at their original locations in the center of their atrios. Without their bases they

109 ATARÁCUARO   110 CIUDAD HIDALGO

248

111 OTUMBA
CALVARIO

112 TIZAYUCA
PARROQUIA

are usually as high as a man or a little higher. Rarely is one more than twice
that (like the impressive monolith from Tepeapulco now set before the Cathedral of Mexico City, scraped smooth of its original reliefs by antiseptic
neoclassic taste). They are almost always large enough, however, to assert
their authority visually in the atrio space, and usually they are raised up impressively and safely out-of-reach on massive bases, often in several tiers
(Jilotepec or Cuautitlán, or Ocuituco and Tiripetío where the bases housed
small chapels).[54] Such elevation served to display the crosses in striking silhouette against the sky or the green of the atrio trees. That at San Felipe de
los Alzati is on an elaborate base with four lesser floreated crosses at the
corners, making an unusually lively silhouette, echoed all around the atrio
wall by little rosettes symbolizing the Host. (Although entirely sixteenth-century in character, this pretty folk-art ensemble may have been executed in the
seventeenth. Michoacán never felt compelled to keep its styles in step with
more up-to-date cities. The cluster of three crosses in the atrio at Atzcapotzalco may also be either sixteenth- or seventeenth-century work.)

Some stone crosses are smooth monoliths of cylindrical section, but more
are enriched with a few episodes of carving, often with the Crown of Thorns
at the intersection of the arms, and dripping patches of Blood where the nails
had been. (That at Metztitlán is typical.) From where the nails pierce it, the
crude and vigorous cross at Ciudad Hidalgo spouts torrents of Blood, so extravagant as to be unintelligible. The Franciscan escutcheon of the Five
Wounds is repeated four times, making a total of twenty-three streams of
Blood on this cross, perhaps devotional but surely as ferocious as much preconquest sculpture. Symbols of the Passion — nails, Blood, Crown of Thorns

249

— were preferred to representations of the Body of the Crucified, which appeared rarely on any kind of cross made by and for the Indians. The only surviving sixteenth-century specimen of an atrio cross with the Crucified Christ is at Maní in Yucatan, now set up inside the church. (The Humilladero Cross at Pátzcuaro has a figure on it, as does one on the facade of Yecapixtla, but these were not atrio crosses.) Perhaps the friars did not want the Body of Christ shown literally, for fear of idolatry or desecration. In view of the Spanish reverence for images, the latter seems more likely. On the other hand, the closing of the preconquest ateliers may so have disrupted the training of sculptors that carving a nude body was too difficult a commission.

Whatever the reason, symbols were preferred to descriptive representation. Although able to show a human form realistically enough, preconquest sculpture had generally favored symbolic stylization or semi-abstraction. A few atrio crosses mix symbolism and reality in the preconquest way, and are curiously half-anthropomorphic in the relation of arms to shaft, with the image of Christ's face from Veronica's veil become a solid, life-size mask at their intersection. (A particularly handsome example at Acolman has reflections at Chiconautla and Teoloyucan; other examples are at El Cardonal and as far south as Teposcolula.) Preconquest in character as this combination seems, there are antecedents for it in Spanish votive paintings and other items of popular art. Sometimes even odder iconography appeared, in isolated aberrations produced by ignorance plus imagination, such as the three little figures in the middle of one of the crosses at Tepeapulco (Christ and the thieves, or the Trinity?), the bodiless human arms on the horizontal part of the cross at Zoquizoquipan, or the base of the cross at Huango-Villa Morelos carved as a bust of God the Father (looking distractingly like Tolstoy). Many crosses have curving flames or lilies sprouting from the ends of the arms

113 SAN FELIPE DE LOS ALZATI

114 CROSSES FORMERLY AT ATZCAPOTZALCO

(Ajusco or Talistac), an ornamental flourish derived more likely from the floral buddings at the ends of portable metal crosses than from the similar terminations of the "Crosses of Jerusalem" of the Knights of the Holy Sepulcher. These flame-lilies vivify the outline and, since the atrio crosses are most often seen in silhouette, they can make a particularly effective enrichment.

Perhaps as an aid to teaching the Indians in the atrios, some crosses have the Instruments of the Passion and symbolic tokens of episodes in its whole drama carved in flat relief on the shaft and arms. No similar iconographical accumulation ornaments monumental crosses in Europe, though occasionally it is encountered in painting and the popular arts. Unsurpassed in Mexican art of the sixteenth century, the crosses at Atzacoalco, Huichapan, and the Villa de Guadalupe are encrusted with low, flat relief, as rich, closely packed, and charged with energy as that of the celebrated Aztec Calendar Stone. Here is proof that some of the aesthetic virtues of Aztec sculpture were vigorous enough to survive a total change in patronage, purpose, and content. There is a similar but slightly coarser cross on a grander scale at Cuautitlán. (The date 1525, said to have been seen on its base, must refer not to the carving

251

116 ATRIO CROSS *of the Franciscan monastery at* HUICHAPAN *carved with Symbols of the Passion: a Nail and Blood on each arm, the Crown of Thorns around the neck framing the image on Veronica's Veil; below this the column of the Flagellation with the cock that crew for Saint Peter on top, flanked by the scepter of the Mocking, and the ladder; below this the Nail for the Feet, with Blood, flanked by pliers and hammer; at the bottom, a Host and Chalice, flanked by the scourge and spear.*

One of the largest of the carved crosses, with its base this towers 20 feet high.

117 ACOLMAN

but to the first appearance of the Franciscans in the town. Perhaps this handsome stone cross is a replacement of a wood one which had been put there by the first friars in that year.) [55]

*

The Indians attributed magic powers to their favorite crosses which, when placed where there had been idols, were often believed to be the heirs of some of the idols' potency. The Franciscans placed a cross on the crown of the pyramid at Cholula as soon as they had pulled down the heathen shrine there. Struck by lightning, the cross had shortly to be replaced, but this and a subsequent substitute were also soon struck down. Exasperated, the brothers dug three deep holes in the platform atop the pyramid, and found hidden idols and a cache of sea-snail trumpets, which they quickly destroyed. Thereafter there was no trouble and the Indians were appropriately impressed. The natives of Jilotepec delighted their friars by exceptional devotion to a large stone cross: they kept garlanding it with flowers and sweeping a broad clean path to it. When a little chapel was made to house it, they protested at building a short paved way where they had been sweeping the path, and when a huge cache of idols was discovered under the path, the garlanding and sweeping were exposed as pagan rather than Christian enthusiasms. It was told how

253

a bejeweled devil appeared to an Indian in a field outside Cuernavaca and demanded obeisance there because no devil could enter the town now that it had a public cross. (This was more likely the cross in the *Calvario* Chapel at the entrance to town than the one in the atrio.) There are many similar tales.[56]

The number of crosses erected is as impressive as their size, quality, and power. They were raised not only in the atrios but often at street corners, entrances to towns, and crossroads. (The most impressive is outside Jilotepec, ill. 80.) The friars placed crosses wherever processions were to stop, and at the boundaries of townships. The native lords raised crosses in the patios of their houses, and wreathed them in flowers and sweet-smelling herbs; there were a hundred in Cuernavaca alone. This profusion of crosses began to disturb the bishops, who decided that the natives should no longer be permitted to have private or family crosses in their patios, but might set them up only in public places (1539).[57] The villages around Lake Pàtzcuaro still have many such crosses at the street corners, and a number of villages, such as Chamula and others in Chiapas, still have dozens of wooden crosses in front of the houses, some as much as 20 feet high. But of all the crosses the Indians made, those in the atrios were the largest, the handsomest, and the most meaningful.

118 ZOQUIZOQUIPAN

VII

MILITARY CHARACTER?

BEFORE examining the two main architectural adjuncts of the atrio — the posa and the open chapel — it may be worth reconsidering some long-held opinions about the architectural precautions taken for the defense of monasteries and towns. Since not only the atrio but the monastery gardens and orchard were commonly walled, the whole monastery has been regarded as a stronghold, with its church the last thick-walled defense. Bristling with battlements, they have often been called "fortress churches." Preconquest towns had rarely been walled or moated, and instead the walled temple precinct had served as a stronghold in emergencies, with the main teocalli the final fortress. (The written symbol for the taking of a town was a glyph of the burning of a temple.) Some have maintained that the walled Christian atrio and the church were meant to be able to serve in the same way, but this idea is not well supported by facts.

Some important people did, however, want churches to double as forts. When Viceroy Mendoza was forwarding Bishop Garcés' request to build a Cathedral in Puebla (1536), he pointed out to the King that "the church will take the place of and serve for a fortress." The citizens had just asked to have the city walled, but both that request and the Viceroy's more economical suggestion were allowed to come to nought, and Father Motolinía was still begging for a fort for Puebla twenty years later, a surprising wish from one so committed to the Indians. This too came to nought. Always apprehensive, Archbishop Montúfar wanted his new Cathedral, which with its cloister and other dependencies was to occupy an entire block, to be guarded by a tower at each corner (1554). Although similarly betowered but unfortified schemes had already been proposed for Salamanca and Seville, in Mexico is was a novel proposal. The project, which also came to nought, was intended to insure defense not against wild Indians but against mistreated city Indians, mestizos, and Negroes.[1]

*

Writing in Michel's *Histoire de l'Art* half a century ago, Louis Gillet characterized the monastery churches as "crenellated masses of abrupt shape, with a single level of windows placed high enough to defy escalade, braced by a series of square buttresses crowned by sentry-boxes [*garitas*] assuring protection of the flanks; the roof is a platform which could serve for artillery. The gargoyles imitate cannon. Sometimes a second platform runs around the building half-way up, like a *chemin-de-ronde,* to assure two levels of fire." [2]

Were such features intended for real defense? Cannon on the roof is an imaginative conjecture, but there is no evidence that any were ever there. (Despite Diego Rivera's "memory" that he had seen one atop the vaults at Tepoztlán, his contemporaries and elders in the town were unable to recall any such occurrence.) What is more, cannon could not have been rolled into effective positions because the top surfaces of sixteenth-century church vaults — there being no roof — undulate too much. The other features are no more meant for practical defense than were the "gargoyles" (waterspouts which, incidentally, were not made in the shape of cannon before the seventeenth century in Mexico).

The rare *chemins-de-ronde,* complete or partial (Cuautinchán, Oaxtepec, Tepeaca, and once at Jalapa [3]), were not needed in their regions, pacified and converted before the churches were built, and luckily not needed for, being without protecting parapets, these *chemins* would have made any "defenders" rash enough to walk out on them into targets as ideally exposed as ducks in a shooting gallery. The occasional ledges at the level of the nave window sills are also unshielded (Tecali, Zacatlán), and are difficult enough just to walk on without also having to try to shoot or dodge the shots of others. It is hard to see why any of these walks was built unless the walls could thus be made economically thinner above while still thick enough below; or perhaps the shelf also was found useful as a walk at a level convenient for the inspection, cleaning, and repair of the walls and windows. Sometimes such walks may have been arranged unmilitarily inside the building (Chiapa de Corzo, Cholula, Quecholac). Equivalent service passages had often been threaded through the thickness of the walls of big churches in mediaeval Europe, and perhaps these in Mexico are no more than routine echoes with little *raison d'être.*

119
ATLATLÁUHCAN
built in 1570's

120
CUAUTINCHÁN
begun 1569

Another common feature was an upper outdoor walkway just inside the parapet at the top of the walls of vaulted churches (Atlixco, Huaquechula, Tecamachalco), put there perhaps because the upper surface of many vaults was too wavy for easy walking. (Circulation without such a walk can be difficult, as anyone can learn who tries to perambulate the top of a church like Acatzingo.) Since the walkway may be there behind the parapet whether merlons punctuate the parapet or not, it shows itself as unmilitary because it does not have to be associated with such military elements.

Besides Tepeaca and Cuautinchán, many churches with other defensive-looking features were built in regions where such precautions would have been supererogatory. The heavy and close-spaced merlons running around the church at Tecamachalco (finished 1557), for example, were not needed against the local Popolocas, for most of them had been converted twenty years before the merlons were made, and those who had not had taken to the hills.[4] The merlons at nearby Tepeaca, which would have been needed even less, are associated with little *garita* sentry-booths too small for any adult defenders, and all surviving *garitas* in Mexico are suspiciously small (as at Cholula, Cuitzeo, Tula, or Yecapixtla), too small for action with bow or gun, though conceivably of some occasional use as supports for scaffolds for the servicing of walls, or windows: habit and a wish for decoration seem more likely explanations. The whole crowning at Tepeaca or Tepoztlán, merlons and *garitas,* proclaims its decorative rather than functional character not only in its main forms but also in its ornamentation: hundreds of little terra-cotta or stone balls, and dozens of medium and bigger balls, all of patent uselessness, and all easy to knock off in a fight since all are stuck on only with mortar.

MILITARY CHARACTER?

121 *GARITAS* AND MERLONS
Tepeaca, 1550's

Even those who were writing when the "fortress-churches" might have been most needed were not concerned with their military practicability. Bishop Zumárraga, for example, at the climax of the worst Indian trouble, wrote nothing about militarizing monasteries or churches, but rather "how I wish I had fifty crossbows and a dozen harquebusses. I have already bought a strong horse, and have sent it on" (1541). When Viceroy Zúñiga asked for a fort (1587) as a protection against the Chichimecas at Mixquiahuala, he cannot have considered the thick-walled monasteries at nearby Actopan, Ixmiquilpan, and Tula as an acceptable defense (a defense for the landowners, for no one was threatening the friars or their towns).[5]

It seems safe to say that none of the sixteenth-century monastery churches in Mexico are properly, practically, and functionally fortified. There are few fortified monasteries in Europe of relevant date because few were being built in threatened territories. Anything like the monastery stronghold on Patmos which the belabored Knights of Saint John were fortifying against the Turks was exceptional because the reasons for building such were already exceptional, even in the East; and this sort of precaution had for some generations been all but unknown in the West. Although the Spanish churches of the military Order of the Knights of Calatrava had been fortified, that had been only as an immediate consequence of the tense conditions of the earlier centuries of the Reconquest, conditions already well past. In the "new towns" planted in once-Albigensian Languedoc two centuries before, there may have been threatening conditions somewhat similar to those in New Spain, and some solutions — military-looking churches in unfortified towns — may now seem similar. Any relation between these and Mexico must remain no more than conjectural, however, for lack of connecting evidence. (It cannot be said too often that apparent similarities in mediaeval art need not indicate a causal relation: that must be proved or shown to be truly probable.) For the first time since Spain had had churches,

258

122 *GARITAS* AND MERLONS
Tepoztlán, 1580's

none was being threatened by anyone save on a few stretches of coast occasionally harried by the Berbers. When a new church was built at Jávea (Alicante), one of the towns which had been so ravaged, it was intelligently fortified: not by being equipped with merlons like the supposedly fortified Mexican churches, but with machicolations set above the only two openings in its high blank walls and with flat roof-platforms for artillery. This unquestionable and rare Spanish fortress-church of the early sixteenth century looks nothing like its Mexican contemporaries and close successors.[6]

THREAT

Whether the seemingly military features were effective or not, many of the friars in Mexico were in contact with a potential enemy, and hence there might have seemed to be better reason to fortify monasteries there than in contemporary Europe. But there must be doubt as to how real these "reasons" were. Although the Spanish minority was often apprehensive, the Indians of the most important, populous, and profitable parts of Mexico — the central parts — never really revolted or seriously planned to revolt. Surprising though this is, it is a historical fact. Charles V had to cope with more numerous and more serious outbreaks in the Old World than in the New.

Fearing an Indian rebellion in the first years, Cortés ordered all Spaniards to keep arms ready in their houses, and the prudent accordingly took precautions. Nevertheless, even when the abuses of the interim government made the provocation greatest, just when the chances for successful revolt were greatest (1525) — when Cortés was off in Honduras with most of the soldiers and horses, and other expeditions had taken most of the rest — the 200 disorganized and frightened Spaniards left in the capital were not attacked by the even more disorganized and frightened 100,000 Indians, who must have been quite aware of the propitiousness of the moment. Bishop Ramírez de Fuenleal, head of the Second Audiencia, asked for a cavalry company of 200 to protect the capital: they were not sent. Yet this was just when pairs of unarmed friars, flanked only by a few Indian boys, were marching out to smash temples and idols with spectacular success. It must have been clear to most of the Indians that the Spaniards intended to keep on bullying them, and not only the city Indians but all those of central Mexico *could* have joined forces to attack their common "enemy" in his moment of greatest vulnerability. The Bishop, nonetheless, could report to the Emperor in 1532 that no insurrections or serious trouble had occurred since Nuño de Guzmán had left: "not one Indian has rebelled." Apparently the Indians, who formerly had fought each other, were no longer — as Cortés had said when they were defending Tenochtitlán — "a united body, strong and quite determined to die," as "determined as was every any race of men." Once, later on, he did think that they were ready to revolt (1535), and that they would join to overthrow the corrupt local government, but there is no evidence for this other than his own conjectures which by this time were not reliable.[7]

When there were threats of trouble, they came not from the civilized centers, but generally from uncivilized mountain tribes on the borders, and these threats were usually scattered, intermittent, and local. There were no massive uprisings except the Mixtón War of 1540–41, in which the whole colony came nearer to being lost than at any other time. Although organized, this was only a border engagement, confined to Nueva Galicia, and an inevitable aftermath of the irresponsible violence of Nuño de Guzmán there. It was put down by Viceroy Mendoza, with 500 Spanish troops, 1,000 horses, and about 50,000 Indian allies — mainly from Tlaxcala, with additions from Cholula, Huejotzingo, Tepeaca, and Texcoco, all Franciscan monastery towns — Indians who must have been so solidly converted and convinced of the desirability of remaining Spanish subjects that they were willing to fight other Indians, not their traditional enemies, the Aztecs, *for* the Spaniards *against* a movement for Indian independence. Another lesser uprising like the Mixtón took place in Yucatan (1546–47), again border warfare, and a final phase of Montejo's cruel conquest. The aroused Mayas killed a few dozen Spaniards, hundreds of converted Indians, and even their imported animals and plants. The Chichimeca warriors in the northern provinces, who fought naked and drunk, kept harrying the pack trains from Zacatecas and other mines, killing a few Spaniards, but never fighting what could be called a war of rebellion. Meanwhile the capital was again left without effective defense and its Spanish population was understandably nervous for some years. They asked (1552) for a cavalry company of 100 or 120 which, again, they did not get. The Indians, however, never really threatened the capital; there was far more to fear there from Negro slaves.

By 1559 careful Inspector Gómez de Cervantes could report that no one bothered to keep arms any more "because New Spain has been so peaceful and orderly and unruffled." In all the sixteenth century the one real revolt was not any Indian affair but a half-baked *criollo* plot centered around Cortés' inglorious legitimate son, don Martín. Conditions seemed so calm in 1571 that Father Mendieta could say: "for many years there has been no threat of rebellion on the part of the Indians, nor any memory of it." [8] There are too many such remarks to believe that they were meant as placebos. In 1580 Viceroy Enríquez, having half-settled and half-bought-off the Chichimecas, could assure his successor that all was safe, even in the north.[9] In 1591 a treaty was signed with Chichimeca leaders which kept the borders fairly calm for another century.

It seems clear that revolt cannot have been feared very much or very often when the only permanent troops in New Spain during most of the sixteenth century were the viceregal guard of two companies of halberdiers, 20 on foot, 20 mounted. They were joined in the last decades by a company or two of infantry called the *compañías de palacio,* who were presumably honor guards. After John Hawkins had raided San Juan de Ulúa in 1568, 50 soldiers were usually stationed there, but serious fortifications were not undertaken for a dozen more years. The handfuls of soldiers quartered strategically here and there, in *presidios* along the frontier, or roads to the mines, could hardly be called parts of an organized army. There never were many such *presidios,* and the scarcity of the notices about them is more revealing than what is said in the few notices there are. While merchants and guilds maintained a sort of militia in some cities, there really was no professional army in the sixteenth century, nor — as a matter of fact — until 1762.

*

One begins to wonder whether, except during the scandalous interludes before the arrival of the Second Audiencia, the lot of most of the Indians was much worse under the alien Spaniards than it had been under the native lords. Although they were surely strong enough to have resisted effectively, the Indians gave up their old religion and took to Christianity with surprising speed. Once converted, they stayed converted, and however large the infidel underground was, after fifteen or twenty years it was no more a fomenter of revolt than the very much smaller Jewish or Protestant undergrounds.

It is doubtful that the natives were happy, though no one knows how unhappy, only that they were not desperate enough to fight. The masses were illiterate and inarticulate, and surviving records represent not their opinion but that of religious and governmental officials: most of it is partisan.

MILITARY CHARACTER?

The main troubles caused by the Indians were frontier engagements waged by unconquered tribes, and once these tribes had been conquered, they hardly fought back at their conquerors. The known reaction of the four or five million conquered Indians to the small but dominant Spanish minority was less actively hostile than might be expected: no more hostile than the reactions of many Indians toward the Aztec minority in power a few years before, the many who joined Cortés in order to throw off the Aztec oppression. Many more Indians revolted then against the Aztecs than ever revolted against the Spaniards.

Under the Aztecs the ordinary Indians did not have anyone who would listen to their complaints: under the Spaniards they had the friars, who tried to defend them from oppression, often and openly. Although resentful and afraid of their civilian masters, the natives rarely resented or feared the friars. Nor did the friars often fear the natives: most of them had no dread even of being martyred, an end so glorious that some had chosen to come among the heathen in the hope of achieving it. Since the Indians did not regard the friars as their enemies, would the friars be likely to feel that they should plan their buildings as fortresses?

ATTACK

Old writers occasionally described raids on monasteries, and almost always these were on the nervous Chichimeca frontier. But while the churches here sometimes did have to serve as strongholds, there is no proof that they had been so planned.

One of the churches specifically cited was at Yuririapúndaro (now Yuriria, built *c*1555–65), unsurpassed even by the luxurious Augustinians in its scale, its profusion of carved ornament, and air of magnificence. In their attack, the Chichimecas gained the atrio but failed to break into the church. Mistaking a statue of Saint Nicholas (or Saint Augustine?) at the top of the facade for a living person, so we are told, they shot at it until an arrow lodged in the stone. With no machines of war more menacing than the bow and the *átl-atl,* or throwing stick, and with no force able to send their arrows as high as the top of the tower, the attackers could do little harm. (Nothing really hurt this church until its own priest made it a furnace to smelt the gold leaf from its rich retables in 1815. The pious women of the town got the fire out, but could not keep part of the vault from falling.) [10]

The raid of the Chichimecas makes an engaging story, but it does not document the kind of attack — and it is the only one recorded for Yuriria — which would demand the building of a fortress. Moreover, the arrogantly splendid church does not look like one. Though out-of-date in his day,

123 YURIRIA, built mainly in the 1560's

Father Grijalva found it "the most superb building imaginable," and could say of it "what Tertullian said of the theatre which Pompey built in Rome: that it was surpassed only by the spirit of him who made it." Even the classicizing eighteenth century could admire it.[11] The elegantly festooned plateresque columns and more than a thousand square feet of carved leafy garlands and twining ribands lavished on the facade would not seem to have been made for a building meant for defense. The walls are thick, it is true, but they would have to be thick to bear the vaults regardless of how near, how many, or how hostile the Chichimecas.

When ever-complaining Doctor de Anguis remonstrated with the Augustinians for building such "sumptuous" and "costly" buildings for two friars or only one (which the Augustinians did not do), he was assured that such buildings would be useful as fortresses.[12] This sounds more like hollow placation than legitimate justification. The Augustinians were so often criticized for their extravagance that they frequently had to exculpate themselves one way or another, but on no other occasion did they try to offer the pretext of military necessity. Whenever the defensive character of a six-

263

teenth-century church is mentioned by a contemporary writer, one finds suspiciously often that special caution is needed in interpreting the evidence.

A defensive character was recorded for the monastery church at Alfajayucan (ill. 89): it was covered with simple vaults "because the country is hot, and perilous with Chichimecas." [13] The house had been founded in 1558, apparently as a sort of security measure, and Alfajayucan is one of the very few cases where this is known. Such assurance can hardly have been needed by the time the existing establishment was being built (after 1570 and before '86) on a new site in a converted region where Spaniards were able freely to graze their sheep.[14] Still "perilous with Chichimecas" or not — the notice is surely too nervous — Alfajayucan was given no features to distinguish it from dozens of other second-class monastery churches built in perfectly peaceful territory far from any peril from Chichimeca bows or *átl-atls*.

Nor are such claims justified by the considerable remains at Etzatlán, another frontier outpost (built mainly in the mid-century). Father Tello wrote that the monastery — he did not mention the church — had been made to serve as a fortress. He knew that a *presidio* had been in the town for a time, sometimes of a dozen soldiers, and that there had been fighting in the neighborhood for a score of years. If any monastery had to be a fort, one would think this might be it. The walls are thick, but so are most sixteenth-century walls of any height; furthermore, these were built in notorious earthquake country where any wall not thick might prove as perilous as Chichimecas. There had been a bad quake in 1566, and there were many minor ones before and after, and fear of those, as much as of Chichimecas, may have been the motive for the sturdy character which made Father Ponce — always cautious with adjectives — qualify the building as "strong." Nothing visible there today has military character.[15]

Father Ponce also noted that the small church in the sierras at Xichú was used by the Christian Otomí Indians to house their women and possessions during attacks by Chichimeca "highwaymen" (and that a garrison of four Spanish soldiers was there to protect the mines, rather than the friars; these men were normally stationed at nearby San Felipe, which had been organized in 1561–62 as one of the very few walled *presidios*). He observed that the church was built of adobe and thatch, certainly not materials which would be chosen for a fortress in a neighborhood with such a good supply of easily workable stone. Xichú had long been a frontier outpost, for the Tarascos had garrisoned it against the Chichimecas in pre-Spanish days. The monastery (begun after 1574, when Xichú was still a visita of Jilotepec) was already finished when Father Ponce saw it in 1586. It cannot have been counted as very strong because a new *presidio* was being maintained only 10 miles away at Palmar de Vega. Never a massive stronghold in its day, the monastery has vanished from the town without leaving any tangible trace or definite memory. No one there now knows where it stood, though a century ago someone still could recall that it had stood right under the present parish church. None of its walls was found worth using again.[16]

One establishment often said to be among the hardest pressed was Xilitla, also on the Chichimeca frontier, in the green Huaxteca Potosina in the last mountains north of Xichú. The Chichimeca raids were such that the peaceful natives fled in 1576, but in three years they were back, and complaining not of what was being done to them by the Chichimecas but by the soldiers sent to protect them from the Chichimecas. But then, according to Father Grijalva, "in the year of '87 the Chichimecas tried to destroy the house and town. They entered the lower cloister, looted the sacristy, and burned all of the monastery that was not vaulted, which was a good part of it. The friars, with some of the Indians who had taken refuge in the monastery, defended the entrance to the second story of the cloister with such valor that they escaped with their lives." [17] (The cloister must have been of wood, for both stories later burned.) This episode does not sound like the storming of a fortress, but more like a raid on a patently nonmilitary building. The main defense was at an upstairs opening in an open wooden cloister, one of the last places intelligent defenders would have chosen had they had a building with any proper defensive features.

Father Ponce indicated that many monasteries built in northwestern regions threatended by Chichimecas were unthinkable as strongholds (Juchipila and El Teul, for example) — small, miserable, and built of adobe. On the southern frontier in Oaxaca, Nejapa was founded (1560) as a garrison town to protect the highroad from the savage Mixes and Chontales,[18] but its monastery, which must have been begun soon after and is still quite well preserved despite later alterations, shows no military features at all. Although frontier monasteries suffered occasional attacks, they were not planned to withstand them. Monasteries in the well-converted central regions were not attacked, and it was these that sct the type for the occasionally attacked frontier houses, not vice versa.

ARCHITECTURAL PRECAUTIONS

FORTIFIED CHURCHES AND ATRIOS

Some modern writers claim that in times of emergency, when unconverted or backsliding Indians were threatening, an entire town and its domestic animals would move into the security of a walled atrio. There is little trustworthy evidence for this, however, and it cannot have been more than an extreme and rare expedient.

MILITARY CHARACTER?

Even though an atrio might occasionally have been pressed into military service, it need not have been built for that. The ordinary atrio guaranteed no effective protection, and it was not considered trustworthy. When Guadalajara was stormed during the Mixtón Rebellion, and the Spanish citizens were forced to withdraw to a fortified enclosure, it was not to an atrio but to a specially built stockade some distance from the atrio and the church (which the Indians were able quickly to destroy).[19] For lack of a fortress, the citizens of Oaxaca constructed a wall around the atrio of their first Cathedral as a protection for their women and children (c1560).[20] This was only a makeshift and afterthought, however, and like most of the other verifiable fortifications it was built *after* the church and atrio types had been fixed, including the character of their circuit walls and useless battlements.

The principal written evidence for the use of the atrio as a fortress comes from Matías de la Mota Padilla, who wrote in the eighteenth century. In describing the monastery of Zapotlán in Jalisco (now Ciudad Guzmán), he noted that its atrio had a "strong crenellated wall of masonry adorned on the inside with six steps all the way around, where separate groups of Indian men and women were taught the Catechism by the Franciscans; and also it served as breastworks or a wall for defense against the assaults of the mountain Indians." [21] Atrio walls were not thus described as defensible by sixteenth- and seventeenth-century writers, who would certainly have been better informed about Indian potential attackers than eighteenth-century Father de la Mota Padilla.

The other notices about Zapotlán are revealing. The monastery had been founded very early, in the 1530's, and had collapsed in the quake of '57. In 1580 the town, or village, consisted of two hundred Indians, attended by a single friar. The monastery must have been of the most primitive kind. When Father Ponce visited it (1587) he said nothing at all about a breastwork-wall, although there were still warm memories of Chichimecas in the neighborhood. Had it been built yet? If built later, would it have been as protection against an enemy no longer there? Father Tello noted the wall and its unusual steps (1653), and explained, without a word about military potentialities, that they were seats for Indians taught in the atrio.[22] Father de la Mota Padilla, writing 90 years later, long after the wall had been built — *it* may have been as remote to *him* as *he* is to *us* — after he had noted the pedagogical purpose assumed a military purpose also. Local conditions had changed so much since the wall had been built that warlike heathen Indians were already more legendary than immanent. It is Father de la Mota, enough of a fantasist to be able even to compose a panegyric on Nuño de Guzmán, who provides the main evidence that the atrio was used as a stronghold, and the evidence is no more defensible than the atrio itself. Nothing survives at Zapotlán, for all was rebuilt in the nineteenth century.

266

The town plaza at Actopan has tiers of seats in the same arrangement, recently built to accommodate the villagers who now listen on Sundays not to Catechism there but to band concerts. The atrios of other frontier houses are no more fortified than those of Zapotlán: at Alfajayucan, for example, once so "perilous with Chichimecas," the walls are indeed thick, but not so much because of the Chichimecas as because they are made of rubble, which could not have been built much thinner and stand.

124 THE ATRIO AT CHOLULA

The battlemented walls around monastery atrios are one of the most striking sights the sixteenth century bequeathed to the Mexican landscape. At Tula, Tezontepec, or Yautepec, they dominate the panorama. The merlons which punctuate their top are usually either so toy-like in scale, or so far apart, that they would be useless as shields. Even if they were usable in themselves — they rarely are — they would be useless *where* they are, for there is no ledge on which a defender could walk around inside the wall at a level where he would be shielded against hostile arrows by the solid merlons, and be able to return fire through the interstices. No military purpose makes merlons run diagonally up from the top of the wall across the gable of an unclosable triple-arched gateway (as at Calpan). These merlons are usually square, with pyramidal tops, a common mudéjar form, more decorative than functional (though occasionally both in a number of Moorish walls and gates built or rebuilt at about the same time as the first Mexican works). Occasionally (as at Tepeji del Río where they have big mouse-like ears simplified from gothic lily- or leaf-cresting) they are of so very fanciful a form that they openly confess themselves pretty trimming, equivalent to the

125 TEPEJI DEL RÍO
*eared merlons on
the atrio wall*

267

126 ACOLMAN
*merlons around
top of church*

fancy scalloped edge with which a contemporary architect as nonmilitary as Palladio might design a nonmilitary monastery wall (San Giorgio Maggiore, at Venice). One cannot consider some of the Mexican examples seriously as functional defensive elements when (as on the church at Cholula) they are gaily studded with colored terra-cotta wind-whistles.[23] Merlons were frankly used as a free decoration to animate the silhouette edge of odd parts of the monastery: they may serrate the skyline with clusters of little cones (at Yecapixtla, Tlayacapan, or Tepoztlán, all in Morelos); they may appear on the bases of crosses in the atrio (Cuernavaca), or on indoor stair-rails (Totolapan), or even on a well-head in the middle of a cloister (Huitzo) — clearly not places planned for defensive engagements.

Equally innocent are atrio gateways, most commonly formed of three arches resting on the ends of the front wall and on two columns between. The lack of cuttings in jambs or shafts, essential to hold doors, gates, bars, or any form of closure, shows that such gateways can never have been securely closed (Calpan, Chalco, Chimalhuacán Atenco, San Andrés Chiautla, Coatlinchán, Coyoacán, Huejotzingo, Tepeapulco, Tepexpan, Tultitlán, Zempoala, etc). Furthermore, who would try more than once to attach gate hinges to cylindrical stone column shafts? Even when instead of columns there are square piers with straight jambs to which doors could easily have been attached, there are no cuttings in the stone to show that any doors, frames, or pivots ever were attached (Acatzingo, Tecali, Tepeaca, and Totimehuacán, all in Puebla, and Hueyotlipan and Tepeyanco nearby, ill. 98).

Old texts tell of other unclosable gates. The *oidores* who kidnapped an Indian from the atrio of San Francisco in the capital (1530) said that the "corral there has no gates and never had." When the Indians of Tehuacán Viejo wanted to keep their friar *in,* so that he could not leave and be replaced by a curate, they "closed all the openings of the atrio and the church with stone and clay mortar, leaving only a small door which locked with a key, so that no one could get in or out."[24] This fortification in reverse would not have been needed if the atrio had already been even half adequately fortified — yet Tehuacán was a frontier house. Written records show that a few atrios did have gates, but not for military use: when Bishop del Toral wrote of the patios of Yucatan which were walled and provided with gates, he explained why: to keep animals out.[25]

Monasteries were not sited on their terrain for military advantage. Most stood on level ground in the center of their towns. Rarely was one set atop a hill, and even here defense does not seem to have been a determinant. When he passed through Zinapécuaro on his way to the Mixtón War, Viceroy Mendoza transformed a native fortification into a Spanish outpost because he thought it such a good defensive site (1540). The existing Franciscan monastery was built later on the same site, but not until a generation after the Chichimeca frontier had been pushed back. The church replaced a temple of Cueravápiri, and the monastery apparently replaced some of Mendoza's fortifications. If there was any reason other than that it was the finest site in town, the establishment would seem to have been put on top of the hill to expunge the pagan sanctuary, in a move typical of the campaign of disorganization and substitution which set so many churches on the sites of teocallis.[26] The monastery at Atlixco was set high on its hill for other nonmilitary reasons: to avoid mosquitoes and to take advantage of a surprising spring. The Augustinians moved their monastery at Metztitlán from its original low site by the river to a spectacular high shelf on the cañon cliff not because it was threatened by Chichimecas but by floods. Cuilapan was moved to a hilltop, but before the monastery was begun there, the hill was cut comfortably *down*, thus cutting also what little defensive advantage it may have had.[27]

127 ATRIO GATEWAY AT TEPEACA
(*The tile-faced lunettes were added at the top c1750.*)

269

128 STAIRWAY leading up to THE ATRIO PLATFORM AT TULA
The church is crested with merlons and garitas of the 1550's.
The top of the bell tower beyond them has been altered.

270

Some writers have thought that the massive platforms on which so many monasteries were reared must have been built to improve defense. Although the particular reasons for expending so much time and effort on these platforms is not often known, when documents do give a reason, it is not military. We know, for example, something about the building of several of the largest and highest platforms in Oaxaca. After a structural collapse, the monastery at Etla was moved from wet land up to a drier and firmer site (where it still is), a platform of earth some 350 by 500 feet. After the first site at Yanhuitlán had developed alarming gullies, a big platform was made in order to arrange a safe base for the large, heavy, and splendid church about to rise.[28] Had they wished, the friars at Coixtlahuaca could have raised their church on any of several neighboring hills, each of which could have been effectively fortified, yet they chose instead to build beside the big plaza on the lowest land in town. The site was so low and so near the river that to make it usable a vast platform had to be built. (This is no longer apparent because the river which once served the large preconquest city has now gone nearly dry: the great city has shriveled to a hamlet of 400.) At Tula, too, the monastery stands on a big platform, some 10 feet high, while there are higher hills nearby which would have been far more effective for defense.

Although atrios raised above the plaza and the adjacent level of the town might be hard to climb into and thus might discourage attackers, they are far outnumbered by atrios on level ground, with walls no more than 10 feet high. Atrios lower than the adjoining terrain (Calpan, Huaquechula, Tecamachalco, Tepeji del Río, Tepeyanco, or Tepoztlán) are too accessible to be reasonably defended; in fact they seem to invite jumping into. At Jalapa, the atrio juts out high over the valley like a serious bastion or "inexpugnable fortress," [29] but one can see that it could not have been so planned if one stops to think where the attackers would come from: it is easily enterable downhill from its one entrance side.

*

Thus for many reasons the atrio cannot be accepted as an intelligently fortified area, and it is difficult to believe that any were so intended. Significantly, there does not seem to be any difference in the arrangements at the frontier monasteries, "missions of penetration," and second-class "missions of occupation" in territory already secure when the monasteries were built.

Largely because their walls are so multiplicately fringed with merlons — at Totolapan and Yecapixtla an ornamental obsession — these forecourts can look so military that scholars have mistaken appearance for fact. Perhaps the bristling battlements are thoughtless echoes of some now-destroyed monasteries of effective military character built during more dangerous early years, but there is no substantial evidence for this; yet since the seignorial houses built early in México-Tenochtitlán did look fortress-like, some lost early churches may have looked fortress-like too. It is somewhat more likely, however, that the military character of churches in Mexico could be a memory of much older military-looking churches in Spain, of which there are still a few striking examples standing today. But it is even more likely that the seeming military character may have been no more than an ornamental preference. The mudéjar and plateresque in Spain had already begun to borrow military motifs and devalue them for decoration. While the Mexican battlements make no defensive sense, they usually make decorative sense. Mexican builders soon found that merlons could make a telling metrical punctuation on the long sweeps of plain atrio walls, and effective staccato accents along the tops of the ponderous bare walls of the monastery churches. At Tlayacapan, Totolapan, Atlatláuhcan, and Yecapixtla, they make otherwise inert walls around the atrio become active, dramatic, and even expressive. Furthermore, they were easy to build, requiring no special knowledge and little supervision. Long before the Spaniards came, the Indians had been building something similar atop the walls of their teocalli patios, and they kept right on building modified merlons for over three centuries, from New Mexico to Bolivia, long after the Chichimecas and their like had evaporated as enemies, long after there can have been any real or good imaginary reason for fortifying churches or atrio walls. Even when the merlons themselves disappeared, something of their decorative animation often remained: the swooping rhythm of the baroque cresting and scalloped silhouettes of many Mexican walls must be a translation into a new language of the old pseudo-military trimming.

129 ENTRANCE TO THE ATRIO AT TEPOZTLÁN

PRECAUTIONS

FORTS AND CIRCUIT WALLS

There are a few other sixteenth-century notices about the desirability of building out-and-out fortresses in certain key towns. Such suggestions, however, do not mention either churches, monasteries, or atrios as fortresses; and furthermore, none of the suggestions was followed.

For example, the citizens of newly founded Oaxaca asked for a fortress (1531), and complained that they had no church, but they did not think of combining their two building needs into one "fortress-church." As nothing was done toward providing a fort for them, they soon asked again and, after an outbreak of the Indians in the surrounding mountains, yet again. Bishop Zárate did not find the situation dangerous, however, and wrote the Emperor (1544) that the local Indians were not really threatening despite what the settlers said. Viceroy Mendoza, a reasonable man, after fifteen years' experience of New Spain, decided that the Oaxaqueños had no need of a fort (1550). He probably agreed with those who believed that whoever was master of México-Tenochtitlán was master of the whole country.[30]

Cortés had begun a pair of forts at the end of the causeway from Ixtapalapa to Tenochtitlán, but they do not seem ever to have been finished — presumably because they were not needed enough — and later they were somehow adapted to serve as slaughterhouses. (One was referred to several times in the late 1520's as a "fortress," but never at all clearly after that. The history of these constructions is far from clear.) The Emperor became concerned about forts for the capital and instructed Viceroy Mendoza (1537) to build a citadel; but the only fortification the Viceroy ever built was a small tower on the island of Ulúa in the harbor of Veracruz. The Royal Attorneys, alarmed to find that there were more Indians for each Spaniard than there were Spaniards in the entire country, told the Emperor (1542, 1544) that the capital ought to be given good fortifications, but the Attorneys were new to the country and had just been scared by the Mixtón War. The municipal authorities also asked several times — without mentioning churches — and again without results. Having been told to make a fort, this time on the Tacuba causeway (1550), Viceroy Velasco had to consider the problem afresh (1552), and as a result he ordered a quite different kind of defense to be built: because the need to protect the city against the recurrent flooding of Lake Texcoco was so much more urgent, he repaired the dikes.[31]

Father Motolinía suggested that in the event of an Indian or Negro uprising it would be a "safeguard for the whole land" if there were a fortress in Puebla (1555): nothing came of the suggestion. When Adelantado Montejo gave the battered pyramids of Mérida, in which he had intended to build two forts, to the Franciscans for their monastery, nothing was said to indicate that the monastery might serve the same purpose as the unbuilt forts. Experi-

273

ence must already have assured him that they need not. When a fort was constructed around the monastery some eighty years later, that was as defense against pirates, and when the monastery itself was finally fortified in the eighteenth century — again against pirates — the friars objected strongly.[32]

A few buildings which were not churches did have an honest military character and purpose. The *Atarazanas,* the combined arsenal, barracks, and naval base, was the first building Cortés ordered (1521) in the rebuilding of Tenochtitlán, immediately after he had taken it. He wrote the Emperor (1524): "Once this building was completed, I considered it safe to proceed with my plan to repeople the city, and therefore I took up my quarters in it, with all of my company." [33] Within a year it was being used not as a fortress but as a jail, because that, presumably, was the more pressing need. There followed repeated requests and orders to substitute a new fortress on the Tacuba causeway for it, but nothing was done. Philip II was told (1567) that the already decrepit *Atarazanas* did not and need not serve as a fortress, for the "true fortress is in your loyal vassals." [34]

The water-girt new Spanish capital did not need walls any more than had water-girt Tenochtitlán or water-girt Venice where, in just these years, Alvise Cornaro kept proposing superfluous battlemented walls with just as little result. Doctor Cervantes de Salazar believed that the potential defense of the capital could be embodied in its houses, "each so well constructed that one would call it a fortress, not a house. Because of the large hostile population, they had to be built like this at first, since it was impossible to surround the city with walls and defend it with towers" (1554).[35] The fortress-houses were designed not so much against any possible invasion by some "hostile population" as against threats of purely local turbulence. Perhaps more important was the pride of the *nouveaux-riches* settlers who wanted grand houses like the nobles' town houses in Spain, houses which had taken the form of strongholds for different reasons and at a different time. Perhaps there was also a wish to impress the Indians with the power of the Spaniards and the permanent character of their occupation by the powerful and permanent character of their dwellings. In the beginning, when houses still were considered a serious potential defense, they were built joined to one another around the periphery of the Spanish quarter of the city and along the old escape route of the Calle de Tacuba — much as they still are in many Andalusian towns — but this wall-like precaution seems soon to have been forgotten. Back in Spain, however, the usual inflexibility, the natural time-lag in communication, and a series of inaccurate reports kept apprehension for the safety of the Spaniards in Mexico warm for quite a while, and as late as 1573, royal ordinances were still demanding that "all town houses are to be planned so that they can serve as a defense or fortress." By this time such ordinances were not, apparently, often observed.[36]

At the end of the eighteenth century there were still some large hummocks in the plaza of Tepeaca believed to be the ruins of a fort from the days of Cortés. If they were, which is questionable, the ruins were probably from some unfinished outlying defense put up when Cortés founded Segura de la Frontera nearby, and not any fort finished and in use in the days of the monastery town, a town about which there is considerable information, even to a description of the plaza (1580) which does not mention any fort: had there been one there, especially one begun by Cortés, it would surely have been noted in connection with the possible need of a fort in neighboring Puebla, a problem many times discussed without, however, any notice of any fort in Tepeaca. In the nineteenth century the tradition of a fort was fastened to the *rollo,* which became known as "the tower of Cortés." [37]

Nowhere did the authorities in the sixteenth century find the Indians threatening enough to make it worth while spending money, materials, and time to build circuit walls or forts for towns in New Spain, with the very minor exceptions of a few Otomí frontier towns, and small garrisons on the way to the mines, which were built not to protect citizens but rather to safeguard convoys of cash. San Miguel Mixquitic, for example, was surrounded by a wall (c1569), but since soon there was no one about from whom to be defended, the town was almost deserted in forty years.[38] There had been some sort of Franciscan establishment here, but no one spoke of fortifications in connection with it. Veracruz, Campeche, and Acapulco became well-fortified ports, but not in a serious way until the seventeenth century, and then not against Indians but against English pirates.

OTHER MEANS OF DEFENSE

HORSES INSTEAD OF FORTS

The learned and experienced *oidor,* Doctor Zorita, who lived in Mexico City from 1554 to '65, after years in Santo Domingo, Cartagena, and Guatemala, and who was professionally concerned with the security of Spanish settlers, did not consider monasteries in the role of fortresses any more than did the others. He had another means of defense: "The very large and very famous city of Mexico is very well planned and very well built, with very long and broad and very straight streets, most of them paved; and it is meet that they should be broad and straight, because the defense and strength of the city is in its people on horseback." He voiced a long-held idea which was repeated again in the Ordinances of 1573: "The streets in cold regions shall be wide; in hot narrow; but for purposes of defense, where there are horses, let them be wide." [39]

It had been noticed during the conquest that the Indians were astounded by horses and horsemen (which at first they thought were a single centauric creature). A lame horse Cortés left behind in Petén struck the Itzáes as such a wonder that they deified it, and made a stone image and special temple for it. Cortés had ordered each important encomendero to keep arms and a horse, on which he was to appear from time to time on pain of losing his Indians (1524). Viceroy Mendoza later gave similar orders, and so did Montejo in Yucatan. It was thought that a good show of horsemen in newly founded Puebla would help keep the peace there (1534). The Indians' fear of horses was allayed by familiarity, however, though it was pointed out with some alarm that since they were no longer afraid enough of *un*mounted white men, it was only their horses that assured the dominance of the Spaniards (1544). There were 520 horses in the capital in 1537; 4000 in 1570. Juan Suárez de Peralta, Cortés' hippophile nephew, and author of a treatise on the arts of horsemanship, was perhaps more enthusiastic than measured when he wrote: "one of the strengths of this land, its horses . . . were of most effect in the Conquest and pacification of the New World." "Nothing .was more feared by our opponents, nor had more effect on them than the horses." He believed it still to be true when he was writing in the late 1580's.[40]

Indians were forbidden on pain of death to mount a horse or mule, and until the end of the century few exceptions were allowed. (One ancient noble was permitted to ride in the capital because though politically strong, he was too weak to walk.) Viceroy Mendoza mounted some of his Tlaxcalteca allies during the desperate Mixtón War, and gave them firearms, both without any bad results; there was, however, cool opposition. Father Motolinía, who was certainly their friend, continued to urge that Indians never be allowed to ride because he thought a monopoly of horses and firearms was still needed by the small minority of Spaniards to maintain their sway over the large majority of Indians (1555). Although in the second half of the century the Indians of Malinalco raised so many horses that they could profitably rent them out, because they were Indians they themselves were not supposed to ride these same horses. Toward the end of the century Spanish ranchers would beg the Viceroy for special permits for their Indian herders to use horses in rounding up tens of thousands of cattle, and permission was not commonly given. Only when they were too far away to be easily disciplined (as in Chiapas by 1568) or when there was some clear advantage to it were they allowed to ride, as with the loyal Tlaxcalteca troops, or the other trustworthy Tlaxcaltecas permanently settled in the north to protect Spanish settlers and gold from the Chichimecas. These last allies were not only allowed but were encouraged to ride, and also to bear arms, and even to preface their names with *don*, and rank as *caballeros* and *hidalgos*. (Philip II, by this time, was selling these same privileges to people who may have done less to deserve them.) Until 1597, when the Viceroy decreed that Indians might ride horses and mules, and might even own these mounts and their saddles, any Indian on a horse must have been an unusual sight. By that date the Chichimecas had managed to get horses of their own, and thereby the Spaniards lost one of their major advantages. Held back for a century, the horsemanship of the Indians and mestizos soon developed into the striking national specialty it remains to this day.[41]

FRIARS INSTEAD OF FORTS

There is no reason to believe that the friars were so apprehensive about the permanence of their conversions that they felt they ought to fortify their own quarters, or when planning monasteries or towns that they ought to think of protecting their Spanish civilian neighbors. Their concern was for their Indians and, had they wanted to build a protection for anyone, it would have been for their own flocks. But there were so very few friars and so very many Indians, converted, half-converted, unconverted, that the friars had to rely on something other than material walls.

How true this was can be learned from Viceroy Mendoza, a statesman who was professionally concerned with security and not professionally involved with the friars: "It became one of his guiding principles to found monasteries in different regions, for he had been convinced by repeated experience that the friars won more influence over the Indians by tolerance and teaching than soldiers ever could by arms." [42] Father Torquemada wrote (c1612): "The King ordered that many fortresses and towers should be put in suitable towns for the greater security of the country; and when this was not done, and monasteries for administering the Faith were put there instead, then the Viceroy, on being charged with this, answered that towers of soldiers were only dens of thieves, while monasteries with friars were walls and castles which were a defense for the whole country, since the friars have won the Indians by their example and holy conversation and advice; and since the Indians now never became restless or rebellious, the monasteries with friars were worth more in the towns than fortresses with soldiers; these monasteries which he had ordered to be built were the stoutest walls with which he had faithfully served his lord, the King." [43]

The unconquerable "Land of War" in the Guatemala highlands was won not by soldiers but by unarmed friars and native singers, directed by Bishop Bartolomé de las Casas — if we can believe his later boasts.[44] When asked by Charles V how to pacify the Chichimecas, Bishop Vasco de Quiroga of Michoacán advised him to withdraw his soldiers, offer amnesty, and admit friars. The Emperor agreed, leaving a long stretch of the border undefended; once the friars moved in, they slowly absorbed more and more Chichimecas into the Spanish State, rolling back the frontier for hundreds of miles.[45] Toward the end of the century, the second Velasco was still dispatching Franciscans to difficult pockets on the frontier in the hope of pacifying the Chichi-

mecas, presumably because he thought friars more effective than soldiers.[46]
Philip II, even after shifting his favor from the regulars to the seculars, had to
admit that the friars could accomplish what no one else could. When curates
refused to stay in hot Valles, he directed his Viceroy to send Franciscans,
"whom everyone loves." If the friars were there, the Indians would come
back, the town would be re-established, and it would be a secure outpost
against the unconverted nomads beyond.[47] Sometimes the attacks on outpost
missions were repulsed just by the authoritative presence of indomitable
friars; the Chichimecas entered Chichicastla and Huango, for example, but
fled when confronted by the unarmed but assured friars.[48]

The friars probably never could have won the country had not the soldiers gone ahead, and beaten and frightened the natives a few times. On the
other hand, the lands taken by the sword could probably never have been
held had not the friars followed. It is not possible to gauge how much of the
friars' success was the result of the Indians' fatalistic fear of the Spaniards.
In many places they may have preferred to accede to the less fearful friars
as a safer submission. They were, of course, right.

The battlements and heavy walls ought, then, perhaps to be interpreted
more symbolically than realistically, more as signs of the militant faith of the
people inside than as military deterrents for keeping unwanted people outside. As symbols, they performed successfully, and were perhaps desirable;
as defense, they could not have performed successfully, and were perhaps unnecessary.

VIII

POSAS

USE, EVOLUTION, AND ARRANGEMENT

Eᴌᴀʙᴏʀᴀᴛᴇ religious processions had been conspicuous in Indian religious ceremonies and, as the Spaniards were more given to outdoor religious parading than any other people in Europe, a double heritage made processions a major event on important feast days in Mexico. Bishop Zumárraga found it worth his really precious time to translate and add to Dionysius the Carthusian's *Brief Compendium treating of the Manner of making Processions* (1544), and see that it was printed in Mexico. Visually they must have been more Indian than Spanish — as some of the enfeebled survivors still are — and full of extravagances which might have looked heathen to Christian eyes had not the occasion for them and most of their symbolism, with a few odd exceptions, been so insistently Christian. The Indians rivaled the Spaniards not only in love of ceremonial, which led to processions, but also in a practiced aesthetic sense which made those processions handsome and visually dramatic. They astonished newcomers from Spain and, as described by eyewitnesses, make us wonder whether they may not have grown bigger than either their American *or* European forebears. We are told, for instance, that 20,000 Indians used to march around the Franciscan atrio in México-Tenochtitlán. In one special feature they did not approach Spanish show, for in sixteenth-century New Spain the religious brotherhoods did not parade with nearly so many *pasos* of life-size polychrome sculptured scenes from the Passion as their Andalusian counterparts were already so enthusiastically and extravagantly doing every Holy Week. The most elaborate processions in Mexico were usually those on Corpus Christi, and for them the Indians learned the special Corpus Christi hymns written by Saint Thomas Aquinas, *Lauda Sion* and *Pange Lingua*.

*

Father Motolinía described one memorable spectacle made by the Indians of Tlaxcala for Corpus Christi (1538) in some detail: "I believe that if the Pope and Emperor had been here with their courts, they would have enjoyed watching it very much. Although neither jewels nor brocades were in evidence, other fineries were just as attractive, especially the flowers and roses

279

that God cultivated on the trees and in the fields, insomuch that it was a pleasure to rest one's gaze on them and to note how a people, until now regarded as brutes, should know how to arrange such a thing.

"The Most Holy Sacrament was carried in procession, together with many crosses and with platforms bearing the images of Saints. The draperies and other trimmings were of gold and featherwork. The statues on the platforms had the same adornments which, because of their exquisite workmanship, would have been prized in Spain more highly than brocade. There were many banners of the Saints, and among them the Twelve Apostles with their various insignias. Many of those marching in the procession carried lighted candles. The entire roadway was covered with sedge, mace reeds, and flowers [a preconquest religious custom], while someone kept strewing roses and carnations. Many different kinds of dances enlivened the procession. On the road there were chapels, with their altars and retables well adorned, where the pauses were made during the procession." [1]

130 A PAUSE, *when everyone kneels to pray and sing, in a modest but typical Holy Week Procession at* SAN PEDRO SACÁN, *Michoacán.*

POSAS AND PROCESSIONS

From this and other texts we know that processions often made pauses at little chapels or oratories in the different barrios of the towns (as they still do at *Pardons* in Brittany). They were not big enough to hold a congregation, but were big enough for an altar before which devout individuals could pray and at which some sort of special ceremonial could be held; crowds could stand outside and sing. Some were temporary, just for festivals, and others were permanent structures of masonry (such as the survivors at Atlatláuhcan, Tlayacapan, and Yautepec nearby, at Tezontepec and Tultitlán, at Tepeyanco, and at Xochimilco, or half-rebuilt at Santa Ana Chiautempan and Acolman). Often each barrio would have a men's religious confraternity, which would care for such a barrio chapel and organize festival processions which would form there to march to the atrio. Only later, in the seventeenth century, did these little barrio chapels develop into parish churches for regular services, and by then they were somewhat larger buildings able to hold the now smaller congregations. Other small but monumental buildings were sometimes made for particular local devotions, such as the raised chapel open on four sides in the plaza at Cocotitlán, or the *Calvarios* at Otumba and Cuernavaca, or the *Humilladero* at Pátzcuaro. Occasionally oratories were built for the Stations of the Cross, leading to a Calvary chapel outside the town, but these did not gain general popularity until the next century.

In addition to these various oratories scattered through the towns, there was often a set of four special chapels in the corners of the atrio, little chapels of a particular kind, for a particular use, in a particular place, and with a particular name. In his *Dialogues* (1554), Doctor Cervantes explained those at Santo Domingo in the capital:

"Alfaro: '. . . in front of the church there is a spacious square, enclosed by walls, with chapels or shrines at the corners, but for what use I do not clearly know.'

"Zamora [expounding the wonders of the new city to his newly arrived friend]: 'An important one you may be sure; as the cloister is too narrow to hold so many people . . . space was made so that when they marched with the cross in front and the images behind, they might stop at each chapel to make offerings and to pray.' " A few pages later Doctor Cervantes mentioned other chapels in the corners of the atrio of San Francisco.[2] Father Burgoa, in describing Etla, wrote that its atrio was "well walled and battlemented, with four roomy wood-roofed chapels in the corners for use in processions," [3] and mentioned similar arrangements at other Dominican houses in Oaxaca. Father Ponce noted them often in Yucatan, and several other chroniclers noticed them here and there all over the country.

Thus it is clear that such corner chapels must have been common in Mexico in the sixteenth century, but not in Spain since Doctor Cervantes thought it necessary to explain them to Spaniards. They were and still are called *posas,* from the verb *posar* applied to the pauses the priest would make at their special altars in the course of outdoor processions around the atrio. More than fifty sets of them are identifiable because they subsist tangibly or else vicariously in documents.

*

Although they were used mainly as adjuncts to processions, posas sometimes had other functions. They might be used by friars teaching separate groups in the corners of the atrio. Individual posas were assigned to the confraternities of the different barrios and, like the little oratories in the barrios, were often dedicated to the same saint or feast as the confraternity. At the Good Friday *encuentro* at Tlacochahuaya, when the townspeople are summoned to the atrio by an officer blowing loud on what appears to be an antique hunting horn, each barrio gathers in the corner by its own posa; then they all march around the atrio, chanting *pésames* for the bereaved Virgin.[4]

POSAS

This custom of the *encuentro,* said to persist elsewhere in Oaxaca, is a remnant of an old procession and play, with pauses at the posas surviving intact. The posas are still so valued by the congregation that one was entirely rebuilt in 1954. Perhaps it is more than a coincidence that the typical atrio had four posas and the typical ideal of a sixteenth-century town had four barrios, heirs of the four equivalent preconquest *calpullis.* Whether originally so intended or not, the posa often came to play an extra role as a sort of neighborhood chapel, regardless of whether the local barrios already had chapels of their own.

DISTRIBUTION

The posa must have taken durable form in stone quite early. The atrio of San Francisco in México-Tenochtitlán may have been given a set by Fray Pedro de Gante,[5] with four posas corresponding to the four Indian *calpullis* or wards, and since San Francisco was better known and more often visited by more clergy than any other monastery, it was presumably an influential model. Unfortunately there is no record of what these posas looked like or when they were built.

Posas were favored by the Franciscans, and of all the surviving posas theirs are the largest, best built, and most richly decorated, sometimes in fact the most richly decorated items of the whole exterior. (There are or were sets at Calpan, Cholula, Huaquechula, Huejotzingo, México-Tenochtitlán, Tepeaca, Tepeji del Río, San Juan Teotihuacán, Tetlán, Tlaquiltenango, Tlaxcala, Totimehuacán, and perhaps also at Alfajayucan, Cuernavaca, Mexicalcingo, Texcoco, Santiago Tlatelolco, and Xochimilco.) In Franciscan Yucatan they were a standard feature but, since the 1910–20 Revolution had such a strong anti-Church character there, all but those at Izamal and one at Motul had been demolished by the time it was over. (Gone are those at Calkiní, Maní, Mérida, Tekantó, Tekax, Tixkokob, Tizimín, and who knows where else?) The Franciscans sometimes built them even for visitas or vicarías (for example, at two little dependencies of Huichapan, San José Atlán and San Jerónimo Aculco).

The Franciscans must have considered posas particularly important or they would not have built so many or, under their usually austere program, have lavished such ornament on them. Cholula, chosen as a model for large Franciscan houses, has posas and so must many of its successors. San Juan Teotihuacán, chosen as model for smaller establishments, has none now, but scars in its atrio walls show that once it did. There may have been something in the Franciscans' ceremonial customs which made posas particularly desirable, perhaps because Franciscan customs in Mexico developed early, when not only conversion but also enormous crowds were ever-present problems. Perhaps the first Franciscans made more outdoor processions with the Host.

We know that Franciscans have a special five-fold ritual revering the Five Wounds of Christ, which might have been performed at the altar of the church or open chapel in the atrio and then at the four posas. It may be relevant that the Franciscan emblem during the sixteenth century in New Spain was a shield displaying the Five Wounds; it was used regularly as a feature in the decoration of Franciscan monasteries.

The Augustinians, though sumptuous to the degree of scandal in some of their churches, built posas less often and treated them more parsimoniously: they are normally vaulted, but plain. A set was built at Tiripetío, their first and most influential house in Michoacán (begun in 1537),[6] possibly in imitation of the first Franciscan set in México-Tenochtitlán. Augustinian posas appear most often in the chain running north into the sierras of Hidalgo (Tezontepec, Epazoyucan, Acatlán, Tasquillo, Zoquizoquipan, Molango, Huejutla, perhaps Actopan and Metztitlán, and also San Lorenzo Ixtacoyotla, though there perhaps not of the sixteenth century). Augustinian posas occur also in Morelos (Tlayacapan, Totolapan, Atlatláuhcan, Yecapixtla, Ocuituco, and in rebuilt form at Zacualpan de Amilpas). The monasteries in these two groups, Hidalgo and Morelos, are on the whole less luxurious (except for Yecapixtla and Actopan) than in Michoacán, yet there, where the churches were richer, posas were rarer. (It is certain that they once existed only at Tiripetío and Cuitzeo, and possible that there was a set at Charo.)[7] Acolman lost its posas when floods silted up the atrio; that just north of the church has been rebuilt. Acolman's poor visita at Tepexpan still preserves three.

Early notices of Dominican posas are rare. There was surely a set at the head house of the Order in Mexico City by 1554, and there may have been earlier examples, though it is known that some monasteries (such as Etla) were *not* equipped with them from their beginning.[8] When the fullest descriptions of important establishments (such as Yanhuitlán or Santo Domingo de Oaxaca) do not mention them, we must doubt any were there. The Dominican posas which survive are the most modest of all. Tepoztlán has the only set with any architectural distinction and, not in proper Dominican territory, Tepoztlán may have been affected by its Franciscan and Augustinian close neighbors. But although their insignificant-looking posas may be afterthoughts the Dominicans must in time have found good use for them, since they took them to monasteries, vicarías, and visitas all over the country (southeast to Izúcar, Tejupan, San Juan Teposcolula, Yolomécatl, Huitzo, Etla, Talistac, Cuilapan, Tlacolula, Teotitlán del Valle, Tlacochahuaya, Mitla, and on to Tecbatán, Tumbalá, and Oxchuc in Chiapas, and as far south as Guatemala, at Santiago Atitlán, San Juan del Obispo, San Pedro de las Huertas, San Antonio Aguas Calientes, and Escuintla).[9] Some of the last examples may have been built in later centuries for Indian communities which were still continuing sixteenth-century ways. Posas were still used for processions in Oaxaca as late as 1670, when Father Burgoa remarked them at Etla and Talistac.[10]

*

By the end of the sixteenth century, however, posas had gone out of use in most of Mexico, and consequently were dropped from the ideal monastery scheme. Some were pulled down: those of the Dominican house in the now-crowded capital must have gone by 1606 when Father Ojea devoted a dozen pages to describing everything connected with the establishment without mentioning them. Once in a while, out in the country, Indians might still build new ones (as at Huehuetoca in the State of Mexico, Santa Ana Chiautempan or Tepeyanco in Tlaxcala, or Santa Maria Tonantzintla in Puebla, Santa Cruz de las Flores in Jalisco, and maybe most often in Oaxaca). In these cases it was presumably because the Indians were still using them and, when the sixteenth-century posas wore out, they replaced them because they needed them. These replacements might be in the latest architectural style. What a surprise are the gay eighteenth-century posas at Zacualpan de Amilpas, baroque and smartly up-to-date even in their new diagonal orientation.

131 ZACUALPAN DE AMILPAS

On the whole, however, people had begun to forget why posas had been built after the Indian congregations had shrunk and had moved into the churches, and when old posas wore out they were more often demolished than repaired or replaced. There is now no way of telling how many sets were destroyed as no longer useful. It is unlikely that, except for replacements, any wholly new sets were put up. When they are built today (one of about 1945 at Mitla, and that of 1954 at Tlacochahuaya), they serve principally as little oratories, much like side chapels in the church, and resume their old role only for big festivals (as on Corpus Christi, or during Holy Week at Calpan, Huejotzingo, Tasquillo, or Tezontepec, or other older towns).

Somehow the posa migrated as far as the shores of Lake Titicaca, 3000 miles from Mexico, for there a full set can be seen at the Augustinian sanctuary at Copacabana, deployed around a big cross on top of a posa-like chapel in the center (an arrangement occasionally found in Augustinian houses in Mexico, as once at Cuitzeo or Ocuituco).[11] The posas stand in the corners of an atrio similar to the Mexican atrios, put there for similar multitudes of converted Indians. Built in the eighteenth century, these posas do not represent a regular feature of Andean architecture but, on the contrary, something special for the very elaborate festivals which drew (and still draw) tens of thousands of Indian pilgrims to the miracle-working shrine. The simple and poor posas in front of a few other churches in the region are imitations of those at this big pilgrimage church. Some Augustinian from Mexico may have carried the idea to Copacabana. Probably related to these were the posas in the churchyards of some of the all-but-inaccessible Jesuit missions of Chiquitos, Mojos, and Maynas, in the tropical rain-forests of the Chaco region east of the Andes.[12] At La Candelaria in Paraguay there were no posas, but crosses in each corner of the atrio, for pauses in outdoor processions.

LOCATION AND NUMBER

By about 1550 a disposition had been standardized: four rectangular chapels were set in or near the corners of an atrio, each widely opened to it on one or two sides. The little buildings emphasized the corners of the big space, and consequently made it more apparent as a defined entity. Because his eye was drawn to the extreme points, the spectator had a more vivid sense of the extent of the area between them.

If they were open on only one side and had only one real front, posas did not face each other in pairs across the main axis, nor all face forward in symmetrical squad formation, as one might expect; instead, each turned toward a procession coming out of the church door and progressing counterclockwise around the atrio. In other words, the orientation was functional, for participants, and not monumental, for spectators. In order that the friars walking around a cloister in meditation might always face a devotional image — usually a scene from the Passion — the niches at the ends of the walk along each side of typical cloisters had been given this same orientation. Some posas still have shallow niches like those in the cloisters. Doctor Cervantes' remark that the cloister of Santo Domingo was not large enough to hold many parishioners, so that they and the friars came out saying their prayers, suggests that this feature of the atrio-and-posa layout may have been a borrowing from cloisters, a feature surely familiar to friars directing the building of the earliest posas. (Townspeople walked around in Dominican cloisters saying special prayers on certain feast days; ordinarily, however, the cloister was not a place for public gathering.) [13]

285

POSAS

Before this scheme was commonly accepted as standard, there were tentative variations. For example, at Tlaxcala, one early posa survives; remains of a similar opening and cornice imply a second; and relief sculpture from a vanished but probable third are embedded in one of the chapels of the existing monastery church. The sure complete survivor stands near the southeast corner of the atrio in a normal location, and the facade of the possible second is set opposite the front door of the church. There is no hint where the lost third stood — if there ever was a third — nor where or whether there once was a fourth: what remains of the layout at Tlaxcala is too abnormal to make any stable base for conjecture.

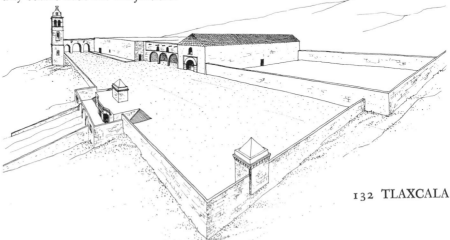

132 TLAXCALA

Father Mendieta claimed that two little chapels in Tlaxcala had the first vaults built after the famous one over the presbytery of San Francisco in the capital. Possibly these were posas, and while this could mean that Tlaxcala boasts the oldest surviving posa, it leaves wide room for doubt. An earlier statement by Father Motolinía said only that there were two early vaulted chapels "in the Province of Tlaxcala"; over a generation later, Mendieta, copying Motolinía, said that they were "at the monastery"; a generation later still, Torquemada, copying Mendieta, put them in the atrio.[14] Such incremental repetition arouses suspicion. Mendieta may have been confused and Torquemada careless in claiming priority for Tlaxcala: both had been Guardians of the monastery, and both may have been swayed by affectionate parochialism.

Inasmuch as what looks like a posa opposite the front door of the church stands on the vault of a chapel set at a lower level (to be discussed in Chapter XI), the vault of this chapel must be earlier than the vault of anything it supports; inasmuch as the putative posa is similar in shape and presumably similar in date to the posa in the corner of the atrio, *no two* of the three

286

vaults can be earlier than the third. If however, the remains of the supposed posa opposite the church — which do not exactly match the survivor though their vaults are similar — if these remains were not really of a contemporaneous posa but of something posa-like built a little later, then the lower chapel and corner posa could be Motolinía's and Mendieta's early vaulted chapels. Such a hypothesis seems, however, more like a sophism fitted to the facts than a deduction drawn from them.

All that can safely be said about the posas of Tlaxcala now is that one is certain (the survivor), and that ambiguous evidence makes either one or two others possible. Whatever way they were arranged was surely abnormal and almost surely early, though probably not early enough to accord with Motolinía's claims. These were more likely made for something else (which will be considered in Chapter XI).

The arrangement of the posas at Epazoyucan, while almost normal in regard to location and orientation, is abnormal in regard to number: there are only three, what ordinarily would be the second, third, and fourth. The place of the first has been taken by a chapel attached to the church facade, beside the main door, a chapel which though small is of novel importance (as will be seen in Chapter XII). Chapel, church, and monastery block are raised above the atrio at the head of a grand stairway. The layout at Epazoyucan was unusual also in that there was no proper plaza in front of the atrio, and the market was held in the atrio instead.[15] The several peculiarities here are probably explained by the early date — 1540-41 — in advance of the definitive standardizations.

At Acatlán, an unpretentious Augustinian establishment near Epazoyucan and built soon after it (1544),[16] the similar arrangement of the three posas is probably an imitation of Epazoyucan. There never can have been a fourth here unless it was right in front of the church, as at Franciscan Tlaxcala and probably also at Augustinian Metztitlán. More likely there was a special chapel beside the entrance to the church, as at Epazoyucan. Since the remains of the church are now barely visible above ground, there is no informative evidence on the spot.

There are only three posas at the much grander establishment at Cholula (ill. 92). The town had six barrios, of which three once were associated with the Aztec dominion, and three not. Possibly the three posas reflect one triad.[17] The other three barrios may have been visitas, for Cholula had a widespread township as well as a concentrated city. Again three posas are disposed so that a procession filing counterclockwise out of the Indian chapel at the back of the atrio arm north of the church could pause at each posa, and then march into the church or back to the chapel. These posas are freestanding; if there ever was a fourth it must have been adjacent or attached to the side wall of the big monastery church, though this shows no scar of it.

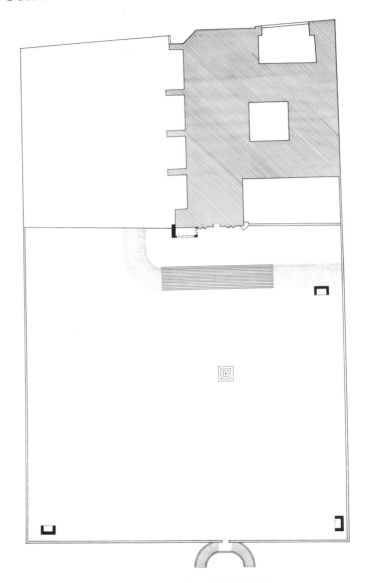

133 *The Augustinian establishment at* EPAZOYUCAN, 1540–41

The posas stand in the northwest, southwest, and southeast corners, but are not joined to the circuit wall as most posas are. The atrio, 315 feet square, is raised 12 feet to a platform, 200 feet long, at the back of which stands the monastery church with a posa-like chapel on its north edge. The entrance to the church, the stairway, the atrio cross, and the single atrio gateway are all on one clear axis. If original, as it may be, the arrangement of the curved double stairway is unique.

288

Another variation appears in the small Augustinian house at Huejutla, founded in the late 1540's after it had been a visita of Pánuco. The hillside site in the sierras of northern Hidalgo was found too unaccommodatingly steep for the standard scheme then taking form. The church (completed with its vaults before 1571) had to be set unorthodoxly north and south, and the narrow atrio — now the town plaza — was tucked under one flank at a lower level. According to a plan drawn in 1580, this arrangement left room for only two posas, in the far corners of the atrio. They are carefully shown in the drawing, and their processional orientation is made clear. Two more posas *may* have been set on the higher level where the church stands, but the Indian drawing which is now our only evidence is far from clear about this.[18]

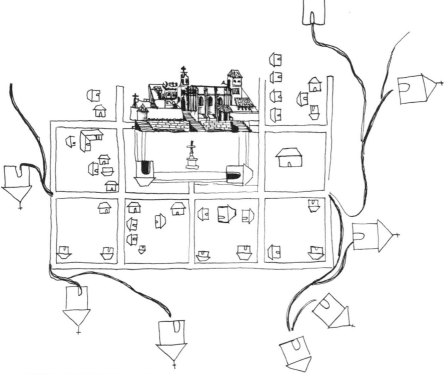

134 THE MOUNTAIN TOWN OF HUEJUTLA (*after a map of 1580*)
The monastery runs along the east side of the narrow atrio and is raised above it, with its church consequently running north-south. Processions filed down the long stairway by the front (north) end of the church to reach the atrio, and there followed the paved walk first to the northwest posa and then past the atrio cross to the southwest posa, after which they must have climbed the stairway at the south end to reach the level of the church. Only the lower part of the town has regular square blocks. Eight visita chapels are indicated, attached to the ends of winding mountain roads.

POSAS

The original arrangement at steep Metztitlán in the same sierra is not clear. Remains against the atrio wall opposite the main door of the church look like a posa, and so perhaps do more equivocal remains in the corner to the left of this and others far back in the corner of the atrio arm beside the church. The relation of these to the church and atrio does not explain itself logically, and it may be involved with the equally peculiar arrangement of the open chapels here (discussed in Chapter XII).

135 POSA, CROSS, AND ATRIO AT METZTITLÁN

Three posas still stand in shabby abandon at Tlaquiltenango, and enough remains to locate a fourth. They mark the corners of a large atrio space in the normal way, but the atrio is not in its normal place in front of the church, but along its left flank. Perhaps the processions went in and out of the church by the elaborate south doorway, awkwardly copied from the side door of nearby Cuernavaca, where the main part of the atrio also flanks the church instead of fronting it. Tlaquiltenango was transferred from the Franciscans to the Dominicans in 1570 against the will of the Indians; in a few years it was given back to the Franciscans, against the will of the Dominicans, who tried to have the Franciscans excommunicated or "suspended." [19] The different proprietors may have built for different outdoor usages, and thus have produced the existing uncoordinated result, or more likely, the layout is too early to be standard. The masonry of the posas is identical with that of the church — rough flat stones laid up almost dry, and surprisingly tight, with cut stones for the corners only — and they could be part of the original ensemble of 1540, and thus perhaps as early as eccentric Tlaxcala (if that really is so early), and only slightly less eccentric Epazoyucan, and possibly of an eccentric early layout at Cuernavaca. All of these cases are exceptional, however, and the great majority of posas are arranged in sets of four in the four corners of an atrio in front of the church, and are oriented for processions.

290

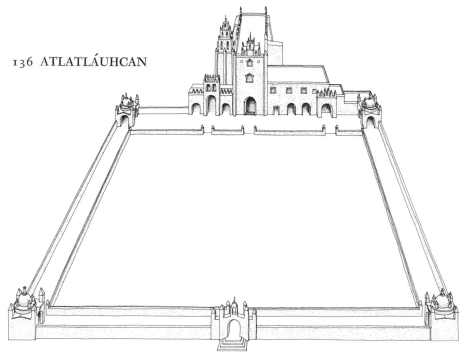

PROCESSIONAL ROADWAYS

As the drawing of Huejutla indicates atrios were sometimes laid out with a special margin for processions: a paved way leading around the edge from posa to posa. At Atlatláuhcan, for example, a flagstone road ten paces wide borders the atrio (370 by 270 feet), just inside its wall. The roadway is separated from the tree-shaded center by a low wall, and by being sunk to a slightly lower level. The combination of corner posas, high outer wall, flat road, and low inner wall emphasizes the edges and hence the sweep of the atrio space as vividly as any arrangement in Mexico.

Traces of a similar roadway survive at Tepoztlán, not sunk but defined and separated from the central square of green by another low stone wall like that at Atlatláuhcan. On Sundays in Lent the townspeople fill the center square, and fantastic beaded and feathered *danzantes* parade around them on the ruined roadway. Occasionally there are less colorful but more orthodox processions here, too.

Sure traces of another road at Totolapan, and probable traces at Oaxtepec show that such processional ways were favored in the neighborhood, and strengthen the supposition that what seem to be similar traces at Cuernavaca may indicate that posas once completed the ensemble there and justified the building of a paved circuit. Other features at Tlaquiltenango have suggested that it may imitate Cuernavaca, and this adds another ounce of probability to the hypothesis of early posas at Cuernavaca. As it was the first house in the region, Cuernavaca may well have been the model for the others. While later chapels have destroyed any possible traces, the very fact that chapels *are* in the corners of the atrio may strengthen the hypothesis that there *were* posas, which the chapels later replaced. (The local story that the eighteenth-century chapel of the Third Order was built by Cortés is preposterous, of course, yet it may be the fossilized memory of an earlier chapel or posa in that corner of the atrio.) Like Huejutla, Atlatláuhcan and Totolapan are Augustinian; Tepoztlán is Dominican; Cuernavaca is Franciscan. In respect to roadway and posas, however, as in respect to several other elements, the homogeneity of the regional manner may be stronger than the individual manners sometimes preferred by the separate Orders. Morelos, where they all are, has one of the few strong and distinct regional manners of the sixteenth century.

One cannot be sure of the handsome green stone paving around the atrio at Etla. Traces of one posa and long stretches of what may have been the original retaining wall are still there. Both are of the same light green stone, but now weathered so differently as to show that the fresh lettuce-colored paving cannot be original; it could as well be a renewal as a modern innovation.

137 IZAMAL, *with a corner posa sunk in later arcades*

There is another such roadway at Izamal, paved with flags from the ruined Maya *mul,* but the arcades added around the edge of the atrio make it hard to ascertain whether the road was part of the original sixteenth-century project or of the later project which produced the arcades (1618?).[20] As there are sixteenth-century posas in the four corners, and there was an abundance of secondhand flat stones available when they were built, such a road might easily have been part of the original scheme (ill. 105). One supposes that the arcades, which dramatize the processional circuit even more than could a bare road, were put up to shade later non-Indian celebrants from the prostrating Yucatecan sun. The Indian congregations may not have expected protection, for the great Maya religious ensembles, under the same sun, had offered nothing to shield their worshippers. For services in the atrios of Yucatan, the friars did provide shade, but in another way shortly to be explained.

ARRANGEMENT

The processional route was sometimes marked by the pattern of tree-planting. This seems to have been the arrangement at San Francisco in the capital and at a number of other Franciscan houses. At Tlajomulco in Jalisco, a pious *cacique* had 116 orange trees planted in the atrio, leaving four open "streets" around the perimeter, and later in the century an Indian friar, educated and ordained in Spain, returned to western Mexico and planted oranges in the atrios of Ahuacatlán and Chapala, "making streets for the processions," perhaps like some Andalusian ex-mosque courtyard he had seen. At their influential house at Tiripetío, the Augustinians had "streets of oranges and cypresses," and sister establishments in Michoacán must sometimes have copied this attractive feature. Dominican Tecomaxtlahuaca in the hot low-lands of Oaxaca also had an atrio "like a great plaza with two rows of orange trees where the processions go." Father Ponce noted a number of paved Franciscan atrios in Yucatan with rows of orange and other trees around the edge, and other notices tell of many similar schemes now destroyed or robbed of their trees. A contemporary item of idealized but garbled visual evidence appears in an engraving of a tree-rimmed atrio made in Italy by Fray Diego de Valadés to illustrate his *Rhetorica Christiana* (1579).[21]

New trees still mark out the old scheme on a small scale at the visita of San José Atlán. On a large scale, the most impressive surviving example is that at Tzintzuntzan, long capital of the Kingdom of the Tarascos, and the main Franciscan site in that important region: all around the enormous atrio stand two rows of the thickset gnarly trunks of what may be the most venerable olive trees in America, close to four centuries old yet still sprouting feathery silver-green branches. (The Spanish authorities soon discouraged and then prohibited the planting of these, fearing that local olives would ruin the profitable export of oil from Spain. As a result the Mexican cuisine developed without oil as a staple. Only in the last decades have olives been planted in quantity.) Old olive trees are almost never seen outside atrios, where the ban against them was not enforced, as we see at Atlatláuhcan, Chimalhuacán Atenco, or nearby Huexotla.

*

Possibly something besides the common-sense reason for planting "streets" of trees around the atrios contributed to the popularity of the scheme: there was a preconquest precedent for it. There were rows of trees around the courtyard of the chief temple of Tenochtitlán. One of the handsomest features of the famous cypress gardens of Prince Netzahualcóyotl at Texcoco was a hollow square of huge *ahuehuetes* ("old man" cypress), and nearby was a similar hollow circle, each making a pleasant shady walk. The trees grew to impressive size, and were a splendid sight a century ago, and even just before the Revolution. Known as "El Contador," today only a few ragged giants still stand, and the pattern and scale of the ensemble is all but lost.[22]

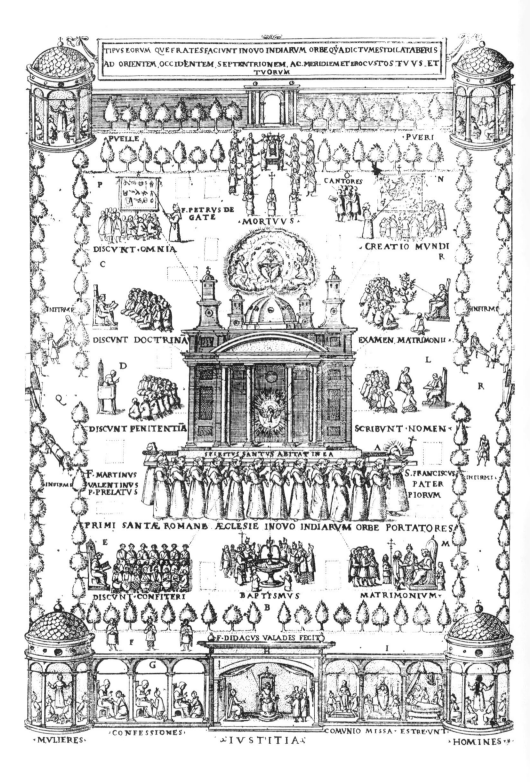

138 THE IDEAL OF THE ATRIO AND ITS ACTIVITIES
illustrated by Fray Diego de Valadés in his Rhetorica, 1579

upper left —   (P) *Fray Pedro de Gante teaching by pictures*
upper middle — *burial*
upper right —   (O) *singers*
                (N) *the Creation, taught by pictures*
middle right — (R) *preparation for Marriage*
                (L) *teaching Indians to write*
lower right —   (M) *Marriage*
lower center — (B) *Baptism*
lower left —   (E) *Confession*
middle left —   (D) *teaching Penance*
                (C) *teaching Catechism*
side borders (roadway between trees) — ministering to the sick
corners — friars teaching girls, boys, men, women, each in a separate posa
across the base — (G) *Confession*
                (I) *Communion, Mass, Extreme Unction*
center — the Church is supported on the shoulders of the Twelve, led by
       Saint Francis and followed by Fray Martín de Valencia. "First to
       bring the Holy Church to Rome to the New World of the Indies."

*

ORIGINS AND HISTORY

Temporary outdoor altars for special fiestas were probably the most directly influential of the antecedents of the posa. Such temporary arrangements are recorded in the second half of the sixteenth century, and Father Mendieta described them several times: "at the four corners which the course of the procession turns, they raise four chapel-like affairs, well canopied and adorned with images and trellises of flowers, with an altar in each one where the priest says a prayer." [23] Before its posas had been built, Archbishop Dávila Padilla noticed that to provide a temporary resting place for the Host on Corpus Christi at Etla (1575), "altars were arranged in a square where the procession would go . . . censed with a thurible by the two priests during the pause when the choir sang some motet or *chançoneta*." (These must soon have been replaced by the stone posas Father Burgoa saw a century later, traces of one of which can be seen today.) [24] The confraternities of the guilds put up temporary posas for the processions where they marched bearing their special emblems, posas which were fanciful constructions sometimes like toy castles. Temporary shrines were still being erected in the 1850's: "On the four sides of the square in front of the church, the Indians construct a green avenue of trees and branches . . . In the four corners, flower-altars are constructed, where the responses are sung; the ground is profusely covered with flowers, and earthenware basins are seen on all sides, in which copal and storax burn." [25]

295

POSAS

The tradition continues. Although liturgical and even devotional religious processions in the streets are now prohibited by Mexican law, they are permitted in the atrios, and for village fiestas one may still sometimes find special temporary altars there. Singing with the reinforcement of a brass band, emphatically punctuated by firecrackers, the marchers will file out of the church, often wearing bright crowns of flowers — daisies, bougainvillaea, or wild pink orchids — and carrying wands of green reed or sugar cane. (In preconquest processions in the teocalli patios, they also carried wands of reed.) [26] In the corners of the atrio the little canopies above the temporary altars are still as intricately decorated as in the time of Motolinía, with real flowers and artificial flowers made of tissue-paper, metal foil, and cellophane; often there are ornamental arrangements of fruit, sometimes stuck with tiny banners of cut tissue-paper lace or even of thin gold foil if the fiesta is important enough to merit the extra expense. Such temporary shrines are still particularly elaborate on the Feast of Corpus Christi, and are often admired by folklorists and anthropologists as examples of the persistence of pre-Spanish decoration: there are, however, clear antecedents and contemporary parallels in Spain.

139

140

139– ATRIO AND ALTARS OF SANTA INÉS ZACATELCO
142 *This unique sixteenth-century ensemble has recently been reported destroyed without — apparently — any objection from religious or civil authorities.*

296

142

Turn the temporary canopies over the temporary near-altars into stone, and the posa comes into being. A transitional stage — transitional morphologically but perhaps not chronologically since the two need not agree in Mexico — could be seen until a few years ago at Santa Inés Zacatelco, near Tlaxcala. Although all but one wall of the sixteenth-century church (an ex-visita of Tepeyanco) [27] had disappeared, there remained four nondescript altar-blocks in the corners of its atrio; one with an atavistically gothic stone Virgin, and the other three with big stone crosses, all turned so that a procession coming out of the church, turning right and marching around the atrio, would always have one altar and a prominent symbol facing it. Similar but cruder altar-blocks presumably still exist at San Jerónimo Coyula, near Atlixco, and at Axocopan, between Coyula and Atlixco, where they are set in the corners of the atrio, both in front and in back of the church which here is in the center of the atrio. Neither set can claim to be of the sixteenth century. (One hears of similar arrangements in eigtheenth-century New Mexico.) [28] At Zacatelco they had no permanent covering, but for the town's chief fiestas, fantastic temporary floral canopies were still contrived.

297

The Indians of the region are so famed for their adroitness with flowers that they are invited to make special decorations for the national shrine of the Virgin of Guadalupe. They carpet whole churches with colored petals, forming figures, symbols, inscriptions, and intricately patterned borders of fragrant carnation, rose, heliotrope, and wild dahlia, a pretty custom which still continues in some towns of southern Spain, the Azores and Canaries.

The posa is an architectural canopy which served the same purpose as the traditional *ciborium* or *umbralacrum*: to give emphasis and dignity to the small and visually insignificant altar, unexpandable beyond table size. The posa is the outdoor equivalent of the indoor ciborium, usually also of stone. There is one difference: a ciborium consists of a canopy on columns, while a posa is a little building with a top supported by walls, cut away by big openings though they may be. It is barely possible that there were once column-borne posas in Mexico: there is record of a stone idol cut up into "four columns on which are the arches of two altars" in the church at Culhuacán. These columns could have been for the support of two table-like altars, but as such altars are otherwise unknown in sixteenth-century Mexico where all known altars are block-supported, it is equally possible that the columns were to support some sort of canopies on arches over altars. Such arrangements are, however, also unknown in Mexican sixteenth-century churches, and no traces remain at Culhuacán to hint at just what was done there. (An elusive hint may appear in a picture in the Códice Azcatítlan of *c*1572 of some incomprehensible happening in *c*1530 involving what looks like a columnar ciborium.) [29]

143 A CHALICE *on an* ALTAR *covered by a* CIBORIUM
(Códice Azcatítlan, *c*1572)
At the right is a funeral bier, with the deceased wrapped in a shroud, set between four giant candles.

A ciborium or some permanent indoor canopy had been mandatory for Early Christian churches, presumably to shield the altar from anything that might fall from a ceiling too high to be easily cleaned. A cross crowned the top of the canopy, but was later moved down to the altar itself, where it soon became a regular item of liturgical equipment. The ciborium also took on symbolic significance as the canopy of Heaven, and from its center hung the receptacle which held the consecrated Host, a receptacle then often in the form of a Trinitarian Dove, but now more often shaped like a lidded chalice.

The forms chosen for the fixed ciborium were sometimes affected by the more splendid forms of movable canopies, later known as *baldacchinos* (from *Baldacco*, the Italian name for Baghdad, whence came the rich textiles of which they were principally made). In accord with antique pagan usage, during the first Christian centuries and intermittently thereafter, baldacchinos were carried over the heads of important personages in religious processions, and also — more relevantly here — over the Host when it was carried outside the church in Corpus Christi processions.

Since the ciborium presupposed a freestanding altar, when the altar table began commonly to be placed against the back wall of the apse in Europe, the ciborium disappeared, and the retable (*retro-tablum*) began to develop instead, though ciboria continued to be used in the Near East, where ritual changed less. A great many ciboria, however, were preserved in Italy as prominent ornaments to their churches. Many were prominent in Rome, and it is conceivable that some Spanish friar who had been to Italy before embarking for New Spain might have been impressed by some prestigious early ciborium there, and half-copied it for a half-new use in Mexico. But as we know of no ciborium inside a Mexican sixteenth-century church, and none outside an Italian church, this hypothesis is thin. The new European interest in ciboria around the middle of the century — Saint Charles Borromeo recommended some canopy over important altars — came too late to affect the morphology of the posa.

In Spain the ciborium had been used since Visigothic times, until liturgical changes in the tenth and eleventh centuries slowly drove it out (except in Catalonia) along with other features of the Mozarabic Rite. It was so obsolescent in the later Middle Ages that one must doubt new ones were being made. Some of the friars who went to Mexico, however, would probably have known one or two of the old ones still standing, most likely the magnificent example over the tomb of Saint James at Compostela; no one is sure enough of its form, however, to make any firm venture as to whether it might have affected posas. The most relevant Spanish examples still visible are those in the Barcelona Museum, and at Zamora, at Rodilla, and particularly those at San Juan del Duero.

San Juan del Duero was originally a small pilgrimage church with one altar in its apse, an arrangement found too cramped when the number of pilgrims multiplied in the twelfth century. Additional priests were needed for additional Masses, and in the thirteenth century additional altars for them were set in the corners at the east end of the nave.[30] These new altars were covered with exotic ciboria which look very much like a number of Mexican posas. That at the left is topped with a small dome; its mate, with a cone. Their curious orientalism is legitimate, for the church was administered by the Knights of Saint John, in close touch with the headquarters of their

Order which was then still in Jerusalem. As there was interchange of personnel, these ciboria could have been designed by someone who had been to Jerusalem, and had seen and admired — there and nearby — not only Near-Eastern ciboria now lost, but also the similar forms of such works as the so-called "Tombs of the Prophets" in the Valley of Hebron. Although there is no documentary evidence, some connection between the ciboria of San Juan del Duero and Mexican posas is possible: the main elements not only look alike but are used for a similar purpose, a purpose for which Spain presented but small variety of other models. If these models embodied any tradition of the Holy Land, no other models, not even Christian Roman ones, would have had more prestige. It may or may not be a coincidence that the ciboria at San Juan and the similar forms in Mexico are set in corners. (It is, of course, possible that other Spanish examples of similar form, now lost, are the antecedents of the Mexican posa if, indeed, it is to ciboria one should look.)

144 CIBORIA AT SAN JUAN DEL DUERO, SPAIN

Here is another of the several odd coincidences involving the Knights of the Sovereign Order of the Hospital of Saint John of Jerusalem which may justify interposing a few paragraphs of discussion.

First, they had settled in Rhodes, which had had the most famous regular town-plan of antiquity. Ousted in 1522, they were given Malta by Charles V in 1530, where they soon proceded to lay out Valleta on a regular scheme as close to Mexican ideals as any city in Europe. This was a little later, however, than the development of Mexico's standard plan.

Second, they fortified their monastery on Patmos and several others against the Turks at about the same time that the "fortress monasteries" were being built in Mexico, and being made to look almost as secure as Patmos really was.

Third, they must have known the Venetian arsenal-boathouses at Candia and La Cannea on Crete, which were apparently more like Cortés' *Atarazanas* than any surviving Spanish examples (such as that at Barcelona).

Fourth, they were responsible for the posa-like ciboria at San Juan del Duero and another very like them in the Cathedral of Paros near Patmos.

Finally, add to this list of coincidences the fact that their Hospice at Rhodes has a courtyard more like a Mexican cloister of the sixteenth century than any preserved cloister in Spain.

Such chips and hints, typical of our knowledge of the international relations of sixteenth-century architecture in Mexico, must remain an inconclusive cluster of coincidences unless it is found that a Knight of Saint John came early to Mexico, or that some friar saw their works in the Mediterranean before he came to Mexico. Only then could these fragments crystallize into a pattern revealing new ancestral relationships for several Mexican forms. Although none is known, such a connection is not impossible. The Knights had strong ties with Spain, for two of their seven divisions were Spanish. Important people in New Spain were aware of the Knights as early as 1538 when, in the elaborate festivities held in the main plaza of the capital to celebrate the Peace between Charles V and Francis I, Cortés and the Viceroy had a "gentleman from Rome" stage a sham battle between "Knights of Rhodes" and "Turks." The only other known connection came too late to have relevance here: don Alonso de Villaseca, rich from mines and encomiendas, sent money to the Knights to help them establish themselves on Malta (probably in the late 1550's).[31]

*

A miscellany of small religious buildings in Spain — wayside *Calvarios, Humilladeros,* cemetery chapels (that at Santa María de Noya, ill. 151, may be an ex-ciborium moved outdoors) — sometimes suggest posas by their form, but without enough family resemblance to claim legitimate parentage. It seems safe to say that while the *need* for the posa came from the number, size, and style of the Mexican religious processions and while the *form* came probably from the ciborium, the posa's immediate development came from temporary festival altar coverings. If the form is related as well to Spanish wayside chapels, it is to those which were themselves adaptations of the ciborium. The closest, perhaps, are the covered crosses of Valencia and its region (for example, that at Jávea). The ciborium, then, is more probably the grandparent than the parent; the temporary outdoor canopy is the parent; the similar little chapels in Spain are collateral relatives.

POSAS

Like the atrios in which they stood, the posas had a preconquest precedent, though not so important and definite a one as the atrio. Father Sahagún found that by the Great Teocalli of Tenochtitlán, the Indians "made many offerings in the houses which were called *calpulli*, which were like the churches of the barrios"; and that here the inhabitants of the barrio would gather to make their offerings. (The word *calpulli* could refer either to the ward or its chapel.) These *calpulli* shrines were in the big patio, set around its edge. Father Torquemada noted the same arrangement.[32] Without knowing more about them one cannot say whether they played any important part in the genesis of the posa or not. Any strong architectual relation seems unlikely since none of the preserved posas shows resemblance to preconquest forms, with one possible exception, the pyramidal roof (to be discussed later). The use of the posa as a chapel for a barrio and a receptacle for its offerings in the court of the main place of worship may, however, involve some organizational or procedural carry-over. This could be another element of the teocalli which was metamorphosed into the monastery.

The posa suggests several other relationships, but on examination they fail to show more than superficial resemblance. A group of kiosk-like domed posas (Acatlán, Atlatláuhcan, Izúcar) bears a curious resemblance to a kiosk of the twelfth century at Palermo, *La Cubola,* sole survivor of the many garden pavilions built by the Arabophile Norman King William II. Others like it may have been associated with Moorish or mudéjar palaces in Spain, and might be the forerunners of Mexican posas, but need not be, for the domed posas are of a form so simple that almost any clever amateur could think it up fresh without having to remember something seen serving a different purpose somewhere else.

There is a yet more exotic (and false) analogue at the temples of the pañchāyatana type in India (Khajurāho), where four subsidiary shrines are set on the corners of temple terraces. The resemblances in this case must be accidental, despite the fact that some Portuguese Franciscans had been in India and other Portuguese Franciscans had come to the New World early in the Great Conversion. Would any Portuguese friar have wanted to use East Indian forms to help make Mexican Indians Christian?

Because so many monuments have been lost, any direct connecting of buildings which *seem* to look alike is even more dangerous here than it is in most other fields in the history of art, where it has become a heady professional game. A closer look shows the resemblance to *La Cubola* as less real than apparent, existing more in photographs than in the actual monuments which, although scholars' photographs can and do make them look alike, are strikingly disparate: *La Cubola* is five times as big as any normal posa, and without photographs, a sixteenth-century builder would not naturally have thought of one while designing the other.

ARCHITECTURAL FORM

The function of the posa was simple: it had only to shelter an altar-block on which the Host, usually in a monstrance, could be set down, displayed, censed, and venerated. Mass was not to be said in a posa, nor was anything to be done which might call for the presence in it of more than one or two persons at a time. Consequently its form was simple and its scale small.

It is not surprising that posas show considerable similarity in form, size, and scale. Most commonly they are about 10 or 12 feet on a side. Virtually all but the meanest are hollow rectangular blocks opened by arches on one or two faces. Some were always open, and some had doors or gates which could be locked. Almost all had wall surfaces kept flat, making the posas appear as much incidents in the atrio wall as independent entities enclosed by it. Like their atrio wall, they were often crested with merlons; like their monastery churches, they were rarely crowned by cornices. What ornament they had — and some had none — was subordinated to the whole, kept close above the surface or sunk a little below it. In only one preserved set, at Tepoztlán, is there an application of major architectural members equivalent to the frontispieces of columns, entablatures, and niches which sometimes emphasized the portals of churches. In other words, in keeping with their minor roles, posas were discreetly recognized as minor architecture.

The refined little boxes at Epazoyucan or Tepeji del Río, and the coarse little boxes at Atlán, Tlayacapan, or San Juan Teposcolula are typical of the simplest type. Some (Epazoyucan or Tetlán) are wood-roofed; others (Yolomécatl, Aculco, Tepexpan, Tlayacapan, Totimehuacán, Tumbalá, or Tlanchinol) are barrel-vaulted; a few are domed.

The effect is often more mudéjar than identifiably late gothic or renaissance plateresque, despite some details in the latter styles. Posas often resemble the tops of minaret-like church towers (such as those destroyed at Teruel in the Civil War), or blocky gateway towers (such as the Puerta de la Justicia at the Alhambra, once the entrance to a *muṣallà*). Mudéjar precedent, however, is here so close to pre-Spanish precedent that one cannot say that the tradition comes exclusively from one or the other. Simple forms look alike all over the world, and a plain block here looks like a plain block there. Mudéjar decorative traditions were sometimes so close to Indian aesthetic preferences that we can no longer always separate them.

The posa most naturally took the form of a square in plan, which suggested symmetry in the architectural treatment, but since the posa must have a definite back wall behind the altar-block and must face front there is an equally natural tendency to oppose a statically symmetrical scheme and encourage an asymmetrically directional one. Square posas, being necessarily symmetrical, recognized this directional need only in their decoration, openings, and the placing of their altar-block, and also in being joined on one or two sides to the atrio wall. Stronger directional quality could be given when posas were not square, and had one long side backed up to the wall and the other opened widely to the oncoming procession. Sometimes the main front was emphasized by a gable (as at Tepoztlán, ill. 129) but the directional distinction which that might give could be vitiated by the use of several gables facing in different directions (as at Cholula, ill. 124).

There often were two openings, one on each of the adjacent sides projecting into the atrio; usually these were archways which cut half or more of the face of their wall, thus making the displayed Host reasonably visible to all. It may be that processions sometimes filed through such posas, each person going in the front opening, reverencing the Host, and then going out the side. Steps on each side suggest this, since they facilitate and emphasize access and egress. (Examples are at Huejotzingo, Izamal, Mitla, Tezontepec, Tlaquiltenango, and Yecapixtla.) At Tepoztlán the arches are of different sizes: a broad one serves as an emphatic proscenium before the altar, and a narrow one as an inconspicuous side exit.

In a few cases, perhaps post-sixteenth-century, the posas begin to lose their identity as buildings. At Tasquillo for example, the body of the posa has been shoved outside the atrio, and nothing shows inside but an archway cut in the straight flat wall, and a blunt point above it which breaks the long level top and interrupts the steady beat of the merlons. This demotes the architectural status of the posa from that of a little building to a pocket in the wall. The posas at Tasquillo ignore processional orientation: the first faces an atrio gate on the opposite side of the church facade; the second and third face each other symmetrically across the west end of the leafy atrio, shaded by walnuts and ashes. There was no fourth, for the atrio gate opposite the first occupies its place. This is charming folk-architecture, difficult to date

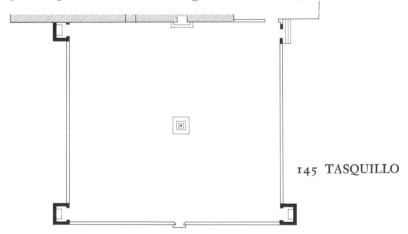

145 TASQUILLO

but quite possibly of the sixteenth century, contemporary with the naïve facade of the little church, a visita of Alfajayucan (though nearer to Ixmiquilpan). The large barrel-vaulted posas of Totimehuacán (16 by 23 feet) are also extruded from the atrio wall, and are also of dubious date.[33] At Zoquizoquipan (over the craggy sierra from Tasquillo, but inaccessible from that side) the strange little pilgrimage sanctuary has an obsessively battlemented atrio with posas reduced to shallow niches in the wall. This is wayward provincial work, also undatable.

146 ZOQUIZOQUIPAN

Like everything else at this remote visita, the posas are diminutive. The altar-block is low, and the arch above it is lower than a man's head. (It is necessary to stoop to enter the equivalent arched gate.) The espadaña *crowning the posa is toy-like, and so are the many pointed merlons.*

TEPOZTLÁN (AND FRANCISCO BECERRA?)

Only the Dominicans in the south had a particular form for their posas, distinct from those of the other Orders. The majority on the Mixteca-Oaxaca-Chiapas-Guatemala chain follow one practical unpretentious scheme: a sloping shed roof rests on the atrio walls where they meet in the corner, and a plain pier holds up the other corner of the roof. These posas are built of large bricks laid up with thick mortar joints like much Moslem and mudéjar work in Spain. Open, economical, and little more than sheds, they are unrewarding architecturally and so styleless as to be undatable. Many may be post-sixteenth-century (Huitzo, Mitla, Talistac, Tejupan, Tlacolula, Tlacochahuaya).

With a more truly architectural scheme and far richer ornamentation and architectural membering, the posas at Tepoztlán make a welcome exception to such Dominican work (ill. 129), and while still complete must have made the ensemble of the atrio there unusually handsome.

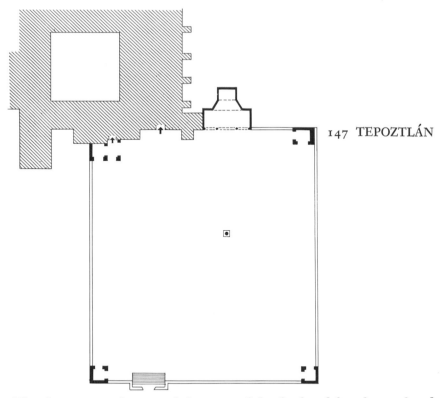

The elegant second posa and the ruins of the third and fourth are placed normally, but the first has been joined — uniquely, as Francisco de la Maza was the first to see — to the portería of the monastery,[34] in one ingeniously subdivided yet clearly articulated composition. Mexican architecture at this time usually kept its functionally separate elements physically separate as well, and rarely tried any complexities in planning compound buildings with multiple functions. Though small, and the resolution of no difficult problem, the combination at Tepoztlán is therefore surprising.

The other posas show other ingenuities. The conjunction of a wide front arch with a narrow side one gives unusual animation and directional emphasis to the important axis of the altar. Also, though some single feature of the decoration may be matched, no other posas offer anything like the combination of engaged fluted columns with near-Ionic capitals, deep niches, vaults with deeply molded ribs springing from ornamental corbels, and crowning cornices with near-pediments. The development of these elements is unusually architectural and plastic, and the vocabulary and the way it is used seem to show the intervention of someone practiced in full-size buildings with some pretentions, more knowing and more independent than the nameless designers of the more generalized works of the time. The design, then, unlike that of any other posas save possibly those at Huejotzingo, seems to reveal the hand of a professional architect.

This may possibly be confirmed by the written record of an important architect active at Tepoztlán. Augustín Ceán Bermúdez, writing in Spain in the eighteenth century, said of Francisco Becerra: "The best architect who went to America in the good period of Spanish architecture . . . [arrived in New Spain] in 1573 . . . built in Puebla . . . two masonry chapels in Totemeguacan and Guatinchan . . . and other [churches] in Tlalnepantla, Cuitablabaca, Tepuzhtlan, and other places in the lands of the Marqués del Valle." [35] Scholars have doubted the accuracy of this list, for it is all but impossible to identify one hand in surviving work executed soon after 1573 in Totimehuacán, Cuautinchán, Tlalnepantla, Tepoztlán, and Cuernavaca. (Or should Cuitablabaca be unscrambled into Cuitlahuaca, now Tláhuac, or — less likely — into Coixtlahuaca, then sometimes called Cuestlavaca? Bernal Díaz called Tláhuac "Cuadlabaca," which may strengthen its slim claim.) Nor is there anything here which can be satisfactorily related to Becerra's other documented work at the Cathedrals of Puebla, Lima, or Cuzco. Furthermore, he must have been kept too busy by his more important commissions in Puebla — he was *maestro mayor* from 1575 — to have had much time left to carry out minor ones in so many widely scattered towns. While Totimehuacán and Cuautinchán could then each be visited in a day from Puebla, the others would have demanded several days of travel across the

mountains. Becerra cannot have supervised work at all these places himself — if, indeed, any work of his was ever built there. He had left Mexico for good by 1580, and must have been regularly very busy in all his seven years there. He was in Quito in 1581, and died in Lima in 1605.[36]

148 THE PORTERIA–POSA
AT TEPOZTLÁN

149 THE SECOND POSA AT TEPOZTLÁN

Could the posas at Tepoztlán, by a hand more sophisticated than those which concocted the half-tequitqui church portal, perhaps be from a design by Becerra? They are not incompatible with his known work, but neither are they so like any of it that they can assure an attribution. If he did have anything to do with these posas, it cannot have been much more than to provide a sketch. The execution is so much less knowing than the design — if we read the evidence right — that it would seem not to have been supervised by the creator of the design. But the design is sophisticated and European, and must have been made by one of the few experienced architects in New Spain. The evidence, both stylistic and documentary, that he may have been Becerra is too thin to support more than a speculation, but it is speculation unopposed by contrary evidence.

150 ATLATLÁUHCAN

DOMED POSAS

The square was used for posas more often than the oblong *parti* with a definite front facade and subordinate smaller sides. It led to elevations little differentiated, if at all, and also to some sort of symmetrical crowning feature on the central vertical axis. Without having to have any exotic precedents in mind, the Augustinians and Dominicans both tried one of the natural consequences of wanting to vault the square posa by putting a dome on top of it (at Acatlán, Atlatláuhcan, Izúcar, Tlacolula, and also at Tepexpan and Tumbalá though perhaps not in the sixteenth century). Despite the invitation to more formal design suggested by the clear, geometric, and centralizing form of the dome, no domed posa shows anything more than the barest architectural treatment. Heavy plain piers support unmolded arches in each case. At Atlatláuhcan, Tlacolula, and Izúcar there is a plain molding for a minimal

309

cornice, and some pointed merlons to enliven the skyline, contrasting with the low dome and continuing the staccato decoration of the atrio wall: the architectural effect, lively but spare, is gained solely by the interplay of these bare geometrical shapes. If its dome is original, the single surviving posa at Motul in Yucatan is the barest of all, without one molding or accent anywhere. Posa domes are too small to be monumental, as domes usually are, but small and clumsy though they may be, some of these are among the first true domes, built in the New World.

The small domes on the posas at Atlatláuhcan (ill. 136) though normal from the outside are curiously ill-defined inside. They are made of small flat stones set in thick horizontal beds of mortar, and start out as flat planes sloping inward from the four flat sides of the little chapel — like the inside of a hollow pyramid — but this shape slowly warps into a cone, and then soon smoothly finishes off like the top of a small hemisphere. The dome over the first posa at Tepexpan also looks like a real dome outside, but shows itself as a clumsy groined vault inside. A similar kind of mixed construction was used in Moslem Spain, but there is no reason to force any relation here, since both constructions probably result from simplified or improvised procedures worked out as the masonry went up. Some adjustment always has to be made when a round dome is set on top of a square space.

Outside, the domes at Atlatláuhcan appear a little less than hemispherical, since they are slightly sunk into their low cylindrical drums, but this potential diminution in emphasis is more than offset by the exclamatory finials of a stubby colonette topped by a stone ball, an echo of those at the corners of the wall of the roadway below. Although the domes are small as domes, the posas they crown are large as posas.

Because of their folk-architecture facades, wider than the body of the posa and almost identical with the atrio gates, the two domes at Tumbalá hardly show themselves. They are so ineffectual that one suspects them of being victims of an inept rebuilding of the facades after the burning of the establishment by rebellious Indians in 1712. The other two posas at Tumbalá are not covered with domes but with barrel vaults.[37]

PYRAMID-TOPPED POSAS

The most successful and widespread of the symmetrical posa schemes was that with a steep pyramidal stone top. The pyramid was hollow, either with a flat-sided corbeled vault on the inside — the natural other side of the outside (as at Totolapan) — or with a more complex concave-sided square cloister vault, ribbed or unribbed. There were probably similar ciboria in Spain, and similar canopies for wayside crosses (as at Jávea or Santa María de Noya). A direct connection with Spanish examples naturally seems probable, but there are no surely enough relevant Spanish prototypes to clinch it. The many pyramidal roofs on Spanish churches — for the most part an inheritance from late Moslem building — are larger, lower, and usually made of tiles on wood rafters; and though they show an undeniable Spanish fondness for the shape of the pyramid as a crowning feature, these would not seem to be directly related to the smaller, steeper, stone pyramidal posa tops of New Spain.

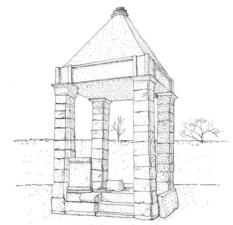

151 CEMETERY SHRINE AT SANTA MARÍA DE NOYA, SPAIN

This probably once sheltered a Calvary Cross or sculptured group. Although intended for outdoors, it imitates the form of an indoor ciborium. The stone pyramidal roof was once crowned with a small stone cross.

Other little buildings with presumably similar tops sometimes stood in the corners of preconquest temple enclosures; and inasmuch as posas stand in the corners of the atrio the coincidence suggests some connection; but since so little is known about these preconquest buildings, no more can be said than that some relation *seems* likely. Since the pyramid, even more than the dome, comes as an apt and natural way to terminate a small cubical building — an almost inevitable form for its roof — it is not necessary to suppose any venerable European or American genealogy for it here. It is possible that the pyramidal posa was the independent invention of some clear-headed early friar. The form was not restricted to posas, and occurred early in Spanish Mexico on one important small monument which was not a posa: the *Calvario* at Cuernavaca, a ciborium-like oratory discussed later (Chapter XI).

The most important group of pyramidal posas is in the neighborhood of Puebla, at the Franciscan houses of Tlaxcala, Huaquechula, Calpan, and Huejotzingo (ill. endpapers). They also appeared sporadically elsewhere, at Augustinian Totolapan and Molango, and as far away as Franciscan Izamal in Yucatan, there doubtless as a reflection of some prominent Franciscan house in the Valley of Mexico or Puebla, perhaps the mother-house of the Order.

311

POSAS

152 IZAMAL

Some are simple to bareness, as for example, the last of the posas at Molango, which has recently been allowed to collapse. The posas at Izamal were also bare, though this is no longer easy to see now that they have been embedded in the arcades built around the atrio in the seventeenth century. The one posa at Totolapan which still has its cover — a surviving mate stands roofless nearby — is also plain except around the top edges of its cube, simply but emphatically crested with the stubby pyramidal merlons epidemic at Totolapan. Two more merlons poke up from the top of the pyramidal roof as exclamatorily as an alert cat's ears.

Huaquechula, Tlaxcala, Cholula

Stylistically the posas of this group around Puebla are interrelated, with the simplest one at Huaquechula essentially close to the most elaborate examples at Calpan and Huejotzingo, and the one at Tlaxcala, though the most distinct, still only a little apart. Although geographically in their midst, the posas at Cholula are different in style from all but the one posa at Tlaxcala. There are stylistic connections also between other elements in the decoration of the church buildings of this group of establishments, with the exception this time of Tlaxcala. There are also known connections in the monastic personnel, civil officials, and encomenderos. The same or closely related craftsmen were probably passed back and forth more than once between these Franciscan houses, and the work they left at the churches of Cholula and Huaquechula, and at the posas of Calpan and Huejotzingo, shows them to have been among the most skilled workmen in sixteenth-century New Spain.

The single surviving posa at Huaquechula is the plainest of the group, even though it is articulated with modeled jambs, and a modeled archivolt enframed in an *alfiz*. Broad and low, the little building would seem to have been carefully proportioned, perhaps as a product of the same building cam-

153 TOTOLAPAN   154 MOLANGO

paign that raised the sophisticated monastery church. (The church must have been partly vaulted and fairly well along to elicit the praise of Doctor Cervantes between 1560 and '67, though not entirely finished since we can see the dates 1569 and 1570 carved high in its walls.) Unlike the neat construction of the church, the masonry of the posa is a sloppy patchwork, and must have been intended to be hidden under stucco. Much of it is of re-used stones. The archivolts of the flattish basket-handle arches and the colonettes of their jambs are of brick, also in part re-used. The stone came more probably from a local teocalli than from the earlier little monastery, but the brick more likely from the latter (which the Franciscans founded and built in the 1530's; it has now disappeared except for the lower story of the cloister). Perhaps when the primitive establishment was dismantled for the handsome one still standing, its masonry was thriftily re-used, not only for posas but also for infill for the new church walls, which were being faced with gaudy but weak pink and orange striated stone; this might date the posas around 1560. Huaquechula, a charming garden village on a flat ridge between ravines, where Doctor Cervantes once found "the best oranges, pomegranates, and figs in the world," was known to have four confraternities in the sixteenth century, and probably each was assigned one of the posas.[38]

155 HUAQUECHULA

156
TLAXCALA

One posa with a pyramidal top still stands in the atrio at Tlaxcala (ill. 132). Motolinía's and Mendieta's texts about early vaults cannot be tied to this posa and some putative mate or mates, as has already been shown, and therefore these texts cannot give reliable dates here, although the little ribbed cloister vault on the existing corner posa and the remains of one like it on the possible posa atop the chapel *look* very early and closely resemble the vault of the chapel on top of which the latter stands; all seem to be among the earliest vaults on the continent. The design of the elevation of the surviving posa *looks* earlier than that of the posas at nearby Huejotzingo, and since it uses the same cornice as the chapel below, it would seem to be contemporary with that, which also *looks* insistently early. While neither the chapel nor posa at Tlaxcala can be dated definitively, one posa at Huejotzingo is fixed firmly in 1550, and as the posa and chapel at Tlaxcala seem to belong to a slightly earlier campaign, before 1550 and well after 1535, they can be assumed to have been made about 1546 or '47, a few years after Father Motolinía had finished writing his *History* and *Memoriales* and after the city had recovered somewhat from the plague of 1545.

The design of the posa at Tlaxcala is not free of crudeness. Its flat facade is almost cut in two by the shelf-like bracketed cornice (quite unlike the cornices at Tepoztlán, which project less, and crown rather than chop). Futhermore, the little attic above this division cannot be happily related to the pyramid, which seems imposed on it rather than to rise out of it. Below the cornice, the square facade is almost all cut away by its big arch, nearly as wide as high. While the coarse archivolt and the stubby pilaster-like imposts from which it springs may strengthen the arch visually, it is at a price, for the impost piers leave only an uncomfortable thin strip of wall at the corners, visually too weak to appear to be able to hold up the crushing mass of the pyramid above. The spandrel sculpture has not been adjusted comfortably to the spaces between the arch and the pyramid. Thus the archivolt, the impost piers, the sculpture, and the cornice all assert themselves individually and independently without cooperating enough to make any legible formal relation with one another. Comparison shows how much more concordant was the design of the posas at Tepoztlán.

157 CHOLULA

Inasmuch as the posas at Cholula (left front endpaper) do not have the pyramidal roofs of Tlaxcala, Huaquechula, Calpan, and Huejotzingo, they may seem little related to them stylistically, though geographically they stand in the middle of the group, and the coeval churches at Huejotzingo and Cholula — one visible from the top of the other — are also closely related. The posas of Cholula do stem directly from those at Tlaxcala, however, though not in the same way as the others. Without any sculpture, they are artlessly animated instead by steep-peaked gables and many spiky merlons, but still they lack integration of design as much as do the posas of Tlaxcala. In both the trimming is done with architectural elements, but the ensemble is naïvely unarchitectural, overdressed with ill-fitting architectural finery.

Cholula had been one of the first Franciscan foundations (mid-'30's), but the present church was not begun until 1549; it was consecrated in 1552.[39] Not strikingly similar or dissimilar to the church, the posas need not belong to the same campaign. Normally they would have been built soon after the church, which in this case would make them a little later than their presumed model at Tlaxcala. Either Tlaxcala or Cholula could have been the model for the one posa discernable in a sketch of Tepeaca by Rugendas; it seems to have been quite similar, but unfortunately it has now disappeared without leaving much trace.[40]

The importance of these posas of Cholula, Tlaxcala, Huaquechula (and perhaps Tepeaca) comes not so much from any architectural quality of their own as from their association with a group in which other examples — the posas at Huejotzingo and at Calpan — show some of the most distinguished architectural design and carving in sixteenth-century Mexico. These merit more detailed examining.

315

158 TEPEACA IN THE FIRST HALF OF THE NINETEENTH CENTURY
*(a sketch by Johann Moritz Rugendas, 1802–58, in the Graphische Samm-
lung at Munich.) The presumed posa is at the right, beyond the organ cactus, and this side of the* rollo, *which he called "the tower of Cortés."*

Huejotzingo

The only firmly dated posa anywhere is one at Huejotzingo ("place of
little willows"): the northeast, or first proceeding counterclockwise from the
church, has 1550 carved in relief on the north face of its pyramidal roof in
bold, incontrovertible, foot-high figures.

The four identical posas are square in plan — 17 feet on a side — and
twice as high as wide, measuring to the top of the pyramid. The two sides
facing the atrio have archways half as wide and half as high as the flat face
they pierce (right front endpaper). Such simple accordant proportions were
probably chosen consciously; there are several other simple geometric relationships in the posa facades, church facade, and elsewhere at Huejotzingo (the
atrio is square), but it is not safe to say that all were willed by the designer,
for some may have been happy accidents, perhaps resulting from the practice
of dimensioning new work with a set of cords or rods, which would naturally
lead to measures in simple multiples. Some *may* have been willed by the
designer, nonetheless, for there are many mudéjar features in these posas,
and simple modular relationships were consciously sought in mudéjar and
late Moslem as well as in late gothic work in Spain. They had long been common in Arab work. Willed or not, the ensemble of the atrio and posas is as
harmonious as anything in sixteenth-century Mexico.

The third or southwest posa, complete except for cresting and cross at the top.

160 CARVING ON
A POSA AT
HUEJOTZINGO

    Whereas the posas at Cholula are uncritical variants of the Tlaxcala scheme, those at Huejotzingo seem to be a critique of it, avoiding its awkwardnesses, and achieving an easy and graceful coherence of form. For example, instead of a divisive cornice, there is a flat frieze framed by a neat flat band, a graceful mudéjar or preconquest way of terminating a building; the pyramid then emerges as a continuation and conclusion of the building below, and not as an abrupt and heavy lid imposed on it, as at Tlaxcala. The jambs and archivolt, though richer and livelier than at Tlaxcala, are subordinated to the block by being recessed into it a little, and they even emphasize the potential strength of the wall which enframes them by revealing some of its thickness.

318

Sculptured accents in bold clear shapes have been very knowingly applied to the harmoniously dimensioned walls of these buildings. The only elements in relief, all these accents were treated frankly as applied ornaments rather than as tectonic or pseudo-tectonic architectural members. They hang on the surface without crowding it in the way that both the sculpture and archivolts do at Tlaxcala, where the sculpture is not only coarser but less adapted to the shape of the spandrels. At Huejotzingo the flying angels with the Instruments of the Passion fit naturally into their spandrels. There must have been 16 of these angels carrying 16 Instruments before those on the southeast posa were chipped off by soldiers billetted there during the revolution of 1910–20. One easily imagines the teaching friars walking their pupils around the atrio, telling the story of the Passion, and explaining its significance, while pointing out the different carvings which illustrate, symbolize, and commemorate it.

Above the arches are shields with the monograms of Mary and Jesus, topped by bold crowns, symbols of Christian majesty, which link the spandrels to the frieze above. Here there are four more shields with the Franciscan emblem of the Five Wounds of Christ, similar to the shields of the posa parapet at Tlaxcala. Now weathered and defaced, bones and a skull denoting Golgotha appear on the front face of the pyramids. While the dedications of the individual posas to the Assumption, Saint John the Baptist, Saints Peter and Paul, and Saint James may have dictated the themes painted inside, they did not affect the iconographical scheme of the exteriors at all, for that refers only to the Passion and to the Franciscan Order. (At Tlaxcala there had been no unified scheme: a Stigmatization is paired with a Saint Dominic.)

A plump knotted rope bounds each arch circumferentially, and then turns outward at the springing, then upward, then over, to form an enveloping rectangular panel into which the arch is set (a mudéjar *alfiz*). From one side of this rope-archivolt depends a fat tassel, or penitential knout. Less expertly handled, this occurs also at Tlaxcala on the arch of the front door of the monastery church, one element of that building which appears to have survived from the early phases of construction.

The knotted rope is, of course, a magnification and translation into stone of the Franciscan cord, often emblematic of the Order, alluding to the rope with which Christ was bound to the column, and symbolic of chastity, temperance, and restraint. It had been used fairly often in similar architectural contexts in Spain, notably at the famous Casa del Cordón in Burgos. It had already appeared also at Santo Domingo, very boldly on the doorway of the Franciscan monastery (c1520–35), and on the Casa del Cordón there,[41] combined with similar shields but without similarities decisive enough to affiliate Huejotzingo. The cord occurs on many other Franciscan monasteries in Mexico, but nowhere else does it perform such disciplinary action in interrelating the rest of the carved ornament as it does here.

Not common in Europe, the shield with the Five Wounds was the regular Franciscan emblem in sixteenth-century New Spain, as an allusion not only to the Wounds of Christ, but also to their counterparts in the five stigmata of Saint Francis. The blood is profuse, and highly stylized in the Indian manner, sometimes (as on the Cross at Ciudad Hidalgo) stylized beyond recognition; it can look more like a flattened pine cone, pineapple, or *chirimoya,* than like rivulets of blood.

161 THE FIVE WOUNDS OF CHRIST *carved on the facade of the church at* HUEJOTZINGO *with the three Nails, all encircled by a Franciscan cord ending in a penitential knout.*

162 ARMS OF PHILIP II *encircled by the chain of the Order of the Golden Fleece, a woodcut used on the title page of Doctor Vasco de Puga's* Cedulario, *printed in Mexico City by Pedro Ocharte in 1563.*

Some of the archivolts at Huejotzingo, many-layered to correspond to their many-shafted jambs, are carved with a flattened chain. The arch of the north doorway of the church is encircled by a different chain, with the B-shaped links of flint and steel of the hyperaristocratic Order of the Golden Fleece. Its presence here would seem to ask for more explanation than the mere fact that Charles V was Grand Master, and had recently called the first meeting in many years (1531), and the fact that the Order was vowed to protect the Church and defend and propagate the Faith. Why does it occur again on the choir windows of Santa Cruz in Antigua (Guatemala)? Such symbolism in Spanish America has been little studied. In Spain, where heraldry was handled like an exact science, its vocabulary would not have been borrowed freely for mere ornamentation. The chain of the Golden Fleece was often used in Spain — properly — to enclose the royal arms on official buildings, and it appears in the same way in many books (for example, Cervantes de Salazar's 1545 translation of Luis Vives; the 1552 Toledo Serlio; Gómara's 1554 *History of the Indies;* or Cervantes de Salazar's 1554 *Chronicle,* all of special interest in New Spain). In Mexico this distinguished chain was well known in appearance, if not in meaning; perhaps it was considered merely as an attribute of royalty, and as such it appeared appropriately around royal arms on the *Casas Reales* at Tlaxcala before 1550, and the printer Ochoa would put it around the arms in Doctor Puga's official *Cedulario* of 1563. It has been claimed — without proof — that the royal favor enjoyed by the Franciscans allowed them to enclose their emblems with the same prestigious chain. Here, however, it encloses only a doorway. Nowhere else, apparently, did the Franciscans use it, save in one imitation of Huejotzingo (at Calpan) where it was so misunderstood as to be all but unidentifiable.

163 CARVING around the arch of THE NORTH DOORWAY AT HUEJOTZINGO

The chains on the posa archivolts at Huejotzingo are plainer than the Golden Fleece chain on the north doorway. Similar simple chains run around the handsome hospital which Ferdinand and Isabella had built at Santiago de Compostela, there alluding specifically to the chains of the Christian captives they had liberated from the Moors of Granada. (On other buildings, the chain seems only to signify that they had slept there.) The armorial bearings Cortés was given with his title were surrounded by a chain, the only part of his new blazon without a clear meaning; [42] probably it is an attribute of nobility or of royal favor. The idea that all such chains must have more than abstract heraldic meaning is denied by the biggest ones in Spain, with links like motorcycle tires, running around the chapel of the Vélez family by the Cathedral of Murcia, unrelated to captives or Catholic Kings; and the idea that they must have some Christian symbolism weakens when one sees them in the *alfiz* of the Puerta de las Armas of the Alhambra. It is not clear what they mean in Mexico if, indeed, they mean anything. Perhaps

321

they are just a pretty pattern, admired and casually borrowed by an un-worldly friar-designer, no more significant than most merlons, or the loosely woven half-mudéjar net which surrounds the doorway leading from the nave of Huejotzingo into its sacristy, or the pretty basketwork bases at Tecama-chalco not far away. Here there is *no* meaning, whereas in Spain, even at Murcia, while not symbolic, they still are elements in systematic heraldry.

164 HUEJOTZINGO
doorway to the sacristy

The sprouts and palmettes radiating from the arch of this north doorway, matching the palmette cresting of the posas, may be an Indianization of mo-tives recently fashionable in Spain, such as those on the Italianate portal of the Medinaceli Palace at Cogolludo (1492–95) or on the Puerta de la Pellejería (1516) and other doorways and tombs at Burgos. Their genesis is half in antique and half in mudéjar foliate patterns. The similarity of the posa ropes to those in the Casa del Cordón has already hinted that someone at Huejotzingo may have known work at Burgos. The sprouts and palmettes of the north door at Huejotzingo seem to be evolving into the rank jungle blossoms of the manoelino, the mudéjar- and perhaps Hindu-tinged late gothic of Portugal; in fact, they look more like those on the Church of the Marvila at Santarem than like any Spanish examples.

The presence of the chains on the archivolts of the posas at Huejotzingo again suggests manoelino, which often used both ropes and chains among other nautical equipment as part of its omnivorous decorative vocabulary. Also, if they were similar to the cross now in the atrio (which may have been one of them), then the crosses atop the posas at Huejotzingo must have used a late-gothic motive common enough in Spain and Germany but a particular favorite with manoelino carvers: twisted vine stalks with all branches cut off. There were several Portuguese among the Franciscans who came to

Mexico early enough to have been effective at Huejotzingo, but there is nothing there which is exclusively Portuguese. Hauntingly like though some motives and the general succulence may be, the resemblance could be fortuitous. Manoelino and Mexican may instead be cousins, descended both from the same international late-gothic and mudéjar lines.

The carving of the relief around the north door at Huejotzingo is lower than that on the posas, although it really needs to be higher because it enjoys sunlight only three weeks in the year; hence it is by no means as effective as the bolder but smaller areas of carving on the posas. The posas, which accomplish more with less, are perhaps a refinement of the work on the doorway, and therefore may be a little later. Furthermore it is unlikely that posas would be built before the church was well along. If this is so, the doorway would have to have been carved before 1550.

One of the two arches of the portería has concentric archivolt bands of the same chain that runs around the posa arches, and thus suggests that the portería (reopened *c*1900/10, and perhaps then patched or rebuilt) [43] may have been carved at about the same time as the posas. The wildly provincial center "column" of the portería — no column at all, but possibly the biggest freestanding baluster in the world — shows the designer's enthusiasm for fancy

165 HUEJOTZINGO
*baluster-column
of the portería*

forms and his naïveté in using them. The hypertrophy of scale suggests that his source lay not in any real architecture that he had seen, but rather in some engraving of architecture that did not make the original scale clear to him. Perhaps he was stimulated by a chapter in Diego de Sagredo's *Medidas del Romano* (1526, 1539, 1542, 1543, and later), provocatively entitled "The Formation of Columns called Monstruous, Candelabras, and Balusters," in which he could have read without having been hampered by many illustrations that such were often found on ancient buildings though not in ancient treatises. Juan de Arfe's later treatise would have done much the same.[44] This, and the miscellany of other decorative elements, tame and wild — the baluster, the different chains, the ropes, the bleeding Wounds, the monograms, the Instrument-bearing angels — most probably came from pictures in books shown to manually competent but unlettered carvers.

Despite the manoelino and plateresque overtones of the closely related north door, the dominant character of the posas is more mudéjar than is at first apparent: the flat strips of wall enclosing the recessed jambs, the *alfiz*

323

enclosing the arch, the flat band enclosing the frieze of shields are all typical mudéjar devices, as must also have been the repeated entwinings of the openwork cresting. The mudéjar character is not just skin deep, nor just a matter of ornament: take away the cresting, the carved symbols, even the pyramid, and a basic Huejotzingo posa could pass as a legitimate cousin of the Puerta de la Justicia of the Alhambra.

Each of the posas is dedicated to a Saint or Mystery and there were confraternities identically dedicated, each of which cared for its own posa. At the end of the seventeenth century each ward of Huejotzingo had its own *ermita* in the corner of the atrio, obviously a posa, obviously still in use. Here they sang on Sundays, and from here they buried their dead. The four-part division seems still to have been by the barrios of the town and not by confraternities, since the latter had already been multiplied beyond four.[45]

Calpan

San Andrés Calpan, once Ixcalpan, "place of many houses," is a pretty village set among walnut groves at the foot of Popocatépetl. In its atrio, half the size of that at Huejotzingo nearby, stand the most ornamented posas in Mexico. They were unknown until studied and published thirty years ago by the historian Rafael García Granados, whose family's vast hacienda included the town.

The confraternities of the village still maintain their rights to individual posas here — each major-domo keeps the key — and they still arrange fiestas on their patron's days. Inside, over the altars, the late sixteenth-century retables remain in place, perhaps largely intact under blankets of inept repaint.[46] The ensemble is unique, and one hopes that it will be better preserved than the cloister, north door, or the inside of the monastery church (which, though ruined by graceless rebuilding, still contains a precious but neglected sixteenth-century feather-mosaic of the *Salvator Mundi*).

Although each of the four posas is different, their basic scheme and much of their decoration relates them closely to one another, and also to the posas at Huejotzingo. Calpan has been considered both the forerunner and the follower but, since Huejotzingo was founded much earlier and was always more important and as its posas show more coherent and disciplined design in both the ensemble and the decoration, Calpan seems more likely the derivative. In preconquest times Calpan had been a subject or a minor ally of Huejotzingo; it had been evangelized from Huejotzingo, and before it was given its monastery it had been a visita of Huejotzingo.

The date of all the work at Calpan is uncertain. Although the source for the assumption is not clear, the monastery is said to have been begun in 1548.[47] (Locally 1548 is accepted, and accordingly there was a quatercentenary celebration in 1948, with ear-splitting band music and fantastic fireworks.) The entire monastic establishment appears to have been built in one campaign, and since the posas would naturally have come nearer its end than beginning, they would presumably have been built some time after 1550, a bit later than the dated posas at Huejotzingo. Laborers and experienced craftsmen could have been sent from neighboring Huejotzingo to work at Calpan and, as they were now already experienced, they may have worked with less direct European supervision. Although more European models were used for the ornamentation of the posas, the models were followed less strictly. The result, consequently, is less European and more tequitqui. If Tepoztlán has the most European posas, Calpan and Epazoyucan can claim the most Mexican.

Whether the same who worked at Huejotzingo or not, skilled craftsmen were surely available for, after having been shown the plans, Calpan Indians were entrusted with building the Old Cathedral at Puebla in 1536. Most of their tribute was remitted for working on this important building, and they had it virtually completed by 1541. Father Motolinía found it "very impressive, stronger and larger than any other yet built in all New Spain." Others found it "sumptuous." The fact that its three aisles were entered from "three richly carved portals" is what may make its possible relation to work at Calpan significant.[48]

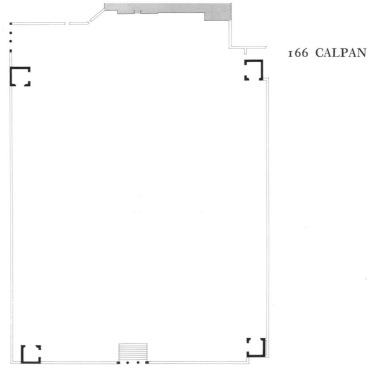

166 CALPAN

POSAS

The posas at Calpan are not rigidly fitted into the plan of the atrio. Those nearest the church do not toe the line of its facade, as is most often the scheme, but stand well out from it, a bit to the west. The first posa is pushed farther along than the fourth, perhaps to make room for a triple gateway at the east end of the atrio wall. The position of this gate, clearly the main access, at the end of the north side wall rather than in the middle of the west end wall (where there is only a smaller gate) may result from the planting of the monastery on an old temple site south of the old *tianguis* or market.[49] These two posas gain greatly in prominence as a result of being pushed out of their corners, because where they are they sharply interrupt the sweep of the walls, and jut more abruptly into the atrio area. The two western posas are not in their corners either, but have been eased out a few feet to positions which make them not only more prominent but more emphatic in the way they face any counterclockwise processions around the atrio. Also, more room is left for the marchers on the right edge of such a procession.

The first posa (left rear endpaper), dedicated to the Assumption, is particularly rich, partly as a result of its peculiar location which exposes three decorated sides, the blank fourth being merged with the atrio wall in the usual way. Like its mates, this posa is edged with mudéjar bands of sparkling tequitqui carving, derived chiefly from the plateresque ornamental repertory, though here mudéjar, tequitqui, and both gothic and renaissance plateresque are all but indissolubly one. The flat surfaces and geometrical blockiness of the whole posa are emphasized by this crisp and delicate flat binding, which also runs around the arches and marks their impost level. Such enframing by ornamental bands, no more structural than a fancy tape edging, is a mudéjar characteristic which may be related as well to preconquest decorative practice: that may be why it was in such accord with native tastes. The strong Indian character of the work need reflect no specific preconquest models, but simply persistent Indian aesthetic preferences.

The pyramidal roof of the first posa is set back from the clean straight edge of the block, and its four ascending angles are emphasized, as at Huejotzingo, by a small but bold torus molding of gothic section. This is no novelty in such a location, for a similar use of the torus can be found in Spain (for example on the pyramidal roof of the covered cross at Jávea). The novelty on this posa at Calpan is that the torus stops suddenly short of the bottom and top to curl back on itself like a fat tendril or uncoiling frond. For this there does not seem to be any Spanish or relevant indigenous precedent. At the apex of the pyramid rises a ferocious Crown of Thorns and a cross (now broken) made of two entwined cactus-like trunks, more probably intended to resemble the type of the late-gothic pruned-vine cross at Huejotzingo than to recall any native flora, as some have thought. The forms which seem to look like local plants here and on the church facade are more probably the result of the innate Indian wish to stylize than of any European-engendered wish to copy natural species. Botanical identification is as difficult or impossible in the half-abstract native decorative tradition as it is in mudéjar or plateresque, and for the same reason: no particular species were usually represented. Again, Indian instinct and Spanish tradition met in agreement.

Apart from this architectural trimming, the main sculptural decoration of the first posa, displayed on the three exposed sides, consists of three extraordinary reliefs: a Madonna with the seven swords of her Seven Sorrows (or with the Seven Gifts of the Holy Spirit?), an Assumption (or Apocalyptic Virgin) amid Seraphim and monstrous abstract flowers, and an Annunciation — all works of such special interest as sculpture that discussion here would make far too long a digression. (A perceptive and rewarding study has been made by Mrs. Weismann in her *Mexico in Sculpture*.) [50]

167 THE FIRST POSA AT CALPAN (opposite)

168 *Looking west from* THE FIRST POSA AT CALPAN *to* THE SECOND, *and on to Ixtaccíhuatl.*

The second posa, dedicated to Saint Francis, has a kneeling figure of him set high on one corner. On the opposite corner kneels another figure, perhaps a donor in unusual prominence, in which case it would be the encomendero Diego de Ordaz Villagómez, heir of the conquistador Ordaz.[51] The tequitqui borders include another chain, its forms naïvely misunderstood from its presumed model, the Golden Fleece at Huejotzingo. The spandrels of the north side have gawky angels with misunderstood drapery, derived most probably from the more conventional, convincing, elegant, and vigorous angels in the spandrels at Huejotzingo. There are many medallions with lively flat decorative carving of the monograms of Jesus and Mary, the name Francis, and the Five Wounds (with sadistically large spouts of blood), some very similar to the more crisply cut medallions on the facade of the monastery church at Huejotzingo. Around the top edge sprouts a cresting still ranker and juicier

328

169 THE SECOND POSA AT CALPAN

than that at Huejotzingo: the dainty anthemions of the Puerta de la Pellejería of Burgos, transplanted to warm and fertile Calpan, have reverted to jungle weeds. Behind them rises a bulging square dome, in construction corbeled like the pyramidal tops at Huejotzingo. Suitably for a chapel dedicated to Saint Francis, the angles are emphasized by a knotted Franciscan cord instead of a plain torus.

It is not clear what crowned the apex: perhaps another cross, or perhaps the Cross-like Seraph who transmitted the marks of the Five Wounds to the Saint kneeling in ecstasy below. Save possibly for the feet, this figure is posed in a receptive attitude for stigmatization more than in one for active prayer, but the lower part of the body is now too eroded for sure evidence. The Mystery of the Stigmatization would be an appropriate climax to the sculptural scheme, and might have been thought a logical complement to the Receiving of the Seven Gifts of the Holy Spirit by the Madonna of the first posa (if that is what is represented there). The Stigmatization had been shown in several

329

familiar books, for example Fray Pedro de Gante's *Reader,* and was the subject of a Franciscan play for Indians (done at Tamazula, 1587); even more significantly, it appears on the surviving posa at Tlaxcala. If this was the subject of the sculpture at Calpan, the donor would have been part of it as a spectator kneeling in perpetual adoration.[52] Rather than Ordaz, the figure might then represent Philip II.

The third posa (right rear endpaper), dedicated to Saint Michael, has a steep pyramidal roof, almost a spire, topped by a papal tiara and a cross of uncertain significance. The angles are edged with a torus even more curiously disposed than those of the first posa: it is cut every foot or so, and the ends of each segment coil back on themselves. The effect is like gothic cresting with buds or knops, but the means are genuinely original, and perhaps come from a misunderstanding of some badly transmitted gothic model, perhaps some decorative work of liturgical equipment in metal rather than anything truly architectural. (Mrs. Weismann has convincingly shown how someone at Calpan was able to improve on inferior European models.) [53]

170 THE STIGMATIZA-
TION OF SAINT
FRANCIS
Woodcut in Fray Alonso de Molina's Náhuatl grammar and dictionary, printed in Mexico in 1571.

171 THE LAST JUDGMENT
Woodcut in Juan de Padilla's Retablo de la vida de Cristo (Seville, 1518), and several other books circulated in Mexico.

The most remarkable feature on this posa is the large Last Judgment in relief, derived ultimately from a German woodcut in the Nürnberg Chronicle of 1493, which was used again in Spain in a grammar of 1498, and reproduced many times in the sixteenth century, most often in the popular *Flos Sanctorum,* a work imported into Mexico in quantities since it was requisite in

172 THE THIRD POSA AT CALPAN

Franciscan libraries.[54] The dedications to the Virgin and Saint Francis of the preceding two posas may have been intended to prepare for this one by first introducing these two compassionate and effective intercessors before the reckoning of Judgment Day. The papal tiara crowning the pyramid might perhaps refer then to Saint Peter, not as the first pope but as the keeper of the gates of Heaven, to which the Blessed are rising. Unfortunately no clearly worked-out iconographical schemes have been traced in sixteenth-century

331

Mexican art, except for the retable of Huejotzingo.[55] Elsewhere, too, the affiliations with late mediaeval art and the scholarly theological background of some friars would probably mean that the choice of themes and saints was not casual or unsystematic. The posas at Calpan may be the clearest instance.

The fourth posa is able to offer us no further clue, for no figure sculpture is there: either it was never executed, or it has been destroyed. The top is like that of the first posa opposite, and the whole may originally have been quite similar, though clearly the work of a different and less skilled carver or carvers. The bordering bands, wider, coarser, and more like embroidery than on the other posas, are contained between more moldings, and look more like run-of-the-mill tequitqui work elsewhere.

*

The relation of the carving at Calpan to Huejotzingo and Huaquechula is complex. The Last Judgment of the Saint Michael posa at Calpan appears again over the fancy north door of the church at Huaquechula, in a much coarser handling. Accompanying it are flying angels in long crumpled robes — intended to be fluttering — like those on the Calpan and Huejotzingo posas. Also, the carving of the tequitqui front doorway of the church at Huaquechula, an increased Indianization of the blossoms on the north door at Huejotzingo, could easily have been done by the same hand which carved the fourth posa at Calpan, but not at all easily by the hand which made the fantastic north portal at Huaquechula. Added to this complicated little net of inter-relationships is the fact that the Huaquechula front door, while carved in the manner of Calpan, borrowed its design from the side door of the monastery church at Cholula, only a few hours' walk away. Clearly there are many connections between these monuments, and clearly they are of more than one kind. It is no surprise to learn that Diego de Ordaz, the encomendero of Huaquechula, was also the encomendero of Calpan and the heir of the first encomendero of Huejotzingo; or that an *alcalde* of Huejotzingo was also the *alcalde* of Huaquechula and Atlixco.[56] Friars were shifted back and

173 FOURTH POSA AT CALPAN

forth between these monasteries. In other words, people in one town were in a position to know well what was being built or proposed in the others, influential people who may have made influential suggestions.

Borrowing of motives of decoration did occur, and was probably facilitated by the circulation of drawings — the Indians had regularly communicated by means of drawings before the Spaniards and their writing came — but what sort of architectural drawings we do not know since none has been preserved. There was probably also considerable borrowing or exchange of the most skilled craftsmen, perhaps itinerant professionals, while the body of less skilled labor may more likely have been local Indians who between times were not engaged in building but in agriculture or some needed local craft.

*

The amount of supervision by Europeans must have varied. Surely there was more of it for the posas at Huejotzingo, where the work must have been done under the direction of someone at least semi-professional. There may have been almost as much at Tlaxcala and Cholula, for they have but little Indian accent, but here the supervisors must have been less schooled professionally because the total design is less coherent, less "correct," and less professional. In other words, though the work is essentially European, it lacks European refinement. There must have been the least supervision by Europeans at Calpan, but this does not result in incoherence as at Cholula and Tlaxcala, for here, apparently, Indian discipline could assert itself enough to substitute for European.

*

It would seem improbable that more than a dozen years separate the posas of Tlaxcala, Huejotzingo, Cholula, and Calpan (and perhaps the lost example at Tepeaca). The posa at Tlaxcala is probably the oldest, and the model for Cholula, which is otherwise unrelated to the group; and also the model for Huejotzingo, which is a critique of it. Huejotzingo, in turn, was the main model for Calpan, but Calpan is not so much a critique of its model as a free fantasy on the soberer theme stated by its model. A severe and conservative country cousin, the posa at Huaquechula is later, and presents no novelties.

Tentatively the following dates may be proposed:

Tlaxcala	c1547
Huejotzingo	1550
Cholula	soon after 1550
Calpan	c1555
Huaquechula	c1560

POSAS

A PARENTHESIS
(THE PROBLEM OF FRAY JUAN DE ALAMEDA
AND FOUR CHURCHES)

While scattered facts are known about a few professional architects who built a few buildings in the sixteenth century in New Spain, less is known about the friar-architects who built voluminously more. One about whom we know the most, and who may have been one of the most active, was Fray Juan de Alameda.[57] He arrived in Mexico with Bishop-elect Zumárraga in December 1528. The next year he moved the old town of Huejotzingo (said to number 80,000 souls) from a gorge at the foot of Ixtaccíhuatl to a more comfortable flat site. Here he proceeded to build something "in a short time." Before the year was over, it was presumably this — whatever it was — that housed not only the friars but Cortés and several important gentlemen who could not have been put in Indian huts. Father Mendieta, and Torquemada and Vetancurt copying him, said clearly that Fray Juan built "the" monastery at Huejotzingo (which may be better understood as "a" monastery). They said also that he was Guardian of the monastery at Tula in 1539, and again two or three times later. There he "put the town in order" and taught the natives "good habits." These same writers said that he completed the monastery at Huaquechula, where he had already built the "sumptuous church," and that he died there about 1570. According to Torquemada alone, he also made the monastery church at Atlixco, which had been begun by Motolinía.[58] These items from the older written sources are not easily related to what is now visible at the monasteries named. (An untraceable legend, of which both the age and reliability are suspect, gives Fray Juan an Indian assistant named Bernardino, who had been trained in the school of Fray Pedro de Gante in the capital.) [59]

It is unlikely that Fray Juan could have begun any substantial work at Huejotzingo as early as 1529 — the year he made the move — or that such work could still have been in construction in 1532, although we know that Indians, already decimated from overwork and forced transplanting, took refuge in something being built at that time. There are puzzling notices, however, of a church "as grand as San Juan de los Reyes in Toledo" and "the most marvelous and sumptuous seen in our times," but they come from minions of Nuño de Guzmán who were testifying to discredit the clergy; such statements made by such "witnesses" under such conditions are not to be trusted. It is possible — even probable — that some older building was adapted and redecorated. 1529–32 was no propitious time for large-scale monastery undertakings: the First Audiencia had made them difficult anywhere, and particularly in Huejotzingo, with which they were in open conflict until the end of 1530; moreover countless Huejotzingo Indians had just died from the effects of being dislocated from their sheltered cañon out to the open plain, and from being forced to carry their tributes of produce 50 miles over the mountains to the capital. Furthermore, it is doubtful if all of them (35,000, over 40,000, 100,000, or 200,000 according to different accounts) could have been moved to the present site by 1529, or that busy Fray Juan could yet have had time to master enough Náhuatl to move very many or build very much.[60]

Possibly there was some preliminary exodus in those years, followed in some months by a major move to the present site, which had meanwhile been being prepared for a permanent settlement. If this did happen, as seems likely, whatever it was that was being built "in a short time," in 1529 would have been no more than an adaptation of an old building, or some sort of new half-improvised monastery. (Some think that fragments of it may survive at nearby Teopanzolco: these shapeless hummocks could be of such a monastery, but they could just as well be almost anything else.) The first provisional building, wherever it was, would not have been pretentious, and Father Motolinía, Guardian at Huejotzingo in 1529, did not find it worth mentioning — at least in any of his preserved writings — and had there been anything worth mentioning, he probably would have done so.[61]

The work known to have been building in 1532, when Fray Jacopo de Testera was Guardian, might, then, have been a *second* monastery, perhaps somewhere in the present town. Although careful Father Motolinía did not mention this either — he had been transferred away — it must have been advanced enough in 1533 to house the small Chapter Meeting held there that year. Furthermore, while in 1536 the citizens of Puebla assented to Viceroy Mendoza's proposal to send Indian masons from Huejotzingo to work on their first little cathedral, such workmen would presumably not have been considered available had they still been busy on their own home church in Huejotzingo. Therefore it was probably this second establishment which was left standing until 1560, during the building of the *third* monastery, that which so handsomely ornaments the town today.[62]

Had this third monastery been built by Fray Juan before he left for Tula in 1539 — as some have thought — it would have to have been built very early in the 1530's or else after 1536 and before 1539. Neither date, however, is acceptable. Early in the 1530's is *very* early for a surviving Mexican building, and no comparable church or monastery can be dated then. Nor can it be believed that anything of importance was built after the workmen left in 1536 and before Fray Juan left in 1539; the life of Fray Martín de Valencia, who was Guardian in 1539, was exceptionally well recorded, and no work of his at Huejotzingo was mentioned by anyone, although unspecified work he did at Tlaxcala was faithfully recorded by Father Mendieta. In view of all these scattered bits of fact and inference, the vague but probable and datable first adaptation of 1529 and second presumably new construction of '32 must be dissociated from the existing buildings, as must anything built before the 1540's.[63]

The existing buildings were more probably begun in the 1540's, perhaps in 1544, just before the plague. There must have been delay during and after the plague, for sometimes hundreds would die in one day, and the city was at times almost deserted (according to Fray Domingo de Betanzos). The Huejotzincos were treated very harshly in the years between the plague and 1550, and can have given little extra service for the friars' building operations.[64] In other words, work may have progressed vigorously in 1544 and into '45, but then only slowly for the next five years.

The first incontrovertible date specifically given to architecture at the monastery is the big 1 5 5 0 so tangibly carved on one posa. There is some reason to think that either the main operations were over in 1557, in time for a Chapter Meeting in 1558 — which would mean that they must have been more energetic in the last years — or else, as Professor Kubler has proposed, that the work was interrupted at about that time or a little later for a few years, and then resumed in a simpler style, and at last concluded in 1571. Some native annals say that the monastery was finished in 1570, which in old Mexican facts and figures may be the same thing. As the population was declining about 1000 a year during the 1560's, it is easy to believe that the work was slowly brought to a modest ending in those years.[65]

Indeterminate though these assembled bits of evidence and conjecture may seem, together they do consistently indicate, without contradiction, that the main part of the present establishment was built c1544–c57, and the rest then finished in about 15 years. Fray Juan, during his recorded stay (1529–39) could not have built any of it. He could, however, already have moved the town, laid out its plan, and put up some sort of *provisional* monastery. He could also have prepared for a more pretentious permanent monastery by beginning the big platform and gathering building materials — good cut stone from local monuments, or from some of the scores of temples or the mountainous pyramid at Cholula.

At Tula, where Fray Juan went in 1539, the handsome church does not importantly resemble that at Huejotzingo except in three stony, structural features: the huge platform on which it stands; the good masonry of which it is constructed; and the ribbed vaulting which covers its nave. This church was not put up until the 1550's — either 1550–54 or 1553–61 according to different records — *after* Fray Juan had surely left Tula for good. Some say it was begun by Fray Antonio de San Juan on orders from Father Motolinía, or by Fray Alonso Rangel (after 1546) and finished by Fray Antonio de San Juan, or else that a church was begun earlier on orders from Bishop Zumárraga, and then (possibly) completed "neatly" by Fray Juan de Alameda.

Apparently contradictory, these notices need not really conflict because they need not all refer to the same building. The last notice could refer to an early preliminary church, which was later turned into a hospital, and whose ruins perhaps are those which still rise on a hill near the Tolteca temples a few miles from the monastery town. No one stated that Fray Juan had anything to do with the big church in town, which could perfectly well have been made by Fray Alonso Rangel and Fray Antonio de San Juan in the 1550's. During his several terms as Guardian of Tula, Fray Juan de Alameda could not only have finished the first little church near the temples, but could also have moved the town from the hillside by the temples to the flat site by the river, where it still is (just as he moved Huejotzingo). Sometime in the late 1540's, he might have begun the platform on which the monastery, the big church, and the atrio at Tula rest (as he may also have done at Huejotzingo), for the platform must have been ready when the church was begun on it in 1550 or '53. Finally, he may also have gathered building materials from the demolished neighborhood temples (as he may already have done also at Huejotzingo). Someone surely did this, for not only is the entire church faced with good ashlar (as at Huejotzingo) but so also is the atrio wall, 14 feet high and some 2,000 feet long; archaeologists have not yet suggested from which preconquest monument of Tolteca Tula this extraordinary subtraction might have been made. Although no notices confirm it, it could also have been possible for Fray Juan to have planned and laid out the fine big monastery church before he left, but he could not have carried it up very far.[66]

Any coordination among the miscellaneous resemblances in the four of the churches associated with Fray Juan could be validated only if it could be shown that he dominated the design of the surviving churches at Tula and Huejotzingo. At Tula he could have controlled the preparatory scheme and perhaps the beginnings of the construction. At Huejotzingo he can hardly have had anything at all to do with the present church if he left for good in 1539. If, however, he had returned there from Tula sometime in the 1540's, then he could have been responsible for much of what is there: he could have begun to build the new monastery in the 1540's, just when we suppose it to have been begun. Although there is no clear documentary evidence that he did, the hypothesis may be strengthened by one curious coincidental but otherwise inexplicable fact: in 1576 some Indians he had trained in making aqueducts were called from Huejotzingo, 6 years after he died. Had he left for good in 1539, they would have had to have been trained 37 years before they were called; but if his training was still fresh enough to be effective, it must have been given less than 37 years before; if men he had trained were young enough to move big stones, it can hardly have been more than about 15 years. This would indicate that he *had* come back, and was at Huejotzingo while the preserved church and monastery were building.[67]

337

POSAS

It would be possible, then, to believe that Fray Juan worked first in some preliminary way on the design of the existing church at Tula, and then successively on the design and construction of the existing churches at Huejotzingo, Atlixco, and Huaquechula, all documented as his. As these last three are all within an easy day's journey of one another, he could easily have gone back to one from another to oversee the completion of any slow work.

While the good masonry and ribbed vaulting of the churches at Huejotzingo and Tula are found also at Atlixco and Huaquechula, is this enough to make all four acceptable as the work of one man? Possibly, but not definitively, for similar cut-stone masonry and rib-vaulting exist elsewhere (for example, at Franciscan Cholula and Franciscan Tochimilco, both close by. Cholula, in addition, is built on a plan which is a close variant of that of Huejotzingo.) While the four churches have much in common, they do not have it in common only with one another, and therefore they cannot be classified together as one distinct stylistic group.

If Fray Juan had been responsible for the main design of the big masonry churches and for some of the monastery buildings at the four sites for which there is written evidence, he would have been kept very busy, and might well have left much of the decoration to other friar-foremen or to Indian carvers. It would be hard to synthesize one artistic personality from all the miscellaneous resemblances in the presumably contemporary decorative work remaining here, but as the discussion of posas has already shown workmen not only could but probably did move back and forth between the Franciscan houses in the fertile valleys near Puebla (though not to distant Tula which, significantly, has entirely different detail).

The relation of Calpan to this group could then be elucidated. Although Calpan has been attributed to Fray Juan in modern times on grounds of style,[68] such an offhand assumption must be based on decorative features only. Without having anything to do with Fray Juan, itinerant craftsmen, here as elsewhere, could easily have repeated ornamental elements from Huejotzingo on buildings designed by someone else. There is no strictly architectural resemblance — as distinguished from decorative — between Calpan and the four churches possibly to be associated with Fray Juan. Cholula could be assimilated more convincingly than Calpan, and a better case could be made for Tochimilco. Hence there is no real reason to connect Fray Juan with Calpan if one believes him to have been the creator of the big vaulted churches at Huejotzingo, Atlixco, Huaquechula, and perhaps the beginnings of Tula.

Of the buildings associated with him, the only two with similar ornamentation are Atlixco and Huejotzingo, and their decoration is similar only in some parts, not in others. The eleven tequitqui medallions on the facade of Atlixco, for example, look like the seven on the facade of Huejotzingo (allusive to the Seven Joys of the Virgin, celebrated in the sevenfold Franciscan Crown or Seraphic Rosary?). In fact, the whole front of Atlixco, if disembarrassed of the later imposition of columns, would be closely compatible with the front of Huejotzingo. Furthermore, the membering around the front doorway of Atlixco resembles parts of the fantastic north doorway of Huejotzingo and the unfinished opening above it. There are also resemblances to the ornamentation of the posas. Close though these similarities may be, the carving does not seem to be by the same hands: Atlixco seems to be trimmed with summary quick copies of finer work at Huejotzingo. There is no substantial reason to assume that these are based on designs by Fray Juan: they have little counterpart in what might be assumed to be the rest of his work. The decorative correspondences in the Franciscan monasteries near Puebla, including parts of Atlixco and Huejotzingo as well as parts of almost all of their Franciscan neighbors, are many, varied, and inconsistent, as already indicated by their posas: these relationships seem to point not to any one guiding hand, but to several, or to several groups, traveling carvers or traveled friars asking carvers to copy admired models.

If, nevertheless, Fray Juan were to be credited with some of the decorative schemes, it would still be impossible to say which, for the blunt gusto of the Indian carvers was too assertive to enable us to distinguish any clear sets of artistic ideas or intentions underneath, like a sauce that makes all meats subordinate and alike in taste. It is far more credible to hypothecate a Fray Juan who made the main design for Tula, Huejotzingo, Atlixco, and Huaquechula, and left their decoration to others. In other words, it is easier to accept him as a strictly architectural architect.

If he was responsible for the main fabric of these three or four fine churches and for some of their more architectural enrichment (as opposed to decorative or sculptural), he was a distinguished architect, but hardly distinguishable from whoever was responsible for the fine Franciscan churches at nearby Cholula and Tochimilco, or even Puebla itself (unless, of course, they are the result of the influence of his expert professional presence in the neighborhood, if not of his actual direction). For the time being, unless new facts are brought out of some archive, it seems better to leave him a ghost, and to go no farther than Professor Angulo in grouping all of these related churches — Fray Juan's and their neighbors — into one coherent but anonymous "School of Puebla." [69] Fray Juan might be called its *chef d'école*, but only tentatively and perhaps temporarily. There is no way of routing the possibility that he was not an architect at all, but just an effective entrepreneur who managed to see that several handsome buildings were built.

IX

THE OPEN CHAPEL

*The patios in this country are very spacious . . . as the number
of people is large and the churches are too small to accommodate
them. The chapels are outside, in the patio, arranged in such a way
that all the Indians can attend Holy Mass every Sunday and feast
day, whereas the churches are used for this purpose during the
week.* — *Father Motolinía (c1540)* [1]

MORE than catechizing or making processions, the celebrating of Masses
was the most important of the uses of the atrio: this was the prime reason
for its existence. Proper celebration of the Mass demanded proper housing
for the celebrant, the altar, and the ritual. The open chapel could provide
this satisfactorily. In view of its role in the religious life of the Indians, and
the fact that it was the Indians' religious life rather than their own which
had brought the friars from Spain to New Spain, it is not surprising to find
that the open chapels were sometimes more elaborate or in a few cases more
spacious than the neighboring monastery churches. In combination with their
atrios, the chapels could contain many more worshipers. Since the combination had been created for the Indian congregations, the chapel was commonly called a *capilla de indios* by contemporary writers.[2] The term now
most often used, "open chapel," was introduced a generation ago by Manuel
Toussaint.

The Spaniards were considered a special group, and were served in
normal churches, intended to be like those they had known in Spain. Increasingly these were administered by the seculars. In the capital, the Spanish families of a neighborhood would go to one of their own parish churches,
while the Indians of the same quarter would go instead to their own *capilla
de indios* at the Franciscan monastery. The same was true in the other cities
built for Spaniards; in Puebla, as many of the Indians as possible were sent
to hear Mass at their own chapel in Indian Cholula nearby.[3] Rejected by the
civilian Spaniards except as laborers, servants, or concubines, the Indians
were welcomed by the friars, and given their own place of worship, their outdoor church, different from the churches of the Spaniards.

340

THE OPEN CHAPEL

When they had no other place to go to Mass, the Spaniards would go to the monastery churches, and some always preferred them. The friars, too, were constantly using their monastery churches for conventual Masses and the offices they had to say daily — Matins, Compline, Vespers, Nones, and so on. Consequently, for the first fifty or sixty years, the Indians' outdoor church was virtually the only place in New Spain where a sizable native congregation could attend Masses regularly on Sundays and feast days.

The open chapel was presumably a regular feature in the first establishments the friars built for their Indians, whether converted, being converted, or about to be converted. In the few towns where they had not built an open chapel — or not yet — the procedure at times of peak load seems to have been much the same as though there already was a chapel: "Those for whom there is not room in the church do not for that reason go away, but they stay outside in front of the doorway; and there in the patio they pray and follow the ceremony like those inside, getting up, kneeling, and making reverence at the same times" (c1540).[4] In such cases the monastery church served — somewhat clumsily — as the chapel for those in the atrio.

Usually, however, some sort of open chapel would be the first building that was put up: in order to protect the provisional altar. At Puebla, for example, one was readied on the Tuesday after the Easter Sunday when the town was founded. Some of these pre-church chapels were little more than huts with thatched roofs, or *xacales*,[5] such as were made at many of the Augustinian foundations in Michoacán (Tiripetío, Tacámbaro, Ucareo, Cuitzeo, Yuriand, and Zacapu). Before there was any church at Chiautla, there was a *xacal* chapel in the atrio with four friars to administer it (1571). Once Fray Juan de San Miguel had founded San Miguel el Grande (now Allende), he made a *xacal*, and it served until a proper church could be built; at Patamba he made a temporary chapel to be used by the town (1557) while he awaited a sign from Heaven to indicate the exact spot on which he should erect the permanent church. When the Franciscans formed the half-Aztec-half-Otomí town of Tlalnepantla (in the 1560's), and established a monastery there, they did not get around to finishing its church for another thirty years: meanwhile, they used an open chapel. Not far away, at San Cristóbal Ecatepec, the Franciscans had a nice stone monastery building, but no church, only something provisional, or "borrowed" as they often said. They did the same at Tepetitlán and many other places.[6]

It is hard to say which were truly proto-open-chapels and which were proto-monastery-churches, for provisional *xacales* served as both until the two functions were separated and given separate buildings; but whichever one it was to lead to, the ordinary *xacal* must have functioned at first more like an open chapel than like a normal roofed church.

THE OPEN CHAPEL

What is most significant here is that when the friars were beginning a friary, whether one of penetration or occupation, they made some sort of chapel as soon as they could because it was the single most important integer in the monastery scheme. They could live in old Indian buildings, recite their offices in them, and even say their own conventual Masses in them; they could teach the Indians their Catechism in old buildings or old courtyards, and preach to them there: but in no building could they suitably celebrate Holy Mass for their Indian converts until they built it themselves. During both the Conquest and Conversion, many Masses must have been said entirely outdoors, or under a temporary shield of cloth, thatch, or wood, because there was no place else to say them, but Masses without a chapel must always have been recognized as a makeshift once the Conversion was well under way.

Only after the arrangements for Mass, Catechism, and the other steps in indoctrination had been satisfactorily made, could the friars begin to build the parts of the monastery where they themselves were to live. Surprisingly, but logically, the church was often the last component of the group to be built, and consequently it was the part most likely to be delayed, postponed, or renounced.

Once the monastery church was completed, or well along, the first temporary open chapel would often be replaced by an architecturally more respectable structure of masonry; or sometimes, if it had not been too flimsily improvised, the first chapel might be kept on as the regular Indian chapel after the monastery church was done. There was such variety in procedures that an open chapel cannot be dated by the date of its accompanying church even in the instances where that is known. As there are even fewer notices of them than of monastery churches, it is not possible to fix exact dates for more than a handful.

The visitas of the monasteries, which functioned like monasteries insofar as the native congregations were concerned, were often provided with both atrios and open chapels. Many had nothing else, for nothing else was needed — there were no resident friars who had to have a place to sleep, eat, or celebrate daily offices — unless there were quite a few Spanish settlers in the neighborhood.

Where there were Indian parishes administered by seculars, the Indians must usually have attended the parish church. Inasmuch as there were few Indian parishes until the last quarter of the century, and even then the congregations were smaller, there cannot have been the same pressures which had brought the open chapel into being in the monasteries. The Council of 1585 effectively prohibited open chapels for seculars when it ruled that their Masses were to be said only in properly consecrated churches and oratories; significantly it was made clear that this rule need not apply to friars.[7] In some cases, however, secular parishes did have open chapels, but these must have

342

been exceptions which imitated monastery forms, perhaps more from inertia than from need. Possibly the Council considered that these *were* churches, and intended its ruling to mean that Masses were not to be said where there was no building at all, but more probably the ruling meant that the open chapels themselves were to be replaced by conventional buildings. As so little secular church building of the sixteenth century survives, and as the contemporary texts mention monasteries about thirty times as often as parish churches — perhaps because there were thirty times more regular than secular writers — it would not be safe to insist on this either way.

EUROPEAN SOURCES?

While European architectural traditions had been adequate for the church and monastery buildings, and native tradition had probably provided the atrio, neither European nor native tradition offered any suitable model for the forms of the open chapel. There are not even any superficially similar antecedents which, as in the case of the atrio, deserve discussion — and dismissal — in more than a few lines. Although there had been open-air worship in Europe, it was only under circumstances too occasional to have engendered any architectural type, circumstances quite unlike those ever-present in Mexico.[8] At the Piazza del Campo in Siena, for example, the outdoor chapel at the foot of the campanile of the Palazzo Pubblico — which might seem at first like an open chapel — had been made as a place for people to venerate a votive Madonna put there after the Black Death: it was no more than a special oratory where occasional commemorative Masses could be said. Never, as in New Spain, was there an open chapel in Europe which was a sanctuary arranged for regular outdoor Masses, with its own congregation which belonged there rather than under the roof of any church.

Although the European architectural vocabulary and either European or native building techniques were used, its *own form* had to be found for this new type of Christian sanctuary. Naturally there was experimentation, and a greater variety of schemes was tried than in other parts of the monastery complex. No single entirely satisfactory architectural solution was found at the beginning, though the need was then particularly acute. Even in the last half of the century, the open chapel never became so standardized as the monastery church — no such august traditions weighed on its growth — and no set scheme can have been included in the standard plans recommended for monasteries. Rarely were open chapels in any "pure" style, in the sense of *late gothic, mudéjar,* or *plateresque.* They often show novel combinations of elements from different stylistic sources, which again perhaps reveal their lack of architectural pedigree. They are provincial, not in the pejorative but in the essential meaning of the word.

343

THE OPEN CHAPEL

LOCATION, PREVALENCE, DISTRIBUTION

Although the open chapel might or might not be physically a part of the monastery building — there are different types and different locations — its use made it functionally a part of the atrio, or vice versa, for it served as the sanctuary of the open-air church of which the atrio was the roofless nave. It was not always set in the same place in relation to the church and monastery building, but in the atrio it was invariably set back of an area large enough to hold a fair-sized congregation.

When not sunk like a deep loggia or apse in the facade of the monastery building, or otherwise closely integrated with it, the open chapel was allowed to stand free as an architectural entity, often on the north side of the church (the monastery building being normally on the more sheltered south). Here, facing parallel to the church, it was kept well back to insure adequate space in front. The atrio then took the form of an L, with one arm in front of the church, big enough for processions and small crowds, and the other arm in front of the chapel, big enough for a congregation. When there is an L-shaped atrio with an ample side arm which does *not* lead to an open chapel (as at Xochimilco, or Culhuacán) we may wonder whether one may not once have been there. Sometimes, such arms may have been related instead to one of those strangely important north doors. Sometimes the north door may have been elaborate because through it came the friar in his priestly vestments, accompanied by attendants carrying the cross, chalice, candlesticks, and other liturgical equipment for a service at the altar of the open chapel. The north door, then, would have been the most important entrance to the outdoor church, for through it would pass the Host.

*

Although there is mention of open chapels in early texts, there are no securely dated early examples. Open chapels were surely in use in the 1530's at some prominent Franciscan monasteries, such as México-Tenochtitlán, and they had probably become relatively common by the 1540's, during the intensive missionary and building campaigns. They must have been found to function well in these conversion drives — days of architectural desperation one would suppose — and they were particularly welcomed because they could be built quickly and with little specially trained labor.

During the 1540's, when they became a familiar component of the monastic complex, two fundamental types took shape:

> the single cell, and
> the portico chapel.

Throughout the century these two types continued dominant, although of course there were variations, some with striking individuality, and a few with startling waywardness.

344

Texts indicate that after the middle of the century every normal Franciscan monastery had some sort of open chapel. Though nothing is left, it may be supposed that San Juan Teotihuacán, for example, must have been so equipped, since it was the chosen model for subsequent monasteries of modest scale. Even the Franciscan houses in cities for Spaniards — the capital and Puebla — were given open chapels facing their atrios. The cathedrals may sometimes have had a similar sort of annex for catechising and preaching to the Indians.[9]

It is not clear whether all Dominican or Augustinian houses had open chapels. Since the Dominicans built one as part of their central house in the south, in the city of Oaxaca (not the superb existing establishment), it seems likely that many other houses were similar in scheme though probably not in details. Father Mendieta specifically said in one passage that *all* the monasteries in New Spain had walled atrios, and that the natives heard their Mass and sermon there on Sundays — presumably from an open chapel.[10] In other passages he seems to have mentioned this as something in the past: there need be no contradiction, for the first passage may have been written early — it could refer to times before the plague of 1576 — and the others may have been written late in the century. It is possible, furthermore, that by "all" he meant only "all Franciscan" monasteries. That would imply that there must have been an open chapel at Xochimilco, for example, as the L-shaped atrio suggests (ill. 93). The church is exceptionally large, it is true, but so is the atrio and so was the population and number of nearby visitas.

There could not be any Mass without an altar, and there could not be any altar in the atrio without the protection of a chapel unless something temporary was set up every Sunday and feast day. While possible in emergencies, the latter cannot have been the weekly procedure in an established town, though we do know that in little-served visitas there were no permanent architectural provisions. It is safe to assume that the great majority of the friaries did have open chapels because they were so imperatively needed for the expanding native congregations — at least until these were diminished by the plague of 1576. Any other arrangement must have been exceptional.

Although standard elements, then, these chapels could still be omitted in the few cases where they were little needed, as for example in the Franciscan and Augustinian houses in Valladolid-Morelia, a town for Spaniards well patronized by those in power but not well populated with Indians. There is no trace of one at the second (present) Santo Domingo in Oaxaca, which has everything else on a grand scale, and none was needed since this establishment was not planned for natives but primarily for white novices. Yet, as has been said, in its earlier days on its earlier site, when there were more Indians and not yet any novices in Oaxaca, it did have one.[11] These three examples have, logically, only small atrios.

There may have been another kind of exception: perhaps the very early three-aisled wooden churches could hold their congregations. Such churches were not only bigger, but the early congregations were not yet so big as successes in the Conversion would soon make them. Around 1540, for example, the neighborhood Indians attended Mass inside the three-aisled church of Santiago Tlatelolco.[12] There may have been equivalent exceptions at monasteries with somewhat later three-aisled churches, at Franciscan Tecali, Quecholac, and Zacatlán, so similar as to suggest that all three were built from the same plan, perhaps a reflection of the first Cathedral of Puebla, a very large, wood-roofed, three-aisled basilica. The Spaniards had already found this a satisfactory type for export, as one can see in the Franciscan church at Santa Cruz on Tenerife in the Canaries (which some Mexican religious surely knew: Father Ponce, for example, visited the monastery).[13] Tecali, Quecholac, and Zacatlán were Indian towns, and their churches may have been made so capacious in the hope of housing the entire local population for Sunday Masses. Why else would they have been built so large? Not for the Spaniards, because they were so few, but perhaps for the Indians, because they were so many? Tecali had a population of about 21,000 in 1565 and 25,000 in 1570; nearby Quecholac had about the same in 1565 but only 17,000 in 1570, of whom a third were in the charge of a secular; Zacatlán had half as many. Tecali had four friars, Quecholac three, Zacatlán two. Tecali had ten visitas, Quecholac four, all of easy access over flat land, and Zacatlán, on its shelf below a mountain and above a cañon in the cataclysmic Sierra de Puebla, had fourteen visitas hard to reach.[14] Three or four thousand standing or kneeling Indians could be crowded into each church in a quite literal pinch (with a scant 5 square feet for each); half that many would be more likely for normal Sundays. One wonders, if most of the country and suburban people were served in the visitas, whether the native townsfolk could have been accommodated inside such churches on Sundays, and if so, at how many Masses. A special reason for trying to fit them under a roof at Zacatlán would have been the *chipichipi*, or endless local drizzle. The congregation there spoke — and still speaks — three reciprocally unintelligible languages. Would there not reasonably have been three Masses, each with its sermon in the intelligible tongue? If so, the three congregations could have fitted themselves successively into the church. Quecholac was a prosperous and well-organized Indian city with considerable communal property — cattle and a full granary — and might have been sufficiently self-governed for the Indians to have built themselves a church big enough for their own use. We know only that it was finished before 1580, perhaps after a fire in 1575, and that the natives chipped in and bought it a bell.[15] Even if these three large churches could and did hold their Indians, they may have had the usual chapel-and-atrio arrangement as well, though if there were such, all traces have since disappeared at Zacatlán, and subsist only equivocally if at all at Tecali and Quecholac. Here and elsewhere there might have been some sort of chapels of wood which have vanished without leaving tangible traces.

There are no traces of an open chapel at the monastery of San Matías at Culhuacán on what was then a point on the Lake of Texcoco. Now a roofless ruin, the church still shows the bases of the columns which made it three-aisled. The fact that it was Augustinian makes an open chapel perhaps not quite so likely as in the aisled Franciscan examples, but this may be contro-verted by the fact that the church is only half the size (c55 by 150 feet) of that at Zacatlán. Culhuacán, once a big city and the capital of the Colhuas, had shrunk after being conquered by the Aztecs, and again after being con-quered by the Spaniards. By the time the church was begun (1552 or '62?), the town was considered a small dependency of Chimalhuacán Atenco, just down the lakeside.[16] Once the church had been built, perhaps the need for a durable open chapel was not insistent.

*

There are occasional notices, written mostly after 1575, which seem to say that the Indians were using roofed churches, though none states so specif-ically. For example, Father la Rea called the monastery church at Uruapan "very large, sumptuous, and capacious for a large congregation"; and he also mentioned nine chapels set at the ends of streets in the nine barrios (1639). Together the large church and the nine chapels might somehow have housed the whole Indian congregation of the town (c17,000 in 1565)[17] if the Masses were short and the friars nimble. But Father la Rea, an unobservant and pedestrian chronicler, may not have known any better than we what local conditions had been eighty or a hundred years before he was writing. Later he wrote of Indians in other churches, but only in his own day. On the other hand, it may be that Fray Juan de San Miguel, who laid out the town with its barrios (1532 or '33), and probably built the church to which Father la Rea referred, did not yet follow the already emerging but not yet standardized atrio-and-chapel scheme. There is still an atrio in front of the church at Uruapan, and a pretty hospital chapel facing the once vast plaza, but nowhere any trace of an open chapel, nor are there any written references to one. (The large church was burned in 1813; the hospital chapel gutted by fire in 1851 and again in 1944.)[18]

Father Mendieta (c1581) quoted Father Motolinía (c1540) in one passage which shows that both church and chapel could be used by one con-gregation on the same day, but it was a special occasion on a very special day — early Christmas morning: "And if they wait to open the church until the throng of people has arrived, there is danger that some might be crushed to death by the force with which they try to get in: since all cannot fit in the church no matter how large it is, many have to stay outside in the patio, where they kneel as though they were in church until, when Matins are over,, a priest comes out to say Mass for them in the patio chapel." [19]

Although there may have been such exceptions, and unknown others, the conclusions are clear: the open chapel was a regular feature of the architecture of the Great Conversion, and nearly every monastery had one. Until about the time of the plague of 1576, the normal Sunday church of the Indians was the atrio-and-chapel, and gradually after that they began to be accommodated within roofed church buildings. By the end of the century the outdoor church must have been obsolete in many regions, obsolescent in most others. Occasionally, however, the Indians would still be segregated outdoors while the Spaniards were inside the church. For example, Father Vetancurt said that the Indians of Cuautitlán heard Mass at their portería, presumably meaning their open chapel, on Saint Nicholas' Day in the 1690's at the same time that the Spaniards were hearing theirs inside; since one sermon was in Spanish and one in Náhuatl, language may have been the chief reason for the division.[20]

Although it has been suggested that the open chapel and posas may have served equivalent functions, and therefore that both may not have been needed in the same monastery,[21] the differences in use already indicated, and the more than two dozen examples in which both either exist or are known once to have coexisted, show that posas were a common but not mandatory supplement to the regular chapel-and-atrio scheme. In many monasteries with open chapels we have no way of knowing whether there ever were any posas, now that the atrios have been remodeled or destroyed, just as in other houses with posas where there is now no open chapel, we cannot safely say that there never was.

Open chapels were built, then, in all parts of New Spain where there were substantial monastery buildings. The Franciscans took them north into Hidalgo, and west into Michoacán and Jalisco. The Augustinians began their great establishments in Michoacán by building chapels. The Dominicans built them from the beginning in their houses extending southeast into Oaxaca, but no surviving sixteenth-century chapels have surely been identified beyond Tehuantepec.

It is doubtful that any true open chapels survive outside Mexico. We know that they once existed at the main Franciscan and Dominican establishments in the capital of Guatemala;[22] but know nothing about them except that they did exist, and were used even in the seventeenth century. There may have been others in Guatemala and in Chiapas before earthquakes shook them down, for the same problem which had brought them into being in central Mexico existed there, and both Guatemala and Chiapas were architecturally as well as ecclesiastically dependent on central Mexico in their architecturally formative years.

348

OBSOLESCENCE

In Guatemala (for example, at Santiago Atitlán) and in Peru, sermons were sometimes preached from balconies in the monasteries to crowds in the atrios, or to crowds in the town plazas, but no unequivocal open chapels serving as the chancels of outdoor churches are known except the two in Guatemala City just mentioned. Nowhere but in Mexico (and here in dependent Guatemala) does there seem to have been an established practice of holding weekly services in an open chapel for a congregation gathered before it in the open air. The outdoor church is thoroughly Mexican, and a major constituent of the architecture of the Great Conversion.

OBSOLESCENCE

Although the need came to an end with the sixteenth century, occasionally one was built in the seventeenth. The "Hospital Chapel" of 1619 at Tzintzuntzan and a few other hospital chapels in western Mexico seem to have been swan songs, for the few open chapels built later were apparently either repairs or replacements for older structures which had deteriorated, but which — in back-country towns or Indian suburbs — remained conservatively in use. Such may be the explanation of the seemingly anachronistic eighteenth-century open chapel in Coyoacán, or of the Churrigueresque scherzo at Axapusco (an old visita of Otumba). Echoes have been seen in the eighteenth-century porterías of the missions of New Mexico, a recently converted frontier region in some ways equivalent to the frontiers of the time of the Great Conversion; but inasmuch as most of these porterías have a doorway in the middle of the back wall where the altar would have to be and a built-in adobe bench all around the walls, and as there are no notices of altars or of any use as chapels, it seems unjustified to accept them as chapels.

Only very exceptionally could a new congregational demand cause the building of a new open chapel: for example at El Arenal (originally a visita of Actopan), crowds attracted by a newly miraculous image made architectural enlargements necessary in 1806–12, and either the old visita chapel was replaced or a new chapel was added to the corner of the little church. No longer the sanctuary of an outdoor church, this chapel cannot, however, be counted a true open chapel: it was and is used only on occasions when crowds of pilgrims create a temporary need. It is more like the open shrines and oratories in Europe already mentioned as distinct from open chapels. Similarly the so-called open chapel of San Pablo Actopa near Toluca is really an oratory for the veneration of the Cross, and it was built (in the eighteenth century) presumably for that and not to fulfill the functions of a true open chapel. So also in Xocoltenango in Chiapas, a new shrine of wood and straw resembling a poor open chapel has recently been put in front of the church so that Masses can be said for the seasonal crowds attracted there by the miraculous image of the Virgén de Candelaria.[23]

THE OPEN CHAPEL

174 EL ARENAL
*Visita church and
open oratory*

After the plague of 1576, while building was slowing down, the need which had brought the atrio-chapel combination into being diminished greatly, and consequently so did the importance of the open chapel. This is perhaps revealed in differences in the writings of Fathers Ponce and Mendieta. Inspector Ponce, who came to New Spain in 1584 and traveled the length and breadth of it until 1589, never explained open chapels except in Tlaxcala and Yucatan where, because of special conditions, they were still visibly in use. The regularity with which his *Relación* refers to them in Yucatan may have come from Fray Antonio de Ciudad Real who did the actual writing of this part of Father Ponce's book, for Fray Antonio had gone to Yucatan before the plague of 1576 when open chapels were even more necessary than in '89 when he accompanied Father Ponce. Although Father Mendieta finished writing later, he had begun earlier, before the plague of '76. He had come to New Spain in 1554, and had seen scores of open chapels in regular use. He mentioned them and explained them oftener and better than Father Ponce, but with inconsistent emphasis: perhaps, as has already been suggested, the fuller explanations were made early in his writing, and the omissions later, when fewer chapels were in use because, as he was aware, the congregations had become much smaller. While Father Ponce was less observant of how things looked, and less curious as to how they worked, his omissions are still remarkable because he so consistently and methodically listed the useful architectural components of friaries. His omission of chapels except in Tlaxcala and Yucatan, and repeated references to them there as something notable imply that at the time he was writing they were little used elsewhere.

The *relaciones* written for a census-taking, mainly in 1580, hardly ever mention open chapels, and when mentioned, they are rarely explained. This seems to show that they were not considered important and were taken for granted: the Indians must have been going to Mass in the usual sort of church in most of New Spain. The *Relación de Tancítaro* may be revealing when it says that the chapel in the atrio there was used only on the most important religious holidays (*Pascuas y fiestas grandes*) when the Indians came from all around in such quantities that they could not fit into the church.[24]

After the sixteenth century people began to forget — quite naturally — what open chapels had been made for. Father Torquemada, writing about 1609 (after some forty years in Mexico, and some forty years after the Great Plague), penned his first half-million words (652 printed two-column pages) without ever mentioning one, and then observed, without additional information or interest, that the Indians were still using their large chapel at San Francisco in the capital.[25] (While this was not precisely an open chapel, still it was used in close conjunction with its atrio unlike any church Torquemada knew in Spain.) His other references to open chapels seem to occur in passages paraphrased from earlier writers, particularly from Mendieta; nowhere did he give fresh information or eyewitness account of activities in an open chapel.

Learned Father Grijalva, writing in 1623, never consciously identified an open chapel, even when describing monasteries where they must still have been eye-catching features. One must read 70,000 words (280 pages) of Father la Rea's dull *Chronicle of Michoacán,* written in the 1630's, before coming on a reference to a *capilla de indios*; he did not explain this one nor refer to any others. Gil González Dávila, Royal Chronicler of New Spain, writing in the 1640's, knew that the Indians had been too many to be fitted into the churches a century before, but he did not bother to tell and perhaps did not know what had been done about it. Ten years later, Father Antonio Tello, the thorough chronicler of western Mexico, passed over all the extant open chapels he must have seen without any notice, and in the same year the same indifference was shown by Father Burgoa, the linguacious chronicler of southern Mexico. Father Matías de Escobar, writing of the Catechism-teaching still going on in it in 1729, called the splendid open chapel at Cuitzeo a portería, though its apse, altar, and retable were in plain sight, and he knew for what they had once been used.[26] Less accurate Father Beaumont, writing in 1777 about the sixteenth century, gave no account of the use of the open chapel. In compiling their chronicles, these seventeenth- and eighteenth-century writers made generous use of earlier texts by men who, having seen open chapels in use, must have discussed them; yet the later compilers did not find such passages important enough to adapt. The open chapel was not a significant reality to them.

Except in big cities, atrios were still regularly laid out with new churches through the entire viceregal period, but by the end they were used only for special fiestas, for religious plays or processions, and for a graveyard. There was no longer the same need for the atrio which had brought it into being and caused it to develop, and there was no need at all for the open chapel. A vital determining ratio had shifted: there were more pastors but smaller flocks; there were more churches, but far, far fewer Indians. Gonzalo Gómez de Cervantes, a conscientious statistician, said in the last years of the sixteenth century that there was only one Indian left for every ten there when the Spaniards came, and the most conscientious and scientific modern statisticians, Professors Cook and Simpson, have shown how the natives had disappeared at a frightening speed.[27] Why, then, build open chapels for the few survivors, who did not need them?

THE ALTAR IN THE OPEN CHAPEL

Little is known about the liturgies used during the formative years in Mexico, and less about the equipment used for them. There are references to a "Mexican Rite," but these are far from clear, and refer presumably to a ritual used by the seculars only. Even after the systematizing pronouncements of the Council of Trent, and the Second and Third Mexican Councils (1565, 1585), some forms in the local liturgy and its equipment must have varied from time to time and from place to place.

The altars of European churches were consecrated, made of stone, permanently fixed, and physically contiguous with a consecrated building. The consecration of its main altar was normally an important part of the dedicatory rites of a new church. Under ordinary circumstances Mass was not to be said except at an altar which had been consecrated by a bishop in a church consecrated by a bishop. In Europe there were only rare exceptions, but for the peculiar conditions which were normal in New Spain, the friars were conceded the right to consecrate their own altars and chalices, and also their own churches and chapels. They had of necessity to do this until the first bishop arrived in New Spain, and they continued for a generation after that, and in some regions for two or even three more. After the middle of the century they generally preferred to have the traditional consecration by a bishop, though of course the four or five Mexican bishops could never get around to all the monasteries, vicarías, and visitas being built by the friars, in addition to the increasing numbers of the parish churches of their own seculars.

From the earliest days Christian altars have been supposed to contain relics (in accordance with Revelations 6:9) or, if relics should be unavailable, a leaf of the Gospel or a consecrated Host. At first only altars with relics were consecrated — others were merely blessed — but by the Middle Ages it was permissible to consecrate an altar which had no relic or symbolic substitute. Though rarely done in Europe, this must have been common in New Spain.

What few treasured relics the Mexican friars had in the first decades were not kept in altars, but safely locked up somewhere near them in the church or in the sacristy. Bishop Zumárraga wrote to Spain to ask for relics for his new churches, and Bishop Quiroga went there to ask for more. The

352

Provincial of the Dominicans, when passing through Cologne — disguised as a *Lanzknecht* to evade the Lutherans — was able to pick up some bones of the 11,000 Virgins which the heretics had been throwing out. (He might have spared himself, for the 11,000 and their relics have since been declared spurious by the Church.) Three of these bones were given to the Franciscan friars, and one to the Franciscan nuns. More relics were imported after the mid-century. Gregory XIII sent a collection to the newly arrived Jesuits, and a special Papal Bull ordered more sent to the Franciscans. The Franciscan church at Guadalajara had a set of little bags of relics of dozens of saints, mostly minor. Xochimilco boasted an arm of Saint Stephen. The head church of the Dominicans displayed a piece of the True Cross presented by Pius V. The Augustinians and Jesuits, not to be outdone, obtained other splinters of *Lignum Crucis,* and soon after them, so did the Cathedral. Even a minor monastery, such as that at Tláhuac, could boast of its own splinter before the century was out.[28]

One cannot imagine any such relics being left outdoors in the altar of an open chapel, or even a consecrated altar being left there, freely exposed to desecration by impious malefactors or profanation by animals. Once consecrated, an altar was sacrosanct, and would surely have had to be vouchsafed proper care. The nature of the altars and the manner of consecrating them must have varied, and there must have been some distinction in the status of those in closed churches and those in open chapels.

*

In the first centuries of Christian worship, the altar had often been made of wood, in obvious symbolic analogy to the table of the Last Supper. Some of the first altars in Mexico must also have been of wood (as they were later under similar circumstances in New Mexico). This would have been from necessity more than from symbolism. Very soon in Mexico as in Europe, altars were made of stone, with a top slab called the *mensa* (table). On or in the mensa was set a small, hard, rectangular stone slab, about 12 by 14 inches: an *ara* which symbolically represented Christ, and was the holiest part of the altar. The chalice and some other equipment would be set on it during the Mass. *Quae tan amplia sit, ut Hostiam et majorem partem Calicis capiat,* according to the Missal. When a consecrated Host was reserved in a tabernacle, or elsewhere — to be taken to the dying in emergencies — it was to be kept in a chalice which stood on an ara. The ara was often a gift from the King, as were the chalice, cruets, and other ritual equipment. The ara was regularly fitted into a special cavity in the mensa (the *sepulchrum*), which might also contain small relics. The mensa was supported by a permanent fixed base or pedestal (*stipes*). During the celebration of Mass, it supported not only the ara and the mensa, but the chalice and cruets which were then standing on the ara, and the cross, missal, and candlesticks on the mensa. As the stipes may contain relics, but often does not, it need not count as a con-secrated part of the altar like the ara and mensa.

The probable arrangement in open chapels now becomes clearer. There could be a permanent unconsecrated stipes, physically fixed to the floor. (A number of these remain, but none is surely of the sixteenth century.) For temporary use, during the celebration of a Mass, a consecrated ara could be set on it, and afterwards be taken away for safekeeping, along with the rest of the liturgical appointments. There would be no need for a consecrated mensa.

From sometime in the Dark Ages or even earlier, a portable ara had become a recognized essential for certain occasions or conditions — before battles or during persecutions, for example — and such portable aras had continued in use throughout the Middle Ages for any kind of Mass which had for any cause to be said where there was no fixed consecrated altar. In-ventories show that they were still common in the sixteenth century, and sacristies and museums in Europe confirm this with several hundred speci-mens, some plain, many sumptuous. Significantly, a portable altar slab had become a recognized essential in the equipment of any religious who was to make a journey into heathen lands.

Portable altars must have been a regular part of the equipment of the friars in New Spain from the beginning. Fray Bartolomé de Olmedo, Cortés' chaplain, must have used a portable altar on shipboard and for his first Masses on land; Cortés ordered "that an altar be made as well as can be in the time," on the island of San Juan de Ulúa, off Veracruz; referring no doubt to whatever the portable ara was to be rested upon.[29] Portable stones must have been used for the altars set up in Tlaxcala, and in the Palace of Axayácatl, which Moctezuma lent the Spaniards when they arrived in Tenochtitlán; here "when Mass was said, we had to place an altar on tables and then dis-mantle it again." [30] A portable stone must have been used on the altar which Cortés forced Moctezuma to approve on top of the Great Teocalli. When Fray Juan Díaz, who accompanied the conquistadores into Oaxaca, said the first Mass there, he "made an arbor, and put the portable altar under a big tree with bright red pods" (an *acacia sculenta?*). The supposed spot, beside the river Atoyac on the road to Xoxo and Cuilapan, was later commemorated by a rustic chapel. When the Franciscans withdrew from the capital because of the outrages of the interim governors, before the arrival of the Second Audiencia, they first "dismantled" their altars; they must have removed the aras and taken them along to Huejotzingo.[31]

Most of the early written evidence for the use of portable aras in the Conversion is either Dominican or Franciscan, and refers to the extreme southeast: Chiapas or Guatemala. Father Remesal, writing in 1615–17 with copious use of earlier documents, mentioned Aras more often than anyone else, always with a capital A. Since the clergy had to travel, "all altar service

354

was portable, and it all fitted into a small chest: Ara, Chalice, Cruets, Chasuble, and Alb, Cross, Candlesticks, and retable." [32] (The retable was painted on a cloth which could be folded for packing.) When Bishop las Casas and a large group of Dominicans were on their way to Chiapas (1545), they were wrecked off the coast of Campeche, and when the survivors were at last safe, "among some trees they hung some cotton cloth, made an altar, and put a frontal and Ara on it, and with much devotion said Mass for the dead." [33] Later he noted that some of these Dominicans, when setting up their first house, at Zinacantán, were lent an Ara by a local official, which they "esteemed as much as a treasure." When Bishop Marroquín of Guatemala visited the Dominicans at San Cristóbal in Chiapas (1546), "he consecrated Aras, because there was a great lack of them." When Father Ponce went to Juchitán (then a visita of Tehuantepec), he "wished to say Mass but could not, because there was no ara." [34]

There is fragmentary evidence for the use of aras in the more central regions. The Franciscans (c1570) recommended putting two responsible Indians who could read and write in charge of visitas, which "they should guard with great precaution, cleanliness, and reverence, and keep the vestments, hangings, ornaments, and other equipment of the church, and never touch the chalice, ara, or corporals with their hands." [35]

Further evidence is shown in one of the engravings made in Rome by Fray Diego de Valadés for his *Rhetorica Christiana* in 1579. (He left Mexico in 1571.) In it, Indian boys who accompany a traveling friar carry a wooden altar base, and a smaller lockable chest which should contain the ara, chalice, cruets, and other liturgical necessities. One boy already displays a chalice, perhaps to show that this essential has been included, or to show that preparations to set up the altar have begun. Only a *donado* would have have been allowed to carry or even touch a chalice.

A few portable altar stones have survived, all small and plain. John Lloyd Stephens, traveling in Guatemala in the 1830's, was shown a venerated "oracle stone" in Tecpán, of "slate" about 14 by 10 inches. This had presumably been cut out of some older object of revered significance, and had been consecrated (after exorcism?) by the first Bishop of Guatemala, and was kept on an altar. Manuel Toussaint discovered a similar stone in a sacristy in the State of Guerrero, a black ara venerated for itself though not used for Masses. What Father Remesal wrote about aras fitted into a traveling chest has recently been given concrete confirmation through the discovery, by Jorge Olvera, of another ara, still kept in its traveling box, in a sacristy in Xocoltenango in Chiapas. It is a polished thin stone slab of about 8 by 10 inches. None of the townspeople now knows what it was made for, but they esteem it reverently and guard it carefully in its box. Neither this nor the ara seen by Toussaint had a hollow for relics or the five crosses customarily engraved on the surface of an ara.[36] All three were small enough to be easily portable yet large enough to support the chalice and Host. (Similar portable altars came into widespread use in Mexico again — semi-secretly — in the years after the Revolution of 1910–20 when Masses were banned by anti-Church factions in some parts of the Republic.)

175 A SCENE OF THE CONVERSION   (Valadés, Rhetorica, 1579)
    A friar (a), with a crucifix hanging on his chest and a big sombrero slung across his back, has walked into the sierras to convert the Indians. Some men (g) and women and children (h) have already been won. He is accompanied by Christian Indian youths (B) probably trained in Fray Pedro de Gante's school. They carry a box with the equipment for Mass, and a pedestal for a portable altar. One youth, who also wears a crucifix (C), guides the heathens to the friar, after having discovered them at some fire rite (f).

Much of the old information is mineralogical. Father Ponce saw near Tecali "a quarry of very beautiful white marble-like stone from which they take out aras, crosses, and other handsome stones which are much esteemed, and these are sent all over New Spain, and even to Old Spain." [37] The *Relación de Tepeaca* (1580) told that aras were made of this pale jasper or translucent white onyx (now called *tecali* from the name of the town), and so also did chroniclers Cobo, Vetancurt, Villaseñor y Sánchez, and geographer Alcedo.[38]

Near Zinapécuaro in Michoacán, Father Ponce noticed a "quarry of black stone from which they have taken many good pieces for aras." In the market there Father Torquemada saw "stones which serve for mirrors, and are very good for making *altares,* razors, and lances." [39] We can still see black stone in the pathways of the Franciscan monastery and all through Zinapécuaro, and can see that it is fine obsidian. (The native word for obsidian, *zinapa,* gave its name to the town.)

Black, hard, and glossy, obsidian — a kind of natural volcanic glass — was particularly esteemed for aras, which statutarily are to be made only of hard stones not liable to "corruption" by cracking, scratching, or chipping. In Europe aras were often of porphyry, serpentine, marble, jasper, or of alabaster or jet, the last two similar to Mexican *tecali* and obsidian. The aras seen by Toussaint and Olvera were of glassy black obsidian, and probably so was the "slate" one seen by Stephens. Oviedo said that he himself had four aras of black Mexican stone in Santo Domingo — he never saw Mexico — and he knew that much of the same stone had already been shipped to Spain (1541). Viceroy Mendoza, to whose papers he had access, had sent the Emperor two black aras with "a vein in the middle, of bright red like a ruby." [40] A fine slab of polished obsidian in the Ethnological Museum in Vienna, labeled "Aztec mirror" may instead be a Mexican ara. (Charles V gave Mexican curiosities to his brother Ferdinand, who added them to the fantastic collections of his *Wunderkammer* at Schloss Ambras near Innsbruck, where they were all displayed until some were transferred with other Hapsburg treasures to Vienna a century ago.) Father Vetancurt saw other altars of *tecali* and obsidian, and in the monastery at Quecholac, an ara of what he called "unpolished emerald" (*esmeralda bruta*), which was probably one of the handsome Mexican jadeites or nephrites.

Although they tell what kind of stone, these passages do not tell specifically which kind of *altar* stone is meant. The earlier texts must refer to portable aras. In the eighteenth century, when Villaseñor and others noted aras, they would have been little needed, except by remote friars going to remoter visitas, and such late notices more likely refer to slabs fixed in the stone mensas of altars inside churches.

Such non-traveling aras set into fixed altar-bases were certainly used earlier as well. Provincial Miguel Navarro gave to San Francisco in Puebla, for example, "a rich custodia, a good organ, a very impressive baptismal font, and a beautiful ara for the high altar" (1570). Father Remesal told how an ara which was *on* the altar of the Dominican church at San Cristóbal, Chiapas, was so shattered by lightning that the scattered bits left on the altar-block looked like broken china (1563). These must have been fixed in the mensas of the high altars, secure inside lockable churches.[41]

THE OPEN CHAPEL

A consecrated altar stone could not be left in a really open open chapel when no Mass was in progress and no priest was nearby. From the descriptions of Father Ponce we know that a few open chapels could be closed: there was a grille, for example, across the chapel at Calkiní in Yucatan; and at San Felipe Ixtacuixtla in Tlaxcala "the church is not done, but is being built; there is next to the portería a pretty chapel in which Mass is said for the Indians and in which the Most Holy Sacrament is kept. There are doors which can be locked with a key for greater security." [42] He noted both of these, however, as unusual arrangements. Since the consecrated ara could not be left outside and since few open chapels could be shut, the ara must generally have been put aside with the Sacrament, sacred vessels, and ornaments in a locked cupboard in some secure part of the building. Friars going to visitas must have taken their aras with them, along with the other equipment, as shown by Valadés, and then must have brought them back when they left the visita unguarded until the next Mass said there.

176
A RURAL ALTAR, *with candles, candlesticks, chalice, and frontal*
(Códice Sierra, c1570)

The ara must have been treated as something sacred, like the chalice — something to be cherished almost as cautiously as the Host it would support. The Council of 1555 ordered that aras must never be sold. Before the Council of Trent decreed that a reserved Host might be kept on the altar in a tabernacle where it could be venerated (1563), following the persuasive enthusiasm of Saint Cajetan in Rome, in New Spain the Host had customarily been kept inaccessible, either in a wall-niche near the altar or in a special cupboard elsewhere, often in the sacristy. Even after the Council's decree, it was kept on the altar only in churches where the members of the congregation would come in for special devotions on weekdays, until the last years of the century, when it was more often on continuous display. The rules for locking the Sacrament are and were so strict that it is unthinkable that one would ever have been left outside in an open chapel. It would be even more shocking than leaving an ara there.

The pedestal or stipes of the altar in an open chapel was, then, no more than a table-like support for the fittings of the Mass, less like a proper altar than like the altar-blocks in posas, which were no more sacred than ordinary church furniture, no more than a pulpit or choir rail, and not vulnerable to desecration demanding full or partial reconsecration. When prepared for Mass, this block might be ornamented with a frontal, painted, embroidered, or made of silver, and when Mass was finished this would be removed and put safely away with the rest of the liturgical equipment.

These exposed altar-blocks may be closely related to another rather loose class of "altars" used in sixteenth-century Mexico: the temporary "altars" which were often set up for special celebrations, many only incidentally religious in character. Father Ponce mentioned these often, for example by the atrio gate at Tlaxcala, where "altars" were to serve somehow during the festivities to welcome a new Viceroy, and he repeatedly wrote of them as having been set up under leafy arbors raised at the entrance of towns which he visited on his long tour of inspection. The typical texts do not make clear just what was done at these "altars," but they do show that it was not the celebration of the Mass. For example: "The Indians had made many arbors and arches, and among them more than twenty very large ones, and in the upper part of each one there was an altar, and next to the altar, a great deal of trumpet music"; or "Each town had made a big arbor on the highway, and in it there was an altar, and beside the altar a table with many bouquets of flowers on it, and plenty of chocolate for those who wished to drink . . . and in some arbors they had wine for the same purpose." [43]

Clearly, then, nothing was consecrated but the ara and the fixed altars in roofed, closed, lockable churches.

MUSIC IN THE OPEN CHAPEL AND ATRIO

> *The music of the Christian Doctrine, intoned in devout chant at sunrise and sunset, makes tender the hard hearts of men and gladdens the angels.* — Father Mendieta (c1580) [44]

Although music had been important to the Aztecs, they had no word for music as such since it had no existence independent of religious ritual. As no preconquest music has survived identifiably intact, knowledge of it today is uncertain. Most scholars assume that the scale was limited, perhaps pentatonically, and thus the music was restricted in melody, although perhaps sophisticated and energetic in rhythm.

There was a wealth of native musical instruments, nearly all percussive except for brisk little whistle flutes, ocarinas, and mournful conch horns. These carried the melodies, necessarily confined to a short rage of notes. Some *teponaxtles* (horizontal wood drums, ill. 10) had two, three, or even four tones, and there were a number of ingenious resonators, such as tortoise shells, or dried gourds floating in water. Accompaniment could be further enlivened by a fantastic variety of rattles and rasps, many made of shell or notched bone.

359

177 INDIAN MUSICIANS (Codex Magliabecchiano, *late sixteenth century*) *One shakes a rattle and beats a tortoise shell with a stick, and another drums a* huéhuetl *with his hands. The hook-shaped glyphs issuing from their mouths show that they are singing.*

The Spanish invaders brought music with them. Cortés had trumpeters during the Conquest, and had clarions and sackbuts played at Mass on his hazardous trip to Honduras. When he came back from Spain with his new title and new wife, he brought a corps of musicians for the lordly household he was planning.[45]

*

The converted Indians took to European music quickly, charmed by its new element of pretty melodies, while the unconverted clung for a while to their old music as a token of resistance. Under the tutelage of the friars, the converts soon learned to perform the new religious music very well. In some ways their ability to master the new music and to create it is closely parallel to their ability to learn and create the new architecture brought by the conquerors, as is also the parallel abandonment of so much of their own accomplishment in the same arts. There is no record of just what the first music was — the music that so immediately beguiled them — but it is safe to suppose that the first friars most commonly sang their Masses in monophonic plainchant. Depending on their earlier musical experience in Europe, for the special occasions when they performed part music, they would have sung either in simple homophonic chordal style or, now and then, in more or less florid counterpoint. This would usually have been *a cappella,* but sometimes the voices might sing one part while the other parts would be played as instrumental accompaniment. There cannot yet have been any instrumental figured basses.

Bishop Zumárraga had been pleasantly surprised by what the Indian singers had already learned from the Franciscans by the time he arrived (1529), and he had an organ and an organist installed in his modest Cathedral within a year. Soon he was asking for music books from Spain for the native boys whom the friars had been teaching, now as charmed by the white men's music as they had once been frightened by their horses and guns. As

Náhuatl is almost sung when nicely spoken — and no people speaks more nicely than the Indians of central Mexico — plainchant came surprisingly easily to the natives. By 1531 they were already singing polyphonic music. "What shall we say of the children of the natives in this land? . . . They sing both plainsong and counterpoint; they make missals and teach music to others; and the joy of religious song is in them" (1533).[46]

Within a few years the Indians were so enchanted that the Bishop complained that music was converting more Indians than preaching, and that the natives were coming "from distant parts to hear music" and "to work in order to learn it" (1540). Viceroy Velasco was of the same mind. Bishop Garcés wrote Pope Paul III that so many natives were so well versed in various sorts of religious music that European musicians were no longer missed. Before 1540 an Indian had already composed a Mass. The relative importance accorded music is implicit in the ratios suggested for monastery help in one of the periodic programs for reform: eight musicians, three acolytes, two gardeners, and one cook. At the memorial Mass for Charles V in 1559, two large choirs sang a long program, part plainsong, part counterpoint in four and five voices, with intermezzi by the choir master and six boy sopranos. There were said to be about a thousand church choirs by 1576, trained to sing the entire service, and so many music-makers at the Cathedral in the capital that they were able by joint guild action to organize the first strike known in American history. (They won.) [47]

Music was exploited to draw Indians to the Church. At a time when the Dominicans were constantly attacking the Franciscans, Dominican Father las Casas asked for Franciscan-trained Indian singers and players to be sent to far-off Guatemala "because with music they can attract the Indians of those regions more quickly to the knowledge of our Holy Faith" (1540).[48] He was said to have penetrated the highlands, where soldiers had failed, with converts who set up musical units in each town to woo the natives melodically to an interest in the new religion. This was done before the friars came in to effect the actual conversion. (There may be reason to doubt these claims of las Casas.) [49] Fray Juan Caro proposed to win the Indians entirely by music, to vanquish the *teponaxtle* with the organ; though almost simple-minded he became through music an astonishingly effective teacher.[50] The importance of European music in native estimation is made plain in one of the few preserved sixteenth-century native accounts, the Chronicle of Chac-Xulub-Chen, when it describes the coming of the Franciscans and Christianity to Valladolid in Yucatan in these brief but revealing words: "1552 was the year when the schoolmasters came, and they sang here in Sisal. They came from the west, and they taught us how to sing Mass and vespers, and with organ and flute and plainsong, none of which did we know before." [51]

361

One of the Franciscan Twelve took the *Pater Noster, Ave Maria, Credo, Salve Regina*, and the Commandments, translated them into Náhuatl, and set them to "graceful plainsong" so successfully that the Indians "were in such a hurry to learn them that they gathered in crowds in the patios of the churches in their barrios, singing and learning prayers for three or four hours; and such was their eagerness that wherever they went, day or night, they went singing the prayers." [52] They had to be forbidden to sing at night. A friar in the Dominican monastery at Tehuantepec composed "verses and songs to make the Indians forget the days of their unbelief." [53] The first and probably the most effective of all the friar-teachers was Flemish Fray Pedro de Gante. After only a few years, he found his pupils worthy of the Emperor's own choir. Having seen that the natives had long had the custom of singing together on important occasions, he made new songs for them to sing on the important new Christian occasions, "very solemn measures on the Law of God and the Faith." [54] These would probably have been set to either the popular or court melodies he knew from musically advanced Flanders. Soon afterwards the melodies of popular Spanish *villancicos, coplas*, and *zéjeles* were made to serve as religious music. Easy, pretty, and catching, these proved to be a wonderfully effective mnemonic aid in teaching Latin prayers to the children. Without some such help, the prayers could not have been readily memorized, but set to music they became "very attractive chants," which the Indians would sing contentedly in their houses by the hour, so that one could not walk through their villages without hearing Latin religious songs. Indianophile Father Sahagún composed a *Psalmodia Christiana* not only with Indian words but also with some Indian melodies, and a few other friars also adapted native tunes.[55] European music seems, nevertheless, quickly to have driven out nearly all native music; the small residuum soon fused with the European, and survived, diluted, only in mestizo popular music.

The Mexican Indians also learned more orthodox liturgical music — even the Mozarabic chant of Toledo and Seville — which they performed *a cappella* or with an organ. Organ-playing was made part of the curriculum at the Indian College of Santiago Tlatelolco, taught not only on the instrument of the Franciscan church next door but also on a *monocordio* (a primitive clavichord) bought for the purpose. Archbishop Montúfar wished the organ alone to be the standard instrument in churches, but often the accompaniment was a choir of flutes or other combinations of instruments which might seem startling now, though less so then, when orchestration was not yet specified for different instrumental voices but left to the discretion of the performers. Soon the Indians were making their own flutes, fifes, flageolets, sackbuts, harps, horns, trumpets, guitars, hautboys, bassoons, rebecs, and other European instruments, as well as their own traditional little flutes and

178 INDIANS DANCING (*Durán*, Atlas, c1580)
to a teponaxtle, *a* huéhuetl, *a clapper, and a rattle.*
The teponaxtle is supported on a European-style pedestal.
One dancer is dressed as a tiger knight, and two as eagle knights.

big drums, vertical *huéhuetles* or horizontal *teponaxtles*. Their organs and flutes of wood and cane or reed were said to be superior to imported ones with metal pipes. Fray Pedro de Gante had been the first to teach them how to make and play these instruments of accompaniment. Although in their old music the limited wind instruments did no more than double the voice in unison, at the octave, or possibly at the fifth, and although they had no part-singing, they had already reached some concept of semi-independent vocal and instrumental phrases in the sense that much of the music of the instruments was rhythmical accompaniment. In the new music, then, an exciting novelty was true part-singing — begun as early as 1527 in Texcoco — at first most commonly in parallel voices, but occasionally in more complex patterns. Soon some of the most gifted pupils were composing in developed counterpoint; some of them wrote entire Masses in four voices.[56]

Spanish music had already absorbed much of the rich and complex Flemish polyphony, and in Mexico additional Flemish influences could have come directly from the Flemish friars, above all from Fray Pedro de Gante. He and his two companions had traveled from Ghent to Seville presumably with the young King Charles and his private choir, and when Fray Pedro later said that his Indian choir was comparable to the royal one, he knew

363

what he was saying. Oviedo, who had served in official capacities in both Spain and Italy, also believed that the native musicians would have been prized in the Old World (1541).[57]

*

The choristers, who were called *Theopantlacatl* ("people of the church"), learned traditional plainsong (*canto llano*) and more modern mensural and polyphonic music (*canto de órgano*) with extraordinary speed, so quickly in fact that it was said that in two months an Indian mastered what took a Spaniard two years. Children of eleven and twelve read music easily. Expert scribes copied and illuminated musical manuscripts in big letters and notes, so that a choir could read them from a distance. (Particularly fine examples are still to be seen at Yuriria and in the Biblioteca Nacional.) [58] Still, most music had to be transmitted *viva voce* until 1556, when the presses in the capital began to turn out singing books. The *Missale Romanorum* of 1561, in red and black, is surely one of the major masterpieces of American printing. Characteristically fearing heterodoxy even here, Philip II prohibited local music printing (1573) after only about a dozen books had been published, but this did not hamper the Indians very much. They could not be stopped. The most gifted singers and players were probably the Tarascos; the fastidious Jesuits asked specially for a Tarasco to teach music in their schools, and to this day fairly pure plainchant can be heard in a few village churches in Michoacán where even the priest may have no music books.[59]

While there can be no doubt about the quantity of religious music performed, some people carped at its vocal quality, for example, Doctor Zorita: "There was much discussion, some saying that they were off key and had thin voices. It is true that they do not have as rich and sweet voices as the Spaniards, and the main reason is believed to be because they go around barefoot, with very sparse clothes, and with their chests bare; and also because their meals are poor and light. Nevertheless, there are good choirs because there are so many of them to choose from." The Franciscans found that "In the towns where there are monasteries, it is the custom to have two choirs of these singers and players of instruments to alternate weekly because, as they are married and want to provide for their wives and children, and must also find something with which to pay tribute, it would be very cruel to make them come to church every day . . . In each of these choirs there are usually fifteen or sixteen Indians, and at least that many are needed because they have weak voices which do not resound unless in a group." (1569) [60]

*

Despite the fact that Indian musicians were not paid, their number became so large that it must have been taken into consideration by anyone conscientiously planning religious buildings. (In European monasteries the monks themselves formed the choirs, and hired instrumentalists only for important occasions.) The choir-balconies of most Mexican churches had to be made large enough not only for the friars who recited or chanted their daily offices there — fewer than in Europe — but also for some dozens or scores of native singers and players who performed every Sunday and feast day.

A few open chapels were of comparable size, and at the others, singers and instrumentalists must generally have been grouped near the chapel at the east end of the atrio, particularly when there were really large choruses and orchestras — not as unusual as one might think. Archbishop Montúfar found that "There are a huge number of Indian singers in the service of the churches: in one monastery we found a hundred and twenty without counting in the sacristans and acolytes and those who play instruments." [61] He found another monastery with "better and more musical instruments than in your Majesty's choir; this is quite common." The Council of 1565 complained of the excessive numbers of singers everywhere, with typical secular jealousy of the regulars' success. [62]

*

Almost every village, even the smallest, would have not only its singers but trumpeters and flutists with Mass which, of course, was often celebrated outdoors. The vicaría of tiny Tejupan in Oaxaca, for example, bought eight trumpets in 1551, and then eight more in 1560. Father Cogolludo said that in remote Yucatan "there is something worthy of attention, and that is that there is not a town, no matter how small, where the divine services are not solemnized with organ playing and a trained choir, as the music demands; and in the monasteries, with contrabasses, *chirimías*, bassoons, trumpets, and organs. [63]

The Indians became so enthusiastic and extravagant that Archbishop Montúfar and the Council of 1555 felt that they must be curbed. "The great excess of musical instruments in our Diocese and Province and the great number of Indians who spend their time in playing and singing oblige us to apply a remedy and to place a limit on this excess. Accordingly, we order that from now on there be no playing of trumpets in church during Divine Service . . . We require that *chirimías* and flutes be stored in the principal towns and be distributed for use in the villages only on the feast days of the patron saints; and as for viols and other instruments, we must also request that they be no longer used . . . The organ is the correct instrument for use in the church." [64]

The order may not have applied to outdoor churches — and anyway it was not obeyed, for six years later Philip had to issue a similar order to curb excessive trumpet and trombone playing. This cannot have been obeyed either, for it was repeated within a few years, this time with an added restriction on drums. The Council of Trent at the same time was prohibiting any "impure" music in churches. Percussive instruments had long been banned in European churches, but again, as so often, minor regulations were ignored in Mexico.[65] Moreover, percussion which could be deafening indoors might be acceptable outdoors, where the sound of the softer instruments would be dissipated. Percussive instrumentation, furthermore, was in the native tradition, and if the Indians were allowed many decibels outdoors, undoubtedly they would sometimes come indoors with the same music unmodified. (Even today Mexican outdoor religious festivals in the country are likely to be louder than in Spain or Italy, brassier and noisier in fact than anywhere else in the Christian world. Firecrackers are regularly exploded in the atrio, and dynamite is not unknown.)

*

A few Indians learned not only sacred but secular music — those who served Viceroy Mendoza were specially trained in minstrelsy and trumpeting — and there were complaints that those employed in the monasteries were learning not only sacred music but also secular vices. Philip II complained that having been trained for nothing else they were often indolent, and even in boyhood were corrupters of the girls and young matrons of the towns. This complaint should perhaps be somewhat discounted, since it sounds so like Philip's usual reactions to the rather sweepingly anti-Indian or anti-Mendicant propaganda fed him by some officials (here perhaps by Archbishop Montúfar).[66]

*

The enthusiasm and aptitude which the Indians showed toward European church music of all kinds, including complex counterpoint, is surprising not only if looked at from the standpoint of the sixteenth century, but also if seen in retrospect from today. The Indians of most of Mexico do not now seem to be particularly musical as active participants although, thanks to the radios in houses and juke boxes in cantinas, thousands are passive consumers. Although they may hear as much, they make less music in their daily life than people in most Mediterranean countries. Outside the cities, they rarely sing at work, except in Michoacán where some farmers sing all day. There is widespread popular music in Mexico now, and much of it is of beguiling character, but it comes from mestizo rather than Indian regions: Jalisco for the compulsive *mariachis*, and the Gulf States for the seductive *huapangos*. There are no still identifiable Indian traits to be found in these. Like tequitqui carving, this music is not Indian nor Spanish, nor half-and-half: it is thoroughly Mexican. Even a century ago perceptive Madame Calderón de la Barca was unaware of any native Indian music at all, but very much aware of mestizo and European when she wrote (1840) that "music in this country is a sixth sense." (There must have been more performers then than now.) Carl Lumholtz noticed the same (*c*1890). The speed and skill with which the Indians mastered European music in the sixteenth century is clear evidence of their innate musicality, which must have been less passive then than now. Their subsequent contribution to music is almost entirely in whatever it was they contributed to mestizo music — *pace* the raveningly nationalist musicians of today — and that contribution was made astonishingly early and early sent to Europe: the *pavane, sarabande,* and *chaconne* all probably came from New Spain.[67]

179 A CEREMONIAL DRUM (Códice Azcatítlan, c1572)
  An Indian (identified by his sandals, short trousers, and coiffure) who is some sort of official (indicated by his staff of office) has duties which have to do with a church and a drum (relation indicated by dotted lines). The drum is a huéhuetl, which is played vertically, but here lies idly on its side. The church is somewhere in Tlaxcala (indicated by the glyph of hands making a tortilla) near a river (indicated by the glyph below the tortilla).

X

THE FIRST OPEN CHAPELS: I

SAN JOSÉ DE LOS NATURALES

SAN José de los Naturales was established in the atrio of San Francisco in México-Tenochtitlán where once had risen the fantastic aviary of Moctezuma. The first chapel made specifically for Indians, it was the ancestor of all open chapels.[1] Built by the Indians at their own expense, it was maintained by their gifts: no royal grants were needed. There were so many in the congregation and they gave so generously that by the end of the century the chapel was helping to support the monastery, its church, and its hundred friars. The chapel had its own visitas, some in the city and some in nearby towns. As the principal church of the Indians, it was accorded privileges normally reserved for cathedrals by both Charles V and Philip II, and its prestige was such that its founder could ask the Emperor to ask the Pope to grant it special indulgences, and its friars could request and obtain plenary indulgence for all buried there, and indulgence so that each Mass said there might release one soul from Purgatory. (It is typical that such requests were sent not directly to the Pope but to the King, and although typical it was improper, for such measure-for-measure release was repugnant to the doctrines of Grace and Purgatory.) Archbishop Montúfar objected to the requests with alarm, perhaps not so much from their impropriety as from fear they might lead the pious to prefer to have Masses said in privileged San José instead of his somewhat less privileged Cathedral. The natives preferred San José to any other church, consistently and enthusiastically, and native writers often referred to it as "our" San José. When some Indians were assigned to the interracial parish church of San Sebastián, made from their old Franciscan barrio church, they boycotted it and joined the other thousands already going to San José. Five out of six Indians of the city regularly went to San José, and once, when ordered to subdivide and attend curates' neighborhood churches, they rioted.[2]

368

SAN JOSÉ

FRAY PEDRO DE GANTE

> *Vir singularis et pietatis, qui omnes artes illis ostendit, nullius enim nescius erat.*   — *Fray Diego de Valadés* (c1578)[3]

The idea for San José was almost surely conceived by Fray Pedro de Gante, an exceptional man who still shines out as a sympathetic European intelligence able to understand many of the problems and to devise humane patterns for the ways of life uneasily evolving in America. Although little of his early history is securely documented, creditable conjectures make it possible to piece together a moderately full biography.[4]

He had been born in Flanders, in a suburb of Ghent, about 1480, and was presumably the illegitimate son of the young Maximilian or the old Emperor Frederick III or perhaps of Duke Philip the Good; thus he was either an uncle or a great-uncle of Charles V, and about the same age as Charles' father, Philip the Handsome. The Indian historian Ixtlilxóchitl, who must have known him personally, called him a cousin of Charles, but Ixtlilxóchitl was often inaccurate, and "cousin" was and still is a curiously elastic term in Spanish. (Charles made all grandees "cousins" of the Crown in 1520.)

Through early manhood Fray Pedro's name was *Peeter van der Moere,* or something similar, which he latinized fashionably into *Petrus de Mura.* He probably was educated at one of the schools of the Brothers of the Common Life and, since concern for his fellows and their education were later to be among his major preoccupations, he may have received there the best training in the Old World for his mission in the New. He must have studied philosophy, theology, mathematics, and probably some medicine and music, either with the Brothers or soon afterwards at the University of Louvain. There he could have heard Erasmus (who had studied with the Brothers), and his later work shows that he knew and concurred with the educational ideals of Erasmus. At the University he could have known the Dean, or Vice-Chancellor, Adrian Florisze of Utrecht, one of the most illustrious of the Brothers, who was soon to go to Spain to become a bishop and the Regent of Castile, and was later to ascend the papal throne as Hadrian VI (1522–23). After the University, Peeter must have gone to Court, but soon he renounced its worldly life to enter the Franciscan monastery at Ghent as a lay brother. Here he must have remained several years, possibly with some time at the Observant house in Bruges.

Aroused perhaps by the abrasive hyperbole of Bartolomé de las Casas, who had recently been preaching at Court, the new Fray Pedro asked to be sent to Mexico (1522), along with an older friar Jehan der Auwera (Juan de Aora in Spanish), and the Guardian of the monastery at Ghent, Johan Dekkers or de Toict (Juan de Tecto). Reports of the new land had come in Cortés' first two letters to the King, and tangible confirmation was to be seen

369

in Antwerp in the startling treasure Moctezuma had sent Cortés and Cortés had sent Charles. The three Franciscans knew, then, that Moctezuma's Empire existed, and that it was strange, rich, populous, and heathen, but they did not yet know that it had fallen to the Spaniards. When permission was granted, they embarked from Ghent, it is said in a convoy with the 22-year-old King which spent six weeks in England while he jousted with his young uncle, Henry VIII, and treated to arrange a marriage (soon rejected) with Henry's 6-year-old daughter Mary (who later married Charles' son Philip II). The party arrived in Spain just in time to hear Cortés' third letter, describing the siege and fall of Tenochtitlán.

The three friars sailed for Mexico on May Day of 1523, and soon arrived in a world which it had been impossible for them to foresee. They witnessed the destruction of the temples, the conquerors' scramble for treasure, and the Indians' confusion, fear, and flight. Cortés — who, curiously, did not mention Fray Pedro in any of his preserved writings — had the three lodged in Texcoco, across the lake from Tenochtitlán, which had not yet been enough rebuilt to accommodate them. Although none knew it yet, the main work of Cortés, political and military, was already over. His successes had been made possible not only by force, but even more by persuading quite a few Indians to collaborate with him. Now the work of the friars, "civilizing" and Christianizing, was about to begin, and they were wise enough to see that this too could not be accomplished by force — of which there never could have been sufficient — but again only by inducing enough Indians to collaborate.

While living in some part of the labyrinthine Palace of the Princes of Texcoco, in the quarters of a converted noble who gave him his sons to educate, Fray Pedro set out to learn Náhuatl. Although a stammerer, he soon mastered it satisfactorily; his friend Bishop Zumárraga said he knew it better than anyone else, and some said he spoke it "elegantly." It must have been better than his Spanish, a language he had only recently learned for, although Spaniards sometimes had trouble understanding him, Indians did not. Possibly Náhuatl was easier for him than Flemish or Spanish because it is spoken with the syllables so much more separated. (Motolinía, who also stammered in Spanish, in Náhuatl also did not.) Fray Pedro succeeded in mastering it well enough to complete a Catechism begun by Fray Juan de Tecto, by writing in the Spanish phonetic near-equivalents of Náhuatl; this was soon published in Antwerp (1528), and was found so useful that it had twice to be reprinted in Mexico. When the Twelve arrived, nine months after the Three, their leader, Fray Martín de Valencia, found that he was able to baptize Prince Ixtlilxóchitl of Texcoco and his chief lords without delay because the Flemings, using Náhuatl, had already managed to teach them the Catechism.

370

Despite the death of his two companions on Cortés' catastrophic campaign to Honduras, Fray Pedro continued to work in Texcoco alone. At first he did not venture into the streets for fear of rousing the natives against the new religion, but kept quietly indoors, instructing their children. He advanced in Náhuatl while teaching the sons of the nobles to sing, and to read and write Spanish. He was the first European to teach in Mexico, and the first to master the language of those he was teaching. He came to use Náhuatl more and Spanish less, as more and more he identified himself with the natives. It was because his Flemish had become rusty in his first six busy years that when he wrote back to his fellow Franciscans in Ghent he used Latin, and asked to have others make translations into Flemish and German. Living for over three years among Indians in a big and busy Indian city of 150,000, and easily able to communicate with them in their own language, he came to understand their temperament, society, needs, and quirks more sympathetically, perhaps, than any Spaniard in Mexico, and therefore he was better equipped than anyone else to plan how to effect the maximum of conversion with the minimum of friction. As a lay brother he could catechize, but not baptize, say Mass, nor administer any of the other Sacraments. He was, notwithstanding, one of the principal devisers of the Great Conversion. He was known to be so effective with Indians that, when the leader of the largest and most dangerous anti-Christian underground, don Carlos Ometochtli of Texcoco, was caught in flagrant political and religious subversion, he was turned over to Fray Pedro to be corrected by quiet talks. (The civil authorities soon decided to deal with Prince Ometochtli in their own way, and burned him.)

Fray Pedro's Christian-humanitarian program was directly opposed to that of the ruthless successors of Cortés. Nuño de Guzmán and his crew saw the Indians either as game to be hunted or chattels to be exploited. Fray Pedro saw the same Indians as Children of God who needed help to be saved from their idolatrous errors and who, once saved, could enjoy the same benefits as other Children of God. Both attitudes determined the future of the Indians, but neither completely: the natives never became part of an integrated society with the Spaniards, as Fray Pedro's program would have made them and Nuño's would not, but they did become Christians.

Probably around Christmastime of 1526, Fray Pedro moved into the monastery of San Francisco in the half-rebuilt capital, and began to carry out a systematic, bold, but quiet program to convert the natives of the whole Valley. As an important adjunct of this campaign he established the chapel of San José de Belén de los Naturales (Saint Joseph of Bethlehem of the Natives). Fray Pedro surely had a voice in formulating its functional program but there is no record of whether he had any hand in the architectural design which embodied this. He may have had both, for later writers somewhat

371

loosely credited him with having been able to teach architecture, without specific reference to any practice of architecture on his part; but perhaps their attribution of architectural knowledge to him was no more than an imaginative item in a eulogistic legend.

Fray Pedro had noticed that the Indians liked to celebrate much that was important to them by dancing and singing, and consequently he began to write Christian songs for them in their tongue, often set to easy European melodies or familiar native ones. He organized festivals in the atrio, where the Indians could jubilate in much their old way. He had them paint special religious symbols on their cloaks, adapting a similar pagan custom, and this made them feel that they "belonged" to something. At times he had them wear special costumes: for example, they dressed as angels on Christmas Eve, and sang alleluias and other songs of joy for the birth of Christ. (In many parts of the country, even in cities as large as Òaxaca, children still dress as angels, with big chicken-feather wings.) One play of the Last Judgment was acted before Viceroy Mendoza and Bishop Zumárraga by eight hundred Indians declaiming and singing in Náhuatl. Fray Pedro must have drawn on his own European experience for organizing such activities, and it may be more than a coincidence that he must have known at first hand the Procession of the Holy Blood in Bruges, one of the most elaborate in Europe, where the Passion and many Old Testament scenes were represented in tableaux, pantomimes, and little spoken plays not unlike the processions and plays described in the Mexican atrios. At the same time he effectively adapted old native customs for his newly Christian Indians in many other ways, as when, for example, he divided them into four major wards corresponding to the four familiar Aztec *calpullis*. For each one he organized its confraternity, which put on its own dances and plays in the atrio of San José. Each soon had its own posa. He built a church in each ward, and these were dependent on San José in much the same way that parish churches were dependent on their cathedral.

"In the daytime I teach reading, writing, and singing: at night I read the Catechism, and preach" (1529).[5] He taught in the school he had founded at one side of the atrio of San José (ill. 138). Each week, fifty of the brightest boys were coached here in the substance of next Sunday's sermon, and then sent out in pairs to announce and explain it among the people. Soon an annex was added for native youths where they were taught many useful trades and crafts which their fathers had not known, such as tailoring, shoemaking, blacksmithing, and Spanish-style stone-masonry, carpentry, and cabinet-making. They were very ingenious and very quick to learn, and their painting was soon particularly admired. (Would the painting Fray Pedro taught them have been in the Flemish tradition — he was a contemporary of Massys, Mabuse, van Cleve, and van Orley — at this time far more advanced than

the Spanish? What survives does not show it. Did he teach arts he himself
had never studied?) The painting pupils made altarpieces and other ornamental fittings for the new churches going up all over. There was also emphasis on music; everyone was taught to sing, and in this school the Indians
were first taught to play European instruments, usually on samples they had
made themselves. Fray Pedro achieved such phenomenal results that he must
have had exceptional musical gifts; it is probably important that he had spent
the first forty years of his life in Flanders, at this time musically the most active and advanced part of Europe, and that he had for many years been at a
Court particularly celebrated for its musicians (where he might well have
known Josquin des Prés).

180 FRAY PEDRO DE GANTE
*below his chapel of San José de los
Naturales and above a nopal cactus* (Códice Osuna, *c1565/68*)
*He is surrounded by the four barrio
churches of Santa María Cuepopan* (la
Redonda, *or* de la Asunción), *San Juan
Moyotlán, San Sebastián Atzacoalco,
and San Pedro Zoquiapan* (or Teopan).
*In the upper right sits Bachiller Moreno
discussing three new bells.*

The program of the school seems to have been pragmatic, with emphasis
on learning by doing, perhaps a reflection of Fray Pedro's own training by
the Brothers of the Common Life. The famous Indian College at Santiago
Tlatelolco (1536ff) was inspired by the school at San José: Bishop Zumárraga wished to complement his friend's vocational school with a Latin
school. His own school was so uniquely Fray Pedro's creation and so dependent on his daily attention that when he died (1572), it was closed. He had
devoted almost fifty years to it, often training five or six hundred pupils at a
time — some said a thousand. They seem to have become devotedly attached
to their master. Once, after he had been banished to the monastery at
Tlaxcala — apparently on mistaken charges — they welcomed him back to
the capital with a sham naval battle, staged as a surprise, and then accompanied him all the way through the city to his cell, with dances and demon-
strations of delight at his return. When he died, many went into mourning.

373

They buried him solemnly in San José, where they had already buried a son of Moctezuma, and put his portrait there; later it was painted together with the Twelve in other friaries. "Pedro de Gante" became a popular name to be taken by a newly baptized Indian, like "Tomás de Aquino."

As a royal relative and a conspicuously successful worker, he had high prestige in the Mexican Church despite his low hierarchic rank. He had chosen to remain no more than a lay brother although three separate licenses were sent to make him a friar-priest: one from the Chapter of the Franciscans meeting in Rome, one from the Papal Legate to Spain, and one from the Pope himself — all apparently at the instigation of the Emperor, who wanted to be able to name him Archbishop. With self-effacement so extreme as to be inexplicable, he several times presented himself to the Emperor in his letters, reminding him how he had been sent, what he had done, what his position was, and discreetly reminding him also of their kinship. Together with his close friend Archbishop Zumárraga, Bishops Quiroga and las Casas, and the first two viceroys, he must be counted one of the saviors of the Indians and true founders of post-Aztec Mexico. A long and outspoken letter to the Emperor (1552) — he could be bluntly aggressive in his last years — contains as forceful a plea for decent treatment as the Indians ever had. The Franciscan Provincial was perhaps not being anti-Dominican or pro-Franciscan when he wrote Philip II that Fray Pedro, who had just died, had done more for the Indians than Bishop Bartolomé de las Casas, and pointed out that Fray Pedro had dedicated the last fifty years of his life to them, while Fray Bartolomé had abandoned them and gone back to Spain to die. The second Archbishop, Alonso de Montúfar, uncharacteristically said: "I am not the real Archbishop of Mexico because that is a lay brother, Pedro de Gante." [6]

THE CHAPEL BUILDING

The Twelve had made some sort of modest church within a year of landing. Father Torquemada and several later writers thought it stood on the Plaza Mayor, near the site of the present Cathedral, but older sources and modern research show that it was where the church of San Francisco now stands, six blocks to the west. [7] At the end of the wood-roofed nave of this small first church, the famous first vault was raised in 1525 over the *capilla mayor* given by Cortés, and beside it Fray Pedro had the Indians build the first San José de los Naturales, perhaps within a year, even before he moved permanently from Texcoco into still half-ruined Tenochtitlán.

The early days of this chapel are not clear. No more than a small, plain, thatched shed, it must have been put up quickly. Within a year or two a big Christmas fiesta for the Indians was celebrated there. Luis Ponce and Marcos de Aguilar (whom Cortés had been accused of poisoning) were probably bur-

374

ied there in 1527, though it is hard to understand why these royal officials should have been buried in an Indian chapel. Its atrio, in which stood the 200-foot *ahuehuete*-wood cross, must have been walled and in use by 1532, when Fray Pedro wrote the Emperor about the *"corrales* and chapel." Presumably this is the same walled *corral* from which the *oidores* of the First Audiencia kidnapped an Indian in 1530, and probably it had been made of the ten lots granted to San Francisco in 1527. Fray Pedro's school for potentially influential boys was soon established on one side of this atrio. Bishop Zumárraga wrote in 1534 of the "patio where Mass is said for the crowd of Indians on Sundays and feast days," showing that San José must by then already have been an *open* chapel. Fray Pedro later referred to it as a "poor portico." [8]

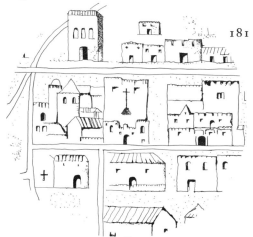

181 SAN JOSÉ DE LOS NATURALES (after the "Santa Cruz" plan) *A very summary representation made c1568 with the atrio and giant cross in front and the church and monastery complex at the left.*

Set beside the north flank of the friars' church, this portico-chapel appropriately turned its back on the Spanish part of the city, and faced some of the Indian quarters, the lake, and the still-wooded country beyond. One reason the friars had chosen this site away from the main center of Spanish life and that they sold the land Cortés had given them on the Plaza Mayor [9] may have been to show from the start that their main concern was not so much with the Spaniards as with the natives.

Insignificant to the eye, perhaps, the hastily improvised portico was nonetheless of enormous import, for it established the open chapel in the Mexican repertory as its most original item, and set an example soon to be followed many times in many different towns. Most of the many "churches" Fray Pedro and others claimed to have built in the next decade were probably no more than similar porticoes. Father Tello's comment about another church building of 1527 may be revealing about the nature of most of these early "churches." "On Palm Sunday a church was built in the town of El Tuito, which was called the Holy Cross of the Palms, and Mass was sung; and then an Indian, one of Father Gante's, was left to teach the Catechism." No more than a thatched portico or shed could be built in one day or — since it was a Sunday and an important feast day — more likely only half a day.[10]

This first portico-chapel may have been transformed into a better and bigger building before 1539, when Bishop Zumárraga wrote his nephew of the "chapel" which was now the "chief sight of the country, with its aisle and chancel suitably arranged [*con el corredor y oratorio en forma*]." [11] While it is not absolutely certain that he was referring to San José, and while the last phrase is not entirely clear, the remark may show that San José was now a portico one bay deep, with an apse set in the middle of its back wall, in an arrangement soon to become widespread, perhaps in imitation of San José. It is possible to be more precise as to the date than the form: one Indian chronicle recorded for 1537 "the biggest earthquake that I have seen, though I have seen many in these parts," [12] and another recorded Indians using wood for something at San Francisco in 1538, and still another said that in that year "the wooden church was raised." Bishop Zumárraga praised a "chapel" in 1539, and soon he planned to add a story to its tower, already with four stories the highest structure in the capital.[13] It is not certain that all these notices refer to the same building — though it is difficult to imagine to what they could refer if they do not — and any conclusions educed from them had best be kept in the subjunctive.

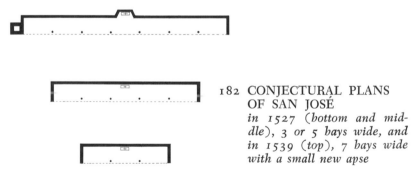

182 CONJECTURAL PLANS OF SAN JOSÉ
in 1527 (bottom and middle), 3 or 5 bays wide, and in 1539 (top), 7 bays wide with a small new apse

To continue in the subjunctive — this San José was perhaps repaired or replaced after another earthquake in 1547, but as the dates in native annals are uncertain or careless, particularly if transposed into the European calendar, it cannot be certain that a quake said to have wrecked San José in 1547 may not be the same as quakes recorded for 1537, '41, or '42 in other annals. Such a suspicion deepens when one sees 1547 crossed out and 1530 substituted at the head of one Indian page noting three earthquakes in one year. (Dates cited by Europeans in the European calendar may often be almost equally insecure, sometimes because of carelessness or sometimes because writers might begin the year either on the Feast of the Annunciation or on the Feast of the Circumcision. Few Mexican dates can be accepted as inflexible facts before the end of the century.) One chronicle states flatly that there was an earthquake *and* that the chapel was begun in 1547, and that not only seems to help fix a date but also suggests rebuilding more than repairs. But when the same chronicle also records a beginning of the chapel in 1556 (as well as "then fish fell") either the credibility of the annals or of our understanding of them begins again to waver.[14] Without additional clarifying information, if anything is to be assumed, the best is that there was important alteration or rebuilding of a wooden open chapel in or about 1538, followed in or about 1547 by a collapse bad enough to call for more repairs or for rebuilding.

183 A leaf of the *CODEX TELLERIANO–REMENSIS* (c1570)
 1547 has been crossed out and 1530 substituted — "when the earth shook three times." (1529 shows Nuño de Guzmán setting out for Jalisco.)

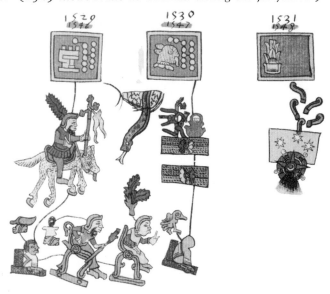

There is another puzzle in the available information about the chapel at this time. After a beginning in 1536–37, followed by an interruption of three years, Father Motolinía finished the writing of his interrelated *History* and *Memoriales* in 1540–42. Any Franciscan building under way in the capital must have been of concern to him, yet although he mentioned the less striking church and atrio he wrote no word about a chapel of San José. This might raise doubts that it had yet been importantly rebuilt, but at almost the same time (1539) his friend Bishop Zumárraga seems to have found the chapel "the chief sight of the country." There would appear to have been some reason to make them appraise the building differently: perhaps they appraised Fray Pedro differently. Like Cortés and Bernal Díaz, Motolinía avoided reference to him. He is not named in the *Memoriales,* where there is generous reference to the Twelve but not to the Three who preceded them. Early teaching at Texcoco and at Fray Pedro's big school are mentioned, but Fray Pedro, the most effective teacher, is not. In the *History* his name appears only once, and then merely in passing: "they brought the news to the Franciscans, one of whom is entrusted with instructing the Indians, and is called Fray Pedro de Gante." More mention is given to Fray Juan de Tecto, who survived only two years in Mexico.[15]

It is possible that Father Motolinía was silent because some biographical notice was to be included in the last treatise in the *History,* devoted to the lives of the first Franciscans in New Spain. (It is not known whether this was ever written; if it was, transformed fragments may survive in Mendieta.) He may, furthermore, have found Fray Pedro difficult — he was nearly sixty — but not yet too important to be ignored. Motolinía may have found him unsympathetic, a foreigner, and an outsider to the little band of Observants centering around the Twelve, already a close and perhaps clannish band which may have been hoping to keep the Conversion and future Province to themselves and to companions from the same part of Spain and the same group within the Order: in other words, Extremeños and Observants.[16] It is not certain that Fray Pedro was an Observant but, even if he was, he was only a lay brother, and he was not Extremeño but Flemish. He was an aristocrat and after his years at Court, probably quite cosmopolitan. There must have been some friction, and this may have been what caused his fellow friars once to banish him to Tlaxcala. It would not be surprising if the ostracism of Fray Pedro in his writing was extended by Motolinía to the building so closely associated with him. In view of these differences, Father Motolinía's silence cannot be taken as strong evidence of anything concerning either Fray Pedro or his chapel. If, on the other hand, the omission was not deliberate, the interruption in Motolinía's writing and the incompleteness of his sometimes confused texts could mean that it was no more than accidental. In either case, then, his silence may be discounted.

In 1552 Fray Pedro wrote the Emperor that the chapel "has been done over again, good [*sic*], and well built, so that the Holy Offices can be celebrated there impressively." This implies recent work, and tends to corroborate a quake in '47 (or to show the effects of another recorded for 1551?). A building of 1538 ought not otherwise to have needed replacing so soon.[17] This recent work could have consisted either of major repairs (including enlargement), or rebuilding (from a new design, or the reproduction or extension of a satisfactory old one). A new building could, of course, have incorporated serviceable parts of its predecessor.

There is no way of knowing how much of it was new or what it looked like since there are no contemporary descriptions of this stage. It must have been large, for the First Council of the Mexican Church met in it in 1555. To be chosen for this important conclave, the building must not only have been roomy, but it must also have had greater preponderance than an ordinary *capilla de indios,* for the Council was not so large that it could not somehow have been accommodated in some other space had San José not seemed appropriate.

After the Council, additional building was documented for 1555, '56, '57, and '58. Native workmen delivered lime for mortar or plastering, and "large stones." Some of this may have been for repairs — there had been floods in 1555 — and some for a new sacristy, but if extensive repairs were needed so often, the chapel at this time was more likely an amalgam of remodelings than one unaltered, unified structure built fresh after a quake of 1547. Fray Pedro now claimed it as the "first church made in the land," when even in its first state it had almost surely been the second, following San Francisco. He also claimed that it could hold 10,000 and its atrio 50,000, but by this time (1558) he was an old man freely given to exaggeration. Cluny, probably the largest church in Europe, held only 40,000 to 50,000. Even if not so capacious as Fray Pedro pretended, San José and its atrio (which was in a way part of the church) must have been one of the three or four largest churches in the world. It surely had great prestige: snobbish Doctor Cervantes de Salazar wrote that it would hold all the Spanish population of the city (c1563), which is another index not only of size but of status, for the Spaniards did not *have* to go to an Indian church.[18]

To prepare for the elaborate obsequies of Charles V in 1559, Viceroy Velasco had the building altered by Claudio de Arciniega, the Cathedral architect. A great amount of lime was needed, and forty more "big stones," now for "heavy pillars" and for arches.[19] After the *Túmulo,* a classicistic catafalque in the atrio, was dismantled and more repairs made (1560), the major phase of the building must have been complete. There are no records of major work on San José for the next few years, years for which documentation of labor elsewhere in the city is particularly full, though some minor work was done on the altars; all were given new bases and steps of Tenayuca stone (1564) and the main altar was given an ara of black obsidian from the sierra of Tlanchinol. By 1569 the floor had sunk below street level, and was sometimes flooded. More quakes were reported for 1561 and 1570. After an elaborate wooden stage put up in 1572 had been broken up in '74, rotted wood members in the chapel were repaired or replaced in 1574 and '79. The sacristy was remodeled in 1588. The facade may have been newly painted in 1589.[20] The repeated little jobs show that the building was held important and kept in trim repair.

379

A new bell-tower was erected at the end of the century. Since its builder, Fray Francisco de Gamboa, had come to Mexico as a page, he cannot have had much architectural experience in Spain, though he built or supervised considerable work in Mexico: a new church of San Francisco next door, a second cloister at Xochimilco, and the completion of the church and monastery there.[21] San José gained new importance in 1590 when it took over some of the major functions of the adjoining monastery church while that was being pulled down to be replaced by Gamboa's grander project. Indian annals recorded that now "the Holy Sacrament was placed in San José de los Naturales, on the right side, where Mass is begun, and the men of Castile were there to see." In other words, instead of to San Francisco, the Spaniards were going regularly to San José. A big new bell, "made by a Spaniard," was installed and tried out after a special sermon had been preached about it (1592). While the new San Francisco was going up, it and San José were somewhat reconciled architecturally by coordinating the runs of their battlements. A side wall, perhaps a party wall of the older church and San José, was pulled down, revealing old confessionals, perhaps like those in the walls at Huejotzingo. One Indian annalist still referred to San José as a *teocalli,* still meaning "house of god," though now a different god.[22]

By the latter part of the century there was already confusion about the history of the chapel. Some writers began to identify the "sumptuous and solemn building" they saw with the first shed put up by Fray Pedro sixty or seventy years before. There is a further confusion possible today, for an old reference to "San José" might mean another chapel dedicated to Saint Joseph, the chancel of the adjacent monastery church, given by Cortés in 1525 and perhaps altered on his orders after his return from Spain. He intended the chapel for a family mausoleum, and accordingly had it decorated with his arms (his old family arms if in 1525, or his grander new arms if after 1529). He planned to have his own tomb *in* the sanctuary, although before this no one not royal would have been buried in a sanctuary; bishops could hope to be buried only nearby in the nave. Cortés' chancel-chapel of San José was pulled down in the 1590's along with the rest of the church. There may by then have been a third San José in the city, belonging to a Confraternity of San José for Spaniards. They had banded together toward the middle of the century, and used to meet in the Cathedral, where soon they had their own chapel, known sometimes as San José de los Españoles. Since these other chapels were smaller, less famous, and not so often called "San José," most unspecified notices of a San José may be presumed to refer to the Indian chapel.[23]

Although, as these conjectural and sometimes incompatible shards of early history show, it is not possible to be sure of the first metamorphoses of the building, better information allows more of its appearance in the second half of the century to be recovered. Doctor Cervantes, who was both interested and informed about architecture, wrote in 1554: "Most pleasing of all, however, is the little chapel which is behind a wooden trellis, yet wholly open and plainly visible from the front. Its roof, high above the ground, is carried by tall tapering columns of wood, the material ennobled by the workmanship . . . It is arranged in such a way that the crowd of Indians, big as it is, which flocks from all around on feast days, can see without hindrance, and hear the priest as he performs the Holy Sacrifice." [24]

184 AN INDIAN IDEOGRAPH OF SAN JOSÉ
(after Codex Mexicanus 23–24, 1570/71)
This occurs above the glyph for the year 1547. The cross on the top may represent either a cross crowning the chapel or the gigantic atrio cross. The four arches (or possibly only two — the original drawing is damaged) need not mean that there were that number on the facade. The criss-cross frieze may refer to the wood lattice, which was far more likely between than above the columns.

Six years later Doctor Cervantes gave further information in describing the memorial Mass for Charles V the year before: "On the left is a chapel called Saint Joseph's, to which one goes up by two steps; it is very large, and supported by many columns which make seven naves . . . they had been painted like marble" for the occasion.[25] Three or four years later he wrote: "It is a sight to see because it is so ingeniously covered with wood over many columns. In front it has a set of stone arches. It is very light because the chapel is high and all open in front, and the stone arches are low, and serve more for ornament than for shelter or support." [26]

While together these do not give a clear image of this strange building, some deficiencies can be reduced by the descriptions of Father Mendieta (*c*1595) and even more by Father Torquemada's compilation from Mendieta and other sources (1608–09): "At the monastery of San Francisco, close by the north side of the church, stands an impressive chapel dedicated to glorious Saint Joseph . . . notable for its most curious building, and for its size and capacity. There is no other church nor other room in all Mexico large enough to hold so many people." "The chapel has seven naves, and for them there are seven altars, all at the east end, with the high altar in the middle and three on either side." The chapel must have reached its maximum size, which was about 200 by 85 feet. A century later Father Vetancurt gave the dimensions of the naves as each about 10 by 30 *varas*, or about 30 by 85 feet.[27] (Probably at the time that the sacristy was being built — 1555–56 — the facade had somehow been extended by the addition of a four-arched portería somewhere on the right, for which some of the "large stones" may have been intended.) [28]

An apparent conflict in Doctor Cervantes' descriptions must be resolved: in 1554 he called San José "little" and in 1560 "very large." It was presumably made larger in the intervening time, perhaps for the Council of 1555, perhaps for the Emperor's funeral of 1559, or immediately afterwards. An open-fronted building made of three walls and a roof on wooden columns ought to have been easy to alter or extend. An added row or two of columns could have made the early "poor portico" or *corredor y oratorio* a bay or two deeper. The chapel need not yet have been deep in '39, when it was perhaps the "chief sight," for Bishop Zumárraga did not say that his chapel was big but only that it was striking. If it was the "chief sight," San José may have been notable not so much for its volume as for its height and its length (perhaps already seven bays). At this time there were still fine cedars, cypresses, and pines on the mountains around the city, and a handsome set of wood columns 30, 40, or 50 feet high would have been obtainable for so important a building. The Indians were able to work timbers of over 100 feet. San José may already have been as tall as the nave of the adjacent church, as the remark about the alignment of their merlons later suggests.[29]

The repeated repairs, alterations, and rebuildings could have made the chapel grow by successive additions of new layers of bays in front, or even in back, but it is not possible to say exactly when such additions would have been made. The building was probably already more than one bay deep in 1555 when the Council chose to meet in it in preference to any church in the city. The lattice Doctor Cervantes mentioned would have screened the Council, which would hardly have convened in a wide-open portico; perhaps the sections of lattice, being of wood, could be taken out to make the chapel suitably open for big congregational Masses.

San José was surely more than one bay deep in 1559, at the time of the Mass for the Emperor. Doctor Cervantes described how a row of benches stretched down each side of the main nave and on out to the *Túmulo*, with special places for the Viceroy, the bishops, the royal and municipal officers, the faculty of the University, and the nobles. Four hundred of the regular and secular clergy filled the sections immediately on either side of the center; beyond them, in the two outer sections at the south sat the Indian lords and officials; in the two at the north, sat the most important ladies. These hierarchical seating arrangements show that the building was already seven bays wide. If two hundred clergy were put in a section 30 feet wide, with reasonable leg- and hip-room, and space to sit and kneel, and if all of them were under cover, then the chapel must have been *at least* 40 feet deep (with a modest 6 square feet for each man), and probably it would have been deeper. If the benches were not all under the roof — and no one said they were — it could have been considerably shallower. Proof that it was more than one bay deep comes from the details of the seating: the Viceroy and ninety-year-old

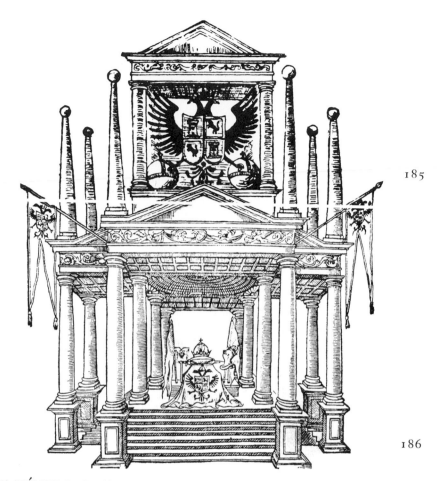

185

186

THE TÚMULO IMPERIAL

Claudio de Arciniega made a model, and after approval by Viceroy Velasco, the full-scale Túmulo was constructed from it in three months.

185 *Although the single known copy of Cervantes de Salazar's Túmulo Imperial lacks the top half of the catafalque, Manuel Toussaint was able to reconstruct it on the basis of the literary description. The obelisks were 30 feet tall. On the apex of each of the lower pediments was a figure of Death, and atop a central element of uncertain form was a still larger Death, Lord of All, wearing the Imperial Crown to show that all of us are his subjects.*

186 *The woodcut (preserved in the Huntington Library at San Marino, California) shows the bottom half. Four stairways rose 8 feet and led to the cenotaph beneath a dome at the center of a cross-shaped roof borne on Doric columns 24 feet high. The shafts had entasis and fluting, which the woodblock omits. The entablature was less "correct," without triglyphs but with a frieze with a running ornament of genii with skulls and trophies of war and death. The pediments did not slope up normally from the corners, but began to rise a few feet in, leaving a level stretch for the bases of the obelisks.*

383

Bishop Quiroga faced one another on special benches draped in black, each in front of a column, and as these can hardly have been the columns of the facade, which would have been too far from the place of honor near the altar, there must have been an interior row of columns running across the chapel behind the facade. There may have been more than one row, for Doctor Cervantes saw "many columns." [30]

This raises a question about the "set of arches" that he mentioned as part of the facade. Describing the preparation of the building for the funeral services of 1559, he wrote: "because there was a set of fourteen very well made arches which hindered the view of the *Túmulo,* [Arciniega] ordered them taken down and moved forward [*los mando quitar y passo adelante*], which gave more grace to the building and majesty to the *Túmulo.*" [31] This arcade was part of the facade described by Doctor Cervantes about three years later. How much earlier it had been made is not known. Perhaps it had not yet been set up in 1558, but already was intended, for some of the stones delivered that year — "large," including "pillars" and stones for arches — may have been ordered for it. Shafts suitable for it would have been monolithic in quake-shaken Mexico, and would have to have been "large." Professor Kubler has proposed that the 14 stone arches had at first lined the central nave, 7 to each side, which would imply that the building was seven bays deep. While possible, this is not the only explanation which can fit the fragments of evidence. [32]

It is also possible that the 14 arches had been intended for the facade from the first, and had been put in place there by 1559, or that enough of them had been set up to show that they made an inescapably unclassical elevation and spoiled the view of the classicistic catafalque from inside the chapel. "To give more grace to the building and majesty to the *Túmulo,*" Arciniega may have chosen to take them down from the facade and set them up some distance across the atrio on the far side of the *Túmulo* (which was too tall to be inside the chapel in the normal place for a catafalque). A relocating of the 14 arches somewhere in the atrio away from the chapel is confirmed by Doctor Cervantes: "the chapel and the rest of the patio was shrouded with black cloths *up as far as the set of arches.*" In other words, part of the atrio between the giant *ahuehuete* cross and the front of the chapel was set apart for the occasion, and its west barrier was made of the 14 arches. The *Túmulo* stood between the chapel and the arches, in or near the center of the black-walled enclosure, hung with Imperial arms and emblems of death. [33]

If the arches had been set up 65, 60, or 55 feet in front of a shallow chapel 20, 25, or 30 feet deep, then after the *Túmulo* was taken down in 1560, the chapel might have been extended forward by adding a few more rows of wood columns until the front reached and incorporated the stone arcade in the new facade. This would have given the chapel a final depth of

the 85 feet indicated by Father Vetancurt who, having been one of its priests
for forty years, knew the building very well. During the obsequies for Charles
V, the participants and important guests would all have been inside the ornamented black enclosure, while the crowd of 40,000 "plebeyos" would have
been outside in the larger part of the atrio beyond the stone arcade. Somewhere, probably within the enclosure, there were forty altars for the four
hundred priests officiating.[34]

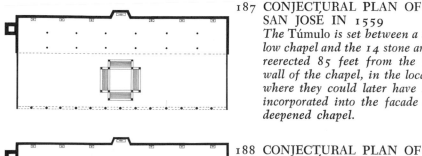

187 CONJECTURAL PLAN OF
SAN JOSÉ IN 1559
The Túmulo is set between a shal-
low chapel and the 14 stone arches
reerected 85 feet from the back
wall of the chapel, in the location
where they could later have been
incorporated into the facade of a
deepened chapel.

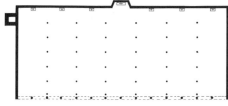

188 CONJECTURAL PLAN OF
SAN JOSÉ IN 1563 *after it had*
reached its final depth of 85 feet
and the 14 stone arches had been
incorporated into the facade, just
in front — presumably — of the
front row of wood columns.

This conjecture, that the arcade was moved forward for the Memorial
Mass and later incorporated into the facade of the chapel which had been
extended forward until it coincided with the line of the arcade, lacks corroboration. The principal objection may be that the *Túmulo* would have been
crowded, with its stairs beginning only 10 feet or less from the stone arches
or the front of the chapel. Compared with the usual cramping of catafalques
inside Spanish cathedrals, however, the objection fades. If the *Túmulo* did
have more space, the stone arches would have to have been set up farther
out from the facade during the ceremonies and could not later have been incorporated into a new facade without being taken down, moved, and set up
again. This is possible: after the *Túmulo* had been dismantled, they could
have been demounted, and then remounted in the new front of the chapel,
with two low stone arches screening each of the seven high wood naves, as
Doctor Cervantes saw and noted about 1563. Each possibility has inescapable
awkwardnesses: the first aesthetic, in crowded appearance, and the second
economic, in inefficient repetition of work. Common sense favors the first,
but twentieth-century common sense cannot necessarily be attributed to the
sixteenth-century people in charge. The known fussiness of Claudio de

Arciniega (which will be revealed in Chapter XV) and the extreme cheapness of labor may favor the second conjecture (in which case the chapel could have had any depth up to 85 feet at the time of the Memorial Mass). Without more information, it seems wisest to leave the two conjectures equal and competitive.

*

Not only is the form of the finished building surprising, but so is the number of its altars. Plural altars were rare in churches in New Spain and rarer in open chapels: seven must have been unprecedented. A new retable for the main altar was installed about 1600, and several painted altarpieces were noted later.[35] The early altars would likely have had either paintings or sculpture from Fray Pedro's craft school; some of the Indians' best work might naturally have been used to ornament their own church next door. The Council of 1555 had decided that only carefully screened masters should be authorized to teach painting to the Indians lest they learn incorrect procedures (and unorthodox iconography?). The Painters' Guild was closed to natives, even as apprentices, but scores of Indian painters were trained in Fray Pedro's school, and surely they turned out scores of altarpieces which were soon set up in Franciscan churches, chapels, and visitas. Although a mestizo, Fray Diego de Valadés was probably an instructor in painting at the school, since he was an artist closely associated with Fray Pedro, for a time as his secretary.[36]

A main altarpiece of San José was painted sometime before 1564 by the most famous of the native artists, Marcos Cipac de Aquino, who had probably also painted the most celebrated and beautiful of Mexican sixteenth-century pictures: the Virgin of Guadalupe. He sometimes collaborated with Pedro de San Nicolás, Pedro Chachalaca, and Francisco Xinmámal, and perhaps was assisted by them on the large and complicated altarpiece for San José. This was composed of two triptychs, one above the other, with a predella below, a mediaeval format less like works currently being made in Spain than like the van Eycks' famous Ghent polyptych (whose double-decker format may have been created by Jan van Eyck after his trip or trips to Spain just a century before), or like Flemish works affected by the Ghent altarpiece, such as the double triptych painted in Antwerp in 1518 for the Marienkirche in Lübeck. Fray Pedro must have been more familiar with Flemish than with Spanish altarpieces, and must have known the already famous one in Ghent at first hand. The type he introduced in his chapel became influential; the over-restored retable still in the open chapel at Zinacantepec, for example, may reflect its arrangement. Elsewhere in San José there was a picture of a genealogical tree, designed to show the natives the degrees of consanguinity within which they were not to marry — a difficult and much argued problem —

189 VALADÉS' TREE OF THE TEMPORAL HIERARCHY, 1579

The Emperor, Viceroy, Judge, and Pater Familias *are on the main trunk, and the punishments of the disobedient on the predella.*

Since Fray Diego de Valadés may have been active in the school at San José as a teacher of painting, and since he was interested in didactic trees of this kind, he may have been in large part responsible for the symbolic genealogical tree at San José.

perhaps similar to the hierarchical trees Father Valadés designed for his *Rhetorica Christiana* or its possible parents in many editions of the *Flos Sanctorum.* Fray Pedro also had a stone replica made of the Virgin of los Remedios for one of the side altars (said still to be preserved at Tepepan. Later opposed as a Spanish patroness to the Indian patroness of Guadalupe, this Virgin cannot yet have become particularly identified with the Conquerors). Soon there were statues also of Saints Francis and Diego, perhaps of wood.[37]

Since over 2,000 could attend Mass inside, as in a normal church, it might be claimed that the finished seven-aisled version of San José ought not to be called an *open* chapel, even though it was open all across its 200-foot front. (As usual, Fray Pedro's figures must be shrunk, for his 10,000 could never have squeezed themselves into 17,000 square feet standing, not to consider kneeling. If space is left for the clergy, the seven altars, and the columns, there could not have been more than 3,000 as a maximum, and 2,000 would be more likely.) To those inside the chapel — whether 2,000, 3,000, or 300 — its function would have been no different from that of an ordinary roofed church but, since its long front was open, and since the chapel could serve other thousands out in the atrio and usually did, most of the time its function was concurrently that of an open chapel.

A MEXICAN MOSQUE

No matter when or how it got its final form, and no matter how it may best be classified, there can be little doubt that the seven-naved San José was patterned on a mosque and its court. Hence it stands out as an exotic among the sixteenth-century churches of Mexico. Although all the big Spanish mosques except Córdoba are now as irretrievably lost as the teocallis of Tenochtitlán, we know that a number, like San José, consisted of a box-like space filled with regular rows of columns, open along one side to a court geometrically dotted with a forest of trees continuing the lines of the forest of shafts within. (The attractive feature of a court with multiplied quincunxes of trees was a Spanish Moslem specialty, established first in the eighth century at the Mosque of Córdoba.) The typical placing of the minaret at a corner of the mosque corresponds to the placing of the tower of San José.

One feature of San José may have been specifically like Córdoba: the low stone arcade running across the facade. If this was easily moved, as it seems to have been, it was probably as unstructural in its original location as it was after it had finally been set up on the facade. Well below the roof, as Doctor Cervantes noticed, and with nothing to support, its arches must have been free-flying, like the pink-and-cream-striped free-flying arches of the Mosque of Córdoba. If classicizing Claudio de Arciniega was willing to use them, even in a subordinate position, it is unlikely that they could have had Moorish details.[38]

Flemish Pedro de Gante cannot have been familiar enough with the architecture of mosques to have had either the fancy or the ability to make a mosque in Mexico. The idea would more probably have come from one of his companions familiar with Andalusia, where a few mosque buildings of this type were still among the arresting sights. One of the Twelve was from Córdoba, another from Seville, and there must have been other southerners in the next groups of Franciscans who arrived before the mosque-like design of the chapel was produced.

Nowhere in Spain, however, not even in mudéjar Andalusia, were churches being made in the guise of mosques at this time, nor had Spanish churches been made so mosque-like, consciously or unconsciously, since the graceful art of the Mozarab refugees had faded six centuries before. There was, of course, a vivid Moorish strain in later mediaeval architecture in most parts of Spain which, having reached its climax in the showy mudéjar art of the late fourteenth century, was still far from extinct in the early sixteenth. This did not make mosque-like churches, however, for the plans and general schemes of mudéjar were orthodoxly Christian: mudéjar delighted not in Moslem plans but in Moslem trimming. Although mudéjar once in a while imitated Moslem structural elements, their structural nature had already crystallized into decorative patterns, as in the typical and dazzlingly intricate *alfarje* ceilings.

Mudéjar art and customs appeared occasionally in Mexico. The Conquest had coincided with persecutions of the unbaptized Mudéjares. Their last mosques were closed in 1525, and the last stragglers were forcibly baptized within a year (and thus made Moriscos) at the same time the first large groups were being baptized in Mexico. Despite the fact that Moriscos were banned, their names tell that a few soon slipped into New Spain among the supposedly pureblooded Spanish immigrants. A special edict in 1543 prohibited the entry of Moriscos "because of the trouble with those who have already come." It was not only these Moriscos who mirrored the late mudéjar phase of Spanish taste: some pureblooded encomenderos liked to sport turbans and engage in Arab-style tournaments. Moorish influence appeared now and then, capriciously here and there, but it did not reach its height until early in the seventeenth century, and even then it never aroused such extravagant enthusiasms as in Colombia or Ecuador.[39]

190 THE ENCOMEN–DERO OF YAN–HUITLÁN IN HIS TURBAN (Códice de Yanhuitlán, c1545/50)

Under the peculiar building conditions of sixteenth-century Mexico, mudéjar forms were usually simplified, and restricted to a few ornamental features on buildings not otherwise mudéjar: pyramidal and stepped merlons, octagonal piers, *alfarje* ceilings, and also — although by now they were thoroughly naturalized elements in Spanish gothic — the *alfiz* (a rectangle of molding enframing an arch) and the scalloped, polylobed, or mixtilinear arch. These elements go back through Spanish mudéjar to the late decorative phases of Moslem work in Spain, work later than about 1200. The characteristic forms of earlier Moslem work were not revived in New Spain any more than they were in Spain: there is not, for example, a single colonial horseshoe arch in Mexico, and none would be expected, since the form had disappeared from the Spanish repertory by the time Tenochtitlán fell.

San José de los Naturales, akin not so much to mudéjar as to actual Moslem building, and not so much to recent work as to the mosques of past centuries, becomes a building as strange historically as it must have been visually. If more were known of later Spanish mosques, such as those built by the Nazarís in the fourteenth and fifteenth centuries, perhaps convincing late prototypes for San José might be found, but this is unlikely because no really large examples are recorded and San José is clearly related to a large mosque. Morphologically it *is* a mosque, and of a type built in Spain only before 1200.

A true mosque was used very differently, not just in the meaning but also in the choreography of the rites. Although there might sometimes be crowds assembled in its patio, they were there only to wash ritually before entering the mosque proper, and not to witness any service emanating from an architectural feature equivalent to an open chapel. The *mihrâb,* in form an apse-like niche, was sunk in the back wall of the typical mosque, and was visible from the courtyard through the rows of columns inside. Its function was only to be a marker or compass-arrow toward the *qibla,* or direction of the Ka'aba at Mecca, and sometimes incidentally to serve as a dignified place to keep the Koran.

The mosque was not held to be the house of God, like the church, but only a gathering-place for prayer, more like the synagogue, which had also influenced its form. There was little difference as far as the meaning or prestige of the building went between one part and another. Except for the *mihrâb* there were no areas specially shaped for special functions. Since Islam had no symbolic ritual equivalent to the Mass, it had no need for any specially consecrated place in its building. There was no nave, sanctuary, or major axis, or any need for one. The roof covered an unfocused area without directional or localized emphasis, and consequently any large interior, such as Córdoba, might bewilder the visitor by its undirected repetitiveness. When the faithful gathered at the only required time, Friday noon, it was for communal praying and for readings from the Koran. They stood in rows to face the *mihrâb* and Mecca. Special merit was accorded the front row and to enable as many as possible to enjoy this the mosque was planned, at variance with the church, for width more than depth.

Although there was considerable formal similarity between the mosque and the chapel-plus-atrio, there was little functional similarity. To anyone who had seen them both animated by the uses which determined their forms, they would have seemed even less like than they do now to us who study them as flattened dead specimens on paper. Only on Fridays, when all Córdoba went to the Great Mosque, and there might be overflow in the orange-shaded patio, was there any significant resemblance in what took place there to what took place in San José.

No one in Mexico would have known this, for there had been no public practice of the Moslem religion in a large columnar mosque in Spain or anywhere else in western Europe for a generation, and before that only in the tiny beleaguered Kingdom of Granada. No Spanish Christian child would have wandered into an active mosque in Granada before 1500 or — if somehow one had — would he have applied what he might remember of it to the solving of a novel church-building program in Mexico several decades later. San José must have been planned by someone who had lived in a city where a big mosque had been expropriated more or less intact to be resuscitated as a big church, as was prominently the case in Córdoba and Granada.

Along with all the other mosques in Granada, the largest and most important had been exorcised and consecrated as a church soon after the city fell. Part was pulled down when the *Capilla Real* was built as a burial place for Ferdinand and Isabella, but most of it stood intact for some decades after 1528 when Diego Siloée began his work on the renaissance cathedral which would rise in time to replace it; part was still in use as a church as late as 1561. A large eleventh-century mosque, 9 by 11 aisles divided by marble columns which continued as quincunxes of lemon trees, it must have resembled the mosque-Cathedral of Córdoba.[40] After they had been made into churches, neither would have been open to its courtyard, or used conjointly with it.

The designer of the mosque-like San José could have known either of these, and since he chose to adopt a type no one in Spain had built for centuries, a type long dead stylistically but here useful in solving a new problem, he is revealed as an independent-minded and ingenious amateur, free from the chronological imperatives limiting contemporary architectural practice.

The earlier thatch-roofed San José was less a mosque than the famous later one, and perhaps more like some preconquest monuments even to a few of its structural details. (The shrines of teocallis commonly had thatched roofs and mosques did not.) The Indian workmen could have approximated a familiar model with more speed and dependability and less supervision than an exotic one, provided that the friars did not think the finished work too evocatively heathen. There were not yet many friars to do the supervising, and those available had more pressing duties. If any lesson from Aztec precedents was heeded in the early San José and retained in the mosque-like successor, then with wonderful historical appropriateness there were put to work ideas from both the religions the Spaniards had fanatically extirpated from their realms, and made to work together for the faith imposed in their place. The result was so different from anything in Spain that it had to be specially explained to newly arrived Spaniards.[41]

Ironically, while the various successive versions of San José were being built, the closest Spanish protoypes were being destroyed. The ex-mosque at Granada was wholly obliterated, and the ex-mosque of Córdoba was being mutilated by Christian efforts to make it into a more usable church: fumbling, insensitive efforts which prompted Charles V, no antiquarian but a lover of then radically modern art such as that of Titian, to say to the Cathedral Chapter, "you have made what could be found anywhere, and you have destroyed what was unique in the world." [42]

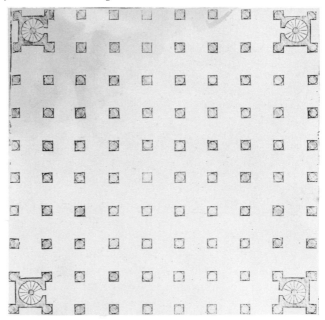

191 SERLIO'S "HALL OF THE HUNDRED COLUMNS"

It is possible that as well as some mosque and some teocalli there was another equally exotic source for the scheme of San José, for a plan very like it appears in Book III of Serlio's architectural treatise. He called it a "hall of a hundred columns," and claimed to have heard descriptions of such a building still visible somewhere in Greece. It was 9 by 9 bays square.[43]

Someone could have seen Serlio's plan in Mexico, and have been struck by the notice that it facilitated services which "could be seen by all the people"; but inasmuch as the trees of San José continued the columnar quadrille of the building beside them, as in mosques in Spain and Spain only, the final scheme of San José cannot have come from Serlio alone. If his plan had any influence, it must have been a year or so after 1540, the year Book III of his treatise appeared in Italy. This could mean that the mosque-like version of the chapel was not yet built in 1538, when the chapel may have been the "chief sight of the country," but that the big seven-naved version must have been the product of some later rebuilding, possibly after the questionable quakes of 1547 and '51. (Since Fray Pedro wrote of a rebuilt building in 1552, it would have been the Italian edition of 1540 that was known, if any; the first Spanish text did not appear until 1552.) It is not certain, however, that this rebuilding was the one that produced the mosque-like version; that may not have been made until just before or after the obsequies of 1559. The most probable dates, then, are either soon after 1547 or '51, or just before or after 1559: in other words, sometime between 1548 and 1562.

SAINT JOSEPH IN NEW SPAIN

The chapel was called *Saint Joseph of the Natives* not only to show that it was theirs but also perhaps to distinguish it from the *capilla mayor* which Cortés gave the adjacent church. Following the prestigious example of San José de los Naturales, later open chapels for Indians were so often dedicated to Joseph, their special patron, that Indians would familiarly call any open chapel a "San José." [44]

*

Joseph had not always been held to merit major reverence. Mark and John had all but ignored him, and only Matthew told some of his story. In the New Testament he is mentioned only once after Jesus' childhood (Luke 4:22). It was the writers of the apocryphal texts, particularly the *Protoevangelium of James* and the *History of Joseph the Carpenter,* who elaborated, extended, and popularized his history. His liturgical cult came late, first in the East, and was promoted in the West in the thirteenth century by refugee Carmelites from Mount Sinai. Despite sporadic further promotion by Saint Bernardino, Saint Thomas Aquinas, and Saint Bridgit of Sweden, in European mediaeval art he had not been allowed more than a supporting role as an auxiliary member of the Holy Family. In the High Middle Ages he had not been venerated for himself: altars were not dedicated to him, and neither statues nor paintings were made of him alone; children were not named for him. Sometimes he had even been represented as a comic character. In the Early Renaissance it was thoroughly exceptional for him to appear in his own right (as he does once in Spanish Sicily in Tommaso de Vigilia's 1486 altarpiece "del duca della Verdura" in the Palermo Gallery, where he is equated with the local saints Lucia, Agata, and Calogero). Although his feast had been put in the Franciscan calendar first, thanks to Bernardino of Siena, Bernardino of Feltre, and Bernardino of Busti (Observants all), and soon thereafter into the Roman calendar by Franciscan Sixtus IV, the Roman Church did not make his feast obligatory. The First Mexican Council made it obligatory in Mexico in 1555, before Rome. They singled out Saint Joseph because of the "great devotion" already accorded him in Mexico, where he was revered in addition as a protector from storms, thunder, and lightning. The Third Council reaffirmed his day as a Feast of Obligation in 1585, but now — surprisingly — only for Spaniards, not for Indians. (Since they had to give so much more time to work, Indians were obligated to fewer feasts.) When Gregory XV finally made Saint Joseph's feast obligatory for the entire Catholic world in 1621, 58 years after it had been endorsed by the Council of Trent, it must automatically have become obligatory for Indians in Mexico, but the obligation was not always observed. Although there has been a movement in recent years to have him included, Saint Joseph's name is not among the 27 saints in the Roman liturgy of the Mass.[45]

Fray Pedro's interest in Saint Joseph might have been awakened during his schooling with the Brothers of the Common Life, for they particularly admired and read the writings of one of his early advocates, the *doctor christianissimus* Jean Gerson, who had eloquently extolled Saint Joseph to the Council of Constance. The Observants of the Flemish Province chose him for their Patron in 1523, and Fray Pedro may likely have heard some of the discussions which led to the choice. He may early have known the important new text exalting Saint Joseph, the *Summa de donis S Joseph,* written by Isidor of Isolanis, a Dominican, and published at Pavia in 1522. Perhaps inspired by Saint Bernard, who was always monastic in his point of view, and by the three Observant Bernardinos, this poem was destined to be of particular interest to friars, for in it Joseph was held up as a model of the very virtues to which they were particularly committed: Poverty, Chastity, and Obedience. Mendicants were exhorted to venerate him, and to dedicate churches and altars to him (which implies strongly that at this time such dedications were rare).[46]

Isolanis' poem had been dedicated to Hadrian VI, who may already have known Peeter van der Moere at the University of Louvain and at Court, while he was Cardinal-Archbishop of Utrecht, and confessor and tutor to Peeter's young kinsman, the Emperor-to-be. Hadrian and Charles had been in correspondence about sending Franciscans to Mexico as early as 1521, while Hadrian was Regent of Castile. He was still in Spain when elected Pope the next year, the year the poem was published. He could, then, have sent Fray Pedro a gift of the new book shortly before or after Fray Pedro left for Mexico. Hadrian must have known that he was going, and must have known the nature of his mission. Before he died (September 1523), Pope Hadrian could have sent the book to the Twelve. He sent them "papers" of some sort which they received in Seville in December, shortly before sailing. The Twelve would already have favored Joseph, for the Observants had become his chief proponents in Spain. They celebrated his feast before other elements in the Church accepted it. Cardinal Ximénez, Archbishop of Toledo, Regent of Spain, Chancellor of the Realm, the restorer of the Mozarabic Rite, and the champion of the Strict Observance, had regularly celebrated the Feast of Saint Joseph in the Cathedral of Toledo.[47]

The first written references to Saint Joseph in Mexico are neither very helpful nor relevant. Fray Pedro, almost certainly the sponsor of the first version of the chapel, wrote (1558) that it had been "called Saint Joseph of Bethlehem because Christ was born there, and therefore it used to be of thatch, like a poor portico," [48] which tells something about the primitive chapel, but not why it was dedicated to Saint Joseph. Fray Juan de Béjar, who came to New Spain only in 1542, after San José was firmly established, was known for his devotion to the Holy Family, Joseph in particular, and was later said to be "the main cause and means, by the excellence of his preaching, by which the glorious Saint Joseph was received as Patron of all New Spain," a claim chronologically unjustifiable. Possibly Father Béjar was instrumental in founding the Confraternity of Saint Joseph for Spaniards, and credit for that was later erroneously extended to the native cult of Saint Joseph. By the time that the Council of 1555 solemnly elected Saint Joseph "Universal Patron of the Province," he had already been venerated in his own chapel for nearly thirty years.[49]

While Béjar and the Council might have been influenced by some movement in the mother country, no real cult of Saint Joseph there is recorded earlier than that in Mexico. The Observants and Cardinal Ximénez celebrated his feast, but did not promote a public cult so far as is known. It was later that Peter of Alcántara (1499–1562) began championing the extremist ideas of the Paschalites (barefoot vegetarians who banned even libraries), and still later (1541) that they were grouped into a *Custodia* dedicated to Saint Joseph, and later still (1559) that it was made a Province dedicated to him. Peter of Alcántara became head of the old Franciscan Province of Extremadura only after the first waves of Mexican Franciscans had already left it, and before that he was not in any influential position. However the known facts of the cult of Saint Joseph are arranged — and the facts are hard to relate — it is Mexico that leads. Veneration of him in contemporary Europe was isolated and sporadic. The widespread cult came only later, fostered by Saint Teresa of Avila, by whose time (1515–82) the cult in Mexico was stronger than ever.

Not only other open chapels but other roofed churches were being put under his patronage in Mexico. The big Franciscan church in Mérida was dedicated to him because the friars had entered the city on Saint Joseph's day (March 19th), and the coincidence was thought worth commemorating. He was made Patron of the City of Puebla and of a large Indian parish church there (1556), after which it was observed with satisfaction that the number of buildings struck by lightning diminished. Indians began to be christened "Joseph" sooner than Spaniards: Chimalpahín mentioned adult Indian lords in the 1540's euphoniously named don Joseph del Castillo Ehcaxoxouhqui, don Joseph de Santa María Teuhctlacoçauhcatzín, and don Joseph de Santa María Panehuayan. They must have been given the name Joseph when baptized a dozen or so years before, in the late 1520's. The Jesuits imported relics of Saint Joseph in 1578 and '94. By the end of the seventeenth century the enthusiasm for him was such that a supplementary feast was celebrated in the capital on the 19th of every month, as well as a special week-long festival offered in gratitude for his saving the city from a deleterious quake in 1681.[50]

In Catholic Europe, meanwhile, churches were not dedicated to him until after the Council of Trent. There is sometimes said to have been an exception in Bologna, but this was probably only a little oratory not transferred to a proper church until 1566. San Giuseppe di Castello was founded in Venice in 1512 by popular request, and staffed by Augustinian nuns from Verona; the devotion to Joseph may have come from the East, like so much in Venice and the Veneto which differs from customs elsewhere in Italy.[51] (Venice could revere as Saints personages not so held elsewhere: Moses, Job, or Samuel, for instance.) The earliest properly Italian church is more probably San Giuseppe degli Falegnami in Rome, established by the Carpenters' Guild in 1538. As Carpenter Saint Joseph is their patron, it is of course possible that other branches of the Guild may have had other chapels or altars dedicated to him before this, but none seems to have been recorded. The handsome statue of him in the Pantheon in Rome (by Vincenzo de' Rossi) was put there by the Congregation of Saint Joseph soon after it was founded in 1545, but this group was not restricted to carpenters.

The members of the Carpenters' Guild in New Spain, Europeans not natives, did not use San José de los Naturales. They were at first affiliated with the local Confraternity of Saint Joseph, also non-Indian, and later, when the Guild had become larger and more independent, it built its own chapel in some other part of the atrio of San Francisco. The guilds of silver and gold workers, of masons, and of carriage makers also took Saint Joseph for patron, but it is not known where they met to venerate him. The big Indian crafts school associated with it from the beginning might well have something to do with the choice of a carpenter saint for patron of the Indian chapel, particularly since Fray Pedro was responsible for both.[52]

In Spain it is said that on every March 19th since the early Middle Ages the carpenters of Valencia have celebrated the day of their patron and the coming of Spring with big bonfires, *fallas,* but although clearly in honor of Saint Joseph there is no record that these annual outbursts were related to any church, chapel, or image. They were originally inspired by sermons of Saint Vincent Ferrer.

The first church of Saint Joseph in Spain was probably at Granada, dedicated in 1525 on the site of the small Mosque of the Hermits which had been pulled down in 1517. This new church of Saint Joseph was building, then, more or less at the same time as the first building of San José de los Naturales.[53] This association with a mosque could be something more than a coincidence if some friar passing through Granada on his way to New Spain stopped to visit the newest churches in town, and then the late or mosque-like San José de los Naturales *could* have an identifiable father, a converted Moslem as it were. The connection is shadowy, and there is no reason to relate the *first* San José de los Naturales to this small, dull, gothic church in Granada of which word would not have reached New Spain until the first San José was well along. No more is there reason to relate the *first* San José to the old mosque serving as Cathedral in Granada which could have affected the *later* building of San José. There is, in fact, no reason to relate the first portico-chapel to any church anywhere in Europe. The Mexican Franciscan chroniclers seem to have been guilty of a rare understatement when they claimed San José de los Naturales as the first church dedicated to Saint Joseph in America: it was probably the second or third Catholic church ever dedicated to him by Europeans and — if the atrio is counted as its nave — the largest.

DESUETUDE AND DESTRUCTION

San José de los Naturales was several times repaired and several times altered after the original need had become less. More than once someone could have said of it what Charles V had said of the Mosque of Córdoba. The building was always such a stranger among contemporary works that writers found it difficult to describe; they called it "a church of various porticoes, but without any doors," or "of many naves without doors, in the manner of a portico." [54]

When the old San Francisco, the first of the friars' churches, the building where the Twelve had preached, the building where the Church had defied the First Audiencia, became so rotted and weak as to be thought unsafe,

397

it was demolished and replaced (1590); meanwhile the Sacrament was transferred to San José, and Spaniards attended Mass there for a few years. San
José, nevertheless, became smaller rather than larger: it was soon narrowed
to five naves, and then, after part of its front fell, nearly all walled in. In
1611 an earthquake wrecked some of the repaired facade. In 1622 the remains of the naves were still serving the Indians, no longer as an open chapel
but now as a normal church. In 1649 it had to be closed for more repairs:
more was pulled down; it is not certain what was taken away and what was
left. The Confraternity planned to rebuild, but did not, and someone pieced
the building together so that it could be reopened in 1653 with a big Indian
fiesta. In 1698 it was still called the parish church of the Indians. New stone
columns were substituted for the remaining old wood ones. In 1720 the
foundations had to be strengthened. Still in 1729 the monastery had a special
post of "vicar for the *capilla de los indios*," but this must have been no more
than a minor post, and the congregation was reclassified as a minor Indian
parish in 1763. Finally, in 1769, nearly all of what was left was pulled down
except one tower. In 1777 Juan de Viera could call San Francisco "one of
the wonders of the New World" in his thoroughgoing description of the
city, and praise its six remaining chapels extravagantly, without being aware
that the most original Christian building in the Americas had once been the
largest of San Francisco's chapels, and that much of it had still been there,
dilutedly serving its original purpose, only eight years before. Some of the
foundations and other salvaged materials seem to have been thriftily re-employed in a new chapel, occupying only part of the site, sold unfinished to
the Servites, dedicated by them in 1791, and finally finished in 1803/04.
This sad and weak echo, still with one altar dedicated to Saint Joseph, was
destroyed by the cutting of a new street in 1861, right after the expropriation of Church property in Mexico. Nothing is visible now.[55]

192 THE DEMOLITION OF THE CHAPEL OF THE SERVITES, 1861

We still have, however, the street that destroyed the last of San José, named — with grim appropriateness — for its creator, Pedro de Gante. The monastery church of Fray Pedro's day has been replaced by another perhaps not too dissimilar. The cloisters were rebuilt in the seventeenth century, and expropriated by Juárez' government in the nineteenth, and have since been used as a Chamber for the Congress, a theater, and finally an awkward Methodist church. The refectory was rented as a livery stable before it was destroyed, and one of the patios was adapted for a circus. The site of the chapel is now occupied mainly by the High Life Department Store, and its atrio by a twentieth-century miscellany of minor shops, a 43-story skyscraper, and the Cucaracha Tourist Cocktail Club.

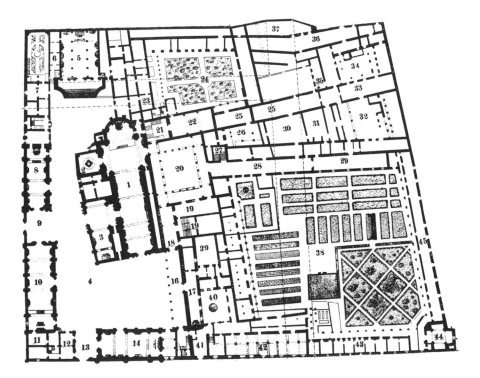

193 PLAN OF THE MONASTERY OF SAN FRANCISCO AT THE TIME OF THE EXPROPRIATION
The dotted lines near the top, behind the apse of the main church (1), show where the new Calle Pedro de Gante *will be cut, slicing off the end of the Chapel of the Servites (5) in the upper left corner. The left edge marks the present* Avenida Madero; *the lower edge the* Calle San Juan de Letrán; *and the dotted lines toward the right show where the* Avenida 16 de Septembre *will be cut.*

399

REFLECTIONS OF SAN JOSÉ

Although the form and the scale of San José de los Naturales were conspicuously abnormal, the prestige of the chapel was such that its form was imitated on a reduced scale in a few other buildings. The *Capilla Real* at Cholula was an out-and-out copy; at Jilotepec there was a more reduced copy; and at Toluca an even more curtailed variation. These were at Franciscan monasteries in close connection with the head house in Mexico City, only 70, 50, and 40 miles away. There was apparently another variation at Etzatlán, half way to the Pacific. In addition, the columnar facade of San José was reflected in quite a few more chapels, and there were scattered reflections of these reflections.

THE CAPILLA REAL AT CHOLULA

Cholula was the venerable Indian city of which nearby Puebla was the new Spanish complement. A chapel for Indians was in use by 1571 on part of the site of a temple of Quetzalcóatl. Little about it is known except that before a decade was over, this or possibly another chapel was similar to San José in plan, though narrower, deeper, lower, and vaulted. It was described in the *Relación de Cholula* in 1581: "There is in this city a monastery of the Order of Saint Francis, the monastery building, cloister, and church very sumptuous and well made . . . As the great concourse of natives did not fit into this church, next to it and within the same circuit of walls, they made a big *cassilla,* almost square, supported by many arches, and with towers at its sides. After it had been vaulted, in order to celebrate a feast in it impressively, the centering of the arches and vaults was taken down; and because the mortar had not set, that night all the vaulting fell to the ground, leaving nothing standing but the walls. It was a miracle that God made it fall at night, for had it been the day before, there would have been great havoc as there were more than four thousand people in the building. It has since lain in ruins because the Indians are now so many less that they have not taken up the work of rebuilding. This structure was the most sumptuous that the Indians have built hereabouts." [56]

Father Ponce saw this chapel five years later, and told the same story: "Beside the monastery at Cholula the Indians made a very large chapel with nine naves, all of stone and mortar and arches, and in this they heard Masses and sermons and received the Most Holy Sacrament; it was sightly and showy, but not very stable or strong as it turned out, for one night all the arches and vaults fell in, leaving the pillars and walls standing the way they are now." [57]

While the history of this building after 1581 or '86 is fairly clear, earlier it is obscure. Francisco de la Maza, who has studied colonial Cholula more thoroughly than anyone, argues that since the *Relación* of 1581 said that the chapel was first built before the Indians became "so many less," the original building was presumably built either before the plague of 1576 or more probably before that of 1544–46, when the population of the newly chartered city was at its height.[58] This earlier plague, according to Fray Domingo de Betanzos, killed 400 to 700 a day. Only a large population could justify so large a building (190 by 170 feet), and it was said that after this disaster only 15,000 Indians were left in Cholula.[59] It seems more likely that San José would have been copied when it was new and still novel than when it was decades old, familiar, and perhaps outmoded. Early vaults, furthermore, would be more likely to collapse than ones built after more experience. These arguments for a date in the 1540's are ingenious and intelligent, and they may be correct, though not everyone agrees with them.

A first objection comes when one remembers that it is doubtful that San José had assumed its mosque-like form before the plague of the mid-1540's. If there was a chapel at Cholula that early, it would more likely have been wood-roofed, possibly imitating an early wood-roofed shed-like San José; and the vaulted chapel at Cholula might then be a replacement which imitated the later mosque-like San José except for its covering. A friary had been founded in Cholula in the late 1520's or possibly the early '30's (1535 according to Zorita), and it was demoted to a vicaría in 1538;[60] it is not known when it became a monastery again, but it must have been only then that a large open chapel would have been undertaken or even proposed. There might not have been time to put up a big vaulted chapel before the beginning of the plague in 1544, and after the plague and subsequent lull, such a work would probably not have been undertaken until 1548 or '49.

The chapel at Cholula had to be large for it was the main Indian church of one of the largest Indian cities. Before the Conquest, Cholula had been a busy religious center with many temples — some said 190, some 300, some 400, some 800 counting small oratories — and a total population of perhaps 200,000 who lived in 50 or 60,000 closely set houses. "More beautiful than the cities of Spain," according to Cortés, Cholula had been half wrecked by him in the Conquest — it was more of adobe than stone — but it was soon renewed enough to be known for "the best houses and the richest people [natives] of all the Indies."[61] It was given the rank of city in 1537, and granted arms in 1540, when there were said to be 37,000 Indians there. Within five years, after the plague, this was down to less than half — 15,000 perhaps — but these figures probably omit women and children, and therefore should be multipled by five, and then enlarged still more if account is to be taken of the Indians in the surrounding cluster of dependent villages. In 1549 the old Indian city must have had advantages lacking in small, new, Spanish Puebla, for it was chosen by the outgoing Viceroy, Mendoza, for conferences with the incoming Velasco. Yet Cholula was overwhelmingly Indian, with never more than a handful of Spanish permanent residents. Although the population kept diminishing — perhaps down three-quarters in the first fifty Spanish years — there were almost surely still some 50 to 60,000 people there shortly before the plague of 1576, living in 18 to 20,000 houses. The congregation cannot have been small if 4,000 were in the chapel the day before it collapsed; and the congregation surely cannot have been poor if even at the end of the century the rich Indian merchants were making such big donations to the Franciscan monastery that it was able to maintain not only itself with thirty friars and the novices they were training, but was able also to make an annual gift to San Francisco at Puebla, which ministered to Spaniards more than to Indians, and had less money. Conditions at Cholula, then, favored religious building: the town was big enough and rich enough to build at almost any time the friars wanted.[62]

The big monastery church was not erected until 1549–52 (according to a lost inscription). It is not planned in any formal relation to the chapel, not built in the same way, and does not have equivalent details: the two do not appear to have been building concurrently. The existing chapel would most likely have been put up a few years after the church. (A few years before would have been the time of the plague.) When the Franciscan Chapter met here in 1568, the establishment was already very large; in 1569 there were five resident friars administering to 60,000 Indians. In the '80's the monastery housed twenty-two friars and administered thirty visita chapels. A very large Indian chapel surely was needed on feast days.[63] In view of all this, an acceptable date for its building would seem to be in the early 1560's.

*

The fact that provisions had to be made for very large Indian congregations must have been one of the chief reasons for taking San José as a model for the Indians' church here, since San José was probably already the largest church in the land and a church specifically for Indians. Moreover, Cholula, as the center of a venerable cult of Quetzalcóatl, may have considered itself the equal or superior of Tenochtitlán — Cholula was considerably older — and deserving of a comparable Indian church. The friars may have had an additional reason for wanting impressive buildings: to supplant memories of impressive non-Christian buildings still prominent in massive ruins all around. It was soon given impressive privileges and exemptions as a *Capilla Real*.

The chapel at Cholula may have been even closer to Serlio's "Hall of a Hundred Columns" than was San José: Serlio's hall was nine by nine bays, the Capilla Real nine wide by seven deep, and San José only seven wide and less deep; probably, at the beginning; Serlio's hall had square stair-towers at each end of the facade, and so did the Capilla Real, but San José had only one.

On the site of an important temple — probably one dedicated to Quetzal-cóatl, part of whose courtyard may coincide with its atrio — the entire monastery had been laid out on an unusually grand scale for the poverty-wed Franciscans, as not only the chapel but also the ample atrio and church still attest. The establishment was the second largest in the land when it was chosen in preference to San Francisco in Puebla for the Chapter of 1568, chosen despite the fact that celebrating a Chapter in an Indian city was not customary when there was a Spanish city so close by.[64]

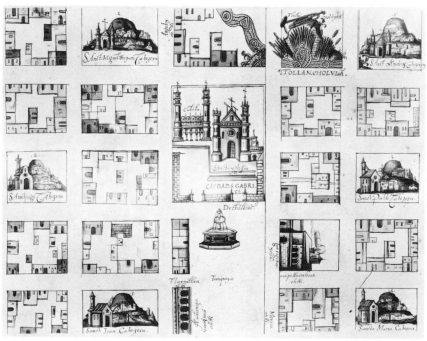

194 THE CAPILLA REAL OF CHOLULA in 1581 (*Relación de Cholula*)
The corner towers, the open arcaded front, the semicircular ends of the barrel vaults above it, and the candelabra finials between them are all indicated, but not accurately described. The monastery church has been correctly located beside and in advance of the chapel, but its facade is not accurately shown. The atrio walls and gates are clear, but the posas have been left out though they must already have been there. On the south (right) side of the atrio runs the portal de peregrinos, *and between it and the church is the entrance to the monastery block.*

In front is the big plaza (labeled tianguizco) *with its public fountain, mayor's house, and arcaded town hall. Out from the plaza the principal streets lead north to Tlaxcala, west to Huejotzingo and Mexico City, south to Atlixco, and east to nearby Puebla. Around the edge are six visita churches, all set beside ex-temple pyramids.*

403

195 THE FRANCISCAN ESTABLISHMENT AT CHOLULA *with the Capilla Real opened up to its typical form of the 1580's. The atrio, with its gates and steps, and the church and monastery block are still today much as they were in the map of 1581 (ill. 194). The three posas are normally placed, but there is none in the southeast corner and probably never was, for it would stand awkwardly isolated between church and chapel or, if against the church, awkwardly isolated from its mates. Church and chapel are raised by a few long steps above the main area of the atrio.*

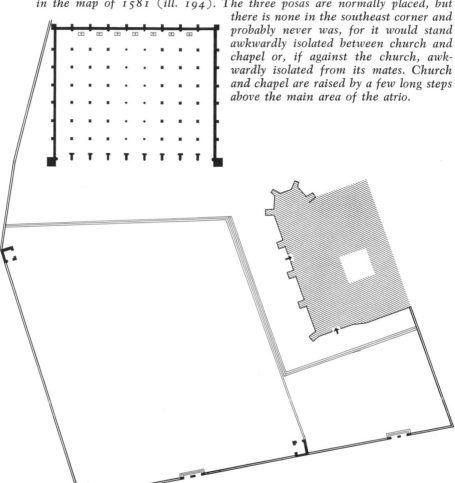

The chapel is peculiarly placed in relation to the church. The atrio is stretched out of shape by trying to accommodate itself to both of them, with its north and south edges determined by the direction of the church, the west by the town plaza, and the east by the front of the chapel. The resulting near-parallelogram makes a sharp bend with the axis of the chapel. As often, the warped asymmetry of the atrio is far more apparent abstractly on a small plan on paper than it is concretely on the actual big plot. The layout of the town is regular, and the chapel is set in accord with its axes. The church alone is at an angle, perhaps in order to be oriented due east, or more likely to take economical advantage of the foundations of an earlier church or of an older temple. Whatever the reason, this reinforces the suspicion that church and chapel were not planned or built in the same campaign. There is no raised platform for the atrio, though there must have been a super-abundance of rubble from the smashed shrines of pagan Cholula, and this reinforces the possibility that it usurps a pagan court even to its pagan paving (ill. 92): the church, then, could well rest on pagan underpinnings.

*

The whole chapel was once covered by nine barrel vaults, running side by side over its nine parallel naves. They were not of stone, as Father Ponce wrote, but of brick, as many traces in the upper parts of the old outer wall still show. The waterspouts to drain the eight long valleys between the nine vaults still pierce the upper part of the rear walls but uselessly now because the new covering is at a lower level and drains another way. Although un-vaulted, the Mosque of Córdoba had (and still has) similar gutters running in the valleys of its parallel rows of pitched roofs, leading to waterspouts. The original barrel vaults of Cholula rested on stone arcades, each with seven arches carried on columns, as the *Relación de Cholula* suggests, and had they not fallen, the vaults would neatly have buttressed each other except at the north and south sides, where they were stabilized by heavy walls with salient pier-buttresses on the outside.

196 ORIGINAL VAULTS OF THE CAPILLA REAL
At the right, in the angle where the modern tile roofing and the old stone wall meet, can be seen the springing of a ruined brick barrel vault.

Even though it collapsed, this chapel was one of the notable vaulting feats of the sixteenth century in Mexico. A huge space, 170 by 190 feet, was covered with thin-shelled lightweight vaults, each only two bricks thick. As these were carried by arches on widely spaced slender columns which made the minimum of interior obstruction, no other vaulted structure of sixteenth-century Mexico could show anything like so low a ratio of solid to void. It would have seemed low at the time in Europe, and surely it was beyond Mexican skills before 1544. Even if built as late as the 1560's, which is probable, the building would have been the envelope of a larger vaulted space than any other in the New World. The novel structural scheme was probably a local invention since the chapel was based on the unvaulted San José and not directly on anything in Spain. (None of the equivalent Spanish mosques still standing then was similarly vaulted.) Although dependent on San José in plan, the Capilla Real far surpassed it in structural ingenuity. A genuine architectural intelligence must have conceived the idea of covering the wide, low, open space with thin-shelled vaults of this kind. This imagination would not seem to have been accompanied by an equivalent structural experience, since the experiment failed to stand up.

197 CONJECTURAL RESTORATION OF THE CAPILLA REAL before 1581 (*based on a drawing by Miguel Messmacher for Francisco de la Maza's* Cholula)

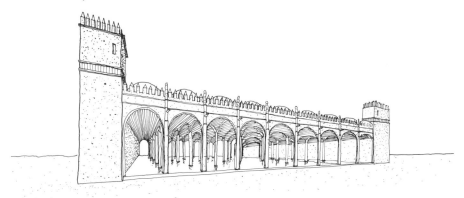

In the National Archives in Mexico City, Heinrich Berlin has recently discovered the name of the architect who rebuilt the chapel after the collapse of the vaults: Luis de Arciniega, younger brother of Claudio de Arciniega, the more famous architect of the Cathedral in the capital. Born in Burgos in 1537, Luis had come to New Spain in the 1550's, and had earned fame as a designer of retables. One still intact at Cuautinchán, begun in 1593 for Tehuacán, is presumably his, and he worked also on retables at Tepeaca, Tula, Mixquic, Malinalco, and Ocuilan, now lost. Possibly the famous and costly retable which once ornamented the monastery church at Cholula was his too. He settled in Puebla, where he made himself so esteemed that he was entrusted with the building of the Cathedral (1589), then a twin and friendly rival of that being built by his brother Claudio in the capital. It was while engaged on this that Luis made his plans for the reconstruction of the Capilla Real at Cholula. He died in 1599 or 1600.[65]

He is known to have done considerable work in Cholula, and might even have been the designer of the vaulted chapel scheme that collapsed (in which case it could not have been begun much before 1560). It could have been designed by an inventive retable-maker who had not yet had much experience in actual construction. If this was so, he might have been called in to take charge of the later repairs because he already knew the building so well. Nothing in his other works, however, resembles that bold, ingenious, and simple system of vaults. Perhaps his hand can be identified more convincingly in details, such as the renaissance plateresque candelabra finials along the skyline which are more akin to retable ornaments. As he was also a sculptor, he might have been particularly interested in the decorative carved elements in architecture. He liked to use such baluster forms, for they appeared both as candelabra and as columns on a temporary monument he put up for Lent in 1595 at the Cathedral of Puebla.[66]

198 A CANDELABRA FINIAL ON THE FACADE OF THE CA—PILLA REAL

Something definite is known about his project for repairing the collapsed Capilla Real, thanks to the researches of Heinrich Berlin. As it had been open to the sky since its vaults fell, the conditions under which the Indian population were using it, every Sunday and feast day from 6 or 7 to 11 o'clock in the morning, were found trying. The sun, rain, and wind were making the congregation so uncomfortable that they would walk out of Mass, or stay away; they complained that the sun had killed some of them. The wind blew out the candles on the altar, and forced the priest to shift from one part of the chapel to another during the service (with a portable ara?). In May and June of 1595, the city governors and other leading Indian citizens petitioned that their chapel be roofed. They pointed out that the adjacent monastery church would hold only a quarter of the Indian congregation; some said only a tenth. (It is one of the largest sixteenth-century churches in Mexico.) Luis de Arciniega made an estimate of the cost of reconditioning

407

the chapel according to a project he had already prepared. He and everyone else thought that the cost would be low because so much of the old building was still there: the walls were standing, and the colonnades were either standing or ready to be stood up again. Building materials needed for the new work were already at hand, and there were plenty of masons and carpenters in the town. The only expenses would be for the transportation of materials (to be paid for in order "to avoid vexing the Indians"), for salaries of a Spanish mason and a supervisor who would visit the job from time to time. Tools and food, but no wages, would have to be given to the Indian workmen, who were thought to be so eager to have their chapel covered that they would work for nothing without being coerced. Everything could be finished in two years or a little more. Arciniega did not plan to vault the building again, for he wrote that he would need strong stone only for columns and arches — some must have been destroyed or damaged — and wood which could be "short and laid flat" for the roof and some sort of mudéjar ceiling.[67]

Now in 1595 the Indians insisted on being sheltered from the weather for their long Catechism, sermon, and Mass. Since this cannot have been common earlier in the neighborhood, some of the Cholultecas, unlike their neighbors at Puebla or Huejotzingo, having once had a large covered chapel must have been so accustomed to worshipping indoors that they did not want to have to worship outdoors. Perhaps they had seen that elsewhere outdoor Masses were obsolescent. It is remarkable that the Cholultecas were still used to spending four or five hours at Catechism, sermon, and Mass every Sunday and feast day. Nowhere in the Christian world can so many people have spent so much time at church as in Mexico.

199 CONJECTURAL RESTORATION OF THE CAPILLA REAL *after the collapse of the barrel vaults and before the building of the domes (photograph reworked by Kenneth J. Conant).*

The result of the Indians' petition is not known, but the wooden roof was nearly done in 1601 and finished (or patched) in 1608, after Luis de Arciniega had died. The wood had begun to rot by 1661, and the center aisle and parts of the others were again open to the sky, except where three small brick domes had been substituted. There was now trouble in getting the Indians to work on the chapel, perhaps because the new project — to dome the entire chapel — was no longer administered by friars but by curates, the monastery having been secularized in 1652. Some Indians, however, wished to cover certain parts in order to protect the graves of their forebears. The work went slowly, and was finished only in 1731, with the now famous quincunxes of tiled domes. Some have thought that this was done earlier but, had they been there many decades before, it seems unavoidable that anyone describing the chapel would have had to comment on the startling spectacle of the densest constellation of domes in the Western world. At the end of the seventeenth century, for example, well-traveled Gemelli Carreri had nothing to say about it at all, and observant Father Vetancurt remarked only on the shortness of the naves.[68]

In Vetancurt's day the outermost aisles had already been divided into chapels like box-stalls, by spur partitions which join the exterior walls to the nearest row of stone columns, leaving seven instead of nine clear naves in the middle. It is surprising that he should have thought the naves "short." [69]

*

The shell of side and back walls, the stone piers of the nine arched openings across the front, and the plain stone towers flanking them probably survive from the chapel whose vaults fell before 1581. At least some of the mudéjar octagonal columns inside are from the rebuilding by Arciniega in the 1590's, since it is recorded that he had some new columns made. While the plateresque candelabra finials could also be from this project, they need not be: they could as well be from the original design of the '60's (if it was made then), for they are too like the plateresque detail of the facade at Acolman (1560) to be very remote from it in date. Arciniega's wood ceiling would probably have been mudéjar, for the pieces of wood "short and laid flat" suggest a typically Islamic patterned scheme. San José de los Naturales had another elaborate wood ceiling which may well have been mudéjar also.

Hispano-moresque character colors much of the elevation as well as the plan at Cholula, but in a far more orthodox manner. (The same may have been true of San José.) For example, before it was walled up, the facade must have looked rather like that of the Mosque of Córdoba, or even more like the simpler Galería del Lagarto at Seville, which stands in the same relation to its Patio de los Naranjos as did San José and the Capilla Real to their atrios. The Moslem character of the latter was recognized as early as

1630 by Father Cobo: writing to a Jesuit friend in Peru, he extolled the city of Cholula, the largest he had ever seen anywhere in the world (although it had already shrunk to a fifth of its preconquest size), and then described its most important building (inaccurately when he noted eight naves) which he recognized as "in the style of the Mosque of Córdoba." [70] He was not able to see, however, that it was not a child but a grandchild of a mosque, because by his time the legitimacy of San José as the immediate parent was unrecognizable: what he saw of San José was a composite, a remodeling of a remodeling, and not any one original complete scheme.

200 THE CAPILLA REAL from the south tower, *showing the line of the sixteenth-century facade, with its merlons and finials, set in advance of the seventeenth-century domes. At the top left is the battlemented atrio wall.*

The chapel at Cholula continued to enjoy fame. In the later eighteenth century it was remarked by the cultured Jesuit, Father Clavijero, only for its many naves and for its door with three hundred different fancy nail-heads. (The voice of the persistently trivial guide echoes unchanged through two centuries: "all made by hand and all different.") In bad repair, the chapel is still perfunctorily cared for, and still occasionally used by the local Indians, though never now on the scale seen 75 years ago by Bandelier, when 3000 attended a festival service.[71]

201 THE INTERIOR OF THE CAPILLA REAL in the 1920's

JILOTEPEC, ETZATLÁN, TOLUCA

At Jilotepec, "hill of tender young corn," the Franciscans made another variant of San José. An Otomí capital on the Chichimeca frontier, Jilotepec had gone over to Christianity early, for its *cacique,* a relative of Moctezuma (to whom he paid a token tribute of three live eagles a year), had become an ardent Christian, effective in converting the Chichimecas around Querétaro.

The chapel at Jilotepec may have been made like San José because of the close connection of the family of one of its encomenderos with the Franciscans in the capital. The town had been given by Cortés to Juan Jaramillo as a pre-wedding present when Jaramillo married Cortés' Indian ex-mistress, doña Marina. On Jaramillo's death it passed not to their daughter but to Jaramillo's daughter by a second wife. This younger girl had paid for considerable building and rebuilding at the Franciscan house in the capital with money from this legacy. She had always favored the Franciscans, and even as a child used to visit their building operations with gifts. For years she was involved in litigation with her older half-sister, Jaramillo's daughter by doña Marina, who felt that her share of the inheritance was disproportionately small in view of the invaluable services her mother had given the Spaniards in the Conquest. Since the suit, mainly over the encomienda of Jilotepec, was still being argued in 1552, if the younger and successful heiress gave much money to the Franciscan monastery at Jilotepec, it would probably have been after 1552, after her title was secure. In that case the chapel would not have been begun before the mid-1550's.[72]

202 THE OPEN CHAPEL AT JILOTEPEC
A sixteenth-century drawing, also showing the encomendero (or mayor?) and a Franciscan friar.

Furthermore, since it resembled the San José described by Doctor Cervantes about 1563, the chapel at Jilotepec must have been designed after the alterations or following the Memorial Mass of 1559 (unless the chronology proposed for San José is faulty). Between the early '60's and 1571 when he went to Europe, Fray Diego de Valadés was active in the neighborhood, evangelizing recalcitrant Chichimecas and serving as Guardian at Tepeji del Río. As he was a disciple of Fray Pedro de Gante, probably his secretary and a teacher at his school, the idea of building a chapel at Jilotepec like Fray Pedro's San José may have come from him. This would reaffirm a date in the late 1560's.[73]

Another reason for making a chapel like San José might have been the size of the congregation. While never so big nor so rich as Cholula — in fact so poor in 1553 that its tribute was reduced — Jilotepec was still populous enough in 1560 to supply 600 Indians for settling a new outpost on the road to the fabulous mines of Zacatecas, appropriately named San Luis Nuevo Jilotepec. (Many of the settlers may have been refugees from lands taken by the rapacious cattle barons all around Jilotepec.) Tlaxcala had refused to supply the men but Jilotepec felt it had enough to spare. In 1574 there were 35,000 natives in the immediate neighborhood. By 1576 the cattle were being kept off the nearby farmlands, and Jilotepec was the hub of a farming region 30 miles around in which there were 25,000 souls served by two busy friars.[74] They would have needed a big chapel.

The stone walls of the sides and back of the chapel are still in place, with enough traces of altar-niches and beam-brackets to indicate that there must have been seven naves, each five bays deep, covered by a slightly sloping wood-framed roof carried on slender wood columns arranged in rows as in San José. Enough remains to show that it was only half the size of its model (100 by 90 feet) and, even clogged as it is by a recent school building, to make us realize how vast that model must have looked. The Jilotepec version must have been impressive too, for Fray Alonso Urbano, sent there by Father Ponce in 1586, called it "a large and sumptuous *ramada* [thatched shed, or porch]," exceptional praise in the *Relación* of phlegmatic Father Ponce, who listed but usually did not describe or try to evaluate the various buildings of the monasteries he was inspecting. (He had shrugged off San José de los Naturales with minimal mention.) [75] The *ramada* of Jilotepec stood north of the church, set back as at San José or Cholula. All three chapels had big atrio areas of their own along one side of the church, bigger than the area in front, thus showing clearly that the main space was for the chapel. Even in these three cases, where the "open" chapel was a roofed church, the atrio was still conceived as an auxiliary to it.

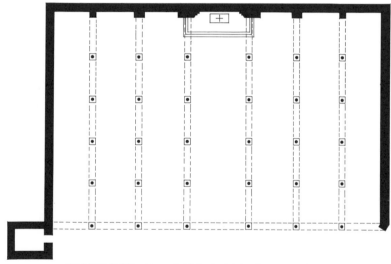

203 CONJECTURAL PLAN OF THE CHAPEL AT JILOTEPEC

Jilotepec gradually lost importance, though there seem to have been sizable Indian congregations: 18,000 in the eighteenth century, outnumbering the combined whites, mestizos, and mulattoes by sixty to one. Later writers do not mention the chapel even when they mention the monastery. Father Vetancurt gave one possibly significant fact relating the chapel to its model — without mentioning the chapel itself — when he wrote that the Indians of Jilotepec still belonged to a Confraternity of Saint Joseph.[76]

*

Another fragmentary reflection of San José de los Naturales is to be found, apparently, at another Chichimeca frontier outpost, Etzatlán, in a sheltered valley among the abrupt sierras of Jalisco. The region had been "prepared by Brother Juan Francisco, a *donado* of our Order, and a pupil of the excellent Fray Pedro de Gante." [77] The Franciscan monastery had been founded in 1534, and it was said in the seventeenth and eighteenth centuries to have been built in the 1540's "of masonry and carved stone" and "in the form which it still has." [78] Since two friars martyred by the Chichimecas were buried in the chancel in 1541, something fairly solid must already have been put up, though it is possible that work on the church was still being carried on in 1554.[79] The evidence that major building was done in the 1540's is respectable.

Life at Etzatlán ("bloody waters" or "bloody gullies") seems to have been hard. The region had suffered badly in the Mixtón War (1540–41), and savage unconverted Indians from the sierras kept harrying it after the revolt had been quelled. They were said to have been calmed only by 1552, by which time many of them were attending Masses at the monastery. A terrible quake in 1566 devastated most of the friaries in Jalisco, though what it did to Etzatlán is not known. In 1569, although it was scarcely distinguishable in size from the others in Jalisco (it had two friars and a thousand tributaries), Etzatlán was considered one of the six towns in Jalisco that could be classified as Indian *and* Spanish.[80]

The monastery was called not only "strong," and "made to be a fortress," "of masonry and carved stone," but also "one of the best in the Province, famous and illustrious . . . for its building." [81] A lay brother was called from Poncitlán "because he was a great architect." [82] The surviving monastery block and church fail to justify these appraisals. The once wood-roofed church has now been vaulted with brick-ribbed adobe, and its thick walls, though "strong," could only by flattery now be called "a fortress," though it is possible to imagine it may have seemed one to people apprehensive in a neighborhood where there was little other material protection. It would take much false flattery to see the crude small church and second-class cloister as "illustrious and famous," or the work of any "great architect." The other houses in the province — today little known, and with little left to know since most were of adobe — must have been sorry examples if this was "one of the best." Only the carved fountain in the middle of the cloister seems to have been of more than commonplace quality. The one distinction of the monastery today is its age, for it is the only one in Jalisco to have survived in fair measure from the sixteenth century.

These eulogistic phrases may not have been intended to refer to the modest church and cloister or to the engaging little fountain, but rather to something else, something big, striking, and pretentious: the Indian chapel. Opposite the church, on the west side of the old atrio now serving as town plaza, there stands — disguised and unnoticed — what appears to be the remains of another quincunx of columns partly re-employed in a seventeenth- and eighteenth-century church of pretty "folk-art" character. Old natives remember that before the Revolution it was connected with an "old" hospital, still there at least as late as 1913. The presumed sixteenth-century structure has been more built into and more radically altered than that at Jilotepec, but more of it still stands: 18 stone columns are visible (or were in 1945), and one can still make out, with a little paleontological patience, a sort of elementary mosque, 5 bays deep and either 5 or 7 wide. It would appear to have been much like Jilotepec in its main disposition.

Inasmuch as there were 10 to 17 or 18,000 natives to be served in Etzatlán in the middle of the sixteenth century, and as there were only three to five friars to do it,[83] making a heavier peak load than at many Franciscan houses with larger buildings, it seems justifiable to identify these fragments — apparently of the sixteenth century — as the remains of a much needed Indian chapel even though it faces the atrio from the west side, opposite the church. No chronicler mentioned a chapel here, but chroniclers were inconsistent in noting open chapels, and often failed to mention even the most striking. Perhaps an extra reason for making a chapel here would have been that the town was Indian *and* Spanish: if the Spaniards were using the small monastery church, they may have wanted the Indians accommodated somewhere else.

Fray Andrés de Córdoba, one of the Twelve, was killed by Chichimecas near Etzatlán in 1567, and his bones were kept in a stone box behind the altar in the chancel of the monastery church together with the bones of four other martyred friars. According to reliable Father Vetancurt, Fray Andrés had been a builder of churches. One of the other friars buried beside him was Fray Francisco Lorenzo, who had been born and reared in Granada. Neither of these scraps of coincidence is tenable enough to make any well-knit connection between the ex-mosque, the ex-mosque-cathedral and the neo-mosque-chapel (Granada, Córdoba, and Mexico City) for it is not recorded whether either friar spent much time alive in Etzatlán before being buried there, or if either had anything to do with building there, or when any part of the monastery at Etzatlán was built, least of all the putative chapel. It is not unshakably sure that the hidden bits of old building were once bits of an open chapel — there are other bits in other buildings in the village — though the odds are perhaps three to one that they were.[84] Whether parts of an open chapel or not, they are surely parts of a hospital chapel. Many were built in Jalisco in the seventeenth century, following the example of Michoacán, and many of these faced east to the church across an atrio or across an atrio and plaza. The best hypothesis for Jilotepec is that a sixteenth-century open chapel was made into a seventeenth-century hospital chapel, which was patched into an eighteenth-century parish church, and then patched and re-patched into its twentieth-century formlessness.

*

204 THE FOUNTAIN AT ETZATLÁN
The water was emitted in thin streams from the four cherubs' mouths. Though of exceptionally small size, this fountain probably first stood in the plaza and not in the cloister where it now is. (Some possibility must be allowed that it may have been carved later than the sixteenth century.)

The chapel at the Franciscan friary at Toluca was almost entirely destroyed in 1874, when the monastery was pillaged and wrecked during the Reform Wars, but enough fragments of information about it can be assembled to show that it, too, reflected San José. Toluca began to be important and rich in the 1540's, from the big cattle ranches in the surrounding high valley. By 1555 there were 150,000 head of cattle there, and 10 leagues of wall had to be built, on orders from the Viceroy, to keep them out of the Indians' fields. There had been an early monastery, which had been begun to be rebuilt in 1550, probably by Fray Andrés de Castro, "the Apostle of the Matlatzincas," on land given not by any of the rich cattle barons but by the converted ruler of the Matlatzincas, don Juan Fernando Cortés Coyotzín. He also gave most of the building materials, which were taken from a repudiated

416

temple and from his own palace. The monastery grew rapidly, and for a while maintained a famous seminary. A few arches embedded in the much altered and deteriorated remains were until recently accompanied by an inscription in Spanish and Náhuatl (spoken locally along with Matlatzinca), associating them with the front of the old church, and dating them between 1552 and '78. The regular monastery church surely once stood next to this arcade, which must have been the facade of the open chapel. This is confirmed by drawings, which show it to have been a portico five arches wide, with the arches running uphill from low ends to a high middle. There were two more arcades behind this front one, and behind them, a back wall. Thus there was made a reduced San José de los Naturales, five arches wide and three bays deep, less dependent on its model, we suppose, than the near-mosques at Cholula, Jilotepec, and Etzatlán, unless it depended more directly on an earlier state of San José when it had not yet become so mosque-like. This chapel at Toluca was influential locally (as will be shown in Chapter XIV) but its offspring resemble San José even less.[85]

THE FIRST OPEN CHAPELS: II

IN his *History of the Indians of New Spain*, Father Motolinía quoted a long letter to the Father Provincial which had been written at Tlaxcala in 1539: "For Easter the Indians had completed the chapel of the patio which, when finished, was a magnificent room: they call it *Bethlehem.*" [1] It was probably given this name because the friars found that *Tlaxcala* could be taken to have the same meaning as *Bethlehem,* "house of bread," and that if they did honor to the early baptism of the chieftains there, they might suggest that Tlaxcala, like Bethlehem, was a birthplace of Christianity. There may also have been an echo of San José *de Belén* de los Naturales, which also gave Bethlehem a prominence unusual at this time. [2]

Father Motolinía's description continues: "They painted the outside in four days, and used fresco because water would not efface it. On one space they painted the works of the first three days of the creation of the world, and on another space the works of the other three days. As for the other two spaces, on one is the tree of Jesse, with the lineage of the Mother of God above it, done very beautifully, and on the other space is our father Saint Francis. Elsewhere is the Church, His Holiness the Pope, cardinals, bishops, and so on, and in another part the Emperor, kings, and knights. Spaniards who have seen the chapel say that it ranks with the most graceful of its kind in Spain. The chapel has well made arches [or richly carved, *bien labrados*] and two choirs, one for the singers and one for those who play instruments. It was all done in six months, and like all the churches they have, it is ornamented and well built." [3]

A puzzling building at Tlaxcala has been identified by some scholars as this chapel. [4] Because of its intrinsic interest and the possibility of a very early date, it demands special scrutiny.

For an early description of a building, Father Motolinía's is exceptionally long, and while it may seem exceptionally explicit too, it tells less about the architecture than it seems to promise. On some points it is definite: there was a "patio" chapel at Tlaxcala in 1539 with notable arches; it had been built in six months, and elaborately painted in four days in what Motolinía thought was fresco; it must have had considerable flat exterior surface for the many painted figures in four major and several minor spaces; somewhere there was architectural provision for two groups of musicians.

418

THE EARLY HISTORY OF THE MONASTERY AT TLAXCALA

Fortunately a miscellany of other items about the building of the monastery has been preserved in Franciscan chronicles. In fact, among histories of sixteenth-century Mexican monasteries, that of Tlaxcala has an unusual number of recorded "facts" and traditions, but not all are to be trusted.

With a population of around 200,000, Tlaxcala was one of the strategic cities the Franciscans chose for their first four monasteries. In 1524 they moved in to Lord Maxixcatzín's palace in the district called Ocotelulco across the river from the modern city. They left, probably in 1527, for new quarters on a hillside called Cuitlixco, also on the edge of the old city, and still on the same side of the river. (Thomas Gage was confused when he thought the monastery in use in 1625 was in Ocotelulco.) This second monastery, at Cuitlixco, was substantially finished in 1529, though some building was still going on in 1532. (Fathers Vetancurt and Suárez de Peredo could see its ruins at the end of the seventeenth century.) [5] In his life of Fray Martín de Valencia, Motolinía, and then Mendieta copying him, said that Fray Martín had been Guardian of Tlaxcala for four years (probably 1527–30/31) just before Motolinía himself first became Guardian; and he went on to say that Fray Martín "erected a friary at Tlaxcala." As Fray Martín was very busy from the time he left Tlaxcala until he died in 1534, if he had time to direct work there, it must have been at this second location at Cuitlixco.[6]

By 1536 or '37, at about the time they were moving the city across the river, the friars began to build another monastery on another hillside just above the new town at a site where they already had a much venerated cross and some sort of small shrine or *humilladero*. This, their third house in a dozen years, was nearly complete by 1540. Presumably it is the basis of the present one: much of its original layout may have survived not only the eruption of Popocatépetl which shook the whole region in 1540 but also the subsequent repairs and changes of individual parts. The plague of 1544–46 attacked Tlaxcala with particular savagery — Father Betanzos said that as many as 1000 Indians died in a day — and there can have been little building for several years afterwards. This indicates an active campaign from about 1536 to 1540 (while Motolinía was Guardian), followed by lesser works until 1544, and a virtual halt from 1544 to '46, with major activity possible again after about 1548.[7] The church was completed in 1564, and its main lines and front doorway apparently are preserved in the present building. By the 1580's, when Father Mendieta was living there, the establishment was larger than average, with seven or eight resident friars and a few more when it was operated as a seminary. In the seventeeth century the church was made higher, and was given the handsome mudéjar wood ceiling which is its chief attraction today.[8]

FIRST CHAPELS II

The existing chapel stands on a hillside at the head of a long and broad ramp which leads up from a large open space below. Although there are unexplored ruins at Ocotelulco on the other side of the river and no record of any preconquest community on this side, it is possible that the chapel stands on what was once an important part of a big pagan sanctuary, as Father Torquemada believed. This could have been one of the reasons why the Franciscans chose it, as well as why the Christian arrangement looks so like a pagan one. Archaeologists do not confirm or deny that preconquest terraces may lie under the existing ensemble. No excavations have been undertaken, and little is known about the general character of the pre-Spanish architecture of Tlaxcala. Whatever the origin of the multi-level site of the monastery may be, the results are not only impressive but remarkably out of the ordinary.[9]

When the Twelve passed through Tlaxcala on their way up to México-Tenochtitlán, they marveled at the crowds, and agreed that more people were gathered in the markets than they had ever seen gathered anywhere. One of the three or four largest of the Indian cities, Cortés had found preconquest Tlaxcala "much larger than Granada, and very much stronger." It must have had many ambitious buildings, and since the city had been little damaged in the Conquest, many must still have been there in Father Motolinía's day, most of them across the river.[10] Like its rival Texcoco, Tlaxcala is now but a shabby memorial of its own crumbled grandeur, post- and preconquest.

The layout of the establishment differs from later ones in several ways. Most striking is the fact that there are two atrios: the larger at the bottom of the hill, in front of the chapel and over 30 feet below it; the more typical smaller one in back of the chapel, 20 feet above its floor but 2 feet below the

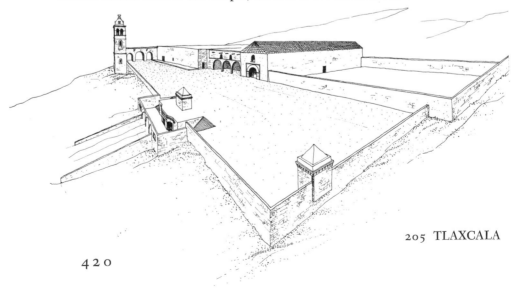

205 TLAXCALA

level of its top. The church and monastery block stand at the back of this upper atrio, which runs across the major east-west axis (church-chapel-ramp) and stretches out so far to the north that it establishes a strong cross-axis. This axis is extended farther north by another long ramp running down to the main part of the new city through the monumental north gateway, whose three arches are set between the monastery block and the freestanding bell-tower. This ramp, made before 1560, once had 63 low steps which a horse could easily go up, according to Doctor Cervantes de Salazar, who puzzlingly also called it "eight sided." [11]

206
The west RAMP at TLAXCALA
*leading up to the triple gateway
and the chapel*

With two big patios, enormous crowds could be accommodated. Father las Casas calculated that he had seen 30, 40, and 50,000 people in the upper atrio, and 80,000 "in the patio" in 1538, but his figures must be deflated. He also noticed a battlemented wall and some stucco paving in the upper atrio which have since disappeared.[12]

Father Mendieta wrote: "I can truthfully say that the most agreeable sight that I have ever seen in my whole life was the two patios of the church at Tlaxcala in days gone by, a high one, and a low one to which one descended by a splendid double stairway like that of the Aracoeli in Rome, the patios and stairways being full of people." [13] Written only about forty years after Motolinía and las Casas, "in days gone by" acknowledges that there were no longer any crowds, and that the spaciousness of the approaches and patios was no longer justified by use. Failure to mention the chapel also suggests that it may not then have been important, visually or functionally. Father Mendieta wrote this probably about 1580, before he had lived at Tlaxcala, and he was referring to something he had seen there a generation earlier. It is as easy to understand his enthusiasm for the amplitude of the atrios and approaches at Tlaxcala as it is to forgive his dim memory of Rome, where the single stairway of Santa Maria in Aracoeli has almost nothing in

421

common with the ramp at Tlaxcala except its tiring length. When he was in Rome the second "stairway" was a dirt ramp, and it led not to the church but to the half-rebuilt Capitoline.

The upper atrio at Tlaxcala now goes around in an L to the south side of the church, and includes the area used as a sports field by the local police and their charges in the little jail installed in the former Franciscan hospital north of the monastery block. (About 1560 the hospital was lower down, at the foot of the north ramp.) On the hillside behind the monastery were the friars' gardens and orchards, both particularly famous. The level rectangle of open space in front of the church still serves as its atrio, now pleasantly shaded by graceful and venerable ash, cassia, and walnut trees. Somewhere by this upper atrio the friars ran a school which by the 1530's and '40's already had 500 or 600 boys.[14]

If the vaulted chapel, which though confused in later walls still stands almost intact at the head of the west ramp, served as an open chapel, this upper atrio could have been used for all the normal functions of an atrio except the main one of an outdoor church. That would have been impossible because the chapel, though in front of the church, is below this atrio, faces away from it, and cannot be functionally associated with it. Inasmuch as the chapel commands the *lower* atrio area, there and there only could the Indians have gathered to hear Mass conducted in the chapel. They would be dissociated not only from the church but also from the monastery block, the portería, the school, and the posas. The situation would have been unique, but neither historically nor functionally impossible. The lower atrio can no longer be perceived as a whole, for what has not been made into a cornfield has been invaded by little houses, shops, and the town bullring.

207 TLAXCALA, through the TRIPLE GATEWAY to the LOWER CHAPEL

208 THE LOWER
CHAPEL AT
TLAXCALA
from the north

These formally imposing but functionally awkward arrangements were not repeated. The closest analogue is at Huexotla, a spacious ensemble which usurps preconquest terraces and, moreover, Tlaxcalteca ones (ill. 103). Huexotla lacks a chapel at the intermediate level between its terraces, and no signs suggest that one was ever there. Clear remains show a large open chapel on the upper level, in a normal position just north of the church. The church has been entirely rebuilt, and only the monastery block and ruined chapel survive from the sixteenth century.

The west or front ramp at Tlaxcala divides where it meets the chapel, and half runs up along each side to reach the upper atrio. Because it goes straight down the middle of the lower atrio, the ramp would cleave any congregation there into two groups, perhaps of segregated men and women.

209 THE LOWER
CHAPEL AT
TLAXCALA
from the south

423

Pushed to one side or the other, everyone would have had only an oblique view of the chapel, a view which would have been hampered further by a gateway of three arches at the top of the ramp and by the fact that the front of the chapel was set back 18 feet behind the arches and the altar 10 feet yet farther back, inside the chapel. If this was used as an open chapel, the functional problems were not solved, nor well understood, and the ensemble would represent a primitive stage of the open-chapel-and-atrio scheme.

THE CHAPEL AND ITS VAULT

A flattened hexagon in plan, the little building seems to be an adaptation of a small European chapel, or perhaps of a polygonal church sanctuary, and it is consequently less a new type than an old type half-adapted to new circumstances with Procrustean unconcern. The front projects like a bay window onto the head of the ramp. Its three flat faces were originally opened up by bold but coarse ogee arches, which could have been closed with wood or metal grilles when the chapel was not in use (as at San José); thus the chancel could have housed a consecrated altar, like a regular church.

The three back sides of the hexagon are sunk into the retaining wall which holds the upper atrio up, and they form a cave-like niche or apse. Half is built out: half is built in. At either end are small irregular-shaped rooms, one probably a sacristy. (They are too small and shut to have been Motolinía's "two choirs.") The hexagon is covered with a strange, ambitious, and clumsy ribbed vault.

This vault has four heavy ribs intersecting at the center, awkwardly adjusted to the space they have to span. The longest, following the long north-south axis of the hexagon, misses the sharp corners from which it might be expected to spring. The shortest, at right angles to it, following the shorter east-west axis, comes down uncomfortably on the point of the entrance arch, and at its other end, not knowing how or where to finish, stops dead on the east wall. Jostled by these, the diagonal ribs do not run in continuous straight lines, but are pushed sideways at the main intersection. A floral pendant tries to hide this clumsiness like a sort of architectural figleaf. Since a posa is still standing on top of it, and since the vault must always have looked much as it does now, the clumsiness cannot be blamed on inexpert rebuilding. As in all early Mexican vaults and many later ones, plenty of mortar and heavy masses of rubble masonry piled up to the haunches of the vault convert it into an almost monolithic shell. Because of its thickness and the fact that it is largely buried in the hillside, the vault creates no problems of thrust or buttressing. Statical problems seem to have been almost paranoically avoided, overcompensated by tons of stabilizing inert matter. Perhaps the builder had been alarmed by a recent quake, and therefore determined to build something that future quakes would not crack.

424

210 The VAULT of the LOWER CHAPEL at TLAXCALA

Traces of figure painting show on the webs of the vault between the ribs, on a skin of plaster so thin that it seems more like thickened paint than a normal plaster coat for fresco. Since Motolinía's frescoes were presumably outside, these undatable patches must be something else. An ornamental zig-zag of stucco runs beside the ribs, and while this appears to be contemporary with the painting, it need not be contemporary with the construction of the vault. (Stylistically it is far older, as old as the twelfth century, as old as romanesque Vézelay or Durham.)

Concerning early vaults, Motolinía wrote in his *Memoriales:* "In the year of 1525 the church of San Francisco was built in Mexico City . . . and the chancel was vaulted . . . Since this the Indians have made two small vaulted chapels in the Province of Tlaxcala. I do not believe that there are others in the country." This notice was repeated half a century later by Mendieta, who added that the two chapels were in the patio of the monastery.[15] Since the vault of San Francisco disappeared long ago, if what Motolinía said was true and referred to this chapel, its odd vault would be the oldest on the American continent. This is far from certain, however, for when claiming priorities for Tlaxcala, his favorite monastery, Motolinía was susceptible to boasting and parochialism as has already been noted in connection with the posas here.

He probably began his *Memoriales* at Tlaxcala in 1536, and might soon have written the lines on early vaults; if working from memory rather than from news, he could have been referring to conditions as far back as 1532 or '33, when there were few vaults for him to see. But while possible, this is not convincing, for he was a conscientious chronicler, and would probably have revised his text before finishing it in the winter of 1541–42.

425

If he wrote about his vaults any time before November 1538, he could not have referred to the existing chapel as one of the two that were vaulted because it was not yet there. (In his *History* he said that it was built in the six months before Easter of 1539.) If he wrote a little later, or revised his information while he was resident in Tlaxcala — either of which is more likely — he would have known the hexagonal chapel and could have referred to it, but he could hardly have claimed one of the first two vaults for it because there were already several cloisters and other buildings with vaults. Even though he cautiously said "I do not believe that there are others," he could not have escaped knowing about quite a few; there were too many to be ignored.

TWO RELATED CHAPELS: ATLIHUETZÍA AND TEPEYANCO

This vault at Tlaxcala was soon imitated in the little open chapel at Atlihuetzía, "where the water falls." The two vaults are so alike in general constitution — though that at Atlihuetzía is not hexagonal but trapeziform — and so alike in the details of the ribs and their ornamental edging, and at the same time so unlike other Mexican sixteenth-century vaults, that the one at Atlihuetzía must be attributed either to the same crew of masons or to a crew directly imitating the work at Tlaxcala. The chapel at Atlihuetzía was built, presumably, while the town was a visita of Tlaxcala. The first license for the friars to build there was issued in 1543, and funds were alotted in 1554 to complete work already under way. If it had not already been built for the visita, which seems likely, the chapel would have been one of the first items to have been built after the license had been issued. Father Motolinía was in the town in 1539, and wrote part of his *History* there; wherever he stopped long enough to write there must have been a well-established visita. The date of the chapel can, consequently, be fixed with probability sometime between 1538 and 1544. It could have been built, in that case, by workmen who had just completed the vault at Tlaxcala (if the not improbably early date for the chapel there is accepted).[16]

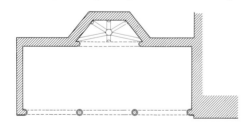

211 THE TRAPEZIFORM CHAPEL AT ATLIHUETZÍA, c1538/44 *with the rectangular space and arcade added in front c1555.*

Atlihuetzía was promoted from visita to monastery in the 1550's, and it would probably have been in the building operations begun soon afterwards that the chapel was extended in depth and width by the addition of the portico of three arches which still stands in front. The adjacent monastery church appears also to have been built mainly at this time. (The Sacrament was first placed there in 1555.) If not then, the chapel might have been given its arcade during a second building campaign when the church was remodeled to make it higher, though the details of the arcade — such as they are — favor a date near 1555.[17]

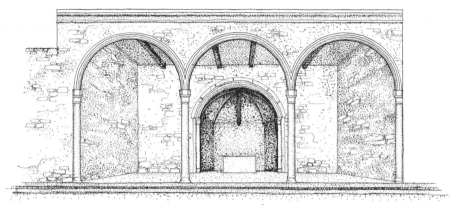

212 THE CHAPEL AT ATLIHUETZÍA *after the addition of the arcade.*

✻

A similar and seemingly related open chapel can be easily identified, though not so easily seen, at Tepeyanco de las Flores, another preconquest town just south of Tlaxcala and once considered its suburb. The plan resembles that of the chapel at Tlaxcala, and the vault, though ribless and slightly domical, is laid up with very much the same sort of rough and ready stereotomy.

Since Tepeyanco was not named as a visita by Father Motolinía, this chapel might have been put up soon after he finished writing in the winter of 1540–41, which would make it a slightly younger near-contemporary of its relative at Atlihuetzía (though both could possibly but less likely be a year or two older if they were counted among the fifty or sixty "small and medium well adorned churches" he claimed for Tlaxcala in both his *History* and *Memoriales*). Tepeyanco was recorded as an Indian visita of Tlaxcala very soon after he finished writing these, and a license to build was issued to the Franciscans in 1543. The church must have been built later than the chapel, after the visita was raised to monastery rank in 1554. (This church was in use by 1558, and before 1600 it had been altered by being made higher, and vaulted.) [18] As at Atlihuetzía, the original chapel was apparently found too small and mean when the visita gained monastery status, and, again as at Atlihuetzía, it was enlarged by adding an arcade in front, in this

427

case a much longer one. Though recently knocked down by an earthquake, the arcade is still almost all there, in fragments hidden under thick brambles.

The three-arched portico at the top of the ramp at Tlaxcala may at one time have been joined to the chapel there by a wooden roof (though the marks in the masonry — probably later than the original construction — do not show when or even surely whether this was done). If it was, then this chapel was extended in a way similar to Atlihuetzía and Tepeyanco, and thus it may a second time have been the model for them.

THE CHAPEL AT TLAXCALA AND "BETHLEHEM"

Whether there were very early vaults at Tlaxcala or not, there surely was a "Bethlehem," and there probably was an open chapel. Whether "Bethlehem" was the open chapel, whether "Bethlehem" was the existing chapel, and whether the existing chapel was an open chapel are all difficult problems. Because of the crucial historical position of this early building or buildings, each possibility has to be studied in detail.

*

In favor of identifying the present chapel as "Bethlehem" and as an open chapel are several facts and suppositions. First, the chapel appears to be of very early construction, possibly as early as 1538–39 when "Bethlehem" was built. Second, "Bethlehem" had "well formed arches" and particularly striking features of the existing chapel are its three sweeping ogee arches which, though perhaps not what might be adjudged "well formed" now, must have seemed more so then. Third, before they were altered these arches made the chapel as open across the front as no kind of chapel except an open chapel would likely be. Fourth, the little chapels at Atlihuetzía and Tepeyanco have vaults which probably imitate that of the chapel at Tlaxcala, and if these chapels imitate the form they may well have been intended to imitate the function, in which case, since they are open chapels, their model would have been one too.

These points fall short of adding up to proof, and there are contrary arguments which together add up to at least as much. First, the possibility that the existing chapel could have been built as early as 1538–39 does not insure that it is identical with a chapel surely built then, for Tlaxcala must have been in a boom of building in those years. Second, Motolinía said that his "Bethlehem" was "of the patio" (*del patio*) but the surviving chapel is between two patios, in neither, level with neither, "of" neither; the position is so peculiar that one would expect him to have explained it in his long description in terms more explicit than *del patio*. Third, the remains above the vault and above the bracketed cornice of the little facade do not allow for the choirs for musicians which "Bethlehem" had.

428

213 TLAXCALA, the embedded POSA (?)

Nothing big enough to hold many musicians could have been fitted above the facade either beside or around the single element surviving at that level: the posa resting on the middle of the chapel vault. This posa has the same sort of bracketed cornice as the chapel and the better preserved posa in the corner of the atrio. It looks like a product of the same building campaign, and hence it has probably been there on top of the chapel since the middle of the sixteenth century at least. The only other space for the choirs would be on the front or side ramps, and that space would have been widely divided and cramped, even worse than a space on top. Although the two choirs might be imagined as wooden affairs somewhere outside the chapel, Father Motolinía's account makes them part of the building. Some cuttings in the outside face of the wall of the chapel, possibly made to receive wooden structural members, appear to be later than the masonry into which they cut, and consequently are more likely to be related to some alteration or addition, perhaps in connection with a roof to the three-arched gateway. Any arrangement of spaces big enough for musicians in contiguity with this chapel is so impractical as to be improbable.

Another argument against the identification with "Bethlehem" is that it is impossible to see where any extensive display of painting could have been spread on the outside of this building, since it has almost no flat wall areas. Even if some lost upper part comprised the musicians' galleries, that could not have added much surface for paintings since extensive exterior surfaces

429

would have shut in the sound. While it might be suggested that the figures in the paintings were so small that many could have been crowded into small areas (as they often had been in preconquest murals, as at Tizatlán just across the river), yet since the technique was supposedly fresco it seems unlikely that whoever knew enough about mural painting to teach the Indians a European technique would have countenanced their using it for tiny figures where only big ones could be read far below by the very crowds for whom the didactic display was being made.

Father Motolinía said "Bethlehem" had arches, but he did not say it was vaulted. It is reasonable to suppose that he would have mentioned any vault over his "Bethlehem" either when writing his long description in the *History* or else when enumerating the vaults of Tlaxcala in the *Memoriales*. (The two texts are closely related, each with some material that is in the other and some that is not.) If as seems likely the vaulted chapel and posas are contemporary, then the chapel cannot have had one of the first two vaults because no two of the vaults at Tlaxcala can be earlier than the third, though one — that of the chapel — could be earlier than the other two.

Father Motolinía's description would not have anything to do with the present chapel if "Bethlehem" had been only a temporary construction put up specially for Easter. If, despite the fact that it ought not to take the Indians six months to put up a small temporary building, "Bethlehem" was only temporary, that might explain why Motolinía did not mention it in his *Memoriales* (assuming that they are not a fragment but a complete text), as well as why Father Mendieta failed to mention it when describing the monastery forty years later. Mendieta ought to have been reminded of it not only by its material presence (if it was there) but also by Motolinía's written praise (which Mendieta surely had close at hand for paraphrasing or quoting). When he took special note of the long ramp, he might have been expected to mention the highly conspicuous painted chapel to which it led — if the chapel was still there in conspicuous condition.

The decisive arguments against the proposal that "Bethlehem" might have been temporary are that it took six months to build, that it had "well formed arches," and that it was painted in fresco. Arches would almost surely have been of masonry; fresco would have to be painted on plastered masonry; masonry would not have been chosen for a temporary building, nor would fresco which, as Motolinía said, had been used because it was *not* temporary. Even though he did not mention it, a "Bethlehem" of masonry must still have been standing by some patio in Father Mendieta's day, unless it had been demolished by the friars or by some natural cataclysm.

In the 1690's, the chronicler Fray Agustín de Vetancurt saw "on the landing of a three-part stairway of sixty steps an *Hermita del Santo Sepulchro*, curious though small, with a *sala* on top with its door on the patio." [19]

Santo Sepulchro, like *Santo Entierro*, could refer either to the dedication of the chapel or to a statue of the Dead Christ venerated there. Such figures were and still are carried in procession on Good Friday (most impressively, for example, at Malinalco). "Bethlehem" was finished for Easter, and if finished purposely for the Holy Week celebrations, it might suitably have housed such a figure. Since the reference was made 150 years after Motolinía, and since the only connection is that both "Bethlehem" and the figure or chapel might have been important in Holy Week, there is not firm cause to identify the *Hermita* with "Bethlehem." Whether "Bethlehem" or not, however, it must be identified with the existing chapel, for the chapel stands on the landing of a "three-part stairway," and it is the only chapel at Tlaxcala that stands there now or could have stood there then.

The *sala* on top might be proposed as "Bethlehem" if the presence of the posa could be explained away. While a priest could officiate at an altar in a posa, a posa would seem too small to have been dignified with the term *sala*, and there does not seem to be room for both a posa and a *sala* on top of the chapel. It is not certain, however, that the little building in the midst of the battered congeries on top of the chapel was no more than a posa. Although its doorway and cornice look enough like those of the posa in the southwest corner of the upper atrio to assign them both to the same building campaign, the two are not identical: the arch of the equivocal *sala*-posa is different, and so are its fluted pilaster jambs. Much is like the posa, but what is different may show that it was more important.

The little building is half ruined, and is embedded in later (?) masonry at the sides and back also now too ruined to be explicity informative. The central posa-like element could have been a small sanctuary for an altar, and there could have been wings opening out from its sides on a scale big enough to justify the word *sala*. Since Father Vetancurt said he saw a *sala* there, a *sala* must have been there at the end of the seventeenth century, and it may have been there earlier. In a passage paraphrased from older writers Father Mendieta mentioned a chapel opposite the church door, where the *sala*-posa is, but it is not unassailably certain that this passage refers to Tlaxcala or to a permanent building.[20]

A chapel here could have served successfully as the open chapel of the monastery though it would have faced west in an orientation which, while reversed and unusual, would not have been unique (if the columns at Etzatlán were what they look like). There are other equally odd elements in the complex at Tlaxcala, such as the grand triple gateway like a triumphal arch at the north end of the atrio, which doubled as a secret bridge, and the bell-tower, freestanding, in direct violation of Franciscan ruling,[21] not to mention the arrangement of the lower ramp, double ramp, and double atrio. In such a context, novelty is not in itself suspect.

431

This brings back the question whether the lower chapel was an open chapel. It is farther removed from the area where its congregation would have to stand than any known open chapel in Mexico, and it is so deep that an altar in the ordinary position against the rear wall would have been invisible to them. As an open chapel, the building could never have served satisfactorily. If it was not a working open chapel, the lower atrio need not have served as the nave of an outdoor church. Only Mendieta wrote of this area as a "patio," and he did not connect it with any chapel-and-atrio combination, but said only that many Indians used to walk up its ramp. Unless a new candidate can be found, a rejection of the lower chapel would leave only the ruined structure on top of it as the possible *sala,* the possible "Bethlehem," and the possible open chapel.

Another candidate can be proposed. After noting his *hermita* and *sala,* Father Vetancurt went on to say "at the south of the church there is a ruined chapel of the Indians, where the Catechism used to be taught to the boys, and where the Indians who were not *caciques* were buried." [22] No traces of building or burials remain to tell its location, shape, or size, but it must have been an open chapel: "chapel of the Indians" and "where the Catechism used to be taught" both apply to an open chapel, and the known general location beside the church is normal for one.

Although it can have been an open chapel, the boys' chapel cannot have been "Bethlehem" because it was not built until eight or ten years after Motolinía wrote about "Bethlehem." The Town Council voted in 1548 to add a chapel for the teaching of children — there were some 500 in the monastery school — and construction was going on somewhere in the atrio in 1550.[23] The atrio chapel Father Vetancurt saw in ruins was for boys; the building authorized in 1548 was for boys; the building under way in 1550 was in the atrio: the three were probably one. When it was finished, about the end of 1550, this chapel could have taken over the role of open chapel from "Bethlehem" or from some other chapel. Although "Bethlehem" had been built only a dozen years earlier, it was just in these years that the decisive experiments in open chapels must have been being tried out — among them could have been "Bethlehem," or the lower chapel, or both — and if any open chapels were rejected for inefficient performance, it would most likely have been one or two of these first experiments.

If something of this sort did happen, the question of the lower chapel must again be reconsidered. It is not difficult to accept it as an open chapel if it need not be an efficient one. The open facade would be hard to explain on other grounds. If it was originally built for an open chapel but then found either so awkward or so damaged by the quake of 1540 that it was abandoned, it could have been adapted as an appropriately cave-like Oratory of the Holy Sepulcher. The square-headed windows blocking its ogee arches show that it was remodeled sometime in the sixteenth century and, unless the result of physical damage, the change in form might naturally have been a consequence of a change in function. The bracketed cornice might come from the same remodeling, which would relate it legitimately to the similarly crowned corner posa. (This posa has already been dated *c*1545–50 on other grounds.) If the remodeling was contemporary with that posa, it would have been contemporary with the problematical *sala*-posa on top of the chapel, and thus confirm a date near 1550 for that. At that time the openings might have been reduced in order to make stronger support for the *sala*-posa about to be put on top. Everything then would agree that the *sala*-posa could have been made at that time, either as a special posa or as a new open chapel to take the place of the unsuccessful one below, though it seems much more likely that it was the boys' chapel which took over the functions of open chapel at this time.

After the lower chapel was made into an oratory there would no longer have been need for close association with an atrio, and the western approach to the monastery might then suitably have been reconsidered. The three-arched gateway might have been set up in front of the ex-chapel then, for though an obstruction to an open chapel, it would not have hampered an oratory; and it could make a grander entrance to the monastery group, which would now be the chief role left to the ramp. If the *sala* on top was built as part of this remodeling campaign, its odd little fluted pilasters would be less exceptional, for they would now be related to the fluted columns of the three-arched gate. The gate cannot give more information, for though its stone lower part is compatible with the proposed date its brick upper part comes from later repairs. Slender and unable to withstand a strong earth shock, the lower part was probably built enough years after the quake of 1540 for its threats to have been half-forgotten. This too would agree with the repeatedly suggested date of around 1550 for a major reworking of this part of the monastery complex.

*

What half-emerges from the foregoing miscellany of notices and inferences is that after 1550 and before the end of the seventeenth century there were three small chapel buildings at the monastery of Tlaxcala, then distinct but now confusable: first, an *Hermita del Santo Sepulchro* apart from the others and at a lower level; second, a *sala* used for festivals in the atrio, opposite the church and atop the *ermita*; and third, a *capilla de indios,* built for boys about 1548–50, beside the church in normal relation to the upper atrio.

Whereas this boys' chapel cannot have been "Bethlehem" because it was not yet built when Motolinía described "Bethlehem," it can have been an open chapel, and it probably was.

Whereas the *ermita* can hardly have been "Bethlehem" because what Motolinía wrote about "Bethlehem" does not match it, it can be the same as the existing vaulted chapel, and it probably is.

The other little building, the *sala*, can have been "Bethlehem," but whereas this hypothesis has the least against it, it has little but inference for it, since it depends on assuming identity between unknowns. Furthermore, there is difficulty in reconciling the known date of "Bethlehem," 1538–39, with the date of this, for it is hard to believe that this was built so early. If it was, then so was the lower chapel which holds it up and the corner posa which matches it in detail, and all must have come through the quake of 1540 fairly intact.

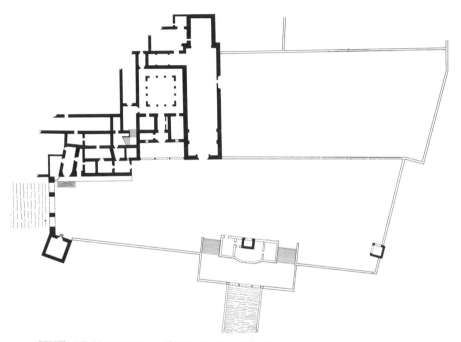

214 THE FRANCISCAN ESTABLISHMENT AT TLAXCALA

At the left, the stepped north ramp leads to the massive triple gateway attached to the belltower at one end and the monastery block at the other.

At the bottom, the long west ramp leads through the lighter triple gateway to a rectangular platform in front of the lower chapel; here it divides, and continues as a pair of stairways on either side of the chapel, leading up to the atrio level.

The possible posa is shown on top of the chapel, on the level of the atrio; it is similar but not identical with the posa in the southwest corner (right).

North of the church is the monastery block, with its small cloister and triple portería; north of these the plan has become confused because of alterations and additions, but three heavy diagonal walls can still be made out.

This reasoning leaves a sure *ermita,* an unsure "Bethlehem," and no open chapel earlier than *c*1550 unless the *ermita* was that before it became an *ermita.* Unsuccessful as it must have been in that function, there may be considerable argument that it was at first so intended.

There is still *another* candidate for both the open chapel and "Bethlehem," but its claims are more difficult to see. A plan of that part of the patched old monastery block that lies beyond the north end of the portería shows odd lengths of three massive diagonal walls. Two of them run parallel to one another and bound a passage cutting obliquely back into the hospital in a way which could be the result of some alteration to improve access to the back; but this fails to explain their heaviness and gives no clue to the obliquity of the third wall. Only some important monumental space can justify the reciprocal dislocation which makes this other wall converge symmetrically on the oblique pair, for there is no reason for it to depart from the strict rectangularity of the neighboring walls if reason is sought in the functional requirements for the arrangement of interior spaces in a monastery building. If instead, space related to the exterior is considered, a plausible large open chapel can be conjured up, with convergent sides like the apse of many contemporary churches and later open chapels.

This phantom can be made to fit Motolinía's description of "Bethlehem," and offer comfortable space for his musicians and murals. The "well formed arches" could have been arranged like those of the adjacent portería. Somewhere about the monastery there must have been more arches like those of the portería, for two extra capitals, matching those on the portería columns, are still lying in the atrio. These capitals, of a type unique in Mexico, could

215 THE PORTERÍA AT TLAXCALA
An extra capital is used as a base for a stone lion behind the tree at the left.

435

be dated around 1538, but also as well in '48, '58, or '68; they seem to be a provincial effort at a sophisticated Spanish model. These capitals could, on the other hand, possibly have been some part of the boys' chapel where Father Vetancurt saw "arcades where confessions are heard." [24]

If an arcade ran across the front of this hypothetical chapel at the north end of the monastery, three arches like the portería arches could have screened its width, and these would have left four spandrels for "Bethlehem's" four sets of wall paintings as described by Father Motolinía.

It is not possible to deduce much about this putative chapel by analogy with the open chapels of other monasteries because so much of the layout at Tlaxcala is peculiar. Still, the layout most analogous, that at nearby Huexotla, probably does reflect it, and its open chapel with an arcaded front just north of the church may be some small argument for an earlier open chapel with an arcaded front north of the church at Tlaxcala.

*

Unsatisfactory as the lower chapel is when seen either as an open chapel or as Motolinía's "Bethlehem," there is not quite enough solid evidence to identify or reject it as either one. Unless more becomes known the best surmise now is that it was *not* "Bethlehem." It cannot be dismissed as a possible early and unsuccessful open chapel. The arrangement is perhaps so peculiar because it was made so early, and because it was affected by pagan work on the site. The altar may have had to purify the spot where some prestigious predecessor had stood, high above a patio from which the rites could be witnessed by crowds. As memories of this weakened, the reason for the difficult location would have weakened too, and after a few years there would have been little objection to moving the altar to a more convenient place. A more convenient chapel could then have been built there.

If "Bethlehem" was not here, and if the existing chapel was built before Motolinía wrote, his "Bethlehem" might have stood on top of it, and the *sala-posa* remains might incorporate parts of it. If, however, the vaulted chapel was built a little later, as seems more likely, sometime after the spring of 1541 when Motolinía finished writing without mentioning it, his "Bethlehem" of 1538–39 must have been somewhere else, possibly north of the portería between the converging walls, and this, then, would have been the original open chapel at the monastery.

It is now possible to winnow all the subjunctive surmises and be left with only four chapel sites and three chapel functions. The most reasonable conclusions seem to be as follows:

> first, a fair-sized chapel between oblique walls, sunk in the monastery building north of the church and portería, built in 1538–39 as "Bethlehem," and possibly used as an open chapel;

second, a lower vaulted chapel, built after the spring of 1541, perhaps originally an open chapel (if the oblique chapel was not), remodeled after about 1550 as an Oratory of the Holy Sepulcher;

third, a boys' chapel just south of the church, built c1548–50, which became the regular open chapel;

fourth, a *sala* on top of the lower chapel and opposite the church, built around 1550 along with the posas and the remodeling of the chapel below, used as a posa and also as some sort of chapel on special occasions.

These are the conclusions that have the least against them. Unfortunately there is not much tangible evidence or documentation to sustain them, and they must remain in limbo as possibilities which cannot be stiffened into probabilities.

TWO OTHER RELATED CHAPELS: TIZATLÁN AND APASCO

On a hill at Tizatlán across the river, amid the ruins of the Palace of Old Xicoténcatl ("a man with a bee at his lips," successor to Xayacamachantlacazcallitecuhtli who was successor to Atzhuatlacazcallitecuhtli), there is another former open chapel, now closed in by later walls and little used. A mile or two from the monastery at Tlaxcala, Tizatlán was another of its old visitas, though once within the limits of the broadly spread preconquest city. There are no signs that any church was connected with the chapel: it must have been a self-sufficient visita unit. Building it may have hastened the ruin of the chief temple of Xochipilli which had been an adjunct of the palace, for not only is the chapel made principally of preconquest stones and bricks but it also stands on extensive preconquest underpinnings.[25]

In addition to being on the chief site of the nation-wide cult of Xochipilli, god of song, dance, spring, and flowers, this particular location at Tizatlán had a special Christian prestige which lent more importance to the chapel than its modest size announced. Legend said that on the night after Cortés had been received in Tizatlán by the newly converted rulers, Maxixcatzín and Xicoténcatl, a large wooden cross had miraculously appeared, and that Cortés and his noble hosts together had planted it upright in the ground to exorcise the now worse-than-useless temple. This was spectacularly successful: after a blinding light which quickly converted their native followers, they saw a devil scurry out of the ex-temple, disguised in the form of a pig. The light in the sky continued to glow miraculously for three or four years, and a column of cloud hovered over the cross until the entire province was converted. (Parts of this legend, which is a confused and variable one, were extended to crosses at Atlihuetzía and Totolac; one variant transferred the cross and legend to the spot in Tlaxcala where the Franciscans finally

437

erected their permanent monastery.) The raising of the cross was made the center of the main scene of the famous big historical painting known as the *Lienzo de Tlaxcala* (c1550, known now only in copies). The cross at Tizatlán was much venerated, and remained standing for many years.[26]

216
*Cortés greets the Lords of
Tlaxcala at the foot of*
THE CROSS OF TIZATLÁN
(*after* Lienzo de Tlaxcala)

The Royal Chronicler, Gil González Dávila, writing a century after the events, said that a chapel had been built in the old temple at Tizatlán or on its site expressly to commemorate the miracle of the cross.[27] This could refer either to the existing chapel or to a predecessor. Something must have been built very early, as early as the time of Cortés, since his chaplain, Juan Díaz, who had baptized the four Lords of Tlaxcala, was said to have been buried here only a few years after the Conquest; his tomb remained one of the chief local sights. At this time important Spanish tombs were not in cemeteries but in buildings, and the only suitable Christian building here must have been the chapel of the cross.[28]

Additional reasons to establish a chapel early would have been to serve the large native settlement around the temple and palace and to occupy the old center of religious and political power with a Christian building. The Spaniards may have had in addition a particular interest in Tizatlán since it had been Cortés' headquarters during the first part of the Siege of Tenochtitlán, and this may have increased the desire to commemorate the spot with a chapel. Although sometimes dated 1571, the chapel may more likely have been built twenty or thirty years before that to replace an earlier makeshift building.

The front, like that of the vaulted chapel at Tlaxcala, is formed of three arches folded outwards into a half-hexagon, like a three-part screen. The building is loftier and more open than that at Tlaxcala, as well as larger. (It is about 16 feet deep by 40 feet long.) Unlike Tlaxcala it has a crypt under the central part — once a jail — and has no vaults, but it does have wings on either side of the polygonal apse, with raised galleries presumably for musicians. There is a profusion of wall-paintings, mostly of the seventeenth century. These are not in true fresco but in something between tempera and *fresco secco*, difficult to analyze or identify because of subsequent superposed daubing. If it was modeled on the lower chapel at Tlaxcala and that was an open chapel, the version at Tizatlán avoids the errors of its model: in fact it could be a criticism of it. Most striking is the change in the chancel, raised above the crypt and made a dramatic stage for the celebration of the Mass.

217 THE CHAPEL AT TIZATLÁN *as it appeared when still open. The wooden galleries for musicians do not show behind the arches.*

Inasmuch as the musicians' galleries and wall-paintings at Tizatlán may give a more vivid image of the "Bethlehem" chapel than does the vaulted chapel at Tlaxcala, Tizatlán may be considered as a copy or reflection of "Bethlehem" or even as "Bethlehem" itself. Father Motolinía said that his "Bethlehem" was *in* Tlaxcala, but the terms "Tlaxcala," "the City of Tlaxcala," and "the Republic of Tlaxcala" were confusingly interchangeable, referring now to the city proper, now to the city and its suburbs, and now to the entire province (about 30 by 50 miles, half the size of the present State).[29] He had explained that as in Spain it was "customary to give the name of the Province to a large town that had smaller towns subject to it." "Tlaxcala" could therefore apply to Tizatlán; Zorita called Tizatlán "a barrio of Tlaxcala," as Motolinía did in one instance; Gómara called it "a street called Tizatlán . . . in Tlaxcala"; and Gage, too, called it an important street in the city.[30]

439

218 TIZATLÁN

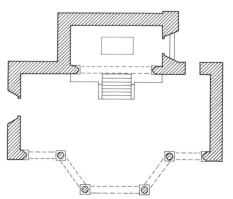

Father Motolinía's account did not place his "Bethlehem" specifically in the monastery of San Francisco, for he said only that it was "of the patio" without designating what patio. Although the chapel at Tizatlán does not now stand in a clear patio — since the chapel's main function has been assumed by a later parish church it no longer needs one — when the chapel was open and needed an atrio it had an unusually splendid one made of one of the several brightly colored courts of the old palace and temple.

The chapel at Tizatlán is unvaulted, but Father Motolinía did not say that his "Bethlehem" was vaulted; the notice about vaults in Tlaxcala is in a different part of a different manuscript. The existing wall-paintings at Tizatlán are not in fresco, not of the sixteenth century, and not of Motolinía's listed subjects; but they could replace a somewhat different sixteenth-century set. Not called "Bethlehem" but now dedicated to Saint Stephen, the chapel could some time in its four centuries have had its dedication shifted, perhaps when its function was shifted and it was walled in. The painting, too, could have been altered or done over then, a new patron calling for a new iconographical scheme.

If the chapel at Tizatlán is not "Bethlehem" — and the arguments for it are not compelling — it is nonetheless closely related. The musicians' balconies and the murals — uncommon though not unique — could reflect those at "Bethlehem" which must have been one of the sights of the neighborhood. The chapel is also related to the hexagonal chapel at Tlaxcala: much of the woodwork supporting the galleries and roof, which appears to be of the sixteenth century, displays a rich system of insistent double brackets unusual in Mexico but akin to the insistent double brackets of the stone cornices at Tlaxcala; the polygonal three-arched open front — even more unusual — is obviously like. Thus what is like "Bethlehem" (balconies and murals) is not like Tlaxcala, and what is like Tlaxcala (polygonal open front, details) is not like anything known about "Bethlehem." If it is not "Bethlehem," which it probably is not, it reflects both "Bethlehem" *and* Tlaxcala, and must be later than both. This hypothesis, which supports the assumption that the surviving chapel at Tlaxcala is not "Bethlehem," seems to be the most acceptable.

Another little chapel, hitherto unrecorded, may be related to that at Tlaxcala and to the posas at Tlaxcala and Huejotzingo. It adjoins the facade of a small sixteenth-century church at Apasco (or Apaxco), a visita of Franciscan Tula. The town was transferred to the seculars in 1569; the carved Franciscan emblems show that both church and chapel had been finished before that. Though small, the town may have preserved some prestige from the legend that the Aztecs had paused there for two years on their wandering but predestined progress toward Tenochtitlán.[31]

The "bay window" front with three open arches is like no other open chapels except Tlaxcala and Tizatlán. The side openings, narrower and lower than the one in the center, have sills a yard above the floor, making them not doorways but windows. The only other windowed front of this kind is at the chapel of Tlaxcala, after it was remodeled, presumably around 1550. There must have been some of the same difficulty in seeing into this chapel as at Tlaxcala, but it has been mitigated by making the front more open. Steps polygonally rimming the bent plan of the facade raise the floor — and altar — a yard above the atrio. The chapel, moreover, faced a smaller congregation in a smaller atrio at a more suitable level. Though the smallest, the

219 APASCO

facade at Apasco is the most developed of the three polygonal fronts. All its openings are arched with richly molded archivolts springing from columnar jambs with renaissance plateresque capitals. The upper surfaces are harmonously enriched by an orderly display of tequitqui carving.

Against the random if not out-and-out haphazard ashlar masonry of tawny pink trachyte, angels in fluttering robes fly over the somewhat freehand arches. They seem to have been derived either from those on the posas at Huejotzingo or from the earlier Annunciate Gabriel of the destroyed posa at Tlaxcala. This relation, plus that of the half-hexagonal front, makes some connection with Tlaxcala very likely. The angels over the side openings at Apasco carry shields with the Franciscan emblem of Five Wounds. Over the center, they hover near but fail to support a defaced royal arms (or an incription?) under a splendid crown, and hover above another shield with the monogram of Christ encircled by the Crown of Thorns. These emblems, too, are close to emblems on the Puebla-Tlaxcala posas. Surmounting everything stands a figure of Saint Francis.

All the carving submits to the architecture in its scale and placing, and in its stiff and emphatically stony character. The three planes of the facade on which it is deployed are each framed by a coarsely but vigorously carved rinceau of grapevines, and crowned by a boldly cut cornice with rows of seraphim set in the hollow of a deep cavetto molding. Above this is a Franciscan cord — again like Tlaxcala, Tizatlán, or Huejotzingo — and a parapet with a niche for a statue, an *espadaña*, and pyramid-topped merlons too restored to be trustworthy.

220 APASCO
Angels and the Franciscan emblem with the Five Wounds

The carving everywhere is flatter, blunter, and coarser than at Huejo-tzingo, or even Calpan or Tlaxcala, but its patent naïveté does not vitiate the surprising sophistication of the general design. If that was based on the chapel at Tlaxcala in its remodeled state with windows, perhaps it is a sort of untutored critique of its model, with an added desire for sculptural enrichment suggested at Tlaxcala and more harmoniously realized at Huejo-tzingo and Calpan. The workmen who carried this out were not as advanced as whoever made the design. Only one other open chapel has such a wealth of representational carving — that at Tlalmanalco — and both, surprisingly, were built by poverty-wed Franciscans, as were the posas at Calpan, comparable and perhaps related in sculptural richness.

The probability that this indubitable open chapel at Apasco reflects the facade of the chapel at Tlaxcala after its remodeling may offer some argument that that was still an open chapel. This argument loses much of its merit when added to the probability that it reflects posas as well. The connection with Tlaxcala and Huejotzingo need not come from any continuation of their programs, from any copying of their forms to serve the same functions: it comes more likely through workmen who knew forms at the big monasteries and copied them in new context at a small new visita.

This brings at last to an end the problems of the chapel at Tlaxcala and its reflections. Except for the four satellites at Atlihuetzía, Tepeyanco, Tiza-tlán, and Apasco, it appears to have been without influence. While this could be an argument for a late date, it makes better argument for an early one and a design so impractical that it had little more than local imitation. The only other early chapels at important and much visited monasteries which did not have much influence were too large, too elaborate, or too difficult to copy. San José de los Naturales, for example, in its most striking form was too large for very successful adapation to more modest establishments, and the early chapel at Cuernavaca was probably too daring in construction.

SAN JOSÉ AT CUERNAVACA

Since San José de los Naturales has been destroyed and the chapel at Tlaxcala was not surely built at the early date often proposed, the large and handsome chapel at Cuernavaca may have claim to be the oldest visible open chapel.

It adjoins a big sixteenth-century church (the Cathedral since 1891) which was built as part of the monastery the Franciscans founded here as their fifth house, in 1525, after a second small group of friars from Spain had joined the Twelve. The natives had at first been slow to accept Christianity, but the extreme piety of one influential noble convert soon set a tide-turning example. After extensive leveling of the hillside site, the friars had built

443

enough of their new monastery by 1529 to be able to move in. The buildings must have been presentable enough by the beginning of 1532 for exigent Cortés and his even more exigent and highborn second wife to have chosen to have one of their children buried there.[32]

The chapel was probably built early in the history of the house, as open chapels often were, but no dependable evidence tells just how early. "Inaccessible documents" and local traditions say that it antedated the first church, and this has led some writers to venture a date as early as 1525–29. No such early date is provable or probable. (Such claims would make the chapel the oldest non-Indian building still standing on the American mainland except to those who still believe in "Lief Ericson's Tower" at Newport.) A church, perhaps no more than provisional, was said to have been finished in 1528, and to have stood on part of the site now occupied by the chapel, which would make it impossible for the chapel to have been built as early as 1525–29; another tradition locates this church on a somewhat removed site where San Francisquito now stands.[33] The character of the existing open chapel and several fragments of evidence and inference concur in suggesting an early date: not so early as 1525–29 but only ten or twelve years later. The difficult problem of the date may involve two other early buildings in Cuernavaca, both associated with Cortés, and they must be considered before conclusions about the chapel can be drawn.

221 THE OPEN CHAPEL AT CUERNAVACA in 1941
(*before the removal of the statue of Bishop Plancarte y Navarrete*)

THE CALVARIO

The *Calvario* stands at the entrance to Cuernavaca on the highway from the capital. Originally it sheltered a cross before which travelers might pray for a safe journey over the mountains, or give thanks for just having concluded one; or pious people might pause here for prayer on their way to the nearby shrine of Tlaltenango. It may perhaps be the chapel built for one of the miraculous crosses found in the trunk of a zapote tree by doña María Salomé, a rich Indian convert (crosses later gathered together with other miraculous crosses in a special chapel in the monastery church). In Spain equivalent *Calvarios* made of a stone canopy over a cross, with or without a figure, were sometimes put on the roads leading in or out of town (for example, at Valencia). Here at Cuernavaca the cross was replaced by a statue of the Virgin of Guadalupe in 1772, and this has in its turn now been replaced by a more modern version of the Guadalupana wreathed in gigantic plastic flowers which light up. The top of the original building has been considerably restored or rebuilt, presumably along its old lines.[34]

The exceptionally fine details of the capitals and moldings are stylistically so like those of the open chapel and so unlike other surviving sixteenth-century work in or near Cuernavaca that it is natural to suppose that the same carvers were employed on one and then the other. Although the general form of the little building is much like that of a posa with a pyramidal roof, particularly like the posas at Huejotzingo, the handling of detail is quite different from that on any extant posas. (The pyramidal posa at Totolapan may result from a provincial degeneration of this design.) The late-gothic details are of an unusually sophisticated character. The capitals and the bold fine-scale moldings, strong enough to assert themselves effectively beside big blank areas of rosy masonry, show refinement and skill in the carving a world removed from the more typical primitive cutting of the middle half of the century, such as for example that at Apasco, Tlaxcala, or Calpan. The carving on the *Calvario* is finer than the spare and blunt ornament on the nearby Palace of Cortés which although presumably only a few years earlier appears to have been made by more naïve hands, native hands less used to European ornament, and tenacious of indigenous shapes and ways of combining them.

The date of the *Calvario* is not securely fixed. A later inscription says that it was built in 1538, and many accept this. A few believe it to have been built a generation later, perhaps between 1563 and '64, by Cortés' legitimate son, Martín, while resident in his late father's palace. Don Martín, born in Cuernavaca in 1532, was interested in the *Calvario* enough to leave money in his will to keep a lamp burning there, which might suggest that he had built it, but could instead suggest no more than filial concern for a work his father had built, or reverence for that particular cross for private reasons.

222 THE *CALVARIO* AT CUERNAVACA
The cartouche above the arch, the firepots on the corners, and the central crowning feature are all post-sixteenth-century work. The rest is original or reliably restored.

The local legend that he was buried in the *Calvario* must also remain only folklore, for he died, semi-disgraced, in Spain. Insofar as dates may be deduced from style — always an unsure business in Mexico — the 1560's seem late: a date nearer 1540 seems more suitable, and the inscription, in view of this and the foregoing, seems acceptable.[35]

446

223 THE *CALVARIO*
Jamb, impost, and archivolts
of a corner pier

THE PALACE OF CORTÉS

The Palace was presumably well along before the *Calvario* and open chapel were begun. Disgusted with affairs in the capital, Cortés may have decided to remove to Cuernavaca as early as 1526, or merely to build a dwelling there such as he was planning in several other towns, all on the same plan. In 1531 there was mention not only of his rebuilt Aztec palace in México-Tenochtitlán (1522–29, the "Old Palace" of Moctezuma) and the huge new palace he was building (on the site of the "New Palace" of Moctezuma), but also of several he already had in other towns: Coyoacán, Texcoco, Chalco, Tlalmanalco, Otumba, and Tepeapulco. Although he had been in Cuernavaca recently, there is no mention of a palace, and he had not yet, presumably, begun to build there by 1531, or had not yet built much. By 1531, nevertheless, he must have maintained some sort of comfortable establishment in Cuernavaca, for a daughter was born there that year and a son the next. Beginning in 1531 his second wife settled there, and she remained there all the time she was in New Spain, most of it in her bed.[36]

By 1533 Cortés had surely begun his palace, for the Indians then protested at being overworked on "the house he is building." They did not include a drawing in their written complaint, as was their custom, because the building was there where everyone could see it. A reference in 1534 already called it a "palace," and told how the marquesa, though ailing, still maintained her ceremonial retainers and large staff of domestic servants.[37]

447

The Palace at Cuernavaca is not only the oldest but, except for the Montejo Palace at Mérida, the only certain and fairly intact specimen of non-Indian domestic building on the mainland earlier than the middle of the sixteenth century. It must have been larger and grander than any private dwelling of European style yet built in the New World, Cortés' palaces in the capital being neither entirely new, entirely private, nor yet entirely built. (He was not able to finish more than a sixth of the newer one which must have been indeed megalomaniacal, spread over 35 building lots, with walls 5 feet thick.) The Palace at Cuernavaca eclipsed that of Columbus' son Diego, at Santo Domingo, which was probably its principal model. Cortés had lived in Santo Domingo until 1511, and likely knew the beginnings of this palace, for work on it had been begun in 1510 or early '11.[38] Perhaps he saw it again in a more impressive state when he passed through Santo Domingo on his way back from Spain in 1530.

These two early palaces, Cortés' and Montejo's, built by the two most successful conquistadores, who had been rewarded with the most land and the largest and most permanent encomiendas, must have been the finest in New Spain. An impressive palace must have seemed an imperative perquisite to each of these men, since each began to build one so soon: Montejo within five years of taking Mérida, and Cortés first within one or two of taking Tenochtitlán, and then soon again at Cuernavaca, within two years of his return from Spain if not earlier. This last palace shows as vividly as any other large surviving building how quickly Spanish architectural ideas of advanced character could be successfully transferred to New Spain, and how quickly Indian craftsmen could come to be more or less at home in European ways.

With two superposed open stories of slender, round-arched, late-gothic arcades forming loggias in front and in back, and with no central courtyard, the palace at Cuernavaca looks untraditional when seen against most other Spanish houses of the time. Although some parts may date from subsequent sixteenth-century remodelings — Cortés' pretentious rich son Martín repaired it expensively — the main elements and the idea of having loggias outside instead of a patio inside seem to go back to the original scheme. Repairs in the 1940's and '50's, after half-ruin from neglect in the eighteenth and from brutal "improvements" in the nineteenth century, have shown that the now four-arched front was once two arches longer, and have exposed a forgotten three-arched loggia on the south side (now over-restored or rebuilt), and have established how very large the sixteenth-century palace was.[39]

The front loggias command a view of the town plaza, once its walled *patio de armas,* which the Palace dominates axially in the same authoritative manner as Conquistador Montejo's palace dominates the plaza at Mérida.[40]

From the back, a more spectacular view — breathtaking even in a land prodigal with spectacular views — sweeps down into the Valley of Morelos, on over its subtropical greenery, and up to the icy peak of Popocatépetl. The Palace may have been oriented to the volcano purposely to take advantage of the view, aimed at the looming white cone as deliberately as the thousands of tourist cameras which now annually try to fix the same melodramatic vista on Kodachrome. Although to our scenery-conscious age this may seem a natural way to set a dwelling in a landscape, it was a novel idea in the sixteenth century, when a love of landscape was yet to show itself clearly in Spanish literature, painting, or architectural orientation.

224 *Loggias of the rear of* THE PALACE OF CORTÉS *at* CUERNAVACA, *now the seat of the local government.*

Such an orientation — which one might call panoramophilic or panoramotropic — seems to have been unprecedented anywhere in European architecture with the single exception of the Piccolomini Palace at Pienza in Tuscany, where the loggias are similarly "aimed" at Monte Amiata. Here the aesthetic orientation was not the idea of the humdrum architect, Bernardo Rossellino, but possibly of his master, Alberti, or more probably of his far-from-humdrum client, the humanist Pope Pius II, who had already written his precocious passages in praise of spacious mountain landscape.

The early loggias on other Italian buildings (such as the quattrocento Belvedere and early cinquecento Farnesina in Rome, the Palazzo Guadagni in Florence, the Villa Candiana near Rovigo, or a score near Verona and Vicenza derived from the mediaeval loggias of palaces on the canals of Venice) are not related to any vistas, axially or otherwise. Could the orientation of the loggias at Cuernavaca, as at Pienza, perhaps have been the idea

449

of another far-from-humdrum client? Cortés may recently have been instrumental in planning another unorthodox building, the *Atarazanas* (completed in the capital in 1524). From written descriptions it is possible to reconstruct that arsenal-boathouse as to many of its main features,[41] and some of these could be related perhaps to the Palace and the chapel in Cuernavaca, both also exceptionally open. (Details and execution would, of course, have been quite different.) This conjecture is, however, too will-o'-the-wispy to pursue.

Away from Venice, houses with airy wide-arched loggias were rare in Italy in the early sixteenth century, and still rarer in Spain, where they were built only under Italian influence. The details of the design in Cuernavaca show nothing Italianate: they are not renaissance but mediaeval, and patently so in the gothic capitals and the mudéjar running *alfiz* enframing the arches of the loggias. The closest Spanish equivalent, at Sarracín on the old road from Burgos to Silos, is not very like, and furthermore it is not early enough to have been influential at Cuernavaca, for it was built probably no earlier and more likely a little later than Cortés' Palace. Moreover, in the sixteenth century, neither this nor any other known Spanish house with loggias was purposely associated with a view. No more does there seem to be much Spanish precedent for superposed arcades. The more the Palace at Cuernavaca is studied, the more remarkable it appears.

Moorish, mudéjar, and gothic palaces and castles in Spain had sometimes had a one-story gallery at the top, where ladies could take the air without being exposed to public gaze. Such galleries, opened by many little arches and set high above a solid wall, were known as *adarves* or sometimes as *azoteas*. They may have been derived from very unfeminine machicolated galleries for military needs. These *adarves* did not take the place of arcaded patios, but supplemented them. Cortés' two-story loggias could have been suggested by a sort of *adarve* atop the palace which he had contrived from the ruins of Moctezuma's "Old Palace" in Tenochtitlán (as shown in a plan of the capital made c1565, ill. 26). Although a document of 1531 mentioned a *suntuoso corredor* above the plaza, it is possible to read this apparent *adarve* as a series of apertures through which guns or cannon could defend the house. Later in the century, too late to have influenced work in Cuernavaca, there surely was a proper *adarve* here with stone columns.[42]

The loggias at Cuernavaca are more advanced than any of their Spanish predecessors which, at best, have little parental claim. These novelties seem to be an American innovation tried first for Diego Colón and then more grandly for Cortés. (They were soon copied in Cuernavaca on houses for the mayor and for a swell of an Indian lord.[43]) The explanation may be that the loggias on Cortés' and Colón's palaces were affected by the fact that the buildings were the official seats of a ruler — Cortés' marquisate was so big and his titles so grand that he could count himself a ruler — and as such the

450

palaces might have assumed the form of an *ayuntamiento, cabildo,* or town hall. In Spain the *ayuntamiento* often already had two stories of open arcading, following the example of the Moorish *alcázar,* and these same features soon appeared on the *ayuntamiento* or municipal palace at Tlaxcala and constantly thereafter on other Mexican *cabildos.* Government palaces had two-story loggias and faced plazas: both Cortés and Diego Colón considered themselves governors: their palaces — and no other private palaces—had two-story loggias and faced open spaces.[44]

CORTÉS AND CUERNAVACA

Major building operations in Cuernavaca during the years of Cortés' residence cannot be satisfactorily understood without considering the effect of his presence. Although ennobled as a Knight of Santiago and as a Marqués, and at last exonerated from the vilifications invented by his enemies, Cortés had been stripped of his official position in the capital when he returned from Spain in 1530. Called Captain General, he was told to stay out of the capital, and to keep at least 10 leagues away until the new Audiencia should be established there. The clergy were forbidden to pray for him publicly. He must have expected — or hoped against hope — that he would be able to return permanently to the great city he had won, and to regain some of his power, for still in 1532 he had hundreds of Indians working on his second palace there, and he was probably at the same time having the chancel of the church of the Franciscans redecorated so that it might serve as his family chapel.

After five miserable and hungry months in Texcoco, and a brief stay in México-Tenochtitlán after the Audiencia was established, he came to live and raise cattle, silk, and sugar (which he knew from Cuba, whence it had been brought from the Canaries) on his rich lands around Cuernavaca, where the topsoil in some places is 10 feet deep. He was, as well as Marqués del Valle, also Count of Cuernavaca, having succeeded in a way to an important preconquest seigneury whose major tribute came from the same rich Tlahuica country, now a large part of the State of Morelos. Cuernavaca, the first town he wanted in his marquisate, remained his feudal headquarters — he had 45 towns round about — from when he established his family there in 1531 until he left Mexico for good in 1540. He never could bring himself to settle down quietly as a feudal lord: he was periodically obsessed by the will to explore and conquer new lands and permanently obsessed by the wish for more money.

The great conqueror appears to have been transformed into a prosperous but harried encomendero. The quick calculations so deadly in the Conquest, and his once all-but-irresistible persuasiveness were inoperative or ineffective in the management of his huge estates. The last decades of his life — he died in 1546 at the age of sixty — were dreary compared to the brief years of his success. The record is largely a snarl of complaints and litigations: he sued the Viceroy and his Indians sued him. Enmity gradually grew between the Marqués and the Viceroy, and became acute when their claims clashed over the rights to "discover" the seven fictitious cities of Cíbola and golden Quivira (in Kansas!). Like many of his illustrious contemporaries, Cortés held to a belief in phantom lands at the very time he was dispelling geographical phantoms by adding to the world's store of geographical facts. Seemingly afraid of allowing him power in the now well-subdued land, Charles V was parsimonious with gratitude, and in time became evasive if not hypocritical, for he secretly instructed Viceroy Mendoza to undermine what power Cortés had left. In his last tragic years, after his final return to Spain, he was excluded from the presence of the sovereign for whom he had gained the largest and richest part of an empire vaster than that of Alexander, Trajan, or Charlemagne.

Except for a fruitless voyage of discovery to Lower California and the bleak Tres Marías Islands (1536–38), Cortés must have been in and out of Cuernavaca during most of his last decade in New Spain. Five of his children were probably born there before 1536. The Dean of the Cathedral Chapter left the capital to serve as chaplain in his Cuernavaca Palace, making him in the eyes of the Church equal in rank with the Viceroy. In his own eyes he was certainly the Viceroy's equal (though when the Viceroy came to dine, Cortés courteously put him at the head of the table; when Cortés dined with the Viceroy there was no head, for each sat equal on either side). He wrote to the King as from one ruler to another, and spoke of his marquisate as of a state.[45]

As he had brought a suite of four hundred as well as his mother and his noble new wife, his residence had to be large, and he felt that it had to be lordly. Just how lordly is told by the records of the tributes paid him, and by the inventories made in 1549, after his death. On the walls he had 22 tapestries and hangings of silk and gold thread, patterned with elephants and kings; on the floors were rugs with lions and leopards. One room was lined with gilded and silvered leather. On the table there could be either gold or silver services. Every week (or fortnight, according to a different document) the town gave his household 750 pounds of corn, 1,600 tortillas, 10 turkeys, and 10 chickens, 10 to 40 patridges or quail, 3 pigeons, and also fruit, salt, chili, wood, and hay; every eighty days they had to deliver 4,800 pieces of cloth, 20 petticoats, 10 damask bedcovers, and 4 cotton mattresses; on feast days there was an extra of 200 eggs and as much fresh fish as needed. From the traditional preconquest tributes of Cuernavaca to which he had fallen heir, he canceled such less useful items as feather ensigns, shields, and 16,000 sheets of bark paper, but he made up for them with material more profitable in trade.[46]

His enterprises were not small, and he must have given a tremendous impulse to building activity in Cuernavaca, activity which was to transform the once large and strong Indian city which he had taken and burned before he demolished Tenochtitlán into a pseudo-European one. Generations before, the local Tlahuica lords had abandoned their old capital, Chicomoztoc, to build a new city, Cuauhnáhuac, so beautiful in site and benign in climate that the Aztecs soon took it over and made country residences with gardens nearby. With its name hispanized to Cuernavaca, it prospered throughout the viceregal period. The mining millionaire, Borda, had elegant formal gardens there in the eighteenth century. The Emperor Maximilian had a favorite country estate there, also with gardens. Today the new lords — politicians, profiteers, countless gringos — as well as the moderately prosperous, have established themselves on the same beautiful site in the same benign climate, and they too have built country residences. Cortés should see his once beautiful city now!

Without being blind to his faults, which had been conspicuous in his youth and still intermittently evident during his first years in New Spain, we must accept the sincerity of Cortés' religious feelings, much as we accept his courage, for the evidence is consistent and copious. He had repeatedly stated that the purpose of the Conquest was the conversion of the Indians, and his actions showed that he meant it. He was more active as a proselytizer than his chaplains, even to the point of rashness during the riskiest moments of the Conquest. Bishop Zumárraga defended him forcefully to the Emperor and took many pages to refute the charges of his enemies.

He would have been seriously concerned with the religious life of Cuernavaca, and that was necessarily dependent on the Franciscans. His connection with the Franciscans was consistently and continuously close: he had had Franciscan chaplains during the Conquest, and on the expedition to Honduras; and when near death on this, he had had a Franciscan robe made for his own burial; on his return he went into a six-day retreat at the head Franciscan house; he had asked the Emperor to send Franciscans to convert the country; he had already several times given them money for their buildings and for other purposes; he sent money for a chapel in the Franciscan church in his home town in Spain; his will directed that his body be sent back to New Spain in ten years, to be buried in a specially founded Franciscan nunnery in Coyoacán, but since that was not built by his heirs, the Franciscans buried his bones instead first in their church in Texcoco, and later in the sanctuary of their church in the capital, not on one side but, like a member of a ruling house or a Prince of the Church, in the center, in a niche immediately behind the high altar. This was the chapel which he had intended as a family mausoleum, which he had decorated with his arms, and which was considered to be part of his estate "not just because he had paid for it . . . but because of the great favor he showed the friars not only in that work, but in everything he gave them." [47] (The chapel fell into ruin and was rebuilt at the end of the century, and at this time, perhaps, the keystone with his arms was sent to his birthplace in Spain, Medellín, where it is said still to be.) He wrote of building for the friars a number of times, and sent plans from Spain for a chapel in Mexico in the last years of his life, still concerned with building and with the Franciscans.[48] Contemporary and later Franciscan writers repeatedly went out of their way to praise him, whereas they were more rarely kind to other encomenderos or governing officials. Surely devoted to the Franciscans, he never did very much for the Dominicans even though the greater part of his marquisate lay in Dominican Oaxaca and his brother-in-law, Antonio de Zúñiga, was a Dominican.

He preferred his Valley of Morelos to his Valley of Oaxaca. He paid for much of the early Augustinian building at nearby Totolapan, and there can be little question that he would have had even more interest in the Franciscans' buildings in Cuernavaca. There is an old but unverifiable tradition that he built them a large church there. He must have been in daily association with them, for the inventory of the second-story chapel in his Palace lists chasubles embroidered with Franciscan cords, which can mean only that he had friars as palace chaplains. One room in the Palace has a carved Franciscan cord running around it just below the *zapata* beam brackets. (Earlier, at Coyoacán, before he moved into ruined Tenochtitlán, he had some sort of quarters built for the Franciscans adjacent to his own so that they could say Mass for him.) [49] Cortés could easily have had not only the wish to promote the construction of a chapel for the Franciscans in Cuernavaca, but also the necessary money and skilled builders at his disposal. He could have made it as advanced architecturally as anything in New Spain, and this is just what the chapel of San José was: as bold as the Palace, as delicate as the Calvario.

THE CHAPEL BUILDING

The vast scale, the lightness of the vaults and their supports, the ingeniousness of the buttressing, and the refinement of the carved and inlaid ornament make this chapel not only strikingly ambitious and elegant, but also precocious, particularly if it was built within twenty years of the Conquest. The chapel at Tlaxcala need not be thought earlier because it is cruder and less successful, for the two do not exhibit differences in degree of evolution so much as differences in artistic quality stemming from different degrees of competence in the designers and builders. San José can hardly have been improvised by an inexperienced friar: the chapel at Tlaxcala can hardly result from anything else. Like Cortés' Palace, the chapel at Cuernavaca is a building which was unprecedented in Mexico, and would also have been unprecedented in Spain. Whoever designed it solved a new architectural problem and conceived the most original and successful work left to us from the first half of the sixteenth century in New Spain.

225 THE OPEN CHAPEL AT CUERNAVACA
Apse and left side compartment

Behind a spacious hall rises a rectangular apse or chancel, closed above by a patterned rib vault. Its floor is raised three steps above the floor of the main hall, and its altar was further emphasized by a large retable of which no trace remains but holes for the fastenings in the back wall. This chancel is flanked by two smaller but similar compartments covered by plain barrel vaults. They communicate with the chancel through wide archways, and were probably railed off from the main space of the chapel in front because no steps lead down from them to its floor. The traces of the original arrangements were blurred when these three spaces were remodeled a century ago into a baptistery, a storeroom, and a bedroom.[50] Since the side compartments were accessible only from the central chancel, their use must have depended on it. Although at first sight they look as though they might have been side apses for side altars, the indirection of access and lack of any scars left by

455

retables or altars suggest that they may have served only for singers and players accessory to High Masses celebrated in the central space. The huge choir-balcony in the adjacent church, covering one third of its nave, shows that music at Cuernavaca was on a grand scale; a balcony much smaller than this 50-foot square would have sufficed for the daily offices said by the handful of friars attached to the monastery, or for a moderate choir of native singers. If the two side compartments of the chapel could not hold all of the music-makers on feast days, they could have occupied part of the main space in front of these compartments.

Here there would have been ample room for extended musical enthusiasm, for the main volume of the chapel is one ample space, 85 feet long and 30 feet wide. It is spanned by a broad and lofty barrel vault, borne on three arches along each side: the back three are the openings to the three rectangular compartments and the front three open out to the atrio. Father Vetancurt found the scale of this vault still impressive a century and half later, after thousands of handsome baroque rivals had been built, and at a time when outmoded mediaeval architecture was not admired.[51] The surface of the vault, which soars some 60 feet above the pavement, is subdivided by two ribs into sections corresponding to the three compartments in back and the three matching arches in front. All of the arches have small but bold moldings of gothic profile, springing from elegantly carved capitals. These are of late-gothic pattern except the two flanking the chancel, which have renaissance details. The craftsmanship is at once bold and exceptionally fine, and decidedly similar to that of the *Calvario*. The contrast of the detail with the space emphasizes the delicacy of one and grandeur of the other. With an inspiring though irrational extravagance so often found in gothic religious buildings, the space seems too big for ordinary people and in more harmonious scale with the symbolic importance of the rites to be celebrated there.

Such a great vaulted hall, crossing the axis of altar and apse and all open on one long side, is a bold innovation in the repertory of Spanish mediaeval church and chapel forms: in fact there are no clear precedents in Spanish church architecture. Possibly some influence was accepted from smaller porches connected with churches or monasteries, or unconsciously from the big open loggias of the *lonjas* or mercantile exchanges of southern Spain. Although several *lonjas* were of loggia form morphologically akin to the chapel, it is difficult to believe in any conscious connection because functionally they were so disparate, not to say hostile: who would chose to model a church on the place of the moneychangers?

There are two likely reasons for this apparent but illogical similarity. First, the designer of the chapel may have known one or two typical *lonjas* well enough to echo the form here without conscious copying. Second, either the designer or Cortés was fond of open facades (in contrast to most contemporary facades in Spain and New Spain), and here where there was functional and climatic justification, may have seized the favored idea and exploited it to the full. Equivalent openness marks the front of the Palace, the *Atarazanas,* and the chapel. Since very little relation to Spanish models can be assumed to have been direct, the idea of the whole chapel should probably be regarded more as an invention than as a conscious borrowing or derivation. By what must be only coincidence, it looks more like the fourteenth-century Loggia dei Lanzi in Florence than anything in Spain, religious or civil.

It was no hasty improvisation, for almost everything is logically integrated. The thrust of such a broad barrel vault must be great, and since the vault is so high, buttressing it was no easy problem. The solution is admirably neat: the three smaller vaults over the apse-like compartments take the thrust at the back, and in front it is received and partly counteracted by two ingenious flying buttresses which spring up to it from the ground. (Unfortunately these have been filled in with masonry reinforcement and, made solid and heavy, now seem more to lean than to fly.) They do not stand out at right angles to the big barrel vault they are stabilizing, as might be expected, but are canted away from one another on slight diagonals so that they might impede the congregation's view of the altar as little as possible, a bold dislocation successful structurally, functionally, and aesthetically. This divergence not only made it easier for people to see into the central section, but also emphasized it visually, pulling their eyes toward the altar through a sort of giant funnel, at the same time serving to screen the adjacent spaces which might be full of distracting musicians.

At the corners of the building there are pier buttresses, set diagonally in the same way that they often were on sixteenth-century Mexican church facades. The hollow main block of the chapel is enlivened by these flaring corner spurs, and even more by the surprising but harmonious accents of the larger flaring-flying buttresses framed by them and parallel to them.

The facade is broad, tall, and open. It consists of the three arches bounding the main space, the bold obliques of the four buttresses at their edges, and, at the top, a band of stuccoed masonry topped by a crenellated parapet. This cresting is interrupted above the center arch by a stone pulpit, small but so dramatically placed that it is hard to imagine a weak or dull sermon coming from it.

Atop one front corner, perhaps both, or all four, there used to be a little bell turret, but as the upper parts of the chapel have undergone alterations and additions — there was a bad earthquake in 1882 and there have been countless lesser ones — it is now impossible to be sure about the original silhouette. Some of the upper parts may be sixteenth-century work a little later than the bold hall below, perhaps contemporary with work on the monastery church.

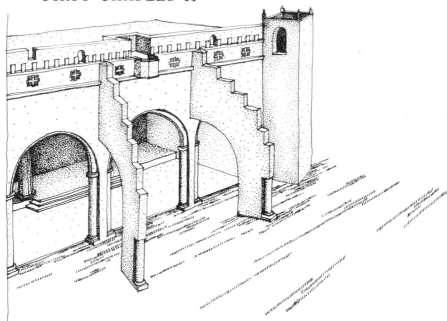

226 RECONSTRUCTION OF THE CHAPEL AT CUERNAVACA

The L-shaped atrio stretches out for 300 feet from the front of the chapel with one of its arms, and runs by the flank of the church with the other. L-shaped atrios were also used early elsewhere, but Cuernavaca has the only one where the open-air "nave" of the chapel crosses in front of the church. This exceptional arrangement may be an indication of a date anterior to the fixing of the standard scheme.

A plain stone cross — at least in part restored — still rises from its original base, on axis with the chapel and in no formal relation to the church which had perhaps not yet been built when the cross was set in front of the chapel. Part of the base with a skull and bones in high relief, indicating Golgotha, seems to have been reworked from a preconquest *cuaxicalli,* a stone box for catching fresh hearts and blood from human sacrifices. In a vivid symbolic humiliation, the old religion was here forced to support the new. The many orange trees which once dotted the atrio must have been set at some distance from the chapel, perhaps around the sides and behind the cross, for a crowd under low trees in front of the chapel would not have been able to see a priest in the pulpit at its top. Once there was also a fishpond somewhere in the atrio, perhaps in the other arm of the L.[52]

San José de Cuernavaca is all but unique: no other buildings show its influence except two low, lumpish, and detailless echoes at Totolapan and Tlayacapan, 20-odd miles away in one of the richest green valleys of Cortés'

Marquisate. Exceptional in form and location, the chapel at Cuernavaca is so exceptional altogether that its essential role as an open chapel has been rejected by one distinguished scholar in favor of its no less certain but supplementary role of portería. While it is true that later writers, Father Vetancurt for example, might call it a portería, they often thus misnamed other open chapels which had ceased to function actively as open chapels. (Surprisingly, for so careful a writer, Vetancurt also said that it was 50 *varas,* or 140 feet, long.) Locally it was still known as the *Capilla de San José* fifty years ago, and the Bishop knew that it had been the Indians' chapel.[53] The accumulation of circumstantial and documentary evidence can leave no doubt that it was built as an open chapel, and that it served as one.

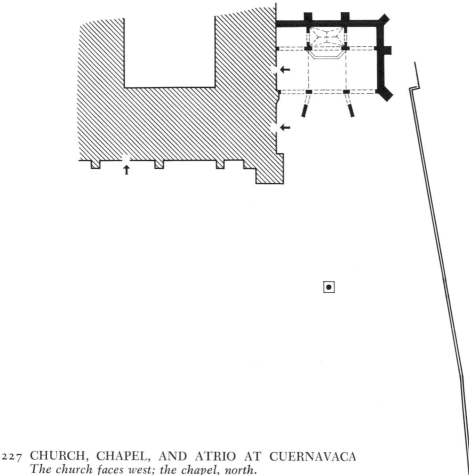

227 CHURCH, CHAPEL, AND ATRIO AT CUERNAVACA
The church faces west; the chapel, north.

459

FIRST CHAPELS II

About 20 feet above the ground the north doorway of the adjacent monastery church is carved with the date 1552. This need not apply to all the work on the doorway, since that does not appear to have been done all at one time, but it shows that much of the building was partly up and that the layout must have been established. Since the provincial style of this doorway is distinct from the sophisticated style of the chapel, and the handling of the masonry cruder, the two presumably come from different building campaigns carried out at different times. The lower part of the west facade of the church and the big choir-balcony inside also differ from the doorway in style and in the character of their masonry.

The local legend that the foundations of the church were allowed to settle ten years before the heavy walls were set on them may be dismissed along with the stories that Cortés worshipped in the existing church and obtained the clock in its tower as a gift from Charles V. All that is certain about the church that is relevant here is that the north doorway was at least partly finished in 1552. The west front would presumably have been begun earlier, perhaps by half a dozen years.

These facts and inferences help date the chapel only if another inference is made from the relative position of the two buildings. Whereas the chapel and the monastery building are coordinately planned to work together — a door at the east end of the chapel is the main entrance to the monastery: they share axes and a wall — the chapel and the church are not coordinated and do not appear to have been planned together. They join only at their corners, and in a clumsy collision where one corner buttress of the chapel overlaps the church facade by a few feet.

It would be difficult to believe that the open chapel was built after the main facade of the church had been begun (some years before 1552, say 1547, just after the plague, or possibly a year or two before) because of the way the chapel's corner buttress overlaps the church and crowds its front door. Had the church been built first, the awkwardness of the jostling buttress could easily have been avoided: the chapel could either have been set contiguous to the church, taking advantage of its mass for stability in buttressing, or it could have been begun a little farther back toward the south, avoiding its mass for clarity of design.

If the chapel was there first, however, already integrated with the monastery building, then when the church came to be erected, that might have taken its normal position with regard to the monastery block when it was begun at the east end, even though that might entail an abnormal and uncomfortable position with regard to the chapel when the west end was reached. The architect of the commonplace church would probably not have minded this as much as the architect of the distinguished chapel.

If the chapel was there first, it would probably have to have been all or nearly completed before the plague of 1544–46, most serious in Cuernavaca from late '45 to '46. Had there been a suitable permanent church building by 1532, Cortés would have buried his child there instead of in the monastery building. Therefore neither church nor chapel was likely built before 1533. Cortés buried his son Luis — more important than an infant daughter — in Texcoco in 1536, which suggests that neither a fitting church nor chapel was yet ready in Cuernavaca. The chapel, if this reasoning is right, was constructed sometime after 1536 and before 1545.

Some date the existing monastery block as late as 1560,[54] but that is more probably the date of remodeling, for part of the building was already considered venerable only a score of years later when Father Mendieta noted the interment of a friar "next to the portería of the old house where he for many years had given food to the poor and needy." [55] This indicates that when

228 NORTH DOORWAY, CUERNACAVA

Mendieta was writing, in 1585 or a little earlier, there was a "new" and an "old" part of the monastery. The portería either adjoined the "old" or was part of it. Since the open chapel served prominently as a portería, it would seem to be the portería mentioned; furthermore, there are clear signs of burials there. A chapel such as this would be a normal place to bury a friar: an ordinary portería would be uncustomary, unsuitable, and — since porterías were not built over consecrated ground — unacceptable. Father Mendieta probably called it a portería because it was being used more as a portería than a chapel when he was writing, and he was, moreover, referring specifically to one of its portería functions (almsgiving) and not to any chapel function. Of all that remains of the monastery at Cuernavaca today, the chapel appears to be the oldest part, and the only part old enough to have been called "old" when Mendieta was writing in about 1585. His comment, then, may reinforce a dating before the plague in the mid-1540's.

If, as is probable though not documented or provable, the chapel is a result of Cortés' presence in Cuernavaca, then it would have been begun, or at least planned, sometime after 1536 and before he left in 1540. This raises a new question: could such a sophisticated and knowingly vaulted building have been designed in Mexico in the late 1530's? It is necessary to consider this question in some detail.

461

Surely one of the first completely vaulted buildings on the continent, perhaps this building may be the first. (San Francisco was vaulted only over the chancel.) If it is, one has again to believe that Father Motolinía, writing between 1536 and '41/42, was mistaken or forgetful when he said that his little vaults in Tlaxcala were the only ones outside the capital. He had visited the monastery at Cuernavaca in 1531 (and had planted there the first two date palms on the continent; they were in flower ten years later).[56] The open chapel cannot have been there then because its vaults are too striking to have slipped his mind. Possibly he had not been back before he wrote, in which case the chapel could have been built at any time after his visit, and he may not have known about it before he began writing. If he was informed about events in Franciscan Cuernavaca and if he kept his manuscript up-to-date, the chapel cannot have been vaulted until after he finished writing in the winter of 1541–42. It could have been begun a year or two earlier, and have been just ready for its vaults when he finished writing. He cannot have been very well informed of recent architectural news, however, because the vaults in several cloisters in the neighborhood were already finished before 1541 as Professor Kubler has shown.[57] There were also two stone-vaulted rooms in a house in nearby Oaxtepec by 1536, recorded in the trial of an idolater. Father Motolinía must have crossed some of the many bridges built by Bishop Ramírez de Fuenleal of the Second Audiencia between 1531 and '35 which, being of stone, must have been vaulted.[58] If Father Motolinía did not notice these other vaults already visible when he was writing about his little Tlaxcala vaults, he may have missed the vaults of the open chapel too; they could have been there since 1538 or '39, before Cortés left.

We are certain of many ambitious vaults built over church sanctuaries and even naves in the 1550's, and vaulting was common enough by 1553 for the Indians of Metztitlán to be asked to build a vaulted house as a matter of course. Doctor Zorita, in Mexico from 1554 to '64, repeated Motolinía's account of the building of the first vault at San Francisco, and then said that *many* had been built since. Doctor Cervantes de Salazar noted without calling it remarkable that the Indians had constructed some 33 vaulted bridges by 1560.[59] In view of these and other like notices, it is clear that quite a few Indian masons had been taught how to construct vaults not long after the raising of the vault over San Francisco in 1525, and that vaulting was an accepted and moderately widespread practice for important buildings within a generation. It seems unreasonable to believe that all this happened only after 1541 with the exception of two little chapels built by Father Motolinía's Indians in his Tlaxcala.

The beneficent Valley of Morelos and its branches, then belonging largely to Cortés, are studded with early monasteries — Tepoztlán, Tlaquiltenango, Tlayacapan, Totolapan, Oaxtepec, Yautepec, Atlatláuhcan, Yecapixtla, Zacualpan de Amilpas, and Ocuituco — most of them with remains of building done during the time of Cortés' residence (1531–40). He gave money for religious buildings in the neighborhood, and it is perhaps no coincidence that in or near his fiefs the cloisters of Ocuituco, Totolapan, and Yecapixtla,[60] Tlaquiltenango, and probably Oaxtepec should all have been vaulted in the years that he was living near them. Even the church at Tlaquiltenango seems to have been fully vaulted by 1540, with a big barrel vault comparable in scale to that of the chapel (ill. 28). The nave walls 8 feet thick show that they must have been intended to carry vaults from the beginning, and hence that the vaults were planned in the 1530's. (It is possible that they were not finished when the inscription "finished in 1540" was put over the door of the monastery block, and it is even possible that the inscription referred only to the monastery block and not to the church — but though possible, not probable.)

The church may be further connected with Cortés' commissions through the stylistic resemblance of some of the carving on its main portal to carving on Cortés' Palace. Both, moreover, are constructed of the same kind of masonry: tight fieldstone rubble with cut stone only at the corners. The fact that in Father Ponce's *Relación* Tlaquiltenango was called a little monastery, a *conventico,* need not mean that the big vaulted church had not yet been built, because Father Ponce never went to Tlaquiltenango, then occupied by the Dominicans. His scribe wrote nothing about the church, only about the monastery block which was and is still small. Furthermore, he said that the monastery had been built "long ago." [61]

The monasteries at Totolapan and Tlayacapan have chapels which seem clearly but clumsily and cautiously to echo the scheme of Cuernavaca. Though they lack the elegance of detail and skill in the handling of vaults and buttresses, they presumably copy the *parti* of three arched openings leading to a broad oblong covered by a transverse barrel vault, a scheme not found in chapels elsewhere. If they were built as early as the evidence of the date of their founding, primitive character, and resemblance to early local cloisters makes probable — the late 1530's or the 1540's — then they may offer additional evidence for an early date for their superior prototype at Cuernavaca.[62]

No such group of vaulted structures as these in Morelos was then to be found elsewhere in Mexico, not even in the capital. There must have been masons at work in the Valley of Morelos who knew how to make vaults, and these men, presumably trained on some of Cortés' first undertakings there, may have been farmed out to the friars building in the vicinity. Cortés' partiality to the Franciscans might explain why the open chapel of the Fran-

ciscans at Cuernavaca and the nave of the Franciscan church at Tlaquiltenango had the services of masons skilled enough to construct the largest
vaults. The other vaults are all smaller, and most are not on Franciscan buildings.

*

The lava "crosses of Jerusalem," or "crosses of the Knights of the Holy
Sepulcher," set into the parapet of the chapel might be construed as allusions
to those bordering the blazon of his grandfather Monroy, which Cortés imposed on the center of the new quarterings granted him by the Emperor in
1525; but the probability is slender, for these heraldic crosses were sometimes
mentioned as "crosses of Saint John" and were not shown with the T-shaped
arms of true "crosses of Jerusalem" in surviving representations. The crosses
on the chapel more probably indicate reference to the Franciscans, who had
assumed such "crosses potent" in 1342, when named guardians of the Holy
Places of Jerusalem, lost by the crusaders but still accessible to the Franciscans
of the monastery there. This type of cross had been associated with crusaders
and with struggles against the heathen, which might have given it special
meaning here at Cuernavaca. (The Franciscans kept on using it in Mexico
later when it must have meant less, for example at Ozumba.) They retained
the sole right to nominate to the Order of the Knights of the Holy Sepulcher,
whose emblem it was. With rich reason to honor Cortés as a fighter of heathens, they might appropriately have conferred this knighthood on him even
though he had not been to Jerusalem, where the dubbing was usually done,
but there is no record of this, and the crosses cannot be used to associate
Cortés with the chapel.

*

In view of all this: of the resemblance of carved detail on the *Calvario*
and open chapel, *if* the Calvario can be dated 1538; of the precedence of
the chapel over the church facade of *c*1544–47, *if* that date is correct; of
the reference by Father Mendieta to a portería by the "old" part of the monastery, *if* it applies to the chapel; of Cortés' known partiality to the Franciscans; of his presumed stimulus to local building activity; of the prevalence
of early vaults in Morelos; of the fact that two early neighboring open chapels
copy Cuernavaca, *if* they do and *if* they are truly early; and of the fact that
building activity is recorded at the monastery during the decade of Cortés'
residence in Cuernavaca; [63] — in view of all this, then, the most likely date
for the design and most of the construction of the open chapel lies within
the period of Cortés' residence in Cuernavaca, and more specifically within
a year or two or three after 1536. (It could of course have been completed
after he left.) Some of the masons who had worked on the chapel may have
moved on to build the next big early vault in the region: the nave of Tlaquil-

tenango. This is equally bold, but much heavier and coarser; its curiously handmade look would be a result of clumsy aping of the vault of the open chapel by second-class workmen or — far less likely — if it was built first, the inexperienced improvisation of workmen who would be more expert on their second try, at the open chapel. It is possible to weigh these several probabilities differently, and reach a different date — a date perhaps later than the one proposed here, about 1538 to 1540 or '41 — but as there are so few hard facts, another date will be only another possibility, not a proved conclusion.

*

What must be stressed even more than the dramatic if early date is the undeniably dramatic and distinguished design. Easy to see in the middle of an easily accessible city, this handsome chapel remains unnoticed by almost everyone — residents, weekenders, and tourists — even including most of those professing an interest in the arts. Cuernavaca offers nothing man-made of comparable quality anywhere else within its now crowded limits.

XII

SINGLE–CELL CHAPELS

NOT only San José de los Naturales but the chapels at Tlaxcala and Cuernavaca must soon have become known to prospective builders, for each was
a prominent adjunct of a much visited monastery. Although their particular architectural forms were imitated in few later buildings, the general
arrangement of these chapels must have given dramatic evidence of how well
the atrio-and-chapel scheme could work. Later examples show so many variations and experiments that it is clear that the open chapel cannot have been
subject to the standards which controlled the morphology of the rest of the
monastery. Perhaps it enjoyed this freedom because it was too unfamiliar to
Spaniards in Spain for them to issue directives for it.

Varied as they are, nearly all open chapels built after the early 1540's can
be classified as either one of two major types:

> the single cell, and
> the portico chapel.

Single-cell chapels were the more common because they were so simple,
effective, cheap, and easy to build. They often correspond in form to the
sanctuary of a church, and if the atrio is regarded as an outdoor nave, the
reason is clear. The little chapels at Atlihuetzía and Tepeyanco were really
apses in function and form. (The analogy can be pushed further, with the
posas likened to side altars; [1] but as earlier discussion has shown, the posas
had a different function, and such an extension of the analogy can be misleading.)

Among existing chapels the nearest to the traditional idea of an apse may
be those at Atlihuetzía and Tepeyanco (without their added porticos) and
that recently discovered at Tarímbaro by Manuel González Galván. In Mexico
the traditional form used at Tarímbaro was a novelty, for the common
European idea of a semicylindrical apse capped by a semidome was uncommon in sixteenth-century Spain, and rarer still in Mexico. Only about half a
dozen churches there adopted the form. The chapel at Tarímbaro is framed
by a large heavy archivolt resting on stubby fluted pilasters. Both archivolt
and pilasters lie in part flat on the front wall of the monastery block and bend

466

in part inward on a blunt angle to make an unorthodox but fully effective transition from the flat plane of the wall to the modeled hollow of the apse-chapel. The altar cannot have been set in its usual place against the middle of the wall in back since a bench runs uninterruptedly around the curve: the altar must have been freestanding, perhaps on the chord of the curve. The date of this odd, sober, and handsome chapel is uncertain. The town had been favored by the ladies of the Tarasco royal house, and their right to it — and its consequent importance — was confirmed by Charles V in 1545. It was early chosen for a Franciscan visita, and soon had the chief infirmary for all the friars of the Province, at least by 1560. The visita became a monastery either just before 1570 or 1583, and its church would presumably have been begun very soon and finished quickly since Father Ponce pronounced the establishment complete a few years later. The chapel might have been made for the early days of the visita, but as far as one can judge from its modestly classicizing style, it appears more likely to have been built somewhat later, perhaps shortly after 1570.[2]

229
TARÍMBARO

UNVAULTED EXAMPLES

An even simpler form is found in many of the small unvaulted chapels which, like Tarímbaro, were sunk in the block of the monastery building, either next to the church or next to the somewhat similar openings of the portería. With their front flush with the front of the monastery building, they showed themselves on this plane like outsize doorways or windows. Something was unsatisfactory when, as often the case (Acolman, Huatla- tláuhca, Yecapixtla), this important component of the conventual group had more the nature of a giant cubbyhole than the dignified architectural entity its liturgical office deserved. The easiest way of emphasizing them was to make them large enough to count as a major element (as at Tepexpan, where the arch spanned 17 feet). Something seemed perverse when the opening was deliberately reduced (as at Zacualpan de Amilpas) by an arch dropped lower than the top of the chapel space behind it. There are many sub-types and minor variations.

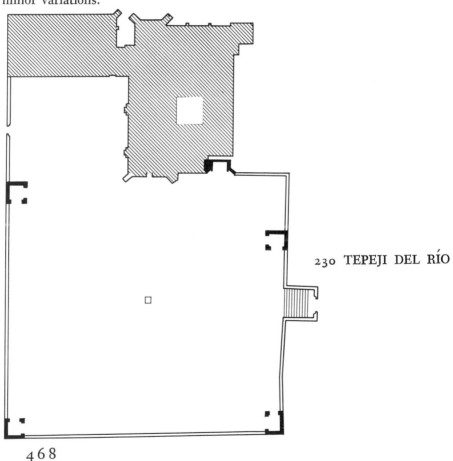

230 TEPEJI DEL RÍO

468

Usually fairly small, these simple chapels were able to function well, and afforded an adequate view of the ritual of the Mass. Efficient functioning, however, is not all that is required of a chapel: it needs also an expressive or formal character appropriate to its religious role.

One special way of emphasizing and dignifying a small and otherwise insignificant-looking chapel embedded in a monastery block was tried at Tepeji del Río. The single cell revealed by the basket-handle arch was made to count more by being pushed back from the plane of the wall of the monastery front, thereby seeming to make that plane bend back on either side to receive and enshrine the little chapel. The flaring diagonals of wall expand the space in front of the chapel to a sort of wedge or broad funnel leading emphatically in. The effective front was increased to 30 feet (from bend to bend) over 13 feet (from jamb to jamb under the arch). The diagonal sections of wall are parallel to the diagonal planes of the corner buttresses on either side of the neighboring church facade and relate the chapel in form to the building to which it is most closely related in function. With equal appropriateness the diagonal sides recall the diagonal sides of an ordinary polygonal apse. Here at Tepeji there seems to have been a wish to relate the chapel also to the posas — they would be used conjointly on festival occasions — for chapel and posas are similar not only in size and shape, but the arches and bands of tequitqui ornament on all of them have been made to match. (The monastery was moved to this site between two old towns in 1558, and Indians from both began the building soon afterwards. Fray Diego de Valadés was Guardian in 1569.) [3]

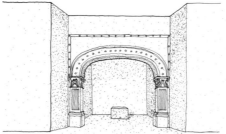

231 TEPEJI DEL RÍO
Elevation of chapel

The recessed arrangement at Tepeji, which seems like an exaggeration of the oblique jambs of the chapel at Tarímbaro, may have been unique. A more common expedient for emphasis was to make the chapel a separate building. This had to be coordinated functionally with the atrio and, for convenience of access, usually with the church or monastery building or with both. Under ideal conditions it might join with them formally in one coherent three-part design; sometimes, however, it did not, particularly when the three constituent elements of the conventual complex were built at different times.

469

232 CHURCH AND CHAPEL AT TEPEJI DEL RÍO

One arrangement, always mechanically practical and often artistically coherent, was to set a small chapel against the flat front of a large church or monastery block, and thus allow the chapel to project and assert itself as an independent little architectural entity backed up by a bigger one. Something of this sort was done with the apse-like polygonal chapel of San Camilo attached to the front of the monastery at Tzintzuntzan, but since this has been walled up the ensemble is no longer legible, and a fresher sense of such a scheme can be gained at Epazoyucan, where a small box-like chapel is backed against the left side of the flat facade of the monastery church (ill. 133). Despite nineteenth-century patching after the church had been struck by lightning, there can be little question that this chapel was not part of any refurbishing for the 91 friars who stayed at Epazoyucan for the Chapter Meeting of 1563 or any later emendation, but part of the original building campaign of seven months and seven days in 1540–41: [4] an original waterspout bonded into the masonry high above the chapel is set obliquely to keep the rainwater it takes from the roof of the church from falling on the roof of the chapel, and shows that the chapel was already there when the upper part of the church was built. Furthermore, the chapel has displaced the main doorway of the church a few feet to the right of center to gain comfortable space for itself at the left. The chapel, doorway, and original belfry are equilibrated into an asymmetrical but subtly coherent ensemble: no one element can be an afterthought or addition since each affects and complements the location of both the others.

Although only 16 by 7 feet inside, the chapel provides enough space for an altar, a priest, and two acolytes, the minimum of celebrants for a High Mass. Despite its insignificant size, the little box is marked as something consequential by its location, its power of dislocation, and by the flickering filigree of its ornament. Renaissance motifs carved in an embroidery-like

233 EPAZOYUCAN

tequitqui cover the archivolt and jambs, and the top edge was once enlivened
with freestanding cresting, sharper and daintier than the bold crowning of
Huejotzingo's posas. The chapel is thus made to seem a precious special place
where something precious and special will be celebrated. It is different in
character from the bigger, plainer, and more imposing church facade in back,
and properly even more different from the yet plainer monastery block still
farther back.

At Epazoyucan there are only three posas, and there never can have been
more. They so closely resemble the slightly larger open chapel in general
form and in details of decoration, and are so placed in relation to it that they
join with it to make one matching set of four little pavilions deployed around
the atrio in an orderly formation. The chapel is related as much to the posas
as it is to the church; to the first by homology and to the second by contiguity.
It is possible that when a procession preceded or followed a Mass held in the
church, the chapel could have func-
tioned as a posa since it would not then
have been called on to function as a
chapel. It need not always have been
exclusively one or the other. The same
altar-block could have served for
either. When Mass was to be said, and
the little building was to be a chapel,
a proper consecrated altar could have
been provided quickly by setting an ara
on the altar-block.

234 EPAZOYUCAN
Elevation of open chapel

47 1

235
EPAZOYUCAN
The ruined open chapel

At Tecbatán in Chiapas and Motul in Yucatan there are open porch-like pavilions attached to the far end of the front of the monastery building north of the church (on the north end here because both are in hot country). Are these at once open chapels and posas, as at Epazoyucan? or just one, or the other, or neither? It is unlikely that they were open chapels. Though now almost invisible, there are conclusive remains of a good-sized walled-up open chapel south of the church at Motul, and the chapel-like pavilion is enough like a posa still surviving there to take its place homomorphically as one of a normal set. The pavilion at Tecbatán is in a region where no open chapels are known, and it is more likely an element of the portería. It is not even surely of sixteenth-century construction.

*

The openings of nearly all open chapel fronts are spanned by an arch. There may be two reasons for this preference, one aesthetic and expressive, the other structural. By the direction of its edge an arch appears to enclose circumferentially and focus radially on the altar below it, and at the same time to emphasize the altar in another and more static way by bounding and giving clear form to the space immediately around it. Moreover, for openings more than 5 or 6 feet wide in the exterior of their monasteries, sixteenth-century builders preferred the arch to a stone or wood lintel. Wood lintels were usual only where well protected inside the monastery building, or in domestic or civil work. Perhaps straight wood lintels were once more common in country church exteriors, but little exposed wood has been able to endure the intervening centuries, and no one wanted to give the time and pains necessary to

472

work the hard and virtually everlasting *zapote* wood which the Mayas had once used so handsomely for lintels, some of which survive in effective use. Mexico does not seem to have been affected by Saint Charles Borromeo's curious contention that round-headed doors were pagan, and only square-headed ones were suitable for Christians.[5]

There are a few exceptions. A wood lintel still spans the simple chapel at San Antonio Oztoyuca near the capital. A more important instance was "discovered" at Angahuan in 1944, when new trails were being explored to take travelers to the newborn volcano at Paricutín in Michoacán. The visita church beside the chapel at Angahuan is dated 1562 on the facade, and probably also 1577 on a pseudo-Cufic inscription inside.[6] Another inscription, around the doorway, announces illiterately that the church was dedicated to Santiago. Nearby was a visita hospital — a specialty of Michoacán — and its chapel also stands intact. The ensemble of little buildings makes a small but unusually complete example of visita architecture of the sixteenth century.

The open chapel is curiously placed at the foot of a squat bell-tower contiguous to the church. As the two-arched gallery above it can be entered only from the choir-balcony of the church, it must have been intended for music makers, which is not surprising since the Tarascos of the vicinity have long been known for their enthusiasm and skill in making both music and instruments.

Although far from monumental the architecture at Angahuan is rich in carving. The tequitqui is at once vigorous, provincial, and arbitrary, and its patterns often recall those of the lively folk-art of the region, particularly the textiles. There can be no doubt that the work was done by local Indians, and

236 ANGAHUAN

473

237 ANGAHUAN
A Palm Sunday procession carrying an image into the visita chapel

little doubt that they quoted some ornamental phrases from the big monastery at Uruapan, 15 miles to the southwest. The doorway was derived from that of the Guatapera or Hospital Chapel there, and other ornamental elements from windows and brackets in the hospital courtyard. The reliefs at Angahuan appear to have been carried out by several different carvers, all less sophisticated in Spanish taste than those who made their models at Uruapan. The men at Angahuan transformed their borrowings, however, by stylizing them into fine-scale, repeated patterns in crisp, low. two-plane relief, curiously like magnified typesetters' ornament. Some of the same men may have worked on the little hospital at Sacán, nearby, for it too is a tequitqui image of Uruapan. The carvers of both Angahuan and Sacán quoted with a strong Indian accent (ill. 130).[7]

Artistically dependent on Uruapan, Angahuan and Sacán were ecclesiastically dependent on the nearer monastery at Sirosto (then usually Tzirosto), but as Sirosto, once celebrated for its splendor, has been shaken and shaken by quakes, whether it was a model for any of the work at Angahuan and Sacán or not would now be hard to say. Since the monastery at

474

Sirosto was founded (c1576) only when the church at Angahuan was presumably under way, Angahuan was somehow dependent on Franciscan Uruapan before being formally assigned to Augustinian Sirosto, and the same seems to hold for Sacán. No student of colonial architecture is known to have visited Sirosto recently. Villagers at Angahuan say that it has no carving like theirs, but praise lacquer doors and retables which — if they exist — might outweigh the trivial discomforts of a horseback trip through a beautiful part of Michoacán. Success is not guaranteed, however, for a century ago a local historian found the church so cracked by quakes that it had been remodeled somehow into a house for the curate, and an archaeologist recently reported new damage from the upheavals of Paricutín.[8]

*

When the one-celled chapel was not embedded in the front of the monastery block, or backed up either against it or the church facade, it might be developed into a more independent unit, sometimes even into a small church. At Izamal, for example, the chapel has a little nave, spanned by diaphragm

238 THE MONASTERY CHURCH AND OPEN CHAPEL AT IZAMAL *behind seventeenth-century arcades and below nineteenth-century espadañas. The horseshoe window in the facade of the church is a nineteenth-century invention.*

475

arches carrying a wooden roof, like a miniature church of the local Yucatecan type of San Juan de Díos in Mérida. It may or may not be the same chapel Father Ponce saw in 1585. Once dedicated to Saint Anthony, it now serves incongruously as a Masonic meeting hall (ill. 105).[9] The facade — no longer open — is set near the middle of the east side of the atrio, in the same plane and close to that of the monastery church which, of course, dwarfs it. The form of this church-chapel cannot have been functionally successful — the altar would have to be placed too far back — and it did not become typical of any part of New Spain.

The independent single-cell chapel more often had the proportions of a chancel, and was set well back on the north flank of the church, where it could have atrio space distinct but not separated from the arm of the atrio in front of the monastery church.

239 JALAPA DEL MARQUÉS
Open chapel and church

BARREL–VAULTED EXAMPLES

Unlike these chapels just discussed, many single-cell chapels were vaulted. This was natural in small chapels which took the form of detached polygonal apses (such as Atlihuetzía and Tepeyanco) but these were never very common, and square barrel-vaulted chapels (like that at Jalapa del Marqués) were a more usual type. They were standard in Yucatan, where easily workable stone for vaults was plentiful and easily workable wood for roofs was not. Elsewhere it was not generally the available supply of building materials that controlled the choice of whether to vault or to roof with wood; nor did the predilection for vaulting come from the tradition that an apse ought to be vaulted — a feeling that the altar ought to be covered by a canopy more durable than an ordinary wood ceiling — for this feeling was already obsolescent in Spain, as many handsome *artesón-* and *alfarje*-covered apses show. Furthermore, if the open chapel did not have to shelter a consecrated altar permanently, this would not have been an imperative consideration. Whether

476

to vault or not must have been determined largely by aesthetic preference, tempered by the availability — or sobering unavailability — of materials, money, and masons. In the best work, the preference was generally for vaulting. Similar preference affected the chancels of monastery churches, for to give aesthetic and expressive emphasis, wood-covered naves sometimes led to a vaulted chancel, and many barrel-vaulted naves to a rib-vaulted chancel. The preference was not for any particular kind of vault as opposed to a wooden covering, but for the special dignity which a shapely vault could give to whatever it sheltered.

A typical small example is at Yautepec in Morelos. Although the end of its vault opens out to the facade with a sizable archway, 15 feet high and 15 feet across, the chapel still lacks authority because it is so belittled by the architectural context: the looming bulk of the monastery church to whose left flank it adheres. No membering or carved ornament was used to give the front of this chapel another kind of emphasis. All is bare and seemingly poverty-stricken, though perhaps once the red-and-black-and-white sgraffito patterns so common in Morelos may have dressed it more brightly and made it look more important. (The church is dated 1567 by an inscription, but there is no date for the chapel which may be ten or twenty years earlier. Dating such nondescript work is particularly difficult and not always significant.)

A number of simple, barrel-vaulted, one-celled chapels were built on a more generous scale and were therefore enabled more suitably to proclaim the authority of their religious function. With a wider arch and vault they were also better adapted to display the full celebration of the Mass.

This can be seen, with a little effort, in the hitherto unrecorded chapel at Izúcar de Matamoros (less correctly but more often called Matamoros Izúcar). At the south end of the benignly fertile Valley of Atlixco, the Dominicans had destroyed pagan Izúcar "of the hundred towers" and raised the first in their long rosary of monasteries from Puebla to Guatemala. Although by 1539 they were well enough etablished in the prosperous market town to try its *cacique* for apostasy, and although they had a church big enough for their Indians to be *in,* the vicaría of Santo Domingo de Izúcar was not officially declared a monastery until 1540. The first Guardian was there by '41. The existing buildings probably replaced the primitive establishment, sometime between 1551, when the Viceroy ordered construction of a "humble and moderate" monastery for which the friars were allotted ample local Indian labor, and 1556, when they had already spent 40,000 pesos. The entire complex is architecturally consistent — exceptionally so — and most of it must have been built in one campaign. The chapel, then, would most likely have been made in the early 1550's.[10]

SINGLE CELLS

The still complete though shabby establishment is all barrel vaulted, and generally as "humble and moderate" as the Viceroy ordered, except in size. The architectural elements are unarticulated, with few moldings, and those few blocky and plain. North of the imposing twin-towered church facade, and flush with it, rises a high, plain, plastered wall with erratically placed windows. Raking light can reveal an arch, 25 feet wide and high, which embraces and crowds the windows and explains their odd location. Before it was filled in, this arch ran back as a barrel vault to cover a square chamber, now a baptistery but once an open chapel. Between it and the nave of the church is the original baptistery (located like that at Chimalhuacán Chalco), now reduced to the role of vestibule. The arch in which the barrel vault terminates was bold enough to hold its own visually beside the church facade. Despite its bareness the ensemble was strongly plastic, with the center of the church facade recessed between its flanking towers.

Above the chapel there is another vaulted room, accessible from the choir-balcony of the church. The scale of this choir, more capacious even than that at Cuernavaca and perhaps the largest left in Mexico, shows that the friars of Izúcar must have found music important, and suggests that the room above the chapel may have been to house music-makers for outdoor Masses. Although one cannot now distinguish in its plastered front wall another arch like that below, some large opening would surely have been necessary to let the music out.

*

There is an even larger barrel-vaulted chapel at Maní, one of the oldest and most important of the friaries in Yucatan, in its general scheme equivalent to contemporary or slightly earlier Franciscan houses in central Mexico. The whole establishment, big in scale, almost all vaulted, and almost all intact, was said to have been built in only seven months (probably in 1548–49, and almost certainly before 1559) by 6000 Indians directed by Fray Juan de Mérida, a conquistador turned friar-architect. It was reported that in 1560 Fray Cristóbal de Rivera tried to use this chapel as part of a new church, and that the scheme came to nought. It is not known why he was planning another church when the normal monastery church had (presumably) just been finished. Some work was done, however, in some part of the monastery in the 1560's. Perhaps the chapel was finished then, and Fray Cristóbal was defeated in trying somehow to change the plans.[11]

The chapel is embedded in the monastery block beside the church, and was once visually linked to the church by the continued arches of the low portería on its front (in Yucatan often called the *racionero*). The chapel itself must have been able to hold its own because of the bold scale of its opening: the arch is the end of a barrel vault 27 feet across and as high as the second story of the monastery building behind. The barrenness of the forms of the chapel, typical of the rest of the monastery as well and of nearly all sixteenth-century monasteries in poverty-stricken Yucatan, seems to rob it of much of the majestic effect its scale could warrant; the fact that it is now walled up robs it of the rest. It was once less bare, however, for Father Ponce saw that "the Indians . . . have their chapel, adjoining the monastery, and it is made of masonry, and with an ornamental vault, and it is called San Francisco" (1585). The ornamentation must have been painted, since the surface of the vault is smooth and the archivolt shows no sign of carving. Although Cárdenas Valencia found the barrel vault of the monastery church "most sightly" in 1639 — he praised everything in Yucatan — he did not mention the chapel, which must originally have been more remarkable than the church; perhaps it had already been walled up. John Lloyd Stephens stayed in the monastery in 1841, and despite its dilapidation and his discoverer's enthusiasm for Maya ruins, he found the church and monastery "among the grandest of these early structures . . . proud monuments of the zeal and labor of the Franciscan friars.[12]

*

In happy contrast to ineffective Yautepec and similar small or medium-sized chapels, the bold flight of the arch over the chapel at Actopan is as arresting as the busy plateresque facade of the adjoining church (c1550). It holds its own visually and symbolically because of the enormous scale of its one element, trumpeted ff. This arch is the front edge of a barrel vault which covers the chapel. The Augustinians, who sometimes indulged in eloquent megalomania — never more extravagantly, single-mindedly, and wonderfully than here — covered the chapel with a vault 57 feet across, 10 feet wider than the vaulted church next to it, wider even than the naves of such proud cathedrals as Paris, Amiens, Toledo, or Seville. It surpassed all vaults in Spain save those of the nave of Gerona, the mightiest gothic vaults in the world. Small wonder that the chapel is locally known as the *bóveda de Actopan,* "the vault of Actopan."

It is expertly built of cut stone kept elegantly thin in the upper parts, which not only makes it look handsome but also reduces the thrust by reducing the weight. The thrust is principally contained by the masonry of two small rooms at either side, one surely a sacristy. Even after four centuries the vault has settled, sagged, or bulged surprisingly little.

The huge opening was given minimal architectural membering, and wisely so, for to be in suitable scale any pilasters on its jambs, for example, would have had to be so big as to be discordantly out of scale with the church. If in scale with the vault, they would have been too fat, for there is only 12 feet of vertical wall for them before the vault begins to spring. The simple archivolt is almost perversely small in proportion, and it was appropriately treated not in Roman fashion, like an active self-sustaining arch with some

240 THE OPEN CHAPEL AT ACTOPAN

structural integrity, but instead like a decorative border unable to hold itself up, passively carried by the working voussoirs behind. The unstructural character of the archivolt is emphasized at its impost, where it is mitered and turned inward, declaring itself as frankly decorative as a picture frame at just the place where a mimetically structural archivolt would need to look its strongest. The treatment is as ungrammatical as on Brunelleschi's Hospital of the Innocents in Florence, where arch moldings behave in the same way. Although the profile of the archivolt is classical, its behavior at Actopan is not and, as at Florence, this comes from lingering mediaeval or otherwise unclassical attitudes toward the character of pseudo-structural classical elements. In contemporary Spain, too, architects were using the repertory of antique forms with almost aggressive indifference to their structural implications.

The smooth inner surface of the vault at Actopan was painted with mock coffers in crimson and black, again small in scale and effective in making the already vast vault look vaster. The pattern was probably borrowed from an illustration in Serlio's Third Book,[13] an illustration he made not from any real coffers but from a coffer-patterned mosaic in Santa Costanza in Rome (to him, a "Temple of Bacchus"). When the original polychrome retable, large in total area and presumably small in the scale of its parts, stood glittering at the shadowy back of Actopan's cavernous chapel, the total effect must have been even more galvanizing than the battered but unforgettable spectacle it presents today.

241 SERLIO'S DESIGNS from A "TEMPLE OF BACCHUS" (Santa Costanza, Rome)
"rich in many different ornaments, but I do not show more than these three inventions . . . some in beautiful stone and some in mosaic."

481

SINGLE CELLS

In the eighteenth century, when there was no more use for it as an open chapel, its front was closed across the bottom by a wall with playfully swooping baroque silhouette. Although the handsome big monastery, on the main Mexico–Laredo highway is much visited today, 19 out of every 20 tourists never walk around to the north side to see its greatest novelty: the chapel and its overwhelming vault.

At Ixmiquilpan, the next Augustinian house north on the old highway to the mines of Zimapán, the open chapel is a denatured variant of that at Actopan. Both houses were founded at about the same time (c1546–50), and both were said to have been built by the same friar, Andrés de Mata.[14] If compared with Actopan, Ixmiquilpan looks like the work of his left hand. Half the size of its model, it counts as less than half, for it is dwarfed by the long flat front wall of the monastery in which it is sunk, and is clumsily jostled by the portería, which competes all too successfully for attention. It is now walled up, but there are said to be plans for clearing it soon.

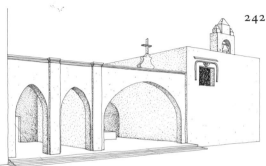

242 IXMIQUILPAN
Portería and open chapel with later infill removed

At Metztitlán there is a curious arrangement of two small barrel-vaulted chapels side by side at the back of the atrio on the left of the church. Although contiguous, they do not appear to represent a concerted scheme: they are separate constructions, unbonded in their masonry, and a little disparate in size. Perhaps they were built a few years apart. The finish is elegant and a little severe like most of the work at Metztitlán. There are crisply molded archivolts, carved rosettes in the shadowy soffits of the arches, and elaborate painted stripes of foliate arabesques on the still more shadowy surfaces of the vaults.

The Augustinians had moved up from a river-flooded site in the valley in 1539; their splendid new church was still in construction in 1553, but was finished before 1569. In 1574 there were 43,000 Indians there, shepherded by five friars. By 1579 there were "churches" of some sort in all the visitas. Once a capital of the Otomí-Chichimecas, Metztitlán had been the center of a belligerently independent pocket not subject to Moctezuma. It

482

had sided with Cortés and the Tlaxcaltecas against its old enemies, the Aztecs; consequently it had not been damaged by the Spaniards, and was entitled to a favorably low tribute. During the years the monastery was building, Metztitlán was prospering pleasantly from the varied crops of its riverside meadows, from silk-raising, and from its trade in textiles. But neither its size, wealth, nor political history explains why the city would have *two* adjacent open chapels. Perhaps some preconquest division was respected by the Spaniards because the Metztitlanos had once been their allies; perhaps there were two chapels because two languages were spoken, though that was not the custom elsewhere. (There were two different kinds of Indians there in the eighteenth century, Aculhuas and Chichimecas, and perhaps the division was an old one.) [15] There is little evidence for the validity of such conjectures, however, and no other town, no matter how large, loyal, rich, or bilingual, is known to have had such an arrangement.

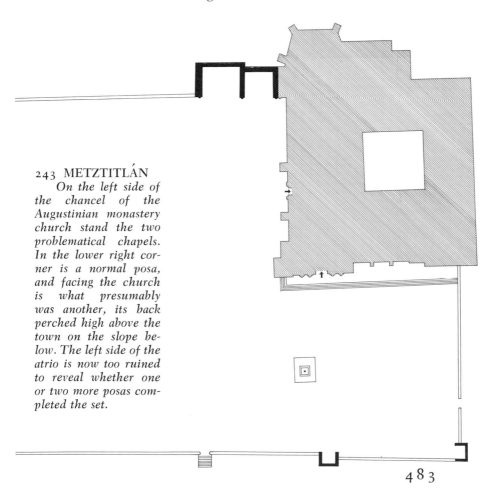

243 METZTITLÁN
On the left side of the chancel of the Augustinian monastery church stand the two problematical chapels. In the lower right corner is a normal posa, and facing the church is what presumably was another, its back perched high above the town on the slope below. The left side of the atrio is now too ruined to reveal whether one or two more posas completed the set.

483

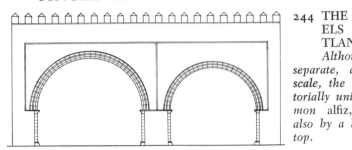

244 THE TWIN CHAP-
ELS OF METZTI-
TLAN RESTORED
Although structurally separate, and disparate in scale, the chapels were pictorially united by their common alfiz, *and apparently also by a level battlemented top.*

Possibly it resulted instead from the peculiarly difficult encomienda divisions of the region of Metztitlán. The three local encomenderos got into an obstreperous conflict with the inspector of tributes in 1551–54. He jailed them and was jailed by them; he had them banished and was banished by them. While the monastery was building the friars and encomenderos were far from friendly, but later, when there were only two encomenderos, there was less trouble.[16] The Indians of each encomienda might for some reason have been given their own separate chapel: perhaps they formed separate confraternities and wanted separate chapels, the way confraternities wanted and got separate posas. This is, however, only a thin conjecture.

Since adjacent chapels could not house simultaneous Masses, it could be that one was intended for musicians; but there is no evidence for that either. A number of other arrangements at Metztitlán are abnormal: the church faces south, and there is what appears to be a posa almost on axis with the front door (ill. 135). Perhaps the smaller of the open chapels, that between its mate and the side of the church, was not a chapel but another posa. It is set in the corner of the atrio like a posa, too close against the precipitous flank of the church to allow a chapel congregation to fan out before its altar, but set satisfactorily enough for a posa's subordinate role in a procession. If it was a posa, it is hard to see why it was big enough to be an open chapel, or why it was made to look so like one. It is, however, somewhat narrower and shallower than its neighbor, and has a somewhat subordinated look; the difference may be slight, but it is undeniable. A suggestion has been made that the lesser of the two barrel-vaulted cells was to serve somehow like the lesser vaulted spaces flanking the single-cell chapels in Yucatan, but since Augustinian Metztitlán is remote from Franciscan Yucatan and both are remote from the capital where architectural ideas might be exchanged, any connection seems improbable.[17] Perhaps the several deviations at Metztitlán come less from a clear program demanding extra chapels or posas juxtaposed to chapels than from the unconventionality of one of the early builders who was more effective when left unhampered in matters of design than when confronted by realistic problems of function.

484

Prosperous Metztitlán soon attracted Spaniards. An English prisoner, Miles Philips, thought he saw 300 there in 1568.[18] Cut off by an unbridged river at the bottom of a deep cañon in the wildest sierras of Hidalgo, Metztitlán remains one of the most beautiful colonial towns in Mexico, and boasts one of the most beautiful monasteries of the sixteenth century (ill. 51). Notable also is the *Tercena* or house for tributes, perhaps a by-product of the feud with the encomenderos, built by the Indians when they had their say about what was their just tribute.[19] (It may be a small remote echo of the *Lonja* at Granada.) Perhaps they also had their say about their chapels: that they wanted and were willing to build two, but whether as confraternity oratorios, or open chapels, or an open chapel and a posa we cannot now tell. No more can we tell when they were built, together or separately, though it must have been after 1539 and probably before 1569.

245 METZTITLÁN, THE LARGER CHAPEL
The beginnings of the alfiz *can be seen at the left.*

There are many more single-cell barrel-vaulted chapels still to be mentioned — for example a few dozen of a special kind in Yucatan — but as the most important ones have peculiarities which put them in separate classifications, they will be better discussed under other headings later in this chapter. One single-cell chapel stands alone, however, and must be discussed in some detail.

485

A RIB–VAULTED CHAPEL AT COIXTLAHUACA

The most elegant of the single-cell chapels is surely that at Coixtlahuaca ("plain of snakes," called "Inguiche" by the local Chochos, and "Yodozocoo" by the Mixtecos),[20] set in the trough of a broad remote valley in the bare sierras northwest of Oaxaca. In the Mixteca the Dominicans had been allowed to own income-producing lands, as the Franciscans never were, and here in the Mixteca Alta they built the grandest of their country monasteries. In them is to be found some of the handsomest and most original architecture in New Spain.

Coixtlahuaca had been the capital of the Mixteca Kingdom until it fell to the Aztecs in the middle of the fifteenth century, and it had long been a large and important trading city, famous for its market and for its goldsmiths. Its wealth is revealed in the lists of annual tribute sent to Moctezuma: 800 skirts, 800 blouses, 800 loin-cloths, 800 bundles of quetzal feathers, 3 feather ensigns, 2 feather shields, 25 gourdsful of gold dust (more than any other single town), and cochineal (more than all the other towns together). Despite the location deep in the Mixteca, the natives still speak Náhuatl, not Mixteco, as a heritage from the Aztec garrison which held the city for three generations before Cortés. Cortés had captured it in 1520, before he took Tenochtitlán. Its industrious Indians, said by Father Torquemada to be "more docile and obedient than those of the Valley of Mexico," continued to prosper under the Spaniards, even after their shallow veins of gold gave out, thanks to the insects that made cochineal and silk. Coixtlahuaca was growing from 1560 to '70 when nearly all the other towns of New Spain were shrinking so tragically, and during these happy years much of the monastery must have been being built.[21]

The Dominicans had been teaching the Indians silk culture as they converted them, and the subsequent silk industry, with its two crops a year — Spain got but one — was so profitable that Viceroy Mendoza complained that buildings for worms to feed and spin in were being favored over buildings for men to pray in. In the 1580's, sometime after the friary at Coixtlahuaca was completed and the population was still large, an increase in local mismanagement and in the availability of inferior but cheaper silks from China and the Philippines ruined the Mixteca silk enterprise. The thousands of mulberry trees which had been so carefully set out and tended died of neglect and drought, or sometimes they were vengefully cut down by the Indians. (The Spanish Government ordered all mulberries destroyed in 1679, and it is rare now to find one in the Mixteca.) In recent years the virtual disappearance of the water supply has been a death blow, and has shriveled once rich and cultured Coixtlahuaca to a sad dusty village, 3000 in 1800 and 1900, about 400 now.[22] It may soon become a viceregal ghost-

486

town, for every season more and more poor families flee the parched neighborhood. Now that there is little reason to visit it except to see its splendid monastery and giant magnolias — which no one does — Coixtlahuaca has for the first time become semi-accessible to wheeled vehicles. A truck can sometimes get through in the dry season if the road has been repaired; usually it has not, and few trucks find reason to make the trip; most of what little travel there is now goes the other way.

The grandiose monastic group is set — atrio and all — on a high platform almost identical with that at neighboring Yanhuitlán; both are about 350 by 500 feet. As we know the latter to have been made specially for the monastery, of earth and rubble from demolished teocallis, we may suppose that so was the impressive mass at Coixtlahuaca. Traces of gray stucco pavement, more likely post- than preconquest, are still visible over much of the top surface.

246 THE OPEN CHAPEL AT COIXTLAHUACA in 1957

The splendid open chapel, dedicated to San Juan Bautista, stands at the top of five steps by the north flank of the church, set well back to gain atrio space. In plan the chapel is a square augmented by a trapezoidal apse. Diagonal buttresses run back from its back corners, and other buttresses set at equivalent angles flare forward from its front corners somewhat as at Cuernavaca. Between them a segmental arch spans the whole chapel front (about 35 feet). Although most of the vault which once covered it has now disappeared, doubtless destroyed by the many quakes which rack the valley, enough of the springing of clusters of ribs remains to show that it was a typically florid late-gothic star, and one of the most sophisticated specimens of cut-stone vaulting in the New World. Anything really gothic in structure is uncommon enough in the Americas, and anything of this quality must have been exceptional. Unfortunately it had already crashed

487

before 1926, when Coixtlahuaca was "discovered" by Manuel Toussaint. No more, apparently, had fallen by 1941, when the next visitors from outside went to see it, but by 1957 a few more pieces had broken off, and all the informative fallen fragments had been cleared away. Fortunately another patterned vault over an adjacent second-story chamber is of expert enough design and construction to show what the still finer lost star-vault must have been. It puts the chapel in quite a different category from the simple barrel-vaulted examples just discussed. (The only other rib-vaulted single-cell chapels known are the little apses at Atlihuetzía, Tepeyanco, and the hexagonal chapel at Tlaxcala perhaps, all in a different class.)

247 COIXTLAHUACA
Proscenium arch and embedded flying buttress

The construction of the chapel at Coixtlahuaca shows many puzzling alterations. In several places extra masonry was added outside the old walls, not bonded to them but just laid up next to them in a supplementary outer layer. In a few places such layers were added twice or three times. Peeled of these additions, what remains of the chapel shows that it was meant to be lighter and airier than it is now; the diagonal flaring buttresses in front, for example, were not always solid walls but once were flying buttresses, lighter than their forerunners at Cuernavaca. One can still make out their arches, now walled in, springing from the same level as the main "proscenium" of the chapel front. One can also see that these flying arches were once surprisingly thin, for their archivolts, preserved on both sides, reveal the original slender section of the working strut of the buttress. These flying arches sprang not from the capital of a column engaged to a massive pier as they do now, but from the capital of a freestanding column. On the side walls of the chapel other arches spring from these same columns, similar to the buttress-arches, and like them now walled up. The whole front half of the chapel was, then, planned to be open, light, and slender.

488

248 CONJECTURAL RESTORATION OF THE CHAPEL AT COIXTLA–
HUACA according to the original design

That this boldly diaphanous scheme was rather suddenly abandoned is shown by the upper parts of the construction, as clearly made for the present thickened arrangement as the lower parts were not. Since the region has so often been shaken by quakes, perhaps some bad shock scared the builder — who must have been an outsider — when the light scheme was half up, and led him to a cautious decision to make the front more resistant by filling in all the open arches except the main arch, the only one that had to be open for practical reasons. Some of the bracing extra layers of masonry must have been added outside the walls at this time; others, one of which interrupts a window, must have been added later. There were surely more quakes, and each of the bad ones has left its layer of stiffening until parts of the chapel and church are now laminated in stone as though by some series of gigantic geological deposits.

One low story up, at the right of the chapel proper, is the chamber with the surviving ribbed vault, opened to the chapel by an 8-foot arch. This room is large enough to hold musicians, but inasmuch as the arched window is not big enough or well enough placed or oriented to transmit their music satisfactorily, out through the chapel to the atrio beyond, the room would seem to have been built for some other use, a use of which the vault asserts the importance. It might have been a sacristy, where the silver and the Host for the chapel were kept between Masses, but unless there was some special reason to keep them upstairs (as they sometimes had been kept upstairs in the monastery building of establishments which did not yet have a church) surely it would have been more convenient to have the sacristy on the same level as the chapel, or to use the sacristy of the adjacent monastery church.

489

It is difficult to think of any reason to open a sacristy to its chapel by an 8-foot arch high in the air. This room was reached by a stairway from a similar room below. Although both chambers adjoin the sanctuary of the monastery church, neither had access to it, and therefore, even though physically joined to it, they cannot have been functionally associated with the church: they must have been planned to serve the chapel.

Most of the architectural vocabulary of the chapel is orthodoxly though provincially renaissance, with none of the fanciful plateresque license of the grand monastery church adjoining. There is some gothic in the profiles of the vault ribs as well as in their pattern, and there is crisp and sparkling tequitqui carving on the Dominican crosses in the spandrel medallions and on the archivolt of the main "proscenium" arch below them. On this threefold archivolt are alternating dragons and pelicans, the former clearly (and heretically though probably not idolatrously) descended from the plumed serpent Quetzalcóatl, and the latter descended more from the family of fierce heathen eagles than the family of mild Christian pelicans, symbols of Christ's sacrifice and the Eucharistic Sacrament (Psalm 102). The pelican-eagles of this archivolt are masterpieces of tequitqui carving, close cousins of such fine birds as that on the heraldic stone of Tecamachalco or on the *Casas Reales* at Tlaxcala. They are outdone by the fancy quarterings of Philip II borne by a double-headed eagle carved over the front door of the adjacent monastery church at Coixtlahuaca, one of the few such heraldic pieces in Mexico not erased during the War of Independence. The curious tequitqui-plateresque side portal of the church displays one of the few samples of the clear survival of a preconquest motif: speech-glyphs issuing from a human head. There is a major difference in style between the chapel and the church, and between the front and side doors of the church. Nothing in the chapel is in the wildly provincial plateresque style of the north door, and nothing resembles the pseudo-antique aspect of the front door surrounded by its many niches derived, perhaps, from Serlio's plate of the Arch of Janus Quadrifons in Rome. The chapel and the exterior of the church do not look like the work of the same designer, and probably were not built at the same time.

Below the dazzling eagle and between the many niches, the architrave of the church door is carved with the date 1576, and contemporary documents also refer to considerable work on the monastery then. Although there is no specific information for the date of the chapel, one may reasonably assume it to be a little earlier, and not only designed but carried out by different hands from those that made most of the church and monastery. Idols were discovered under the atrio cross in 1576,[23] perhaps because it was then being set in line with the recently completed chapel (as its shapeless base still is). Since the masonry of the chapel is not bonded with the church, the chapel

490

must have been built at a different time, and that would have been more probably before than after the church. The monastery had been founded in 1544. If the date of some bad quake in the 1560's or '70's were known for this region, that could be a clue to when the construction of the still unfinished chapel was changed to something thicker. The monastery wing, on the other side of the church, would probably have been in good shape by 1564 when the Dominicans held their Chapter there. They would not have needed the big chapel. At their next meeting here (1583), ignoring their surroundings (by now including the palpably lavish church), the friars declared that all monasteries under construction should be "finished as quickly as possible, restraining all superfluities, in accord with our station and poverty." Money was not to be squandered on retables.[24] Such resolutions seem tacitly to admit past extravagance, and Coixtlahuaca and Yanhuitlán are eloquent testimonials to it. Perhaps extravagance was not so difficult to renounce in 1583 when prosperity had gone from so much of the country and so much of the labor supply had died in the plague a few years before. The renunciation was not enforced, however, and the grandest of all Dominican establishments outside the capital, that at Oaxaca itself, continued to rise and accumulate magnificence.

249 COIXTLAHUACA
Facade of the monastery
church

250 SERLIO'S ARCH OF
JANUS QUADRIFONS

*

The monastery at Yanhuitlán, half a day's ride over the mountains, has the handsomest sixteenth-century church in Oaxaca if not in all Mexico.[25] Right on the Pan-American Highway, it is now as easy to reach as Coixtlahuaca is difficult. Questionable tradition explained its size and grandeur by the grand ideas of the local encomendero, a cousin of Cortés. He or his son was rumored to have sent to Spain for architects, even for men experienced on Philip's Escorial — Becerra has been suggested as one of them — but no tangible evidence corroborates this, and the dates of construction make it impossible for anything except late touches or repairs.[26] In its forms Yanhuitlán embodies the stylistic ideals of two or three generations earlier than the Escorial.

The church at Yanhuitlán shows so many similarities to the church at Coixtlahuaca that one is led to suppose that both follow the same model or that one is modeled on the other. Both stand south of big atrios raised on high platforms; both are similarly rib-vaulted throughout; many details are similar, particularly renaissance plateresque and gothic ones. (There is less pure renaissance and no tequitqui at Yanhuitlán.) One seems to see the same guiding hand at work on many parts of both, for example in the strange north portals, not only like each other but unlike anything else. Many lesser doorways and other details are similar in general disposition, individual moldings, and a distinctively personal and eccentric flair for design. Professor Toussaint, who "discovered" both, convincingly ascribed both churches to the same master. (Might he have been Fray Antonio de la Serna?) Perhaps some of the workmen went with the master from one job to another. Something at Yanhuitlán was begun in 1550; it was big enough for a Chapter Meeting in 1558; and building continued for about twenty years with crews, it was said, of 400 to 600 out of a labor pool of 6000. The main part of the establishment must have been comfortably complete by 1570 when the Dominican Chapter met there again.[27] Much of the work on the two houses must have been contemporaneous: they were surely aware of one another, and ideas and even workmen probably went both ways.

In view of these relationships, it is tempting to conjecture that some sort of arrangement like the chapel at Coixtlahuaca may have been considered at Yanhuitlán, though probably not built. It was not the deep portería beside the church, similar to that at Coixtlahuaca, as has been suggested, for there is a contemporary doorway just where the altar would have to have been, and there is very little atrio space in front.

Father Cobo wrote admiringly of the church and monastery at Yanhuitlán in 1630 without mentioning any open chapel, and had there then been anything as handsome in the atrio as the chapel of Coixtlahuaca, he probably would have mentioned it. He stayed there three days. Father Burgoa, who knew the whole establishment particularly well and was inclined to boast about it (he had been prior twice) wrote a long and thorough description of the building complex in 1670, noting the atrio, its wall, and its stairway, but not any chapel or posas. Had they been there, he would doubtless have described them.[28]

ELEVATED CHAPELS

From information in earlier documents then in the monastery library, Father Burgoa gave an account of the building operations of a century before. One peculiar item may be revealing: during some technical difficulties which delayed the construction of the church, "although the friars knew the objections to keeping all those recently converted neophytes exposed to the sun and wind every day, and though they themselves shared in the discomfort, they did not dare to rush the work." [29] Can this mean that it was intended to house the Indians under cover during divine services in the 1560's or '70's? Would it have been intended to have them in the church or under some sort of shed in front of an open chapel? The church is one of the largest: could it have been planned for the Indians? All the answers seem to be negative, since friars elsewhere had no such concern (with a few exceptions connected with sheds, to be discussed later). It is unlikely that the church was meant for them since the very similar church at Coixtlahuaca in a similar climate and with a similar congregation was supplemented by an open chapel for the Indians. Conceivably some sort of open chapel of wood could have been planned for Yanhuitlán. There was a local tradition of fine carpentry which produced the choir-balcony of the church (a particularly splendid example which has just been restored after a long neglect which had allowed 15 percent to fall in 15 years). But this does not seem to be a satisfactory explanation either. So far as its atrio is concerned, neither the sixteenth-century intentions nor practices at Yanhuitlán are now clear. Father Burgoa had a truly messy mind, and perhaps here he was inappropriately applying seventeenth-century standards to sixteenth-century practice.

ELEVATED OPEN CHAPELS

Raising the level of the chapel floor well above the level of the atrio had been tried by 1540 at Epazoyucan and perhaps also at Tlaxcala and Ocuituco. The chapel at Epazoyucan stands with its church at the head of broad steps which climb 15 feet above the level of the atrio spread out before them in the usual way. Though small, the chapel was thus enabled to dominate the entire atrio at its feet, and to present the symbolic ritual impressively to everyone below, even to those in the backmost rows. At Ocuituco the ground where the chapel may have stood is raised in somewhat the same way (but rebuilding prevents proof a chapel was surely there). At Tlaxcala a chapel may have been raised still higher, at the head of that ramp like a teocalli stairway. The early dates of this one virtually certain and two possible examples strongly suggest that the idea of elevating the chapel may have come from fresh memories of preconquest architecture, along with those memories which had probably contributed so importantly to the whole concept of open-chapel-and-atrio.

SINGLE CELLS

While the friars did not erect churches on the tops of pyramids, as guides and guidebooks repeatedly tell us, they did make other use of these high places, particularly in the first years when the pressures to convert to the new religion and devalue the old were the greatest, when the supply of pyramids was the greatest, and of monasteries the smallest. Masses were said atop the teocallis of Tenochtitlán and Tlatelolco as soon as the conquistadores had smashed the shrines there.

The little chapels or shrines the friars sometimes put on the top of teocallis after their tutelary *demonios* had been exorcised may be a link between the raised pagan shrine and the raised Christian chapel. These pyramid-chapels were not used for the weekly Masses said before a big congregation; most of them must have been more in the nature of occasional oratories, supplemental rather than essential to the architectural program of the Conversion. There seem to have been quite a few of these: for example at Sotuta in Yucatan there was not only "the monastery of San Francisco where two friars reside and administer the Sacraments . . . but they have also an *hermita* of Our Lady of the Immaculate Conception in a room high on a platform or embankment up thirty steps, and there they say Mass on all the feasts of Our Lady" (1581).[30] In other words, celebrations were held there from time to time on special occasions, and not as a weekly function.

Mass said in a high place, novel in Spain, must soon have been fairly familiar in New Spain. The idea of a raised sanctuary cannot have been a complete novelty to all the friars from Spain, however, for some must have known arrangements like those at Santo Tomás at Avila, San Francisco at Baeza, and a few other Mendicant churches where the altar was on a balcony or something like a balcony, above the level of the nave. Take away the nave, and the equivalent of an elevated open chapel would be left. There are no other clear European models: Mexican raised open chapels do not seem to bear relation to chancels raised over crypts, nor to the balconies sometimes found on the exterior of European churches where relics were displayed to an outdoor crowd on special occasions.[31] The Mexican open chapels were sanctuaries where Mass was regularly celebrated: though superficially similar, the European relic-balconies were not. While it is certain that some of the friars responsible for the first elevated chapels must have known the preconquest equivalents all too well, it is far from certain that they would have known the rare and not very close parallels in Europe.

The adaptation of the pagan models altered not only the details, as would be expected, but it also reduced the elevation. The friars celebrating Masses wanted to be in closer rapport with their congregations than the priests celebrating human sacrifice did with theirs. Open chapels were therefore not raised more than 15 or at most 20 feet (except at Tlaxcala if that chapel ever was an open chapel).

494

All the identifiable elevated open chapels are either Franciscan or Augustinian. Perhaps the Dominicans disapproved of separating the congregation from the celebrant, but probably not, since they had already done so with less practical reason at the parent house of the Order, San Domenico at Bologna, and in Spain at Santo Tomás at Avila. Santo Tomás however, was a royal tomb-chapel in a monastery and not a church with a large and consequential congregation. The Masses said there were less for the living than for the dead. There may have been one temporary Dominican elevated chapel in New Spain, made at Etla for the Corpus Christi celebrations of 1575; we know that an altar was put at the end of a high wooden gallery which collapsed the only time it was used.[32]

*

A number of single-cell chapels were raised even higher than that at Epazoyucan which, while above the atrio, was still on the same level as the church. At Yecapixtla and Acolman (both presumably before 1550), at Tecamachalco and Tlaquiltenango, and also at Tacámbaro, the chapels are level with the second floor of the monastery and conveniently entered from it. A small proscenium arch opens them wide to the atrio below. This scheme, irreducibly the simplest, is hardly more than a big hole in the wall with a small exposed room behind it.

251 CHURCH, ELEVATED CHAPEL, AND PORTERÍA AT ACOLMAN

SINGLE CELLS

The chapel at Acolman, possibly but not surely part of the very early Franciscan monastery, must still be a dozen or more years earlier than the plateresque church of the Augustinians, completed there by 1560. Allowed no more than a plain *alfiz* to enframe its plain arch, the chapel now looks severe and a little mean. Once its interior was enlivened with mural painting, of which a life-size Saint Catherine is still an attractive reminder that many other chapels were enriched in much the same way. Saint Catherine was chosen probably because there was an important Indian barrio of Santa Catalina (to which the parish was later transferred).[33]

*

The chapel at Tecamachalco is simpler and coarser than the Franciscan church (1551–57–61) of this once cochineal-rich town, and it must have been built by different hands, probably at a different time. It is not clear whether the chapel was what was still called a *capilla de los naturales* in the 1690's in one of the rare late references to such chapels.[34] Its segmental arch echoes the arch of the portería just below and respects the same vertical axis, but beyond the obvious repetition of forms and axial continuity, there is no integration of design. Someone at Tecamachalco was interested in the visual organization of varied elements, however, for the adjacent church facade has one of the few examples of a portal and choir window worked into one inclusive composition.

*

The arrangement at Tacámbaro appears to have been similar, with the individual elements made heavier as a consequence of anti-earthquake precautions. The portería, axially below what was presumably the chapel, is an imitation of the portería at famous Tiripetío, from which Tacámbaro had been founded as a visita in 1538 and a friary in 1540, and on which its forms were consciously modeled in the main building campaign in 1553–56. The chapel at Tacámbaro could, then, reflect an earlier one at Tiripetío. The superposition at Tacámbaro, in any case, is a result of an early change of mind, for the whole monastery had at first been built in only one story because of recent quakes. A new church was finished in 1667, but the ruins of the old one were still visible two hundred years later; much of the establishment was altered in the nineteenth century along unarchaeological lines,[35] and as a result, it is not possible to be entirely sure of its hitherto unrecorded open chapel.

*

The small open chapel at Tlaquiltenango, also unnoticed until now, was originally set above the monastery portería in much the same way, and it may be part of the conventual ensemble completed in 1540 (according to a lost inscription).[36] A one-story vestibule-porch was added in front of the portería fairly soon afterwards, impeding the view of the altar and the priest if services were still celebrated inside the chaped. The terrace of the roof of the vestibule might have seemed a better location, like the terrace on top of the pavilion at Tecbatán; both may look theatrically ideal to modern eyes, until they notice in both places that there is a doorway just where the altar would have to be. Furthermore, there is no evidence that uncovered roof terraces were ever used as open chapels. (The chapel at Cacalac in Yucatan was described as on some sort of *azotea,* which might have been a roof terrace, though it is not clear what was meant or whether the arrangement was permanent.[37]) An altar where Mass is said must by custom stand below some sort of cover, either of wood or stone, or a temporary cloth canopy. This tradition was already old and strong, and presumably it was respected. As there is no reason to think that the friars would set up and then take down a canopy over an altar every week, it must be assumed that altars were under some sort of architectural covering.

Perhaps after the vestibule interfering with it had been built, the open chapel at Tlaquiltenango was no longer used — it was soon walled in — and the outdoor church was moved to the south side of the main church, where there is more atrio space and where the posas are. The new south door (later than its dated model of 1552 at Cuernavaca) may be part of the same rearrangement. The Franciscans were active proselytizers here: they were reproved in 1559 for having roughed up the curate of nearby Zacatepec who, they thought, had been poaching for souls in their territory. Possibly the rearrangement of the chapel and vestibule is related instead to the transfer of the town from Franciscans to Dominicans in 1570.[38] If the Dominicans did not use elevated chapels, as apparently they did not, they might not have hesitated to render this one useless by adding the little vestibule below and filling in the then useless proscenium arch.

*

The walled-up chapel at Yecapixtla was equally simple, and set above the portería in much the same way as at Tlaquiltenango, Tacámbaro, and Tecamachalco. While perhaps not dating from the time of Cortés — who made gifts to the friars and occasionally stayed with them — as Manuel Toussaint proposed, still it must be early, probably as early or 1540 or very soon thereafter.[39] It is similar to that at Tlaquiltenango, which is in the same vicinity, and one may have been modeled on the other.

*

It is possible that all these raised chapels — modest, early, and widely scattered — were inspired by some striking early example at an important monastery, perhaps Tiripetío for the Augustinians, but there is no prototype to propose for the Franciscans (unless they borrowed the idea from the Augustinians).

252 THE MONASTERY CHURCH AT YECAPIXTLA *and, beyond the simple portería arch, at the extreme right, the walled-up* ELEVATED OPEN CHAPEL. *Except for the nineteenth-century tombs and the restored atrio cross, everything in the picture is from the sixteenth century.*

The individual independence of the separate parts, chapel and portería, which shows in the general composition of these non-ensembles in monastery facades — their only willed relationship would appear to be axial — is characteristic also of much Spanish architecture of the sixteenth century, and of much preconquest work. The two traditions ran parallel, and again the guiding architectural disciplines of the originals lost force in the derivatives. In Mexican design of the sixteenth century, while separate parts were often juxtaposed along an axis, they were rarely correlated through repetition, interaction, or any other such disciplinary directives whereby the whole would affect the parts. The simplest lining-up of disparate elements — door, window, gable — seems to have been a standard procedure for organizing church facades. The open chapel was even less coherently integrated into controlled large designs in cooperation with its neighboring portería, church facade, or the fenestral scheme of the monastery building.

*

Both dangers, insignificance and discongruity, were avoided in the design of a few Franciscan raised chapels in the neighborhood of Puebla (which may add some strength to Professor Angulo's proposal of a sixteenth-century

"School of Puebla").[40] While at Tecamachalco the single opening of the chapel was put directly over the single opening of the portería, at Huaquechula and Tochimilco the single openings of the chapels are placed over the center arches of three-arched porterías, making a more strongly organized pattern and dominant accent in the monotonously long and flat monastery wall. At Tochimilco the heavy low portería acted as a sturdy visual base for the big arch of the chapel it carried (until the chapel, hitherto unnoticed, was walled up). The bold scale of the whole compound motif was happily refined and emphasized by the delicate but effective scale of the archivolt running around the arch of the chapel. A winding stair, fitted into the corner buttress of the adjacent facade of the church, led not only to this chapel but also to the little outdoor pulpit used in conjunction with it.

Most unfortunately the chapel at Huaquechula (c1565) is now also closed in, but once it must have made a uniquely handsome effect with its broad and intricately patterned vault seen sharply from below. The most elaborate gothic vault in Mexico which has survived complete, in quality it is comparable to what remains of the big vault at Coixtlahuaca. The slender but deep and sharply profiled ribs must have carried well visually, though high and in shadow, and must have given vigor to the flower-like interlace of softly waving and sharp straight lines. The profiles and rib-pattern had to be strong here not only because of the shadow but also because of the competition given by the pattern of the veins in the outlandish building stone: pink, yellow, and rusty orange, in striations not so much like marble as like marble cake. The rib pattern of the vault was probably further reinforced by painting and perhaps gilding. The monastery church was supposedly built

by Fray Juan de Alameda, who died here about 1570.[41] The church must have been entirely or nearly finished by then, for among the masons' marks high on the flank and rear are the dates 1569 and 1570. The similarity of their vaulting suggests that church and chapel were made in the same campaign. Fray Juan might then have been responsible for the design of the chapel as well as of the church, and its vault might then be his masterpiece.

*

253 HUAQUECHULA
Vault of the elevated open chapel

499

SINGLE CELLS

An ingenious variation of single-arch chapel over triple-arch portería was worked out in what was the largest and grandest of the elevated chapels: that at Calkiní, half way between Mérida and Campeche. This chapel so impressed Father Ponce's secretary in 1586 that he took time to write an exceptionally long description: "This monastery has no church, but instead there is placed against one of its walls a large and sightly chapel . . . very strong and high, all built of good masonry, and closed with a smooth half dome. [What little remains looks more like the beginning of a ribbed groin vault or half a star-vault.] Under the main chapel there are three other vaulted chapels next to one another, filling the whole width of the chapel above; these are framed by columns of delicate and curious stone. Below each of their vaults is an altar . . . and in the big upper chapel is the main altar, somewhat high up, but with plenty of room for the celebrants; here too is the Tabernacle, and the Most Holy Sacrament, and to one side, the choir of the friars. One enters to this altar and choir from the upper level of the cloister [One can still discover this access.] . . . Across the entire width of the chapel there is an iron balcony rail, very thin and open so that it will not hinder the Indians below from seeing the Mass. The chapel is 42 feet wide and 52 feet deep, and it has a high and strong iron grille which, for safety, is locked with a key at night . . . The chapel and *ramada* are located in a good patio, surrounded by orange and avocado trees . . . and the whole monastery is set on a *ku* or *mul* of the ancients." [42]

Calkiní had been raised from visita to monastery in 1555 or '61, and dedicated to San Luis Obispo (Saint Louis of Toulouse). The large chapel must have been built soon after that. The monastery was said to have been built by Fray Martín (or Miguel) Vera, about whom nothing else is known except that he came to Yucatan in 1553 and became Guardian of Izamal in 1561. There does not seem to have been anything unusual about the town which would explain why it had this extraordinary chapel. Once a lesser capital and tribute-collecting center (turkeys, cotton, corn, cochineal, honey), Calkiní had continued in importance under the Spaniards. Streets were "opened" from 1579 to '82, and the hospital, second only to that of Mérida, was signaled for special praise from the King in 1598.[43] Yet this was on the peninsula of Yucatan, where even in bigger, more prosperous, and politically more important cities — Mérida, Maní, Valladolid, Campeche — no chapel of such pretentiousness was attempted.

What is most remarkable now at Calkiní is one of the largest barrel vaults in Mexico, over the refectory (seventeenth century?), and one of the smallest cloisters (sixteenth century) only two arches to a side, so very small that a larger cloister was later added nearby. Unfortunately, only pitifully little survives from the chapel and, except for a baptismal font, what does remain has been so battered and patched that nothing is to be learned from it

500

that cannot be learned better from Father Ponce. His description, incidentally, is one of the very few to mention an altar, and this mention, like the others, does not tell much.

Only one Spanish monument seems to be related to the remarkable scheme of Calkiní: San Francisco at Baeza, a masterpiece of Andrés de Vandelvira (built probably 1540–46). Here too, three small barrel-vaulted apses carried the floor of the main presbytery, richly ornamented and decorated in one of the best organized ensembles of all the Spanish plateresque, infinitely more sophisticated than anything in Yucatan. An earthquake and French soldiers destroyed half of it early in the last century. Luckily it was shown in a romantic lithograph soon afterwards, before half of the remaining half collapsed. Little known, little published, the chancel now rises superbly from the garbage pits of local tenements, cut off from its former nave now reduced to an abandoned movie theater.

A connection with Calkiní is possible: Fray Francisco del Toral, a native of Ubeda (a few miles from Baeza), became a friar of the Franciscan Province of Andalusia before going to Mexico; he returned to Spain in 1553–54 and again in 1561–62, and would therefore have had opportunity to see the new church of his Order at Baeza. He could have transmitted some of his admiration to the builders at Calkiní when passing through in 1562 on his way to take his post in Mérida as Bishop of Yucatan. He had earlier been Guardian at Tecamachalco, where he would have seen the raised chapel in use, and this may have awakened his interest. He maintained close connections with Tecamachalco to the end of his life. Fray Martín, the supposed builder of the chapel at Calkiní, was said to have left for Izamal in 1561, which would mean that he was no longer in Calkiní when Bishop del Toral passed through in 1562. If knowledge of Baeza was transmitted to Calkiní through the Bishop, it must have been before 1562 (perhaps after he returned from Spain in 1554) or else there is an inaccuracy of a year or so in the data given by the chroniclers of his life and that of Fray Martín (or Miguel) Vera. Such inaccuracies are not at all unlikely, but while they permit, they do not support this otherwise plausible hypothesis.[44]

*

The most engaging of all raised open chapels is surely that at Tlahuelilpa, a small dependency of the Franciscan friary at Tula.[45] With an austerely grand church, Tula allowed surprisingly gay visitas: here, at Apasco, Atotonilco, and Tequisquiac. Tlahuelilpa (in Otomí, Huantax, or "irrigated field") was more than an ordinary visita: it was a vicaría with a resident friar and all the architectural elements of a monastery, but on the small scale of a visita and, like a visita, administratively dependent on a monastery, and without a vote in the Provincial Chapter.

SINGLE CELLS

Looking surprisingly like a little opera box, this chapel anticipates the gaiety of the eighteenth century, a gaiety rarely found in Mexico or Spain in the sixteenth. This feeling is enhanced by the pretty color of the mauve-rosy trachyte of which it is built. The exotic design must have been the product of some inexperienced but imaginative provincial master who, having had access to pictures of the sophisticated plateresque of Spain, and having an understanding of the practical problems of the open chapel, went straightforwardly ahead to create an original design, unhampered by tradition and innocent of orthodoxy.

254 VISITA CHURCH AND OPEN CHAPEL AT TLAHUELILPA

The jamb colonettes do not quite touch the arch they "should" support; the oval medallions of the arch, enclosing flowers and the Instruments of the Passion, look like an engraved design for a straight border, long panel, or pilaster, bent freely around to form a scalloped arch, a form often mudéjar but here more likely spontaneously produced. Above it are five spots of carving: a pair of friars, Saint Francis, and two angels holding the shield with the Five Franciscan Wounds enclosed in a Crown of Thorns. They wear fluttering robes as much like nightgowns as Franciscan habits, and are closely related to those on the chapel at Apasco nearby (ill. 220). All is enclosed in an *alfiz* made of a Franciscan cord. Here is a sort of folk style in the sense that much Breton gothic or Bavarian rococo is a folk style. Except in the little figures, it is not tequitqui: though the forms are not pure, their impurity is not the result of any indianizing metamorphosis, but simply of gay naïveté. Here, as happens now and then in folk art, architectural innocence is close to bliss.

This little scherzo dominates the complex of vicaría buildings at Tlahue-lilpa not only because it is in itself so eye-catching, but also because everything else that might compete is so small. (There were only about 380 Indian households in the village in 1571.) [46] Other small window- or stage-like chapels are usually inexpressive of their important function yet at the same time too assertive as a black hole to be easily assimilated into the general design of the monastery. Here these aesthetic pitfalls are evaded, and all the elements are happily reconciled. The friars in charge of the building of the vicaría must have liked the odd touch of the designer, for he was given a free hand in the charming cloister and the unusually elaborate chancel arch of the tiny church, only 19 feet wide, just as wide as the open chapel beside it.

255 TLAHUELILPA

Some scholars have thought that an elevated open chapel was sometimes put over the front door of a church [47] on a small balcony entered directly from the big choir-balcony just inside. It is impossible to accept any example advanced for this assumption — none is surely of the sixteenth century — for the entrance to such "chapels" is always in the middle of the back wall, leaving no place for an altar where an altar ought to be. These balconies must have been built for religious activities not requiring altars, though probably not for altarless benedictions of special crowds, like the important large loggias over the doorways of Saint Peter's, the Lateran, and the Escorial, as has been proposed. They were more likely for preaching to people in the atrio in much the same way that this was done from the pulpit above the main arch of the chapel at Cuernavaca (ill. 226) or from the raised outdoor pulpits on the churches at Tochimilco, Huaquechula, and Atotonilco de Tula. These are separate enough from their open chapels so that preaching from them could have been independent of the celebration of the Mass.

503

SINGLE CELLS

The rustic balconies over the doorways of the Dominican churches at Nejapa and Chamula are still sometimes used for preaching on festival days, but neither is of the sixteenth century. Mass is not and could not be said on them. What may be a related preaching-balcony of the sixteenth century still in use can be seen yet farther south, on the Franciscan monastery church at Santiago (founded 1541, finished before '71), the former capital of the Zutugil kings on Lake Atitlán in Guatemala.[48] This hitherto unnoticed balcony is not over the doorway but at one side of the facade in the base of a stone belltower; it cannot have been an elevated open chapel because the space is too small for an altar and priest and it is not covered, yet since it is accessible only from the church, it must have had some churchly function. Raised high above the atrio in front, it would appear to have been made for preaching, as an activity independent of the celebration of the Mass (which would require an altar). Probably all these balconies in Mexico and this example in Guatemala served similarly.

There are various European precedents for Mendicant preaching outdoors without altars. Sometimes it was done from temporary wooden pulpits (as shown in Lotto's picture of Saint Dominic preaching, or Erri's Saint Vincent Ferrer, both in the Vienna Gallery), or sometimes from permanent stone pulpits attached to churches (as at Santo Stefano at Bologna or San Francisco at Viterbo). The idea does not seem to have been particularly Spanish or particularly Mendicant, and there is little reason to assume close relationship between the American and European examples. What relation there is, is general and multiple. High outdoor pulpits attached to churches were not very common on either continent, but were common enough for friars to remember as something they had seen somewhere or other in Europe and could adapt for local needs in America.

There are other elevated chapels, at Atotonilco el Grande, Huejutla, and perhaps Huejotzingo, but as a study of them also involves the question of why they·face sideways to their churches, it will be postponed to the following section which is concerned particularly with that peculiarity.

ABNORMAL ORIENTATION

Until the influential Jesuits discarded it after the Council of Trent, European churches were supposed to have a fixed orientation with the apse toward the east. Mexican monastery churches respected this tradition all through the sixteenth century, with few exceptions: Metztitlán and Huejutla had to face sideways on precipitous terrain (ill. 134); Tehuacán Viejo and Tepetitlán were set into old towns sideways; Tzintzuntzan was fitted in backwards between a lake, a swamp, and the mounds of a ruined preconquest city; and at Tajimaroa (now Ciudad Hidalgo), the church was similarly reversed in adjusting itself to the plaza of the old Tarasco town.

Orientation with the altar at the east was also felt proper for open chapels, and there are few exceptions. At Cuernavaca the chapel faces north, across the east-west axis of the church (ill. 227). The whole monastery with its atrio was set on a hillside and raised on a special terrace which, though no longer noticeable in the overbuilt modern city, is still distinguishable in the retaining walls — only half hidden by the houses — which run down the sloping streets. The limited site affected the location of the chapel in the first place: it was put at the far south end, across the atrio from the main gate which led to the center of town, on the one side which the hill made inaccessible except through the atrio, the one location which could command maximum atrio space without interfering with the church.

At Etzatlán, where the presumed chapel stood face to face with the front of the monastery church on the opposite side of the atrio, there is no clear reason for the reversed orientation unless this was the only way of coordinating the large square area of the chapel with the edge of the atrio and the rest of the town layout without coming into collision with important existing buildings, the monastery, the hospital, or whatever was there.

Shattered bits at Calkiní show that the chapel used to face south, but do not show why. Possibly here too the remains of the preconquest town imposed limitations.

If the battered block of masonry abutting the northwest corner of the church at Oaxtepec is the base of an open chapel, as seems likely, then that chapel must have faced north. The atrio had been made on that side of the church because springs and slope prevented a normal location in front, and the chapel, if there was to be any, was forced to face sideways by the same natural peculiarities.[49] In all of these cases the problem may have been, on a smaller scale, the same as that of fitting atrios and plazas into preconquest towns: something of the ideal had to surrender to material peculiarities.

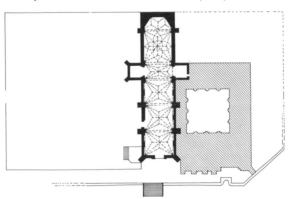

256 THE DOMINICAN ESTABLISHMENT AT OAXTEPEC
The platform at the left of the facade of the church may be the altered base of an open chapel. The north side door is farther from the chancel than is normal, and this would have made easier access to the chapel for the clergy and their helpers carrying liturgical equipment.

SINGLE CELLS

In a few instances more certain than that at Oaxtepec, the open chapel was built out sideways to the flank of the church, making an L with the axis of the chapel at right angles to that of the church from which it branched. For example, at Valladolid in Yucatan, the monastery of San Bernardino, built by Fray Juan de Mérida in the Indian suburb of Sisal (1552–60) [50] had what is presumably an open chapel running south from the west end of the nave of the church. The chapel is formed of one barrel-vaulted cell so big in scale that it looks like a slice of the nave turned at a right angle. To leave space for an altar in a normal position in the middle of the back wall of the chapel, the door communicating with the nave was kept to one side. Above this door is another, which opens into the choir-balcony of the church and shows that there must have been a choir-balcony in the chapel too, though all trace but this doorway has vanished. As usual in Yucatan, there is no ornament: no carving, no moldings. Its original use having atrophied, the chapel has been walled in, whitewashed, and assigned a new use as baptistery.

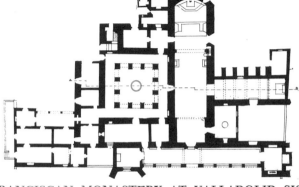

257 THE FRANCISCAN MONASTERY AT VALLADOLID–SISAL
The open chapel is at the right of the front of the church, in back of the entrance portico and in front of a later longer chapel.

No reason is apparent for the sideways orientation; in several places a normally oriented chapel could have been arranged with the requisite area in front and with convenient connection with the choir-balcony of the church. It could not have been put next to the church on the same side with the monastery building, as chapels often were, because of the long portico running across the church and monastery to a little chapel at each end (if this portico is coeval with the church, as seems probable). In the seventeenth century Cogolludo mentioned two small chapels at either end of the portico as well as three chapels *in* the church and one outside its wall, this last presumably the big barrel-vaulted one now identified as the real open chapel. Father Ponce saw it fronted with a big thatched shed for shade.[51]

506

The monastery's ample land ought to have been firm enough for the foundations of a church or chapel anywhere inasmuch as the entire establishment had been moved to specially chosen solid ground here in Sisal after a first site in Valladolid had been found too damp. What looked solid, however, was found perhaps not entirely solid, for Father Ponce and fifty years later Cárdenas Valencia saw that the monastery was built over a *cenote*, or opening in the limestone shelf made by an underground river. Perhaps some discovery of an underground pool led to a change in plans. A curious sixteenth-century well-house behind the monastery draws on what must be a large subterranean supply of water. The conventual complex has suffered so many repairs that its history here is not decipherable. Bad fires were set by bad encomenderos in 1562 and '67.[52]

258 THE MONASTERY AT VALLADOLID–SISAL *with the open chapel projecting from its right flank, behind an arcade running across the facade to supplementary chapels at either end.*

At Tzintzuntzan, when the Hospital Chapel was added in 1619, it was put on the north side of the atrio: its portico — the chapel is not monocellular — therefore faced sideways to the church, which faces east at the west end of the atrio. In near ruin a century ago, the chapel has since been repaired, altered, walled in, given a new entrance, and now (1962) it is being disencumbered to reveal again its original state. It still stands in its own small atrio separate from the main atrio of the monastery.[53] Why was it built so late? Possibly because it was intended for the inmates of a hospital who for reasons of health would be put in an airy atrio rather than in a covered church, a reason which no longer had a parallel in the case of the Indians who were not sick and went to the adjacent monastery church. Tzintzuntzan,

507

the ancient Tarasco capital, had very briefly been the seat of a bishopric, but the town began to shrink when that was transferred down the lakeshore to Pátzcuaro. Perhaps when Pátzcuaro began to shrink later in the century, after the seat had been transferred again (to Morelia), Tzintzuntzan began to recover: it had about 50,000 souls in 1554, 40,000 in 1565, was made a city in 1595, and was chosen by the Franciscans for their big Provincial Chapter Meetings in 1589 and 1601.[54] Clearly the monastery was considered a major one.

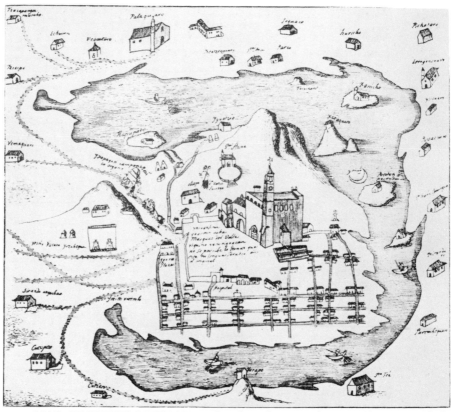

259 MAP OF TZINTZUNTZAN, *said to have been made c1545 but more likely made a generation later, perhaps on the basis of an earlier map.*
The Franciscan monastery is in the center, with its church and large atrio, below which is the hospital, with its own chapel, small atrio, and cross, surrounded by the regular blocks of the town. To the left are preconquest yácatas (mound temples), and above the monastery is the chapel of Santa Ana, with its unusual round atrio. Lake Pátzcuaro (reduced in size) surrounds the town. On its far shore, little buildings indicate the towns of Pátzcuaro (upper left), Erongarícuaro (upper right), and Santa Fe (lower right), all with monuments which will be discussed in later chapters.

508

The monastery church is small (or perhaps one should say *was* small since, already half ruined in the nineteenth century, it was deliberately burned on Good Friday Eve in 1944, and everything but the shell of the walls destroyed). It may have been found too small for the Indians when they were beginning to be allowed to use it on Sundays in the early seventeenth century. As the old seat of the Tarasco court, Tzintzuntzan had been chosen by the Franciscans for their first settlement in Michoacán. Set opposite the big preconquest *yácatas* (mound-temples), their first establishment was small and architecturally poor, until Fray Pedro de Pila rebuilt both its church and monastery building before he went to France in 1579. As the great linguist, Fray Maturino Gilberti, was buried in the presbytery in 1572, and his body was "found" there in 1580 and subsequently moved to the sacristy, the rebuilding of the church was probably carried out in the late 1570's.[55] While it has been suggested that the monastery's open chapel of San Camilo is its oldest surviving element (which might mean that it was devalued when the new church rose in the 1570's), it is more likely that this chapel was built in the same campaign as the church. If so, the addition of another and larger open chapel some forty years later would indeed seem an odd extravagance unless its use was different. Everything seems to say that it was: that it was built for the hospital's particular needs. It may replace an earlier hospital chapel on or near the same spot, as suggested by the old map here reproduced. Hospitals and hospital chapels were a familiar regional specialty, as Uruapan, Angahuan, and Sacán still testify.

260 THE HOSPITAL CHAPEL AT TZINTZUNTZAN
inscribed CVSI MAIVS 17 — 1619 AÑOS

SINGLE CELLS

A few of the elevated chapels do not face the same way as their adjoining churches. At Atotonilco el Grande and Huejutla, geographically but not architecturally related houses on the Augustinian circuit in Hidalgo, the chapels are fitted between salient buttresses on one flank of the church. As both churches are vaulted, their buttresses are heavy and deeply projecting — 10 feet at Atotonilco — and easily able to accommodate a small chapel. Each of the chapels is borne on an arch raised above the heads of the congregation, and each is thus made conveniently enterable from the choir-balcony on the other side of their common wall. The one at Atotonilco was probably built before 1546, a date once inscribed on the vaults of the church [56] which, being higher than the chapel, would normally have been completed later.

261 THE ELEVATED CHAPEL AT ATOTO–NILCO EL GRANDE *between the buttresses on the north flank of the church.*

The layout at hard-to-reach Huejutla is unique (ill. 134). Difficult terrain, steep slopes, and a river made the friars discard orthodox orientation for the church: its apse is at the south. The chapel, at right angles to the axis of the church, is on its west flank, and this inevitably puts *its* altar at the east, where by custom it should be. The chapel is therefore oriented abnormally with relative respect to the church and normally with absolute respect to the compass. The establishment, which is vaulted throughout, was probably built from 1545 to '48, when Fray Juan de Estacio was Provincial of the Augustinians. Resident at Huejutla off and on from 1540, he founded the church and monastery in 1545 to replace what had been a modest visita, and he seems to have cared for them with particular solicitude, which might have encouraged major building.[57]

*

Over the extravagant north doorway of the church at Huejotzingo (ill. 163) there are puzzling fragments which show some drastic change in sixteenth-century intentions, though a shift from what to what is not now clear. A large opening, wider than the doorway below, was begun with a fancy enframement of carved shafts rising from late-gothic prismatic bases. The opening was never completed, for the aperture between the multiplied jambs was soon walled in, the jambs stopped half way up, and the upper part finished off plain, like any other section of the blank masonry wall of the flank of the church.

Such a location over a doorway is not normal for an open chapel but a few others are located on the side of a church, and a few over doorways of porterías, but not front doors. Whatever the opening at Huejotzingo opened into would have been on a level easily accessible from the choir-balcony inside the church, as is usual with elevated open chapels, and it would have to have been entered from one side, leaving the center of its back wall free for an altar. There are passages in the thickness of the opposite wall of the church, some to give access to confessionals, and a particularly important one which led to the choir-balcony; and they show that something similar could have been contrived to give access from the choir-balcony to the putative chapel (ill. 29). The chapel would have been shallow, but probably not too shallow.

If not for a chapel, it would be hard to say for what such a large and richly enclosed opening was intended: it is too large for a window, and probably too elaborate for either a window or a preaching balcony. If nevertheless it was destined for a preaching balcony, this would have been the fanciest one in New Spain. There is space in the monastery grounds at this side of the church for a sizable congregation below a chapel or balcony, for the main atrio wall stands well back to the north. Such a balcony would be remote if used just as a place for preaching, with its crowd probably having to move around in front of the church for the rest of their Sunday duties. Any friar who wanted a preaching balcony — and few did — would more likely have had the sense to ask for it over the front door of the church or over the adjacent portería.

Established in 1524, Huejotzingo was one of the first four monasteries in the country. The others, México-Tenochtitlán, Tlaxcala, and Texcoco, had early open chapels (though one cannot say just how early in Tlaxcala or Texcoco). It seems reasonable to propose that Huejotzingo might have had one too.

After the move to the present site, many Huejotzincas died in the plagues, above all that of 1545, and when their tributes were transferred to the unhappy survivors, many moved away. The population was said to be 50,000 in 1560, 45,000 in 1565, and 40,000 in 1571, before the plague of 1576 swept Huejotzingo with special savagery. Prosperity collapsed with the collapse of the cochineal trade at the turn of the century, after the enraged Indians cut down the *nopal* cactus on which the cochineal *coccus* lived. By 1612 there were only 5,000 people left, 2 percent of what there had been before the Spaniards came.[58] After one of these disasters, when active construction of the church was resumed, the putative unfinished chapel, no longer needed for the shrunk congregation, might have been abandoned and walled up. No traces of any other open chapel have been discovered though they have been conscientiously hunted. The flat roof over the portería, level with the second floor of the monastery, has been suggested, but an unroofed chapel on a terrace cannot be accepted without proof, and there is none. The walled-up opening in the middle of the south atrio wall might seem to be the remains of an open chapel set like the Hospital Chapel at Tzintzuntzan. It does not match the other gateways, and as there is already one gateway in the south wall near this, it cannot be satisfactorily explained away as a gate. Because it was not a gate, however, does not mean that it was a chapel. There is nothing about it which is convincingly like a chapel, and the fragment over the north door of the church makes a more credible candidate.

262 THE NORTH DOORWAY AT HUEJOTZINGO

263 THE NORTH DOORWAY AT HUEJOTZINGO *with conjectural indication of the form of the upper opening.*

513

Assuming that the atrio platform was started and building materials were collected by Fray Juan de Alameda by 1539, construction of the buildings we see today was almost certainly being carried out on a grand design in the late 1540's, perhaps after a lull following the plague, and still being carried out vigorously in the early 1550's. One posa was complete by 1550, and the entire friary must have been in respectable picked-up condition when Viceroy Velasco chose to hold a Council in the atrio soon after. It is probable that the ensemble was completed by 1570. Professor Kubler has convincingly proposed that the present buildings were begun in 1544, and finished in 1571, after some interruption and change in program to a plainer cheaper scheme in the 1560's.[59] This would not contradict the hypothesis of an open chapel begun early but eliminated when work was reactivated in the 1560's.

Perhaps the change in program was coincident with drastic economic changes a little earlier than the 1560's. It was reported in 1556 that the Indians could pay more tribute (they had hitherto been favored as ex-allies against the Aztecs) and a year later, after an inspection, their tribute was raised. By 1558 it had been octupled from 1000 to 8250 gold pesos, and it was raised again in 1560. Meanwhile, the population was going down, even between plagues. With such tax quotas to be filled, perhaps there was neither spare money nor spare labor for the elaborate project which had already produced the posas, the fancy north door, and may have begun the chapel above it which would then have been abandoned, a victim to the new tribute. Again in 1562 it was reported that tribute could be augmented, and though there is no record whether it was or not, that could as well as 1558 be the date for the reduction of the ambitious original scheme. In the eighteenth century, geographer Alcedo found the "exquisite" monastery in disrepair in a depopulated town, and reported that it had been the "work of the first architects the Emperor Charles V sent to these parts" which, if based on anything more than speculation or hearsay, might reinforce a date before the plague of 1545 for the grand design.[60] (At the time of the shift, whether in 1558 or '62, some of the carvers who had been working on the ornamented original scheme could have gone to some of the other Puebla establishments, Calpan, Atlixco, or Huaquechula, where some of the detail reveals stylistic likenesses to Huejotzingo.)

An objection to the idea that economy changed the scheme might be seen in the elaborate ribbed vaults of the church, resting in part on the plain wall where the chapel was stopped but, having been planned as a major feature of the church, the vaults may have been kept in the project while something which already seemed less important — an open chapel — was given up. On the other hand, the tribute could have been raised in '58 and '62 because the town had become very prosperous. Then there would have been plenty of money for building, and nothing would have had to be relinquished for financial reasons. Huejotzingo, though large, was not a wealthy community before the Conquest. Thanks to cochineal culture, it became one later, but since prosperity is recorded only in the last quarter of the century, it would not have affected building soon after the middle.[61] To assume that prosperity came in time to pay for the elaborate vaults shortly after the open chapel had been abandoned for lack of money would be neat and convenient, but that would be fitting the facts into a hypothesis rather than educing it from them.

Unfortunately all the hypotheses about Huejotzingo involve apparent inconsistencies which, though they can be individually more or less explained away, interfere with any one entirely convincing, consistent explanation. Nevertheless, that a chapel was intended above the emphatically decorated doorway is easier to believe than that the unfinished element there was intended for anything else, of necessity less important. As the doorway and the supposed chapel low in the cliff-like side wall of the church, and show similarities to the posas, securely dated 1550, it seems probable that all were produced within a decade, before either the workmen or their style would have had time to change very much.

The conclusions are that an open chapel was planned over the north doorway, perhaps as part of the original main project, in the late 1540's, that it was begun, perhaps around 1550, and that it was abandoned a few years later, perhaps when the tributes were raised and the population had declined, but that there was enough money still to complete the upper part of the monastery church with the handsome vaults originally planned.

CHAPELS INSTEAD OF CHURCHES — TLAXCALA

> . . . next to the portería [at Ixtacuixtla] there is a pretty chapel in which Mass is said for the Indians, and in which the Most Holy Sacrament is kept, and it has doors which can be locked for greater security; in this province they make use of these same chapels in the monasteries where there is no church; . . . and even if there is a church at the monastery, they also have similar chapels in the patio, to say Mass, and preach to the Indians. — Father Ponce (1585) [62]

There was a curious practice in Tlaxcala of setting up visitas and even monasteries that had no walled and roofed church for congregational worship: the outdoor church took its place. The friars must have said their conventual Masses and their offices in the sacristies, refectories, or whatever room in the monastery was found suitable. As the congregations were all Indian or very nearly so — Spaniards were not supposed to own property or live in Tlaxcala — perhaps it was thought there was little call for roofed churches. As late as 1585 Huamantla, Santa Ana Chiautempan, San Felipe Ixtacuixtla, and San Juan Totolac had no proper churches although they were fully functioning monasteries with resident friars.[63] In the 1540's, while they were visitas, Atlihuetzía and Tepeyanco, like Tizatlán, had open chapels but no churches; they appear to have got their churches only after having been elevated to conventual rank in the 1550's. At the establishments in Huamantla, Chiautempan, Natívitas, and Ixtacuixtla, churches were finally built only several decades later.

There was no church at Hueyotlipan either, and still only a one-room monastery there in 1585, though one would have thought that the Spaniards might have wished to provide better for the citizens of the town where Cortés and his men had been assured safety and desperately needed military support after their disastrous flight from Tenochtitlán. At Hueyotlipan there still stand the remains of a third-class brick monastery building, made soon after 1585, complete with a cloister but with no trace that any church was ever built or intended. (The present parish church is 200 years and 200 yards removed from the monastery building.) There must, therefore, have been an open chapel, though no traces of it remain.

With the arrangements in the city of Tlaxcala already described, this accounts for all the sixteenth-century Franciscan houses in the Province except Atlancatepec, a miserable affair of adobe. It was founded late (c1573/80), the monastery building was ruined in the seventeenth century, and little is now left but the layout. The church is a patchwork, mostly modern, and reveals nothing of any sixteenth-century predecessor. Calpulalpan, nearby but in Texcoco territory, also had a chapel but no church.[64]

Tlaxcala had been converted early and easily. Although the legend of the baptism of the four leading lords within a few days of their defeat by Cortés perhaps may not survive examination as anything more than a legend, some Tlaxcalteca nobles did become Christians very quickly. Their sons began to smash idols as early as 1525, and all went so well that little was heard of idolatry there after the early 1530's. Churches, whether roofed or open, must have been needed soon and often.

Viceroy Mendoza heard that the Franciscans were already building 35 stout churches when he stopped in Tlaxcala on his way up to the capital to assume office in 1535; apprehensive of their suitability, he ordered work suspended until he could investigate. Within five years Father Motolinía was able to write of 50 or 60 small and medium churches in Tlaxcala, and in 1560 Doctor Cervantes de Salazar wrote that there were already over 400. Again in 1570 it was said that Tlaxcala had "many churches," that the entire Province was "sown" with them, so many already built or building that the Indians could not support them. Father Mendieta found many of these more "huts" than "churches." Cervantes' figure of 400 must be shrunk, and even then taken to include every shelter where Mass was said, regardless of whether any specialized building had been put up. Because no certain traces survive and because there are no later notices, most of these "churches" must be demoted to something like visita chapels, probably open chapels made of wood and thatch. Father Fidel Chauvet has made a reasonable estimate that besides their 10 friaries, the Franciscans built about 120 lesser churches or chapels in Tlaxcala during the sixteenth century.[65]

The dispensing with roofed churches in visitas and monasteries may be a demonstration of Franciscan thrift in the "Republic" of Tlaxcala which as the indispensable ally of the Spaniards in the Conquest — the Tlaxcaltecas may have been even better fighters than the Aztecs — was exempt from encomiendas and all but token tribute. The Indians had not been moved into towns and, not forced to work for tribute, they worked less.

Cold and dry, Tlaxcala had been poor before the Conquest; it continued poor; it is poor today. There was little money when the church-building campaign got under way and there was less later, nothing like what could and did come in the sixteenth century from the more fertile Morelos, Michoacán, Puebla, or Oaxaca, in spite of the fact that the population of Tlaxcala was denser and the rate of declines lower. There were no important sources of income: no big-scale agriculture, cattle raising, or mines. The head of the Second Audiencia, Bishop Ramírez de Fuenleal, ordered the Tlaxcaltecas to raise cochineal for export and to increase their production of it above preconquest quotas, but though there was a cochineal auction every Sunday, cochineal brought prosperity only for a short time and only to a few.[66] Though some natives raised sheep and goats, no successful wool industry was established until the end of the century. The more profitable work of raising horses and cows was supposedly restricted to Spaniards in New Spain, and since there were no encomiendas — Tlaxcala was directly under the Crown — there were no Spaniards except squatters, poachers, and a few officials. None of these peculiar conditions was beneficial to the Franciscans' building program.

Spanish officialdom seems to have valued Tlaxcala less and less as the accumulating years diluted the memory of the brave allies who had saved the Spaniards' hearts from being torn out on the teocallis of Tenochtitlán, years that brought into disturbing prominence the fact that Tlaxcala was not profitable. Taxes were gradually raised, and Spanish squatters were able, unpunished, to take more and more land. The dwindling of Tlaxcala's prestige was made clear quite early: it began when the officials of nearby Puebla began to plot to have the seat of the Bishop transferred to the new stone church they were planning (1535), and became clearer when the Emperor finally ordered this done (1539, and again in 1541, '43, and '48). Although Puebla was much smaller, it was much more Spanish, and more promising of progress and profit. By the middle of the sixteenth century, Puebla had eclipsed Indian Tlaxcala, and by the end of the seventeenth century that once great city could be described by travelers as a "village" or "hamlet." [67]

The most important cause of architectural poverty must have been the agricultural impotence, for Texcoco and Huejotzingo, other ex-allies with reduced tributes, show no signs of architectural poverty. Huejotzingo, in fact, has one of the most richly ornamented of all Franciscan monasteries. Here, as at Texcoco, since lands were richer, the Spaniards moved in sooner; any specially favorable treatment given to old companions-in-arms seems to have disappeared even faster than it did in Tlaxcala.

It is not surprising to find, then, that none of the surviving Franciscan monasteries in Tlaxcala was luxurious in the sixteenth century: the church at Atlihuetzía is a patchwork of disparate building materials, some of them second-hand; the cloister at Hueyotlipan is of the coarsest brick, badly made and badly laid up; none of the churches had vaults until Tepeyanco and Ixtacuixtla were given theirs at the very end of the century. Even chapels were made without vaults in most places. The Franciscan church at Tlaxcala itself is like a barn, and its only costly attractions — retables and mudéjar ceiling — are from subsequent centuries. If anything sets the sixteenth-century establishments in Tlaxcala apart as a group, it is their common poverty. The lack of money and of the need to provide for exigent Spanish congregations were excuses enough for not building regular churches when an outdoor church could be made to do for the Indians. Nowhere else where sixteenth-century monasteries survive is architectural poverty so widespread and so characteristic with the single exception of Yucatan.

CHAPELS INSTEAD OF CHURCHES — YUCATAN

There were many open chapels on the peninsula of Yucatan (including the modern State of Campeche and Territory of Quintana Roo), the Maya U Lu'umil cutz u Lu'umil ceh, "land of the turkey, land of the deer." As at Tlaxcala there were many Indians — perhaps 300,000 settled in 200 towns — but relatively fewer Spaniards than in most of central Mexico, perhaps about 300. As at Tlaxcala there was relatively less income. Except for beeswax for the extravagant quantities of candles burned in Mexico — church candles must be at least half pure beeswax — there was little to export: small amounts of dyewood, salt, honey, and cotton cloth. Indigo became briefly profitable, but as it endangered the Indians' health they were soon forbidden to raise it. Cochineal culture was tried, but it failed. There were no mines at all.[68]

Although Yucatan, which for many years the Spaniards believed an island, had been the first part of New Spain they discovered, they never became as enthusiastic about it as about the more profitable mainland. After finally conquering most of it on their third try (1535–48), they half-forsook it for more rewarding regions. Bishop del Toral wrote that his diocese was poor (1563), and that there were few clergy and few Spanish settlers, but that the latter were the most decent in New Spain and got along well with the Indians who were, however, restive about their tribute because they had no money. He wrote about the shortage of almost everything, particularly friars: "this land without them is like land without water." [69] Complaints about "sumptuousness" were nonetheless sent to complaint-loving Philip II even from here where church-building was more reduced in quantity and quality than in any comparable part of Mexico. If empty space can be counted a luxury, as it often is today, then Izamal had that one luxury; the other houses lack even that. The pinched group of churches that actually was built owes its existence to the converted Mayas: the encomenderos, no matter how "decent," did not help. [70]

After a 15-year campaign of building monasteries according to the standard scheme in five key centers — Mérida, Campeche, Maní, Izamal, Valladolid — the Franciscans, who were the sole Order there, began instead to put up monasteries and visitas without any church building and — more surprising — none envisioned. There is no indication that any churches were planned for the dozens of establishments mentioned in the *Relaciones de Yucatán* of 1579–80, and although it was ordered in 1583 that all churches be built of stone within two years, there is no sign that stone churches were planned for the score of establishments which Father Ponce noted as having chapels but no churches five years later. Travelers pass additional sad churchless examples today, even in remote Quintana Roo. [71]

At the end of the century it was said that "all the other churches of the parishes for Indians in these parts are of thatch except for the chancels where Mass is said, and those are of stone; but all the main body of the church is, as I say, thatch. The Indians have got along with these ever since the land was discovered, and it does well enough for them." The same was said by Cárdenas Valencia as late as 1639. [72] The total evidence for the forswearing of enclosed churches is copious and irrefutable. Retrenchment was more drastic and extensive than in Tlaxcala, where churchless convents presumably hoped someday to have churches if there should ever be money enough.

After the completion of these first five monasteries (with Dzidzantum possibly six), real churches were built only in the city of Mérida and in the neighborhood of Valladolid, according to the *Relaciones* of 1579–80, which speak of *yglesias* rather than *capillas* there, and praise some of the *yglesias* for having retables painted in oil. The reason for these *yglesias* is that Mérida and Valladolid were considered not Indian but Spanish towns, and they had not friars but secular curates to serve not Indians but Spaniards (1565).

There were monasteries there too, but they served the Indians. In Yucatan the division between Indian and Spanish settlements seems to have been even stronger than in central Mexico.[73]

On his 760-mile inspection trip of Franciscan houses in Yucatan in 1588, Father Ponce (or his secretaries) often noted the peculiar local religious arrangements. His first and fullest description is this: "The monastery at Tizimín was all completed, with its two-story cloister, cells, and dormitories, all stoutly built of stone and mortar. Off the upper cloister there is a large and very good hall in which they keep the Most Holy Sacrament, and this room serves also as a choir in which the friars recite the holy offices. There is this same arrangement in all the monasteries of the province where there is no church . . . In the enclosure or patio of the monastery of Tizimín (which is square and paved, with four chapels in the corners, one in each, and with many oranges and other trees in orderly rows), there has been made a *ramada* of wood covered with the thatch of the branches of a certain kind of palm, which are very wide and long. This is big enough for many people, and so ingeniously made that in all of it there is neither nail nor rope. It is very strong, and rests on some forked sticks or posts of very strong wood tied together with canes like flexible willow withes. It has no walls, and is therefore more comfortable, for the air comes in from all sides. In this *ramada,* the people gather to hear the sermon and Mass which is said in a big chapel at the head of the *ramada.* The Indians officiate from the choir, which is at one side of the chapel, and there the baptismal font is generally kept, and on the other side is the sacristy. All the towns of the province have arrangements like this, whether there is a monastery or not, for it is necessary because of the heat there." [74]

264 MOTUL, A TYPICAL OPEN CHAPEL OF YUCATAN (freed of later alterations)

The chancel is flanked by subordinate spaces: a choir at the right and a baptistery at the left. All three are barrel-vaulted. The monastery church was begun at the end of the sixteenth century and completed in the middle of the seventeenth. Beyond it to the left (north) is the monastery block with its arcaded portería, and in the corner of the atrio is one of the few posas still standing in Yucatan.

265 SANTIAGO AT MUXUPIP

A typical Yucatecan open chapel of the sixteenth century, once a visita of Motul. The chancel and flanking chambers are vaulted in stone. The chapel proper has now been adapted as the sanctuary of a tin-roofed church, and one of the side chambers serves as a sacristy.

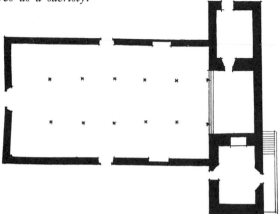

Although almost nothing of what Father Ponce saw at Tizimín is left, there is enough elsewhere to show that this was the regular scheme in Yucatan after 1562; it was noted over and over again by Father Ponce — at Tinum, Tekantó, Conkal, Hunucmá, Oxkutzcab, Tekax, Umán, Homún, Hocabá and elsewhere — and it was repeatedly noticed by the chroniclers of the seventeenth century, Cogolludo, Cárdenas Valencia, and Lizana.

Since big timbers were scarce and good building stone was plentiful, many chapels were vaulted. The commonest scheme was a barrel-vaulted chancel buttressed on either side by smaller barrel-vaulted rooms, one a combined sacristy and storeroom, the other a combined baptistery and choir. In front there would be a light *ramada* of small wood members and thatch. The skin of soil above the limestone shelf underlying Yucatan can only rarely sustain big shade trees — often not even small ones — and as the unrelenting sun and occasional violent rains made some sort of shelter seem imperative to the friars (as it had not seemed to their pagan predecessors) a welcome solution was found in the thatched shed made of the small wood members available.

All that there usually was at a visita was one of these stone chancels, perhaps with small side chambers and probably with a light wood *ramada;* at a monastery there would be additional rooms for the friars and a very small heavy cloister. Only a few chapels were large, such as that at Oxkutzcab 30 feet wide and 40 high, and only a few *ramadas,* such as that at Calkiní 233 feet long.[75] Nails were not used because they were such a luxury,

521

handmade one by one; they must have been particularly rare in Yucatan which had no natural metal and very little money. The *ramadas* must have been put together with much the same ingenious nail-less technique that had been used for the thatch-roofed shrines on top of some Maya pyramids or for Maya houses (where it is still to be seen in simplified survival).

Outdoor congregational worship must have been more comfortable in the shed-shaded atrios of Yucatan than it was during most of the year in cold, bleak Tlaxcala, 5,000 to 10,000 feet higher. Though they were sometimes constructed (there was one at Huamantla), *ramadas* were not considered necessary there because, as Father Ponce observed, it was possible to say Mass outdoors "without fear of getting wet, because in that part of the country it is a great surprise to have it rain in the morning." Father Mendieta described services as being all finished by nine o'clock "before the heat of the sun" except on big fiestas which might last until noon.[76] (If one knows how vehement Mexican rains can be, it is impossible to imagine what happened in climates where it did rain in the morning.) Rows of trees were common, and offered some protection from the sun and light rains, but as this shelter would be inadequate in many parts of the country, it is possible that *ramadas* may have been commoner than old texts indicate, even in mild Puebla, Michoacán, or Jalisco, where it rains only during three or four months and then rarely for more than an hour. Notices of ramadas in parts of the country other than Yucatan show that they were often considered no more than a temporary expedient.

*

It is not possible always to be sure what the Augustinian chroniclers of Michoacán, such as Father Basalenque, meant by the *xacal* they often noted in the atrios. *Xacal* means "thatched roof" in Náhuatl, and the word had often been extended to designate the thatched shrine building atop a pyramid. The friars borrowed it to designate a small shed-like open chapel, usually a cover for the altar rather than for the congregation, but sometimes large enough to shelter both (in which case it was a *ramada* as well as a *xacal*). *Ramadas* must have been put up very often in the hot, humid, and very poor country along the Pacific coast.

This odd arrangement of churchless friaries and visitas was found less satisfactory in Yucatan in the seventeenth century, and by then it was less necessary. The pressure to evangelize the Mayas and establish monasteries for them had been reduced, and there were more resident religious, both proportionately and in actual numbers. Not only were new churches then built in Yucatan with normal covered naves for the Indians, more or less like poor, plain, simple churches elsewhere, but often new naves were added in front of old open chapels, replacing the *ramadas*. Some were of stone; others were of a local kind of adobe; still others were only the old straw- or palm-roofed sheds closed in with some convenient sort of wall. They show how the population had shrunk, for most naves are on a smaller scale than the sixteenth-century chapels which became their apses (for example, Hocabá, Hunucmá, Kinchil, Mama, Muxupip, Oxkutzcab, Sotuta and its visita Sudzal, Tekantó, Tekax, Temax, and Tixkokob. At Motul and Umán, the small sixteenth-century chapels are, by exception, overshadowed and downgraded by the big seventeenth-century churches beside them.)

266 KÁUA, YUCATAN
The sixteenth-century open chapel was later used as the sanctuary of a narrower-naved church, now in ruins.

Although occasionally the open chapel and atrio entirely replaced the monastery church elsewhere in Mexico, except in Tlaxcala and Yucatan such an arrangement resulted not from chronic conditions but from accidental or temporary ones where the friars had not yet been able to get around to building a proper church. In towns too poor to build any church an open chapel might substitute indefinitely, but this presumably was a desperate, minor, and local expedient and not the accepted policy for any large regions save Tlaxcala and Yucatan.

Curates sometimes served their visita parishes in similar churchless arrangements. For example, near Tepozotlán "the churches and little oratories are all unroofed except the church in the main town, which is roofed; and the sanctuaries of these churches are roofed, some with wood and some with thatch" (1567).[77] If this practice was widespread in secular parishes and visitas, as would seem likely despite the Mexican Church Councils' theoretical opposition to Masses in the open air, it would help explain why so very few secular churches from the sixteenth century are left.[78]

There must also have been pitiable cases where no open chapel nor even any *ramada* was built. Some of the remoter visitas, served no more than once or twice a year, may have had no interim architectural arrangements at all, or nothing more than a plain patio with a wooden cross in the middle. Everything needed for the infrequent Masses was either brought by the circuit-riding religious or improvised locally for the occasion. It is probable that such faceless sanctums were more commonly the visitas of curates than of friars.

XIII

PORTICO CHAPELS: I

ALTHOUGH the single cell was the type of patio chapel chosen most often, its artistic range was restricted: despite such exceptions as Actopan and Coixtlahuaca it could not easily be expanded to grand scale or accept much architectural elaboration since it was constituted of only one architectural element. While Calkiní, by embracing three small openings under its big one, might have led to rewarding developments, it remained instead a unique exception.

With the striking example of San José at Cuernavaca before their eyes, and the presumably no less striking early version of San José de los Naturales, builders soon began to experiment with chapels fronted by porticoes of several arches. An arcade would be open enough to allow the congregation outside to see what was happening inside, and it could discreetly emphasize and dignify the ritual. Such porticoes would not only be longer than a facade with a single opening, but because of their greater number of elements they would present more opportunities for richer compositions of forms and spaces, for richer play of light and shade, as well as for more carved or painted embellishments. The portico chapel could become not only a larger and more dominating entity in itself but it could also be more effective in enlivening and organizing the composition of the whole monastic group — an advantage rarely grasped by sixteenth-century designers, who were generally more concerned with episodes than ensembles.

When Atlihuetzía and Tepeyanco, for example, had been raised to monastery rank, and their single-cell chapels seemed too small and mean, porticoes were added in front. This made these chapels more impressive, and also gave more covered space for the additional celebrants who had become available now that several friars would be living in the monasteries and training more altar boys, acolytes, and musicians. The primitive chapel at Atlihuetzía, 25 feet wide, was doubled to 50 by the arcade, and given 18 more feet of depth (ill. 212). At Tepeyanco the modest 18-foot chapel was extended to a grand 120 by a new front of five arches, set 30 feet out from the old front, and brought into proper scale with the 65-foot facade of the new church it now adjoined. (Part of this arcade survives, flat on the ground, invisible under brambles.) Although such portico chapels were rarely more than one bay deep, besides the celebrants and choir and instrumentalists sometimes they could shelter some select part of their congregation. At Tepeyanco, the enlarged chapel could hold more than a third as many worshippers as the church, perhaps six hundred if they were herded in with 6 scant square feet each. It is unlikely that this would happen often, however, and usually there must have been plenty of empty space in the region around the altar.

A space as big as an atrio demands that any building which is to keep it in its subordinate role of forecourt must be interesting enough to attract and hold the spectator's attention. If its visual magnetic pull is inadequate, the chapel will count as no more than an ornamental episode in the surrounding walls: it will be part of the setting instead of what is set. Thanks expressly to their porticoes, easily emphatic beside their church facades and monastery blocks, a number of chapels set back on one side of the church are able to assert themselves successfully as architectural and liturgical entities (Erongarícuaro, Otumba, Puebla, Tecómitl, Tehuantepec, Tepeyanco, Teposcolula, Tlalmanalco, Zempoala, and Zinacantepec, among others). Even when they are flush with the facade of the church — which, being taller, offers stronger visual competition — they can be made to hold their own (Tlamaco near Apasco, and probably also the now ruined chapels at Huexotla, La Concepción Atzcapotzalco, or San Bartolo Naucalpan near Mexico City).

267 PACHUQUILLA SU—
PERPOSED ARCADES

The certain portico chapels are no more than a step or two above the level of the atrio, but exceptionally one may have been set on top of a portería in a kind of composition which would be related to the somewhat simpler arrangements of single cells above triple porterías tried at Huaquechula or Tecamachalco. The result would be a striking double loggia, a form which seems natural enough, without signs of striving after novelty. The two stories of arcades at Pachuquilla, now disfigured by later masonry closing two of its upper openings, may seem a bit pretentious as a portería and chapel for this small village, yet the village could perhaps claim special prestige because the Indian governor of the entire region of Pachuca had his residence there in the eighteenth century, and presumably in the seventeenth and sixteenth. There was no monastery at Pachuca itself until the end of the century: the mines had not yet made it important.[1] Through no more than a minor work, pretty rather than grand, it is able to suggest pos-

526

sibilities for so much more imposing compositions that one is led to wonder why the scheme was not developed elsewhere. Such speculation cannot be substantiated, for even this one candidate is slightly suspect since its upper arcade, while possibly an open chapel, was not surely built for one. It may instead be a small-size reference to the two-stories of arcades common on *cabildos*. Unless other examples are identified, it will be safer to assume that portico chapels were confined to ground level.

TYPICAL SIMPLE EXAMPLES

The chapel at San Mateo Atlatláuhcan is a small separate building standing to the left of the big Augustinian church (ill. 136), which it may antedate if it served when the town was still only a visita of Totolapan, after a few years as a visita of Ocuituco. (The monastery church was probably not built until 1570 or a little earlier.[2]) Three arches on plain square piers give into a trapezoidal space whose side walls converge to a small box of an apse at the back.

268 THE OPEN CHAPEL AT ATLATLÁUHCAN
The side openings have been walled in, and the center opening has been reduced in height and width. The processional roadway around the atrio is set off from the central area by a low wall, interrupted by a gateway on axis with the chapel.

Spare to asceticism like its neighboring posas, without columns, moldings, archivolts, or tangible marking of the spring of the arches, the chapel gains its architectural effect solely from the simple relationships of its basic elements: the three arches (aAa), the stepped silhouette enlived by geometric merlons, and the three miniature arches of the *espadaña*. The blocking of the lower arches has now destroyed the bold pattern of solid versus void, light versus shade. The spareness is not so barren as that of Yucatan, thanks to the greater variety of contrasting forms, and thanks also to the exceptional emphasis put on non-figural mural painting, outdoors as well as indoors. Black, white, and red patterns simulating stonework and woodwork were lavished on the outside surfaces. (Such decoration may partially explain the flat austerity of individual forms in so much Morelos building. The unpunctuated flatness is so consistent that it amounts to an identifiable characteristic of regional style.) The barrel-vaulted interior, now a smelly storeroom, was made exceptionally colorful: its vaults were painted with gold straps edged with red, interlacing in front of a light blue ground in a never-ending mudéjar maze. Through what remains of the starry interstices, appear cherubim with green wings, a gold sun, and a silver moon.

269 SAN GERÓNIMO TLAMACO

The small chapel at San Gerónimo Tlamaco [3] was built for a visita of Tula, but was transferred to the seculars in 1563. From the beginning it was apparently associated with the small church beside it, like the other Tula visitas at Apasco and Tlahuelilpa. Less interesting than Atlatláuhcan in its general form, and never vaulted, Tlamaco's now roofless chapel is a plain rectangular box, opened to its atrio by three semicircular arches on columns. Its architecture is more developed in detail than that of Atlatláuhcan, with the different parts articulated by simple moldings. Relief decoration not unlike that at Apasco, Tlahuelilpa, or Atotonilco de Tula, is confined to the doorway of the church, which specifically resembles the presbytery arch of the little church at Tlahuelilpa. Perhaps these sister visitas, though small, were given handsomer decoration than many others because their towns were so venerable, and perhaps still rich with the prestige of legend, for the wandering Aztecs were said to have rested for some years in each on their way to found Tenochtitlán.

The three-arched portico chapel at Tlayacapan was perhaps the only church in the town while it was a visita and then a vicaría of Totolapan (1534–54–60). It is larger than the chapel at Atlatláuhcan, also built as a visita of Totolapan, but a little later. The heavy ribbed barrel vault at Tlayacapan runs crosswise to the axis of the altar, and is smaller, lower, and heavier than that at Cuernavaca which, nearby and morphologically similar, was likely its model. The vault at Tlayacapan is homogeneous also with the barrel vaults of the very early cloisters roundabout in Morelos. A few years later, perhaps when the church was building (c1569–72?), another portico was added in front of the one already there holding up the vault, perhaps in order to bring the chapel into easier relation with the front of the new church. It would have been probably at this time that the new walls and barrel vault were fancily frescoed in the manner of Atlatláuhcan.[4]

270 CUAUTINCHÁN

At Cuautinchán the same scheme was used on a bolder scale, over 30 feet wide. The portico chapel, the portería, and the facade of the church run in a row, interrupted only by the slight salience of the twin towers, an arrangement perhaps related to the bolder, coarser, and earlier example at Izúcar not far away. Everything at Cuautinchán was kept to a restricted *purista* character, with ornament and even moldings eschewed deliberately, not just as a negative consequence of poverty or as a background for sgraffito patterns, but more likely as a positive expression of ascetic stylistic ideals.

Although there are no specific dates for these last chapels, it may be supposed that Tlayacapan, the only vaulted one, is the oldest, and the other three were built between 1550 and '75. Tlamaco was called an "old" establishment in 1570, which may or may not have applied to the chapel building. Cuautinchán may be younger: most of the monastery was built by the townspeople for their beloved Franciscans after the unfortunate attempt to substitute Dominicans in 1554, and built quickly enough so that the church could be dedicated in 1565.[5]

271 TEPOZTLÁN
Dominican church, and the back arch of the ruined OPEN CHAPEL.
(The tops of the towers are later additions.)

Not far from Atlatláuhcan, on the other side of the wild weather-bitten crags of the Tepozteco, the monastery at Tepoztlán had an open chapel built on the same general scheme, but at a grander scale and with more developed details. Only a sad ruined fraction stands today. The big arch still visible just south of the church, half as wide as its facade, was the opening of the chancel of the chapel, formed like that at Atlatláuhcan with diagonal walls leading back to a small rectangular apse. Although the chapel at Tepoztlán is now too badly ruined to make the original use of some second-story openings in these walls immediately explicit, comparable buildings show that they must have been for twin pulpits of the Gospel and Epistle. In front of the big arch, one jamb and the base of one column supply just enough for a paleontological reconstruction of a slender portico of three arches embraced by a long *alfiz*. This made vivid contrast with the church: the low and horizontal chapel versus the high and vertical church, the openness of the unvaulted chapel versus the solidity of the cliff-like facade of the vaulted church, and the rich light and shade of the chapel versus the shadowless even light on the church's flat front.

530

The atrio cross stands on axis with the chapel, and not with the church which seems pushed to one side. If the cross is still in its original position, as seems likely though its base has been rebuilt, then the atrio, whose hub it is, was designed to depend on the chapel rather than on the church, possibly because the atrio and chapel were laid out together before the church was built or definitely planned (ill. 147). The chronology of everything at Tepoztlán is such a laminated puzzle that no dates are sure. There is no reason to connect the chapel with the far more sophisticated posas, or the less sophisticated tequitqui church facade. It seems to be the project of a third designer.

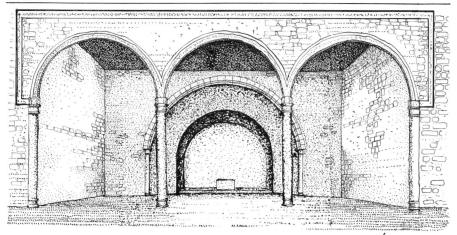

272 RESTORATION OF THE OPEN CHAPEL AT TEPOZTLÁN
Perhaps its floor should be raised a step or two above the level of the atrio. The pulpits are not shown.

The somewhat similar chapel of San Juan Bautista in the city of Puebla was probably built along with the Franciscan monastery church it adjoins. The city, founded in 1531 as a Spanish settlement, was definitely laid out on its present site only in 1541. Near the large Indian cities of Tlaxcala and Cholula, but not immediately adjacent to any sizable native town, Puebla had to import much of its labor force. Each Spanish settler was allowed to have his own Indians living in the city, sometimes as many as fifty. Within a generation there were so many that native barrios had to be created, and so many that architectural provision had to be made for their religious life.[6]

There cannot, however, have been anything like so many natives at this house as at monasteries founded in or among Indian towns, founded there expressly because there was such a large native population. Although there may have been plenty of domestic servants in Puebla, there was a

531

shortage of labor for big undertakings, and crews from Calpan and elsewhere had to be brought in to work on the Cathedral. So many Negro slaves were imported and converted that they soon had a special jail, and later a chapel of their own (not open) dedicated to the Blessed Benedict of Palermo, probably the only Negro chapel or church dedicated to a beatified Negro on the North American mainland. There were over 20,000 Mexican Negroes by the middle of the sixteenth century, and in surprisingly many regions they outnumbered the whites. By 1580 there were 8,000 Negro slaves in the capital alone, as many as free Spanish citizens. By 1599 they had their own religious confraternity of "Benedict the Dark-skinned." Puebla, however, did not become a particularly Negro city, and there were only 500 there in 1570 or 1580. Negroes and mulattoes were taught Christianity in much the same manner as the Indians, but less urgently even though Negroes were generally considered more corrupt and more dangerous. (In Puebla they were not allowed on the streets at night.) They were treated worse, and only rarely given any specialized building for worship, in contrast to their somewhat better lot in much of South America.[7]

In 1571 there were only about two hundred houses in the Indian barrio of Puebla — Indian families could not live within the Spanish *traza* — and the city then had five hundred Spanish houses, most of them sheltering not only Spanish families but a dozen or more Indian and Negro servants who "lived in." There were said to be 3000 Indians altogether. Father Ponce found in 1585 that the Franciscans in Puebla had few Indian charges. If the modern road along the north side of the atrio, leading out of town to Veracruz, coincides with the old highroad to Tepeaca, as it very probably does, it shows that the atrio can never have been large, which would be natural where there was no large native population to put in it. (The highway had been moved to pass through Puebla at the instigation of the friars.) [8]

The congregation of Indians could probably have been fitted into the main monastery church, but the Spaniards of Puebla, who made up the smaller but more important part of the congregation, may not have wished to have Indians sharing their space during Masses. By the time the chapel was built (the church may have been begun c1544, was probably well under way by 1550, and was being finished in 1567),[9] the idea of an open chapel and open court as the church of the Indians was already so fixed in people's minds that it seemed the natural provision to make for an Indian congregation even if there were not enough of them to need it. In the latter part of the century there were enough more Indians in Puebla to necessitate more chapels — presumably open and associated with atrios — at the Cathedral, at the parish church at San José, and at Santo Domingo. They survived through most of the eighteenth century but there are no remains of them now, and almost nothing is known of their architectural form.[10] (Open chapels connected with cathedrals or secular churches in cities must have been rare.) The chapel at San Francisco, fortunately, is still there. Walled up, by 1833 it was said to look more like a storeroom than a place of worship.[11]

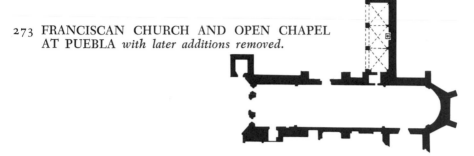

273 FRANCISCAN CHURCH AND OPEN CHAPEL AT PUEBLA *with later additions removed.*

It adjoins the monastery church far back on the north side, and was conveniently accessible through a doorway from the nave for the one friar out of the dozens in the monastery and associated seminary who was assigned to minister to the Indians.[12] The chapel is of a normal type, with three vaulted bays, each about 15 feet square and once open to the atrio through a simple three-arched portico. On one of the piers a stone pulpit is still in place, and in the back wall there is a large flat sinkage for the retable. Three extra bays and a solid wall have been added in front, and although almost everything but the congregation is still there, these additions make such an effective disguise that no one connected with the church now recognizes its open chapel. The small ruined chapel of San Agustín Zoquipa in the southeast section of Mexico City must once have been quite similar to this chapel at Puebla, though somewhat later in date; probably it served instead of a real church for a poor suburb now absorbed into the slums of the city.[13]

*

A number of chapels were worked out with more complex plans. For example, the portico chapel at Zempoala on the bare plains of southern Hidalgo has a plan compounded of an apse beyond an apse. Here a normal-sized half-hexagonal apse with a flat back and flaring sides is set in the middle of the flat back of a larger half-hexagon with similar flaring sides. The long front of the larger space is screened by a portico of three light arches resting on severe classical columns. The other details of the chapel also respect the academic canons of renaissance purism. This portico is a motif large enough to make the chapel dominant, and keep the atrio subordinate despite its size.

533

Just as the trapezoidal or half-hexagonal apse in a church seems to be the spatial climax as well as the definite end of the nave in front of it, so does this large trapezoid seem to draw together the great unfocused and undirectional space in the atrio in front of it, and at the same time focus and stop it. The big apse is in scale with the atrio, the small apse with the altar, and the two are in a happy formal relationship, with one echoing the other. The smaller apse seems to be a concentration of the general space and the climax of the ensemble. The altar is thus the heart of the composition, visually as well as liturgically. Originally it was further emphasized by the ribbed vault above it, and by an eye-catching polychrome retable behind it. (Some carved oak fragments in the sacristy of the monastery church may be parts of this retable: it must have been one of the finest in the country.)

The monastery church was begun about 1570 and had four friars by 1580, but the chapel may have been erected first, soon after the Franciscans took over an early visita which the Augustinians had established in Zempoala. Although the walling-up of the chapel (perhaps to adapt it for a confraternity of Spaniards dedicated to the *Santo Entierro*) and the desolate condition of the atrio now make their visual virtues hard to revive, patience and a few minutes of looking permit one to see how the ensemble once was a skillful resolution of the many varied functional, expressive, and aesthetic demands of the outdoor church.[14]

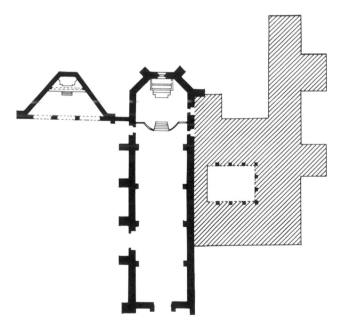

274 ZEMPOALA

275 THE ARCHES OF TLALMANALCO
at the beginning of this century

TLALMANALCO

Similar to Zempoala in its flaring trapezoidal plan, but larger in area, more opulent in decoration, and far grander in conception, is the open chapel at Tlalmanalco. The most arresting features are the portico of five arches of cinnamon-colored stone springing from multishafted gothic piers, and the deep layer of carving lavished over its archivolts, capitals, and pilasters. No surviving monument of sixteenth-century Mexico is richer, nor are any lost rivals known which could have surpassed it. Despite the generous supply of skilled and semi-skilled carvers available to them throughout the sixteenth century, neither civilians nor clerics would often attempt such a rich ensemble. Someone concerned with the design of the chapel must have come recently from Spain, fresh with enthusiasm for the most lavish plateresque, a plateresque of many small motifs juxtaposed as densely as in the patterns of textiles, a plateresque like that in the palaces of the Dukes of Alba or Medina Sidonia in Seville, or San Pablo at Peñafiel; or perhaps someone had stopped to admire the extraordinary piers of the beautiful church of the *Jerónimos* in Lisbon, a closer equivalent and — one would suppose — an unforgettable one.

Tlalmanalco, "place of pounded earth," had been an important center for Aztec sculpture, as is still attested by the arresting red stone figure of Xochipilli now in the National Museum at Mexico City. The low and intricate floral reliefs which cover this god of flowers, if compared with the floral reliefs of the chapel, may suggest that the skill of the local carvers could pass from the pagan ateliers into the Christian ones without much dissimilation — a phenomenon long familiar in the history of Christian art.

535

The change is one of vocabulary more than of artistic conception, for the latter seems to have varied no more than one would expect in the lapse of a few decades, or with the shift from fine to coarse-grained stone, from moderate to somewhat larger scale, from low to the high relief demanded by the new architectural context. The new clients were perhaps less concerned with artistic conceptions than with the symbolism of some of the decorative vocabulary — a religious interest — and with the general effect of richness — perhaps a more worldly one. Furthermore the Xochipilli is a masterwork made by one artist, and what would have been destroyed first in the disruption of the pagan ateliers would have been the specialized and concentrated training of such masters; the more generalized skill of the secondary carvers in the shops would perhaps have been more likely to have persisted. Unlike a masterpiece made by an individual, the chapel is a big decorative assembly of many episodes, carried out by many hands. Made to be seen from a greater distance, the carving of the chapel is properly coarser and bolder than the Xochipilli. Often as vigorous as Spanish work, carving in Mexico was generally less refined.

276 XOCHIPILLI
god of flowers and dance
(México, Museo Nacional)

The decoration manages to reconcile passages of renaissance plateresque, late gothic, mudéjar, and what may be indigenous ornament in an exuberant and original synthesis, more plastic than planar, too bulgingly carved to be typically tequitqui,[15] yet with such unmistakable indigenous flavor that it could never be mistaken for Spanish work. The varied motifs submit to one uniform and emphatic kind of carving, and all of them are fitted into a repetitive, sparkling, coloristic light-and-shade pattern — half-Indian, half-European, all-Mexican — synchronizing the dense never-ending rhythms of the native and mudéjar with the more phrased meter of the plateresque. Most of the pattern consists of renaissance arabesques in brocade-like designs crowded tightly within thin enframements (as in printed book borders).

277 Jambs of the sanctuary of THE CHAPEL AT TLALMANALCO

Although the relief seems great for the many small motifs if they are considered individually, it seems uniform and relatively flat when seen as an ensemble. The many motifs of disparate ancestry seem to have been almost forcibly stuck together, victims of *horror vacui,* or perhaps beneficiaries of it. Their coherence is enhanced by the sharp enframements and by the contrast of zones of flat bare masonry round about, a dramatic juxtaposition with distinguished artistic ancestors in both Seville and Tenochtitlán.

A similar handling of concentrated carving embellishes the north doorway of the Franciscan church at Texcoco and, even more strikingly, one of the gateways of the atrio of the Dominican monastery at Coyoacán, a single arch moved (c1880) and re-set in a *rejoneado* wall to serve as the entrance to the little cemetery beside the church. One can equate but one cannot identify any single hand or specific crew of carvers in these or other works seemingly akin to Tlalmanalco: it remains superbly unique.

Set far back on the north side, the five great arches of the portico quite eclipse the commonplace monastery church. The plan shows that like most of the other large open chapels Tlalmanalco's was self-sufficient, able to

537

function independently of the church which it did not even touch. Now up two steps — once perhaps three — the stage-like space of the trapezoidal chancel allowed generous room for the celebrants, for many musicians, and perhaps for some specially favored Indian gentry. Scars on its wall and the high level of its tabernacle niche show that the big box-like apse at the back of the trapezoid was raised yet another five or six steps above the floor of the chancel. This apse is framed in front by a carved arch of culminating luxuriance, and at the side it has a special entrance from what must have been a sacristy, though that is now too badly wrecked to be identifiable by anything more than its location.

278 RELOCATED ATRIO GATE
      AT COYOACÁN

279 TLALMANALCO

538

Under a rebuilt arch in the right diagonal side wall of the chancel is a ruined niche suited in size and shape to hold a big round baptismal font; such a font is preserved in the adjacent church. Above and a little to the east of the niche there are traces which explain themselves only if one looks at the corresponding place on the opposite diagonal wall, where a stairway leads up in the thickness of the masonry to what must once have been a stone pulpit. There were, then, twin raised pulpits, one for the Epistle and one for the Gospel, as at Izúcar and Tepoztlán.

Both levels of the chapel at Tlalmanalco were paved with polished crimson stucco, and the atrio with less emphatic gray, some of which may survive from a pre-Spanish shrine. Stones from a demolished temple were used in the monastery church, and probably also in the chapel. The Franciscans burned and smashed the teocalli of Tlalmanalco and converted the town in 1525, and in 1532/33 they finished some sort of early church, perhaps using old materials.[16] A possible 1560 in Náhuatl glyphs has been deciphered,[17] and the chapel may have been begun a year or two earlier. (The date need refer only to the part of the work where it was put.)

Why the renunciatory Franciscans in this cold mountain town at the foot of icy Ixtaccíhuatl came to build such a sumptuous Indian chapel remains unexplained. It has been suggested that it was intended to care for the crowds attracted there by the relics of the beloved Apostle of the Indians, Fray Martín de Valencia, who had been buried in Tlalmanalco in 1534, and that the work — which appears to be unfinished — was stopped in 1567 when the horrified friars discovered that his coffin had been emptied and there was nothing left to keep on attracting such big crowds. But Fray Martín had been buried in the chancel of the early church, not in this chapel. Also, although there is a great supply of early texts about Fray Martín, there is nowhere any record of any such cult at Tlalmanalco: they tell only that the coffin was opened several times so that other religious might see the body — a Spanish custom — and that such a cult did exist at another time and at another place, Amecameca. Furthermore, there is exceptionally full information about happenings in the region, about the Franciscans and Fray Martín, thanks to the Annals compiled by a pious and snobbish Indian lord of the local ruling house, don Domingo Francisco de San Antón Muñón Chimalpahín Cuauhtlehuantzín. He noted other events for these years, but never mentioned the chapel or any cult of Fray Martín, though he mentioned him often in other connections. (Often what was left out of sixteenth-century chronicles can be as informative as what was put in.) Long after the body had vanished a large new church was begun, sometime after 1585, and it was finished by 1591. Perhaps the old and presumably small early church had had to be replaced after the bad earthquake of 1582.[18]

280 TLALMANALCO

In view of these facts and inferences, the ingenious hypothesis that the work on the chapel was stopped in 1567 because of the theft of the body cannot be accepted, though it may be that the presence of this relic had until then attracted an exceptional number of gifts to the monastery. If that was so, the large income might have led to a large and elaborate chapel. It would be surprising if the Franciscans undertook it without some such special circumstance.

Work on the chapel may have ceased shortly before 1564, for in the 18 months before that about half the population of the region — Tlalma-nalco, Chimalhuacán Chalco, Amecameca — had died. There may not have been the need, the labor, or the energy to carry on such a large and elaborate undertaking. A terminal year close to 1564 would correlate well with the date of 1560 which some have made out in the carving of the chapel. If

540

the ambitious big project was not completed for and by the survivors after 1564, they could either have used it unfinished or they might somehow have been fitted into a church. If only a church was used, it would have been the one in which Fray Martín had been buried, the predecessor of the church there now. After the truly terrible plague in this neighborhood, in the winter of 1576–77, and the accompanying famine and six weeks of unprecedented frosts, the population must have been reduced yet more, but the natives managed to finish the monastery building in 1582, after the bad earthquake.[19] Since the idea of building open chapels was obsolescent, the harassed Indians may then have put their efforts into building a large, simple, new monastery church rather than into finishing an unneeded, large, and complicated old chapel.

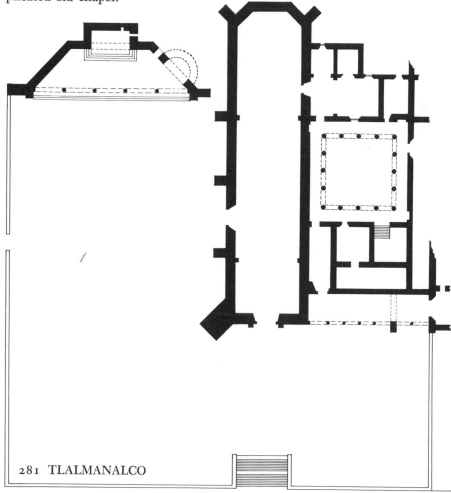

281 TLALMANALCO

This hypothesis is more convincing than the supposition that the chapel must have been built after Father Ponce was there in 1585 because he failed to mention it. The chapel was probably not in use in 1585, having for some years been left unfinished. Granted that it is one of the most striking buildings of his century, still Father Ponce could have failed to record it just as he failed to record many other eye-filling architectural sights. He was not interested in monuments as monuments, particularly if they were not being used, nor in open chapels as open chapels, except in Tlaxcala and Yucatan, where he could see them in use. He was not an art-historian taking architectural notes, but a Franciscan Commissioner General inspecting the equipment of his working force. Furthermore, when he visited Tlalmanalco he was in a hurry and he was ill.[20]

Here at Tlalmanalco, as at a number of other chapels, one may be reminded of the relation of San José de los Naturales to its church in both plan and in elevation — a portico set far back on the north side of the church — and one begins to realize that many if not all of the long portico facades may derive in part, directly or indirectly, from that first, most important, and then best-known of colonnaded chapel fronts. Tlalmanalco may reflect San José specifically in still another way: above the clustered columns which carry its carved arches, appear corbels which support the beginning of other clustered shafts, and these shafts may have been intended to carry either a second tier of arches or the wooden beams of a roof. In either case — and it is hard to imagine what else the upper bundles of shafts could have been intended to carry — the existing carved arches would have been independent, curving from pier to pier without carrying anything, like the free-flying arcades inside the Mosque of Córdoba and like what the facade of San José may have been after Claudio de Arciniega had remodeled it to include 14 stone arches, sometime after the Túmulo had been taken down in 1559.

If the arches at Tlalmanalco were arranged in this way — and it is not a certainty — a date of c1560 would be still more probable for the beginning of the chapel there. The chapel cannot safely be dated by its stylistic character or by its iconographical scheme (which seems unintelligible and may be nonexistent) as might have been feasible with a European work. The evidence, though fragmentary, is consistent, and it all indicates a work of the early 1560's, uninterrupted, and lasting no more than a few years. Although unfinished, the chapel is well enough preserved to make this convincing.

It long enjoyed a special reputation, often confused but always approving. The geographer Alcedo found the monastery "magnificent" (1789), surely because of the chapel, for the rest of the establishment, while serviceable, is far from handsome. The chapel was admired as a romantic ruin in the Romantic Period, and was prettily lithographed as such. Manuel Rivera

Cambas, a widely read recorder of his country's past, described it in his *México pintoresco* without having any idea what it had been made for (1880). Father Vera, the antiquarian of nearby Amecameca, wrote in 1909: "Notable in the cemetery of Tlalmanalco are some magnificent arches about whose origin nothing is known." Fray Luis del Refugio de Palacio who anticipated even Manuel Toussaint in his interest in sixteenth-century monasteries — he was himself a Franciscan — still did not know in 1918 for what the arches of Tlalmanalco had been raised. José Juan Tablada wrote in 1927 that they were part of some sort of unfinished church. Manuel Toussaint was the first in modern times to recognize the true meaning of this spectacular monument.[21]

282 THE RUINS OF TLALMANALCO *c*1875

TEPOSCOLULA

Except for the Capilla Real at Cholula, the largest open chapel still in anything like its original state is San Juan Bautista at Teposcolula.[22] It is also the most complex in organization and, after Tlalmanalco, the richest in ornament.

Despite an economic flurry during the last war, when it became accessible over an all-weather but short-lived road rushed through from the Pan-American Highway to the mica mines of Tlaxiaco, the town of Teposcolula is poor and without any regular means of approach for travelers, though during the dry season a truck still sometimes manages to reach it over 30 miles of

543

the retrograded road. The fortunate few who have penetrated to the chapel and with their own eyes have seen its fanciful arcades of caramel-colored limestone agree in acclaiming it one of the masterpieces of colonial art in Mexico.

The town of Yucundaa ("place of carved copper axes"), Teposcolula's native parent, had been moved to the steep green valley deep in the sierras of the Mixteca Alta at the suggestion of Viceroy Mendoza; he soon decided that the ground was too damp, and tried unsuccessfully to move it once more. The Dominican monastery of San Pedro y San Pablo was founded about 1538 by friars who had moved away from Yanhuitlán because of troubles with its Spanish encomenderos and its Indian "converts" still covertly pagan. Permanent building was probably not attempted for a dozen years.[23]

One of the first centers for the raising of silk, Teposcolula soon prospered, and by 1552 was leading the region: esteemed Teposcolula worms were bought by other towns; salt was mined profitably; and cochineal culture — Yucundaa-Teposcolula had paid part of its tribute to Moctezuma in cochineal — brought additional prosperity. There must have been a boom, for the town's tribute was more than quintupled in the generation after 1550, including the years when the chapel was most probably building. Testimonials to this pleasant prosperity, a monastery and a church must have been complete enough to have been acceptable to the Provincial Chapter by 1561, since that year they chose to meet there. They would have had no need of an open chapel, and it was probably built for the most part sometime after the meeting of 1561 and before the plague of 1576. In these years the population would surely have needed an open chapel for it had grown to something above 10,000, perhaps as high as 20,000, and was served by four friars.[24]

As in most cities, the population began to decline, and right after 1576 there was the usual tragic drop. In 1579 the labor of a hundred Indians working on the "church" was diverted to some private enterprise. This "church," which could be either the modest monastery church or the far-from-modest open chapel, may have been largely completed by the year before (1578), when Simon Pereyns and Andrés de la Concha, the two leading painters of the day, made a retable for Teposcolula. As at Coixtlahuaca (a steep but short day's journey over the sierra to the northeast), the prosperity so vital to building all but vanished when the silk industry all but vanished during the next decades, and when the plagues of the latter part of the century raged in the Mixteca with special virulence. The population began to drop again, sometimes as much as 8 percent a year, and it is doubtful that much could have been built in the years following the main construction campaign: little could have been built, that is, in the late '70's or '80's or even in the '90's. The friary was kept up nonetheless and still considered important; it had six friars as its regular complement in 1603. Cochineal was still a source of income in the eighteenth century.[25]

The scheme is basically that of a double portico chapel, double because a second arcade runs behind the long arcade of the facade and divides the chapel into two long parallel spaces running north-south across the east-west axis of the altar. Although it is two bays deep and 140 feet long, and hence big enough to shelter several hundred people, the chapel was not made to house a congregation but, like Tlalmanalco, it was conceived as a sort of grand liturgical stage with architectural scenery. Since it is only two bays deep and, though capacious, not arranged so that people in it would be in a comfortable congregational relationship to the altar, it is a true open chapel.

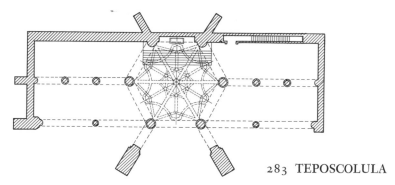

283 TEPOSCOLULA

The scheme is more complicated than just a double portico or a space two transverse aisles deep. In order that the short east-west axis and — more important — the altar it led to might dominate the north-south axis, four times as long but leading to nothing, an arresting special feature was interpolated: the two transverse aisles are interrupted in front of the altar by a hexagonal space, 40 feet wide and as deep as the two cross aisles together. The hexagon thus emphatically fills the building to its full depth from facade to retable wall. Its front and back edges continue in line with the front and back walls of the whole building, and the side points meet the line of the intermediate arcade (which divides the rest of the building into its two aisles). A hexagon was, then, worked in with the arcaded aisles here in a way superficially similar to the more famous but less expert arrangement at the crossing of the Cathedral of Siena,[26] though there can be little likelihood that the designer of Teposcolula was aware of this precursor. The Mexican solution is neater, probably because the building was conceived and executed in one campaign, whereas the Sienese hexagon was a later interpolation forced into a building already built. The Mexican reconciliation of aisles and polygon is comparable in quality more to that of the aisles and Octagon at Ely, surely unknown to anyone at Teposcolula.

545

PORTICO CHAPELS: I

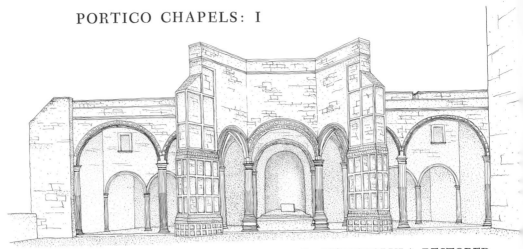

284 TEPOSCOLULA RESTORED

The main arch of the facade, opening to the hexagon, makes another strong centralizing accent, for it interrupts both the level and the rhythm of the thinner and plainer arches of the rest of the portico and, at the same time, vigorously links them. This main arch not only emphasizes but also opens up the space in front of the altar, and makes it more visible to those in the atrio. The altar was further accented by a gilded and presumably colored wood retable. Holes for its supporting timbers in the back wall are the only traces remaining, but they show that it was impressively large. Could it have been the one made in 1578 by Pereyns and Concha? The chapel was worthy of their work.

The front arcade is high, 40 feet to the crowns of the arches; the inner arcade is lower, hardly more than half the front, for its arches carry a second story, a wall with windows opening to upstairs rooms of uncertain purpose. Though closed in, these rooms may have been intended for music-makers, since the one on the right communicates directly with the choir-balcony of the church. Yet this use, while possible, is not certain: through the small windows only a few singers or players could have made themselves heard. The space is a walled room and not an open gallery. There is plenty of space for musicians below, on the ground floor of the side wings, where they could certainly have made themselves better heard. Perhaps then, like the upstairs room at Coixtlahuaca, one of these rooms may have served as a sacristy. If it did, the other may have been for storing musical instruments or other valued equipment. Behind locked doors and well above the dampish ground, anything stored there could have been kept secure and dry. These rooms are reached by stairways in the thickness of the back wall, like the stair leading to the elevated chamber at Coixtlahuaca or those leading to the pulpits at

546

Tlalmanalco. Neither at Teposcolula or Coixtlahuaca are there now any traces of pulpits. They cannot have been on top, as at Cuernavaca, nor can they have been at the head of the stairs or related to the upstairs chambers. They must have been downstairs, and must have been designed as pieces of furniture. Probably, then, they were of wood.

The big hexagonal space was crowned by a star-ribbed dome of a florid late-gothic pattern, based ultimately on Moslem precedent of a kind often used in Spain at the crossing of large churches or over important private chapels. The lost star vault at Coixtlahuaca was probably similar. Manuel Toussaint saw most of the dome still in place at Teposcolula in 1926, though one of its six supporting piers and a piece of vault above it had already fallen. This weakened it so much that by 1944 all but the outer edge of the dome had crashed, most of it in the quake of 1933. It was still in the same sad condition in 1954.[27] (No one interested in the chapel seems to have visited it since.)

285 THE CENTRAL ELEMENT AT TEPOSCOLULA

No more skillful vault had been built in the Americas. It was perhaps the finest example in the New World of mediaeval craftsmanship on a grand scale which survived to our time. Not any structural fault in support or buttressing, but minor earthquakes and major neglect brought the dome down more than 350 years after it was raised. No recent losses of early work are more lamentable. (If the *Dirección de Monumentos Coloniales* of Mexico

547

had 1 percent of the money spent on the preservation of later and often far less distinguished buildings in the United States, it could not only restore this and Coixtlahuaca, but also rescue many other fine works from the collapse already threatening; or if it were given 10 percent of the funds yearly spent on preconquest excavations, some admittedly minor, artistically undistinguished, and unthreatened, it could preserve much more of the handsomest artistic heritage of the sixteenth, seventeenth, and eighteenth centuries of any country in the Americas.)

286 INSIDE THE CHAPEL AT TEPOSCOLULA, *looking out to the northwest from under the dome. One of the paneled buttresses shows at the left, and the arcade and windows of the central dividing cross-wall at the right.*

Intricately and expertly constructed, this hexagonal vault was ingeniously buttressed. In front there are two showy flying buttresses, projecting some 30 feet, and spread apart like those at Cuernavaca and Coixtlahuaca in order to make optimum sight lines for a maximum of people in the atrio. At Teposcolula the angle of the buttresses coincides with the direction of the outward radial thrust of the dome, whereas at Cuernavaca the canting, justified visually, is arbitrary and somewhat inefficient mechanically. The middle (north and south) corners of the vault at Teposcolula were buttressed by the intermediate arcade and wall; here the arches nearest the dome suddenly ramped up to act like lesser flying buttresses, also radial to the dome, and again, like their mates in front, making for our eyes a vivid play of forces in concert with it; the low arcade leaps up to the high dome which interrupts it and at the same time becomes its climax. Pier-buttresses project from the back wall at the same angle as the flying buttresses in front, and thus all six buttresses at all six points of the hexagon are radial and of maximum efficiency. The entire construction is also graceful, light, and open, even more than the early project which had to be abandoned at Coixtlahuaca when quakes called for immediate reinforcement. This taut slenderness is the more remarkable because the earth at Teposcolula, too, is subject to many tremors.

287 THE RUINED DOME OF TEPOSCOLULA

The chapel is a composite type, formed of a portico chapel doubled in depth and interrupted in the middle by one large hexagonal cell. The facade is composite, too, for the portico arcade is interrupted by both the buttresses and the single motif of the big arch opening into the hexagonal space (aaAaa), a proscenium of the same grand scale as some of the larger single-cell chapels such as Coixtlahuaca. The long facade fronts a large atrio, wider than deep. The stump of a stone cross still stands in the center, on axis with the dome. The monastery church, now oddly rebuilt with some re-use of sixteenth-century material, is off at one side, unassertively subordinate to the chapel.

549

288 *The paneled pier of one of the flying buttresses at* TEPOSCO-LULA

Except on the dome, the detail shows sober and standard renaissance forms, not so free as plateresque yet not so academic as *purista*. Nearly all the ornament is strictly architectural in character; it is abstract, geometrical, and repetitive — dentils, balls, diamond bosses, and oblong panels — all sober, consistent, and coherent, and all sharply effective in the Mixteca sunlight. The ornament is vigorous and appropriately stony, with marked resemblance to the non-tequitqui parts of Coixtlahuaca. There is no sign of Indian influence, though all the labor in this remote but well-populated valley must have been Indian.

Although the individual architectural details are for the most part in themselves "correct," many are used with "incorrect" freedom. For example, the capitals and bases are formed of strong simple moldings which, despite their orthodox profile, ignore the canons of proper Roman or renaissance orders because their abaci and plinths are round in plan. This can be justified on special grounds, for the center columns have to carry an uneven bouquet of arches spraying outward at divergent angles, and such an asymmetrical ramification would not be easy to fit on the square of an orthodox abacus.

Not only the canonized forms but also some of these unclassical variations are probably derived from books. It must not be forgotten how attracted many sixteenth-century architects — Serlio for one — were to the surprisingly non-"classical" aspects of antiquity. Diego de Sagredo in his *Medidas del Romano* of 1526 not only countenanced round plinths for column bases but made them normal for Tuscan on the authority of Vitruvius.[28]

But while the Venetian editions of Vitruvius of 1511 and '24 illustrated a round plinth for the base in clear perspective, no authoritative book had sanctioned a round abacus for the capital. This might have come without sanction from a misreading of several of the plates in various later editions of Vitruvius or Serlio, which presented the Tuscan capital in direct elevation, without shading, and with no demonstrated distinction between what was round and what was square. It might as well have come from an error in some editions of Serlio, where the maker of the woodblock of the capitals in direct elevation inadvertently shaded the abacus to make it look round like the other parts of the capital and base.

It is just as likely, however, that the round abacus may be a lingering mediaevalism transmitted through the plateresque, in which it had quite often appeared. (There are similar cylindrical piers with cylindrical abaci in a number of churches in Spain, for example at Santa María at Villena near Alicante. Many renaissance designers in Spain showed an impulse to simplify while classicizing even though the result might have to be unclassical.) [29]

289 *A ramping arch buttressing the dome at* TEPOSCOLULA

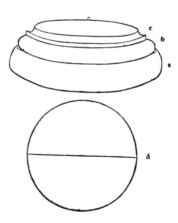

290 VITRUVIUS' TUSCAN BASE (*Venice, 1511*)

The designer of the chapel at Teposcolula seems to have been closer to Serlio than to any other printed source. Diamond-pointed blocks, dentils, and rectangular panels appear in a number of Serlio's plates, and though his taste was fancier than that of the designer of Teposcolula, perhaps the latter hunted for the simpler forms because of his Indian carvers' limited experience of the European repertory, and also because of the granular structure of the stone at Teposcolula, unsuited to delicate modulations or fine detail. Ideas from books are no more than minor episodes at either Coixtlahuaca or Teposcolula, and as usual it was the illustrations rather than their texts which were relevant. (It should be remembered in this connection that Spanish architectural books generally had fewer illustrations than Italian.)

*

The scheme at Teposcolula went far beyond the original open scheme at Coixtlahuaca. Nowhere else in sixteenth-century Mexico was there created such spatial complexity as here, in the relation of the high dome to the two lower aisles of unequal heights, or in the integration of the oblique sides and the points of the hexagon with these same spaces. Any spatial complexity is rare in Mexico, and such knowing spatial intricacy as this is unique. (The nearest approach was perhaps in an ungainly sixteenth-century fountain in Texcoco, recently destroyed and then "restored.") Nowhere else is there such rhythmical tension or such disciplined linear interplay as in the arches of different heights and lengths ramifying out — animated and orderly — from the central ring of columns. Nowhere is there such unity of effect, yet with many diverse parts all clearly differentiated. Nowhere is there such coincidence of structure and design.

The scheme must have been contrived by someone who had both architectural experience and natural ingenuity. Such controlled three-dimensional complexity would be unlikely in the first efforts of an amateur, and such neatness in the coincidence of structural, functional, and aesthetic solutions as in the projecting diagonal buttresses or the buttressing of the intermediate angles of the dome by the interior wall would seem unthinkable for an unpracticed designer. Yet, knowing tradition, he cannot have borrowed his ingenious solutions from it for so far as is known, they are new. Nonetheless, they are worked out in traditional forms, most expertly in the case of the web of the gothic vault, which was thin, neatly jointed, and reinforced by elegantly slender and deep ribs in a way uncommon in New Spain and based necessarily on some years of practical experience, presumably in Europe. Whether the designer was a gifted amateur or an innovating professional, either he or someone working for him must have had some sort of earlier experience with gothic vaults.

At the same time, the handling of many of the renaissance details exposes amateurishness. Nowhere, for example, do the archivolt moldings end

291 TEPOSCOLULA 292

neatly and properly; they have to be stopped before they meet their supports because otherwise they would meet each other first and collide, cross, and cut each other off. The condition is particularly awkward where a high and low arch of the front arcade, a diagonal buttress arch, and a diagonal hexagon arch all swing in together to the top of each of the two front center columns: here the carving of archivolts and soffits stops, and projections of unfinished stone are left instead, blocky lumps on which the ornament has not yet been carved because there seems to have been no way to make it come out right; the several archivolts would inevitably slice into one another and cut one another's ornament. A simple explanation could be that the normal voussoirs of the main sweep of the arches, where there were no such difficulties, had already been carved except for the final finish while the stone was still on the ground, and that the lowest voussoirs, irregular because of their difficult multiple directionality, were to have been carved only after they had been raised into place and conjoined to their divergent arches. Even the soffit ornament stops where the archivolt ornament does, and there can be no other reason for stopping this, for here the carving does have room to continue, and could perfectly well have gone on to its natural termination where the soffit meets the abacus of the capital. If, however, all the moldings on the blocks at the springing were to have been carved after the blocks had been put in place —

553

archivolts *and* soffits — then everything might have been given up in discouragement when it was found that the collision and intersection of the archivolts could not be avoided or resolved. Since the work is unfinished, either someone was discouraged with the work itself, or perhaps discouraged by the plague of '76, or possibly discouraged when workmen who were to do the final finishing were diverted to private undertakings in '79.[30] The dome above the unfinished blocks must have been put up after they were and, puzzlingly, it shows no discouragement or amateurishness.

Whoever was in charge of carrying out these unresolved details would seem to have been impatient, irresponsible, or inexperienced; he left his problems unsolved in plain sight. This does not seem the same disciplined mind that planned the whole work, including the dome. Although it is set right above the irresolution of the archivolts, the dome could have been finished first, and the carved detail below it then finished bit by bit, working downward as the scaffolding was removed. Perhaps by the time the archivolts were reached the master was no longer in Teposcolula; perhaps he had left the execution of the last details to a foreman illiterate in the syntax of classical moldings; or perhaps the master was well versed in the gothic repertory he had used in his dome — where problems of this kind would not occur — and not at all versed in the renaissance repertory. Whatever it was that happened, it seems doubtful that the same man could be responsible for both the sloppy execution and the fastidious design. Perhaps, however, we ought not to be too hard here, for equivalent though less clumsy irresolution sometimes appears in the best Spanish plateresque. (There is trouble for example, with the archivolts on the portals of the beautiful Escuelas Menores and of the Colegio del Arzobispo at Salamanca.)

The detail, the vaulting, and the buttressing at Teposcolula are so like work at Coixtlahuaca that Professor Toussaint convincingly attributed both chapels to the same master.[31] The vaults were similar and unlike any other work in the neighborhood (compare the rib-vaulted nave of Tlaxiaco or the coffered chancels of Yanhuitlán or Cuilapan), nor even like other ribbed vaults elsewhere in Mexico. They are so suggestive of firsthand knowledge of Spanish precedents that one suspects the intervention of a master mason or an experienced friar, someone trained at least partly in Spain.

The similarities between the work at the two monasteries do not stop here: a number of specific small details are also identical. There are other strong resemblances to work at some of the other great Dominican houses of the Mixteca in decorative abstract detail only: to some severe parts of Yanhuitlán, or to the front door of Tlaxiaco (ill. 45), and to work in the neighboring Valley of Oaxaca, at Cuilapan, Etla, and Huitzo, and even as far southeast as Tehuantepec. While none of these except Coixtlahuaca can boast anything approaching the spatial and structural achievements at Tepos-

554

colula, all share a common vocabulary of sober, geometric renaissance detail — strictly architectural — and a similar freedom (and occasional clumsiness) in using it.

There might therefore be a question of both a local school and a specific master: the school a lively, provincial, and anti-plateresque manifestation of the renaissance, which played with sober forms of abstract ornament without always understanding their traditional meanings and accepted syntax, and without always being able to manage neat junctures; and the second a bold master, sure of his architectural fundamentals, particularly vaulting and buttressing, while somewhat impatient or negligent of renaissance details. Either he had had little training except in vaulting and gothic detailing, or else he left his classical detailing to some less skilled practitioner, perhaps a native foreman with access to a copy of Serlio.

*

The chapel of San Juan Bautista at Teposcolula seems to have no European prototype and only partial prototypes in Mexico. The high-arched portico and the flaring-flying buttresses were anticipated at Cuernavaca but the dome and the details have no equivalent there. Perhaps the view of an inner arcade through an outer one could have been suggested by the developed version of San José de los Naturales or one of its imitators. The chapel at Toluca had parallel arcades with a higher arch in the middle, which might at first seem to suggest Teposcolula, but it is improbable that they looked at all alike or that Franciscan Toluca, far from Dominican territory, could have been influential in the Mixteca.

The chapel at Teposcolula is not a pastiche, nor even a synthesis of Cuernavaca, San José, and Coixtlahuaca: it shows instead an originality which cannot be discounted. Nowhere else in Mexico is there anything like the combination of its high hexagon — domed and centralizing — with widespread open wings. (Any resemblance to troglodytic Tlaxcala seems no more than a coincidence, without meaning, and more apparent on paper than in reality.) Nowhere else is there a spatial composition like that of the wings, with their quick sequence from the lofty front arcade (a plane almost all transparently cut away), to the intermediate arcade (a plane with its lower half open and its upper half opaquely walled), to the plane of the back wall (unpierced and shut with complete finality).

Despite its incidental clumsinesses, this is a building with claims to mastery. It would have been notable in Spain, and it appears as phenomenal as a comet in New Spain. It was the unanticipated first sight of this chapel, which he was the first to rediscover, that animated Manuel Toussaint to devote the rest of his life to the study of the colonial art of his country. He became its most distinguished, comprehensive, and readable scholar, and he discovered singlehanded its sixteenth century for our twentieth.

PORTICO CHAPELS: I

TEHUANTEPEC

Beyond Teposcolula and beyond Oaxaca on the chain of Dominican houses which led to Guatemala stand the church, monastery, and open chapel of Tehuantepec. Now accessible on the Pan-American Highway, not far from a pseudo-Californian Motel, the strange early buildings remain unpublished and all but unknown. Miguel Covarrubias' full-length study of the art and culture of Tehuantepec ignored the entire establishment. The sharp-eyed Abbé Brasseur de Bourbourg, though he saw and noted the church in 1860, missed the chapel. Even the otherwise full *Descripción* of 1580 ignored monastery, church, and chapel.[32]

Historically in the first category, artistically the chapel was in the second, and in its present patched state only in the third. The town of Tehuantepec (Yutañaña, or "tiger hill"), once extolled as a terrestrial paradise, fertile, populous, and rich, has also lost most of the beguiling character it had managed to preserve through wars, cholera, and economic collapse; the folkloric charms of its way of life have not been able to survive the assaults of what the Pan-American Highway has brought. What so attracted Sergei Eisenstein and Diego Rivera forty years ago is preserved better in their pictures than in the town itself.

The Franciscans had preached here very early, before the Dominicans came to stay (c1538/41). The monastery the Dominicans soon built (1544–50?) was important not only because Tehuantepec was a major Pacific port and a stopover on the highway to Guatemala, but also because there were so many Indians in the vicinity — about 100,000 in 1550. The town was transferred from the marquisate of the Cortés family to the Crown in the 1560's after long litigation. So much of the native population had died that by 1570 over half was gone — some said five-sixths — and there were only some twenty poor Spanish households; yet the duties of the monastery towards the 12,000 to 15,000 Indians still in the town were too heavy for the four friars, and two more were needed. In 1580 there were only fifteen Spaniards left, but the monastery was still so important that when the Dominican houses of Oaxaca were assembled into a Province in 1592–96, it was one of the five to be made a priory, along with the establishments at the City of Oaxaca, Cuilapan, Yanhuitlán, and Tlaxiaco, all already endowed with notable buildings on a grand scale (which survive in fair condition). Tehuantepec must, then, have been thought more important than Teposcolula or Coixtlahuaca, neither of which was elevated at this time.[33]

In the beginning Cortés built ships here, but no church, and the local encomenderos provided the town with only a mean straw-roofed affair. Generous funds for a new monastery were donated in 1544 by Prince Cosijopii, a nephew of Moctezuma, child of a political marriage arranged to seal an

Aztec-Zapoteca treaty. Already rich from tributes of gold, jade, feathers, and furs, he may have been stimulated to make this handsome gift by Fray Bernardo de Alburquerque, then Guardian, and soon to become Bishop of Oaxaca. Cosijopii was a spectacular nabob who had been elaborately baptized in the presence of Cortés with the new name of don Juan Cortés Cosijopii. When he symbolically surrendered his jeweled gold diadem for a Spanish cloth hat, he bent to the inescapable by submitting gracefully to Charles V in return for political security and a regular cash allowance. Security and allowance both came to an end when he was caught officiating at the old Zapoteca rites with the Huijatóó and the Copavitóó, refugee high priests from Mitla whom he had hidden in a remote part of his vast palace. His apostasy was discovered through the greed of a Spaniard who followed Indians he saw going to the palace at night because he thought they might be receiving largesse from the princely treasury. Denounced and apprehended, Cosijopii was jailed by the Dominicans in the monastery he had just built them. His subjects threatened revolt to get him back until he pacified them in an abject public confession. As a prince or "king" who had ceded to another king, he was accorded special judicial treatment, and conducted to the capital for a star-chamber trial by the Audiencia (1562/63–64). His considerable properties were confiscated, and the Huijatóó and Copavitóó were executed at an *auto de fe.* Cosijopii died on the trip back to Tehuantepec, from apoplexy said to have been brought on by despair and rage. Meanwhile, the construction of the monastery had been pressed forward by his old friend, Father Alburquerque, who had remained in Tehuantepec until 1553, nine years after Cosijopii's big gift. Viceroy Velasco wrote of the establishment in 1554 as though it had been completed, which it almost certainly was by 1555, when it was made part of the Diocese of Oaxaca by the Dominicans of Guatemala-Chiapas (to whom it had been assigned in 1550, just before they set up their Province in 1551). Funds were still being sought for the new monastery in 1555, perhaps for running expenses, or perhaps for completing details of the building now that it had finally been assigned to Oaxaca; perhaps extra funds were needed for the furnishings and liturgical equipment. It seems clear that most of the establishment must have been built in one fairly continuous campaign between 1544 and 1554/55. (The town was not transferred from the Cortés Marquisate to the Crown until after this, and although the monastery is the earliest surviving one in Oaxaca, it shows no connection with Cortés. He helped houses near Cuernavaca where he lived, but not in the region of Oaxaca from which he took his title.) [34]

The only writer, living or dead, who has discussed the open chapel is Father Burgoa, though even he did not know what it was. No one writing as late as 1670 was likely to recognize or be interested in what open chapels had been a century or so before. He did note how the Dominicans had "kin-

557

dled devotion to the most Holy Rosary, so that the men and women would all say their prayers together in a very capacious church, under the patronage of Saint Peter, which ministered to the Indians; only a single wall divides it from the main church for the Spaniards." [35] Inasmuch as there is no room for any other church or chapel contiguous to the monastery church, this must refer to the ex-open chapel.

It was later abandoned, probably in the early nineteenth century. The Abbé Brasseur de Bourbourg, between billiard games with the dashing young governor, don Porfirio Díaz, saw what he considered ruins on the chapel site in 1860.[36] The chapel has now been patched up and closed in by a big cheap front addition with a corrugated iron roof supported on pipe columns, a grim sort of machine-age *ramada*.

The whole chapel was set back on the south side of the monastery church because the cloister and cells were given the comfortably cooler north, as so often in hot country, for example at Nejapa nearby, and farther south in Chiapas and Yucatan. The facade consists of three heavy low arches: the segmental center one is 30 feet across, wider than those on either side, and comparable to Coixtlahuaca in scale if not in quality of design.

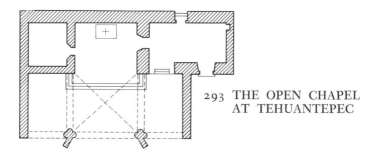

293 THE OPEN CHAPEL
AT TEHUANTEPEC

Flaring out diagonally from the two middle piers are two deep buttresses, similar to those at Teposcolula except that they are solid and do not fly. To-day they can hardly be seen, for they have been partly replaced and partly encased in sheaths of brick hastily put up after a series of alarming quakes in the early 1940's. Big buttresses had been needed from the beginning to take the thrust of the square groined vault behind the front arch. Broad and low, this awkward vault is like that under a choir-balcony, but bulged up in the middle as though trying to become a dome, and thus also like a vault over a chancel. While the scale is grand, the effect is not, for the construction (consciously anti-earthquake, much repaired, or rebuilt?) is obviously very heavy, and the thinned-out Teposcolula-style detail is ill-adjusted to it. The stone paneling on the buttresses, for example, was ineffectual where it was —

558

it is concealed now — perhaps too like the wood paneling from which it had borrowed its forms, maybe directly, maybe by way of Serlio. Examination of this gawky country cousin vividly points up the elegant assurance of the chapel at Teposcolula.

*

Related domical groin vaults on pointed gothic ribs cover the first three bays of the monastery church beside this chapel. Curious throwbacks to the first gothic vaults in Spain constructed four centuries before, these may resemble their remote forebears because both were conditioned by similarly limited skills. Both are examples of that coarsening and simplification which often modified the evolved French gothic forms when work far from France was given to masons not experienced in the construction of developed French gothic vaults. (The same atavism appeared in many corners of Europe: a number of vaults in Prussia, Friesland, or Apulia look like close cousins of those at Tehuantepec because all have retrogressed about the same amount from the same type.)

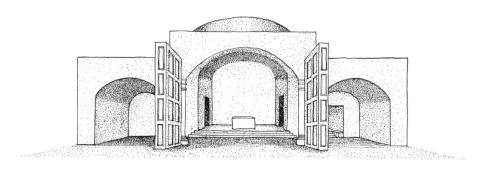

294 THE CHAPEL AT TEHUANTEPEC, *disembarrassed of later additions, as it appeared when it was still open.*

Even more remarkable is the vault that covers the sanctuary at Tehuantepec: an octagonal dome, lightly gored, and carried on an even more old-fashioned element, a set of arched squinches. These too are forms which have Spanish equivalents in the twelfth and thirteenth centuries. They could be the result of the same kind of atavistic simplification, or they could have materialized from the memories of a friar nostalgic for some twelfth-century monastery that had sheltered him in Spain. It is easy to assume the last, particularly for the squinches, but it is known — exceptionally — that for at least part of the time there was an important builder here who was *not* a friar.

559

PORTICO CHAPELS: I

295
MONASTERY CHURCH
AT TEHUANTEPEC
Ribbed vaults of the nave

For a few years, 200 pesos were taken annually from the income of Cortés' estate to pay a *"maestro español* who will supervise the work of the monasteries of Tehuantepec and Jalapa." [37] (Cosijopii's gifts cannot have been large enough.) What is left at Jalapa del Marqués, an isolated town of Cortés' marquisate up the river from Tehuantepec, is detailless and virtually undatable, but it is all vaulted (ill. 239). The church vaults, however, are the result of later restorations, and the little open chapel bears no resemblance to the big one at Tehuantepec. Cosijopii's daughter, doña Magdalena, gave desirable properties to the Dominicans here, but Jalapa never prospered; in fact it declined in the 1560's and, eclipsed by neighboring Tequisistlán, it was cut from a staff of four friars to only two.[38] Consequently, the *maestro español* must probably have done his work there sometime before 1560/65, though just what that work was, one cannot now say.

*

A new monastery *was* at Tehuantepec in the 1550's and an old monastery *is* at Tehuantepec in the 1960's. How much of the first can be found in the second?

Although Father Ponce in 1586 and Friar Gage in 1626 passed through the city without mentioning it, the monastery must have been more impressive then than it looks today, for well-traveled, sophisticated Jesuit Father Cobo wrote in 1630 that it was "the most sumptuous monastery I have seen since leaving, all built of bricks and mortar, and vaulted . . . very tall." Father Cobo was fresh from the capital of Guatemala and from visits to the big Dominican houses in Chiapas (Copanabastla, San Cristóbal de las Casas, Chiapa de Corzo) which he had found "very sumptuous" or "better than our church in Lima," showing that the church in Tehuantepec must have been at least as ambitious then as it is now if not more so. Father Burgoa saw that it was vaulted, and declared it "sumptuous" in 1670, "one of the foremost in the Province." [39] The vaults may be part of this impressiveness, and the dome alone was striking enough at that time to evoke praise.

In 1851 an American engineer, surveying the Isthmus for a railway, observed "the venerable Parruquia built by Cocijopi . . . in 1530 . . . somewhat Saracenic . . . its ruined dome fast crumbling to decay"; and in 1860 the Abbé Brasseur de Bourbourg saw a "coupole demi-moresque." [40] The thick plaster and many coats of whitewash and sky-bluewash all over the vaults, and the frequency of quakes vitiate any assumption that these are all exactly the same as Cosijopii's church or the same as each other. There surely have been repairs, and perhaps rebuilding or replacing of part or all of the original structure.

The pointed arches may help limit the dates of alterations: it would be unlikely that pointed arches would have been built as such a dominant element at any time between 1600 and about 1850. They must almost surely be either genuine late gothic or else neo-gothic. Inasmuch as "Saracenic" and "demi-moresque" elements were seen in 1851 and 1860, it seems likely that there were pointed arches there then. Since they were not new, they were likely built before 1600, and if before 1600, most likely between 1544 and '54, for though possible it is not probable that a church built in the 1540's would have been rebuilt in a markedly primitive gothic style before 1600 (though it is possible that a gothic church might have had to be patched in this terrestrially epileptic region). Unless there have been extensive changes since 1860, it may be presumed therefore that the vaults in their main lines still conform to their original shape.

There may, however, have been changes since 1860. There could have been an impulse to "improve" the old church when it was made a cathedral in 1892; or perhaps in the first years of the present century when, despite endemic yellow fever, Tehuantepec was at the peak of its prosperity, thanks to the Trans-Isthmian Railway, which had not yet been forced into obsolescence by the Panama Canal. The vaults could have been done over after the quake of 1897, which flattened much of the town, or the quake of 1902. Although rebuilding within a decade of 1900 is possible, this too seems improbable: the work looks consistently older, and there appears to be no record of recent work in the obvious contemporary sources, or in the memories of older townsfolk (questioned in 1940). Furthermore the heavy pseudo-twelfth-century style was not one used in Mexico by any known neo-gothicist.

*

Although style alone is an unreliable guide for dating buildings in Mexico, and although the forms of these vaults (including the dome) are unique there, it is still not imprudent to suppose that they survive substantially from the mid-sixteenth century as to their general form, though much of their substance may have been restored from time to time.

PORTICO CHAPELS: I

A DIGRESSION ON DOMES

Although there cannot be as many church domes in any other country as there are in Mexico today, in the sixteenth century the dome was not yet the familiar and attractive sight that it now is through so much of the countryside and the older cities. Its multiplication did not take place until the baroque taste of the seventeenth and eighteenth centuries called for the contrast and richness which the form and color of a glossy globe of tiles could give to the top of a church. While some small domes were built early, they were novel accessories rather than a standard item in the architectural repertory. A few were on posas, others were over the corners of the corridors of monastery buildings (as at Ocuituco), and a few more were scattered elsewhere. A small dome, presumably of wood, capped the *Túmulo Imperial* which Claudio de Arciniega raised at San José de los Naturales, another little dome capped the tower of the mother church of the Dominicans (before 1579), and another was over the stairway of the first Jesuit College.[41] All these were minor, probably atypical, and certainly small. Even rarer must have been any domes of more than a dozen feet in diameter.

296
TEPOZTLÁN
Domical vault over the chancel

More common than true domes are near-domes, groined vaults of more or less domical shape bulging upwards in the middle as though about to balloon into domes, though not yet in form hemispherical enough nor in structure built enough in concentric rings of voussoirs to be classifiable as true domes. (One has already been mentioned at the chapel in Tehuantepec.) Such vaults had occurred often in late gothic plateresque in Spain, perhaps as a consequence of its fondness for semicircular, segmental, and depressed arches, or perhaps in recognition of the reduced thrust of the domical form. They were often chosen in New Spain to emphasize the important space immediately in front of the apse and altar by pushing it up higher than the long level-topped nave. These upward-swelling vaults at the east end made a climactic spatial expansion, suitable to a sanctuary because differentiated from the nave without becoming too separated from it. Typical examples are not rare (as one sees at Acatzingo, Chimalhuacán Chalco, Ixmiquilpan, Izamal, Tepoztlán, Yautepec, or dozens of other vaulted churches).

562

A church might be covered with a row of domical ribbed groin vaults: they hump up over the nave of the peculiar church at Tehuantepec, and were handled more gracefully over the more sophisticated nave at Tecamachalco, there of brick in a bold 36-foot span, and strongly reminiscent of the "Angevin" vaults of Poitou and their Spanish reflections (as at the cathedrals of Ciudad Rodrigo, Murcia, or Santo Domingo de la Calzada). But though domical, such vaults in Mexico cannot properly be classified as domes (with the possible exception of the sanctuary vault at Acolman, which is not only more dome-like in form but is also in part constructed like a true dome despite its ornamental star of gothic ribs).

297 ACATZINGO *Domical ribbed vault over the chancel*

There was an exceptional group of domes in the Dominican south, of which six large examples are known. First, that of the open chapel at Coixtlahuaca. Second, that at Teposcolula, both with magnificent sixteenth-century cut-stone ribbed vaults of strikingly dome-like form; though technically not pure domes because not built up in concentric rings of fairly uniform wedge-shaped voussoirs, nevertheless, since they were more like domes than like normal groined vaults, they may reasonably be classified as domes. Third, the dome on squinches over the church at Tehuantepec (the crude dome on crude squinches at Malinalco is a freak of questionable date, not to be considered along with this, and the lumpish dome at Nejapa is a copy of that at Tehuantepec, and not earlier than the seventeenth century). Fourth and fifth, two domes at the east end of the Dominican church at Chiapa de Corzo. Sixth, the dome of the monumental fountain beside the church at Chiapa.

563

298 SAN AGUSTÍN ACOLMAN *Domical ribbed vault over the chancel*

The dome of the public fountain in the plaza of the large Indian city of Chiapa de Corzo is octagonal, with the sections sharply separated by thin but prominent ribs in much the same way as on the dome at Tehuantepec. The dome at Chiapa is also of brick, but of thinner and more expert construction. When it was about fifty years old, Father Remesal wrote that the fountain was "one of the best and best planned in all the Indies; Fray Rodrigo de León planned it and commenced it, and in his absence a Spaniard continued the work until the water was brought in the year 1562; and when the Indians saw it rise they thought at first it was a miracle so great that the old ones dropped to their knees and beat their breasts as though seeing something divine." The Indians of Chiapas seem to have liked seeing miraculous fountains, so much so that they became a local specialty: one at Chamula was said to rise and fall twice every day and twice every night, and there were two near San Cristóbal de las Casas which would gush for three years and then dry up for the next three.[42]

It is hard to see how the water which comes from a spring on flat land could have risen in much of a jet at Chiapa. Jet fountains were rare in 1562, even in Europe. If the water rose in a real jet, as Father Remesal implied half a century later, the Indians may have been quite right to think it a miracle. The first indisputable jet of which there is word in Mexico was a temporary fountain made by the Jesuits in 1576 for a fiesta celebrating the reception of 250 relics sent from Rome by Pope Gregory XIII.[43] Perhaps some of the cosmopolitan Jesuit fathers had seen some of the new jet fountains recently inaugurated in Rome, fed by the repaired aqueducts of the emperors. (Pope Gregory had been responsible for a good part of the new hydraulic display.) This was followed in Mexico by some sort of lesser jet at the big public fountain in the main plaza of Pátzcuaro, but that town is on a hillside, and its water came conveniently from above, and not from flat land as at Chiapa.

299 THE PUBLIC FOUNTAIN AT CHIAPA DE CORZO

300 CHIAPA DE CORZO
Inside the fountain house

Father Ponce — phlegmatic, tired, old, and not easily impressed — was much struck by the fountain at Chiapa in 1586, and he noted specifically that the water *fell* in many streams.[44] That sounds not so much like anything with a rising jet as like the normal type of sixteenth-century public fountain, which he noted a number of times elsewhere, where thin streamlets dropped into a basin from a central standard — the streamlets for those who wanted to catch water in a cup or jar and the basin for those who chose to dip. As far as can be made out now, the internal arrangements of the fountain at Chiapa could store water a little above the level of where the streamlets issue from the standard, but not enough above it to ejaculate what would now be classed as a true vertical jet.

This common European type, probably common in sixteenth-century Mexico too, can still be seen in action at Tochimilco and Ocuituco. Even more important, it can be seen at Chiapa in what is either the original hydraulic arrangement or one very close to it. (This was soon copied at Zinacantán in Chiapas and Chimaltenango in Guatemala: it must have been admired.) Passing through Chiapa in 1612, Father Vázquez de Espinosa found the fountain not only "excellent" but also "very beautiful." We can understand the admiration it evoked, since it has been well cared for (probably because it has for centuries been the main water supply for much of the town. The river is sometimes repellent with mud, snakes, or alligators.) Careful consolidations were made in 1944 to caulk recent earthquake cracks.[45]

This curious, handsome, and influential monument has not yet had all the study it demands. The octagonal domed element, which is what is most relevent here, probably comes ultimately from the Moslem repertory. Though no clear ancestor survives in Spain, some older ones perhaps do in European Turkey and the Dodecanese, and there is a mudéjar cousin in the cloister of Guadalupe in Extremadura. If this feature is not as closely related to European fountain architecture as one might expect, the example at Chiapa may instead be closer to mudéjar *cimborios,* low brick lantern towers over the crossings of churches (as at La Seo in Zaragoza, the Cathedral of Teruel, or Tarazona). A flight of someone's imagination has become fossilized to survive in Chiapa in the tradition that the whole structure represents the Crown of Spain.[46]

More surprising than the big, thin, brick dome is its abutment: eight flying buttresses radiate from it as from an English gothic chapter house (or perhaps a reflection of one in Portugal, since there was a Portuguese friar-builder, Pedro de Barrientos, at the neighboring monastery).[47] This is the only known complete set of flying buttresses in sixteenth-century Spanish America, and the only other knowing, mature, original use of them is in the flaring pairs on the open chapels at Cuernavaca and Teposcolula, and those begun at Coixtlahuaca. (The pairs on the north flank of the church at Chimalhuacán Chalco and on the flat apse at Totolapan are most likely later misapplied imitations of Cuernavaca, and the single mammoth on the apse at Yanhuitlán is a cautionary addition of the seventeenth century. Those at Yuriria and Copándaro are also afterthoughts.)

The less spectacular fourth and fifth of the southern domes are on the Dominican church at Chiapa de Corzo, between the fountain and the river: two brick domes at the east end, heavier and far less expertly managed than that over the fountain. The ends of the transepts are covered with domical ribbed groin vaults like those over the nave at Tehuantepec. The cornerstone of the church at Chiapa was laid by Bishop Marroquí of Guatemala in 1547, but the real building was done from just before 1554 to 1572. The two domes would have been among the last features built, possibly by some of the same workmen who had finished the nearby fountain in 1562 or, more likely, by amateurs who wished to imitate it. (Portuguese Fray Pedro de Barrientos is said to have completed the monastery.)[48] It is possible, however, that these domes are replacements or additions after an earthquake. This is another building that needs more study.

It is possible to postulate an evolution which would clarify the relation between the most important of these domes, beginning with the knowingly built fountain dome and its buttresses: this could be the starting-point of a sequence which led through Coixtlahuaca to Teposcolula. The "Master of Teposcolula" would, then, have worked earlier at Chiapa. Can one postulate securely on the coincidence that both the fountain and chapel display ornament developed in a geometrical and strictly architectural vocabulary (rare), that both have octagonal ribbed domes (rarer), braced by flying buttresses (rarer still)? No other monuments have this combination of features, nor any one of these features so well developed as in these two examples. The handling of ornament is similar but not identical, but since the fountain is a workaday affair of brick and the chapel an elegant Sunday structure of stone, it would be natural to expect differences very like the actual differences one sees.

The chapel at Coixtlahuaca could then quite naturally be dated sometime between the fountain at Chiapa and the chapel at Teposcolula. The domes on the churches at Tehuantepec and Chiapa would stand outside the direct evolution, the latter as awkward offsprings of the fountain, more in the nature of a retrogression than a development from it. The dome on squinches at Tehuantepec would stand entirely outside the evolution as an unclassifiable sport, perhaps an early one. If there is a connection between the fountain at Chiapa and the sophisticated domes of Coixtlahuaca and Teposcolula, and the "Spaniard" who finished the Chiapa dome is the "Master of Teposcolula" — all in the most hypothetical subjunctive — he could then also be the *maestro español* who had been active at Tehuantepec, where work was presumably finished just before the fountain at Chiapa was begun. The known dates and the style of the monuments do not vitiate the hypothesis. Further speculation about this conjectural master can add to his biography some professional connection with the Dominicans which might have led him to visit their houses in Morelos on a trip which incidentally showed him the flaring-flying buttresses of Cuernavaca. He might have been interested in them enough — they were major novelties — to borrow ideas from them later in Tehuantepec, Chiapa, Coixtlahuaca, and Teposcolula. Not brought up in earthquake country — he was Spanish — he did not realize that flying buttresses were risky in it. A quake at Coixtlahuaca made him (or someone he had left in charge) change from flying to solid buttresses when flying ones were half way up. Perhaps those at Teposcolula were already done by then, for it would seem perverse for the same man to change from flying to solid in one place and then in the same region start out again with another pair of flying buttresses. His biography can be made quite long, but it cannot get out of fiction into history.

*

The domes over the chancels at Tehuantepec and Chiapa (and perhaps Malinalco), and the bulging groined vaults over the east ends of many other sixteenth-century churches look ready to develop into the hemispherical domes in the same location which will become so pleasantly omnipresent in the baroque seventeenth century. But that was not to be the evolution of the Mexican church dome, nor has the Chiapa-Coixtlahuaca-Teposcolula episode anything to do with it, for after achieving its two masterpieces this line came to an end when gothic ribs began to go out of fashion in Mexico toward the end of the sixteenth century. The true ancestors of the thousands and thousands of baroque domes in Mexico are not to be found in Oaxaca or Chiapas or anywhere else in the New World, but in Europe. The dome was again brought across the sea, in a new form and as a new feature, perhaps first to one of the influential lost mother churches of the Orders in Mexico City. (Santo Domingo had a "dome" of wood, perhaps mudéjar. The Templo de Jesús or San Pedro y San Pablo, begun in 1576, perhaps had proto-baroque domes in brick or stone.) The oldest still visible is that soaring over the Cathedral of Mérida in Yucatan, proudly inscribed: "The master of this was Juan Miguel de Agüero, the year 1598." At the same time, the new church of Santiago Tlatelolco in the capital was beginning to show the typical scheme of church and dome which would dominate the Mexican baroque through the seventeenth and eighteenth centuries. These domes, Mérida and Tlatelolco, really belong with the next century.

XIV

PORTICO CHAPELS: II

PORTERÍA *AND* CHAPEL

SOMETIMES the open chapel coalesced with the portería, and could be considered as located *in* the portería, or vice versa. It cannot always be said which is which since that might depend on the use of the moment. Whenever the portería and chapel were merged, it was behind a portico: the portería chapels are therefore a subdivision of the group of portico chapels. There are many examples: Atzcapotzalco, Atocpa and Ostotepec near the capital, Alfajayucan, Calimaya and its unrecorded echo at San Lorenzo Natívitas, Coatlinchán, Coyoacán, Cuitzeo, Erongarícuaro, Jonacatepec, Malinalco, Otumba, Tecómitl, Tepeapulco, Tlalnepantla, Tlayacapan in its second state, Totolapan, Zinacantepec, and doubtless many more. All were either Franciscan or Augustinian: almost none Dominican. Not enough is known of the rituals and observances in Mexico to determine whether differences in ceremonial had anything to do with differences in architectural program, nor whether it is more than a coincidence that the Dominicans also, apparently, rejected elevated chapels.

As with ordinary porterías, the usual arrangement for portería chapels was to have an arcade either sunk into the facade of the monastery block like a loggia or set in front of it like a porch. The entrance to the monastery would usually be behind the arch nearest the church, so that through-traffic would be kept to that end. The altar would be set axially behind the center arch, flat against the back wall or perhaps recessed in a niche (as at Cuitzeo, Otumba, or Zinacantepec). On the wall behind the altar-block there was often fixed a painted wood retable, or a substitute painted on the surface of the wall; if none was permanently there, something portable, of canvas and wood, might be temporarily set up each time Mass was said, along with a frontal and other ornamental accessories.

A small baptistery sometimes adjoined the portería chapel at the end away from the church and monastery door (as at Calimaya, San Lorenzo Natívitas, Cuitzeo, Otumba, Zinacantepec). Such baptisteries were built some years after 1550, when the most urgent days of the big mass baptisms were past, and when the dispute about the days on which Baptism might properly be administered had finally been settled. Before this, when there were baptisms of more than a few dozen Indians, the rites must have been held outdoors in association with the open chapel. If there were not two fonts, one for the church and one for the chapel, sending the Indians one by one to the font inside the church would have been awkward; possibly the font would have been moved outside for the occasion, though that would in many cases have been difficult because fonts were very heavy.

Occasionally the portería was specially equipped for religious functions other than the Mass. Father Basalenque had a stone confessional made in the portería at Charo — it is still there — and Father Vetancurt told that confessions were heard in the porterías at Tlaxcala and Xochimilco.[1] Extreme Unction was often given in the portería to Indians who had come there especially to die. Unlike Baptism, these Sacraments could be administered independently of a church or chapel.

*

One important portería chapel has already been considered, that at Cuernavaca, where a door in one end was the main entrance to the monastery (ill.227). San José at Cuernavaca may be not only the oldest surviving portico chapel but also the oldest portería chapel. There is no conflict between the two functions here because the space is so ample; the entrance to the monastery is well removed from the altar. Furthermore, while the altar was being used nothing else would be going on, and when there was no service plenty of space would be free for all the activities normal to a portería; yet the altar still remained suitably apart, raised above the main floor level, set back, secluded and enshrined in its special compartment. The apparently useless prodigality of space which is one of the most handsome and expressive features of the chapel at Cuernavaca turns out to have this one psychological-practical justification. If the portería and chapel were ever to be combined in a small space, there would be an incongruous friction; even in its off hours a small chapel cannot comfortably serve as a public thoroughfare, or vice versa.

An early, simple, and more typical example is the portería chapel at Totolapan. Behind the three arches of its portico a heavy barrel vault runs crosswise to the axis of the altar, as at the early portico (but not portería) chapel at Tlayacapan nearby. The vault here at Totolapan is buttressed in back by the monastery block and in front by extra masonry on the stout piers, which are prow-shaped like the upstream side of bridge piers, or the piers of the typical early Morelos cloisters such as the one here at Totolapan. The chapel projects indecisively some 6 feet in front of the church, which it probably antedates by a generation, having more likely been built along with the primitive cloister and monastery block soon after the founding in 1536 but later than the chapel at Cuernavaca which it reflects, simplified, coarsened, and reduced in size. (If this is so, it can be added to the arguments for an early dating of Cuernavaca.) As so often in Morelos, the exterior of the chapel at Totolapan is decorated by reticulated mock-masonry patterns in sgraffito.[2]

Often, as at Totolapan, the portico-portería arches were all alike, undifferentiated in size or shape to mark either the doorway to the monastery or the axis of the altar. Most often there were three or five arches; at Alfajayucan (ill. 89) there were six, one for the monastery entrance and five for the chapel, with the altar behind the middle arch of the five; at Malinalco (nearly finished by 1571) there were seven.[3] The longer porticoes best kept the monastery doorway and its stream of everyday traffic disengaged from the zone of the chapel.

301 PORTERÍA CHAPEL AT MALINALCO
The arches were walled up in the nineteenth century.

Sometimes, however, the arches of portería chapels would be varied in size in order to differentiate and give more space to the bay in front of the altar, and consequently more emphasis to the service, the altar, and its ornaments. At Jonacatepec the rhythm is in a meter which one could write as aAa, and at Calimaya, aAaa. At Tepeapulco (ill. 107) the longest arch, a clumsy affair with a flat middle span, is perversely set in front of the monastery door, and the altar seems little enhanced by the architecture, set as it is behind a narrow arch identical with two more on either side; this goes Aaaaaa. At Tlalnepantla (largely finished by 1583, probably including

572

portería, though church still building in 1587) the central arch of the seven rests on heavier square piers while the three on either side are on lighter cylindrical columns; both these trios of arches are more open and linked to one another than to the rather pinched middle; this goes AAAaAAA. One trio may have screened the monastery entrace and the other the chapel, with the middle only a subordinate connective, in an arrangement which would then be more a portería-*and*-chapel than a portería-chapel. Perhaps, however, there may be another explanation here: since the town had been compounded by the Spaniards from separate Aztec and Otomí settlements — it was on the border — and long kept a duple character with two groups speaking two languages, each AAA may have been the front of a chapel, one for Náhuatl, one for Otomí.[4] If that was so — and it is only an unsubstantiated guess — Tlalnepantla would have had the only double chapel other than the doubtful pair at Metztitlán. (Here it may be well to remember, however, that Calkiní had four altars, and San José de los Naturales seven.)

The simplest portería chapels are fronted by bare arcades, and these are generally either early work or, more often perhaps, economical later work at second-class houses such as Tecómitl or Alfajayucan. Tecómitl was then and is still a dormitory suburb for some of the capital's commuting labor pool. The monastery (finished by 1581) was always small and poor, and it had to provide for a large and poor congregation; consequently it had a large and cheap chapel facing a large court. Alfajayucan was a second-class frontier house with no architectural pretensions (built probably c1576–86).[5] Its main attractions now are its wild mimosas.

Occasionally the running motif of a cloister arcade would serve also for a portería chapel facade. At Tlayacapan, the design for the new portico which was added in front of the older chapel (transforming it into a portería chapel) is similar to one side of a typical prow-buttressed Morelos cloister, as also at Totolapan. No new form, but a form familiar from a different function, was put to new use without noticeable change. The new portico, aAaaa, had its largest arch on axis with the altar, as had the earlier aAa chapel; consequently the two A's are in line. Tlayacapan had been a visita of Totolapan from 1534, soon after which the cloister and primitive aAa chapel both have been built. The chapel is clearly an echo of that at Totolapan which was probably an echo of Cuernavaca. The visita of Tlayacapan was raised to monastery rank in 1554, and additional building, including the new portería arcade, may soon have been undertaken (perhaps c1555–65), and at about the same time more pretentious decoration in the form of frescoes was applied to the older building. All the work of this second phase at Tlayacapan is in the Augustinian grand manner, sophisticated and decidedly metropolitan, and unexpected here at the foot of the cataclysmic crags of the Tepozteco.[6]

302 PORTERÍA CHAPEL AT CALIMAYA

A roof has recently been put over the battlements. The entrance to the monastery block was presumably from one side of the small raised chancel (behind the largest arch), an unusual arrangement. The didactic murals on the back and side are said locally to be "reconstructions" of sixteenth-century predecessors.

Some porticoes had much lighter supports which made them more transparent and the services behind them more readily seen. "Correct" classical columns, interposing the minimum of visual obstruction, carry "correct" triple-fascia archivolts at Calimaya and Zinacantepec; here all is as pure and "grammatical" as the plates in an academic treatise, except that the columns are as unclassically far apart as with pre-academic Brunelleschi. Coincidentally, the archivolts at Calimaya fold out sideways at each end, unstructurally, in the manner of the early Brunelleschi, much as they did at Actopan. (Founded in 1557 for Matlatzincas, Calimaya may have been built in the 1560's. Zinacantepec, "hill of bats," for Otomíes, was in construction from 1570 to '85, and longer.) [7]

The chapel at Zinacantepec (ill. 100) is virtually complete, with its long airy portico, its baptistery and font, and its altar-block and even its painted retable still in position. As one stands back in the atrio, observing not only the pretty chapel but also its relation to the atrio, church, and monastery building, one is given as complete a picture of this whole sixteenth-century type as Mexico now can offer. Though modest, the ensemble is revealing. A closer look, alas, shows the retable to have been all but ruined by recent repainting.

303 ZINACANTEPEC

Both Calimaya and Zinacantepec had been visitas of the monastery at Toluca, a house well known to those Franciscans who had tried to master the formidable Matlatzinca language in its seminary. Such friars would naturally have been assigned to houses in the Matlatzinca- or Matlatzinca-and-Otomí-speaking region round about, including both Calimaya and Zinacantepec. The portería chapel at Toluca had a portico of five arches, high in the middle and low on the ends, aaAaa,[8] which may have been the model for the almost-elegant portería chapels at Calimaya and Zinacantepec, each with one raised arch, and it also may have been the model at second-hand for Calimaya's imitative visita chapel at San Lorenzo Natívitas.

The portería chapel at Otumba has the same general scheme, probably without reference to Toluca but perhaps with reference back to San José de los Naturales (surely before 1585, probably before 1569).[9] The light columnar arcade is exceptionally open and airy. One of the largest of portería chapels, it dominates its church and easily rules its atrio. Both Spanish and Indian architects had long delighted in juxtapositions of ascetic and exuberant, and here at Otumba such European and native traditions are again in concurrence. A vocabulary of a few purist forms — a sort of academic patois — was used for the arcades and vaulted apse, while a wild tequitqui in unanticipated contrast to this — a plateresque pidgin — was applied to other elements such as the doorway to the monastery building. Although the tequitqui vocabulary used here was derived from gothic and renaissance plater-

575

esque, one cannot imagine its Indian carvers speaking proper Spanish, or perhaps any Spanish at all, whereas one can almost hear the Latin ancestry of the Spanish spoken by the designer of the correctly elegant portico. There must have been two differently trained crews at Otumba.

In neither of its styles is the chapel at Otumba close to other work which has survived in the neighborhood. The supervisors and workmen were probably brought from outside, and not all from the same place. Originally subject to the monastery at Texcoco, Otumba may have been partially dependent on it artistically. Though the portería chapel at Texcoco is unrelated, as the next pages will show, there may be some significant similarity between the side doorway of the Franciscan church at Texcoco and the doorway of the open chapel at Otumba, and perhaps a closer relation to the tequitqui doorway of the barrio chapel of "La Conchita" (officially but not locally known as La Concepción).

304 OTUMBA

576

305 OTUMBA
Sanctuary during repairs

TEXCOCO

Famous for the herb gardens on its fertile lakeshore, and its orchards of peaches, nectarines, and apricots, Texcoco had long been admired for its literary culture as well, and for the purity of its spoken Náhuatl. Athenian Texcoco had had enlightened rulers unhappy under the tyranny of their ally, Roman Tenochtitlán. The first city to cast its lot with him after Tlaxcala, Texcoco was an incalculable asset to Cortés, and he seems never to have forgotten it. Taking advantage of its location on the lake across from Tenochtitlán, he had launched his main campaign there, backed by legions of local warriors. Fray Pedro de Gante and his two Flemish companions had been able to begin their work here before México-Tenochtitlán was picked up and rebuilt. The Spaniards soon felt as confident at Texcoco as at Tlaxcala because the natives had been good allies and because they had so early and easily become Christians (with one spectacular exception in the princely house, burned alive in the plaza in 1539).

The monastery was the first founded outside the capital. It was dedicated to Saint Anthony of Padua because on his feast day the Twelve had entered the city, had been greeted deferentially by Cortés and Prince Ixtlilxóchitl, and had then celebrated an impressive and symbolically triumphal High Mass. The monastery was established at first in part of an old palace, where there was soon also established a sort of annex to care for converted young noblewomen. There may have been an open chapel here very early to care for the large Indian population, said to be 150,000 in the 1520's, twice that of Tlaxcala. The court alone consisted of over 26,000 people (who ate 400,000 tortillas a day). Right after the Conquest it was still so populous — larger than devastated Tenochtitlán — and so prestigious, that the Spaniards might have begun to build on a scale and in quality second only to the capital, though not in comparable quantity since Texcoco's old buildings had not been wrecked. Many stood for a long time; in 1582, don Juan Bautista Pomar admired houses and palaces already two hundred years old. As a postconquest

577

city Texcoco was able to keep its preconquest importance for about fifty years, but then like Tlaxcala it began to wither and, no longer a capital with a court, its importance was sapped by too-near México-Tenochtitlán. As a consequence, anything built by the Franciscans before the plague of 1575–76 might likely be of the first category: anything later, of the second. By the end of the eighteenth century the once great city was described as "today almost destroyed for lack of trade." [10]

While the portería chapel at Texcoco looks very early, its style is not enough like familiar datable early work to be interpolated chronologically. One cannot say with certainty when any of the surviving parts of the six-teenth-century monastic complex was built.[11] For such an important establish-ment in such an important city, something must either have been put up immediately, or else — more probably — quickly adapted from something already there. In either case, this would have been done so soon and so hurriedly that it likely would have had to be replaced after a few years. Fernando de Alva Ixtlilxóchitl, a writer of the princely house too partisan to be trustworthy on local matters, said that a church begun in Texcoco in 1524 was still standing a century later. Motolinía said that the Sacrament was installed in Texcoco in 1525, which means that there must have been some-thing — old or new — which could be used acceptably as a church. If these dates are correct, this "church" cannot have been any part of the present monastery, for this was not located on its present site until 1527 or '28. Ixtlilxóchitl was probably inaccurate, however, and may rather have meant that he still could see whatever the Franciscans first built on their new site about 1527–28. Many natives began to accept conversion in 1527, according to Father Mendieta, and "gathered every day in the patio of the monastery," perhaps a patio of one of the old palaces. (The new monastery was close to the palace of Prince Netzahualpilli, which was still standing at the end of the seventeenth century.) Soon after the new monastery was built there were so many converts that important visitas were set up in Huexotla, Coatlinchán, and Coatepec Chalco. The old atrio has now been erased by streets and little houses, and its former extent cannot be determined. Perhaps the pretty folk-art stucco chapels at what may have been its east end are replacements of posas. (There used to be four big confraternities here.) [12]

There must, however, have been something architecturally respectable in Texcoco as early as 1530 because Cortés, then resident for a few months, reburied his first wife and later buried his mother there. In 1536 he chose to bury a son in Texcoco although his family was already firmly established in Cuernavaca.[13] Lordly Cortés could choose the best in the land — outside the capital which, although he had a sort of family chapel in San Francisco, was still somewhat taboo to him; he would not have chosen a second- or third-rate building for his family tombs just because it happened to be in the same place

578

where he once had briefly lived. Long the second city of the land, Texcoco must still have been the best city outside the capital. There is good reason, then, to assume that important building may have been carried out at Texcoco before Cortés left Mexico in 1540.

The portería chapel and the lower parts of the cloister are both surely from the sixteenth century, though the cloister has since been substantially repaired and in part rebuilt. There is no evidence, internal or external, to date them as early as 1530, which was when Cortés buried his mother and first wife somewhere in the monastery. He could have given money then for some sort of building, which would probably have been constructed within a few years, perhaps in time for the burial of his son in 1536; or he could have given money at that time. If Cortés cared at all to improve the site of the family tombs, as one would expect of a proud new-rich new-grandee, he must have done so before 1547, the year he made his will, for in it he left nothing to the friars of Texcoco, despite having by then given up or having been forced to give up the idea of family tombs in the chancel of San Francisco in the capital. Instead of México-Tenochtitlán or Texcoco, he was thinking of having the family mausoleum in a special Franciscan nunnery in Coyoacán, where nuns could say countless Masses for the family's souls. The nunnery was never built, and when Cortés' body was sent back in 1566 it was first buried — temporarily — in Texcoco.

The main group of teocallis at Texcoco, notably handsome and high, was not destroyed until 1535. Such big-scale demolition might have supplied the friars with an abundance of building material just when monumental building became possible. Sometime between 1536 and '47, then, seems the most reasonable date for early major building at Texcoco, and it is in no way incompatible with the style or technique of the existing portería chapel. Perhaps this date can be narrowed to 1536–45, since it is improbable that major work would have been undertaken at the height of the plague. Whether the chapel was among them or not, some parts of the monastery had very probably been built by then, for cautious Father Ponce considered the monastery "old" in 1585, and he would not have classed as "old" any work of the 1550's or later, such as the work done unwillingly on the "church" by Indians of Calpulalpan in 1566.[14] (Conceivably, by "old" he might have referred to the founding of the monastery in 1525 rather than to any part of the then extant building, but that seems unlikely.) If the chapel was built before c1545, which is not unlikely, then it must be included with Cuernavaca, Tlaxcala, and their early echoes at Totolapan, Tlayacapan, Atlihuetzía, and Tepeyanco, among the oldest open chapels standing.

It was recorded that Father Motolinía built a church in Texcoco and had the body of Flemish Fray Juan de Aora reburied in it; but very probably this would have been after 1542, after the completion of the *History* and the

579

Memoriales, for he made no mention of it in those texts. Local conditions would have been favorable then, and Motolinía was said to have been a builder, active earlier at Tlaxcala and later at Atlixco (where he began a church and probably built the hilltop chapel dedicated to his patron Saint, Toribio). The cloister and portería at Atlixco, older than the existing church, cannot convincingly be associated with the porteria chapel or any other early work existing at Texcoco, nor can anything existing at either site today be convincingly associated with Motolinía.[15]

A few years after Father Ponce visited it, and found the "old" monastery "complete" (1585), Father Mendieta mentioned the portería in a chapter on the ravages of the great plague of 1576, because it had served as a dispensary while the atrio was serving as an infirmary.[16] As there was no reason to mention the portería's chapel function in this connection, Father Mendieta's silence about that means little. The portería may or may not still have been being used as a chapel in his day.

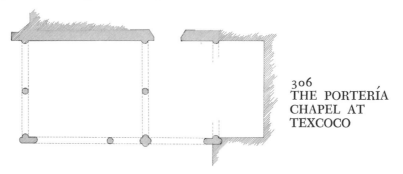

306
THE PORTERÍA
CHAPEL AT
TEXCOCO

Its curious double form attests that it had originally been built for the double function of portería and chapel. The chapel and the monastery entrance were equally emphasized by an odd weak-centered arrangement, AaA. The chapel was given the larger space, for it includes the small connecting link, and its Aa is separated from the monastery entrance's A by two small arches running back to the rear wall, aa, matching the small a between the two big A's on the front. This logical but complicated and visually unclear arrangement is unique. Rather than the monastery doorway, the chapel, by exception, was next to the church. The chapel crowds the church, a difficulty encountered early at Cuernavaca, and the conclusion at both places is that the chapel was built before the church. It surely was built before the existing church at Texcoco, for that dates only from the seventeenth century, and it was almost surely built before the church known to have been under construction in 1566, though the location of that is too uncertain now to raise the question of its relation to the chapel.

307 THE PORTERÍA CHAPEL AT TEXCOCO, *now altered from the original scheme by an upward extension of the walls into a parapet pierced on the south side by slots which allow drainage to stain the wall in stripes.*

The detail at Texcoco or, rather, the archaic absence of plastic detail, has some curious features. Arches of different spans, with fat semicylindrical soffits but without archivolts, have obvious difficulty in adjusting themselves to the compound piers from which they spring at different levels; the junctures are unresolved and crude. With the same repertory of forms more smoothly and knowingly combined, the cloister manages to achieve a restrained elegance. The problems in this cloister, where the arches are all the same size and all spring from the same level and run on the same plane, are fewer and simpler, but even discounting that, the difficult and clumsy portería still appears to be more primitive and probably older than the cloister, which seems in some ways to be a successful criticism of it.

581

308 THE CLOISTER AT TEXCOCO

This type of arch, semicircular in section as well as in elevation, is not rare in the neighborhood. Those in the cloisters at Huexotla and Coatlinchán must be small-town reflections of something admired at the head house of the neighborhood, Texcoco. This archivoltless fat-soffited arch, possibly of Salamantine origin, had come early to Mexico: it is seen on Cortés' palace at Cuernavaca, the cloister of La Comunidad at Metztitlán (1537–39), and soon at Etzatlán.[17] It could have appeared early at Texcoco, between 1536 and '45, the limits here proposed for the building of the chapel. The form was favored for cloister arcades, and appears in three separate families of them: Augustinian in Hidalgo (Metztitlán, Molango, Atotonilco el Grande, and Acolman just over the border in the State of Mexico), Franciscan in Michoacán (Zinapécuaro, Ciudad Hidalgo), and Dominican in Oaxaca (Cuilapan, Huitzo, Yanhuitlán, and several others). The portería chapel at Texcoco seems to be independent of these and related directly only to its own descendants in its own neighborhood. The other cloisters may derive from some prominent lost examples, perhaps in the capital. The use of this form on the chapel at Texcoco and the palace at Cuernavaca, and the possibility that Cortés paid for the chapel as well as the palace is not a coincidence sturdy enough to support any conclusions. Like the strange chapel at Tlaxcala, that at Texcoco is separate from any line of development traceable today.

309 CORTÉS' PALACE AT CUERNAVACA

CUITZEO, COPÁNDARO, ERONGARÍCUARO, AND "FR IO METL"

A few of the more pretentious portería chapels had elaborate renaissance arcades, their piers enriched with engaged columns in that kind of attenuated Roman Arch Order often favored by the plateresque. The handsomest example is at Cuitzeo, which is not only the grandest of the Augustinian portería chapels, but perhaps the most sophisticated in its details of any in Mexico. Here the piers are delicately paneled, and their slim columns are fluted, set on paneled pedestals, and topped with leafy capitals carrying a full entablature which breaks out "correctly" above each one.

The northernmost bay stops against the church, and its arch, the first of six, leads to an opulently molded doorway which leads in turn to a vestibule and thence to the cloister. The five other arches front the chapel space. Behind the center one is a semicylindrical apse with fluted jambs and a pretty little semidome with ribs punctuated by floral bosses and terminated by a skillfully carved floral pendant. Unfortunately a doorway has been cut through where the altar once stood. The little apse was a sort of prelude to the fine ribbed apse of the monastery church, which may have been its principal model, and perhaps also a model for the ribbed semidome apse of the open chapel at Franciscan Tarímbaro nearby (ill. 229), unless that was derived directly from the chapel at Cuitzeo. (Such specific borrowing of a

583

design from one Order by another would be rare.) At the far south end of the portico at Cuitzeo there is a shabby chamber, now inaccessible from out-doors to all but bats, but when open to the chapel it served as its baptistery in an arrangement similar to that at Zinacantepec.

310 THE PORTERÍA CHAPEL AT CUITZEO with the apse restored

Cuitzeo had been one of the oldest native towns of Michoacán. After having been burned by Nuño de Guzmán, it was newly laid out with straight streets and many neat little adobe houses for the poor and grander ones of stone for the rich. When the monastery was begun (1550 or '51) the town had a population of about 10,000. A prime assertion of Augustinian sumptu-ousness and refinement, the monastery was finished sometime before 1579. (There have been several subordinate additions and remodelings since.) It was soon recognized as "something sumptuous," and "one of the most illus-trious edifices in New Spain"; it was still praised in the eighteenth century when enthusiasm for sixteenth-century works was rare.[18] Even now, no other house can surpass the grace and strength of its details.

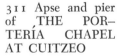
311 Apse and pier of ‚THE POR–TERÍA CHAPEL AT CUITZEO

312 Church portal and ‚THE POR–TERÍA CHAPEL AT CUITZEO
(opposite)

584

Once garden-like, the great atrio has now become the field of a long slow struggle between exhausted roses and drought. More than half the area has been made a municipal desert, in one corner of which a sad small market meets on Sundays. The atrio has lost its defining wall, its posas, and the odd vaulted chapel beneath the giant cross which once marked its center.

Until twenty years ago, one saw the monastery overtop its trim white town of cubical houses, and of magnolias, jacarandas, and tamarisks, much as it must have been when new, and the buildings and trees rise picturesquely on their near-island at the end of a stone causeway stretching half a mile across a lake; and the ensemble could thus suggest in miniature that water approach to shimmering Tenochtitlán which had so struck the conquistadores, and had survived for decades the metamorphosis of Tenochtitlán into Mexico City. The lakes around the capital have now all but vanished, and the lovely Lake of Cuitzeo, once 30 miles long, was drained in the 1940's to become a mud-flat in the rainy season and a dust-flat in the dry. In the sixteenth-century it was a nice source of income for the town and for the friars because, in the very middle of the country, equidistant from Atlantic and Pacific, it produced not only fish (*mixtlapiques*), but salt.[19]

585

PORTICO CHAPELS: II

The monastery at Santiago Copándaro, once a fishing-village vicaría of Cuitzeo at the west end of the ex-lake, has a much smaller triple-arched portería which may also have doubled as an open chapel. Copándaro had been founded in 1550 or '51 by the same learned Fray Alonso de la Vera Cruz who had founded Cuitzeo, but the building campaign began only in 1560, and was concluded in 1567. Cuitzeo was building at the same time, and those parts which are echoed at Copándaro — the portal, the cloister, and perhaps the portería — must therefore antedate 1567. The fine quality of the work at Copándaro, particularly its charming little cloister, makes one suspect that despite the small size of the village the house had been marked for promotion even when the building was begun, though the actual elevation to monastery rank came only in 1566. The establishment was still admired in the eighteenth century, and singled out for its architectural refinement by French Father Beaumont.[20]

*

The architecture of Copándaro is tied to that of Cuitzeo in a peculiar way. At Cuitzeo and Copándaro the churches were not only commissioned by the same friar but also, according to Father Basalenque, built by the same *"oficial* from Mexico City." [21] His name may be recorded in an inscription on the portal of Cuitzeo: *Fr Io METL ME FECIT.* Only the last two words are immediately intelligible. The first three cannot refer to an Indian Fray Juan Metl as there were not yet Indian friars, and Metl cannot be a Spanish name. It is not likely to be the name of an otherwise unknown friar translated into Náhuatl, as has been suggested, since names were not translated from Spanish into Náhuatl, certainly not friar's names (though *very* exceptionally a friar might take an Indian name, as Motolinía had). But Tarasca and not Náhuatl was the language of the neighborhood, and Metl cannot be Tarasca since Tarasca has no *L.* Furthermore, Metl is the Náhuatl word for the big "century plant" agave now always called *maguey,* the name the Spaniards brought from the Antilles. No one would have called himself "Brother John Century Plant." Perhaps *Fr Io METL* ought better be read as *Francisco Juan Metl,* a plausible name for a baptized Náhuatl-speaking Indian or mestizo.

Oficial can hardly have meant "official" in our sense — no Indian would likely have risen to that — but more probably indicated someone engaged in an *oficio,* meaning a craft or trade. *Oficial* would be applied specifically to a craftsman who had completed his years of apprenticeship but had not yet passed the examinations given by a guild to those wishing to become *maestros.* Since Indians and mestizos ordinarily did not become *maestros,* though Viceroy Mendoza had ordered that they should not be prevented, and though there were increasing irregularities, the most skilled Indians were usually only *oficiales.* A few years before the work at Cuitzeo was begun, the Augustinians at nearby Tiripetío were having their Indians trained by

Spanish *oficiales* from the capital. These Indians, however, were local Taras-cos, and none could have been called *Metl:* but if the Augustinians were training Indians in the capital in the same way, one trained there could have been an *oficial* called Francisco Juan Metl. He could have learned his renaissance plateresque vocabulary in some sophisticated Augustinian work-shop such as that which in 1560 was completing the very pure plateresque portal of Acolman just north of México-Tenochtitlán; he could have brought this knowledge, delicately and sympathetically tempered by an exceptional Indian sensibility, to the design of the important new Augustian house at Cuitzeo. Nowhere else, save possibly at Yuriria and Acolman (ills. 123, 251) — both also Augustinian and both stylistically related to Cuitzeo — were buildings signed, and though it may be hard to accept such a simple explanation here with such scant reinforcement from contemporary archi-tectural or literary sources, it seems to be even harder to find any other ac-ceptable explanation. (Some work at Cuitzeo was directed by a Fray Fran-cisco de Villafuerte at about this same time, but it cannot be said how much his direction had to do with the design, if at all, nor with what part of the building.) [22]

*

The general design of the portal of the church at Cuitzeo is Spanish, and of exceptional quality; the detailed execution is Indian, and also of ex-ceptional quality. The execution must be by native craftsmen trained by Spaniards, who may in addition have used some Spanish or Spanish-inspired drawing. That the Augustinians used to send drawings from monastery to monastery is proved by the appearance of identical schemes at widely sep-arated towns in works clearly executed by different workmen: for example, the facades of Yuriria and Acolman, or Acolman and Metztitlán (ills. 51, 123, 251), or the cloisters of Acolman, Atotonilco el Grande, and Molango, all removed from one another by several days' journey over several steep sierras. Acolman may have been the most copied because it was the most Spanish, and it may have been based on fresh drawings from Spain. These drawings, or drawings of Acolman itself, could have been given to the local artisans at the other houses.

The designer of the church portal at Cuitzeo — Metl or not — probably did not design the portería as well. Even allowing for the difference in the architectural problems presented, it is hard to find anything that betrays the same hand in either the design or the execution. Both portal and portería are of high quality, but not the same quality. They need not have been built at the same time, for the *xacal* which would have been put up first could have continued in use as an open chapel after the church was finished — as was common practice — and the portería (which is ill-coordinated with the openings of the monastery block) could have replaced it some years

313 The main portal of THE MONASTERY CHURCH AT CUITZEO

later. The detailed investigations of a local antiquarian, José Corona Nuñez, tend to confirm this.[23] When the church facade was building, some sort of adjacent portico must surely have been foreseen, however, for the stonework of the two is bonded together. While the portería cannot then very well be a late afterthought — even the nineteenth century has been suggested — it need not be strictly contemporaneous: it may, rather, be a postponed element of the original scheme. The masonry of the edge of the church facade could perhaps have been left raw, anticipating later bonding with the portería, whenever that should be built. Because such a procedure may not have been usual, it need not be rejected as improbable here, for those who were in charge at Cuitzeo could change their minds abruptly: the cloister, we know, was vaulted in stone just after it had been given wooden ceilings.[24] The portería chapel fronts the cloister, and is as likely related to some building campaign there as to the one that produced the church. Church portal and chapel portico were not necessarily designed on the spot;

588

drawings may have been sent from an outside source, and if drawings for both were sent, they need not have come from the same source and need not have been coordinated in design on the spot. More important than whether they were built together or not is the strong likelihood that they were not designed together.

*

Erongarícuaro, "place of vigilance," or "place from which to see the front," at the west end of Lake Pátzcuaro, has a very open triple-arched portería chapel. Its broad and high openings make it a smaller Cuernavaca in general proportion, though not in style, and since it is not vaulted it is even lighter than Cuernavaca. As at Cuitzeo, the arcade rests on compound piers, but here with paired columns engaged on each pier. The whole is further complicated by the columns, which show two kinds of fluting before coming to an end in pidgin plateresque capitals (which, by contrast, make Cuitzeo look more metropolitan and much more Spanish). All three arches are fitted into one long *alfiz*.

It has been suggested that this engaging, wayward, pseudo-sophisticated but naïve design may have been the work of the same *"oficial* from Mexico City" who built Cuitzeo and Copándaro, then a day's journey to the north-west.[25] There are several objections to such an attribution: first, Erongarícuaro was Franciscan while Cuitzeo and Copándaro were Augustinian; second, while the church facade may be by the *oficial,* the chapel at Cuitzeo is probably not by the same designer as the facade; third, the plateresque repertory was manipulated far less knowingly at Erongarícuaro than anywhere at Cuitzeo.

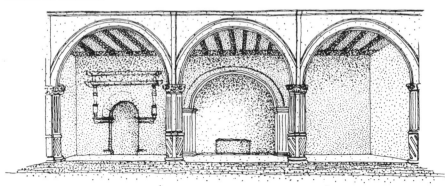

314 THE PORTERÍA CHAPEL AT ERONGARÍCUARO RESTORED

Several important differences need to be classified here. First, *Fr Io METL,* the presumed designer of the church facade at Cuitzeo, was archi-tecturally a mestizo who achieved a handsome creative synthesis between

Spanish design and Indian carving. Second, the designer of the chapel at Cuitzeo was more academic than was Metl, and also more academic than whoever executed his design, for what little is Indian in the chapel is in the details of the execution and not in the basic design. Third, the maker of the chapel at Erongarícuaro avoided stylistic friction between Spanish and Indian not in the synthesizing manner of Metl, but by so reducing the Spanish discipline in the relation of his forms that they were freed for improvisatory and non-European juxtapositions, which might then achieve coherence in a new way. He may have been illiterate in Spanish, but he was rudely eloquent in his own dialect. One cannot believe that the European tradition was close enough to anyone working here for it to have been seen clearly enough to be followed. Therefore, Professor Angulo is probably right in associating Erongarícuaro not with Cuitzeo but with Tzintzuntzan [26] at the other end of Lake Pátzcuaro, for Tzintzuntzan is equally exuberant, equally wayward, stylistically equivalent, and geographically close. Moreover it was at this time the parent house of Erongarícuaro.

The entrance to the monastery building plays only a minor part in the chapel at Erongarícuaro: it is a small door in the left end bay of the portería, set off in a fantastic *alfiz* improvised with oversize plateresque balusters for its sides. While this may at first seem naïve, it need not therefore be called Indian, for the same arrangement occurs in Spain (for example on the side doorway of Santo Domingo at Ubeda); both are not so much illiterate as innocent and provincial, like so much plateresque on both sides of the Atlantic.

315 ERONGARICUARO in 1954

The opening of the apse at Erongarícuaro was three times as wide as the opening of this door, and almost unobstructedly visible, thanks to the lightness and openness of the facade. The main arches of the portico are over 20 feet high, enough to permit a wooden musicians' gallery at the left end. One wonders whether here at Erongarícuaro, and at Teposcolula and Cuernavaca, the broad space at either side of the central bay, if not used for musicians, may not have served, as sometimes did the chancels of monastery churches, as a special place where dignitaries and first families might assist at Mass, symbolically set apart from the ordinary townsfolk outside in the atrio. This was and still is the custom in many villages in Spain, and occasionally, though less commonly, the municipal officers in Mexico are still favored with a special place near the altar. At Erongarícuaro and Teposcolula, such an élite would then have been Indian.

The chapel at Erongarícuaro must be later than 1552, for in that year Philip II refused the Franciscans permission to build a monastery there on the pretext (supplied by anti-Franciscan Bishop Quiroga of Pátzcuaro) that there already was one Franciscan house in the "City of Michoacán" (Quiroga's Pátzcuaro, where the monastery was small and unfinished), and that Erongarícuaro was no more than a suburb (although it was half as big as Cuitzeo, and 15 miles away from Pátzcuaro by water and 20 by land). Its open chapel seems too pretentious for a mere visita, and it probably was not built until Erongarícuaro was established as a monastery, sometime after 1563, and probably after 1571 when it was still called only a *doctrina*. Work may not have begun until a few years after the troublesome Bishop died (1565), and perhaps it was carried out by some of the workmen then released from his big Cathedral project. This would make the chapel a year or two later than the portería at Copándaro, and contemporary or probably a little later than that at Cuitzeo (since the arch order at Erongarícuaro may be a pretentious provincial parody of that at Cuitzeo). All this indicates a date in the 1570's, which may be strengthened by the fact that some sort of construction was surely going on at the monastery in 1575–76, despite the plague. The whole establishment was completed by 1586.[27]

PORTERÍA *OR* PORTERÍA CHAPEL

Portería chapels were not always given an architectural treatment different from that of porterías which were not chapels. Many sixteenth-century porterías look as though they might also have served as chapels, even though they now show no traces of an apse, retable, or other adjuncts of an altar. Even if the now-portería-now-chapel had had a little apse, that could easily disappear during alterations after it had lost its reason for being. To perform as a chapel, a portería need not have had any apse or niche: an altar-pedestal could be set up against the back wall behind one of the arches without affecting any of the architectural elements which have survived its disappearance, and a retable might have been painted on the wall, or have been something movable, foldable, or rollable, which could be set up when needed and taken down and put away when not. After there was no longer use for open chapels as chapels, the liturgical accessories which had made the weekday porterías into Sunday chapels would have been taken away, and need not have left any telltale scars in the stonework. Consequently, one cannot now say from physical evidence alone whether some porterías were ever chapels or not.

The portería at Coyoacán (perhaps built by Fray Lorenzo de la Asunción) appears to be no more than an ordinary portería, but Father Ojea recorded that a friar had been buried "in the chapel of the portico of the portería" in 1603. The chapel was perhaps called back into use because the old church was being repaired after the bad quake of 1588 and was temporarily unusable.[28] Where no similar records give information, the general arrangement may offer suggestions. At Etla (Ñuunduchi, "place of beans") there is a normal four-arched portería in the normal place in front of the monastery block and beside the church. Behind the arch nearest the church a door leads to the cloister as usual; behind the other three arches there are now successively a window, a door, and another window, all of later manufacture.

316 THE PORTERÍA
AT ETLA

The middle arch may once have framed a view of the retable and altar of an open chapel, and the later doorway now there may replace part of a former apse-niche. All the portico arches are broad and high, and the columns are elegantly slender for earthquake country: the visibility of the service would have been ideal. This is, nonetheless, no more than conjecture.

On top of the hill of Tultepec, on the back road from Tultitlán to Ecatepec, there is a small three-arched portería which, for its size, is as rich as any in Mexico. There is no reason why this little visita, hitherto unnoticed, would have so elegant a portería unless it was also to be a setting for the Mass. The carving would not be unseemly for a chapel, but would be presumptuous if it ornamented arches leading only to simple rooms which were hardly ever occupied in a visita so close to its head house (Franciscan Cuautitlán). Tultepec had a curious status for, despite its location only a few miles north of the capital, it was juridically a part of Michoacán, three days' journey to the west. While still an island in the 50-mile lake in which the capital stood, Tultepec had been given its first church by Vasco de Quiroga while he was an *oidor* of the Second Audiencia; when he became Bishop of Michoacán San Pedro Tultepec became part of his See, an island of Michoacán in a lake in the Diocese of Mexico. Sometime later it became a Franciscan visita, and two carved Franciscan emblems show that the portico must have been ornamented then, and that this must have been during the sixteenth century. Perhaps the illustrious patronage of Bishop Quiroga explains the elaborate architecture, but such interest from this constant quarreler with the Franciscans would be surprising at any Franciscan visita. The explanation may be that it was begun and endowed shortly before he died in 1565, and soon afterwards transferred to Cuautitlán and finished by its friars.[29]

At Yuriria and Acatlán, alterations have obscured what might have been evidence but, since remains of the porterías can now explain themselves perfectly well as portería chapels despite the lack of any informative traces of altars or retables, it seems no more arbitrary to accept than reject them. Now that the large four-arched portería at Yuriria has been opened up (1957–58), it appears to be basically more a sixteenth-century than a seventeenth-century work. Although it was repaired and altered in the middle of the seventeenth century, the main arches appear to be of the sixteenth. Despite some recutting, the loss of some carving, and the addition of thick reinforcing arches inside the original arches to hold up a new, heavy, vaulted second story, the portería in its present state looks like some element more spacious and grand than an everyday portería, yet since so much at Yuriria is overtly spacious and grand, these qualities alone are not wholly valid arguments to prove that anything was made to be a functionally useful rather than a luxuriously semi-useless space. On the other hand, since Yuriria was a close ally and friendly rival of equally grand Cuitzeo, a dozen miles away, one may surmise that anything one had the other might have, or hope to have, too. Furthermore, the atrio at Yuriria, like that at Cuitzeo, is huge. (It is now the shadiest laurel-park in Mexico.) There were a great many Indians to fill it — once perhaps 40,000, down to something like 4,500 in 1579 [30] — and an open chapel is surely possible.

There are many equivalent cases. For example the portería arcade at Atlixco (Aaaaa) seems to ask to be de-remodeled back into a portería-and-chapel despite the fact that the Indian congregation is known to have been small. There was, however, a definite and separate Indian congregation (which still had a bilingual priest in the eighteenth century). While the largest arch of the portico, that nearest the church, clearly marks the main entrance to the monastery, the four smaller arches might be made to explain themselves as an extended portería or as a *portal de peregrinos;* but either of these would be half useless here, and the arches seem more reasonably to be the front of an open chapel.[31] The portería is on axis with the atrio gate, but at an angle to the church, and was probably built at a different time from the church, perhaps earlier.

At the end of the seventeenth century Father Vetancurt noted that there was a Mass for Indians in the portería at Cuautitlán concurrent with a Mass for Spaniards inside the church. Since the portería was then serving as a chapel, it may have been built as a chapel in the first place; Father Vetancurt had earlier said that the Indians at Cuautitlán had their own chapel, and that chapel and the portería are probably the same. Later writers, even when they knew their purpose, usually called portería chapels nothing more than porterías: for instance, Father Vetancurt described the chapel at Cuernavaca in detail, and Father Escobar described even the chapel function of the portería chapel at Cuitzeo, in neither case calling them anything but porterías.[32]

One cannot be any more certain about the surviving portería arcades or traces of arcades at Amecameca, Apam, Calpulalpan, Charo, Chiconautla, Ciudad Hidalgo, Santa Clara Coatitla near Ecatepec, Chimalhuacán Chalco, Coatepec Chalco, Mexicalcingo, Molango, Ocuituco, Singuilucan, Teotitlán del Valle, Tepeaca, Tezontepec, Totimehuacán, or Tula; nor at Quecholac, Tecali, or Zacatlán despite the exceptional roominess of the churches there; Tláhuac and more doubtfully Ozumba could have been the same. Raúl Flores Guerrero and others have seen a possible chapel in the ruins of the portería of Calpan, some as a chapel in the portería, some as a chapel elevated above it.[33] There are no other traces of open chapels at these sites.

317 SANTA CLARA COATITLA

Perhaps the lost original portería at Xochimilco, where confessions were held, was also the open chapel which the scale of the congregation and the establishment (including its huge atrio) seems to demand. There were also very large Indian populations in and around Chiconautla and Ciudad Hidalgo, and if the large porterías there did not double as open chapels, then there must have been other open chapels provided somewhere, although no traces show now. At Ciudad Hidalgo, the sixteenth-century monastery church of San

318 CIUDAD HIDALGO

José, though remodeled, still shows itself so small that the friary (founded 1550, church built 1598) could not have operated without some sort of open chapel, unless there was once a larger church there, which is unlikely.[34] The handsome portería is suggestively large. Size alone, without knowledge of the needs of a large Indian congregation, is not a sure sign, however, for there was a long Spanish tradition of large porterías. (That at Las Huelgas near Burgos, for example, has five very big arches, not for use — because there was any numerous congregation outside — but for show — because there were numerous noble nuns inside.) Furthermore, even in Mexico there were very large porterías which surely were not chapels: the one at Tlalmanalco has seven arches and is almost as broad as the huge open chapel on the other side of the church. Such extended porterías were sometimes *portales de peregrinos,* serving for pilgrims attracted to the church by some favorite image or relic.

The porch of the monastery of San Francisco at Campeche, a fragment not swept into the sea with most of the rest of the establishment at the end of the sixteenth century, may once have been a portería chapel, more like a porch than a vestibule. The other early monasteries on the peninsula of Yucatan had open chapels, and it is clear from remains such as those at Izamal, Maní, and Valladolid-Sisal that a greater variety of forms was tried in this element than in any other part of the Yucatecan monasteries. It is known that at Campeche (founded in 1546 perhaps on a different site; church complete before 1562) there was once the common arrangement of a chapel for the Indians with a *ramada,* adjacent to the monastery church used by the Spaniards. Around 1570 there were something like 10,000 adult Indians and only a handful of Spaniards. The Indian chapel must have been passable architecturally, for when the church was wholly wrecked in the seventeenth century, the local Spaniards heard Mass in the chapel; and this must have been an exceptional substitution.[35] While the same thing

595

happened in 1590 at San Francisco in Mexico City, San José de los Naturales was a very much grander Indian chapel than anything imaginable at Campeche. No other certain portería chapels are known in sixteenth-century Yucatan, however, and the arches surviving at Campeche may instead be no more than the remains of a portico that was no more than a portico, like those fronting the churches at Maní and Valladolid-Sisal.

319 THE RUINED PORTERÍA AT CAMPECHE

Perhaps it is not alway necessary to distinguish portería chapel from non-chapel portería, for on occasion an ordinary portería could be drafted into service as a chapel though it had not been built expressly to be one. Such seems to have been the case at San Felipe Ixtacuixtla, an Aztec and Otomí town near Tlaxcala. In 1585 Father Ponce visited it, before he had become very familiar with the functioning of open chapels such as those he was about to see in churchless Tlaxcala and Yucatan. He had just passed Calpulalpan and had called its portería chapel a provisional or "borrowed" church (*de prestado*). Of Ixtacuixtla he said: "The church is not done; next to the portería there is a pretty chapel where Mass is said to the Indians and where the Most Holy Sacrament is kept; it has doors which can be locked with a key for greater safety; outside this chapel there is a big portico which serves as a church where the people congregate." [36] This sounds as though the portico was borrowed by the chapel when needed. The chapel has been rebuilt and domed, and the portico — made one bay deeper — is now the rear half of a strange church five bays wide but only two bays deep. The center transverse row of arches still shows the continuous *alfiz* which must once have been a feature of the portico facade. The whole is so insignificant-looking now that even sharp-eyed Bishop Vera y Zuria, writing about all the churches of his diocese in 1924, went by without noticing it. The big monastery church, unfinished in Ponce's day, has now become a mound of ruins. It must have been abandoned soon after the friars left, when Ixtacuixtla was secularized in 1640; the seculars chose then to build a new church instead of taking over the monastery church, still perhaps unfinished. Once rich, the town like so many others in Tlaxcala became poorer and poorer; it was called "miserable" in 1801.[37]

*

The First and Third Mexican Church Councils (1555, 1585) ordered seculars not to say Mass in the open air.[38] Had they not been doing so, they would not have been told not to, and since they were, they must have had some suitable place: that may have been some sort of single cell, portico, or portería chapel, though almost nothing survives or is known about open chapels at secular parish churches. The triple portico beside the church shown on the plan of Tenango del Valle made in 1582,[39] for example, could be a portería leading to the curate's quarters and no more than that but, topped by a cross as it is, it could as well be a chapel. There are other similar cases, none of them clear. The drawings of Indian towns made by Indian artists are not realistic descriptions but ideographs, intended to show where a church was by means of a symbol rather than to tell what it looked like by a graphic representation. Information about secular chapels is inadequate for any conclusions or generalizations.

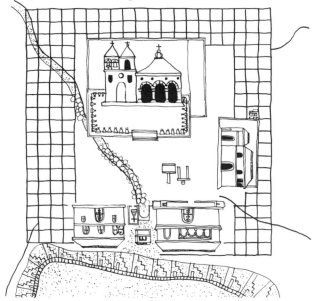

320 TENANGO DEL VALLE (after a map of 1582)

Parish church (with bells in an espadaña) *and portería face an atrio enclosed by a battlemented wall and raised a few steps above the plaza, which has a gallows (indicated with a skull on top) and a column at the foot of which justice was administered. The cross is by the west entrance (as at Acolman), between the mayor's mansion and the arcaded town hall.*

597

XV

A POSTSCRIPT:
TWO UNUSUAL CHURCHES

SPECIAL efforts to solve the architectural problem presented by too many Christian Indians and too few Christian priests resulted in three buildings arrestingly unlike the ordinary types of open chapel: one was the mosque-church of San José de los Naturales in the capital; one is part of the Dominican monastery of Cuilapan in Oaxaca; the third was begun as the Cathedral Church of the Diocese of Michoacán. Since none of the three was primarily or fully an open-air church or chancel-chapel, though each offered an equivalent but divergent answer to the dilemmas which had led to the invention of the open chapel, none can in the strictest sense be classed as an open chapel. Since San José was open across all of its wide front, it has stronger claim than the other two; furthermore, it probably affected the arcaded facades of many true open chapels of the portico type. Each of the other two was unique, unimitated, even freakish, and they can neither be comfortably lumped with the normal open chapels nor comfortably left out. Consequently they are appended here in a postscript.

THE "BASILICA" AT CUILAPAN

Cuilapan (in Náhuatl, Coyolapan, "river of the coyote," in Mixteco, Sahayuco, "at the foot of the mountain") had been a city which the Mixtecas took over from the Zapotecas two centuries before the Spaniards took it over from them. The founders of the Spanish city of Antequera or Oaxaca, eight miles away, hoped to seize Cuilapan and its fertile fields from Cortés to whose Marquisate of the Valley of Oaxaca it had been awarded by the Second Audiencia. The town was not administered by the Cortés family agents like the other towns of the Marquisate but, after a few years as a secular parish, by the Dominicans. They claimed more rights there than Cortés had wanted to give them, but despite many lawsuits the town remained firmly in the Cortés estate, mainly because Charles V for once backed Cortés' claims.

598

The friars moved it from the foot of Monte Albán to the top of a gentle hill near a river, a hill they made gentler by having the Mixtecas slice down its top, and a river they brought nearer by having them move its bed. The site was oddly cut by barrancas, whose meanderings made parts of the town plan irregular. The friars managed to draw such profits from its lands — in pomegranates, dates, figs, silk, and cochineal — that they could undertake to build one of the largest monasteries in Mexico, which they dedicated to the Patron of all Spain, Santiago Matamoros, Saint James the Slayer of Moors. By 1565 it had 24 dependent visitas, and its own aqueduct, reservoir, and flour mill. In 1571 it had 14 farms and ranches of its own, and it shepherded some 30,000 Indians; it was listed in the diocese as second only to the huge Dominican house in Oaxaca itself. Its pleasant walnut groves became a favorite place of recreation for Oaxaqueños on summer evenings. There was also a grove of seventy date palms which made it, like Elche, resemble an oasis, though not in a desert but amid fertile farms. Shorn of its profitable botanical charms, Cuilapan is now just another dusty Indian village, noteworthy only for the ruined hulk of the monastery which, since exclaustration a century ago, has served as a rural school, barracks, and a jail.[1]

Although lavish in adornment and scale, most of its main elements conform to the standard monastery plan. Exceptional features connected with its church are a freestanding bell-tower in back, a long arcaded portico projecting from the front, and — most exceptional and most important — a supplementary church projecting at right angles from its north side. This secondary church is commonly known as the "basilica," and because it is convenient though not exact, this term will be used here to distinguish it from the handsome big monastery church it adjoins.

DATE

The dates of construction at Cuilapan are difficult to fix, but an approximation can be reached. One source tells that a church was begun before 1550, but this may be inaccurate or may not refer to any part of the existing monastery, for the town was probably still a secular parish until about 1548 (so attractive a one that Viceroy Mendoza was interested in acquiring some land there for himself). The Dominicans quickly organized their establishment, which was formally "accepted" in 1550 and formally "founded" in either 1553 or 1555.[2]

A stone set low in the west wall of the basilica is carved with 1555 in Arabic numerals and Mixteca glyphs, and with 1568 in Mixteca alone. This may not, however, be relevant information, for it is not clear what the inscription refers to or certain that the stone (which has been moved at least once) was originally part of the building. Any dating by inscription was rare

321 THE BASILICA AT CUILAPAN *from the dome of the unfinished monastery church*

in sixteenth-century Mexico, and a dated inscription inside a church rarest of all. (Where besides Tula, Cholula, and the Cathedral of Mérida?) According to Father Burgoa and a *Relación* of 1581, the Dominicans began their real mission at Cuilapan in 1555; the town was moved then, and work on the buildings of the monastery was begun the next year. As to many of Father Burgoa's dates, a year or two may be added or subtracted. A firmer date is 1559, when the Dominicans held their Provincial Chapter Meeting in Cuilapan. Since the delegates cannot have slept in the fields or in the Indians' huts, a substantial part of the monastery must already have been fit for them to sleep and meet in. Unless there was acceptable provision they would not have chosen to meet there. Since the main monastery church is unfinished — stopped at cornice height by the Audiencia during a suit with the heirs of Cortés — if there was any usable church other than a thatched shelter for the Chapter in 1559, it must have been the basilica, and it must already have been finished enough to be roofed. Hence 1559 is a possible and fairly plausible terminal date for most of its construction.[3]

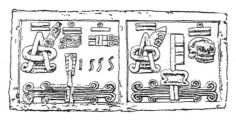

322 THE DATED INSCRIPTION AT CUILAPAN

Another conjecture may fix the beginning. Considerable work on the first building of the Cathedral of Oaxaca came to an end in 1555.[4] Some of the workmen then released may have been taken by the Dominicans to the big project they were beginning at nearby Cuilapan. The unvaulted, three-aisled, columnar Cathedral could have been a model for the unvaulted, three-aisled, columnar basilica. Its aisles are separated by heavy cylindrical columns which could reflect the monolithic shafts of the Cathedral (found worthy of notice as early as 1544). Oaxaca was known for its good stone, easy to cut or carve and available in unflawed blocks big enough for lintels or columns (dramatically demonstrated at the ruins of Mitla). Though clumsily stumpy, and more romanesque than classical in appearance, these columns of the basilica may also reflect one of the plates in Serlio, since except for their round abaci they fumblingly respect the precepts for his simplest column, the Tuscan.[5] (The only surviving church interior which reflects Cuilapan, and thus perhaps the Cathedral, is a clumsy copy at San Juan Teposcolula.)

The friars might have been able to speed their basilica to completion with some of the Cathedral workmen, if they could assign them to some type of work already familiar. The main monastery church was not the same type as the basilica or the Cathedral, and because of its ribbed vaults, well developed moldings, and rich ornamentation, it demanded special skills which could not be summoned into being overnight. Hence it seems reasonable to assume that the basilica was built — at least in its essential parts — between 1555 and 1559, independently of the monastery church.

Not only were the two churches at Cuilapan probably not built at the same time or by the same workmen, they were probably not designed by the same man. The basilica shows such particularity that it cannot be interpolated with the stylistic phases of the rest of the monastic complex. This is true not only of the interior but also of the facade, which exhibits quite a divergent style. If this church was rushed so that the Chapter of 1559 could use it, the ornamenting of the surface of the facade might have been postponed a few years. It is an elaborate frontispiece crisply carved in more or less renaissance plateresque detail. (The main church is late gothic on the inside, provincial *purista* on the outside, and has no plateresque features anywhere.) The facade of the basilica displays engaged columns with swag-draped capitals and a big Dominican heraldic emblem flanked by little Dominican dogs (*Domini cane,* similar to those being carved at about the same time over the door of the Dominican church in Valencia). The scheme underlying this plateresque trimming is not plateresque; instead it seems to echo the round-towered Poitevin facades of romanesque Castile (San Martín de Frómista, or San Isidro de Dueñas) or perhaps renaissance revisions of this scheme (San Salvador at Ubeda). Such connections insist on remaining remote, and any more than accidental relation to a Spanish monument would have to be the result of the nostalgic memories of some Dominican friar-builder, memories not necessarily accurate.

323 The FRONT of the ruined BASILICA at CUILAPAN

324 SERLIO'S "PRISON OF ORLANDO"

The facade may reflect instead the illustration of a fanciful city gate shown by Serlio as "The Prison of Orlando." [6] Besides this and the "Tuscan" columns inside, a few other features at Cuilapan and at some of its neighbors suggest that a copy of Serlio was often consulted — if not always well understood — by someone concerned with Dominican building in the Valley of Oaxaca and the Mixteca. Inasmuch as copies of Serlio are known to have been imported in quantity later in the century, it would not be surprising if one had got to Oaxaca while Cuilapan was building. An example of the Spanish edition of 1552 could have arrived in time to affect the nave columns as well as the facade.

INCONGRUITIES

Study of the ruined building exposes a number of incongruities. Not consistent in style with the adjoining church, the basilica is not stylistically consistent in itself. The plateresque parts of the front find no counterpart in the body of the building, and are particularly disparate with the heavy romanesque-looking nave columns. In their massiveness these are disparate even with their immediate surroundings, the thin and much-pierced outer walls. The emphatic heaviness is less likely the result of someone's memories of romanesque columns, however, than of someone's ill-informed wish to be classical or someone's well-informed precautions against earthquakes, then so much more frequent than now that for generations even the most pretentious Spaniards in the City of Oaxaca did not dare make their palaces more than one story high; by 1580 the quakes had been so strong, so lengthy, and so many that the citizens had dedicated a special chapel to San Marcial, the advocate against them.[7] If this was a consideration, the columns of the basilica may recall not only those of the vanished Cathedral but also the stout cylindrical supports at preconquest Mitla farther down the Valley, exaggeratedly anti-seismic in much of its construction. The columns of Cuilapan withstood all threats until after the Revolution of 1910–20, when the building lost its roof and suffered so many miscellaneous damages that the terrible quake of 1931 was able to shake down half a dozen and weaken others so that several have fallen since. As a result, the building which only in our time has been made a ruin is now as romantically venerable-looking as the mediaeval churches wrecked by Henry VIII, who may have been pulling them down while this was being put up.

325 CUILAPAN
Colonnade of east aisle of the basilica, looking south to the main monastery church

In addition to such stylistic and structural incongruities, there appear to be functional ones. There seems now to be no sanctuary, though in the late seventeenth century Father Burgoa saw one "handsomely adorned with a retable," and covered with a "beautiful ribbed vault." [8] This sanctuary can be recovered, fortunately, in a ribbed vault with four pineapple pendants over a dark square chapel to the left of the main monastery church. The nave of the basilica now ends in a broad, high, bricked-up archway whose springing coincides with the springing of this fancy vault on its other side. At the bottom, three steps, such as were commonly used to raise the sanctuary above the nave, still show on the basilica side, leading up to the level of the floor beneath the vault beyond the wall. Clearly the chapel was once the sanctuary of the basilica. The vault does not look like anything else in the basilica, but does look like gothic work in the unfinished main church. Since the chapel is embedded in the main church complex, it could have been built by the designer of that church rather than by the designer of the basilica. Like the facade, it need not have been made at exactly the same time as its nave.

Some of the other peculiarities are less easy to explain. The pulpit is oddly set half way down the nave and not by the chancel where a priest would traditionally have stood during his sermon, facing a congregation facing him. The sermon was considered to be of particular importance for new converts, and the Dominicans in Mexico, like their brothers in Europe, were particularly noted for their preaching. As the Cuilapan Indians would have been standing in the nave and aisles during the sermon, they could all have turned phonotropically on their axes to face a pulpit in their midst. No one's ears would then have had to be so far away from the preacher's lips as half would have been if he were in a pulpit at the end of the nave. Such a dislocation of the pulpit for audio-visual advantage might seem like contemporary practice in Reformation Germany where there was equal if not greater stress on sermons and where the pulpit was often set in the center of the congregation. But it is so difficult to see how or why German practice would come to the

Valley of Oaxaca that the arrangement there seems more likely to be the result of a long-established Mendicant custom, to be seen for example at San Petronio in Bologna, where a big movable wood pulpit is still kept half way down the nave. Even so, it seems less likely that the placing of the pulpit was determined by functional reasoning than from unreasoning habit; for while the nave is long, it is so narrow that no sizable crowd could ever find room to gather about its pulpit. Functionally the location cannot have met the needs.

There are other incongruities. The basilica is long (13 bays, 215 feet) but its nave is narrow (24 feet). The arches of the nave arcade which are nearest the chancel are larger than the others. They cannot have been made larger as part of any arrangement for the choir, as one might guess, for Father Burgoa recorded that the choir was somewhere else, "in the middle, as in a cathedral." [9] (Small column bases in the fourth bay must be remains of its stone furnishings. It blocked the narrow free area near the main portal from joining the only slightly less pinched area around the pulpit and chancel.) A "choir as in a cathedral" would have justification in a cathedral with many canons who chanted sacred offices almost all day, or in a big monastery church where friars did the same, but there would be no call for such a

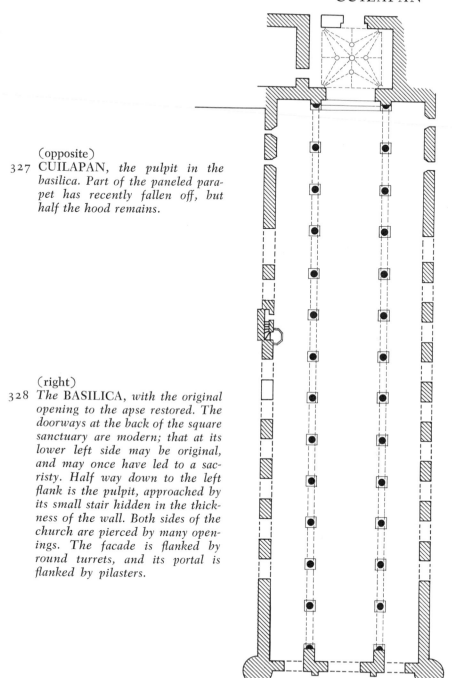

(opposite)
327 CUILAPAN, *the pulpit in the basilica. Part of the paneled parapet has recently fallen off, but half the hood remains.*

(right)
328 *The* BASILICA, *with the original opening to the apse restored. The doorways at the back of the square sanctuary are modern; that at its lower left side may be original, and may once have led to a sacristy. Half way down to the left flank is the pulpit, approached by its small stair hidden in the thickness of the wall. Both sides of the church are pierced by many openings. The facade is flanked by round turrets, and its portal is flanked by pilasters.*

choir in a supplementary church made for the passive needs of an Indian congregation rather than for the active needs of chanting friars. The reason here must be that the main monastery church, which would have been for the friars, was never finished, and their needed choir was put here instead, as an afterthought, without fresh thinking how to adjust it to its new context. This choir may be another echo of that lost first Cathedral and, if it is, the larger arches may also be an echo: they may open the space of the nave to a transept which is not there.

Above the nave arcade on either side are four small windows, which open from high in the nave to high in the aisles. They admit no light or air because they are below both nave and aisle roofs (which the end walls show to have been of different pitches with no clerestory between). They led only from indoors to indoors. They may be meaningless repetitions of real clerestory windows in the Cathedral, or they may have been made meaningless only at the last minute from some change in the roofing scheme, perhaps related to the upper part of the facade then being completed.

ARCADED FLANKS

The most curious problem is presented by the long outside walls. That of the west flank, facing the atrio, is pierced by nine arched openings, plain, without moldings for archivolts or imposts, and without cuttings to receive doors. Opposite, in the east wall, there is a series of identical openings, but only eight, since the pulpit and its stair block the place of one. In striking disagreement, the three generous openings in the adjacent plateresque facade have elaborately molded jambs and reveals, carefully rabbeted to receive big doors; the holes for their pivots are also still visible.

329 THE BASILICA *looking north from west flank. The arches lead from the atrio to the right-hand aisle. The turret at the end contains a spiral stairway.*

330
THE BASILICA, *looking north from the end of the east aisle, toward the inside of the facade, showing the spur wall ending in an engaged half-column. The bull's-eye window recalls Serlio's "Prison of Orlando"* (ill. 324).

The spacing of these doorways in the long sides does not correspond to that of the openings of the nave arcades next to them. They are too out of phase with one another to be reconciled; nine doorways take the same space as eight intercolumniations plus a narrow extra fraction. Perhaps the lateral walls were built first, without much forethought about the arcades which would go inside, and later a different foreman rushing the church to completion, divided the nave neatly into equal bays with an extra wide one at the sanctuary end and two little spur walls at the other end, butting into the back of the facade. These spur walls were not, as one might suppose, intended to help support a choir balcony unless that choir "in the middle" was an afterthought which took the place of a choir balcony abandoned for it. The change in the thickness of these walls half way up suggests a change in program when the facade was half way up. Perhaps the spurs were intended to stiffen the facade, which is taller and thinner than the side walls, but this was hardly necessary when the facade was flanked by such stout turrets and when the long unstiffened side walls could stand safely despite their repeated piercing.

An inadequate explanation for some of these incongruities was given in 1670 by Father Burgoa, the most prolix, self-indulgent, and disordered of the Mexican religious chroniclers: "There is in the patio of the church another second one, which was made wider and longer, also all of masonry, with lengths of wall made of open arches so that the multitudes of people who have come to Catechism may enter easily; it is of three naves, with heavy marble columns and a beamed ceiling; the choir is in the middle, as in a cathedral which it resembled from all over the valley . . . Because of the lack of people, and the troubles which come from distrust and suspicion, the openings of the arches were walled up outside, leaving empty spaces inside adequate for chapels, which were all adorned with altars of Saints for the devotions of the natives." [10]

Although longer and more detailed than any chronicler's description of any equivalent building except San José de los Naturales and the chapels at Tlaxcala and Calkiní, this is unclear and inaccurate. The columns are not marble; they do not even look like marble. (Professor Kubler has suggested that by *marmol* Burgoa meant "column," and thus generously excuses him.) [11] In view of Father Burgoa's many other carelessnesses with facts, the rest of his remarks must be also taken with generous dubiety until they can be confirmed by others or by the evidence of the building itself. Conscientious Father José Antonio Gay, who wrote in the 1870's while the basilica was still in regular use, saw the arches of the flanks still closed, and thus confirmed some of what Father Burgoa had written two hundred years before.[12] A few old people in the village said they remembered (1947) going to Mass in the building fifty years ago, when it still had a roof, but were uncertain whether the arches were then walled or open. (Inasmuch as the church was being used, one may suppose that it was walled.) After it was despoiled during the Revolution it had to be abandoned as a place of worship. Half of the big unfinished church was then patched — in part with material taken from the basilica — and some of the altars were salvaged and moved into the new makeshift.[13] The bricks from the side arches must have been taken out at this time, and some used to fill the chancel arch. Unfortunately none of the local reminiscences can be verified, and nothing — local memories or published texts — yet explains why so many arches were put in the flanks of the basilica in the first place.

*

A crowd from the atrio could easily enter the building through the nine doorless doorways, as Father Burgoa pointlessly pointed out: in fact they could easily come in through fewer. Subdivided into groups suitable for teaching, they could have entered the basilica in successive shifts to attend successive Masses. Father Burgoa said they came *into* the basilica for catechizing, however, which would have been contrary to the sixteenth-century practice of rehearsing Catechism in the atrio; but since he was writing more than a century later and did not state unequivocally just what had been done where, it may be that he did not know. Whether catechized in the atrio or not, all the local Indians could not have attended one Mass, for at the time the basilica was built the town was too large, 15,000 to 30,000 (now only 5,000).[14] As the long narrow building would hold only about 1,500 or perhaps 2,000 with crowding and some overflow, there would have had to be ten or more Masses every Sunday. Priests in Spain were limited to one Mass a day; friars in New Spain could say more, and they must have said more here; but ten in one place would have been improbable.

Not only are there these nine openings to the atrio, there are eight identical openings in the other wall. Indians had easy access through the nine doorways from the atrio, but why equivalent egress opposite? When both sides were unalterably open, why did the basilica have closable wooden doors in the facade between them?

It might be thought that with one flank giving onto an atrio which was walled and the other flank onto a garden which was also walled, neither side wall of the basilica itself would need to be able to be closed as yet another barrier against the extra-monastic world. The outer circuit of walls might already give enough protection. This would presuppose that the facade, being lockable, faced some public space outside the monastery complex and its walls. A road might have run past the facade, and the monastery walls might have run along this road to join the corners of the facade. Everything could then be explained and justified except one archway next to the pulpit which shows pivots for big doors. Such a hypothesis, however, does not survive scrutiny.

Father Burgoa's statement that the basilica was "*in* the patio" of the church of the monastery would deny it, and this is a statement which can be corroborated on the spot. Battered foundations mark the location of a posa and of the northwest corner of an atrio, which extended a couple of hundred feet in front of the facade and a similar distance in front of the facade of the other church. A few old villagers still remember a *capillita* with an altar inside, which stood a couple of hundred feet in front of the northeast corner of the basilica, in the northeast corner of the present all-purpose atrio-cornfield-cemetery; old photographs in the files of the *Dirección de Monumentos Coloniales* show a small, shapeless, confirmatory hump of rubble there. The *capillita* must have been another ex-posa, and it marked another corner of the atrio. A cross on a ruined base of masonry like that of the first ruined posa stands just where the old atrio cross ought to have stood in relation to the two posas and basilica. An eighteenth-century drawing (Escorial *ms* F 340R) shows the whole monastery in summary synopsis, set well inside a complete circuit wall which agrees with the atrio wall predicated by the posas. The

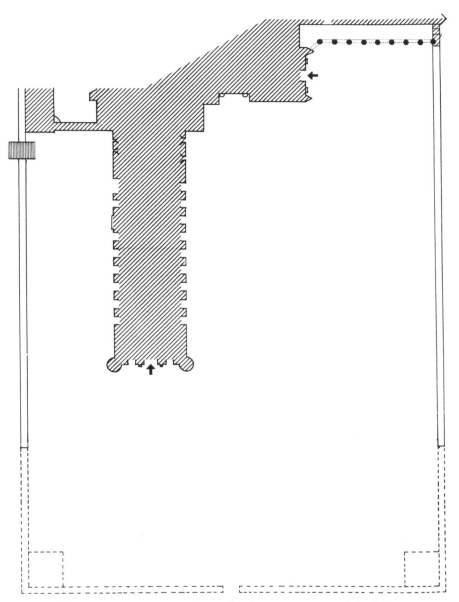

331 THE ATRIO AT CUILAPAN, with adjacent conventual buildings.

The old north wall of the atrio and the two corner posas are shown at the bottom by dotted lines. The basilica projects into the atrio, and west of it (at the right) is a corner of the big monastery church. Beyond its facade, which faces west in normal fashion, is the portería, closing the south end of the atrio.

original atrio, it now is clear, was L-shaped, bent around the long west and short north sides of the basilica, approximately coterminous with the dusty atrio-cornfield-cemetery of today. The facade with the lockable doors stood not on any public road but back inside the atrio, then prettily planted with quincunxes of orange and small coconut trees watered by the monastery's private aqueduct.[15]

The plausible explanation is that the facade openings were the only public entrance left when the side openings were bricked in, and at that time their jambs were rabbeted to receive doors. The single rabbeted doorway by the pulpit would have been a private entrance for friars taking a rear shortcut from the monastery. The lockable wooden doors would have been precautions against those "troubles which come from distrust and suspicion" mentioned by Father Burgoa as a reason for closing the side openings. If the main monastery church was never going to be finished, as must already have been clear, and the basilica was going to serve the now reduced congregation regularly, there may have been a decision to make it into a more normal church by walling it in. Then it could be locked and safely left with its consecrated ara, reserved Host, and sacred vessels, without fear of desecration by human or animal marauders.

*

While this can explain how there came to be adjacent openings with and without provision for doors, it does not explain their extraordinary number. Since not all 20 openings $(9 + 3 + 8 = 20)$ can be functionally justified as doorways, it must be doubted they were all planned for human traffic. It could be that the basilica was conceived as an open shed, a half-outdoor church, roofed but half wall-less because of the climate, a monumental stone equivalent of the wood *ramadas* used in hot Yucatan and other hot regions.

Although such a half-open stone church may seem freakish now, in the sixteenth century it would not have been unique in the region, for the unpublished, unlovely, and all-but-unknown Dominican churches at Tequisistlán and Nejapa, in hotter country southeast of Cuilapan, both had side walls similarly perforated.

Tequisistlán was a "conventico," a small mission for the Chontal Indians set in a tropical valley, beside the Tehuantepec River in what Father Burgoa, whose family seat it was, vaingloriously found "like Hebron in its deliciousness," with plenty of parrots, and crops of chocolate, vanilla, coconuts, and bananas. It drew off a substantial part of the population of equally hot Jalapa del Marqués, of which it had once been a visita; as it grew larger it came to need a new and larger church. One was built in the last quarter of the sixteenth century, though by that time the town had dropped from 2000 to 640 Indian families, plus the inhabitants of half a dozen dependent villages.[16]

UNUSUAL CHURCHES

Santiago de Nejapa (Yutanuyaa, "river of ash") had been founded earlier, in about 1550 or '60, to protect the Tehuantepec highway from the untamed Mixes and Chontales (who were holding out against Christianity because they could not understand its God, who not only allowed them no fun after working hours, but also did nothing to the Spaniards who maltreated them and even kept the converts from Mass). The thirty founding Spanish families who had been moved down to Nejapa from the Villa Alta de San Ildefonso soon went back because — they said — of the sudden cold winds. This must have been a fabricated pretext because, according to the natives, cold winds do not blow in hot Nejapa. The Dominicans began a "sumptuous church" in 1560. The adjoining monastery must have been well along by 1561 because five or six friars were already living in it.[17] Turncoat friar Thomas Gage, working to make everything in southeastern Mexico sound like bait for an English conquest, claimed in 1626 that the monastery was "very rich" and the town "absolutely one of the wealthiest." Jesuit Father Cobo found it hot in 1630, and remarked that the monastery was all vaulted (which cannot have been true, as one can see today). The town was busy with trade in indigo, sugar, and cochineal until ravaged by a plague in 1736. (It has never recovered.) In the old church there are traces of an early barrel vault above the lower substitute which now covers the nave. This first nave vault had already collapsed by 1670 when Father Burgoa saw a termite-riddled wood ceiling on what with shameless local patriotism he called "one of the most capacious and beautiful churches in the Province." It had showy retables of termite-repelling cedar, and these must have impressed him, for the architecture could not.[18] It had, nevertheless, other unusual features he did not note.

Both here and at Tequisistlán there are heavy arcades along the flanks, whose masonry runs through the thickness of the walls and shows its arches on the inside face. The arcades at Nejapa are of an aqueduct-like heaviness on the south side, easily able to carry and buttress their original vault. They are lighter on the north, where the mass of the cloister could help buttress. They are such an abnormal support for a nave vault, and must have called for so much more material and skilled labor to build, that someone must have had an insistent wish to have them instead of an ordinary, simple, plain wall. No one would go to the expense and trouble of building such arcades if they had been intended to be walled up from the beginning. These churches must once have had open flanks similar to Cuilapan, perforated for cross-ventilation. Neither Burgoa, Gage, nor Cobo pointed out such use, but perhaps it was not then enough of a novelty in the region to have seemed worth noting.

There are other examples of similar planning for heat in the Dominican south. The church at Ostata in Chiapas has six doors on each side,[19] surely put there more to admit refreshing breezes than Chiapanecas easily able to

614

go in and out the front door in the usual way. The monastery building at hot Jalapa del Marqués is laid out as an H, doubtless to gain maximum perimeter and cross-ventilation (ill. 239). There were eighteenth-century churches with arcaded flanks in Haiti,[20] and there may be one at San Germán in Puerto Rico. (Within the past dozen years churches with ventilating open flanks have been built at Cataño, Puerto Rico, and Varadero, Cuba.)

What might appear at first to be similar construction at Etla, just north of Cuilapan and Oaxaca, was not built as an open flank for the church. After the collapse of some temporary construction during the performance of an allegorical play in the atrio of the old church, a new church was begun, 500 paces up the hill. The Indians made the main body of this new church (complete before 1586) so big that they thought spanning it with a vault would be unsafe. To reduce the span of the nave they built deep arcades inside the already completed walls, forming side chapels. Now narrowed and precautiously ready for a vault with irreproachable support and buttressing, the nave was not given one: the natives (frightened by a recent quake?) called a Spanish carpenter from Oaxaca to make a thrustless and relatively weightless wooden ceiling, a mudéjar *artesonado* "with moldings so delicate that they looked as though made of wax." [21] At nearby Huitzo (then still called Guaxolotitlán), this chapel-forming arcade was soon imitated on the north wall of the monastery church, presumably as a brace (again for fear of quakes?). In the 1950's the opposite wall was given a similar arcade, for the sake of symmetry, and the nave was then covered with a new barrel vault, with the result that the interior of Huitzo now looks as Etla was once intended to look.

The archways in the flanks of the basilica at Cuilapan are plain, with no moldings marking imposts or archivolts. They thus make striking contrast to everything else, particularly to the elaborately carved facade and to the big church adjoining. The archways look like something of simple utilitarian function, such as ventilation, rather than important portals through which the faithful were to enter the House of God. Even if the freshly catechized Indians in the atrio could and probably did enter the basilica through them, the real doorways in the traditional and symbolic if not the utilitarian sense were certainly those in the proper facade.

AN OPEN CHAPEL?

Even though it was so open across its west flank, and even though it was recognized as a church for Indians by Burgoa, the basilica was not, as has sometimes been said, intended to be an open chapel: it is a complete church and not an augmented sanctuary to an atrio. No crowd in the atrio could witness the celebration of a Mass *in* the building, for its sanctuary and its altar were around a corner and out of sight. From the atrio they might have heard something of the music made by the choir "in the middle," but sermons preached from the pretty pulpit, even reinforced by its little accoustical hood, could hardly have reached many of them intelligibly across the intervening aisle and through the arches in the outer wall. It cannot have been an open chapel because even with its many openings it was not open enough. Furthermore it was not big enough for the local population for whom it would have been made. The question arises whether some other provision may not have been made for them, perhaps with a more usual scale and relationship of chapel and atrio.

332 THE MONASTERY CHURCH AND PORTERÍA AT CUILAPAN

From the south corner of the facade of the unfinished church projects a portico which runs west, at right angles to the facade, marking the south end of one arm of the L-shaped atrio. It may have had more than one use: an entrance porch to the monastery behind, a porch for pilgrims or *racionero* (like those of Tochimilco, Cholula, and San Francisco at Puebla), and perhaps also an open chapel. If it was a chapel, the monastery at Cuilapan was arranged with three different places for public celebration of the Mass: the main church, the basilica, and this portería chapel. Since the main church was not finished, only two of the three can have been used, and two would be normal. Since the basilica and portico are unlike the big church in style and like each other, they are probably products of the same workmen and the same building campaign. That might mean that two places were made for

616

Indian Masses and none for the regular conventual Masses the friars were obligated to celebrate daily. Unless the friars intended the basilica for themselves from the beginning, which is improbable, *if* the portico was also a chapel, it became so as an afterthought. The role intended for the basilica may have changed while it was building — the big church planned from the beginning having been abandoned half finished — and this shift in function may have led to unforeseen changes elsewhere in the building, changes which resulted in some of the inconsistencies still so striking. The extreme length and the location of the pulpit and choir could be the result of some improvised changes in the program of work not yet completed.

The portico by the big church might then have been adapted to serve as a portería chapel, with its one larger arch (that adjoining the church) leading to the door of the monastery in the usual way, and the remaining arches defining a portico chapel at one end of the atrio arm also in the usual way. No traces of an apse or verifiable holes in the back wall for the support of a retable confirm this, but such are not necessary. The limits of the role of this portico, whether portería, *racionero,* or chapel, cannot any longer be precisely determined. It surely was the first; it may also have been either the second or the third; perhaps it was all three.

DOMINICAN DESIGNERS IN OAXACA

There is enough documentary and circumstantial evidence to encourage exploration into questions of the authorship of the design of the basilica and its relation to other buildings, but not enough to arrive at sure answers.

According to Father Burgoa, the town was moved by Fray Domingo de Aguiñaga, a youthful friend of Ignatius Loyola who had come to Mexico soon after the Conquest and had taken the Dominican habit in 1539. Known for both his learning and his manual skill — he could repair clocks and he could sew — he must also have been an effective organizer of labor, for he directed the moving of the town half a league and the moving of the river. With an independent mind inexperienced in architecture (he came to Mexico in his teens), he could have been the author of the main lines of the basilica and could have carried out a good part of it — Father Burgoa said that he "began, and gave form and splendor to this town and monastery" — before he was transferred to Yanhuitlán in 1559, where he might also have been responsible for some of the work. (The language spoken at the two towns was identical.) He rose in the hierarchy to become *provincial, vicario general,* and confessor to the Viceroy. At Cuilapan he was succeeded by Fray Bernardo de Alburquerque, who had already supervised building at Tehuantepec. Having been trained at architecturally sophisticated San Esteban at Salamanca, Father Alburquerque may have had tastes more elaborate than anything realized at Tehuantepec except perhaps the minor feature of the paneled buttresses. Such tastes would have been more elaborate than anything at the basilica except its facade and stone furniture (pulpit, stoups, choir). Father Alburquerque cannot, however, have given much time to the works there because he was busy serving as Bishop-elect of Oaxaca in the years he was at Cuilapan. There is little reason to connect him with any of the design.[22]

*

Accompanying him at Cuilapan was a Portuguese lay brother named Antonio Barbosa. "The best architect who has been seen in these parts," "very ingenious," "expert in carpentry and architecture, he served his Order and Province admirably in building monasteries and churches . . . working on them with his own hands," according to Fathers Burgoa and Franco.[23] As he died in 1608 when he was nearly a hundred, he must have been in his late twenties or very early thirties when he arrived in Mexico about 1541, and consequently, though he may have had some sort of youthful training in Spain, he cannot have had much practical experience there. (Father Burgoa considered that he was "without previous experience.") Before joining the Dominicans in 1548, he worked for a few years in Campeche as a carpenter, and this suggests that his training — if any — may have been in carpentry rather than in building.[24]

While nothing still visible in the main church or the monastery block at Cuilapan betokens an ex-carpenter or ex-Portuguese, signs of both appear in the interior of the basilica. The peculiar location of the pulpit has Portuguese antecedents, and its panels and moldings suggest wood joinery more than stone masonry. This might seem to conflict with the supposition that the basilica was built largely from 1555/56 to 1559, for Father Barbosa arrived in Cuilapan with Father Alburquerque only in 1559. He might, however, have been asked to work on the stone furnishings of a building which had already been carried well along by Father Aguiñaga. The pulpit would have been made only after the walls were well up, and it may be an unprepared interpolation, for the pulpit together with its little stairway is neatly fitted into the space of one of the doorless doorways, and would probably not have been fitted into that precise space as a new construction unless the opening was there already. The pulpit may postdate the Chapter Meeting of 1559. Since Father Barbosa came to Cuilapan from Tehuantepec with Father Alburquerque who had been supervising building there, it is possible that the odd joinery-style paneling on the buttresses of the open chapel at Tehuantepec was a late embellishment in the work there but an early effort in the architectural career of Father Barbosa. As such paneling was not common in New Spain, the relation may be a real one. (The equivalent paneling on the buttresses at Teposcolula was made later, around 1570.)

Sometime in the second half of the sixteenth century a Gallego friar named Agustín de Salazar pushed the building campaign with energy. He was said to have inspired the Indians to work "like angels" and "as though of their own free will." But as he, like Father Alburquerque, came from San Esteban at Salamanca, if he had anything to do with the design of Cuilapan, it might have been for the sophisticated main church, the handsome cloister, or perhaps the plateresque facade of the basilica. There seems to be no reason to connect him with the rest of the basilica or with the portería.[25]

*

As well as these different men who can be conjecturally involved in the design of Cuilapan, there are several different stylistic episodes which can be distinguished in it. If trained workmen came from the early Cathedral of Oaxaca in 1555, some of the details at Cuilapan would reflect its style, but just what that was is hard to see since the building has been destroyed. Many episodes which presumably reflect it — moldings, round bases and capitals, stubby shafts — as well as the unornamented and strictly architectural character of the interior, seem to herald the more mature style of Coixtlahuaca and Teposcolula, a day or two's journey over the mountains. Together all these might constitute the evidence for a Dominican "School of the Lost Cathedral of Oaxaca."

Proto-Teposcolula, plateresque, pseudo-romanesque, and Serliesque, the basilica is richly mongrel, unlike the elegant church and monastery it adjoins, where there is nothing at all of the "School of the Lost Cathedral" except the portico of the portería. This and the nave of the basilica, both ill-assimilated into the rest of the general scheme, are likely the creations of the same amateur, who could have come from some old-fashioned and severe provincial house in Spain, or could have had uncomprehending access to a copy of Serlio. Much of the determinedly elementary vocabulary of the nave and portico is similar to that in other Dominican houses of the region: in many details of Etla, in the cloisters of Coixtlahuaca and Huitzo, in a few parts of Tlaxiaco, of the chapel of Tehuantepec, and even of the lower parts of the chapels of Coixtlahuaca and Teposcolula (in slightly awkward incidentals easily separable from what is so expert there). It is easy to imagine a crew of masons — some of whom had worked earlier on the Cathedral — passed from house to house among the actively building Dominicans of Oaxaca for twenty or twenty-five years. In addition, drawings by the architecturally sophisticated may have been passed from house to house and eventually to the hands of the architecturally innocent. Some of the most innocent of all were at Cuilapan, for surely there can be few buildings as pure in design as the large church there which are as wayward in their stereotomy (ill. 47).

UNUSUAL CHURCHES

Although such naïve detail is a regional characteristic of Dominican Oaxaca, none of it appears in the handsomest of the contemporary churches of the region, Yanhuitlán and Coixtlahuaca. Here is sensed instead a different and far more sensitive hand, a hand not manifest in the basilica, even on its facade, though perhaps it is traceable in the big unfinished church.

*

Thus most of the principal Dominican buildings of Oaxaca are interwoven in a net of possible stylistic relationships, with only the facade of the basilica and all of Santo Domingo in the City of Oaxaca apart from it — the first perhaps and the second surely the work of a later generation. It is possible to unravel some of the main strands in this network. There seem to be three artistic personalities: *first,* the "Master of Teposcolula," responsible for the fountain at Chiapa de Corzo (as an early work), the open chapel at Coixtlahuaca, and the open chapel at Teposcolula; *second,* the "Master of Yanhuitlán," responsible for the fine church at Yanhuitlán, the equally fine church at Coixtlahuaca, the unfinished monastery church at Cuilapan perhaps, and also its cloister; *third,* the "Master of Cuilapan," not trained as an architect, possibly Domingo de Aguiñaga (less likely Antonio Barbosa), responsible for the nave of the basilica at Cuilapan and the portico by the facade of the big church there.

*

This by no means accounts for everything. Equally important may be a "School" consisting of crews of workmen from the Cathedral of Oaxaca, responsible for many similar details on the basilica and portico of Cuilapan, and many details at Etla, at most of Huitzo, at the monastery block and cloister at Coixtlahuaca, and at a few subordinate parts of Yanhuitlán, Teposcolula, and Tlaxiaco; and when they were very tired they might have built the visita church of San Juan Teposcolula. This group or entity could be called the "School of the Lost Cathedral of Oaxaca" as has already been said.

*

Without knowing better the conditions out of which the basilica grew, we cannot entirely understand it now (as is much more often true in the study of the history of architecture than is commonly recognized). We need to know but cannot be quite sure for what it was intended or how it was used, in what order it was built, and if, how, when, or why it was altered. It does not appear to be a building which was well enough thought out for its particular functions to give clear clue now as to what its functions were. Moreover, its functions almost surely were changed while it was being built. Usages must have been unusual, and the building is unusual; but we cannot match the unknown unusual usages to the known unusual shape.

> In órder to pacify these natives, and to attract and not frighten
> them, in my opinion we should not fight them but instead seek
> them out. More effective than the rigors and inhumanities of war,
> slavery, and ransom, would be the fodder of good works, once the
> natives had been sought out, and thereafter converted, cherished,
> and kept in the fold.   — Bishop Vasco de Quiroga [26]

The most peculiar of all the solutions to the problem which had produced
the outdoor church was that proposed by the aged Bishop of Michoacán, don
Vasco de Quiroga. The immediate conditions — physical, spiritual, financial,
and political — are better known than at Cuilapan, as there is more documentary information for Bishop Vasco's Cathedral than for any other building of the sixteenth century in Mexico except the Cathedral in the capital.
Thanks to this, a building even less normal than the basilica at Cuilapan can
be better understood.

QUIROGA'S HOSPITALS: UTOPIA IN NEW SPAIN

The most important years of Vasco de Quiroga began in his sixties, after
he had arrived in New Spain. Earlier he had served in the Audiencia at
Valladolid, and although not an ordained cleric but a Doctor of Canon Law,
he had served also in some capacity at the Cathedral of Granada. Because
of his distinguished legal career, he was named to the Second Audiencia of
Mexico, with which he arrived in México-Tenochtitlán in January 1531.
Shrewd in the investigations of the malfeasances of the First Audiencia conducted by the Second, he soon showed another side of his character as an
advocate and compassionate friend of the Indians. He went so far in their
behalf as to remind the Emperor that the royal claim to America, based on a
papal grant, was predicated not on the exploitation but *only* on the evangelization of the natives.

Don Vasco quickly understood the Indians' plight, acute at this time,
and within a year of his arrival he acted with great resourcefulness to alleviate it: by founding a model Christian community or "hospital" in the hills
near the capital. After a trip to investigate a report of the discovery of gold
in Michoacán — the mines turned out to be inferior — and a sight of the
ravages wreaked by Nuño de Guzmán in the region, he took some restitution
upon himself by founding another Christian "hospital" there (1534).

333 ACÁMBARO   334 URUAPAN

HOSPITAL CHAPELS

A number of large and handsome charity hospitals had recently been built in Spain under the patronage of Ferdinand and Isabella. The Aztecs had had big hospitals before the Spaniards came, with staff doctors some thought superior to their European counterparts. With this dual heritage it was natural that hospitals should soon have been built in Mexico. Not only the sick but often the destitute were given shelter in them. Cortés' Hospital de Jesús was the first, and the friars' first was probably at Uruapan, founded by Fray Juan de San Miguel in the 1520's. Thanks to its well-made buildings, put up a generation later, it is one of the best preserved. It was soon imitated not only at other Franciscan but at Augustinian monasteries, and in hospital-conscious Michoacán, even at parish churches. Hospitals were soon established at Veracruz and halfway along the highway to the capital for those suffering from the effects of the new climate and new diet. Many more were built during and following the plague of 1545. The Church Council of 1555 — which don Vasco attended — went so far as to order one constructed in every town where a church had been built, and subsequently hospitals were ordered for every town in Michoacán (1563, 1571). Villages of less than five hundred Indians often had their own hospitals. Some establishments could care for as many as four hundred people, and some served also as hospices. From the remains in Michoacán, or at establishments such as those at Tlaxcala or Oaxtepec, it is to be surmised that the hospital had no standardized architectural scheme equivalent to that of the monastery, though some, such as Cortés' Hospital de Jesús or the Guatapera at Uruapan, were elaborated in special architectural treatment, and others, such as that at Acámbaro, were given their own attractive chapels.

622

Even in a land so rich in hospitals, the two founded by Vasco de Quiroga were exceptional. He bought the land for them, and sold his clothes, his sheep, and other worldly goods for funds to launch them. Both were called Santa Fe, *Santa Fe de México* in the hills southwest of the capital where there were exceptionally abundant springs, and *Santa Fe de la Laguna* at one end of Lake Pátzcuaro. Both were entirely practical in their operations, and at the same time untrucklingly idealistic in their program. Some saw them as a renewal of the spirit of the early Apostolic Church and, while don Vasco was surely sympathetic to such an idea, the immediate basis for the ordinances on which they were run was not so old. It was radically modern: it was the *Utopia* of Saint Thomas More. There were several editions he could have read, Louvain 1516, Paris 1516–17, Basel 1518. Perhaps he used Bishop Zumárraga's copy (now preserved at the University of Texas). Chancellor More was a scholar, a lawyer, a statesman, and a profoundly religious man, in several ways like Magistrate Quiroga, who admired him as "an illustrious man of more than human genius." Having read Vespucci's descriptions of the New World, More had referred to America several times, and had implied that his ideal state was not far from it. Prompted perhaps by these references (as Silvio Zavala showed some years ago), don Vasco chose Sir Thomas for his guide. In Europe the *Utopia* was considered a politico-philosophical speculation, a serious fantasy, anything but a practical manual for running a big community. Instead of turning to More, perhaps the loftiest Christian political idealist of the Renaissance, many contemporaries who wanted a practical guide for running such an enterprise might have turned to someone more pragmatic — such as Macchiavelli.

Originally intended for over 60,000, but of necessity reduced to half that, each hospital was a model Christian socialist colony, a school for vocational and humanistic studies, an orphanage, old people's home, and hospital in the modern sense. The social unit was the family, in clan-like clusters of about 40, each ruled by a patriarch. One of don Vasco's reasons for founding the first establishment had been to provide a home and work for the Indian youths trained in the friars' schools, youths who might revert to their parents' ways if returned to their parents' homes. Boys were married at 14, girls at 12, and they lived with the young husband's clan. As in Utopia the women and girls wove and tailored everyone's clothes, all of unadorned natural white cotton or wool, and all alike to avoid the sin of envy. The women had to cover their bodies to the elbow and cover their heads; the men had to wear trousers to the knees.

Everyone spent alternately two years on communal farms and two years in community buildings in the town. As in Utopia everyone worked for six hours a day — men and women, old and young — and the products of their labor were distributed free, according to individual needs. Part of any sur-

623

plus was saved for hard times, and the rest distributed outside the hospital to orphans, widows, and the sick. Property was communal, and the hospital itself was the owner of all lands and cattle. Families were permitted small private gardens, with usufruct but not ownership of the land.

Plainsong and other religious music was taught to the whole community, and they sang many times during the day and night, often accompanying themselves on instruments they had made in the hospital workshops. On great holidays there were community banquets for general religious rejoicing, like the *agapes* of the early Church. There was a variety of organized religious activities all the time, supervised by a resident curate. (The first one at Santa Fe de México was Fray Alonso de Borja, close kinsman of Pope Alexander VI and Saint Francis Borgia.) Remarkable enough to us now, these peaceful Christian communities of Indians with no encomendero or other Spaniard profiting from their labor were far more remarkable then.

*

Unfortunately little is known of their architecture. It must have been simple, yet from the beginning there were complaints that the buildings were too good for Indians, who could have been kept content with huts. In addition to the big main church at one side, the hospital building at Santa Fe de México had a chapel in the center of its big courtyard, open on the sides so that the seriously ill patients in the adjacent wings could attend the Masses without having to be moved. This arrangement seems to have been an ingenious variant of the recently contrived open-chapel-and-atrio scheme of the friaries combined with memories of similarly accessible chapels which were often part of the scheme of recent Spanish hospitals, the most important in Europe (such as those at Santiago de Compostela, Granada, or Toledo). Although *tepetate* (a soft building stone which hardens on exposure to the air) abounds on the site of Santa Fe de México, in order to provide additional materials for the buildings, devoted Indians carried adobe (which is less strong) and other stone all the way from the capital on their backs. The buildings were architecturally modest: the houses were small, and the church seems to have been made of a remodeled older building. (Everything there now is the result of later rebuilding.)

*

The Queen and Prince Philip looked with favor on both the establishments, and granted land for vineyards and .an olive orchard. (The wine and oil necessary for church ritual were costly to import.) The two hospitals functioned effectively for over forty years, until after don Vasco's death. They became the model for many of those which the Augustinians and Franciscans established in Michoacán. These last, however, were simply hospitals, without the many social and religious activities of don Vasco's enterprises.

Don Vasco saw his work as that of teaching his Indians to live in ideal communities, not only like those of Plato, and of Platonic and Erasmian More, but also like his image of the ideal communities of the primitive Christians. By reviving some of its social forms, he hoped to recover some of the lost spiritual values of the early Church, and he hoped to accomplish this without transplanting European society to America. The New World, the unimagined continent, was easy to associate with an imaginary land, Utopia, for one need seem no more unreal than the other. He *believed* in Utopia and in the possibility of organizing his innocent natives into Utopian communities better than anything in old and spiritually shabby Europe.

*

Judge Quiroga was not so theoretical an idealist that he refused to use less-than-ideal means to achieve his ideal ends. At times he used unpaid Indian labor, just as the other Spaniards did, and he accepted the encomienda and its drafting of labor as an institution which would assure evangelization. He had pointed out to the Emperor that their paganism was no justification for enslaving Indians, and he defended more rights for the natives than did all but a handful of his fellow Spaniards. Like More, however, he condoned slavery as a punishment for wrongdoers, in this case apostate rebellious Indians, none of whom were allowed to contaminate his hospitals by their presence. It is surprising to discover, by reading of their manumission in his will, that he himself had household slaves.

*

The regime in the Utopian hospitals was the admirable opposite of the exploitation practiced by most of the encomenderos and mine owners. Learned, wise, resourceful, devout, kindly, but sometimes cranky, don Vasco saw the Indians differently from most of his contemporaries: he considered them uncorrupted children of nature, like Man before the Fall. He knew of Lucian from reading More, and saw in his Indians the men of Lucian's Golden Age of Saturn. In other words, he saw them not only in the mediaeval way as children of God, but also with the new renaissance feeling for the dignity of Man. Many of his contemporaries recognized his compassionate charity, but some of them doubted his practical ability to make it work: "he is a virtuous man, and jealously concerned with the welfare of the Indians, but he is timid and cautious; that is why he is more fitted to carry out orders than to direct operations," wrote Licenciado Salmerón (1531),[27] perhaps with prejudice. Time would show that don Vasco was far from timid. His success in making Christian idealism work seems even more dramatic if compared with what little we know of Bartolomé de las Casas' complete disaster with his idealistic colony on the Pearl Coast of Venezuela, or with what may have been las Casas' one success, the peaceful conversion of the war-like Indians of Tuzutlulán, "Land of War," now la Verapaz, "True Peace," in Guatemala.

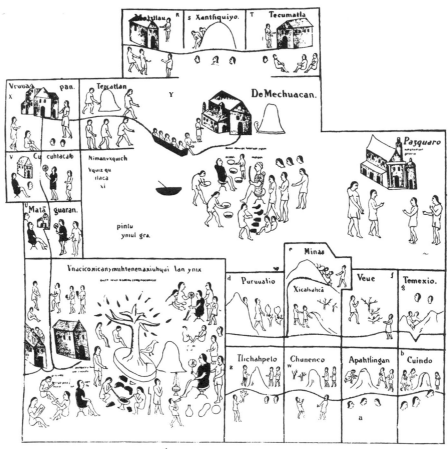

335 TZINTZUNTZAN, PÁTZCUARO, AND NEIGHBORING TOWNS
(after a map in the *Lienzo de Jucutácato*, *c*1545, in the Instituto de Geografía y Estadistica, México)

Tiripetío (lower left) has an important big tree, a yácata (mound-temple), and two churches, the primitive one and a new one being finished by Indian workmen on (above) the roof. Augustinian friars (dark clothes) hold Hosts like pinwheels, and one has a thurible at his feet. All are teaching Indians, some of whom are already able to read from books.

Uruapan (upper left) has the most complex cluster of buildings because it already has not only a monastery but a hospital.

"Tezcatlan" (Erongarícuaro, at the right of Uruapan) still has a yácata but not yet friars or a church, and consequently its citizens go across the lake by boat to

"Mechuacan" (Tzintzuntzan, in the center) with its big church next to its big yácata. A Franciscan is teaching Indians, who have no books but who bring food. The large seated figure in a patterned garment may be Bishop Quiroga, and his odd hat may be intended for his biretta (cf. ill. 259)

At the right is Pátzcuaro, with an elaborate church (the primitive Cathedral, or perhaps an ideograph of its still unbuilt successor). There are Indians here, but no friars.

626

QUIROGA, BISHOP

Because of his exceptional successes with the natives, Judge Quiroga was raced through Holy Orders in one compressed composite ceremony and then consecrated by his friend Archbishop Zumárraga as the first Bishop of Michoacán. The Diocese, which had been erected by Pope Paul III in 1536, was much larger than now, for as well as Michoacán itself it embraced Guanajuato, Jalisco, and considerable indefinite lands to the north, an area easily half that of Spain. Before he died, Bishop Quiroga was said to have traveled over 20,000 miles in administering it. Beautiful mountain-girt Michoacán was potentially so profitable that Cortés had tried to get grants of land there. In the eighteenth century, Father Beaumont still found it "the most populous and flourishing diocese in all America," and Father la Rea a *"hortus conclusus* like paradise." It is still surely one of the most beautiful parts of the world.[28]

Most of the Indians of the new See were Tarascos — they called themselves *Purépechas* in their own language — a particularly sympathetic and responsive race. The Spaniards, who did not often admire the mien of the natives, recognized that the Tarascos were handsome — they are tall, elegantly fine-boned, and green-eyed — and the Spaniards also approvingly observed that they were "brave, diligent, and very intelligent," "peaceful and affectionate," excellent bowmen, stronger than most other Indians, and particularly hard-working. The Tarascos were less aloof than the Aztecs who, incidentally, had never conquered them. Some of the diocese was peopled with Chichimecas, and most of it, when don Vasco arrived as Bishop soon after Nuño de Guzmán had burned the Tarasco King alive, was as anti-Spanish as any Chichimeca land. Don Vasco left it one of the most stable and prosperous regions in New Spain. Father Motolinía declared after a visit in 1549 that no other part of the country was half so Christian, perhaps not even a third. Father Acosta found them "the best Indians and truest Christians in New Spain." The penances they afflicted on themselves were said to produce "pools of blood," and in the eighteenth century, Father Moreno still found them "given to excesses of religion even more than the people of our [Spanish] pious nation" and believed this to be a direct heritage from the good Bishop.[29] Some of the credit should, however, be shared with Fray Juan de San Miguel and the first Franciscans.

With the Hospital of Santa Fe de la Laguna as a sample demonstration, and still inspired by the *Utopia*, the new Bishop set out determinedly to organize his vast See for the best benefit of his Indians. He conceived of it as a "Republic of Hospitals," and planned its economy by arranging for particular products to be the exclusive specialty of particular towns, which would then trade with one another and enjoy a symmetrical and stable economy. All advantage would be taken of their local resources of mining,

627

handicrafts, and agriculture, freely augmented by such remunerative novelties as silk, several kinds of bananas, and less successfully by grapes and olives through special permission of the King. He even taught them how to fish in Lake Pátzcuaro more effectively with a traditional Spanish technique. He had his nimble-fingered Tarascos taught new occupations which would be reciprocally useful and necessary: they learned carpentry, shoemaking, metalworking, how to make Spanish-style pottery and bread, and they were at the same time encouraged to continue their highly developed local crafts. Some villages in Michoacán are still busy at the same activities don Vasco chose for them: Patamba and Tzintzuntzan are famous for pottery, Uruapan for lacquer, Erongarícuaro for sombreros, Cocupao (now called Quiroga) for wooden boxes and chairs, Paracho for musical instruments. Some towns preserve such pleasantly incongruous religio-industrial names as Saint Clara of Copper, Saint Philip of the Blacksmiths, or Saint John of the Bedspreads (though this last in recent years has been almost lost, thanks to the *National Geographic* magazine and others who insistently published it in connection with the nearby baby volcano of Paricutín as San Juan Parangaricútiro, an official name rarely heard on the spot). Bishop Vasco accomplished an amalgamation of indigenous and European cultures in everyday occupations; at this level an amalgamation was possible, while it probably would not have been at a higher artistic or intellectual level, where both cultures were too involved with their religions.

The original seat of the Bishopric was Tzintzuntzan on the shore of Lake Pátzcuaro (ill. 259). The name was derived from the onomatopoetic word for hummingbird, and was given to the city dedicated to the hummingbird god. Both town and lake were known in Náhuatl as *Michoacán,* "place of fish." Tzintzuntzan had been chosen as a Christian religious center because it was the venerated capital of the Tarascos, and because it abounded in freshly abandoned pagan sites the new Cathedral could replace and expunge. As Bishop-elect, don Vasco had already obtained permission from the Emperor and an order from the Queen to build a Cathedral here (1537), and to use tithes and unpaid labor for it "with as little vexation as possible."

He soon decided that the low and sometimes swampy shore of the lake, where the Franciscans already had an adobe and thatch church, was unsuitable for his new Cathedral. He took formal possession of his See in Tzintzuntzan in August 1538 in order to comply to the letter with the terms of Paul III's Bull of Erection — don Vasco was a lawyer and correct — but immediately transferred the Cathedral to Pátzcuaro — as a lawyer he had been farsighted enough to obtain royal authorization to move. The transfer was for a time merely statutary and he remained for some months in Tzintzuntzan.

Several miles away by water or land, Pátzcuaro, "place of delights" or "place of the dyers," on paper was nevertheless a barrio of Tzintzuntzan. Art gave it its fame, for it was said to be the center for the finest of all preconquest featherwork. Although a summer retreat for the Tarasco kings, it had less than a score of substantial houses. Objections to moving there were voiced by the local encomenderos because their lands were handier to Tzintzuntzan, but not by most of the Indians, as sometimes has been said, for the flower of the Tarasco nobility, including the royal heir, supported the new Bishop in his wish to move to the higher site down the lakeside.

Here he tried to create a major Indian city, calling natives from all around until he had, or was said to have had, his ideal number of 30,000 in the 15 barrios of the city itself, and 70,000 in "Greater" Pátzcuaro, including its other barrios. He encouraged building actively, and did all he could to establish Pátzcuaro as a real city. In order to swell its population he kept annexing neighboring villages (until Pátzcuaro became a sort of proto-Los Angeles, made up of 75 barrios, some of them 20 or 25 miles away). He insisted on having it known as *the City of Michoacán,* hitherto one of the titles of the old capital, Tzintzuntzan.

A grand plaza was laid out, over 500 feet on a side, and some years later it was equipped with a fountain, "very well made and curious, with eight showy spouts; six of them are gentlemen carved in stone, who stand looking at each other at equal distances about a round basin; they spout water into it through their mouths; from the crown of a carved eagle set on a column in the middle of the basin another jet goes up and then falls into the same basin; the eighth spout is a lion, likewise carved of stone, and set on another pillar, lower than the eagle and in front of it, facing outwards on the outer edge of the basin; the water comes out of an escutcheon on his breast, and spurts out for over three yards into another basin" (Ponce, 1586).[30] This wonderful ornament was still spouting as late as 1862, but nothing now remains of the old plaza, alas, but blank space.

THE CATHEDRAL FOR 30,000

At about the time of the move to Pátzcuaro, probably at the end of 1540, Bishop Quiroga had the extraordinary idea of building a Cathedral big enough to hold all his 30,000 Indians at once, three times as many as can fill a great gothic cathedral such as Notre Dame in Paris. While the other cathedral churches of the sixteenth-century Mexican Sees are architecturally the proud daughters of the cathedrals of Spain, that of Pátzcuaro was not. (Also, it is the only one never finished.)

During the first years at Pátzcuaro a temporary wooden building was used, with liturgical equipment contributed by Archbishop Zumárraga who already had a surplus in the capital. It is not known exactly when Bishop Vasco began either to plan or to build his permanent Cathedral. It cannot have been before he established his See in Pátzcuaro, but it must have been before 1544, the year of the earliest preserved reference to it. (Unfortunately sometime between 1545 and '48 almost all the early Cathedral records were burned.) Bishop Quiroga was away for about nine months in 1542–43, trying to get to the Council of Trent (his boat leaked so badly it had to turn back), and work most likely was begun soon after he returned, begun in late 1543 or early 1544. It is possible that a strong letter from Prince Philip in 1543 urging him to care for his Indians was a spur to the undertaking, though even at 73 Bishop Quiroga does not seem to have been one likely to sit idly waiting for a royal prod before beginning to build what he wanted.[31]

In 1545, when it cannot have been far above ground, the building was already being criticized by local Spaniards. Although the site was high above the lake on a hillside, they condemned it as damp and unhealthy, good enough perhaps for Indians, but not for Spaniards. Outnumbered more than five hundred to one in the intended congregation, the Spaniards still wanted to dictate what and where the church should be. In the familiar Philistine way they complained that they could not understand the plan at all because it was so different from what they were used to.[32] At the bottom of their bad temper, now and later, was resentment at don Vasco's championing of the Indians and slighting of the Spaniards' pretentions. From a man so distinguished, this must have been particularly exacerbating.

He continued to have trouble with them, for they began to move to a new non-Indian city 40 miles away, beside the old Pirinda village of Guayangareo, a settlement which had been fostered by Viceroy Mendoza as early as 1537 and officially "founded" by Fray Juan de San Miguel in 1541. Streets and lots were laid out by a surveyor named Juan Ponce. Given the title of "city" in '45, and arms in 53, it was peopled with Spaniards, "fifty noble families," and to serve them, Indians from Tzintzuntzan, Pátzcuaro, and Tiripetío (where the Augustinians, on the invitation of Bishop Quiroga, were building their first house in Michoacán). Viceroy Mendoza had found that the site, which is still benevolent and pleasing, not only reminded him of Valladolid in Spain, for which he named it, but also fulfilled "the seven conditions which Plato said a city should have." At the same time he pronounced Pátzcuaro not healthy for Spaniards, and ordered the Cathedral built in Valladolid (in 1541, showing that it had probably not yet been begun in Pátzcuaro). Favorite projects of rival powers, civil and ecclesiastical, the two cities were predestined to become rivals — to the benefit of neither.[33]

The Bishop found the site of Valladolid anything but Platonic, "a high bleak plain, a desert, windy and barren of people, far from food and water." [34] He tried to keep its settlers from having any priests or from building any church. His chief fears were that if the Spaniards left Pátzcuaro, the income for his big new building would be cut, and that if they set up their own church, it would be cut even more. He claimed that he had taken the right to the title of *the City of Michoacán* with him from Tzintzuntzan to Pátzcuaro. This, he insisted, could be only where he, the Bishop of Michoacán, was and where he had his Cathedral. The Spaniards, consequently, had to try to content themselves with Mendoza's name, Valladolid. (Nationalists annulled that for *Morelia* in 1828.) [35]

Unperturbed, the citizens of Valladolid wrote the King to ask for the income from nearby towns for their own city, which they kept calling *the City of Michoacán*. They asked him to tell the Bishop to move the Cathedral there because they had no proper church.[36] (This was just what the Viceroy wanted, and he may have suggested the idea to them.) They did have some sort of adobe church in the Franciscans' temporary quarters but, "because it is very small, Mass for the Spaniards is often said outdoors, in the country, so that the Indians may hear it too." [37] The Spaniards did not like such an arrangement, particularly when in nearby Pátzcuaro a large Cathedral was being built for the Indians. One of the deep-rooted antagonisms causing decades of conflict must have been just this question of whether the Cathedral church was to be in a city of Indians, as its Bishop insisted, or whether like other Mexican Cathedrals, it should be in a city of Spaniards, and as Spanish as possible. (The same rivalry had torn Indian Tlaxcala and Spanish Puebla a decade earlier, and here the Spaniards had easily won the Cathedral for their own town.)

Despite the local campaign against it and the absence of its Bishop, work on the new building at Pátzcuaro went fitfully ahead. Don Vasco had gone to Spain (1547) to recruit clergy to serve in his Cathedral, to settle his dispute with the insistent citizens of Valladolid, to collect relics, and to conduct other business of a secret nature. In order to show the Spaniards what civilized Christians they could be, he took several exemplary Indians with him. While there, he obtained the final authorization for the moving of his Cathedral to Pátzcuaro, some ten years after he had actually moved it. He probably asked for this supererogatory authorization as a weapon in his jurisdictional war with the citizens of Valladolid, but it was not effective in putting an end to their demands or complaints. In Spain he debated the problem of perpetual encomiendas with Bishop Bartolomé de las Casas, and made a great impression with his eloquence and forcefulness. He was offered the miter of Mexico or of Puebla, but he refused both, saying that he wanted only to get back to his own Michoacán. Why he stayed away seven years is not explained.[38]

While in Spain he heard of the missionary success of Francis Xavier in India and of the Spiritual Exercises of Ignatius Loyola. Don Vasco had for over a decade had some connection with the Jesuits through Fray Alonso de Borja, the head of his Santa Fe de México. General Loyola expressed to don Vasco an interest in the opportunities for missionary work in America, but died before translating it into action. His successors promised to send four Jesuits to Michoacán; all four fell suddenly sick at the last minute and could not sail, but they recovered surprisingly soon and sailed to India instead. (No Jesuits came to New Spain until 1571. Two came to teach in Michoacán in 1573, and a Jesuit College was established in Pátzcuaro in 1576.) [39]

HERNANDO TORIBIO DE ALCARAZ

AND THE HUMILLADERO PLAN, 1550–54

Sometime in the winter of 1549–50, work on the Cathedral was put under the direction of Hernando Toribio de Alcaraz, the first professional architect in New Spain whose name we know (assuming that early friar-architects such as Juan de Alameda were amateurs or not architects at all; most of the known friar-builders were active *later*). Documents tell that a Toribio de Alcaraz had practiced architecture in Spain as early as 1535, which might lead one to assume that it was he who came to Mexico, but other documents tell that a Toribio de Alcaraz was practicing in South America after a Toribio de Alcaraz had died in Mexico. Professor Wethey has recently resolved this seeming contradition by revealing that there were two Spanish architects with the same uncommon name active in the New World at the same time. [40] Perhaps they were cousins.

Probably Bishop Quiroga hired the Mexican Toribio shortly before leaving for Spain in 1547, soon after Toribio had arrived in Mexico. Viceroy Mendoza may have proposed Toribio to him, for Mendoza later recommended him warmly to the incoming Viceroy Velasco (1550). During his architectural activities in New Spain, his professional competence was sometimes under fire, and in Pátzcuaro he was almost always in trouble. Neither he nor any of the earlier builders were good enough for threnetic Archbishop Montúfar when in 1555 he asked the Council of the Indies to send over "a *buen maestro* because here there are none." Once a controversial figure, Toribio is now an elusive one. Some have even denied his role as an architect, despite respectable though scattered affirmative evidence. [41]

In 1550 Bishop Quiroga obtained definite orders from the Queen to expedite work on his Cathedral, now surely under the direction of Toribio de Alcaraz, and assurance that it was to be financed in the usual way: one third from the Crown, one from the encomenderos, and one from the Indians. The order was repeated in 1553 and 1555 perhaps because there was trouble putting it into effect. [42]

336 TZINTZUNTZAN

(after a map published by Father Beaumont in the 1770's, presumably copied from one drawn in the 1540's or a decade or two later)

top center — Pátzcuaro, with the Humilladero at the left

top right corner — Erongarícuaro

upper middle — the chapel of Santa Ana, with its round atrio

right middle — the monastery at Tzintzuntzan, with its cross and olive-planted atrio in front, adjoining the big plaza where markets were held. The hospital is on the side opposite the monastery, below a hill with yácatas. (It is the only component which has been moved.)

left middle — Indians carry a bell and organ to Pátzcuaro (cf. ill. 259)

633

In 1554 or '55 the Bishop returned from his unaccountable seven years in Spain and formally set up the hierarchical organization of his still unbuilt Cathedral. He wanted nine canons and a complement of curates, and was incensed when six or seven canons who had just visited Pátzcuaro pronounced the establishment so poor that they did not care to serve there. They perhaps objected to the temporary wooden Cathedral rather than to the far-from-finished stone one. (It must have been for this temporary church that Indians had just carried an organ and bells on their backs two leagues from Tzintzuntzan to Pátzcuaro.) The Bishop was not left shorthanded, however, since as far back as 1540 he had foresightedly founded the Colegio de San Nicolás in Pátzcuaro to train Spanish boys to serve in his Cathedral, and he managed to have it staffed and fully organized by 1554.[43]

The school, which was transferred to Valladolid in 1580 and there merged with another Colegio de San Nicolás, still exists and enjoys the dignity of being the oldest educational establishment in the Americas, a decade older than the University of Mexico. (Both have survived short interruptions.) It was organized as a seminary to train Spanish youths over twenty to become priests, and to learn to speak Tarasca, and also to train Indian boys in the Christian doctrines and to learn to speak and read and write Spanish. The student body was, thus, daringly interracial, though each race had a different curriculum. One of the most distinguished of the early Indian students was don Antonio Vitziméngari y Mendoza, last King of Michoacán, son of Calzontzín, and godson of Viceroy Mendoza in whose house he had been reared. He was given a special curriculum: reading Spanish, Latin, Greek, and Hebrew. His son, don Pablo, was probably, as has already been said, the first Indian to be ordained. In his will, don Vasco endowed the College with two farms, an hacienda, his horse, a picture of Saint Ambrose, and 626 books.[44]

*

Pátzcuaro, now officially *the City of Michoacán,* had been given its armorial bearings in 1553. In place of the "church on a peak" specified by the College of Heralds, the plan of the new Cathedral became the center of the escutcheon and, as such, was carved on the base of an *Humilladero,* or wayside Calvary Cross, still standing near the old entrance to the city on the spot where the Indians had made their definitive surrender to the Spaniards. Exactly when this plan first took shape is not known, but it was already enduringly recorded on the stone cross in 1553, before don Vasco returned from Spain. He is reported to have brought the municipal arms back with him in 1554, but that was probably only in some formal sense, since they had been carved there in stone the year before, with the church plan already substituted for the "church on a peak" (a substitution which sounds like his own idea).[45] The date 1553 *might* refer to the year of the

634

granting of the arms, in which case they could have been carved later, but more likely it refers to the year the cross was carved.

Here at last we can see what was causing such a stir. Five naves are shown converging on one sanctuary. Three, at right angles, form a T; the other two are fitted diagonally between the arms of the T. Five navefuls of Indians were thus aimed at one altar, so that all 30,000 of them might attend the same Mass in the same building at the same time. This resulted in a wildly original and seemingly unprecedented scheme, outside any known tradition of church building. If related to anything in Spain, which is far from certain, it might possibly have drawn an idea from Diego Siloée's Cathedral of Granada (according to Professor Kubler) where the high altar could be seen not only from the main nave but also, with some difficulty, through several tunnel-like passages radiating from it to the large ambulatory. This peculiar arrangement (according to Professor Rosenthal) was probably a renaissance "copy" of the Church of the Holy Sepulcher in Jerusalem.[46]

The basic plan of Pátzcuaro must be the product of an independent and practical mind, and probably of one not trained in architecture. Familiarity with tradition might have hampered the invention of such an *un*architectural scheme. It probably was not the creation of architect Alcaraz but may well have been conceived by non-architect Quiroga. He had arrived in New Spain in 1531, and although he had been connected with the Cathedral of Granada, that was before Diego Siloée had begun his scheme (designed 1528–32). It is conceivable that he had heard about the many vistas this would provide toward the main altar — pinched though they are — from some old associate. He could have written to ask about the building of a big church in Granada after he knew that he himself would be building a big church in Pátzcuaro. It is not at all likely, however, that he had any clear idea of what the Cathedral of Granada would look like; it was no more than half up while he was planning, still half unroofed, and full of scaffolding; the scheme for Pátzcuaro shows no signs of any understanding of the properly *architectural* features of Granada. The possible resemblance is in theory only, a theory of maximum visibility for large numbers of people, but the resemblance is doubtful even there. Although it would surely have been attractive to him had he known of it, the idea of reproducing the Church of the Holy Sepulcher was not — so far as anyone knows — then in anyone's mind in Mexico.

Bishop Quiroga had already dealt with a similar problem — how to deploy crowds of Indians under cover so that all could see and follow Mass celebrated at one necessarily small-scale central point — in the open chapel in the patio of his Hospital de Santa Fe de México, and there too he had arrived at a bold and practical solution, though not an original one. It may sound farfetched to suggest that the plan of a Cathedral was influenced by

ESTAS·SON·LAS·AR
MAS·QVE·DIO·EL·REI·

ESTA CIVDAD DE
MECHVACÁN

636

that of a hospital, but two more-than-coincidental facts must be conceded: the propounder and the problem were the same in each case. When Bishop Quiroga began his Cathedral, his only other architectural undertakings had, presumably, been the hospital buildings. It is not the form of the hospital which may have affected the Cathedral so much as the thinking that had chosen that form.

No more than the basic scheme could be the Bishop's. The *Humilladero* plan of 1553, carved about six years after he had left Michoacán for Spain, presumably shows his notion translated concretely into architectural terms by whoever was the first executant in charge, and perhaps subsequently modified by professional Toribio de Alcaraz who had been in charge since 1549/50.

Not only the whole but also some of the few discernible details show bold and original thinking. The interior buttresses which stiffen the nave walls are sliced off at such an angle (on the edge towards the congregation and away from the altar) that they offer only minimal visual obstruction to a congregation facing the altar. Together with their wall they are like widely spaced teeth on a saw. Obviously the determinant controlling such an unorthodox detail was the visual comfort of the congregation. Vasco de Quiroga's religio-humanitarian idealism may have affected even architectural forms.

(opposite)
337 CARVING ON THE PEDESTAL OF THE *HUMILLADERO* CROSS, 1553
"These are the arms the King gave [above a map of Lake Pátzcuaro and a plan of the Cathedral] to this city of Mechuacán."

INVESTIGATIONS, DELAYS, AND INFLUENCE, 1554–65

In 1554 the *oidor* Lebrón de Quiñones was sent out from the capital to report on Michoacán and to "moderate" the personal service of Indians working on building and provisioning the new city of Pátzcuaro. He calculated that there were 15,000 able-bodied men in the city and immediately subject towns, and that 3,000 of them could be spared to work in Valladolid during the next two years. He declared Quiroga's work quotas too high, and reduced them as much as half or two-thirds. His report was hostile to the Cathedral, probably on purpose. Meanwhile the citizens of Valladolid were still trying to wreck the project. They wrote the King (1555) that the Bishop wanted to locate his church "in a barrio of Indians where he has his own house." They hoped to have the orders to build it rescinded, and they instituted a suit to try to take from him the right to the title of *the City of Michoacán*.[47]

In 1555 the new Viceroy, Velasco, visited Pátzcuaro, saw the beginnings of the Cathedral, took alarm at its size and its strangeness, and ordered all work stopped and an investigation started. (Don Vasco, meanwhile, had to be away for some months at the First Mexican Church Council, meeting in San José de los Naturales.) The soil where the building stood was declared improper for its foundations, and cracks were pointed out in the walls. In view of the structural troubles anticipated, it was decided to cover the naves with wood and vault only the chancel. This must mean that earlier it had been intended or proposed to vault the naves, and although later texts also suggest an original scheme with vaults, it is hard to believe that any practiced builder had accepted this, for the central nave was 66 feet wide. The diagonal naves, were 40, and the transverse 30,[48] and had they all been designed for vaults, the arrangements at the juncture of the naves would have been inescapably awkward. Buttressing vaults of such spans would involve problems beyond local skills.

The critical new recommendation also said that the work was to be "without any carving or sculpture, but plain, smooth, and well-made."[49] The church was not long bare, however, for soon there were some large carved shells on it, symbols of pilgrimage, set between pairs of columns, and there were "pedestals and floreated and fluted cornices in a perfect Ionic style" (sic), carved in pink and white stone. The white stone came from excellent quarries only two leagues to the west, and the pink must be the lovely rosy trachyte of which so much of colonial Morelia is built.[50]

The Franciscans, who had recently rebuilt their monastery in Pátzcuaro, had so long had so many houses in this part of Michoacán that they had come to consider it as territory exclusively theirs, and they began to attack the instrusive Cathedral project with most un-Franciscan virulence. The Bishop had already had trouble with the Franciscans, quite possibly of his own making. He had given Tiripetío and Cuitzeo to the Augustinians, and the Franciscans may have resented them as poachers. In 1552, still in Spain, he had persuaded Philip II to forbid the Franciscans to build a monastery at Erongarícuaro, where they already had established a visita of Tzintzuntzan. The pretext was that they already had two houses in the City of Michoacán (Tzintzuntzan and Pátzcuaro) and that Erongarícuaro — 20 miles away at the other end of the lake — was just a barrio, though it had a population of around 5000.[51]

There were also complaints to the Crown that he was ordaining mestizos and creoles as secular priests, and giving minor orders improperly. The Crown promptly commanded him to give such orders and the tonsure only to properly prepared youths of more than 14, and of pure Spanish blood. In 1560 he was ordered to stop refusing to ordain friars because of his "passion against them." Franciscan Bishop del Toral wrote the Council of the Indies

(1558) that Bishop Quiroga was now very old — he was 88 — and that he no longer "understood matters of Ordination nor of the other Sacraments, but only lawsuits, quarrels, and tithes." [52] He was also having trouble with the Augustinians. They complained to the King that he was encroaching on the land which he had given them, at which he fought back and accused them of setting up monasteries without his authorization. Like many reformers, always sure that he was right, he seems to have become so intractable that it is small wonder the friars were hostile. [53]

The King was warned in 1560 that the Cathedrals of Mexico City and of Michoacán were costing him much more than he knew because of the tricky ways in which moneys were being allotted. Francisco de Mena, the Franciscan Commissioner General and an avowed enemy of the nonagenarian Bishop, wrote the King to "stop this Babylon of a church in Michoacán, for in it is being spent the wealth of your Majesty and that of the Spaniards and Indians, and not only their wealth but also the lives of many poor souls who meet their death working on it; and as has been said, and truly said, the Indians do not need churches with roofs nor churches with five naves." (This is a strong contrast to the attitude of compassionate and far more truly Franciscan Father Motolinía who, when in Pátzcuaro a dozen years before, had said when he saw the size of the crowds of Indians that he understood why such a large church was wanted.) [54]

Perhaps as a result of these complaints and their effect on susceptible Philip II, Viceroy Velasco ordered another investigation. In 1560 he sent his chosen architect, Claudio de Arciniega, to inspect the work and make a report. Claudio, the older brother of Luis de Arciniega of Puebla and Cholula, had arrived in Mexico only about five years before (more probably than around 1545 as has sometimes been supposed). Although his beginnings were modest, as a mason and maker of fountains, he was soon successful, and was kept very busy in the capital with important commissions, particularly that of the very Spanish Cathedral. He seems to have become the leader of the *purista* movement in Mexico. He made the famous classicistic catafalque for Charles V in anti-classical San José de los Naturales (ill. 185), and perhaps also a circular church at Chapultepec; later he built new quarters for the University. [55] Hernando Toribio de Alcaraz, in contrast, would seem to have held the freer architectural ideas of an older generation. Favorite architects of successive Viceroys, and advocates of successive and rival styles, inevitably they clashed.

Arciniega's report was generally unfavorable and particularly unfavorable to Alcaraz, who was forced to dig up ten feet of soil to expose the old foundations, though they had already been twice inspected and passed. Arciniega further overstepped his duties by slipping in suggestions for redesigning the building more to his own academic taste — no ornament —

and he accompanied his suggestions with drawings to show how he would "correct" the scheme. He recommended abandoning all four of the supplementary naves and finishing only the main one, and suggested adding some sort of ambulatory behind its main altar "for processions." Clearly he was thinking of a proper cathedral in the conservative Spanish fashion and not of any tradition-defying affair for 30,000 Indians. (There were now 300 Spaniards in Pátzcuaro.) [56]

The loyal local party said that he was trying to discredit Toribio's work so that he could get the job for himself. If that is true, it would not be the only time Arciniega ran down a building with an eye to a job: in 1564 he made a report on the Cathedral of Puebla, suggesting that it be pulled down and replaced, though it was still stout enough to stand for another hundred years. (This was, of course, before his brother Luis was put in charge of the Cathedral works at Puebla.) [57]

When Claudio's evaluation of Toribio's work at Pátzcuaro was received, construction was ordered suspended again. Feeling harassed, Bishop Quiroga wrote directly to the King (1561): the entire Mexican Church, he said, was being harmed by so many disputes outside and bitternesses inside; the attacks on his Cathedral were rash and prejudiced; the Franciscans had been unfair. He pointed out that the building had already been officially examined and approved twice, and that an official license had been issued to complete the work as it had been begun. Why then had Arciniega been sent to examine it a third time? He was, moreover, but "a stonecutter, and not a prominent one" and not to be trusted to give an unprejudiced report.[58]

Later in 1561 the work was resumed, with precautionary orders that expenses be kept as low as possible, and with the acceptance of some of Arciniega's ideas. Trouble now came from a new source: in 1562 the Indians began to grumble and to make their grumbles heard. Those of Tzintzuntzan objected to being subject to upstart Pátzcuaro, and those of Pátzcuaro threatened to leave because their tribute was so high. There had been ill-tempered rivalry between the two towns before.[59]

In 1563 more complaints were registered by Fray Maturino Gilberti, an influential Franciscan who accused the Bishop of exhausting his Indians by overwork on his Cathedral, making them travel 15 or 20 leagues carrying their food and children on their backs to work on a building "which would never be finished" and which even in its unfinished state was already an example of "improper sumptuousness and great confusion." Some Indians were jailed and condemned to six months of labor on the Cathedral "from which cause their wives and children suffer great detriment." [60] Old Bishop Quiroga seems to have forgotten his major goals for a time while concentrating so hard on the minor one of a building to help achieve them. Nonetheless, work did manage to go slowly forward.

THE END OF THE CATHEDRAL OF UTOPIA

Bishop Vasco died in 1565 at the age of 95, and he was buried, fittingly, in his Cathedral. The Indians came to venerate him like a saint, and affectionately treasured his staff, hat, and chair, which still are shown like relics at Santa Fe de la Laguna. All idea of completing the full scheme of his Cathedral was abandoned, and in accord with Arciniega's recommendation, only the main nave was finished. Even that was done as simply as possible, with a plain wood roof.

Disagreeable Doctor Luis de Anguis, Bishop Montúfar's Notary of the Inquisition and a secret agent of Philip II, complained to his master in 1571 about undue sumptuousness in San Agustín in the capital, and then went on to report: "I say the same of the church of Pátzcuaro . . . which has neither head nor tail, and never in the life of man will it be finished, nor be good for anything in the end; nor is there any reason why Your Majesty should spend so many thousands of pesos on it every year for the three or four Spaniards who live there [there must have been 100 or more]; and as for the Indians, any simple thing would be better for them." At this same time the Dean and *Cabildo* of the capital were denouncing Doctor de Anguis as unscrupulous and unreasonable, and as a creature of Archbishop Montúfar who should be banished from New Spain. Philip granted a permit that same year to move the Cathedral and seat of the See of Michoacán from Pátzcuaro to Guayangareo (Valladolid) "where it is now," showing that Anguis' letter was effective even though misunderstood. Philip's permit may never have been sent; if it was, it produced no effect for some years. Dead only six years, don Vasco still exerted power.[61]

The plague of 1575–76 killed two-thirds of the people of Pátzcuaro. Don Pedro Cuinvrapati, last of the royal Tarasco line, nursed the sick, caught the plague, died, and was buried in the unfinished Cathedral. The new Bishop, Morales de Molina, was able to accomplish but little. Though he planned to move the See to Valladolid, and planned a seemingly official document to assure it, he never got so far as to begin the move. The one roofed nave served as a Cathedral for only seven years, however, for in 1579, fourteen years after don Vasco's death, the third Bishop, Molina Rincón, definitely and officially moved the See to Spanish Valladolid, hardly yet a city, though already the seat of both Augustinian and Franciscan monasteries. Only 40 Spaniards were living there, served by 50 Negro slaves and 50 horses. There were now only 50 Spaniards left in Pátzcuaro, with 25 slaves and 40 horses, and some 5000 tribute-paying Indians.[62]

The Indians, many of whom had left their villages to live in don Vasco's Cathedral town, resisted the Spaniards who wanted to rob them of the distinction of having a Cathedral. When agents tried to carry off the bell don

Vasco had blessed and the Indians themselves had paid for, they objected, and kept their bell. When other agents tried to steal don Vasco's body in the middle of the night to rebury it at the new Cathedral going up in Valladolid, they were stopped by 1000 angry natives. To make sure that the body would not be spirited away some other time, they set on the sepulcher an enormous stone, so heavy that only a big crew of men could raise it. (The body was not moved until 1897.) [63]

338 DOORWAY OF SAN FRANCISCO AT PÁTZCUARO, 1577

339 CHAPEL OF SAN CAMILO AT TZINTZUNTZAN

During the 1570's, when work on the Cathedral was greatly curtailed, workmen must have been released from the shops in Pátzcuaro, and some must have found jobs elsewhere in the vicinity. Something of the quality of the carving on the Cathedral may be mirrored in the cloister doorway of San Francisco at Pátzcuaro (carved with the date 1577) for its design is far more sophisticated than anything else in the neighborhood. Even though the Franciscans were hostile to the Bishop's project, they might not have been averse to using accomplished carvers trained on it. Perhaps the shells and fluted pilasters of the Chapel of San Camilo and the church facade at Tzintzuntzan may also be reflections of the Cathedral, but at one stylistic remove further than the doorway at San Francisco. Fray Pedro de Pila rebuilt almost everything at Tzintzuntzan and also rebuilt Fray Jacobo Daciano's early buildings at Zacapu (ill. 50), in a sophisticated style, both presumably before he went to Paris in 1579, in just the years when the Cathedral carvers might likely have been seeking new jobs. The apse-like open chapel at Tarímbaro (ill. 229) is very like the Chapel of San Camilo in several important features, and may consequently be a reflection of a reflection of the Cathedral, as well as a more direct reflection of work at Cuitzeo. The more naïve work at Erongarícuaro might also be two removes from the Cathedral ateliers, as would the Hospital Chapel of 1619 at Tzintzuntzan with its shells, sun, and moon (ills. 260, 315). Three removes might account for several charming folk-art portals, such as those at Aranza and other towns around Lake Pátzcuaro. This may be the genesis of the widespread pidgin plateresque of Michoacán, late and with a peculiar enthusiasm for cockle shells known nowhere else in Mexico. Though no such shells could be found in the lake, stone ones could be seen on the Cathedral. Professor Angulo's "School of the Master of Tzintzuntzan" should perhaps be renamed the "School of those Dismissed from the Cathedral of Pátzcuaro." [64]

Although there were only thirty houses of Spaniards there in the early 1570's, and only 150 tribute-paying Indians, Valladolid waxed as Pátzcuaro waned. After the first Cathedral of Valladolid (begun in 1580) burned down in 1584, Indians from all around were sent to work on a new one, presumably because of powerful favoritism for Valladolid at the viceregal court; 200 were brought from Pátzcuaro, more than from any other town, presumably from the opposite of favoritism. The eclipse of Pátzcuaro threatened to become total soon after the transfer of the title of Cathedral, and further humiliation came when Pátzcuaro was reduced to a barrio of Valladolid. After similar humiliation as a barrio of Pátzcuaro, old Tzintzuntzan regained autonomy and was promoted to the status of city in 1590. Pátzcuaro, down to about 3500 at the end of the century, and apparently no longer a threat, was also allowed to regain independent municipal status, and even to remain the titular head of the Province for three centuries.[65]

OBSOLESCENCE AND CONFUSION

Soon people began to forget what the original scheme had been, and to misunderstand the unfinished parts they still could see. Careful, unimaginative Father Ponce was not clear about it when he visited Pátzcuaro in 1586, only sixteen years after the church had been put into use. "The Bishop of Michoacán . . . began to build a very large church with ten or twelve naves, so strange and ingenious that from all of them one could see the main altar, and the Masses said there, for all the naves give into the chancel, to the middle of it where the altar is; a great deal of work has been done, and if it were to be finished, it would be a notable thing." [66]

Although he himself was still well remembered, the ideas of don Vasco faded and blurred during the next century. The Carmelite chronicler, Antonio Vázquez de Espinosa, found only the fish and boats of Pátzcuaro worthy of mention (c1620). He paid no attention to the looming fragment of the Cathedral, but wrote only: "The Cathedral church was founded in Tzintzuntzan, which was the court of the kings of that land, and then it was moved by its first Bishop, Vasco de Quiroga, in the year 1544, to where it now is" (i.e., Morelia-Valladolid).[67]

As by so much else, Father la Rea was confused by it. "The Bishop moved the See to the City of Pátzcuaro, where he at once laid foundations and began his church, following the plan of Saint Peter's of Rome, with the grandeur and ostentation which Italy esteems and the world admires." Romanophile la Rea could invent no greater praise than to say something Mexican was worthy of comparison with something Italian; he found that the pretty subtropical town of dirt streets and thatched houses which Fray Juan de San Miguel had laid out in Uruapan was "an arrangement not to be bettered by the aristocracy of Rome," and that the churches at Cuitzeo and Yuriria were "so sumptuous and excellent that they could compete with those in Italy." [68] It is to be assumed that his reference to Saint Peter's is also ignorant provincial boasting, and that it is not based on any actual similarities seen by Father la Rea or consciously borrowed by Bishop Quiroga or architects Alcaraz or Arciniega.

Ten years later (c1649), Gil González Dávila borrowed his boast and promoted it to a fact: "following the plan of Saint Peter's in Rome, which is one of the wonders of the world," but he did not recognize the one standing nave as part of the ex-Cathedral. Some eighty years later, Father Escobar took it as an established truth that the Cathedral was made "after the exemplary fashion and plan of the great temple of Saint Peter in Rome," which he himself had never seen (1729).[69]

In the 1640's, only a few years after la Rea, Father Basalenque wrote more cautiously that don Vasco "tried to make the Cathedral church . . . begun in masonry with five naves all facing the main altar, all vaulted, and arranged so that those in one nave could not see those in the others. It was a work such as no one had ever seen in this land, and was being built with such grandeur that, finished, it might have been the eighth wonder of the world in buildings . . . The middle nave was built with a timber roof and not with a vault, and one sees its handsome trusses today; the church is so big that the entire town, both Indians and Spaniards, cannot fill it in the biggest concourse of the year, which is on Holy Thursday." [70] He shows that more had been forgotten than in the days of Father Ponce who at least knew for what multiple naves were meant, though he multiplied the multiple naves. With Indians, mestizos, and Spaniards now going to the same Masses together, and with the town become so much smaller, there was no longer reason to know why the extra spaces had been intended.

José Antonio de Villaseñor y Sánchez, an official and mathematician, and an observant and accurate man, saw "that the church has only one nave but the foundations are arranged for five, in the shape of a hand," [71] a clear description of a difficult shape but again with no explanation of why such a shape had come into being (c1747).

Father Juan José Moreno, in his biography of Bishop Quiroga published twenty years later, proceeded with the conscientiousness of a good modern historian. He corrected some of the fictions of his predecessors, including several which had been boosted to the status of facts because they had been so often repeated. He was cautious about the Cathedral: "Of those who re- member it, some say that it followed the plan of Saint Peter's in Rome, others that it was of five naves covered with vaults and all ending at the High Altar . . . and everyone agreed that it would have been the Eighth Wonder. And truly the vestiges of it which remain are the admiration of all those who come to Pátzcuaro and are interested in antiquities" (1766).[72]

It is hard to see how it could ever really have been intended to vault this church. The naves were of different widths and heights and their walls were not thick enough to carry the weight of wide vaults. Their buttresses were in- side where they were effective enough as a simple stiffening for walls but would have been inadequate as abutment for the uneasy thrust of the dif- ferent vaults in quaky country. Perhaps some early project for vaulting the church, rejected by the investigations of 1555, came to later writers' atten- tion.

The chronicler Beaumont, after borrowing and repeating many of the now traditional errors, went on to make some first-hand observations (1777): "There remained only some spiral stairways going up the towers, and their workmanship is the admiration of all who see them, the stone being very much burnished, and the mortar of singular consistency; it seems like some- thing lacquered, for the Tarascos use some clayey earth which formerly was plentiful in the mountains, and which, mixed with sand and lime, makes a sort of resin, smooth and transparent like varnish . . . Another monument of the early days of this church which has survived is a ciborium of stone so delicately carved that it seems to be an exquisite work in wax, cast with the greatest art." (Was this ciborium a receptacle for the Host, or a canopy?) He found the whole church "sumptuous." [73]

In another text Father Beaumont gave another description, including a confused notice of the ambulatory proposed by Arciniega: "The Parish Church is in the same place where the old Cathedral was, and there can be recognized the remains of a sumptuous construction of five naves which must have had the shape of a cross with two extra arms." He then mentioned some unfinished work by the old chancel, showing "that there must have been a passage around the head of the cross, of a round form to embrace the high altar which must have been in the middle, leaving a space beyond the cross for the Altar of the Kings," [74] which is traditionally at the end of important Spanish Cathedrals. At some time before don Vasco died, a start must have been made to build Claudio de Arciniega's ambulatory. As Toribio de Alcaraz was on the job until after don Vasco died, he must have been forced to accept this idea of his hostile critic.

Father Beaumont gave another piece of information, extraordinary information if based on the truth, confusing misinformation if not. He displayed the plan of the building twice. Once he showed it as it appears on the arms of the city, like the *Humilladero* plan, but smaller and in some parts reduced to a meaningless pattern, with the buttresses not understood as buttresses but transformed into brushstrokes which persist in remaining no more than brushstrokes.[75] This must be the original scheme of don Vasco as developed by Toribio de Alcaraz by 1553, before the intervention of Arciniega. Father Beaumont showed a second plan which appears to be an ingenious baroque fantasy based more on accounts of the varying schemes than on knowledge of the foundations of the incompleted parts.[76] He may have had access to information or drawings now lost which showed earlier variants of the scheme. In any case he was inconsistent, for the star-like arrangement of five radial naves is incompatible with his reference to the shape of a hand or the town arms. (The original scheme was older to Beaumont when he wrote in 1777 than Beaumont is to us; furthermore, he was far from dependable.)

The one element which may relate meaningfully to his written description is the pentagonal ambulatory, vaulted somewhat like the mediaeval ar-

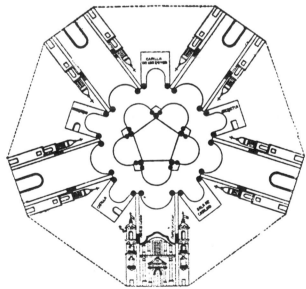

340 BEAUMONT'S PLAN OF THE CATHEDRAL OF PÁTZCUARO

rangement at the Cathedral of Toledo. Since the Toribio de Alcaraz of Pátzcuaro may be the same Toribio de Alcaraz who in 1535 had a commission in Alcaraz in the diocese of Toledo,[77] the ambulatory in the plan *might* reflect his mediaevalizing translation of an idea of anti-mediaeval Arciniega (who first proposed an ambulatory). But since the rest of the star plan, though ingenious, is inaccurate, it seems unrealistic to strain through two subjunctives to try to validate Father Beaumont's freakish ambulatory, and more sensible to lump it with the other fantasies that don Vasco's Cathedral engendered in such numbers.

In his *Geographical Dictionary* of 1786–89, Antonio de Alcedo praised the beauty of the streets and plazas of Pátzcuaro, and its "delicious and agreeable countryside." He knew that the Cathedral would have been remarkable if it had been completed, but of what he could see he singled out only the "two beautiful spiral stairways." One was apparently single and built of particularly fine masonry, and the other was a double affair of two entwined stone helices. Here prankish Indians would astound visitors by suddenly letting go their hold at the top and then whirling themselves dizzily down the entire corkscrew drop of the smooth inner curb.[78]

*

Earthquake shook down much of the surviving early work in 1806, '37, and twice in '45. The roof fell, and in 1844 lightning shot off the top of the tower. The remaining raw hulk, patched and shored, was reopened in 1857, but another quake in 1858 knocked much of this flat.[79] Hardly anything of what is standing shows anything of what was originally hoped, though the foundations make it preserve the ambitious size. That is still impressive, even though it is only one fifth of the old scheme, and that fifth patched, pieced, altered, and denatured.

While his church has been forgotten, don Vasco has not. Clavijero, in the mid-eighteenth century, wrote of "the incomparable don Vasco," and Father Florencia found that the local Indians, a century and half after he died, would not allow the fruit and nut trees in the Jesuits' College to be cut down because, they said, don Vasco used to go to pray among them.[80] Two centuries after his death, a patriotic Mexican cleric, Juan José Moreno, wrote his biography and made it such a eulogy, so packed with accounts of his virtues and of miracles worked by his relics, that one begins to suspect that it might have been intended as propaganda for a canonization. (There was then only one American saint, Rose of Lima.) The author was not above tampering with old documents to credit don Vasco with hospitals founded by Franciscan Fray Juan de San Miguel. A century later, Fanny Calderón de la Barca found don Vasco still venerated in Pátzcuaro,[81] and even today, almost four centuries after his death, he remains alive in Indian memory,

647

648

gently faded into folklore as *Tata Vasco* (Grandpa Vasco), a benevolent *genius loci*. Every few years an eager young anthropologist returns from some back pocket in the mountains of Michoacán to report the discovery of some all-but-inaccessible Indians who believe that he is still alive somewhere in some other mountains, ready one day to come down and make everything fine again.

The battered and patched wreck of his church still stands, "raide et ascétique," as Eliot said of an older sad church, "Vieille usine desafectée de Dieu." [82]

341 THE CATHEDRAL OF PATZCUARO in 1845
There were many repairs in the seventeenth century, including the resurfacing of the walls, and more in the eighteenth, including most of the decoration of the facade, a new ceiling and roof, and a new little baptistery (at the left). Following repeated quakes, there were more in the nineteenth. This painting in the Museum at Morelia shows the new belfry (under construction in the 1840's) collapsing in the second quake of 1845. No more than the core of some of the walls dates back to the Cathedral of Bishop Quiroga.

GLOSSARY

BIBLIOGRAPHY

NOTES

INDEX

GLOSSARY

The definitions which follow are limited to the particular meanings relevant to this book. Many of the listed terms have additional meanings in different contexts or in different parts of the Spanish-speaking world. Some readers may find a few words here which seem to need no definition. I have perhaps been somewhat schoolteacherish in including them, but it was with the hope that to nonprofessionals generous definitions might make clear and more precise the meanings of some words often loosely or only half understood.

The linguistic derivation of some terms not commonly used in ordinary English has been indicated in parentheses right after the terms: A for Arab, C for any of the Caribbean languages, F for French, I for Italian, M for any of the Mexican languages, S for Spanish, and SA for native South American.

PRONUNCIATION

Mexican pronunciation, derived principally from the Andalusian of a few centuries ago, is simple, clear, and musical. It differs from classic contemporary Castilian only in the pronunciation of some consonants. The vowels are the same, all with pure, clear sounds:

a as in f*a*ther
e approximately like *a* in *a*ny, but somewhat more like *a* in m*a*te when accented and like *e* in m*e*t when not
i as in pol*i*ce when accented, but a bit more like poult*i*ce when not
o as in h*o*tel when accented, but more like H*o*ttent*o*t when not
u always like *oo* in h*oo*t.

Consonants are pronounced as in English except:

c like *k* before *a, o,* and *u,* but like *ss* before *e* and *i*
ch (a separate letter in the Spanish alphabet) always as in *ch*oke
g as in *g*o before *a* and *o,* or before *u* followed by a consonant; like *h* before *e* and *i; gu* before a vowel is like *w;* and *gü* like *woo*
h always silent
j like a somewhat strong *h*
ll (a separate letter) like *y,* except in Indian words where it is like *l*
ñ (also a separate letter) like *ni* in on*i*on
qu like *k* (with the *u* entirely silent)
rr always rolled
s always like *ss,* never like *z*
x like English *x* in words derived from Latin; in Indian words, originally like *sh* (Cuauh*x*icalli), now often modified to *ss* (Mi*x*teca) particularly at the beginning of a word (*X*ochimilco) and sometimes eroded to an *h* (Oa*x*aca)
y before a vowel like *y,* otherwise like *ee* in ch*ee*k
z always like *ss*

Stress is given to any syllable marked with an orthographic accent ('). If there is no accent, stress falls on the last syllable of all words except those ending in a vowel or the letters *n* or *s,* in which case it falls on the next to last syllable.

GLOSSARY

There are no exceptions. The written accent is considered part of the spelling and may be omitted only on capital letters. It is not always used on Indian words, and some purists prefer to omit it. It has been used here in order to facilitate pronunciation.

A*bacus* — the top member of the capital of a column, normally a plain square slab for the Tuscan and Doric orders.

adarve (A) — a walkway around the top of a building, protected by a parapet, and occasionally under arcades.

adobe (S) — a large brick or building block of dried but unbaked clay.

ahuehuete (M) — *Cupressus disticha* or *Taxodium mucronatum,* a kind of giant cypress, sometimes over a hundred feet high and hundreds of years old.

alabado (S) — a hymn or motet in praise of the Sacrament beginning with the words *Alabado sea.*

alcázar (A) — the palace (often fortified) of a Spanish Moslem ruler.

alfarje (A) — a ceiling of many small pieces of wood worked into a repetitive interlacing design, often found in Moslem and mudéjar work.

alfiz (A) — a rectangle of molding embracing an arch, a rectangular label or hood molding, found in Moslem, mudéjar, and plateresque work.

amate (M) — *Ficus petiolaris,* a native tree of the mulberry family from whose cortex "bark paper" is made; also paper made from this tree.

anthemion — a conventionalized palmette and/or floral ornament found in antique and plateresque decoration.

ara — a portable altar stone; or a consecrated hard stone slab (symbolically representing Christ) set permanently on the mensa of an altar.

architrave — the lintel or horizontal beam which is the lowest member of the entablature of the classical orders.

archivolt — the architrave-like molded band on the vertical face of an arch curving circumferentially around its opening.

artesonado (S) — a wooden ceiling with coffers (*artesones,* usually square or polygonal) sunk between its beams.

ashlar — masonry of dressed rectangular stones laid in regular horizontal courses, usually with a regular pattern of joints.

átl-atl (M) — a throwing stick or board which increases the force of darts or small javelins propelled with its aid by extending the effective length of the throwing arm.

atrio (S) — the large walled forecourt of a Mexican church; in Spain a paved space by a church, usually raised, and in the Middle Ages often enclosed by a low wall; see Chapter VI.

attic — a small story or band of wall above the main cornice of a building.

audiencia (S) — a regional court or high tribunal with some administrative powers; or the district under the jurisdiction of such a body.

auto de fe (S) — now generally accepted to mean the public execution by a civil tribunal of a sentence previously pronounced by the tribunal of the Inquisition. (Strictly the term applies to the meeting of the Inquisition at which suspected heretics could abjure their errors in a public "act of faith.")

auto sacramental (S) — a Spanish equivalent of the English morality play, usually in praise of the Eucharist and performed on Corpus Christi after a procession carrying the Host through the streets of a town.

654

avocado or *aguacate* (M–S) — *Persea americana* (*gratissima*), a subtropical tree of the laurel family; or its fruit.

ayuntamiento (S) — an elected municipal council or *cabildo;* or the building where it meets.

azotea (A) — a roof terrace on which one can walk, usually with a parapet or rail, and sometimes with a covering.

Baldacchino (I) or *baldaquin* — a canopy over an altar or throne, either suspended or borne on movable poles; the canopy carried over the Host in processions.

barrio (S) — a major division of a town, a ward or precinct.

basilica — a type of church with a single nave flanked by aisles and lighted by clerestory windows above them.

battlement — a serrated parapet (alternating merlons and gaps) put at the top of a wall for defense.

Cabildo (S) — a municipal council or *ayuntamiento;* or the building where it meets.

cacique (C) — the chief of a native town.

calpulli (M) —a social or religious organization of the men of one part of a preconquest city; or the quarter of the city where they lived.

Calvario (S) — a raised Calvary Cross or Group, usually a tall Crucifix flanked by a mourning Virgin and Saint John; a chapel containing such a Cross or Group.

canto llano (S) — *cantus planus,* plainsong, Gregorian Chant, the chant of the Roman Church as distinguished from the Milanese, Gallican, or Mozarabic — unaccompanied, monophonic, and rhythmically free.

canto de órgano (S) — mensural music, often polyphonic, written with differentiated notes indicating different durations.

capilla mayor (S) — liturgically the principal part of the church, the space for officiating clergy and altar, usually the same as the chancel or presbytery.

capillita (S) — a little chapel.

catechism — oral instruction in the Christian Doctrine by means of question and answer; a written or printed manual of the Christian Doctrine.

catechumen — an adult or adolescent undergoing training and instruction preparatory to Baptism.

cathedral — the chief church of a diocese containing the bishop's throne or *cathedra.*

cavetto (I) — a concave molding approximately a quarter-circle in section.

cenote (M) — a deep hole in the limestone shelf of Yucatan with a potable water supply below serving as a community well or reservoir.

chancel — the space reserved for the officiating clergy, immediately in front of the apse and usually separated from the nave by a chancel rail.

chançoneta or *chanzoneta* (S) — a short ballad or festive song sung on a religious festival, most commonly at Christmastime.

chemin-de-ronde (F) — an exterior walkway around the upper part of a building, arranged for purposes of defense and usually shielded by a battlemented parapet.

655

GLOSSARY

Chichimeca (M) — a generic name for the wild nomadic tribes north and north-west of the Valley of Mexico.

chinampa (M) — a small Indian garden plot surrounded by little waterways, often artificially built up of mud and reed mats, but never floating.

chirimía (S) — a small clarinet-like wind instrument of wood with a single-reed mouthpiece and six to ten holes.

chirimoya (SA) — *Annona cherimola,* a tropical or subtropical fruit borne on the chirimoyo tree, sometimes called the "custard-apple."

choir — in architecture that part of a church which accommodates the singers (canons, monks, friars, or regular choir), in Europe often located between the transept and apse, in Mexico usually on a balcony at the west end of the nave.

chrism — a mixture of olive oil and balsam balm consecrated by a bishop on Maundy Thursday, used in the rites of Baptism, Confirmation, and Ordination, and for the consecration of altars, chalices, fonts, bells, and churches.

ciborium — in architecture a fixed canopy over an altar, carried on wood or more usually stone columns.

cimborio or *cimborrio* (S) — a dome over the crossing of a Spanish church, usually raised on a drum with windows; also the space under such a dome.

clarion — a kind of shrill trumpet with a long narrow metal tube.

cloister vault or *bishop's hat vault* — a square (occasionally oblong) vault whose four sides curve up to a common apex, and form a hollow pyramid with bulging sides.

coatepantli (M) — the circuit wall of an Aztec sacred enclosure often crested with carved serpents; also, a rack for the skulls of sacrificial victims.

cochineal — a carmine, crimson, magenta, or purple dye or paint made of the dried bodies of the *coccus cacti* insect which lives on nopal cactus.

codex or *códice* (S) — a preconquest manuscript or postconquest one made by natives; also a manuscript volume of miscellaneous related texts (such as the *Códice franciscano*).

coffer — a box-like sinkage in a ceiling or in the soffit of an arch or beam, commonly square or polygonal.

colonette — a small column, usually more decorative than structural.

Compline — the last of the canonical services of the day.

console — a kind of bracket or corbel often used ornamentally in a cornice, usually formed with an S-shaped scroll below.

copla (S) — a popular song or ballad formed of short verses, often couplets.

corbel — a block of stone projected outward beyond the face of the stones below in order to support or help support something above.

cornice — a projecting group of moldings usually used to crown a building or some important part of a building; the top element of a classical entablature immediately above the frieze.

corporal — a square linen altar-cloth on which the Chalice and Host are placed, used also to cover the Chalice.

coscomate (M) — a vase-shaped corncrib or small silo of wattle-and-daub topped by a conical thatched roof.

crenellation — a battlement, merlon, or short section of parapet between two open notches; or a series of such, with the solids for protecting a defender from hostile fire and the gaps for allowing him to return it. (The gaps are sometimes called *crenelles*.)

656

criollo (S) — a creole, someone of Spanish blood born in a Spanish-American or other colonial dependency.

cu (C) or *ku* (in Yucatan) — a native temple or pyramid, a *teocalli*.

cuauhxicalli (M) — a vessel or box to receive fresh hearts torn out in human sacrifice, usually carved in some kind of lava stone.

custodia (S) — a monstrance or tabernacle for the display of the Host; also a subdivision of a Mendicant Province (a Franciscan term occasionally extended to similar divisions in the other Orders).

D*anzante* (S) — a native performer in a public religious dance, preconquest or postconquest.

dentils — a row of smallish tooth-like rectangular blocks often used as a molding in classical cornices.

donado (S) — anyone (usually a native) who lived in a monastery, gave his services to the friars, and wore a version of the monastic habit, but was not ordained.

drum — in architecture one of the cylindrical stones or sections which make up the shaft of a column; also a hollow cylinder of wall carrying a dome.

E*jecutorial* (S) — an order to carry out the sentence of a tribunal; or a royal order to observe the directives in a Papal Bull.

encomienda (S) — a royal grant of native labor to a Spanish settler; the tract of land where the natives bound in encomienda to an encomendero were settled.

encuentro (S) — a type of rural religious community celebration held in the atrio, most commonly in Holy Week.

entablature — that part of a classical order above the column, normally consisting of an architrave, frieze, and cornice (the frieze occasionally omitted).

ermita (S) — a small independent chapel or oratory used only on special occasions, not usually located in a town.

espadaña (S) — a short wall pierced with arches in which bells are hung.

F*inial* — an ornament placed at the top of a pediment, roof, or any architectural composition, usually with a highly characterized silhouette.

flageolet — a small end-blown wind instrument similar to a recorder, a whistle flute, usually with six holes in front and a thumb hole in back.

fresco (I) — mural painting on plaster; *"true" fresco* painted with pigment mixed with water and applied on fresh wet plaster which on drying incorporates the pigment into the wall behind a film of carbonate of lime; *fresco secco* with pigments compounded with glue, gum, honey, or egg binder, applied to dry plaster or to old plaster specially dampened.

friar — a brother in one of the Mendicant Orders (in Mexico in the sixteenth century, Franciscan, Dominican, Augustinian, and at the end, Carmelite).

frontal — a movable ornamental covering for the front of an altar, made of cloth, wood, or metal, also called an *antependium*.

657

GLOSSARY

Gallican Rite — the non-Roman rite of the early Church in Gaul and Spain.

garita (S) — a sentry box, or sentry-box-like feature often used as an episode on a battlemented wall.

garth — an enclosed yard beside a building.

groin vault or groined vault — a square (occasionally oblong) vault formed like the intersection of two barrel vaults at right angles.

guava or guayaba (M) — Psidium guajava, a tropical tree of the myrtle family; or its fruit.

Hacienda (S) — a landed estate, usually a plantation given over to agriculture or a ranch given over to cattle raising.

hautboy — an ancestor of the oboe, a wooden wind instrument with a double reed mouthpiece, made in various sizes for various ranges of pitch, often in sets of up to seven.

hermita (S) — obsolete for ermita.

hidalgo (S) — a person belonging to the Spanish nobility by birth.

Huaxteca (M) — the region of northern Veracruz, southern Tamaulipas, and eastern San Luis Potosí, inhabited by related Huaxteca-speaking tribes.

huéhuetl (M) — a vertically cylindrical wooden drum with a taut skin head, struck presumably with the fingers.

Huitzilopochtli (M) — "Hummingbird wizard," god of war, one of the main solar dieties of the Aztecs, and chief god of Tenochtitlán.

humilladero (S) — a wayside chapel or shrine containing a Calvary Cross or image, usually at the entrance to a town; also, a wayside Calvary Cross.

hyssop — a bushy herb the twigs of which had been used to asperge in Hebrew rites and occasionally in Spain in the mass conversions of Moslems.

Iconography — a system of representing or suggesting important subject matter or personages (usually religious and significant beyond what is immediately visible) by the categorical use of pictorial symbols.

impost — the molding, band, or other top member of the pier or wall on which rests the lowest part of an arch (the springing).

Jacal or xacal (M) — a thatched hut, commonly with adobe walls.

jamb — the side post or wall of a doorway or window, particularly the surface facing the opening.

Knop — a rounded protuberance resembling a knob, boss, or bud.

Lectern — a high desk or stand for the books from which the Gospel and Epistle are read during Mass, or for chant-books.

lonja (S) — a public exchange building, often with an open lower floor, where merchants met for business and trade.

Machicolation — a projecting balcony or shallow gallery, usually high above a doorway or other entrance, supported on corbels between which are holes through which stones, molten lead, or some burning substance could be dropped on assailants; or one of those openings.

madroño (S) — *Arbutus unedo,* sometimes called the "strawberry tree."

maguey (C) — *Agave americana* or *mexicana,* the large aloe or "century plant."

mamey (C) — *Mamea americana,* a tropical fruit tree; or its fruit, sometimes called the "mammee-apple."

manoelino (P) or *manuelino* (S) — the late gothic style of Portugal which flourished especially during the reign of Manoel I (1469–1521), tinged with exotic influences from mudéjar, African, and perhaps Indian art.

Matlatzinca (M) — the principal tribe of the Valley of Toluca and of the region around Charo in Michoacán; or their language.

Mendicant — applied to the religious Orders dependent on alms (in sixteenth-century Mexico the Franciscans, Dominicans, Augustinians, and later the Carmelites).

mensa — the flat stone slab constituting the top of an altar, generally marked with the five crosses of its consecration; also, a similar but smaller stone set into the top of an altar temporarily or permanently.

merlon — a single battlement, the short section of a military parapet between two gaps.

mestizo (S) — a person born of one Spanish and one Indian parent, or with other mixture of Spanish and Indian blood.

metate (M) — a slightly concave slab of lava stone used for grinding corn.

mihrâb (A) — a recess in the rear wall of a mosque marking the direction of Mecca and the direction in which the faithful at prayer must face.

mimbar (A) — the pulpit in a mosque from which the Koran is read.

mitote (M) — a native religious dance involving scores of costumed *danzantes.*

Mixteca (M) — a large region of southeast Puebla and northwest Oaxaca, much of it thickly populated by Mixteca-speaking tribes.

Mixteca Alta (M + S) — the part of the Mixteca in the Sierra Madre Occidental around Tlaxiaco, Yanhuitlán, and Coixtlahuaca.

monocordio (S) or *monocord* — originally the name of a mediaeval musical instrument with one string stretched above a resonator, which soon became polychordic, and evolved by the sixteenth century into the early clavichord.

monstrance — an *ostensorium,* a receptacle for the display of the Host on an altar, or in a procession through the streets as on the Feast of Corpus Christi.

Morisco (S) — a converted Moslem who had accepted Christian Baptism, usually an ex-Mudéjar.

motet (F) — an unaccompanied choral composition, generally on a sacred subject and written in imitative counterpoint.

Mozarab (A) — a practicing Spanish Christian living under tolerant Moslem rule and adopting Moslem social and cultural patterns.

mozarabic (A) — Spanish Christian art of the ninth to eleventh centuries under strong Moslem stylistic influences, the art of the Mozarabes.

Mozarabic Rite — the rite prevalent in Spain from the fifth through the eleventh centuries, in some regions until the fifteenth (misnamed because used by the Visigoths and not related to the Mozarabes), in Latin America now persisting only in marriage rites.

mudéjar (A) — art in Moslem or Moslem-influenced style made for Spanish Christians, chiefly from the thirteenth to the fifteenth centuries; also a tribute-paying Moslem living under Spanish Christian rule — the opposite of a Mozarab.

mul (M) — a pyramid-temple of Yucatan, a *teocalli.*

muṣallà (A) — a walled but unroofed religious precinct in Moslem Andalusia, usually at the edge of a city, serving principally for mass meetings to pray for rain.

Náhuatl (M) — the common language of the Aztecs and some of their neighbors, the widespread official language used even in non-Aztec parts of the Aztec "Empire."

narthex — a vestibule or portico at the entrance of an Early Christian church to which catechumens and penitents were relegated during Mass.

nopal (M) — *Nopalea cocinellifera,* a cactus cultivated for the support of the cochineal insect; *Opuntia ficus indica,* the "prickly pear" cactus, sometimes cultivated for its fruit (the *tuna*).

Observants — a reformed branch of the Franciscan Order (from 1368) which followed Saint Francis' strict rule to the letter (as opposed to the more liberal Conventuals), divided in the sixteenth century into the Capuchins and Recollects.

obsidian — natural glass, dark vitreous lava or volcanic rock (the Náhuatl *zinapa*) used for aras, blades, mirrors, and miscellaneous small precious objects.

ogee — a pointed arch with S-curved sides, concave below and convex above.

oidor (S) — a judge who was a member of an *audiencia.*

opus incertum — a Roman wall surfacing of small stones inserted in a core of concrete or of rubble and lime.

orans or *orante* — a figure with arms outstretched like a cross, often painted in the Roman catacombs to represent a Christian in the act of prayer, or perhaps his soul in perpetual prayer.

oratory — a small chapel not the principal place of worship for a fixed congregation but for some special group.

ostensorium — see *monstance*

Otomí (M) — a group of tribes (some nomadic) in the region north of the Valley of Mexico (in Guanajuato, Querétaro, Hidalgo, and México); also their common language.

Pange Lingua — a hymn still sung to one of the few melodies surviving from the extinct Gallican Rite.

Pánuco (M) — the region of the broad valley of the River Pánuco and the adjacent coastal plain (in northern Veracruz and southern Tamaulipas).

papaya (C) — *Carica papaya;* or its melon-like fruit sometimes called "paw-paw."

parti (F) — the essential scheme or distribution of the principal elements in an architectural composition.

paso (S) — a sculptured group representing a scene from the Passion, usually colored and life-size, carried through the streets in Holy Week.

patronato real (S) — the right of the king of Spain to name bishops and other religious to cathedrals, churches, and other benefices.

pediment — the triangular gable end of a building outlined by cornices, or a similar arrangement of the same shape used decoratively.

pésame (S) — a condolence delivered personally to a recently bereaved family, often in connection with the telling of the Rosary by a group.

pilaster — a decorative pseudo-support having the same elements as a classical column (base, shaft, capital), a shallow rectangle in plan with one long side attached to a wall.

Pirinda (M) — a branch of the Matlatzinca tribe living around Charo in Michoacán; also their peculiarly difficult language.

pisé (F) — construction of earth, usually clayey (sometimes mixed with rubble) rammed between board forms and there allowed to harden.

plateresque — a kind of Spanish architecture which flourished c1470–1550: divided into *gothic plateresque* (the decorative late gothic manner often elaborated into flattish dense patterns of mudéjar character, also called *Isabelino* or *Isabelline*); and *renaissance plateresque* (the early renaissance manner with italianate ornamental details organized similarly to gothic plateresque, and like it featuring patterned areas akin to mudéjar but without mudéjar detail).

polyptych — an altarpiece made of a planned combination of several related pictures or reliefs, sometimes equipped with folding wings.

portal de peregrinos (S) — a portico where pilgrims are received, adjacent or close to a church, sometimes identical with a portería or *racionero*.

portales (S) — porticoes, arcades, or colonnades, particularly those facing or surrounding plazas.

portería (S) — the porch or vestibule at the main entrance to a monastery.

posa (S) — a small chapel-like building in the corner of an atrio at which outdoor religious processions made a pause; see Chapter VIII.

predella (I) — a long narrow picture set at the bottom of an altarpiece often forming its base.

presbytery — the sanctuary or eastern part of the chancel where the altar stands; also called a *capilla mayor*.

presidio (S) — a garrison of soldiers; also their fort or fortified settlement.

pulque (M) — a drink made of the fermented sap of magueyes about to flower.

purista (S) — a strict academic renaissance style of the mid-sixteenth century.

Qibla (A) — the axis of the direction towards Mecca, marked in a mosque by the mihrâb.

qubba (A) — a monumental Islamic tomb, often square and topped with a dome.

Quetzalcóatl (M) — "Plumed serpent," the god of the air, the wind, the evening star, commerce, and knowledge, presumably a deified Tolteca king (who later appeared in Yucatan as Kukulcan).

quincunx — a symmetrical arrangement of several items equal distances apart.

Rabbet or *rebate* — a groove cut on one surface, such as the jamb of a door or window, to receive the edge of another piece (sometimes movable), such as a door or window.

racionero (S) — the portico of a monastery where alms are distributed, sometimes identical with the portería (especially in Yucatan).

ramada (S) —a walless thatched shed.

GLOSSARY

rebec (A) — a primitive, pear-shaped, bowed instrument usually with three strings.

rejoneado (S) — a native masonry technique.

relación (S) — a report (often official) about local conditions.

retable — a set of decorated panels of sculpture or painting rising above the back of an altar.

reticulated — arranged in a pattern resembling a net.

rinceau (F) — a running pattern of foliate spirals.

rollo (S) — a cross, or a cylindrical or polygonal tower in a town plaza, from the base of which judicial sentences were pronounced.

rubble — coarse masonry made of a conglomerate of undressed stone and mortar which is poured or dumped rather than laid in courses, generally used as filling.

rustication — masonry with sunk joints arranged in a regular pattern, usually with natural or naturalistically rough surfaces on the exposed face of the individual stones.

S*ackbut* — a mediaeval trombone with a slide for changing the pitch.

Sala de Profundis (S) — a chapter hall, so called from the first words of Psalm 130 read at the close of meetings held there.

Salve Regina — "Hail Holy Queen," one of the oldest antiphonies of Our Lady, often sung by friars after Compline.

sanctuary — the east end of a church, specifically the apse and space immediately in front of the altar.

sărīa' (A) — an open court similar to a *muṣallà*.

sepulchrum — a shallow cavity in the upper part of an altar (in the stipes or the mensa or between them) where relics were placed during the act of Consecration.

sgraffito (I) — a technique of decorating a wall by scraping through a thin surface layer of plaster to a lower coat usually of a different color.

soffit — the exposed underside of an architectural member, particularly of an arch or lintel.

spandrel — the triangular space left between the outer edge of an arch and a vertical member beside it, or the triangle between two adjacent arches.

squinch — an arch, niche, or beam carried across the corner of a square or polygonal space to help support a dome or other covering.

stereotomy — the arrangement or pattern in which structural cut stones are fitted together in a wall or vault.

stipes — the lower part of a fixed altar which supports the mensa, statutarily of stone.

T*apia* (S) — a kind of *pisé* wall construction of earth (sometimes clay or mortar and stones) rammed between boards and allowed to harden.

Tarasco (M) — pertaining to the Tarasca-speaking nation inhabiting the modern State of Milchoacán, and having their traditional capital at Tzintzuntzan.

tecali (M) — a translucent alabaster quarried principally near the town of Tecali in the State of Puebla.

tejocote (M) — *Crataegus pubescens* (*mexicana*), a small tree of the family of the rosaciae; or its cherry- or plum-like fruit.

662

temascal (M) — a small building for native sweat baths.

teocalli (M) — a native temple on a pyramid, a *cu* or *mul.*

tepetate (M) — a porous conglomerate stone which can be cut with a saw but hardens on exposure, used for building walls in many parts of central Mexico.

teponaxtle (M) — a horizontally cylindrical wooden drum with an H-shaped slit on the upper side forming two tongues toned a fifth apart, played with special sticks.

tequitqui (M) — postconquest art (relief sculpture in particular) using European motifs combined with an Indian sense of pattern.

Tezcatlipoca (M) — "Smoking mirror," a powerful solar deity of the Aztecs appearing in many varied aspects.

thurible — a censer, a metal cup with a pierced cover for the ceremonial burning of incense, usually suspended on chains.

tianguis (M) — a native public market, or the plaza where it was held (commonly once a week).

Tlāloc (M) — "He who makes things sprout," the Aztec rain god.

tonalámatl (M) — the Aztec calendar-almanac.

Tonantzín (M) — the Aztec goddess of motherhood.

tortilla (S) — a thin disc of unleavened cornmeal, a staple in both the preconquest and postconquest Mexican diet.

torus — a molding of convex semicircular section.

trachyte — a volcanic rock with a gritty surface, usually pink, tan, or gray.

traza (S) — a regular town-plan; a drawing of such a town-plan; any architectural drawing of a plan; also the regularly planned zone of México-Tenochtitlán or Puebla reserved for the houses of the Spaniards.

triptych — a common format for an altarpiece with painting or reliefs arranged in three panels, often hinged so that the sides fold over the center.

tuna (M) — the "prickly pear" fruit of the *nopal* cactus.

V*ara* (S) — a measure of 33.6 inches, usually divided into 3 *pies* (feet) or 4 *palmos* (palms).

vicaría (S) — a town in the jurisdiction of a monastery where a few friars resided but which did not rank as a monastery and had no vote in Chapter Meetings; also the building of such an establishment.

villancico (S) — a popular song (often accompanied by a lute) sung on religious occasions such as Christmas.

visita (S) — a town in the jurisdiction of a monastery where friars did not live but which they visited periodically to say Mass.

volador (S) — a native religious flying game or dance performed by men whirling outward in descending spirals on ropes attached to the top of a tall central pole, still performed in the mountains of Veracruz and Hidalgo.

voussoir (F) — one of the wedge-shaped blocks which constitute an arch or vault when arranged in an organized series.

W*attle-and-daub* — a framework of poles and interwoven twigs smeared over with clay or mud, used for the walls of humble buildings.

GLOSSARY

X*acal* — obsolete form for *jacal*.

Xochipilli (M) — "Flower prince," the Aztec god of flowers and the dance (with an important sanctuary at Tizatlán), the patron also of springtime, song, gaming, feasting, pleasure, and frivolity.

Y*ácata* (M) — a mound-temple of the Taracos.

Z*apote* (M) — *Diospyros ebenaster,* the *zapote prieto,* a large subtropical tree of the persimmon family, and also its fruit; *Sapota achras,* the *chicosapote,* a somewhat larger tree with smaller fruit (sometimes called the "sapodilla") from the sap of which chewing gum is made.

Zapoteca (M) — a nation inhabiting the Valley of Oaxaca, with religious centers at Monte Albán and Mitla and a political center at Zaachila.

zéjel (A) — a Spanish Moslem verse form.

zinapa (M) — the Náhuatl term for obsidian.

664

BIBLIOGRAPHY

BIBLIOGRAPHICAL NOTE

I have drawn from as many contemporary and near-contemporary sources as were pertinent and available, though limiting them to those published. In little-explored archives there must be revealing papers and parchments awaiting some alert researcher. It has seemed proper to draw from the chroniclers of later centuries who often drew from earlier writings now lost. I have used the newer editions of the older books which have been republished because of their availability and valuable scholarly notes.

Because of their still unsurpassed accumulations of facts, more recent secondary sources have proved valuable, particularly those of the historians of a few generations ago, such as García Icazbalceta and Orozco y Berra. I have drawn on partisan modern writers, such as Fathers Bravo Ugarte and Cuevas, but less often and more warily, and sometimes with partisan counterweights from another side. To show which are the older and primary sources in the ensuing list, parentheses have been appended with dates and, while most of these figures are documented, some could probably accept refinement of a year or two.

Occasionally I have used whatever edition was available where I happened to be working — Mexico or Massachusetts, Rio or Rome — and consequently a few peripheral references are to "popular" editions. When they contained pertinent material I have used some works which may seem more popular than scholarly, such as nineteenth-century travel books, because of their descriptions of monuments now altered or destroyed.

Since the comments of their editors sometimes compete with the texts themselves in interest — for example, Wigberto Jiménez Moreno's notes for the *Códice de Yanhuitlán* — I have put their names in the listing, or listed the text under the name of its editor. Important works which have been issued as parts of a series of otherwise little-related texts (such as Motolinía's *Memoriales*) are listed under their authors; or under their titles if author is unknown or if authorship is questionable or irrelevant (as in documents where the writer is less an author than a hired scribe). Cross-references ought to clear confusion.

Works whose title might lead to mistaken identity or uncertain classification are often listed under their editors: Father Cuevas' volume of *Documentos inéditos del siglo XVI para la historia de México,* for example, is cited and indexed under Cuevas, *Documentos* . . . in the hope that thus it may less likely be confused with the 36-volume *Documentos inéditos o muy raros para la historia de México,* or with the *Documentos históricos de Méjico.*

Abbreviations, which are necessary in undisciplined titles more than twenty words long, will be found at the beginning of the notes.

Double surnames are listed in full, and indexed under the first, in accord with Latin-American and Spanish practice, even when the last name is better known than the first: hence for Icazbalceta, see García Icazbalceta. Only for a few Indian writers, such as Fernando de Alva Ixtlilxóchitl, have I subordinated the first, or patronymic, as he did, and stressed the second, or metronymic, his royal native

665

BIBLIOGRAPHY

name, Ixtlilxóchitl; for similar reasons, Hernando Alvarado Tezozomoc will be found under *T*. When the full names are known but were rarely used in full, the semi-superfluous elements are in parentheses: hence Gonzalo Fernández de Oviedo (y Valdés).

Good usage and consistency do not always agree about surnames introduced by *de* or some form of the definite article. Inasmuch as the good but variable usage in Spanish is not accessible to everyone, while consistency is, all such names are ruthlessly listed here *without* the preposition but *with* the definite article, and arranged alphabetically without heed to either: Bishop Bartolomé de las Casas (or Las Casas), will consequently be found among the C's as *las Casas, Bartolomé de*. (Such usage is less customarily imposed on modern authors, who might now appear in some library catalogue or telephone directory as *Casas, Bartolomé de las*. Customs vary from country to country.) To avoid confusion, I have used one system for everyone, living or dead, Spanish or Mexican, and I hope that Francisco de la Maza and some of our common friends will not feel that they have been typographically treated as dead — *la Maza, Francisco de* — and instead take it as a tribute that I list them in the same way as writers who have been established as long as Bishop las Casas.

In the hope that they may help the pronunciation of readers unfamiliar with Spanish, accents have been used, even on Náhuatl terms which do not have to have them, and on the titles of old books which did not originally have them.

To a work on a subject about which I have claimed that so little has been written, it may seem odd to append so long a bibliography; but it is because so little is listed elsewhere that I have made it so long. Outside the writings of Toussaint, Angulo, Kubler, la Maza, and Flores Guerrero, 99 per cent of the items listed are not primarily concerned with Mexican architecture of the sixteenth century. Each work does contain, however, something pertinent, though perhaps only peripherally. (How is one to know the extent of the center if one does not scan the periphery?) The following list is of the books and articles which I have used and hope may be useful to others. If some important works are missing, it is because I have not read them.

666

BIBLIOGRAPHICAL LIST

Acosta, Jorge R., and Gorbea Trueba, José, and Martínez del Río, Pablo. *Tula, Guía oficial*. México (Instituto Nacional de Antropología e Historia), 1957.

Acosta, José de (c1539–1600). *De procuranda indorum salute* (1575–   ), translated, with introduction and notes, by Francisco Mateos. Madrid (España Misionera), 1952.

——— *The Natural and Moral History of the Indies* (1st ed. 1588–89), reprinted from the English edition translated by Edward Grimston, 1604, edited, with notes and introduction, by Clements R. Markham. London (Hakluyt Society), 1880, 2 vols.

Acosta Saignes, Miguel — see Sahagún, *Historia* . . .

Adams, Eleanor B. — see *Advertimientos* . . . ; *Documentos para la historia de Yucatán*; Domínguez, *Missions* . . . ; *Memoria de* . . . *Nuño de Guzmán*; *Proceso contra Tzintzicha* . . . ; Scholes and Adams, *Don Diego Quejada* . . .

Advertimientos generales que los Virreyes dejaron a sus sucesores para el gobierno de Nueva España, 1590–1604, edited by France V. Scholes and Eleanor B. Adams. México (Porrua), 1956.

Aguayo Spencer, Rafael. *Don Vasco de Quiroga, documentos* (includes Moreno biography, *Ordenanzas*, Will, etc.). México (Polis), 1939 (1940).

——— *Siluetas michoacanas, cinco ensayos*. México (Bosque), 1941.

Aguilar, Francisco de (1479–1571). *Historia de la Nueva España* (1560), edited by Alfonso Teja Zabre. México (Botas), 1938.

Aguilar, Gilberto F. *Hospitales de Antaño*. México (Hospital Juárez), 1944.

Aguirre Beltrán, Gonzalo. *El proceso de aculturación*. México (Universidad), 1957.

——— "The Slave Trade in Mexico" in *H A H R*, XXIV (1944).

——— See also Marroquín, *Ciudad mercado* . . .

Aiton, Arthur Scott. *Antonio de Mendoza, First Viceroy of New Spain*. Durham, N.C. (Duke University), 1927. See also Wilgus, *Colonial Hispanic America*.

Ajofrín, Francisco de, and Olite, Fermín de. *Diario del viaje que hicimos a México* (1763–   ). México (Robredo), 1936.

Alamán, Lucas. *Obras*. México (Agüeros), 1899–1901, 5 vols.

Alcedo, Antonio de (1736–1812). *Diccionario geográfico-histórico de las Indias occidentales o América*. Madrid (Cano-González), 1786–89, 5 vols.

Alcolea, Santiago. *Granada*. Barcelona (Aries), 1960.

Aldana, Cristóbal de (1735–   ). *Crónica de la Merced de México*, introduction and notes by Jorge Gurría Lacroix. México (Biblioteca Nacional), 1953.

"Alegato de Fr. Diego de Osorio en favor de la parroquia de San José de los Naturales" in *Memorias de la Academia Mexicana de Historia*, XV (1956).

(Alessio Robles, Miguel). *Cuernavaca (Monografías mexicanas, Estado de Morelos)*. México (Cultura), 1934.

Almoina, José. "Citas clásicas de Zumárraga" in *Historia mexicana*, II (1953/54).

BIBLIOGRAPHY

Alonso de San Juan — see Ponce, *Relación* . . .

Altolaguirre y Duvale, Angel de. *Descubrimiento y conquista de México*. Barcelona (Salvat), 1954.

Alva Ixtlilxóchitl, Fernando de — see Ixtlilxóchitl, Fernando de Alva.

Alvarado, Francisco de. *Vocabuiario en lengua mixteca* (1592), introduction by Wigberto Jiménez Moreno. México (Instituto Nacional Indigenista e Instituto Nacional de Antropología e Historia), 1962.

Alvarado Tezozomoc, Fernando de — see Tezozomoc, Fernando de Alvarado.

Alvarez, Manuel F. *Apuntes biográficos de arquitectos mexicanos*. México (Vargas Rea), 1955.

Alvarez Barret, Luis — see Pedro de Gante, *Cartilla* . . .

Anales antiguos de México y sus contornos — see *Anales mexicanos–uno pedernal diez caña; Anales mexicanos–1589–1596*.

Anales de Cuauhtitlán — see *Códice Chimalpopoca*.

Anales mexicanos–uno pedernal diez caña, anónimo en lengua mexicana, traducido al español por el Lic. Faustino Chimalpopoca. México (Vargas Rea), 1949.

Anales mexicanos–1589–1596, ms inédito en la Biblioteca del Museo, tomo I, *Anales de México y sus contornos*, anónimo de lengua mexicana traducido al español por el Lic. Faustino Chimalpopoca Galicia. México (Vargas Rea), 1954.

Anales de Quauhtinchán — see *Historia Tolteca-Chichimeca*.

Anales de Tarécuato (1666). México (Vargas Rea), 1953.

Anales de Tecamachalco (1590) in *Colección de documentos para la historia mexicana*, edited by Antonio Peñafiel. México (Secretaría de Fomento), 1903.

Ancona, Eligio — see *Antología de la historia de Yucatán*.

Anesagasti, Jaime de. *Tonalá ayer y hoy*. Guadalajara (Navarrete), 1941.

Angeli, Diego. *Le chiese di Roma*. Rome, 1904.

Anglería, Pedro Mártir de — see Pedro Mártir de Anglería.

Angulo Iñiguez, Diego. *Arquitectura mudéjar sevillana de los siglos XIII, XIV, y XV*. Seville (Universidad), 1932.

——— "La capilla de Indios de Teposcolula y la Catedral de Siena" in *Archivo español de arte*, XXV (1952).

——— *Las catedrales mejicanas del siglo XVI*. Madrid (separata del *Boletín de la Real Academia de Historia*), 1943.

——— *Historia del arte hispanoamericano*, I, II, with chapters by Enrique Marco Dorta and Mario Buschiazzo. Barcelona (Salvat), 1945, 1950.

——— "The Mudéjar Style in Mexican Architecture" in *Ars Islámica*, II (1935).

——— *Planos de monumentos arquitectónicos de América y Filipinas existentes en el Archivo de Indias*. Seville (Universidad), 1933–39, 4 vols. and atlas.

——— See also Calderón Quijano, *Fortificaciones* . . .

Anonymous Conqueror — see Conquistador Anónimo.

Antigüedades mexicanas, published by the Junta Colombina de México en el IV Centenario del Descubrimiento de América. México (Secretaría de Fomento), 1892, 2 vols.

Antología de la historia de Yucatán, articles by Ancona, Cámara Závala, Carillo y Ancona, Esquivel Pren, Molina Solís, and Morley. México (Cultura), 1951.

Antonio de Ciudad Rodrigo — see Ponce, *Relación* . . .

Appleton's Guide to Mexico — see Conkling, *Appleton's Guide* . . .

Archivo mexicano, Documentos para la historia de México . . . — see *Sumario de la residencia* . . . *Cortés.*

Arenas, Atanasio. "Cuilapan" in *Mapa,* #71 (1940).

────── "Cuitzeo" in *Mapa,* #74 (1940).

Arfe y Villafañe, Juan de (1535–1603). *Varia comensuración para la escultura y arquitectura* (1585).

Argensola, Bartolomé Leonardo y — see Leonardo y Argensola, Bartolomé.

Arillaga, Basilio — see *Concilio III* . . .

Aristotle. *Politics.* Cambridge, Mass. (Harvard, Loeb Library), 1950.

Arlégui, José (de). *Crónica de la santa Provincia de nuestro P San Francisco de Zacatecas.* México (Hogal), 1737.

Armas Medina, Fernando de. "Evolución histórica de las doctrinas de indios" in *Anuario de Estudios Americanos,* IX (1952).

Armillas, Pedro — see West and Armillas, "Las chinampas . . ."

Arriaga, Antonio. "La relación geográfica del pueblo de Charo" in *Anales del Museo Michoacano,* IV (1946).

Arroyo, Esteban. *El monumental convento de Santo Domingo de Oajaca.* Oaxaca (author), 1955.

Ars Hispaniae — see Chueca Goitia, *Arquitectura del siglo XVI,* Gudiol Ricart and Gaya Nuño, *Arquitectura y escultura* . . . ; Torres Balbás, *Arte almohade* . . .

"El arte en México en los siglos XVI y XVII," special number of *Archivo español de arte,* XXXI (1935) — see García Granados, "Capillas de indios . . ."; Toussaint, "Supervivencias góticas . . ."

Ascensio, José. *Cronistas franciscanos.* Guadalajara (Gráfica), 1944.

Atl, Dr. (pseud. for Murillo, Gerardo) — see Toussaint, *La arquitectura religiosa* . . .

Augustine (Augustinus, Aurelius, Saint). *The City of God against the Pagans.* Cambridge, Mass. (Harvard, Loeb Library), 1957.

"Auto de posessión del título de la ciudad de Zintzuntzan Vitzitzilan" (1590) in *Anales del Museo Michoacano,* II (1889).

Autos y coloquios del siglo XVI — see Rojas Garcidueñas, *Autos* . . .

Azcoitia, Francisco Xavier. *Reseña de la ciudad de Xalapa.* Jalapa (Talleres gráficos del Gobierno de Veracruz), 1943.

The Badianus Manuscript (Codex Barberini, Latin 241), *an Aztec Herbal of 1552,* translated, with introduction and notes, by Emily Walcott Emmart. Baltimore (Johns Hopkins), 1940.

Bandelier, Adolph Francis. *Report of an Archaeological Tour in Mexico in 1881, Papers of the Archaeological Institute of America,* II. Boston (Cupples, Upham), 1884.

Barlow, Robert H. "El Códice Azcatítlan" in *Journal de la Société des Américanistes,* XXXVIII (1949).

────── "Dos relaciones antiguas del pueblo de Cuilapa, Estado de Oaxaca," edited, with an introduction, by R. H. Barlow, in *Tlalocan,* II (1945/48). See also Steck, *El primer colegio de América* . . .

Barth, Pius Joseph. *Franciscan Education and the Social Order in Spanish North America 1502–1921* (published dissertation). Chicago (Chicago), 1945.

Basalenque, Diego de (1577–1651). *Historia de la Provincia de San Nicolás de*

BIBLIOGRAPHY

Tolentino, de Michoacán, del Orden de N P San Agustín (–1644).
México (Barbedillo), 1886.

Bataillon, Marcel. "La Vera Paz, roman et histoire" in Bulletin Hispanique, LXIII (1951).

——— "Zumárraga, reformador del clero seglar" in Historia Mexicana, III (1953/54).

Baxter, Sylvester. *La arquitectura hispano-colonial en México,* translated, with introduction and notes, by Manuel Toussaint. México (Departamento de Bellas Artes), "1934" (appeared 1943).

——— *Spanish-Colonial Architecture in Mexico,* photographs by Guillermo Kahlo; drawings by Bertram Grosvenor Goodhue. Boston (Millet), 1901, 1 vol. text, 9 portfolios illustrations.

Beaumont, Pablo de la Purísima Concepción. *Crónica de la Provincia de los Santos Apóstoles S Pedro y S Pablo de Michoacán, de la regular observancia de N P S Francisco* (1777–78). México (Archivo General de la Nación), 1932, 2 vols.

Bello Martínez, Ernesto. *La fundación de Puebla de los Angeles.* Teziutlán (author), 1945.

Belmar, Francisco. *Breve reseña histórica y geográfica del Estado de Oaxaca.* Oaxaca (Imprenta del Comercio), 1901.

Beltrán, Antonio. *Valencia (Guías artísticas de España).* Barcelona (Aries), 1953.

Beltrán y Rózpide, Ricardo. *América en tiempo de Felipe II.* Madrid, 1927.

Benavente, Toribio de — see Motolinía, Toribio (de Benavente).

Benítez, Fernando. *La vida criolla en el siglo XVI.* México (Colegio de México), 1953.

Benítez, José R. *Alonso García Bravo, planeador de la Ciudad de México y su primer director de obras públicas.* México (Cía. de Fomento y Urbanización), 1933.

——— *La fuente monumental de Chiapa de Corzo.* Guadalajara, 1941.

——— *Morelia.* México (Talleres Gráficos de la Nación), 1935.

Benzoni, Girolamo (c1519–72). *History of the New World* (1555), edited and translated by W. H. Smyth. London (Hakluyt Society), 1857.

Berlin, Heinrich. "Artífices de la Catedral de México" in *Anales del I I E,* XI (1944).

——— "El convento de Tecpatán" in *Anales del I I E,* IX (1942).

——— *Fragmentos desconocidos del Códice de Yanhuitlán y otras investigaciones mixtecas.* México (Robredo), 1947.

——— "The High Altar of Huejotzingo" in *The Americas,* XV (1958/59).

——— See also *Historia Tolteca-Chichimeca.*

Bernal, Ignacio. *Introducción a la arqueología.* México (Fondo de Cultura), 1952.

——— *Monte Albán — Mitla,* translated by Pablo Martínez del Río. México (Instituto Nacional de Antropología e Historia), 1958.

——— *Tenochtitlán en una isla.* México (Instituto Nacional de Antropología e Historia), 1959.

Bernal Jiménez, Miguel. "Música nuestra, breve ensayo sobre la música mejicana" in *Estudios Americanos,* I (1948/49).

Bevan, Bernard. *History of Spanish Architecture.* New York and London (Scribner), 1939.

Biblioteca colonial americana — see *Relaciones geográficas de Indias.*

Blethen, John F. "The educational activities of Fray Alonso de la Vera Cruz in sixteenth century Mexico" in *The Americas*, V (1948/49).

Blom, Frans (Ferdinand). *The Conquest of Yucatan*. Boston (Houghton Mifflin), 1936. See also Tomás de la Torre, *Desde Salamanca* . . .

Blunt, Sir Anthony. *Artistic Theory in Italy*. Oxford (Clarendon), 1940.

Bopp, Marianne O de. "Autos mexicanos del siglo XVI" in *Historia Mexicana*, III (1953/54).

Borah, Woodrow (Wilson). "The collection of Tithes in the Bishopric of Oaxaca during the sixteenth century" in *H A H R*, XXI (1941).

—— *New Spain's Century of Depression*. Berkeley (California), 1951.

—— "The New World" in *The Americas*, XII (1955/56).

—— *Silk Raising in Colonial Mexico*. Berkeley (California), 1943.

—— See also Cook and Borah, . . . *Population* . . .

Bosch García, Carlos — see *Homenaje a Silvio Zavala* . . .

Bourne, Edward Gaylord. *Spain in America*. New York (Harper), 1904.

Braden, Charles S. *Religious Aspects of the Conquest of Mexico*. Durham, N.C. (Duke), 1930.

Brandi, Karl. *The Emperor Charles V*, translated by C. V. Wedgwood. London (Cape), 1954.

Brasseur "de Bourbourg," Charles Etienne (1814–74). *Voyage sur l'Isthme de Tehuantepec, dans l'état de Chiapas, et la république de Guatémala, executé dans les années 1859 et 1860*. Paris (Bertrand), 1861.

Braudel, Fernand. "La vita economica di Venezia nel secolo xvi" in *La civiltà del rinascimento*, Venice (Sansoni), 1958.

Braun, Joseph. *Der christliche Altar in seiner geschichtlichen Entwicklung*. Munich (Günther Koch), 1924, 2 vols.

Bravo Ugarte, José. *Historia de México*, vol. II, *La Nueva España*. México (Jus), 1941. See also Motolinía, *Carta al Emperador*.

Brenner, Anita. *Idols behind Altars*. New York (Payson, Clarke), 1929.

Bruman, Henry J. "Early Coconut Culture in Western Mexico" in *H A H R*, XXV (1925).

Burgoa, Francisco de (1605–81). *Geográfica descripción de la parte septentrional del polo ártico de la América, y neuva Iglesia de las Indias Occidentales y sitio astrónomico de esta Provincia de Predicadores de Antequera, valle de Oaxaca* . . . México (Publicaciones del Archivo General de la Nación), 1934, 2 vols.

—— *Palestra historial de virtudes y exemplares apostólicos* . . . México (Publicaciones del Archivo General de la Nación), 1934.

Burland, C. Arthur. *Art and Life in ancient Mexico*. Oxford (Cassirer), 1948.

Burrus, Ernest J. "Pioneer Jesuit Apostles in New Spain — 1572–1604" in *Archivum Historicum Societatis Jesu*, XXV (1956).

Buschiazzo, Mario. *Estudios de arquitectura colonial hispanoamericana*. Buenos Aires (Kraft), 1944. See also Angulo Iñiguez, *Historia* . . .

Byne, Arthur, and Stapely, Mildred. *Spanish Architecture of the XVI Century*. New York and London (Putnam, for Hispanic Society), 1917.

Cáceres López, Carlos. *Chiapas, Síntesis geográfica e histórica*. México (Forum), 1946.

Cajigas Langner, Alberto. *Monografía de Tehuantepec*. México (León Sánchez), 1954.

BIBLIOGRAPHY

Calderón de la Barca, Frances Erskine (Inglis) (1802–82). *Life in Mexico.* New York (Dutton), 1931.

Calderón Quijano, José Antonio. *Historia de las fortificationes en Nueva España,* foreword by Diego Angulo Iñiguez. Seville (Escuela de Estudios Hispano-americanos), 1953.

Camargo, Diego Muñoz — see Muñoz Camargo, Diego

Camón Aznar, José. *La arquitectura plateresca.* Madrid (Instituto Velázquez), 1945, 2 vols.

Camps y Cazorla, Emilio. *Módulo, proprociones y composición en la arquitectura califal cordobesa.* Madrid (Instituto Velázquez), 1953.

Cantón Rosado, Francisco. *Historia de la instrucción pública en Yucatán.* México (Secretaría de Educación Pública), 1943.

Caravaglieri, Giorgio. "Outline for a History of City Planning from Prehistory to the Fall of the Roman Empire" in *Journal of the Society of Architectural Historians,* VIII (1949).

Cárdenas, Juan de (1563–   ). *Problemas y secretos maravillosos de las Indias* (1588–89). México (Museo Nacional), 1913.

Cárdenas (y) Valencia, Francisco de. *Relación historial eclesiástica de la Provincia de Yucatán de Nueva España escrita el año de 1639.* México (Robredo), 1937.

Carranza, Baltasar Dorantes de — see Dorantes de Carranza, Baltasar

Carreño, Alberto María. "The Books of Fray Juan de Zumárraga" in *The Americas,* V (1948/49).

—— *Don Fray Juan de Zumárraga, Documentos inéditos.* México (Porrua), 1941.

—— *Fray Domingo de Betanzos, fundador en la Nueva España de la venerable Orden dominicana.* México (Victoria), 1924 (1934).

—— "La marquesa, doña Juana Zúñiga, esposa de Hernán Cortés, y el boticario Diego Velázquez" in *Memorias de la Academia Mexicana de Historia,* XI (1952).

—— *Nuevos documentos inéditos de D Fr Juan de Zumárraga y cédulas y cartas reales en relación con su gobierno.* México (Victoria), 1942.

—— See also *Un cedulario desconocido . . . ;* Gemelli Carreri, *México en 1697;* Gómez de Cervantes, *La vida económica . . . ;* Gómez de Orozco, *El convento de Cuernavaca.*

Carrera Stampa, Manuel. *Los gremios mexicanos; la organización gremial en Nueva España, 1521–1861.* México (Ibero-americana), 1954. See also *Memoria de . . . Nuño de Guzmán.*

Carrillo y Gariel, Abelardo. *Técnica de la pintura de Nueva España.* México (Universidad), 1946.

Carrión, Antonio. *Historia de la ciudad de Puebla de los Angeles.* Puebla (Dávalos), 1896.

Cartas de Indias. Madrid (Ministerio de Fomento), 1877.

Cartas de religiosos de Nueva España, 1539–1594, introduction by Joaquín García Icazbalceta. México (Chávez Hayhoe), 1941.

Cartas y relaciones de Hernán Cortés — see Cortés, *Cartas y relaciones . . .*

Cartilla vieja de . . . Puebla — see López de Villaseñor, *Cartilla . . .*

Cartografía de Puebla en el Archivo General de la Nación. Puebla (Centro de Estudios Históricos), 1958.

Casarrubias, Vicente. *Rebeliones indígenas en la Neuva España.* México (Educación Pública), 1945.

las Casas, Bartolomé de (1474–1566). *Apologética historia de las Indias* (after 1551, before 1566). Madrid (Bailli, Baillière), 1909.

—— *Breve relación de la destrucción de las Indias Occidentales,* foreword by Servando Teresa de Mier Noriega y Guerra; notes by Ignacio Romerovargas Yturbide. México (Luciernaga), 1957.

Cascajo Romero, Juan. "La medicina en la vida de Cortés" in *Anuario de estudios americanos,* IV (1947).

Caso, Alfonso. *El pueblo del sol.* México (Cultura Económica), 1953.

Castañeda, Carlos Eduardo — see Cervantes de Salazar, *Life in the Imperial . . . (Dialogues)*

Castelo, María (de) — see Zavala, *Fuentes . . .*

Castillo, Cristóbal del (1519/26–1606). *Fragmento de la obra general sobre historia de los Mexicanos,* translated by Francisco del Paso y Troncoso. Florence (Salvador Landi), 1908.

Castillo Ledón, Luis. *La conquista y colonización española en México, su verdadero carácter.* México (Museo Nacional), 1932.

Castillo y Piña, José — see *Un desconocido cedulario . . .*

Castro Morales, Efraín. "Luis de Arciniega, maestro mayor de la Catedral de Puebla" in *Anales del I I E,* XXVII (1958).

Catálogo de construcciones religiosas del Estado de Hidalgo, edited by Justino Fernández, with a foreword by Manuel Toussaint. México (Secretaría de Hacienda), 1940, 1942, 2 vols.

Catálago de construcciones religiosas del Estado de Yucatán, edited by Justino Fernández, with essays by Jorge Ignacio Rubio Mañé, José García Preciat, Alfredo Barrera Vázquez. México (Secretaría de Hacienda), 1945, 2 vols.

Catálogo de pasajeros a Indias. Madrid (Espasa-Calpe for Ministerio de Trabajo), 1930.

Ceán Bermúdez, Agustín — see Llaguno y Amírola, *Noticias . . .*

Cervantes de Salazar, Francisco (before 1515–after 1575). *Crónica de Nueva España que escribió el Dr D Francisco Cervantes de Salazar, crónista de la Imperial Ciudad de México* (c1558–). Madrid (Hispanic Society of America), 1914.

—— *Dialogues* — see *Life in the Imperial . . .*

—— *Life in the Imperial and Loyal City of Mexico in New Spain and the Royal and Pontifical University of Mexico, as described in the Dialogues for the Study of the Latin Language* (1554), here cited as *Dialogues;* facsimile of 1554 edition, translated by Minnie Lee Barrett Shepard; introduction and notes by Carlos Eduardo Castañeda. Austin (Texas), 1953.

—— *Túmulo imperial de la gran Ciudad de México* (1560); facsimile of 1560 edition; prologue by Federico Gómez de Orozco. México (Alcancía), 1939.

—— *Homenaje . . .* — see Islas García and Varela

Cetto, Max (L). *Modern Architecture in Mexico.* New York (Praeger), 1961.

Chamberlain, Robert Stoner. *The Conquest and Colonization of Yucatan 1517–1550.* Washington (Carnegie Institute), 1948.

Champlain, Samuel de (1567–1635). *The Works of Samuel de Champlain,* translated and annotated under the direction of H. P. Biggar. Toronto (Champlain Society), 1922–36, 6 vols.

673

BIBLIOGRAPHY

Chapman, Charles Edward. *Colonial Hispanic America.* New York (Macmillan),
1933.

Charencey, (Charles Félix) Hyacinthe (Gouhier, Comte de). *Vocabulario tzotzil-español.* Orléans (Jacob), 1890.

Chauvet, Fidel de Jesús. "The church of San Francisco in Mexico City" in *The Americas,* VII (1950/51).

—— *Los franciscanos y sus construcciones en Tlaxcala.* México (Talleres Junípero Serrá), 1950 (sobretiro de los *Anales de la Provincia del Santo Evangelio*).

—— *Iglesia de San Gabriel Cholula.* México (Talleres Junípero Serrá), 1953 (separata de los *Anales de la Provincia del Santo Evangelio*).

—— *Tlatelolco, Interesante recopilación histórica.* México (Parroquia de Santiago Tlatelolco), 1945.

—— See also Mendieta, Oroz, and Suárez, *Relación* . . .

Chavero, Alfredo (1841–1906). *Los azteca o mexica, Fundación de la Ciudad de México Tenochtitlán.* México (Biblioteca Mínima), 1955.

Chávez, Ezequiel A. *La educación en México en la época precortesiana.* México (Jus), 1958.

—— *Fray Pedro de Gante.* México (Jus), 1943, 2 vols.

Chávez Hayhoe, Salvador. *Historia sociológica de México.* México (Chávez Hayhoe), 1944, 3 vols.

Chávez Orozco, Luis — see *Códice Osuna*

Chevalier, François. *La Formation des grands domaines au Méxique, terre et societé au XVIe–XVIIe siècles.* Paris (Institut d'Ethnologie), 1952.

—— "Signification sociale de la fondation de Puebla de los Angeles" in *Revista de Historia de América,* XXIII (1947).

Chimalpahín, Domingo Francisco de San Antón Muñón. *Annales, sixième et septième relations* (1258–1612), publiées et traduites sur le manuscrit original par Rémi Siméon. Paris (Bibliothèque Linguistique Américaine), 1889.

Chimalpopoca (Galicia), Faustino — see *Anales antiguos de México y sus contornos; Anales mexicanos–uno pedernal diez caña; Anales mexicanos–1589–1596; Códice Chimalpopoca*

Chueca Goitia, Fernando. *Andrés de Vandelvira.* Madrid (Instituto Velázquez), 1954.

—— *Arquitectura del siglo XVI* (Ars Hispaniae XI). Madrid (Plus Ultra), 1953.

Ciudad Rodrigo, Antonio de — see Ponce, *Relación* . . .

Clavijero, Francisco Xavier (1721–81) — see *Tesoros documentales* . . .

Climacus, Saint John — see Joannes Climacus, Saint

Cobo, Bernabé (1582–1657). "Dos cartas inéditas" in *Revista histórica* (Lima), VIII (1928); reprinted in Vázquez de Espinosa, *Descripción* . . .

Codex — here not alphabetized separately, but interpolated with *Códice*

Códice Aubin (1576), (cuarto cuaderno, *Colección de documentos para la historia mexicana,* edited by Antonio Peñafiel). México (Secretaría de Fomento), 1902.

"Códice Azcatítlan" — see Barlow, "Códice Azcatítlan."

Códice de Calkiní, edited by Alfredo Barrera Vázquez. Campeche (Gobierno del Estado), 1957.

Códice Chimalpopoca, Anales de Cuauhtitlán, y Leyenda de los soles, translated by Primo Feliciano Velázquez. México (Universidad), 1945.

Códice de Cuernavaca — see *Códice municipal de Cuernavaca*

Códice Florentino (1564/65, as illustrations to Sahagún, *Historia*). México, 1926.

Códice franciscano (1569–71), introduction by Joaquín García Icazbalceta. México (Chávez Hayhoe), 1941.

Códice Gómez de Orozco (*Un ms novohispano del XVI–XVII*), edited, with a study and notes, by Alfonso Méndez Plancarte. México (Imprenta Universitaria), 1945.

Codex Magliabecchiano, Manuscrit mexicain post-colombien de la Bibliothèque Nationale de Florence reproduit en photochromographie au frais du duc de Loubat (c1553). Rome (Danesi), 1904.

Códice Mariano Jiménez (1549), *Nómina de tributos de los pueblos Otlazapan y Tepexic en geroglíficos azteca y lenguas castellana y náhuatl,* edited by Nicolás León. México, 1904.

Códice Mendieta, documentos franciscanos, siglos XVI y XVII, edited by Joaquín García Icazbalceta (*Nueva colección de documentos para la historia de México,* IV, V). México, 1892, 2 vols.

"Codex Mexicanus 23–24, Bibliothèque Nationale de Paris" — see Mengin, "Codex Mexicanus . . ."

Códice municipal de Cuernavaca (*Anónimo del siglo XVI*). México (Vargas Rea), 1951.

Códice Osuna (1565), edited by Luis Chávez Orozco. México (Instituto Indigenista Interamericano), 1947.

Códice Plancarte, with notes by José Corona Núñez. Guadalajara (Colección "Siglo XVI"), 1959.

Códice Ramírez (manuscrito del siglo XVI intitulado *Relación del orígen de los indios que habitan esta Nueva España*) (by Juan de Tovar?), edited by Manuel Orozco y Berra (in vol. with Tezozomoc, *Crónica . . .*). México (Ireneo Paz), 1878.

Códice Sierra (c1570) (including *Relación de Tejapa*), edited and translated, with explanatory text, by Nicolás León; introduction by Federico Gómez de Orozco. México (Museo Nacional), 1933.

Codex Telleriano-Remensis (manuscrit méxicain du cabinet de Ch. M. Tellier, archevêque de Reims) (c1570). Paris (Hamy), 1899.

Códice de Tlaltelolco — see Steck, *El primer colegio . . .*

Códice de Yanhuitlán (c1545–50), with a study by Wigberto Jiménez Moreno and Salvador Mateos Higuera. México (Museo Nacional), 1940.

Cogolludo, Diego López (de) — see López (de) Cogolludo, Diego

Colección de documentos inéditos para la historia de España. Madrid (Calero), 1842–95, 112 vols.; here cited as C D I España.

Colección de documentos inéditos para la historia de Ibero-América (some vols. have title *Colección de documentos inéditos para la historia de Hispano-América*). Madrid (Cía. Ibero-América), 1927–32, 14 vols.; here cited as C D I Ibero-América.

Colección de documentos inéditos relativos al descubrimiento, conquista y organización de las antiguas posesiones españoles de América y Oceanía, sacados de los archivos del reino, y muy especialmente del de Indias (also known as

Colección de documentos inéditos de Indias). Madrid (Real Academia de Historia), 1864–84, 42 vols.; here cited as *C I D Indias.*

Colección de documentos inéditos relativos al descubrimiento, conquista y organización de las posesiones españolas de ultramar (2nd series of preceding title). Madrid (Real Academia de Historia), 1885–1900, 13 vols.; here cited as *C D I Ultramar.*

Colección de documentos para la historia de la formación social de Hispano-América 1493–1810 — see Konetzke, *Colección* . . .

Colección de documentos para la historia mexicana, edited by Antonio Peñafiel. México (Secretaría de Fomento), 1897–1904. See also *Anales de Tecamachalco; Códice Aubin.*

Colección de documentos para la historia de México, edited by Joaquín García Icazbalceta. México (Andrade), 1858–66 — see Mendieta, *Historia* . . . (reprint); Motolinía, *History* . . . (reprint)

Colección de documentos para la historia de Oaxaca. México (Museo Nacional), 1933; here cited as *C D H Oaxaca.*

Colín, Mario. *Toluca, Crónicas de una ciudad.* Toluca, 1955.

Collis, Maurice. *Cortés and Montezuma.* New York (Harcourt), 1955.

Concilios provinciales primero y segunda de México (1555, 1565) — see Lorenzana, *Concilios* . . .

Concilio III provincial mexicano, celebrado en México el año de 1585, notes by Basilio Arillaga. México (Maillefert), 1859.

Conkling, Alfred Ronald. *Appletons' Guide to Mexico.* New York (Appleton), 1884.

El conquistador anónimo (Alonso de Ulloa?), *Relación de algunas cosas de la Nueva España y de la gran Ciudad de Temestitlán México, escrita por un compañero de Hernán Cortés* (c1535?). México (Editorial América), 1941.

Constituciones del arçobispado y provincia de la muy ynsigne y muy leal Ciudad de Tenuxtitlán México de la nueva España (1555). México, 1556.

"Contrato que hicieron los naturales del barrio de San Pedro con los pobladores del pueblo de Patamban con intervención de Fray Juan de San Miguel" (1557) in *Anales del Museo Michoacano,* III (1944).

Contreras y López de Ayala, Juan de — see Lozoya, *Historia* . . .

Conway, George Robert Graham. *An Englishman and the Mexican Inquisition 1556–60.* México (privately printed), 1927. See also Cortés, *Postrera voluntad y testamento* . . .

Cook, Sherburne Friend. "The Incidence and Significance of Disease among the Aztecs and related Tribes" in *H A H R,* XXVI (1946).

—— *Soil Erosion and Population in Central Mexico.* Berkeley (California), 1949.

—— and Borah, Woodrow. "The Rate of Population Change in Central Mexico, 1550–70" in *H A H R,* XXXVII (1957).

—— and Simpson, Lesley Byrd. *The Population of Central Mexico in the Sixteenth Century.* Berkeley (California), 1948.

Córdova, Juan de — see *Vocabulario castellano-zapoteco* . . .

Cornaro (Corner), Flaminio. *Notizie storiche delle chiese e monasteri di Venezia.* Padua (Seminario), 1758.

Cornejo Franco, José. *Guadalajara.* México (Monografías Mexicanas), 1946. See also Tello, *Crónica* . . .

Corona Núñez, José. "Fray Juan de San Miguel, fundador de Uruapan," in *Universidad Michoacana*, #25 (March 1959).

—— *Rincones michoacanos, leyendas y breves datos históricos de algunos pueblos de Michoacán*. México (Cámara de Diputados), 1938.

—— See also *Códice Plancarte; Relaciones geográficas de Michoacán*

Cortés, Hernán (Fernando, or Hernando) (1485–1547). *Carta de Hernán Cortés, Marqués del Valle, a su pariente y procurador ad litem, el Licenciado Francisco Núñez* (1532). México (Vargas Rea), 1944.

—— *Cartas y otros documentos de Hernán Cortés*, edited by Mariano Cuevas. Seville (Díaz), 1915.

—— *Cartas y relaciones de Hernán Cortés al Emperador Carlos V*, edited by Pascual Gayangos. Paris (Chaix), 1866.

—— *Documentos inéditos relativos a Hernán Cortés* — see *Colección de documentos inéditos para la historia de España*, I

—— *Documentos inéditos relativos a Hernán Cortés y su familia*. México (Archivo General de la Nación), 1935; here cited as *D I Cortés*.

—— *Escritos sueltos de Hernán Cortés*. México (Escalante), 1871.

—— *Five Letters*, 1519–26, translated, with introduction, by J. Bayard Morris. London (Routledge, Broadway Travellers Series), 1928; here cited as *Five Letters*.

—— *Letters of Cortés* (1519–26) (*The Five Letters of Relation from Fernando Cortés to the Emperor Charles V*), translated, and edited, with notes, by Francis Augustus MacNutt. New York (Putnam), 1908, 2 vols.; here cited as *Letters*.

—— *Nuevos documentos relativos a los bienes de Hernán Cortés* — see *Nuevos documentos . . .*

—— *Postrera voluntad y testamento de Hernando Cortés, Marqués del Valle*, introduction and notes by George R. G. Conway. México (Robredo), 1940; here cited as *Testamento*.

—— *Will* — see Cortés, *Postrera voluntad . . .*

"Cortés y los franciscanos" — see Editors of *Archivo Ibero-Americano*

Couto, José Bernardo. *Diálogo sobre la historia de la pintura en México* (1860–61). México (Cultura Económica), 1947.

Covarrubias, Miguel. *Mexico South, The Isthmus of Tehuantepec*. New York (Knopf), 1946.

Crónicas de la conquista de México (including Chronicle of Chac-Xulub-Chen), edited by Agustín Yáñez. México (Universidad), 1939.

la Cruz, Juan de — see Juan de la Cruz

la Cruz y Moya, Juan José de (1706–60). *Historia de la santa y apostólica Provincia de Santiago de Predicadores de México en la Nueva España* (1756–57). México (Porrua), 1954, 1955, 2 vols.

Cuevas, Mariano. *Documentos inéditos del siglo XVI para la historia de México*. México (Museo Nacional), 1914.

—— *Historia de la Iglesia en México*. México (Cervantes), 1942, 5 vols.

—— See also Cortés, *Cartas y otros documentos . . .* ; *Tesoros documentales . . .* ; Vázquez de Espinosa, *Descripción . . .* ; Zerón Zapata, *La Puebla de los Angeles . . .*

677

BIBLIOGRAPHY

Dávila Garibí, José Ignacio. *Ocotlán*. México (Cultura), 1948. See also Espinosa, *Crónica* . . .

Dávila Padilla, Agustín (1562–1604). *Historia de la fundación y discurso de la Provincia de Santiago de México de la Orden de Predicadores, por las vidas de sus varones insignes, y cosas notables de Nueva España* (1st ed. 1596). México (Academia Literaria), 1955.

Delgado, Jaime — see Sigüenza y Góngora, *Piedad heroyca* . . .

Un desconocido cedulario del siglo XVI pertenecente a la Catedral Metropolitana de México, foreword and notes by Alberto María Carrillo; introduction by José Castillo y Piña. México (Victoria), 1944.

Descripción de Antequera, por Pedro Gutiérrez de Verdiga (1580). México (Vargas Rea), 1957.

Descripción del Arzobispado de México hecha en 1570 y otros documentos, edited by Luis García Pimentel. México (Terrazas), 1897.

Descripción de Atlatlauca, por Gaspar de Solís (1580). México (Vargas Rea), 1957.

Descripción de Cholula — see *Relación de Cholula*

"Descripción de la Ciudad de Pasquaro" (1581) in *Anales del Museo Michoacano*, II (1889); (reprinted also in *Relaciones geográficas de* . . . *Michoacán*).

Descripción del Obispado de Michoacán — see León y Gama, *Descripción* . . .

Descripción de la Provincia franciscana del Santo Evangelio de México hecha en el año de 1585 — see Mendieta, Oroz, and Suárez, *Relación* . . .

"Descripción de Tehuantepec" (1580) in *Revista Mexicana de Estudios Históricos*, II (1928), appendix.

Desfontaines, Pierre, and Durliat, Marcel. *La España del Este*. Barcelona (Juventud), 1958.

Díaz, Victor Miguel. *Las bellas artes en Guatemala*. Guatemala (Diario de Centro América), 1934.

Díaz del Castillo, Bernal (1492–1581?). *The Discovery and Conquest of Mexico, 1517–1521*, edited by Genaro García; translated, with introduction and notes, by Percival Maudslay. London (Routledge, Broadway Travellers Series), 1936.

—— *Historia verdadera de la conquista de la Nueva España*. México (Porrua), 1960, 2 vols.

Diffie, Bailey W. *Latin-American Civilization, Colonial Period*. Harrisburg, Pa. (Stackpole), 1945.

División de la Nueva España en obispados (1534). México (Vargas Rea), 1953.

Documentos, etc. — see also *Colección de documentos* . . . ; *Nueva colección de documentos* . . .

Documentos de arte colonial sudamericano — see *El santuario de Copacabana* . . .

Documentos históricos de Méjico — see Motolinía, *Memoriales; Relación de los Obispados* . . .

Documentos para la historia de México (*Archivo Mexicano*) — see *Sumario de la residencia* . . . *de Cortés*

Documentos para la historia de Yucatán, edited by France V. Scholes, Eleanor B. Adams, Ignacio Rubio Mañé. Mérida (Menéndez), 1936–38, 3 vols.

Documentos inéditos del siglo XVI para la historia de México — see Cuevas, *Documentos* . . .

678

Documentos inéditos o muy raros para la historia de México, edited by Genaro García and Carlos Pereyra. México, 1905–11, 36 vols.; here cited as *D I H México.*

Documentos inéditos referentes a . . . Quiroga — see León and Quintana, *Documentos . . .*

Documentos inéditos relativos a Hernán Cortés — see *Colección de documentos inéditos para la historia de España,* vol. I

Documentos inéditos relativos a Hernán Cortés y su familia. México (Archivo General de la Nación), 1935; here cited as *D I Cortés.*

Documento del siglo XVI. México (Vargas Rea), 1953.

Documentos sobre Toluca (1533–48). México (Vargas Rea), 1953.

Domínguez, Francisco Athanasio. *The Missions of New Mexico, 1776,* translated end edited by Eleanor B. Adams and Angélico Chávez. Albuquerque (New Mexico), 1956.

Domínguez Assayn, Salvador. "El calvario de Cuernavaca" in *Mapa,* #124 (1944).

Don Vasco de Quiroga, documentos — see Aguayo Spencer, *Don Vasco de Quiroga . . .*

Dorantes de Carranza, Baltasar (fl1550–1604). *Sumaria relación de las cosas de la Nueva España* (1601–04) (including also Orozco y Berra, *Los conquistadores de México*), introduction by Luis González Obregón. México (Museo Nacional), 1938.

Dorta, Enrique Marco — see Marco Dorta, Enrique

dos Santos, Reynaldo — see Santos, Reynaldo dos

Dubois, Cardinal Louis Ernest. *Saint Joseph.* Paris (Lecoffre-Gabalda), 1927.

Durán, Diego (c1538–88). *Historia de las Indias de Nueva España y islas de tierra firme* (1579–81), edited by José F. Ramírez. México (Andrade y Escalante), 1867–1880, 2 vols. and atlas.

Echanove T., Carlos A. "Izamal" in *Mapa,* #26 (1934).

Echeverría y Veytia, Mariano Fernández (de) — see Fernández (de) Echeverría

Edificios coloniales artísticos e históricos . . . que han sido declarados monumentos — see (Encisco, Martínez Cosío, and Rosell), *Edificios . . .*

(Editors of *Archivo Ibero-Americano*). "Cortés y los franciscanos" in *Archivo Ibero-Americano,* VIII (1948).

Emmart, Emily Walcott — see *Badianus Manuscript*

Enciclopedia yucatense. México (Gobierno de Yucatán), 1944, 8 vols.

Encinas (Enzinas), Diego de. *Cedulario indiano, provisiones, cédulas, capítulos de ordenanzas instrucciones, y cartas* (1596). Madrid (Cultura Hispánica), 1945–46, 4 vols.

(Enciso, Jorge, and Martínez Cosío, Leopoldo, and Rosell, Lauro). *Edificios coloniales artísticos e históricos de la República Mexicana que han sido declarados monumentos.* México (Instituto Nacional de Antropología e Historia), 1939.

Ensayos históricos hispanoamericanos — see Steck, *Ensayos . . .*

Enzinas, Diego de — see Encinas, Diego de

Epistolario de Nueva España 1505–1818, edited by Francisco del Paso y Troncoso. México (Robredo), 1939–42, 16 vols.

Escalante Plancarte, Salvador. *Fray Martín de Valencia.* México, 1945.

Escobar, Matías de. *Americana Thebaida, Vitas patrum de los religiosos hermita-*

ños de N P San Agustín de la Provincia de S Nicolás Tolentino de Michoacán (1729). México (Victoria), 1924.

Escritos sueltos de Hernán Cortés — see Cortés, Escritos sueltos . . .

Espinosa, Isidro Félix de (1679–1755). Crónica de la Provincia franciscana de los apóstoles San Pedro y San Pablo de Michoacán (–1751), notes by Nicolás León; prologue and notes by José Ignacio Dávila Garibí. México (Santiago), 1945.

Esquivel Obregón, Toribio. "Factors in the Historical Evolution of Mexico" in H A H R, II (1919).

Esteva, Cayetano. Nociones elementales de geografía histórica del Estado de Oaxaca. Oaxaca (San Germán), 1913.

Estrada, Genaro — see Orozco y Berra, Historia . . .

Essays in Pre-Columbian Art and Archaeology — see Kubler, "On the Colonial Extinction . . ."

Fernández, Justino. Uruapan, su situación histórica, y características. México (Talleres de impresión de estampillas y valores), 1936.

—— See also Catálogo de . . . Hidalgo; Catálogo de . . . Yucatán.

—— and O'Gorman, Edmundo. Santo Tomás More y "La Utopia de Tomás More en la Neuva España." México (Alcancía), 1937.

—— and Gómez de Orozco, Federico, and Toussaint, Manuel. Planos de la Ciudad de México, siglos XVI y XVII. México (Universidad), 1938.

Fernández (de) Echeverría y Veytia, Mariano (1718–80). Historia de la fundación de la Ciudad de la Puebla de los Angeles en la Nueva España (c1749–79). Puebla (Labor), 1931.

Fernández de Oviedo (y Valdés), Gonzalo (1478–1557). Sucesos y diálogo de la Nueva España (1526–49), edited, with a foreword, by Edmundo O'Gorman. México (Universidad), 1946.

Ferrer de Mendiola, Gabriel. Nuestra ciudad, Mérida de Yucatán, 1542–1938. Mérida (Basso), 1938.

Feuchtwanger, Franz, and Groth-Kimball, Irmgard. The Art of Ancient Mexico. London (Thames and Hudson), 1954.

Filarete — see Holt, Literary Sources . . .

Florencia, Francisco de (1619–95). Historia de la Provincia de la Compañía de Jesús de Nueva España (1st published 1694), foreword by Francisco González de Cossío. México (Academia Literaria), 1955.

Flores Guerrero, Raúl. Las capillas posas de México, foreword by Manuel Toussaint. México (Ediciones Mexicanas, Enciclopedia mexicana de arte #15), 1951.

—— "El convento de Charo" in Anales del I I E, XXII (1954).

Focher, Juan (–1572). Itinerario del misionero en América (c1570, revised by Diego de Valadés, 1st published 1574), texto latino con versión castellana, introducción y notas del P Antonio Eguiluz. Madrid (Suárez), 1960.

Foster, George M. Culture and conquest, America's Spanish Heritage. Chicago (Quadrangle, Viking Publications #27), 1960.

—— and Ospina, Gabriel. Empire's Children, the People of Tzintzuntzan. México (Nuevo Mundo, for Smithsonian), 1948.

Franco, Alonso (–1659). Segunda parte de la Historia de la Provincia de

Santiago de México (1637–45) (continuation of Dávila Padilla, *Historia* . . .). México (Museo Nacional), 1900.

Franco, José Cornejo — see Cornejo Franco, José

Fuentes para la historia del trabajo en Nueva España, edited by Silvio Zavala and María (de) Castelo. México (Fondo de Cultura Económica), 1939ff, 7 vols.

Gage, Thomas (c1600–56). *The English-American, a New Survey of the West Indies* (1st published 1648). London (Routledge, Broadway Travellers Series), 1928.

Galindo y Villa, Jesús. *Historia sumaria de la Ciudad de México.* México (Cultura), 1925.

Gante, Pablo C. de (pseud.). *La arquitectura en México en el siglo XVI.* México (Porrua), 1954.

Gante, Pedro de — see Pedro de Gante

García, Genaro. *Carácter de la conquista española en América y en México.* México (Fuente Cultural), 1940. See also *Documentos inéditos o muy raros para la historia de México*

García Bravo, Alonso — see *Información de méritos . . . de Alonso García Bravo*

García Cubas, Antonio (1823–1912). *Cuadro geográfico estadístico, descriptivo e histórico de los Estados Unidos Mexicanos.* México (Secretaría de Fomento), 1885.

—— *El libro de mis recuerdos* (1904). México (Patria), 1945.

García Granados, Rafael. "Calpan" in *Universidad de México,* I (1930/31).

—— *Capillas abiertas.* México (Ediciones de Arte, Colección Anáhuac), 1948.

—— "Capillas de indios en Nueva España" in *Archivo español de Arte,* XXXI (1935).

—— *Filias y fobias.* México (Polis), 1937.

—— "Reminiscencias idolátricas en monumentos coloniales" in *Anales del I I E,* V (1940).

—— *Xochimilco.* México (Talleres Gráficos de la Nación), 1934.

—— and MacGregor, Luis. *Huejotzingo, la ciudad y el convento franciscano.* México (Talleres Gráficos de la Nación), 1934.

García Gutiérrez, Jesús. *Apuntamientos de historia eclestiástica mejicana.* México (Victoria), 1922.

—— "Un documento guadalupano del siglo XVI, la información contra el Padre Bustamante" in *Memorias de la Academia Mexicana de la Historia,* XIV (1955).

García Icazbalceta, Joaquín (1825–74). *Bibliografía mexicana del siglo XVI,* edited by Agustín Millares Carlo. México (Cultura Económica), 1944.

—— *Colección de documentos para la historia de México.* México (Andrade), 1858–66 — see reprints of Mendieta, *Historia* . . . ; Motolinía, *History* . . .

—— *Fray Juan de Zumárraga, primer obispo y arzobispo de México.* Buenos Aires (Espasa-Calpe), 1952.

—— *Nueva colección de documentos para la historia de México.* México (Andrade y Morales), 1886–92 — see *Cartas de religiosos; Códice franciscano; Códice Mendieta;* and Pomar and Zurita, *Relación* . . .

—— *Obras.* México (Agüeros), 1896–99.

BIBLIOGRAPHY

García Icazbalceta, Joaquín. *Opúsculos y biografiás,* edited, with a foreword, by Julio Jiménez Rueda. México (Universidad), 1942.

García Maroto, Gabriel — see Yáñez and García Maroto

García Pimentel, Luis — see *Descripción del Arzobispado de México;* Motolinía, *Memoriales; Relación de los Obispados . . .*

García Prada, Carlos — see Wiley and García Prada

García Preciat, José. "Historia de la arquitectura" — see *Enciclopedia Yucatense, IV; Cátalogo de . . . Yucatán*

Garciadueñas, José Rojas — see Rojas Garciadueñas, José

Gardiner, C. Harvey. "Tempest in Tehuantepec, 1529" in *H A H R,* XXXV (1955).

Gay, José Antonio. *Historia de Oaxaca* (1st published 1881–82), foreword by Jorge Fernando Iturribarría. México (Venero), 1950, 2 vols., each in 2 books.

Gaya Nuño, Juan Antonio. *La arquitectura española en sus monumentos desaparecidos.* Madrid (Espasa-Calpe), 1961.

Gayangos, Pascual de — see Cortés, *Cartas y relaciones . . .*

Gemelli Carreri, Juan Francisco (Giovanni Francesco) (1651–1725). *México en 1697, las cosas más considerables vistas en la Nueva España,* translated by José María de Agreda y Sánchez; foreword by Alberto María Carreño. México (Xóchitl), 1946.

Ghyvelde, Frédéric de. *Saint Joseph, sa vie, son culte.* Quebec (Franciscan Mission), 1902.

Gibson, Charles. *Tlaxcala in the Sixteenth Century.* New Haven, Conn. (Yale), 1952.

Gillet, Louis. "L'art dans l'Amérique Latine" in Michel, *Histoire de l'art depuis les premiers temps jusqu'à nos jours,* VIII/3. Paris (Colin), 1929.

———— *Histoire artistique des Ordres Mendiantes, étude sur l'art réligieux en Europe du XIII au XVII siècles.* Paris (Layrens), 1912.

Gillow (y Zavalza), Eugenio (Gregorio Clemente). *Apuntes históricos del Obispado de Antequera.* México (Sagrado Corazón de Jesús), 1889.

Gómara, Francisco López de — see López de Gómara, Francisco

Gómez de Cervantes, Gonzalo. *La vida económica y social de Nueva España al finalizar el siglo XVI* (1599), foreword by Alberto María Carreño. México (Porrua), 1944.

Gómez de Orozco, Federico. *El convento franciscano de Cuernavaca.* México (Centro de Estudios Franciscanos), 1943.

———— "Don Hernando Cortés" in *Miscelanea Americanista,* II (1951).

———— "Monasterios de la Orden de San Agustín en Nueva España, siglo XVI" in *Revista Mexicana de Estudios Históricos,* I (1927).

———— See also Cervantes de Salazar, *Túmulo imperial . . .* ; *Códice Sierra;* Fernández, Gómez de Orozco, and Toussaint, *Planos . . .* ; *Mapa de Xochítepec;* Suárez de Peralta, *Tratado . . .*

Gómez Hoyos, Rafael. *La iglesia de América en las leyes de Indias.* Madrid and Bogotá (Institutos Oviedo y de Cultura Hispánica), 1961.

Gómez Moreno, María Elena. *Catálogo de la exposición de Carlos V y su ambiente.* Toledo, 1958.

Gonzaga, Francesco (1546–1620). *Carta de avisos y apuntamientos de nuestro Reverendíssimo Padre Fray Francisco Gonçaga . . .* (1579). México (Porrua), 1939.

BIBLIOGRAPHY

González de Cossío, Francisco. "Libros mexicanos," in *Boletín del Archivo General de la Nación*, XX (1949).

⸺ *Xalapa, breve reseña histórica*. México (Talleres Gráficos de la Nación), 1957.

⸺ See also Florencia, *Historia* . . . ; *El libro de las tasaciones* . . . ; Martínez, *Repertorio* . . . ; *Nuevos documentos relativos a los bienes de Hernán Cortés;* Villaseñor y Sánchez, *Theatro* . . . ; (Villerías), *Relación* . . .

González Dávila, Gil (1577–1658). *Teatro eclesiástico de la primitiva Iglesia de la Nueva España en las Indias Occidentales* (1647–49). Madrid (Porrua Turranzas), 1959, 2 vols.

González de Eslava, Fernán (1534–c1601). *Coloquios espirituales y sacramentales,* edited, with foreword and notes, by José Rojas Garcidueñas. México (Porrua), 1959, 2 vols.

González Obregón, Luis. *México viejo*. México (Bouret), 1900. See also *Libros y libreros* . . .

González Peña, Carlos. *Historia de la literatura mexicana desde los orígenes hasta nuestros días*. México (Cultura y Polis), 1940.

Gorbea Trueba, José. *Culhuacán*. México (Instituto Nacional de Antropología e Historia), 1959.

⸺ *Tepeapulco*. México (Instituto Nacional de Antropología e Historia), 1957.

⸺ *Yanhuitlán*. México (Instituto Nacional de Antropología e Historia), 1962.

⸺ *Yuriria*. México (Instituto Nacional de Antropología e Historia), 1960.

⸺ See also Acosta, Gorbea Trueba, and Martínez del Río, *Tula* . . .

Grijalva, Juan de (1580–1638). *Crónica de la Orden de N P S Augustín en las provincias de la Nueva España* (1623). México (Victoria), 1924.

Groth-Kimball, Irmgard — see Feuchtwanger and Groth-Kimball

Gudiol Ricart, Josep, and Gaya Nuño, Juan Antonio. *Arquitectura y escultura románicas* (Ars Hispaniae VI). Madrid (Plus Ultra), 1948.

Guerrero Moctezuma, Francisco. *Las plazas en las ciudades de la Nueva España en relación con las ordenanzas de nuevas poblaciones de Felipe II*. México, 1934.

Gurría Lacroix, Jorge — see Vázquez de Tapia, *Relación* . . .

Habig, Marion Alphonse. "The Franciscan Provinces of Spanish North America" in *The Americas*, I (1944/45).

Hakluyt, Sir Richard (1552?–1616). *A selection of the principal voyages, traffiques, and discoveries of the English Nation*. New York (Knopf), 1926.

Hanke, Lewis. *Bartolomé de las Casas, Historian*. Gainesville (Florida), 1952.

⸺ *The First Social Experiments in America. A Study in the Development of Spanish Indian Policy in the Sixteenth Century*. Cambridge, Mass. (Harvard), 1935.

⸺ "Free Speech in Sixteenth-century Latin America" in *H A H R*, XXVI (1946).

⸺ "Pope Paul III and the American Indians" in *Harvard Theological Review*, XXX (1937).

d'Harcourt, Raúl (Raoul). *América antes de Colón, las civilizaciones desaparecidas*. México (Biblioteca Mínima), 1955.

Haring, Clarence H. "Ledgers of the Royal Treasurers in Spanish America in the Sixteenth Century" in *H A H R*, II (1919).

⸺ *The Spanish Empire in America*. New York (Oxford), 1947.

BIBLIOGRAPHY

Harth-Terré, Emilio. "Francisco Becerra, maestro de arquitectura" in *Miscelanea Americanista*, III (1952).

—— *Francisco Becerra, maestro de arquitectura, sus últimos años en el Perú.* Madrid (Instituto "Gonzalo Fernández de Oviedo"), 1952.

—— *Las tres fundaciones de la Catedral del Cuzco,* reprinted from *Anales del Instituto de Arte Americano,* #2 (1949).

Haupt, Albrecht. *Geschichte der Renaissance in Spanien und Portugal.* Stuttgart (Paul Neff), 1927.

Hawks, Henry — see García Icazbalceta, *Obras,* VII

Heliodoro Valle, Rafael — see Valle, Rafael Heliodoro

Hernández Serrano, Francisco J. "Atlatlahucan" in *Mapa,* #117 (1944).

—— "Xochimilco" in *Mapa,* #77 (1940).

Herrera Carrillo, Pablo. "La conquista musical de América por España" in *Boletín de la Sociedad Mexicana de Geografía y Estadística,* LXIII (1947).

Herring, Hubert. *A History of Latin America from the Beginnings to the Present.* New York (Knopf), 1955.

Heydenreich, Ludwig. "Pius II als Bauherr von Pienza" in *Zeitschrift für Kunstgeschichte,* VI (1937).

Hijuelos F., Fausto A., ed. *Mérida, monografía.* México (Secretaría de Educación Pública), 1942.

Historia Tolteca-Chichimeca, Anales de Quauhtinchán (c1544), edited by Heinrich Berlin, with Silvia Rendón; foreword by Paul Kirchhoff. México (Porrua), 1947.

Holmes, Jack D. L. "El mestizaje religioso en México" in *Historia Mexicana,* V (1955/56).

Holt, Elizabeth Gilmore, ed. *Literary Sources of Art History.* Princeton, N.J. (Princeton), 1947.

Homenaje a Silvio Zavala, estudios históricos americanos, salutación de Alfonso Reyes. México (Colegio de México), 1953.

Howe, Alice. *Cuernavaca, Museum Capital of Morelos.* Cuernavaca (author?), 1952.

Hughes, J. Quentin. *The Buildings of Malta during the period of the Knights of St John of Jerusalem, 1530–1795.* London (Tiranti), 1956.

Humboldt, Alexander, Freiherr von (1769–1859). *Essai Politique sur le Royaume de la Nouvelle Espagne.* Paris, 1811, 5 vols.

Hvidtfeldt, Arild. *Teotl and Ixiptlatli.* Copenhagen (Munksgaard), 1958.

Icaza, Francisco A. de. *Diccionario autobiográfico de conquistadores y pobladores de Nueva España.* Madrid ("El Adelantado de Segovia"), 1923, 2 vols.

—— "Miscelánea histórica" in *Revista Mexicana de Estudios Históricos,* II (1928), appendix.

Icazbalceta, Joaquín García — see García Icazbalceta, Joaquín

Iglesia, Ramón. *Cronistas e historiadores de la conquista de México, el ciclo de Hernán Cortés.* México (Colegio de México), 1942.

Iglesias de México — see Toussaint, *La arquitectura religiosa . . .*

Información apologética de los dominicos en México en 1578 (published with Ojea, *Libro tercero . . .* but with separate pagination). México (Museo Nacional), 1897.

Información de méritos y servicios de Alonso García Bravo, alarife que trazó la Ciudad de México (1604), edited by J. I. Mantecón, foreword by Manuel Toussaint. México (Universidad), 1956.

Instrucciones que los virreyes de Nueva España dejaron a sus sucesores. México (Imperial), 1867.

Iturribarría, Jorge Fernando. *Ensayo histórico sobre la industria de la seda en Oaxaca.* Oaxaca (Imprenta del Gobierno), 1933.

—— *Oaxaca en la historia.* México (Stylo), 1955.

—— See also Gay, *Historia* . . .

Ixtlilxóchitl, Fernando de Alva (1568–1648). *Décima tercia relación de la venida de los españoles y principio de la ley evangélica* (c1610). México (Robredo), 1938.

—— *Obras históricas (Relaciones, Historia Chichimeca)* (c1610), notes by Alfredo Chavero. México (Secretaría de Fomento), 1891–92, 2 vols.

Jarnés, Benjamín. *Vasco de Quiroga, obispo de Utopia.* México (Atlantida), 1942.

Jiménez, Francisco — see Ximénez, Francisco

Jiménez Moreno, Wigberto. "La colonización y evangelización de Guanajuato en el siglo XVI" in *Cuadernos Americanos,* III (1944).

—— *Estudios de historia colonial.* México (Instituto de Antropología e Historia), 1958.

—— See also Alvarado, *Vocabulario* . . . ; *Códice de Yanhuitlán; Vocabulario castellano-zapoteco* . . .

Jiménez Rueda, Julio. *Estampas de los siglos de oro.* México (Universidad), 1957.

—— *Herejías y supersticiones en la Nueva España, los heterodoxos en México.* México (Universidad), 1946.

Joannes Climacus, Saint. *The Ladder of Divine Ascent,* translated by Archimandrite Lazarus Moore. London (Faber), 1959.

Johnson, Frederick — see *The Maya and their Neighbors*

Jones, Willis Knapp. *Breve historia del teatro latinoamericano.* México (Studium), 1956.

Juan de la Cruz. *Doctrina Christiana en la lengua guasteca.* México, 1571.

Juarros, Domingo (1752–1820). *Compendio de la historia de la Ciudad de Guatemala.* Guatemala (Tipografía Nacional), 1936, 2 vols. in 1.

King, Georgiana Goddard. *Mudéjar.* Bryn Mawr (Bryn Mawr College), 1927. See also Street, *Some Account of Gothic Architecture* . . .

Kirchhoff, Paul — see *Historia tolteca-chichimeca*

Kirkpatrick, Frederick Alexander. *The Spanish Conquistadores.* London (Black), 1946.

Konetzke, Richard, ed. *Colección de documentos para la historia de la formación social de Hispano-América, 1493–1810,* Vol. I. Madrid (Consejo Superior de Investigaciones Científicas), 1953.

Krautheimer, Richard. *Die Kirchen der Bettelorden in Deutschland.* Cologne (Marcan), 1925.

Kubler, George. "Architects and Builders in Mexico: 1521–1550" in *Journal of the Warburg and Courtauld Institutes,* VII (1944).

—— *Mexican Architecture of the Sixteenth Century.* New Haven, Conn. (Yale), 1948, 2 vols.

BIBLIOGRAPHY

Kubler, George. "On the Colonial Extinction of the Motifs of Pre-Columbian Art" in Samuel K. Lothrop et al., *Essays in Pre-Columbian Art and Archaeology.* Cambridge, Mass. (Harvard), 1961.

—— "Mexican Urbanism in the Sixteenth Century," *Art Bulletin,* XXIV (1942).

—— "The Name Tenochtitlán" in *Tlalocan,* I (1943/44).

—— *The Religious Architecture of New Mexico in the Colonial Period and since the American Occupation.* Colorado Springs (Taylor Museum), 1940.

—— "Two Modes of Franciscan Architecture: New Mexico and California" in *Gazette des Beaux-Arts,* XXIII (1943).

—— "Ucareo and the Escorial" in *Anales del I I E,* VIII (1942).

—— See also *Studies in Latin American Art.*

—— and Soria, Martin. *Art and Architecture in Spain and Portugal and their American Dominions, 1500–1800.* Baltimore (Penguin, *The Pelican History of Art*), 1959.

Kuri, A. Miriam Nicolás — see Nicolás Kuri, A. Miriam

Lacas, M. M. "The encomienda in Latin-American History: a Reappraisal" in *The Americas,* VIII (1951/52).

Lamadrid, Lázaro — see Vázquez, *Crónica* . . .

Lampérez y Romea, Vicente. *Arquitectura civil española de los siglos I al XVIII.* Madrid (Calleja), 1922, 2 vols.

—— *Historia de la arquitectura cristiana española de la edad media según el estudio de los elementos y los monumentos.* Madrid (Espasa-Calpe), 1930, 3 vols.

Landa, Diego de (1524–79). *Landa's Relación de las cosas de Yucatán* (1566), translated and edited, with notes, by Alfred M. Tozzer. Cambridge, Mass. (Peabody Museum), 1941; here cited as Landa (Tozzer).

Lanning, John Tate. "Cortés and his First Official Remission of Treasure to Charles V" in *Revista de Historia de América,* I (1938).

La Rea (Larrea), Alonso de — see la Rea, Alonso de

Larson, Orville K. "Ascension Images in Art and Theatre" in *Gazette des Beaux-Arts,* LIV (1959).

Latorre, Germán, ed. — see *Relaciones geográficas de Indias*

Lavedan, Pierre. *L'architecture gothique réligieuse en Catalogne, Valence, et Baléares.* Paris, 1935.

—— *Histoire de l'urbanisme.* Paris (Laurens), 1926–52, 3 vols.

Lebrón de Quiñones — see *Lo que proveyó el licenciado Lebrón* . . .

Lee, Raymond L. "Cochineal Production and Trade in New Spain to 1600" in *The Americas,* IV (1947/48).

—— "Grain Legislation in Colonial Mexico, 1575–85" in *H A H R,* XXVII (1947).

—— "The Viceregal Instructions of Martín Enríquez de Almanza" in *Revista de Historia de América,* XXXI (1951).

Lees-Milne, James. *Baroque in Italy.* London (Batsford), 1959.

—— *Roman Mornings.* London (Wingate), 1956.

Legislación del trabajo en los siglos XVI, XVII, y XVIII, foreword by Genaro V. Vázquez. México (Departamento Autónomo de Trabajo), 1936.

Legueu, Françoise. "Impressions mexicaines" in *Revue des Deux Mondes,* VIII (1955).

686

Leicht, Hugo. *Las calles de Puebla, estudio histórico.* Puebla (Mijares), 1934.

Lejarza, Fidel de. "Las borracheras y el problema de las conversiones en Indias" in *Archivo Ibero-Americano,* I (1941).

León, Nicolás (1859–1929). "Fray Maturino Gilberti y sus escritos inéditos" in *Anales del Museo Michoacano,* II (1889).

—— "La relación de Michoacán" in *Revista Mexicana de Estudios Históricos,* I (1927).

—— "Reyes tarascos" in *Anales del Museo Michoacano,* I (1888).

—— *El ylmo señor don Vasco de Quiroga, primer obispo de Michoacán.* México (Sucesores de F Díaz de León), 1904?

—— See also Espinosa, *Crónica* . . .

—— and Quintana, José Miguel. *Documentos inéditos referentes al ilustrísimo señor don Vasco de Quiroga.* México (Robredo), 1940.

León y Gama, Antonio de. *Descripción del arzobispado de Michoacán* (1753). México (Vargas Rea), 1957.

Leonard, Irving A. *Books of the Brave. Being an Account of Books and of Men in the Spanish Conquest and Settlement of the Sixteenth-Century New World.* Cambridge, Mass. (Harvard), 1949.

Leonardo y Argensola, Bartolomé (1562–1631). *La conquista de México* (1st published 1630 in *Anales de Aragón*), introduction and notes by Joaquín Ramírez Cabañas. México (Robredo), 1940.

Las leyes nuevas (1542–43), reproduced in facsimile, with notes by Antonio Muro Obregón, in *Anuario de Estudios Americanos,* II (1945).

Leyes y ordenanzas nuevamente hechas por su Magestad para la governación de las Indias. Seville, 1543.

El libro de las tasaciones de pueblos de la Nueva España, siglo XVI, foreword by Francisco González de Cossío. México (Archivo General de la Nación), 1952.

Libros y libreros en el siglo XVI, edited by Francisco Fernández del Castillo; introduction by Luis González Obregón. México (Archivo General de la Nación), 1914.

Lienzo de Tlaxcala — see *Antigüedades Mexicanas*

Lizana, Bernardo de (—1631). *Historia de Yucatán.* México (Museo Nacional), 1893.

Llaguno y Amírola, Eugenio (—1799). *Noticias de los arquitectos y arquitectura en España desde su restauración,* with notes by Agustín Cean-Bermúdez. Madrid (Imprenta Real), 1829.

Lo que proveyó el licenciado Lebrón en la Ciudad de Michoacán (1554). México (Vargas Rea), 1945.

López, Atanasio. "Misiones y doctrinas de Michoacán y Jalisco (Méjico) en el siglo XVI, 1525–85" in *Archivo Ibero-Americano,* IX (1922).

López (de) Cogolludo, Diego (1610–86). *Historia de Yucatán* (1656). Mérida (Aldana Rivas), 1867–68, 2 vols.

López de Gómara, Francisco (1510–60?). *The Conquest of the Weast India* (Vol. II of the *Historia General de las Indias,* 1st published 1552), translated by Thomas Nicholas (1578). New York (Scholars' Facsimiles and Reprints), 1940.

López González, Valentín. *El palacio de Cortés en Cuernavaca.* Cuernavaca (Universidad de Morelos), 1958.

López de Priego, Antonio — see *Tesoros documentales* . . .

BIBLIOGRAPHY

López Velarde, Benito. *Los misiones en México, 1524–1798*. México (Jus), 1957.

López de Velasco, Juan. *Geográfica descripción universal de las Indias* (1571–74). Madrid (Fortanet), 1894.

López de Villaseñor, Pedro (1710–85). *Cartilla vieja de la nobilísima Ciudad de Puebla* (1781), edited by José I. Mantecón; introduction by Efraín Castro, Jr. México (Imprenta Universitaria), 1961.

Lorenzana (y Butrón), Francisco Antonio (1722–1804). *Concilios provinciales, primero y segundo, de México, celebrados en la muy noble y muy leal Ciudad de México . . . 1555 y 1565*. México (Hogal), 1769.

Lorenzetti, Giulio. *Venezia e il suo estuario*. Rome (Instituto poligrafico dello Stato), 1956.

—— *Onoranze a Jacopo Sansovino*. Venice (Comitato per le Onoranze Sansoviniane), 1929.

Loughran, E. Ward. "The First Episcopal Sees in Spanish America" in *H A H R*, X (1930).

Lozoya, Marqués de (Juan Contreras y López de Ayala). *Historia del arte hispánico*. Barcelona (Salvat), 1931ff., 5 vols.

Lumholtz, Karl. *Unknown Mexico*. New York (Scribner), 1902.

Lyon, George Francis (1795–1832). *Journal of a Residence and Tour in the Republic of Mexico in the Year 1826*. London (Murray), 1828, 2 vols.

McAndrew, John. "Fortress Monasteries?" in *Anales del I I E*, XXIII (1955).

—— Review of Kubler, *Mexican Architecture* in *Art Bulletin*, XXXII (1950).

—— See also *Studies in Latin American Art*.

—— and Toussaint, Manuel. "Tecali, Zacatlán, and the *Renacimiento Purista* in Mexico" in *Art Bulletin*, XXIV (1942).

MacGregor, Luis. *Actopan, Official Guide*, translated by Pablo Martínez del Río. México (Instituto Nacional de Antropología e Historia), 1957.

—— *Actopan* (Memorias del Instituto Nacional de Antropología e Historia, IV). México (Instituto Nacional de Antropología e Historia), 1955.

—— *Estudios sobre arte colonial mexicano*. México (Publicaciones Mundiales), 1946.

—— *Huejotzingo*, translated by Pablo Martínez del Río. México (Instituto Nacional de Antropología e Historia), 1957.

—— *Tepoztlán*. México (Instituto Nacional de Antropología e Historia), 1958.

—— See also García Granados and MacGregor, *Huejotzingo*

MacNutt, Francis Augustus — see Cortés, *Letters* . . .

Madariaga, Salvador de. *The Fall of the Spanish American Empire*. London (Hollis and Carter), 1947.

—— *Hernán Cortés, Conqueror of Mexico*. London (Hodder and Stoughton), 1942.

—— *The Rise of the Spanish American Empire*. New York (Macmillan), 1949.

Magdaleno, Mauricio — see Sahagún, *Suma indiana*

Magner, James A. "Fray Juan de Zumárraga, his Social Contributions" in *The Americas*, V (1948/49).

Malagón, Javier. "Las *Ordenanças y Copilación de Leyes* del Virrey Mendoza para la Audiencia de Nueva España" in *Revista de Historia de América*, XVI (1954).

Mâle, Emile. *L'art réligieux de la fin du xvi siècle, du xvii siècle, et du xviii siècle, étude sur l'iconographie après le Concile de Trente.* Paris (Colin), 1951.

Malvasia, Carlo Cesare (1616–93). *Pitture, scolture ed architetture delle chiese, luoghi pubblici, palazzi e case della città di Bologna e suoi subborghi,* edited by Bianconi, with Zanotti notes of 1706. Bologna (Longhi), 1792.

Mapa de Xochítepec, with an explanatory text by Federico Gómez de Orozco. México (Vargas Rea), 1952.

Marasovič, Tomislav, and Marasovič, Jerko, and Petricoli, Ivo. Untitled articles in *Urbs,* 1958.

Maravell, José Antonio. "La utopia politico-religiosa de los franciscanos en Nueva España" in *Estudios Americanos,* I (1948/49).

Marco Dorta, Enrique. "Atrios y capillas abiertas en el Perú" in *Archivo Español de Arte,* XLIII (1941).

—— "Francisco Becerra" in *Archivo Español de Arte,* XVI (1943).

—— *Fuentes para la historia del arte hispanoamericano.* Seville (Escuela de Estudios Hispano-Americanos), 1951.

—— "Iglesias del siglo XVIII en Bolivia" in *Arte en América y Filipinas,* IV (1952).

—— "El santuario de Copacabana, de la Paz a Tiahuanaco" (*Documentos de arte colonial sudamericano,* VII). Buenos Aires (Academia Nacional de Bellas Artes), 1950.

—— See also Angulo Iñiguez, *Historia del arte hispanoamericano*

María y Campos, Armando de. *Representaciones teatrales en la Nueva España (siglos XVI al XVIII).* México (Costa-Amic), 1959.

Mariscal, Federico E. *La patria y la arquitectura nacional.* México (Stephan y Torres), 1915.

Markman, Sidney D. "Santa Cruz, Antigua, Guatemala, and the Spanish Colonial Architecture of Central America" in *Journal of the Society of Architectural Historians,* XV (1956).

Márquez Rodiles, Ignacio — see Pedro de Gante, *Cartilla* . . .

Marquina, Ignacio. *Arquitectura prehispánica.* México (Instituto Nacional de Antropología e Historia), 1951.

—— *Templo mayor de México,* translated by Pablo Martínez del Río. México (Instituto Nacional de Antropología e Historia), 1957.

Marroquí, José María (1824–98). *La Ciudad de México.* México ("La Europea" de J. Aguilar Vera), 1900–03, 3 vols.

Marroquín, Alejandro. *La Ciudad mercado, Tlaxiaco,* introduction by Gonzalo Aguirre Beltrán. México (Universidad), 1957.

Martí, Samuel. *Instrumentos musicales precortesianos.* México (Instituto Nacional de Antropología e Historia), 1955.

Martínez, Henrico (1550?–1632). *Repertorio de los tiempos e historia natural de Nueva España* (1606), foreword by Francisco de la Maza; bibliographical appendix by Francisco González del Cossío. México (Secretaría de Educación Pública), 1948.

Martínez Burgos, M. "Nicolás de Vergara, cantero" in *Archivo Español de Arte,* XXIII (1950).

Martínez Cosío, Leopoldo. *Heráldica de Cortés.* México (Jus), 1949. See also (Encisco, Martínez Cosío, and Rosell), *Edificios* . . .

BIBLIOGRAPHY

Martínez Gracida, Manuel. *El rey Cosijoeza y su familia (reseña histórica y legendaria de los últimos soberanos de Zaachila).* México (Secretaría de Fomento), 1888.

Martinez del Rio, Pablo — see Acosta, Gorbea Trueba, and Martínez del Río, *Tula*

Mártir de Anglería, Pedro — see Pedro Mártir de Anglería

Mateos, Francisco — see Acosta, *De procuranda* . . .

Mateos Higuera, Salvador — see *Códice de Yanhuitlán*

The Maya and their Neighbors (by the Students and Colleagues of Alfred Tozzer). New York (Appleton-Century), 1940.

Mayer, Brantz. *Mexico as it was and as it is* (1841–42). New York (Winchester New World), 1844.

la Maza, Francisco de. "Arte colonial de México" in *Cuadernos Americanos,* VIII (1949).

—— *La capilla de San José Chiapa.* México (Instituto Nacional de Antropología e Historia), 1960.

—— *La Ciudad de Cholula y sus iglesias.* México (Universidad), 1959.

—— "Fray Diego de Valadés" in *Anales del I I E,* XIII (1945).

—— *El guadalupanismo mexicano.* México (Porrua), 1953.

—— *Los retablos dorados de Nueva España.* México (Ediciones Mexicanas, *Enciclopedia Mexicana del Arte* #9), 1950.

—— Review of Torres Balbás, "Musallà y šaría" in *Anales del I I E,* XVII (1949).

—— See also Martínez, *Repertorio* . . .

Mazihcatzín, Nicolás Faustino. "Descripción del Lienzo de Tlaxcala (1778)" in *Revista Mexicana de Estudios Históricos,* I (1927), appendix.

Means, Philip Ainsworth. *History of the Spanish Conquest of Yucatan and of the Itzas.* Cambridge, Mass. (Peabody Museum), 1917.

Mecham, J(ohn) Lloyd. *Church and State in Latin America.* Chapel Hill (North Carolina), 1932. See also Wilgus, *Colonial Hispanic America.*

Medina, Fernando de Armas — see Armas Medina, Fernando de

Medina, José Toribio. *Ensayo bio-bibliográfico sobre Hernán Cortés.* Santiago de Chile (Fondo Medina), 1952.

Memoria de los servicios que había hecho Nuño de Guzmán desde que fué nombrado Gobernador de Pánuco en 1525, study and notes by Manuel Carrera Stampa. México (Porrua), 1955.

Méndez Arceo, Sergio. "Contribución a la historia de don Vasco de Quiroga" in *Abside,* V (1941).

—— "Documentos inéditos que ilustran los orígenes de los obispados Carolense (1519), Tierra Florida (1520), y Yucatán (1561)" in *Revista de Historia de América,* IX (1940).

Méndez Plancarte, Alfonso — see *Códice Gómez de Orozco;* Ramírez, *Memorial de Pedro Plancarte* . . .

Mendieta, Gerónimo (Jerónimo) de (1525–1604). *Historia eclesiástica indiana* (c1574–96). México (Chávez Hayhoe), 1945, 4 vols.

—— See also *Códice Mendieta*

—— and Oroz, Pedro, and Suárez, Francisco. *Relación de la descripción de la Provincia del Santo Evangelio que es en las Indias Occidentales que llaman la Nueva España* (1575–85), introduction and notes by Fidel de Jesús Chauvet. México (Aguilar Reyes), 1947.

Mendizábal, Miguel O. de. *"El lienzo de Jucutácato,"* su verdadera significación. México (Museo Nacional), 1926.

Mendoza, Antonio de — see *Ordenanzas y copilación de leyes* . . .

Mendoza, Vicente T. *Panorama de la música tradicional de México.* México (Universidad), 1956.

Menéndez Pidal, Gonzalo. *Imagen del mundo hacia 1570.* Madrid (Ultra Alcalá), 1944.

Mengin, Ernest. "Codex Mexicanus, Bibliothèque Nationale de Paris, 23–24," in *Journal de la Société des Américanistes,* XLI (1952).

Merriman, Roger Bigelow. *The Rise of the Spanish Empire in the Old World and the New,* vols. III, IV. New York (Macmillan), 1925, 1934.

Michel, *Histoire de l'art* — see Gillet, Louis, *L'art dans l'Amérique* . . .

Millares Carlo, Agustín. *Apuntes para un estudio biobibliográfico del humanista Francisco Cervantes de Salazar.* México (Universidad), 1958.

Miozzi, Eugenio. *Venezia nei secoli, la città.* Venice (Libeccio), 1957, 2 vols.

Miranda, José. *El tributo indígena en la Nueva España durante el siglo XVI.* México (Colegio de México), 1952.

Moedano Koer, Hugo. "Tizatlán, asiento del señor Xochipilli" in *Cuadernos Americanos,* II (1943).

Molina, Alonso de (—1585). *Vocabulario en lengua castellana y mexicana* (facsimile of 1st edition of 1571). Madrid (Cultura Hispánica), 1944.

Molina Hipólito, J. *Guía monumental de Baeza.* Baeza (Diario "Jaén"), 1959.

——— *Guía de Ubeda.* Ubeda (La Loma), 1959.

Molíns Fábrega, N. *El Códice Mendocino y la economía de Tenochtitlán.* México (Libro-Mex, Biblioteca Mínima), 1956.

Monroy, Melitón Salazar — see Salazar Monroy, Melitón

Monumentos coloniales de México — see (Enciso, etc.) *Edificios coloniales* . . .

Moreno, Juan José (Joseph). *Vida de don Vasco de Quiroga, primer obispo de Michoacán* (1766), including also the *Ordenanzas* (both republished also in *Don Vasco de Quiroga, documentos, q v*) Morelia (Martínez Mier), 1939.

Moreno Villa, José. *La escultura colonial mexicana.* México (Colegio de México), 1942.

——— *Lo mexicano.* México (Colegio de México), 1948.

Morison, Samuel Eliot. *Christopher Columbus, Mariner.* Boston (Little, Brown), 1955.

Morris, J. Bayard — see Cortés, *Five Letters*

Moses, Bernard. *The Spanish Dependencies in South America.* New York (Harper), 1914.

la Mota y Escobar, Alonso de (1546–1625). *Descripción geográfica de los Reinos de Nueva Galicia, Nueva Vizcaya, y Nuevo León* (material gathered 1602–05). México (Robredo), 1940.

la Mota Padilla, Matías de (1688–1766). *Historia de la conquista del Reino de la Nueva Galicia* (1742), edited, with notes, by José Ireneo Gutiérrez. Guadalajara (Gallardo y Alvarez del Castillo), 1924, 2 vols.

Motolinía, Toribio (de Benavente) (de Paredes?) (—1565). *Carta al Emperador* (1555), *refutación a Las Casas sobre la colonización española,* introduction and notes by José Bravo Ugarte. México (Jus), 1949.

——— *Motolinia's History of the Indians of New Spain* (c1536–c1541/42), translated and annotated by Francis Borgia Steck. Washington (Academy of American Franciscan History), 1951.

BIBLIOGRAPHY

Motolinía, Toribio. *Memoriales* (c1536–c1542?) (*Documentos Históricos de Méjico*, I), edited by Luis García Pimentel. México-Paris-Madrid, 1903.

Moyssén, Xavier. "Las cruces de Toluca" in *Anales del I I E*, XXVII (1958).

Muñoz, Diego. "Descripción de la Provincia de los Apóstoles San Pedro y San Pablo en las Indias de la Nueva España" (1583) in *Archivo Ibero-Americano*, IX (1922).

Muñoz Camargo, Diego. *Historia de Tlaxcala* (end of XVI). México, 1947/48.

Muraro, Michelangelo. *Les villas de la Vénétie*. Venice (Neri Pozza), 1954.

Muriel, Josefina. *Conventos de monjas en la Nueva España*. México (Santiago), 1946.

Murillo, Gerardo ("Dr. Atl") — see Toussaint, *La arquitectura religiosa* . . .

Muro Obregón, Antonio — see *Las Leyes Nuevas* . . .

Navarro, José Gabriel. *Los franciscanos en la conquista y colonización de América*. Madrid (Cultura Hispánica), 1955.

Neasham, V. Aubrey. "Spain's Emigrants to the New World" in *H A H R*, XIX (1939).

Neumeyer, Alfred. "The Indian Contribution to Architectural Decoration in Spanish Colonial America" in *Art Bulletin*, XXX (1948).

New Laws — see *Las Leyes Nuevas* . . .

"Newe Zeitung von dem Lande das die Spanier funden haben ym 1521 Iare genant Jucatan" in *H A H R*, IX (1929); (reprinted with Spanish translation by Universidad Nacional de México, 1940).

Nicolás Kuri, A. Miriam. *Fray Pedro de Gante como precursor de los grandes pedagogos Pestalozzi y Froebel*. México (Escuela Normal Superior), 1952.

Noel, Martín S. — see *El santuario de Copacabana* . . .

Noyes, Ernest. "Fray Alonso Ponce in Yucatán, 1588" in *Middle American Research Papers*, IV (1932).

Nueva colección de documentos para la historia de México, ed. García Icazbalceta. México (Andrade y Morales), 1886–92 — see *Cartas de religiosos; Códice franciscano; Códice Mendieta;* Pomar and Zurita, *Relación* . . .

Nuevos documentos relativos a los bienes de Hernán Cortés, introduction by Francisco González de Cossío. México (Archivo General de la Nación), 1946.

Nuttall, Zelia. *Ancient Mexican Feather Work at the Columbian Historical Exposition at Madrid*. Washington (Government Printing Office), 1895.

——— *Documentos referentes a la destrucción de templos e ídolos, violación de sepulcros y las remociones de indios e ídolos en Nueva España durante el siglo XVI* (reprinted from *Centenario de la Sociedad Mexicana de Geografía y Estadística*). México (Cultura), 1933.

——— "The gardens of ancient Mexico" in *Smithsonian Institution Annual Report 1923* (Washington, 1925).

——— "Royal Ordinances concerning the Laying out of New Towns" in *H A H R*, IV (1921), and V (1922).

——— See also Sahagún, *Colloquios* . . .

Obregón, Gonzalo. "La iglesia del Colegio de Niñas" in *Anales del I I E*, XX (1952). See also Viera, *Breve compendiossa naración* . . .

Ocaranza, Fernando. *Capítulos de la historia franciscana*. México (author), 1933, 1934, 2 vols.

—— *El imperial Colegio de Indios de la Santa Cruz de Santiago Tlaltelolco*. México (author), 1934.

Ochoa V., Angel S. *El convento de San Francisco de Guadalajara 1554–1954*. Guadalajara (Font), 1959.

O'Gorman, Edmundo. *Reflexiones sobre la distribución urbana colonial de la Ciudad de México*. México (XVI Congreso Internacional de Planificación y de la Habitación), 1938. See also Fernández and O'Gorman, *Santo Tomás More* . . . ; Fernández de Oviedo, *Sucesos* . . .

Ojea, Hernando (–1615). *Libro tercero de la historia religiosa de la Provincia de México de la Orden de Santo Domingo* (before 1608) (written as a continuation of Dávila Padilla, *Historia* . . .). México (Museo Nacional), 1897.

Olite, Fermín de — see Ajofrín and Olite

Olvera, Jorge. "Copanaguastla, joya del plateresco en Chiapas" in *Ateneo*, I (1951).

Ordenanzas y copilación de leyes por el muy ilustre señor don Antonio de Mendoza (1548). Madrid (Cultura Hispánica), 1945.

Ordenanzas del trabajo, siglos XVI y XVII, edited, with notes, by Silvio Zavala. México (Instituto de Historia de la Universidad Nacional), 1947.

Orosa Díaz, Jaime. *Yucatán, panorama histórico, geográfico y cultural*. México (Secretaría de Educación Pública), 1945.

Oroz, Pedro — see Mendieta, Oroz, and Suárez

Orozco y Berra, Manuel (1816–81), *Los conquistadores de México* — see Dorantes de Carranza, *Sumaria relación*

—— *Historia de la dominación española en México* (1849), with note by Genaro Estrada. México (Porrua), 1938, 4 vols.

—— See also *Códice Ramírez*.

Ortega, Angel. "El convento de San Francisco de Belvís de la Provincia de San Gabriel de Extremadura, sus orígenes, fundación, y primeros moradores" in *Archivo Ibero-americano*, IV (1917).

Osorio, Diego de — see "Alegato de Fr. Diego Osorio . . ."

Ots Capdequí, José María. *El estado español en las Indias*. México (Colegio de México), 1941.

Oviedo (y Valdés), Gonzalo Fernández de — see Fernández de Oviedo, Gonzalo

Padden, Robert Charles. "The Ordenanzas del Patronazgo, 1574" in *The Americas*, XII (1955/56).

Palacio (y Basave), Luis del Refugio de. *Joyas franciscanas en Puebla y Tlaxcala*. México (Centro de Estudios Históricos Franciscanos), 1944.

—— *Visita de curioso al convento de Huexotzinco, Cholula — Parrangón*. Guadalajara (Font), 1937

—— See also Tello, *Crónica* . . . ; Torres, *Crónica* . . .

Palacios, Enrique Juan. *Puebla, su territorio y sus habitantes*. México (Secretaría de Fomento), 1917.

Palm, Erwin Walter. "Las capillas abiertas americanas y sus antecedentes en el occidente cristiano" in *Anales del Instituto de Arte Americano*, VI (1953).

—— "Estilo y época en el arte colonial" in *Anales del Instituto de Arte Americano*, II (1949).

—— *Los hospitales antiguos de la Española*. Ciudad Trujillo (Secretaría de Estado de Sanidad y Asistencia Pública), 1950.

BIBLIOGRAPHY

Palm, Erwin Walter. *Los monumentos arquitectónicos de la Española, con una introducción a América.* Ciudad Trujillo (Universidad de Santo Domingo), 1955, 2 vols.

——— "Plateresque and Renaissance monuments of the Island of Hispaniola" in *Journal of the Society of Architectural Historians,* V (1945).

——— "Tenochtitlán y la ciudad ideal de Dürer," in *Journal de la Société des Américanistes,* XL (1951).

Panofsky, Erwin. *Early Netherlandish Painting: Its Origins and Character.* Cambridge, Mass. (Harvard), 1954, 2 vols.

Papeles de Nueva España, edited by Francisco del Paso y Troncoso. Madrid (Rivadeneyra), 1905–06, 7 vols. (vol. II never published). See also *Relaciones geográficas de la Diócesis de Michoacán.*

Paredes Colín, Joaquín. *Apuntes históricos de Tehuacán* (1910). Tehuacán, 1953.

Parkes, Henry Bamford. *A History of Mexico.* Boston (Houghton Mifflin), 1938.

del Paso y Troncoso, Francisco, ed. (1842–1916) — see Castillo, *Fragmento . . .* ; *Epistolario de Nueva España; Papeles de Nueva España*

Pazos, Manuel R. "Los franciscanos y la educación literaria de los indios mejicanos" in *Archivo Ibero-americano,* XIII (1953).

——— "Reducciones franciscanas en Méjico" in *Archivo Ibero-americano,* XIII (1953).

——— "El teatro franciscano en Méjico durante el siglo XVI" in *Archivo Ibero-americano,* XI (1951).

Pedro de Gante (Petrus de Mura) (c1480–1572). *Cartilla para enseñar a leer* (facsimile of 3rd? edition, México, Ocharte, 1569), introduction by Luis Alvarez Barret; introductory bibliographical note by Ignacio Márquez Rodiles. México (Academia Mexicana de la Educación), 1959.

Pedro Mártir de Anglería (Pietro Martire d'Anghiera) (1459–1526). *Libros de las décadas del Nuevo Mundo* (1511–26), translated, with notes, by Agustín Millares Carlo. México (Secretaría de Educación Pública), 1945.

la Peña, Francisco Javier de — see Villa Sánchez, *Puebla . . .*

Peñafiel, Antonio. *Ciudades coloniales y capitales de la República Mexicana.* México (Secretaría de Fomento), 1914. See also *Códice Aubin; Anales de Tecamachalco*

Pereyra, Carlos. *Hernán Cortés.* Buenos Aires (Espasa-Calpe), 1953.

——— *Historia del Pueblo mejicano.* México (Ballesca) (c1908), 2 vols.

——— *Las huellas de los conquistadores.* Madrid (Consejo de la Hispanidad), 1942.

——— *La obra de España en América.* Madrid (Aguilar) (c1925).

——— See also *Documentos inéditos o muy raros para la historia de México*

Pérez, Lorenzo. "La Provincia de San José fundada por San Pedro de Alcántara" in *Archivo Ibero-americano,* IX (1922).

Pérez Verdía, Luis. *Historia particular del Estado de Jalisco.* Guadalajara (Escuela de Artes y Oficios del Estado), 1910–11, 3 vols.

Peterson, Frederick A. *Ancient Mexico, an Introduction to the Pre-Hispanic Cultures.* New York (Putnam), 1959.

Phelan, John Leddy. "Free versus Compulsory Labor: Mexico and the Philippines 1540–1648" in *Comparative Studies in Society and History,* I (1959).

——— *The Hispanization of the Philippines, Spanish Aims and Filipino Responses,* 1565–1700. Madison (Wisconsin), 1959.

694

—— *The Millenial Kingdom of the Franciscans in the New World, a Study of the Writings of Gerónimo de Mendieta (1525–1604)*. Berkeley (California), 1656.

Pineda, Vicente. *Historia de las sublevaciones indígenas habidas en el Estado de Chiapas*. Chiapas (Tipografía del Gobierno), 1888.

Plancarte, Salvador Escalante — see Escalante Plancarte, Salvador

Plancarte y Navarrete, Francisco. *Apuntes para la geografía del Estado de Morelos*. Tepoztlán, 1909.

Plato. *Laws*. Cambridge, Mass. (Harvard, Loeb Classical Library), 1946.

Pleito entre d Francisco Velázquez de Gijón, gobernador de Yucatán, y el Obispo Fray Diego de Landa, año de 1574. Guadalajara (Colección "Siglo XVI"), 1960.

Pol, Ferrán de. *Cuernavaca*. México (Edición de Artes, *Colección Anáhuac*), 1948.

Pomar, Juan Bautista. *Relación de Texcoco* (1582) with Zurita (Zorita or Çorita), Alonso de (1511/12–after 1585). *Breve y sumaria relación de los señores de la Nueva España* (c1557–64, 1574) and *Varias relaciones antiguas*, introduction by Joaquín García Icazbalceta. México (Chávez Hayhoe), 1941; here cited as Pomar and Zurita. See also Zorita, *Historia* . . .

Ponce, Alonso (supposed author). *Relación breve y verdadera de algunas cosas de las muchas que suciederan al Padre Fray Alonso Ponce en las provincias de la Nueva España, siendo Comisario General de aquellas partes . . . escrita por dos religiosos* (probably Alonso de San Juan and Antonio de Ciudad Real) (1584–c1588). Madrid (Calero), 1873, 2 vols.

Ponz, Antonio (1725–92). *Viaje de España* (c1771--91), edited by Castro María del Rivero. Madrid (Aguilar), 1947.

Powell, Philip Wayne. "The Chichimecas, Scourge of the Silver Frontier in Sixteenth-century Mexico" in *H A H R*, XXV (1945).

—— "Presidios and Towns on the Silver Frontier of New Spain, 1550–80" in *H A H R*, XXIV (1944).

—— "Spanish Warfare against the Chichimecas in the 1570's" in *H A H R*, XXIV (1944).

Prentice, Andrew N. *Renaissance Architecture and Ornament in Spain in 1500–1560*. London (Batsford), 1893.

Priego, Antonio López de (López de Priego) — see *Tesoros documentales* . . .

Proceso contra Tzintzicha Tangaxoan el Caltzontzín formado por Nuño de Guzmán, año de 1530, edited by France V. Scholes and Eleanor B. Adams. México (Porrua), 1952.

Procesos de indios idólatras y hechiceros. México (Archivo General de la Nación), 1912.

Puga, Vasco de. *Provisiones, cédulas, instrucciones para el gobierno de la Nueva España* (1563). Madrid (Cultura Hispánica), 1945.

Quevedo, F. G. de. *Así es Oaxaca*. México (Font), 1948.

Quiñones, Lebrón de — see *Lo que proveyó el licenciado Lebrón* . . .

Quintana, José Miguel — see León and Quintana, *Documentos inéditos referentes al . . . Quiroga*

Quiroga, don Vasco de, Documentos (includes Moreno Biography, *Ordenanzas, Will*), edited by Rafael Aguayo Spencer. México (Polis), 1939 (1940).

BIBLIOGRAPHY

Quiroga, Documentos inéditos referentes al . . . — see León and Quintana

Quiroga, Vida de . . . — see Moreno, *La vida de* . . . *Quiroga*

Quiroz y Gutiérrez, Nicanor. *Historia de la aparición de Nuestra Señora de Ocotlán y de su culto en cuatro siglos (1541–1941).* Puebla, 1940.

Radin, Paul. *The Sources and Authenticity of the History of the Ancient Mexicans.* Berkeley (California), 1920.

Ramírez, Diego. *Carta al Emperador de Diego Ramírez haciendo relación de lo ocurrido en la visita que había hecho a diez pueblos (1552).* México (Vargas Rea), 1953.

Ramírez, Félix C. *Ireti Khatape, ensayo de una interpretación de la Relación de Michoacán.* México (Casa Ramírez), 1956.

Ramírez, Francisco. *Memorial de la santa vida y dichoso tránsito de el buen beneficiado Pedro Plancarte, cura de Capácuaro (1627),* edited, with notes, by Alfonso Méndez Plancarte. México (Abside), 1947.

Ramírez, José Fernando. *Perigrinación mexicana.* México (Vargas Rea), 1945.

—— *Vida de Fray Toribio de Motolinía.* México (Porrua), 1944.

—— See also Durán, *Historia* . . .

Ramírez Aparicio, Manuel. *Los conventos suprimidos en México.* México (Aguilar), 1861.

la Rea, Alonso de. *Crónica de la Orden de N Seráfico P S Francisco, Provincia de San Pedro y San Pablo de Mechoacán en la Nueva España (1639).* México (La Voz de México), 1882.

Recopilación de leyes de los Reinos de las Indias (1681). Madrid (Boix), 1841, 4 vols.

Redfield, Robert. *Tepoztlán, a Mexican Village.* Chicago (Chicago), 1930.

Rees, T. Ifor. *In and Around the Valley of Mexico.* Aberystwyth, Wales (Cambrian News), 1953.

Relación or *Relaciones,* arranged below alphabetically by town or subject, disregarding prepositions, articles, *"Pueblo de,"* etc.

Relación del Pueblo de Atenco por Juan de Padilla (1579). México (Vargas Rea), 1957.

Relación de Ayusuchiquilazala (1580). México (Vargas Rea), 1956.

Relación breve de la venida de la Compañía de Jesús — see (Villerías), *Relación* . . .

Relación breve y verdadera de . . . *Alonso Ponce* — see Ponce, *Relación* . . .

Relación de Celaya y su partido, año de 1570 (includes Acámbaro, Yuriria). México (Vargas Rea), 1945.

Relación de las ceremonías y ritos, población, y gobierno de los indios de la Provincia de Mechoacán, hecha al illmo Dr D Antonio de Mendoza, in C D I *España,* LIII.

"Relación de Cholula" (or "Descripción de Cholula") by Gabriel de Rojas, 1581 in *Revista Mexicana de Estudios Históricos,* I (1927), appendix.

Relación de los pueblos Coçautepeque, Teotzacualco y de Amoltepeque (1580). México (Vargas Rea), 1956.

"Dos relaciones antiguas del pueblo de Cuilapa . . ." — see Barlow, "Dos relaciones . . ."

Relación de Culhuacán — see *Relación de Puctla* . . .

Relación de la descripción de la Provincia del Santo Evangelio . . . — see Mendieta, Oroz, and Suárez, *Relación* . . .

"Relación de Epaçoyuca" (part of "Relación de Zempoala y su partido") in *Tlalocan*, III (1949/57).

Relaciones geográficas de la Diócesis de Michoacán 1579–1580, notes by José Corona Núñez. Guadalajara (Colección "Siglo XVI"), 1958, 2 vols.

Relaciones geográficas de Indias (1560–82) (Vol. IV of *Biblioteca Colonial Americana*), edited by Germán Latorre. Seville (Zarzuela, for Centro Oficial de Estudios Americanistas), 1920.

Relaciones geográficas del siglo XVIII. México (Vargas Rea), 1945.

Relación hecha en Michoacán . . . — see *Relación* . . . *Michoacán*

Relaciones . . . *de Indias* — see *Relaciones geográficas de Indias*

Relación de Instlahuaca (1580). México (Vargas Rea), 1956.

Relación de Iztapalapan (1580). México (Vargas Rea), 1957.

"Relación hecha en la Provincia de Mechoacán en el año de 1603" by P. de Vera in *Colección de documentos para la historia de España*, C (1891). See also *Relación de las ceremonías* . . . *de Mechoacán; Relaciones geográficas de* . . . *Michoacán*

Relación de Mistepeque por Andrés Aznar de Cozar (1580). México (Vargas Rea), 1956.

Relación de los Obispados de Tlaxcala, Michoacán, Oaxaca y otros lugares en el siglo XVI (*Documentos Históricos de Méjico*, II), edited by Luis García Pimentel. México-Paris-Madrid, 1904.

Relación de Pátzcuaro — see *Descripción de la Ciudad de Pásquaro*

Relación de los pueblos de Peñoles (1579). México (Vargas Rea), 1956.

Relación de Puctla y Relación de Culhuacán (1580). México (Vargas Rea), 1956.

"Relación de Tancítaro" in *Tlalocan*, III (1949/57).

"Relación de Tehuantepec" in *Revista Mexicana de Estudios Históricos*, II (1948), supplemento.

Relación de Tejupa — see *Códice Sierra*

Relación de Teutitlán (Teotitlán del Camino and other towns) (1580–81). México (Vargas Rea), 1957.

Relación de Texcoco — see Pomar and Zurita, *Relación* . . .

Relaciones de Yucatán (1579–81), vols. 11 and 13 in *C D I Ultramar*

Relación de Zacatepec (1580). México (Vargas Rea), 1956.

"Relación de Zempoala y su partido, 1590" (including Epazoyucan) in *Tlalocan*, III (1949/57).

Relaciones, miscellaneous typescripts in Museo Nacional, Mexico. See also *Descripción de* . . . ; *Papeles de Nueva España*.

Relazioni degli ambasciatori veneti. Florence (Alberi), 1839–63, 3 vols.

Remesal, Antonio de (*fl.* 1593–1613). *Historia general de las Indias Occidentales y particular de la Gobernación de Chiapa y Guatemala* . . . (1615–17). Guatemala (Sociedad de Geografía e Historia), 1932, 2 vols.

Revilla, Manuel Gustavo. *El arte en México en la época antigua y durante el gobierno virreinal*. México (Secretaría de Fomento), 1893.

Reyes, Alfonso. *Ultima Tule*. México (Imprenta Universitaria), 1942.

—— *Visión de Anáhuac*. Madrid (Indice), 1923.

Reyes Hurtado, Salvador. "Contribución a la historia de la vida de Vasco de Quiroga" in *Anales del Museo Michoacano*, IV (1946).

Ricard, Robert. "Apuntes complementarios sobre la plaza mayor española y el 'rossio' portugués," in *Estudios Geográficos*, XIII (1952).

BIBLIOGRAPHY

Ricard, Robert. *La 'Conquête spirituelle' du Méxique, Essai sur l'apostolat et les méthodes missionaires des Ordres Mendiants en Nouvelle-Espagne de 1523/24 à 1572*. Paris (Institut d'Ethnologie), 1933.

—— "Un document inédit sur les Augustins en 1563," in *Journal de la Société des Américanistes*, XVIII (1926).

—— "L'incorporation de l'indien par l'école au Méxique," in *Journal de la Société des Américanistes*, XXXIII (1931).

—— "La plaza mayor en España y en América" in *Estudios Geográficos*, XI (1950); reprinted from *Annales Economies-Sociétés-Civilizations*, IV, 1947.

—— "Remarques bibliographiques sur les ouvrages de Fr. Toribio Motolinía," in *Journal de la Société des Américanistes*, XXXV (1933).

Rico González, Victor. *Hacia un concepto de la conquista de México*. México (Instituto de Historia), 1953.

Ríos, Eduardo Enrique. *Fray Juan de San Miguel, fundador de pueblos*. México (Cuadernos Franciscanos), 1943.

—— "Una obra ignorada de Simón Pereynes" in *Anales del I I E*, IX (1942).

Rippy, J. Fred. *Latin America, a Modern History*. Ann Arbor (Michigan), 1958.

Rivera Cambas, Manuel. *México pintoresco, artístico y monumental* (1880). México (Editora Nacional), 1957, 3 vols.

Rivero Carvallo, José. *Totimehuacán, convento y templos franciscanos*. Puebla (López), 1961.

Robertson, Donald. *Mexican Manuscript Painting of the early Colonial Period, The Metropolitan Schools*. New Haven, Conn. (Yale), 1959.

Robles, Vito Alessio — see (Alessio Robles), *Cuernavaca* . . .

Rodríguez Familiar, José. *La conquista de Querétaro*. Querétaro (Cimatario), 1944.

Rodríguez Prampolini, Ida. "El arte indígena y los cronistas de Nueva España" in *Anales del I I E*, XVII (1949).

Rohde, Francisco José. "Angahuan" in *Anales del I I E*, XIV (1946).

Rojas, Gabriel de — see "Relación de Cholula"

Rojas (Rodríguez), Pedro (Mario). "Copándaro" in *Anales del I I E*, XXII (1954).

—— *Tonantzintla*. México (Universidad), 1956.

Rojas Garcidueñas, José. *Autos y coloquios del siglo XVI*. México (Universidad), 1939.

—— "Fiestas en México en 1578" in *Anales del I I E*, IX (1942).

—— "Fray Juan de Alameda" in *Abside*, XI (1947) (references here are to offprint, pp. 8–36).

—— See also González de Eslava, *Coloquios* . . .

Romero, José Guadalupe. *Noticias para formar la historia y la estadística del Obispado de Michoacán*. México (García Torres), 1862.

Romero Flores, Jesús. *Historia de la Ciudad de Morelia*. México (Morelos), 1952.

—— *Iconografía colonial*. México (Museo Nacional), 1940.

—— *Michoacán histórico y legendario*, foreword by Rafael Heliodoro Valle. México (Talleres Gráficos de la Nación), 1937.

—— *Tacámbaro*. México (Talleres Gráficos de la Nación), 1939.

Romero de Terreros (y Vinent), Manuel (Marqués de San Francisco). "El antiguo convento franciscano de Topoyanco" in *Memorias de la Academia Mexicana de Historia*, XII (1953).

—— *Arte colonial*. México (Robredo), 1918–21, 3 vols.

698

—— *Los artes industriales en la Nueva España*. México (Robredo), 1924.
—— *Atlatláuhcan*. México (Instituto Nacional de Antropología e Historia), 1956.
—— *Ayotzingo*. México (Instituto Nacional de Antropología e Historia), 1959.
—— "El convento dominicano de Chimalhuacán Chalco" in *Anales del I I E, XXX* (1961).
—— "El convento franciscano de Ozumba y las pinturas de su portería" in *Anales del I I E, XXIV* (1956).
—— *Hernán Cortés, sus hijos y nietos, Caballeros de las Ordenes Militares*. México (Robredo), 1919.
—— *Historia sintética del arte colonial en México*. México (Porrua), 1922.
—— "Huexotla" in *Anales del I I E, XXVI* (1957).
—— *La iglesia y convento de San Agustín*. México (Instituto de Investigaciones Estéticas), 1951.
—— "La iglesia de San Francisco de México" in *Anales del I I E, XX* (1952).
—— See also Vázquez de Tapia, *Relación* . . .
Romerovargas Yturbide, Ignacio — see las Casas, *Breve relación* . . .
Rosell, Lauro E. *Iglesias y conventos coloniales de la Ciudad de México*. México (Patria), 1946. See also (Enciso, Martínez Cosío, Rosell), *Edificios* . . .
Rosenthal, Earl E. *The Cathedral of Granada*. Princeton, N.J. (Princeton), 1961.
—— "The Image of Roman Architecture in Renaissance Spain" in *Gazette des Beaux-Arts, LII* (1958).
—— "A Renaissance 'Copy' of the Holy Sepulchre" in *Journal of the Society of Architectural Historians, XVII* (1959).
Roys, Ralph L. — see Scholes and Roys
Rubio Mañé, Jorge Ignacio. *Introducción al estudio de los virreyes de Nueva España 1535–1746*. México (Universidad), 1955, 1959, 2 vols.
—— See also *Catálogo de* . . . *Yucatán; Documentos para la historia de Yucatán*.
—— and Toussaint, Manuel. *La casa de Montejo en Mérida de Yucatán*. México (Imprenta Universitaria), 1941.
J(ohann) M(oritz) Rugendas (1802–55) *en México*. Catalogue of an Exhibition in Mexico, 1959, with essays by Peter Halm and Federico Hernández Serrano. Munich (Prestel), 1959.

Sagredo, Diego de. *Medidas del Romano necessarias a los oficiales que quieren seguir las formaciones de las bases, colunas, capiteles, y otras pieças de los edificios antiguos* (facsimile of 1st edition, 1526). Madrid (Asociación de Libreros y Amigos del Libro), 1946.
Sahagún, Bernardino de (1499/1500–1590). "Colloquios y doctrina christiana con que los doze frailes de San Francisco . . ." (1564), introduction by Zelia Nuttall, in *Revista Mexicana de Estudios Históricos, I* (1927), appendix.
—— *Historia general de las cosas de Nueva España* (c1540–77), notes, etc., by Miguel Acosta Saignes. México (Nueva España), 1946, 3 vols.
—— *Suma indiana* (selections from the preceding) edited, with a foreword, by Mauricio Magdaleno. México (Universidad), 1943.
—— See also *Códice Florentino*.
Salazar, B. *Los Doce, primeros apóstoles franciscanos en México*. México (Centro de Estudios Franciscanos?), 1943.

BIBLIOGRAPHY

Salazar Monroy, Melitón. *Convento franciscano de Huejotzingo*. Puebla (López), 1944.
—— *Convento de San Francisco y Capilla de Tercer Orden en la Ciudad de Tlaxcala*. Tlaxcala (Oficina de Turismo del Estado), 1938.
Salinas, Miguel. *Datos para la historia de Toluca*. México (Muñoz), 1927.
—— "Doña Juana de Zúñiga, primera Marquesa del Valle" in *Revista Mexicana de Estudios Históricos*, II (1928).
—— See also Cólin, *Toluca* . . .
San Juan, Alonso de — see Ponce, *Relación* . . .
Sancho, Hipólito. "Notas y documentos para la historia de la arquitectura de las Ordenes Mendicantes" in *Archivo Ibero-Americano*, XII (1952).
Santiago Cruz, Francisco. *Las artes y los gremios en la Nueva España*. México (Jus), 1960.
—— "Estampas chiapanecas" in *Abside*, XVIII (1954).
Santos, Reynaldo dos. *O estilo manuelino*. Lisbon (Academia Nacional de Belas Artes), 1952.
El santuario de Copacabana, de la Paz a Tiahuanaco (*Documentos de Arte Colonial Sudamericano*, VII). Buenos Aires (Academia Nacional de Bellas Artes), 1950.
Sartorius, Christian. *Mexico and the Mexicans*. London (Trübner), 1859.
Scholes, France Vinton — see *Advertimientos que los virreyes* . . . ; *Documentos para la historia de Yucatán; Proceso contra Tzintzicha* . . .
—— and Adams, Eleanor B. *Don Diego Quijada, alcalde mayor de Yucatán 1561–1565*. México (Robredo), 1938.
—— and Roys, Ralph L. *Fray Diego de Landa and the Problem of Idolatry in Yucatan*. Washington (Carnegie Institute), 1938 (reprinted from *Cooperation in Research*).
Scholes, Walter Vinton. *The Diego Ramírez Visita*. Columbia (Missouri), 1946.
Schubert, Otto. *Geschichte des Barock in Spanien*. Esslingen (Neff-Schreiber), 1908.
Seitz, Josef. *Die Verehrung des heiligen Joseph in ihrer geschichtlichen Entwicklung bis zum Konzil von Trient*. Freiburg-im-Breisgau (Herder), 1908.
Seler, Eduard. "Die alte Bewohner der Landschaft Michoacán" in *Gesammelte Abhandlungen zur Amerikanischen Sprach- und Altertumskunde*, III, Berlin (Asher), 1908.
Serlio, Sebastiano (1475–1554). *Regole generali di architettura* . . . Venice, 1537, 1540, 1544, 1551, 1559, 1560, 1562, etc. (different editions contain different books, I–V, in differing combinations); also Antwerp, 1545; Paris, 1545, 1547; Toledo, 1565 (books III, IV).
Shepard, Minnie Lee Barrett — see Cervantes de Salazar, *Life* . . .
Siebenhüner, Herbert. *Das Kapitol in Rom: Idee und Gestalt*. Munich (Kösel), 1954.
Sigüenza y Góngora, Carlos (1645–1700). *Piedad heroyca de don Fernando Cortés* (1691–93), introduction by Jaime Delgado. Madrid (Porrua Turranzas), 1960.
Simpson, Lesley Byrd. *The Emancipation of the Indian Slaves and Resettlement of the Freedmen, 1548–53*. Berkeley (California), 1940.
—— *The Encomienda in New Spain, the Beginning of Spanish Mexico*. Berkeley (California), 1950.
—— *Many Mexicos*. New York (Putnam), 1941.

———— "The Population of 22 Towns in Michoacán in 1554" in *H A H R*, XXX (1950).

———— *The Repartimiento System of Native Labor in New Spain and Guatemala.* Berkeley (California), 1938.

———— *Studies in the Administration of the Indians in New Spain.* Berkeley (California), 1934.

———— See also Cook and Simpson, *The Population of Central Mexico* . . .

Smith, A. Ledyard. "The Corbelled Arch in the New World" — see *The Maya and their Neighbors*

Smith, F(rancis) Hopkinson. *A White Umbrella in Mexico.* Boston (Houghton Mifflin), 1889.

Smith, Robert C. "Colonial Towns of Spanish and Portuguese America" in *Journal of the Society of Architectural Historians*, XIV (1955).

Smith, Robert Sidney. "Sales Taxes in New Spain, 1575–1770" in *H A H R*, XXVIII (1948).

Sobre la necesidad que hay de haberse de enseñar y predicar a los indios en su propio idioma la Doctrina Christiana (c1770). México (Vargas Rea), 1948.

Sodí de Pallares, María Elena. *Historia del traje religioso en México.* México (Stylo), 1950.

Soler Alonso, Pedro. *Virreyes de la Nueva España.* México (Secretaría de Educación Pública), 1945.

Soria, Martin. "Colonial Painting in Latin America" in *Art in America*, XLVII (1959).

———— "Notes on early Murals in Mexico" in *Studies in the Renaissance*, VI. New York (Renaissance Society), 1959.

———— See also Kubler and Soria, *Art and Architecture in Spain* . . .

Sotomayor, Arturo. "Huaquechula, esplendida joya colonial" in *Magazine de Novedades*, April 1961.

Soustelle, Jacques. *La vida cotidiana de los aztecas,* translated by Carlos Villegas. México (Fondo de Cultura Económica), 1956.

Specker, Johann. "La política colonizadora eclesiástica y estatal en Hispanoamérica en el siglo XVI" in *Estudios Americanos*, XIII (1957).

Spell, Lota M. "Music in the Cathedral of Mexico in the Sixteenth Century" in *H A H R*, XXVI (1946).

Spinden, Herbert J. *Ancient Civilizations of Mexico and Central America.* New York (Museum of Natural History), 1928.

Stanislawski, Dan. "The Anatomy of Eleven Towns in Michoacán" in *University of Texas Institute of Latin American Studies*, X (1950).

———— "Early Spanish Town Planning in the New World" in *Geographical Review*, XXXVII (1947).

———— "The Origin and Development of the Grid-pattern Town" in *Geographical Review*, XXXVI (1946).

Steck, Francis Borgia. *Ensayos históricos hispanoamericanos.* México (Abside), 1940.

———— *El primer colegio de América, Santa Cruz de Tlaltelolco,* with a study of the *Códice de Tlatelolco* by Robert H. Barlow. México (Centro de Estudios Franciscanos), 1944.

———— See also Motolinía *History* . . .

Stephens, John Lloyd (1805–52). *Incidents of Travel in Central America, Chiapas and Yucatan.* New York (Harper), 1841, 2 vols.

BIBLIOGRAPHY

Stephens, John Lloyd. *Incidents of Travel in Yucatan.* New York (Harper), 1843.

Stevenson, Robert Murrell. *Music in Mexico, a Historical Survey.* New York (Crowell), 1952.

Stier, Wilhelm. *Die Marienkirche zu Lübeck.* Lübeck, 1957.

Street, George Edmund (1824–81). *Some Account of Gothic Architecture in Spain,* edited by Georgiana Goddard King. New York (Dutton), 1914, 2 vols.

Studies in Latin American Art, edited by Elizabeth Wilder (Weismann). Washington (American Council of Learned Societies), 1949.

Suárez de Peralta, Juan (1536–   ). *Tratado del descubrimiento de las Indias* (1589) (*Noticias históricas de Nueva España*), introductory note by Federico Gómez de Orozco. México (Secretaría de Educación Pública), 1949.

Suárez, Francisco — see Mendieta, Oroz, and Suárez

Sumario de la residencia tomada a D. Fernando Cortés, Gobernador y Capitán General de Nueva España . . . (1528, 1529). (*Archivo Mexicano, Documentos para la historia de México*). México (García Torres), 1852–53, 2 vols.

Tablada, José Juan. *Historia del Arte en México* (1922). México (Aguilar), 1927.

Tello, Antonio (*fl.* 1596–1652). *Crónica miscelanea de la sancta Provincia de Xalisco* (first pub. 1653), foreword by José Cornejo Franco and notes by Luis del Refugio de Palacio. Guadalajara (Font), 1942, 1945, vols. III, IV.

———— *Libro segundo de la Crónica Miscelanea* (1st book is lost). Guadalajara (Guevara, República Literaria), 1891.

Ternaux-Compans, Henri. *Voyages, relations, et mémoires originaux pour servir à l'histoire de la découverte de l'Amérique.* Paris (Bertrand), 1837–41, 20 vols.

Tesoros documentales de México, siglo XVIII: Priego, Zelis, Clavijero, edited, with a foreword, by Mariano Cuevas. México (Galatea), 1944.

Tezozomoc, Hernando (Fernando de) Alvarado. *Crónica mexicana* (*c*1598), edited by Manuel Orozco y Berra. México (Ireneo Paz), 1878 (in same volume with *Códice Ramírez*).

Thompson, J. Eric S. *The Rise and Fall of Maya Civilization.* Norman (Oklahoma), 1954.

Toro, Alfonso. *La cántiga de las piedras.* México (Patria), 1943.

———— "En el silencio del viejo convento" in *Revista de Revistas,* January 1919.

Torquemada, Juan de (1563/65–1624). *Monarquía indiana* (–*c*1612/15). México (Chávez Hayhoe), 1943, 3 vols.

la Torre, Tomás de. *Desde Salamanca hasta Ciudad Real Chiapas, diario del viaje 1544–45,* foreword and notes by Frans Blom. México (Editora Central), 1945.

Torres, Francisco Mariano de. *Crónica de la sancta Provincia de Jalisco* (mid-XVIII), notes by Luis del Refugio de Palacio. Guadalajara (Colección "Siglo XVI"), 1960.

Torres Balbás, Leopoldo. *Arquitectura gótica* (*Ars Hispaniae,* VII). Madrid (Plus Ultra), 1952.

———— *Arte almohade, arte nazarí, arte mudéjar* (*Ars Hispaniae,* IV). Madrid (Plus Ultra), 1949.

———— "El estilo mudéjar en la arquitectura mejicana," in *Al-Andalus,* VI (1941).

—— *La mezquita de Córdoba y Madanat al-Zahra.* Madrid (Plus Ultra), 1952.

—— "Muṣallà y šarīa' en las ciudades hispanomusulmanes" in *Al-Andalus,* XIII (1948).

—— "Naves de edificios anteriores al siglo XIII cobiertas con armaduras de madera sobre arcos transversales" in *Archivo Español de Arte,* XXXII (1959).

—— "Plazas, zocos, y tiendas de las ciudades hispanomusulmanes," in *Al-Andalus,* XII (1947).

Toscano, Salvador. *Arte precolombino de México y de la América Central,* foreword by Manuel Toussaint. México (Universidad), 1944.

—— "Chiapas, su arte y historia coloniales" in *Anales del I I E,* VIII (1942).

—— "Una empresa renacentista de España: la introducción de cultivos y animales domésticos euroasiáticos en México" in *Cuadernos Americanos,* V (1946).

Toussaint, Manuel. *Acolman.* México (Ediciones de Arte, *Colección Anáhuac,* #16), 1948.

—— *Acolman, guía oficial.* México (Instituto Nacional de Antropología e Historia), n. d. (1949).

—— "Angahua" in *Journal of the Society of Architectural Historians,* V (1945).

—— "El arquitecto de la Catedral de Cuzco, Perú" in *Anales del I I E,* VII (1941).

—— "Arquitectura agustiniana" in *Artes Plásticas,* II (1939).

—— *La arquitectura religiosa en la Nueva España durante el siglo XVI* (*Iglesias de México,* VI, ed. "Dr. Atl" and José R. Benítez). México (Secretaría de Hacienda), 1927.

—— *Arte colonial en México.* México (Universidad), 1948.

—— *El arte flamenco en Nueva España.* México (Aldina), 1949.

—— *Arte mudéjar en América.* México (Porrua), 1946.

—— *La Catedral y las iglesias de Puebla.* México (Porrua), 1954.

—— "El convento de Cuitzeo" in *Arquitectura,* VI (1940).

—— "The Convent of Jonacatepec" in *This Week Esta Semana,* XVI (1952).

—— "El convento de Zinacantepec" in *Caminos de México,* III (1955).

—— "El criterio artístico de Hernán Cortés" in *Estudios Americanos,* I (1948).

—— "Huaquechula" in *Caminos de México,* II (1955).

—— "Huellas de Diego de Siloée en México" in *Anales del I I E,* XXI (1953).

—— *Oaxaca.* México (Cultura), 1926.

—— "Oaxtepec" in *Caminos de México,* I (1954).

—— *Paseos coloniales.* México (Universidad), 1939.

—— *Paseos coloniales* (new edition with new material), introduction by Justino Fernández, edited by Xavier Moyssén Echeverría. México (Imprenta Universitaria), 1962.

—— "Paseos coloniales: Huaquechula" in *Universidad de México,* VI (1952).

—— "Paseos coloniales: Zinacantepec" in *Universidad de México,* II (1948).

—— *Pátzcuaro.* México (Instituto de Investigaciones Estéticas y Escuela de Arquitectura de la Universidad Nacional), 1942.

—— *La pintura en México durante el siglo XVI.* México (Mundial, *Enciclopedia ilustrada Mexicana*), 1936.

—— *Pinturas murales en los conventos mexicanos del siglo XVI.* México (Ediciones de Arte, *Colección Anáhuac*), 1948.

—— "La Relación de Michoacán, su importancia artística" in *Anales del I I E,* I (1937).

BIBLIOGRAPHY

Toussaint, Manuel. "Santa Caterina de Acolman" in *Anales del I I E*, III (1939).
—— "Supervivencias góticas en la arquitectura mexicana del siglo XVI" in *Archivo Español de Arte*, XXXI (1935).
—— "Toribio de Alcaraz, arquitecto de la Catedral de Pátzcuaro" in *Novedades*, April 21, 1943.
—— "Yuririapúndaro" in *Excelsior*, August 6, 1950.
—— See also Baxter, *La arquitectura colonial* . . . ; Fernández, Gómez de Orozco, and Toussaint, *Planos* . . . ; Flores Guerrero, *Las capillas posas* . . . ; *Información de* . . . *García Bravo;* McAndrew and Toussaint, *Tecali, Zacatlán* . . . ; Rubio Mañé and Toussaint, *La casa de Montejo* . . . ; Toscano, *Arte precolombino* . . .
Tovar, Juan de (presumed author) — see *Códice Ramírez*
Tozzer, Alfred M. *A Comparative Study of the Mayas and Lacandones.* New York (Macmillan, for the Archaeological Institute of America), 1907. See also Landa, *Landa's Relación* . . . ; *The Maya and their Neighbors*
Trens, Manuel B. *Historia de Chiapas desde los tiempos más remotos hasta la caída del Segundo Imperio.* México (Talleres Gráficos de la Nación), 1957.
Trueba, Alfonso. *Don Vasco.* México (Campeador), 1954.
—— *Fray Pedro de Gante.* México (Jus), 1959.

Ugarte, José Bravo — see Bravo Ugarte, José
Ulloa, Alonso de (possible author) — see Conquistador anónimo
Ulloa Ortiz, Berta. *Los documentos más antiguos del Archivo del Ayuntamiento de Puebla.* Puebla (Centro de Estudios Históricos), 1959.
Unwin, Rayner. *The Defeat of John Hawkins.* London (Allen and Unwin), 1960.

Vaillant, George Clapp. *Aztecs of Mexico; Origin, Rise, and Fall of the Aztec Nation.* Garden City (Doubleday Doran), 1941.
—— "Native Mexican Manuscripts from Tlaquiltenengo, Morelos" (c1931). Typescript in American Museum of Natural History, New York.
Valadés, Diego de. *Rhetorica Christiana ad concionandi et orandi usum accomodata* . . . Perugia (Petrumiacobum Petrutium), 1579.
Valle, Rafael Heliodoro — see Romero Flores, *Michoacán* . . .
Valle-Arizpe, Artemio de. "El caballo en América y su importancia en la conquista de México" in *Cuadros de México.* México (Jus), 1943.
—— *Historia de la Ciudad de México según los relatos de sus cronistas.* México (Robredo), 1939.
—— *En México en otros siglos.* Madrid (Espasa-Calpe), 1950.
—— *Por la vieja calzada de Tlacopan.* México (Cultura), 1937.
Vallejos, Raúl. "El Colegio de San Nicolás de Hidalgo y la enseñanza de la filosofía" in *Universidad Michoacana*, #25 (March 1959).
van de Velde, Mr. and Mrs. Paul. *Guide to Oaxaca, Monte Albán, Cuilapam, etc.* Oaxaca (authors?), 1933.
Varela, Juan de Díos — see Islas García and Varela
Vargas, Fulgencio. *El Estado de Guanajuato.* Guanajuato (Talleres Gráficas del Estado), 1933.
Vargas Lugo (de Bosch), Elisa. "La vicaría de Aculco" in *Anales del I I E*, XXII (1954).
Varona, Esteban A. de. *Oaxaca.* México (Unión Gráfica), 1957.
Vasco de Quiroga, Documentos — see *Quiroga, Documentos* . . .

Vázquez, Genaro V. — see *Legislación del trabajo* . . .

Vázquez, Francisco (1647–1713/14). *Crónica de la Provincia del Santísimo Nombre de Jesús de Guatemala* (1681–c1712), foreword and notes by Lázaro Lamadrid. Guatemala (Biblioteca "Goathemala" de la Sociedad de Geografía e Historia), 1937–44, 4 vols.

Vázquez de Espinosa, Antonio (–1630). *Descripción de la Nueva España en el siglo XVII por el Padre Fray Antonio Vázquez de Espinosa y otros documentos del siglo XVII,* foreword by Mariano Cuevas. México (Patria), 1944.

Vázquez de Tapia, Bernardino. *Relación de méritos y servicios del conquistador Bernardino Vázquez de Tapia, vecino Regidor de esta gran Ciudad de Tenustitlán, México* (1544), edited by Manuel Romero de Terreros; foreword by Jorge Gurría Lacroix. México (Robredo), 1953.

Vázquez Santa Ana, Higinio. *Apuntes geográficos e históricos del Estado de Tlaxcala.* Tlaxcala (Gobierno del Estado), 1927/28.

Velasco y Mendoza, Luis. *Estampas del Estado de Veracruz.* Jalapa, 1940.

Velázquez, Primo Feliciano, trans. — see *Códice Chimalpopoca* . . .

Vera (y Talonia), Fortino Hipólito. *Itinerario parroquial del Arzobispado de México, y reseña histórica, geográfica y estadística de las parroquias del mismo Arzobispado.* Amecameca (Colegio Católico), 1880.

Vera y Zuria, Pedro. *Cartas a mis seminaristas en la primera visita pastoral de la Arquidiócesis.* Barcelona (Luis Gili), 1929.

Verlinden, Charles. *Précédents mediévaux de la colonie en Amérique.* México (Instituto Panamericano de Geografía e Historia), 1954.

Vetancurt, Agustín de (1620–c1700). *Teatro mexicano, descripción breve de los sucessos exemplares, históricos, políticos, militares, y religiosos del Nuevo Mundo occidental de las Indias; Menologio franciscano de los varones más señalados; Tratado de la Ciudad de México; Tratado de la Ciudad de Puebla.* México (Benavides, viuda de Ribera), 1697–98 (New edition in press: Madrid [Porrua Turranzas], 1960ff.)

Since the parts of this work are not always arranged in the same way nor bound in the same order, nor even always included together as parts of one work, for the sake of clarity they are here cited as separate works, as follows with original pagination):

I. *De los sucessos naturales* (2 tratados), pp. 3–66

II. *De los sucessos políticos* (3 tratados and 1 manifiesto), pp. 1–100

III. *De los sucessos militares* (2 tratados), pp. 101–168

IV. *De los sucessos religiosos,* or *De la fundación de la Provincia del Santo Evangelio de la Nueva España,* but generally known and here cited as the *Chrónica* (5 tratados, of which 1 = pp. 1–23; 2 = pp. 24–90; 3 = pp. 91–104; 4 = pp. 105–115; 5 = pp. 115–135

Associated with the *Teatro mexicano,* but not among its named and numbered parts are the 3 following:

(a) *Menologio franciscano de los varones más señalados* . . . (including *De los ilustrissimos Señores Obispos; De los Comissarios Generales; De los R Padres Provinciales*)

(b) *Tratado de la Ciudad de México* (pp. 1–45)

(c) *Tratado de la Ciudad de Puebla* (pp. 45–56)

Veytia, Mariano José Fernández de Echeverría y — see Fernández de Echeverría, etc.

Viera, Juan de. *Breve compendiossa naración de la Ciudad de México, corte y cabeza de toda la América Septentrional* (1777), foreword and notes by Gonzalo Obregón. México-Buenos Aires (Guaranía), 1952.

Villa Sánchez, Juan. *Puebla sagrada y profana* (1646), with notes by Francisco Javier de la Peña. Puebla (Campos), 1835.

Villaseñor y Sánchez, José Antonio de. *Theatro americano y descripción general de los Reynos y Provincias de la Nueva-España* (1746–48), foreword by Francisco González de Cossío. México (Editora Nacional), 1952, 2 vols.

(Villerías, Gaspar de). *Relación breve de la venida de los de la Compañía de Jesús a la Nueva España* (1602), edited, with a foreword and notes, by Francisco González de Cossío. México (Universidad), 1945.

Violich, Francis. *Cities of Latin America.* New York (Reinhold), 1944.

"Visita de doctrinas de Puebla (1653)" in *Anuario de Estudios Americanos,* II (1945).

Vitruvius Pollio. *De Architectura,* translated by Frank Granger. London and New York (Heinemann, Putnam, the Loeb Classical Library), 1931–34, 2 vols.

Vocabulario castellano-zapoteco del Padre Córdova, introduction by Wigberto Jiménez Moreno. México (Museo Nacional), 1942.

Wagner, Henry Raup. "Early Silver Mining in New Spain" in *Revista de História de América,* XIV (1942).

—— "Fray Juan de Zumárraga, his Social Contributions" in *The Americas,* V (1948/49).

—— "The *Proceso*" in *Revista de Historia de América,* V (1939).

—— *The Rise of Fernando Cortés.* Los Angeles (The Cortés Society), 1944.

Wagner, Max Leopold. "Die spanische Kolonialarchitektur in Mexiko" in *Zeitschrift für bildende Kunst,* N F XXVI (1914/15).

Waldeck, Jean Frédéric Maximilien, comte de (1766–1875). *Voyage pittoresque et archéologique dans la Province de Yucatan.* Paris, 1838.

Ward, Sir Henry G. *Mexico.* London (Colburn), 1829, 2 vols.

Wauchope, Robert. "Domestic Architecture of the Maya" in *The Maya and their Neighbors.*

Weckmann, Luis. "The Middle Ages in the Conquest of America" in *Speculum,* XXVI (1951).

Weise, Georg. *Studien zur spanischen Architektur der Spätgotik.* Reutlingen (Gryphius), 1933.

Weismann, Elizabeth Wilder. *Mexico in Sculpture, 1521–1821.* Cambridge, Mass. (Harvard), 1950. See also *Studies in Latin American Art.*

West, R. C. *Western Liturgies.* London (Society for Promoting Christian Knowledge), 1938.

West, Robert C., and Armillas, Pedro. "Las chinampas de México" in *Cuadernos Americanos,* IX (1950).

Westheim, Paul. *Arte antiguo de México.* México (Fondo de Cultura Económica), 1950.

Wethey, Harold E. *Colonial Architecture and Sculpture in Peru.* Cambridge, Mass. (Harvard), 1949.

—— "Hispanic Colonial Architecture in Bolivia," I, II in *Gazette des Beaux-Arts,* XXXIX (1952), XL (1952).

—— "The Problem of Toribio de Alcaraz" in *Gazette des Beaux-Arts,* XXXI (1947).

Wilder, Elizabeth — see Weismann, Elizabeth Wilder

Wilgus, A(lva) Curtis, ed. *Colonial Hispanic America.* Washington (George Washington), 1936.

Willey, Norman L., and García Prada, Carlos. "El embrujo de las chinampas" in *H A H R*, XIX (1939).

Williams, Bernice Davis. *La historia del primer convento franciscano en México.* Published dissertation. México (Universidad), 1947.

Williams, John Jay. *The Isthmus of Tehuantepec.* New York (Appleton), 1852, 1 vol. text, 1 vol. maps.

Wilson, Robert A. *Mexico: including California and Central America; or Residence, Travels, and Historical Researches.* New York (Harper), 1855.

Wittkower, Rudolf. *Art and Architecture in Italy, 1600–1750.* Baltimore (Penguin, *The Pelican History of Art*), 1958.

Wroth, Lawrence. *Some Reflections on the Book Arts of Early Mexico,* foreword by Philip Hofer. Cambridge, Mass. (Harvard College Library), 1945.

Ximénez, Francisco (c1666–1722). *Historia de la Provincia de San Vicente de Chiapa y Guatemala de la Orden de Predicadores (–1721/22),* foreword by J. Antonio Villacorta. Guatemala (Biblioteca "Goathemala" de la Sociedad de Geografía e Historia), 1929–31, 3 vols.

Yáñez, Enrique, and García Maroto, Gabriel. *Arquitectura popular de México.* México (Instituto Nacional de Bellas Artes), 1954.

Zaldívar G., Sergio. *Arquitectura* (Jalisco en el Arte, 8). Guadalajara and México (Ediapsa), 1960.

Zavala, (Arturo) Silvio. *Aspectos religiosos de la historia colonial americana.* Guadalajara (Estudios Históricos), 1959.

——— *La encomienda indiana.* Madrid (Imprenta Helénica), 1935.

——— "Las encomiendas de Nueva España" in *Revista de Historia de América,* I (1938).

——— *De encomiendas y propriedad territorial en algunas regiones de la América español.* México (Porrua), 1940.

——— *Ensayos sobre la colonización española en América.* Buenos Aires (Emecé), 1944.

——— *Idearío de Vasco de Quiroga.* México (Colegio de México), 1941.

——— *New Viewpoints on the Spanish Colonization of America.* Philadelphia (Pennsylvania), 1943.

——— "Sir Thomas More in New Spain" in *Diamante,* III (1955).

——— "La Utopia de América en el siglo XVI" in *Anales del Museo Michoacano,* IV (1946).

——— *La "Utopia" de Tomás Moro en la Nueva España y otros estudios,* foreword by Genaro Estrada. México (Robredo), 1937.

——— See also *Fuentes para la historia del trabajo . . .* ; *Homenaje a Silvio Zavala; Ordenanzas del trabajo . . .*

Zelis, Rafael de — see *Tesoros documentales . . .*

Zerón Zapata, Miguel. *La Puebla de los Angeles en el siglo XVII* (end of XVII), with letters from Juan de Palafox, and from Manuel Fernández de Santa Cruz; foreword by Mariano Cuevas. México (Patria), 1945.

Zorita (Zurita or Corita), Alonso de (1511/12–after 1585). *Breve y sumaria*

BIBLIOGRAPHY

relación de los señores de la Nueva España and *Varias relaciones antiguas* — see Pomar and Zurita

—— *Historia de la Nueva España* (*c*1584–85). Madrid (Victoriano Suárez), 1909.

Zumárraga, Juan de (before 1468–1548). *The Doctrina Breve (1544) in facsimile,* with forewords by Zephyrin Englehardt and Stephen H. Horgan. New York (Catholic Historical Society), 1928. See also Carreño, *Documentos de . . . Zumárraga; Nuevos Documentos . . .*

PERIODICALS

Abside, revista de cultura. México, 1937–
Al-Andalus, revista de las Escuelas de Estudios Arabes de Madrid y Granada. Madrid, 1933–
The Americas. Washington (Pan-American Union), 1944–
Anales de la Provincia del Santo Evangelio de México. México, 1949–
Anales del Instituto de Arte Americano (e Investigaciones Estéticas). Buenos Aires (Universidad), 1948–
Anales del Instituto de Investigaciones Estéticas. México (Universidad Nacional), 1937– ; here cited as *Anales del I I E*
Anales del Museo Michoacano. Morelia, 1888–89, 1944–
Annales Economies-Sociétés-Civilizations. Paris, 1946–
Anuario de Estudios Americanos. Seville (Universidad), 1944–
Archivo Español de Arte (y Arqueología). Madrid (Centro de Estudios Históricos), 1925–
Archivo Ibero-Americano. Madrid, 1914–
Archivum historicum Societatis Iesu. Rome, 1932–
Arquitectura. México, 1938–
Ars Islamica. Ann Arbor (Michigan), 1934–
Art Bulletin. New York (College Art Association), 1905–
Art in America. New York, 1913–
Arte en América y Filipinas. Seville (Laboritorio de Arte, Universidad), 1935–36
Artes Plásticas. México (Instituto Nacional de Bellas Artes), 1939–
Ateneo. Tuxtla Gutiérrez, Chiapas, 1951–
Boletín del Archivo de la Nación. México (Secretaría de Gobernación), 1930–50
Boletín de la Real Academia de Historia. Madrid, 1843–
Boletín de la Sociedad Mexicana de Geografía y Estadística. México, 1884–
Bulletin Hispanique, revue des Universités du Midi. Bordeaux, 1898–
Caminos de México. México, 1954–
Comparative Studies in Society and History. The Hague, 1958–
Cuadernos Americanos, la revista del Nuevo Mundo. México, 1942–
Diamante. London (The Hispanic and Luso-Brazilian Councils), 1953–
Estudios Americanos. Seville (Escuela de Estudios Hispano-Americanos), 1948–
Estudios Geográficos. Madrid (Instituto "Juan Sebastiano Elcano"), 1950–
Estudios Históricos. Guadalajara, 1943–45
Excelsior (newspaper). México, 1926–
Gazette des Beaux-Arts. Paris, 1859–
Geographical Review. New York (American Geographical Society), 1916–
Harvard Theological Review. New York and Cambridge (Harvard University Theological School), 1908–

708

Hispanic American Historical Review. Baltimore and Durham, 1918–   ; here cited as *H A H R.*

Historia Mexicana. México (Colegio de México), 1951

Journal de la Société des Américanistes. Paris, 1911–

Journal of the Society of Architectural Historians. Louisville, 1941–

Journal of the Warburg and Courtauld Institutes. London, 1937–

Mapa, Revista de Turismo. México, 1934–

Memorias de la Academia Mexicana de Historia. México, 1941–

Middle American Research Papers. New Orleans (Tulane), 1926–

Miscelanea Americanista. Madrid (Consejo Superior de Investigaciones Científicas). 1951–

Novedades (newspaper). México, 1911–

Revista de Historia de América. México (Instituto Panamericano de Geografía e Historia), 1938–

Revista Histórica. Lima (Instituto Histórico del Perú), 1920–

Revista de Revistas. México, 1910–36

Revista Mexicana de Estudios Históricos (now *Estudios Antropológicos*). México (Sociedad Mexicana de Antropología), 1927–

Revue des Deux Mondes. Paris, 1829–1944, 1948–

Smithsonian Institution Annual Report. Washington, 1881–

Speculum, a Journal of Mediaeval Studies. Cambridge, Mass. (Mediaeval Academy of America), 1926–

Studies in the Renaissance. New York (Renaissance Society of America), 1953–

This Week Esta Semana en México. México, 1936–

Tlalocan, a Journal of Source Materials on the Native Cultures of Mexico. Sacramento, 1945–57

Universidad de México, revista mensual. México (Universidad Nacional Autónoma), 1930–38, 1952–   ; (from 1936–38 called *Universidad*)

Universidad Michoacana. Morelia, 1956–

University of Texas Latin American Studies. Austin, 1940–

Urbs. Split (Urbanisticki Biro), 1950?–

Zeitschrift für Bildende Kunst. Leipzig, 1866–1932

Zeitschrift für Kunstgeschichte. Leipzig, 1932–

ABBREVIATIONS

In the notes many titles are given in shortened form, but always with the key words which ought to make identification not only clear, but certain. The few abbreviations of titles which have been compressed down to letters are given below.

Anales del I I E	*Anales del Instituto de Investigaciones Estéticas*
Burgoa, *G D*	Burgoa, *Geográfica descripción de la parte septentrional* . . .
C D I España	*Colección de documentos inéditos para la historia de España*
C D I Ibero-América	*Colección de documentos inéditos para la historia de Ibero-América* (including volumes substituting *Hispano-América*)
C D I Indias	*Colección de documentos inéditos relativos al descubrimiento, conquista y organización de las antiguas posesiones españoles* . . . *Indias*
C D I Ultramar	*Colección de documentos inéditos relativos al descubrimiento, conquista y organización de las posesiones españolas de ultramar*
C D H Oaxaca	*Colección de documentos para la historia de Oaxaca*
D I Cortés	Cortés, *Documentos inéditos relativos a Hernán Cortés y su familia*
D I H México	*Documentos inéditos o muy raros para la historia de México*
H A H R	*Hispanic American Historical Review*
Kubler, *M A*	Kubler, *Mexican Architecture of the Sixteenth Century*

NOTES

Almost all the notes are for bibliographical information only. If information seemed pertinent, it was put into the text: if not, it was omitted. The pious early chroniclers, whose often self-indulgent and prolix accounts have been my principal printed source of information, often took facts or pages from one another. As a consequence, a note for one item is sometimes given with several sources. There is multiple corroboration also for evidence given by writers suspected of bias or carelessness. To keep the notes in the hundreds rather than thousands, and because so many paragraphs are the result of weaving factual wisps from many sources, I have often put several references in one omnibus note toward the end of the paragraph.

FOREWORD

1. La Cruz y Moya, I, 26.

I. THE SPANISH MASTERS

1. Madariaga, *Fall,* 16.
2. Díaz del Castillo, *Discovery,* 150–51.
3. Aguilar, *Historia,* 93.
4. *C D I Indias,* XLI, 142; Cortés, *Letters,* II, 202–03.
5. Motolinía, *History,* 91–92.
6. Pedro de Gante, quoted in Chávez Hayhoe, III, 87.
7. Motolinía, *History,* 101.
8. *Cartas de religiosos,* 26.
9. Simpson, *Encomienda,* appendix II, 212–13
10. Florencia, 309.
11. García Icazbalceta, *Documentos,* II, 213.
12. Chávez, *Pedro de Gante,* II, 63ff.
13. Cuevas, *Documentos,* 421–22.
14. Zorita, I, 281.
15. *Cartas de religiosos,* 39–40.
16. Pomar and Zurita, 101.
17. *Cartas de religiosos,* 4.
18. *Cartas de religiosos,* 38–39; Mendieta, III, 13.
19. Carreño, *Nuevos documentos,* 70, 80; *Cartas de religiosos,* 35; Cuevas, *Historia,* II, 132; *Instrucciones,* 228.
20. *Epistolario,* VII, 246.
21. *C D I Indias,* XLI, 179.
22. Mendieta, IV, 45, 46; Vetancurt, *Chrónica,* 1.
23. López de Velasco, 187; Mendieta, III, 207–08; Ponce, I, 85; II, 383.
24. Mendieta, III, 211.
25. Motolinía, *History,* 249.
26. Espinosa, 335.
27. Cuevas, *Documentos,* 245.
28. Vázquez, II, 225.
29. Cuevas, *Documentos,* 311.
30. Grijalva, 223.
31. Escalante Plancarte, appendix, xvi.
32. Hawks, in García Icazbalceta, *Obras,* VII, 136.
33. Corona Nuñez, "Fray Juan de San Miguel," 16.
34. Mendieta, II, 184.

II. THE GREAT CONVERSION

1. García Icazbalceta, *Opúsculos,* 6.
2. Chimalpahín, 203; *Códice franciscano,* 206, 214.
3. Chimalpahín 239; *C D I Indias,* XLI, 93; Cortés, *Cartas y relaciones,* 540; *Escritos sueltos,* 209; García Icazbalceta, *Documentos,* II, 41; Motolinía, *History,* 174.

4. *Cartas de Indias,* 55; *Códice franciscano,* 162; *Códice Mendieta,* II, 185; Escobar, 723; Espinosa, 100; Franco, 424; Mendieta, II, 114; III, 14, 45–46, 86; Motolinía, *History,* 182–83; Torquemada, III, 456.

5. Mendieta, II, 12.

6. *Anales de Tecamachalco, passim; Códice Mendieta,* II, 33.

7. Cuevas, *Documentos,* 68.

8. MacNutt, in Cortés, *Letters,* I, 203 n1; Wagner, *Cortés,* intro., vi.

9. Ojea, 8; Torquemada, III, 232–35.

10. *Códice Mendieta,* II, 28–29; Nicolás Kuri, 158.

11. Acosta, *History,* II, 530–31; Nicolás Kuri, 158.

12. Acosta, *History,* II, 353; Mendieta, IV, 112–13.

13. Augustine, ch. viii; Mendieta, IV, 51.

14. Acosta, *History,* II, 528.

15. Moreno, 116 n2.

16. "Descripción de Pásquaro," 44.

17. Mendieta, II, 95–96.

18. *Códice franciscano,* 59.

19. Muñoz, 417.

20. *C D I Indias,* XLI, 84; Escalante Plancarte, appendix, xvi; Motolinía, *Memoriales,* 130.

21. García Icazbalceta, *Obras,* III, 22.

22. García Granados, *Filias,* 239–48 (inc. letter from Ricard); García Icazbalceta, *Bibliografía,* 104.

23. Mendieta, II, 95.

24. Remesal, I, 219.

25. Mendieta, II, 123.

26. Motolinía, *Memoriales,* 95, 110; Torquemada, III, 223.

27. Grijalva, 286–89; Puga, ff191r, 193r, 194.

28. Phelan, *Millenial Kingdom, passim.*

29. Grijalva, 320–25.

30. Gonzaga, *passim.*

III. NEW TOWNS

1. Espinosa, 142; Lorenzana, 148.

2. *Cartas de religiosos,* 24.

3. Espinosa, 142–43.

4. Cortés, *Escritos sueltos,* 92.

5. Guerrero Moctezuma, 5ff, or Nuttall, "Ordinances," in *H A H R,* IV, 743ff; V, 249ff.

6. López de Villaseñor, 72, 75, 96, 298.

7. *Papeles de N E,* V, 23.

8. Chauvet, in Mendieta, Oroz, and Suárez, 168 n188; Kubler, *M A,* I, 170, 209 n77; Peñafiel, 61; Zorita, I, 119.

9. Corona Nuñez, in *Universidad Michoacana,* #25 (Mar '59), 16; Espinosa, 148–50; la Rea, bk 1, ch. xxv.

10. *Relaciones de Yucatán,* I, 50.

11. La Rea, 109.

12. Florencia, 235; López de Villaseñor, 84.

13. Blom, 93.

14. Gibson, 128–29; Toussaint, *Mudéjar,* 11, 27.

15. Angulo Iñiguez, at 1961 International Congress of the History of Art, did not entirely agree; Foster, 43–47, partly disagrees; Kubler, "Urbanism," 167–68, disagrees; Smith, "Colonial Towns," 3; Stanislawski, "Town-planning," 94 n2; "Grid-pattern," 118.

16. Foster, 43–47, partly disagrees; Palm, *Española,* I, 59, 62, 79.

17. Hughes, 15, 21, 26, 27.

18. Ricard, "Apuntes," 230, 231, 232; "Plaza Mayor," 324.

19. Filarete (Averlino), in Holt, 145; Kubler, *M A,* I, 99–100; Stanislawski, "Grid-pattern," 113ff.

20. Basalenque, I, 198; Cervantes de Salazar, *Dialogues,* 42; in Islas García and Varela, 41; Escobar, 340, 361; *Libros y libreros, passim;* Millares Carlo, 127.

21. Palm, "Tenochtitlán," 64.

22. Torquemada, I, 282.

23. Kubler, *M A,* I, 73–74; Paredes Colín, 48, 53–54; Robertson, 79, 83, and at the 1961 International Congress of the History of Art.

24. Muñoz Camargo, 251.

25. Chimalpahín, 203.

26. Cortés, *Letters,* II, 200–02.

27. Benítez, *García Bravo, passim; C D I Indias,* XLI, 73; Fernández, Gómez de Orozco, and Toussaint, 21, 149; Icaza, *Pobladores,* I, 55–56; *Información de García Bravo, passim;* Kubler, *M A,* I,

73–74; Orozco y Berra, in appendix to Dorantes de Carranza, 384, 394, 404; Stanislawski, "Town-planning," 97–98; Toussaint, intro. to *Información de García Bravo*, 5ff; Wagner, *Cortés*, 396; Willey and García Preciat, 83–86.

28. Motolinía, *Memoriales*, 139.

29. *Instrucciones*, 240; López de Gómara, 352–53.

30. Conway, 20, 21; Ponce, I, 174; Tomson, in García Icazbalceta, *Obras*, VII, 85.

31. Champlain, I, 38, 41; la Cruz y Moya, I, 83; Gemelli Carreri, 42; Ojea, 6; Vázquez de Espinosa, 117.

32. Cervantes de Salazar, *Dialogues*, 38–39.

33. Conquistador Anónimo, 43.

34. Beaumont, I, 535–36.

35. Díaz del Castillo, *Discovery*, 302.

36. Conquistador Anónimo, 43; Cortés, *Letters*, I, 257; II, 87; Díaz del Castillo, *Discovery*, 300, 307, 560; López de Velasco, 192.

37. Cervantes de Salazar, *Dialogues*, 41.

38. Guerrero Moctezuma, 16–19; Venturi, in conversation.

39. Ricard, "Plaza mayor," 322.

40. Gage, 89.

41. *Tesoros*, 88, 99, 318.

42. Cited in Valle Arizpe, *Ciudad de México*, 443.

IV. NEW MONASTERIES

1. *Epistolario*, X, 36.

2. Ancona, in *Antología de Yucatán*, 146; Beaumont, III, 59; López de Cogolludo, I, 261.

3. Motolinía, *Memoriales*, 140.

4. Alessio Robles, 41; *C D I Indias*, XLI, 88; Howe, 49; McAndrew, in *Art Bulletin*, XXXII, 195–96; Vaillant (quoting Spinden), in *Mss from Tlaquiltenango*; (Vaillant), in *Tlalocan*, I, 362; information kindly supplied by George R. G. Conway and Herbert Spinden.

5. Angulo Iñiguez, in *Archivo español de arte*, XVII, 381; *Historia*, II, 364; Basalenque, I, 126, 318; *Catálogo de Hidalgo*, I, 248; *Descripción del Arzobispado*, appendix, 442; Gómez de Orozco, "Monasterios de San Agustín," 47; Grijalva, 157–58; McAndrew, in *Art Bulletin*, XXXII, 195–96; Motolinía, *Memoriales*, 140; Toussaint, *Arquitectura XVI*, 34.

6. Kubler, *M A*, II, 473; Motolinía, *History*, 193; Paredes Colín, 50.

7. Kubler, *M A*, II, 346–47, 515.

8. Kubler, *M A, passim*.

9. Discussed in Chapter XI.

10. Burgoa, *G D*, I, 303; *Instrucciones*, 239; Kubler, in *H A H R*, XXIII, 113, disagrees about Alcaraz; Toussaint, in *Novedades*, April 21, 1943, answering Kubler; Wethey, "Alcaraz," 165ff.

11. *Códice franciscano*, 137; *Códice Mendieta*, I, 80; Franco, 165–68; *Fuentes de trabajo*, II, 388; Ojea, 57–58.

12. Benítez, *García Bravo*, 24ff; Carrera Stampa, 22, 103; Icaza, *Pobladores*, I, 56: II, 310; *Instrucciones*, 239; Kubler, "Architects and Builders," 7ff; Toussaint, "Criterio de Cortés," 66–67.

13. Focher, 373; Grijalva, 225; Kubler, "Architects and Builders," 15; Mendieta, Oroz, and Suárez, 106; Motolinía, *History*, 234, 240; Ortega, 18–24; Vetancurt, *Menologio*, 93–94.

14. Basalenque, I, 120, 317–18; Franco, 165–68; Kubler, "Ucareo," 8; Tello, III, 80.

15. Icaza, *Pobladores*, II, 140.

16. Ramírez, *Plancarte*, appendix I, 161.

17. *Libros y libreros*, 471.

18. *Códice franciscano*, 58.

19. Mendieta, III, 80; Pomar and Zurita, 157; Torquemada, III, 215.

20. Puga, f96v.

21. *C D I Ibero-América*, I, 189–90; Haring, 197; Ramírez, *Carta*, 24.

22. Motolinía, *Memoriales*, 141.

23. Vera y Zuria, 25.

24. García Granados, *Xochimilco*, liv; Mendieta, III, 42; Vetancurt, *Chrónica*, 57.

25. Soria, "Colonial Painting," 32; "Notes on Early Murals," 236, 240.

26. Angulo Iñiguez, *Historia*, II, 354ff.; Carrillo y Guriel, 57, 67–70; Kubler and Soria, 305–06, for a different view; *Libros y libreros*, 471; Soria, "Notes on Early Murals," 240; Toussaint, *Pintura en México XVI*, 39–40; *Pinturas mu-*

rales, *passim;* Wroth, *passim;* information kindly supplied by Elizabeth Jones, Fogg Museum.

27. Carrión, I, 99; la Cruz y Moya, I, 262; Nuttall, "Feather Work," 332, 335; Obregón, in Viera, 110 n118; Tomson, in García Icazbalceta, *Obras,* VII, 79–80.

28. Escobar, 574; Grijalva, 525; Toussaint, *Arte colonial,* chs. iv, viii.

29. Torquemada, III, 224.

30. Berlin, "Tecbatán," 6; Ferrer de Mendiola, 73; Motolinía, *History,* 262; Toussaint, *Arte colonial,* 21.

31. Cook, "Soil Erosion," *passim; Instrucciones,* 228; López de Gómara, 353; Martínez, 180; *Ordenanzas del trabajo,* 75–77.

32. Motolinía, *Memoriales,* 184.

33. Torquemada, III, 36; Vetancurt, *Chrónica,* 32; Zorita, I, 296.

34. Vázquez, I, 181, 220.

35. Romero de Terreros, *Arte colonial,* III, 14.

36. Chauvet, *Tlaxcala,* 14; D I México, XV, 25; Díaz del Castillo, *Historia,* II, 177; Mendieta, III, 61; Romero de Terreros, "Topoyanco," 302.

37. Carrión, I, 92; Salazar Monroy, *Huejotzingo,* 10.

38. Gemelli Carreri, 137; la Maza, *Cholula,* 67 n10; Rivero Carvallo, 70.

39. Gorbea Trueba, *Yanhuitlán,* 37; Paredes Colín, 50ff.

40. *Tesoros,* 331; Villaseñor y Sánchez, I, 249.

V. THE NEW ARCHITECTURE AND THE OLD

1. *Libros y libreros,* 264ff; Santiago Cruz, *Gremios,* 79.

2. Escobar, 736–37.

3. Mendieta, II, 102.

4. Torquemada, III, 107.

5. *Códice franciscano,* 52.

6. *Cartas de Indias,* 106; Cuevas, *Documentos,* 245.

7. Arroyo, 75–76, 80; Carreño, *Betanzos,* 204; Zumárraga, in Ternaux-Compans, XVI, 141.

8. Epistolario, XII, 18.

9. Kubler, "Ucareo," 8; Romero, 126.

10. D I H México, XV, 83ff.

11. Grijalva, 221–22.

12. Díaz del Castillo, *Discovery,* 269–70; Pedro Mártir, Dec. V, bk 4, ch. ii.

13. Cortés, *Letters,* I, 285; II, 107.

14. Mendieta, IV, 86; Vetancurt, *Menologio,* 93.

15. Carreño, *Nuevos documentos,* 66; D I H México, XV, 47–48, 65; Díaz del Castillo, *Historia,* I, 232; Nuttall, "Destrucción," 294.

16. Mendieta, I, 91; Motolinía, *History,* treatise I, ch. xii; Torquemada, III, 208.

17. Torquemada, I, 303; II, 146.

18. Ancona, in *Antología de Yucatán,* 121–23; Calderón Quijano, 216; Landa

(Tozzer), 175–77 (inc. notes 922, 923, 924).

19. Ponce, II, 414; Stephens, *Yucatan,* I, 92ff; Waldeck, 18.

20. Ponce, II, 407, 414, 420.

21. Stanislawski, "Anatomy of Towns," 21.

22. Pomar and Zurita, 63.

23. Cervantes de Salazar, *Dialogues,* 39; Cortés, *Letters,* I, 162–63.

24. Gorbea Trueba, *Yanhuitlán,* 13; Kubler, *M A,* I, 167.

25. Torres, 56–57.

26. Bandelier, 247; la Maza, *Cholula,* 71, 142; Palacio, *Huexotzinco,* 80, 84.

27. Cetto, 12.

28. *Epistolario,* XII, 124; Mendieta, III, 62.

29. Pedro Mártir, Dec. IV, bk 9, ch. i; Dürer, quoted in Holt, 300; Sahagún, *Historia,* II, bk 10, chs. vii, viii, x, xii, *passim.*

30. Cuevas, *Documentos,* 60; Torquemada, III, 211.

31. Motolinía, *Memoriales,* 181–82; la Rea, 38; Zorita, I, 229.

32. Moreno Villa, *Escultura,* 16–18.

33. Robertson, *passim.*

34. Kubler, "Colonial Extinction," 16–17; Neumeyer, 104ff.

VI. THE ATRIO

1. Mendieta, III, 70, 72.

2. C D I Indias, XLI, 9, 12, 14, 24,

33; Cuevas, *Historia,* I, 261; Ternaux-Compans, XVI, 97.

3. Torquemada, III, 224.
4. Mendieta, III, 70.
5. *Concilio III*, 305.
6. *Concilio III*, 323; Cuevas, *Historia*, I, 430; Lorenzana, 84.
7. *Códice franciscano*, 7; *Epistolario*, XII, 25.
8. Mendieta, III, 156–57.
9. *Anales de Tecamachalco*, 56–57.
10. Motolinía, *History*, 240; Torquemada, III, 404.
11. *Códice franciscano*, 56.
12. Escobar, 154, 661–62; Tello, IV, 24.
13. *Códice franciscano*, 56; Juan de la Cruz, 18, 22, 27, 32.
14. Basalenque, I, 84.
15. Mendieta, III, 71.
16. Rojas Garcidueñas, intro. to *Autos*, xix–xx; Vetancurt, *Chrónica*, 42.
17. Grijalva, 141.
18. *Códice franciscano*, 76.
19. Mendieta, III, 90; Zorita, I, 210–11.
20. Burgoa, *G D*, I, 387; *Concilio III*, 23; Cuevas, *Historia*, I, 430; II, 489; Jiménez Rueda, *Herejías*, 20–21; Lorenzana, 146; la Maza, "Valadés," 32.
21. Acosta, *History*, II, 444; Mendoza, 39; Ponce, I, 525.
22. Ponce, II, 39–42.
23. Motolinía, *History*, 157–59.
24. Rivero Carvallo, 61; Salinas, *Toluca*, 62.
25. Chauvet, in Mendieta, Oroz, and Suárez, 100 n105; Cortés, *Letters*, II, 53; Emmart, intro. to *Badianus Ms*, 73–74; Ponce, I, 171–73; Simpson, *Repartimiento*, 86; Rivera Cambas, II, 456ff; Vetancurt, *Chrónica*, 56–58; Villaseñor y Sánchez, I, 165.
26. *Códice franciscano*, 23; *Códice Mendieta*, I, 63, 240–41; Torquemada, I, 315, 321.
27. Arroyo, 5, 17, 67; inscription in portería of Santo Domingo, Oaxaca.
28. Pedro Mártir, Dec V, bk 6. ch. v.
29. *Historia Tolteca-Chichimeca*, 125.
30. *Catálogo de Hidalgo*, II, 464ff, 559ff; Grijalva, 125.
31. Ajofrín and Olite, 27; Alcedo, V, 349; Azcoitia, 12–13; González de Cossío, 41, 270; Lyon, II, 200; Wilson, 53 illus.

32. Jiménez Moreno, intro. to *Códice de Yanhuitlán*, 30.
33. *Catálogo de Yucatán*, II, 191 and passim; Stanislawski, "Anatomy of Towns," 21.
34. *Códice franciscano*, 15; Ponce, I, 218.
35. Recently discovered by Jorge Olvera.
36. Cervantes de Salazar, *Dialogues*, 64–65.
37. "Relación de Zempoala," 39.
38. Palm, "Capillas abiertas," 47, disagrees.
39. Mendieta, III, 86.
40. López de Villaseñor, 134–35.
41. La Maza, in *Anales del I I E*, XVII, 88–89; Torres Balbás, "Musallà," 167ff.
42. Motolinía, *History*, 136–38.
43. Díaz del Castillo, *History*, 300, 412.
44. Dávila Padilla, 75; la Maza, "Valadés," 19, 23, figs 15, 16, disagrees in part; Motolinía, *History*, 136.
45. Mendieta, II, 61.
46. *Catálogo de Yucatán*, I, 237ff; Echanove, in *Mapa*, April 1934, 20; García Preciat, in *Enciclopedia Yucatense*, IV, 477ff; Hijuelos, 25–26; Landa (Tozzer), 68; Lizana, I, chs. ix, xiii; Landa, I, chs. ii, iii, x; López de Cogolludo, I, 290–91, 338, 424; Ponce, II, 414; inscription in monastery at Izamal.
47. Jiménez Moreno, intro. to *Códice de Yanhuitlán*, 22, 30; Mendieta, IV, 104; Torquemada, I, 282ff; information kindly supplied by Dr. Isabel Kelly, the guardian at Huejotzingo, and the parish priest at Tula.
48. *Catálogo de Hidalgo*, I, 247ff; Grijalva, 158; "Relación de Zempoala," 37, 39.
49. Motolinía, *History*, 177.
50. Motolinía, *History*, 215.
51. Beaumont, II, 150.
52. García Granados," "Reminiciencias," 54–56; Ixtlilxóchitl, *Obras*, II, 370; Kubler, "Colonial Extinction," 27; Mendieta, II, 161; Torquemada, III, 202; Weismann, 7–13, 189–91.
53. Ajofrín and Olite, 27; Beaumont, III, 214–17; Castillo, 106; Cervantes de Salazar, *Dialogues*, 54; *Túmulo*, f2r; *Códice franciscano*, 207, 215; Franco, 236;

García Cubas, *Recuerdos*, 72; Rodríguez Familiar, 8; Torquemada, I, 303; Vetancurt, *Chrónica*, 41, 59.

54. Escobar, 154, 661–62; Gorbea Trueba, *Tepeapulco*, 21.

55. Vera, 103; Weismann, 8–11, 189–90.

56. Las Casas, *Historia*, 347; "Relación de Cholula," 168–69; Vázquez, II, 93; Weismann, 12–13, 190, 192; Zorita, I, 147, 161.

57. *Códice de Cuernavaca*, 4, 23–24; García Icazbalceta, *Zumárraga*, 112.

VII. MILITARY CHARACTER?

1. *Epistolario*, VII, 307; Motolinía, *Carta*, 76–77; Ulloa Ortiz, 16.

2. Gillet, in Michel, VIII/3, 1026.

3. Ward, II, frontispiece.

4. Kubler, *M A*, II, 472.

5. *Fuentes de trabajo*, III, 82; Zumárraga, in *Códice franciscano*, 269.

6. Desfontaines and Durliat, 238–39; Kubler, "Urbanism," largely disagrees; Lampérez, *Arquitectura cristiana*, III, 292, proposes merlons at Jávea; Wethey, in *Art Bulletin*, XXIV, 384–86, disagrees with Kubler.

7. Alamán, IV, 110; Cortés, *Cartas y relaciones*, 546; *Letters*, II, 107, 117; García Icazbalceta, *Documentos*, II, 142; Ramírez de Fuenleal, in Ternaux-Compans, XVI, 255.

8. Gómez de Cervantes, 97; Mendieta, in *Cartas de religiosos*, 110.

9. *Instrucciones*, 242.

10. Basalenque, I, 256–57; Kubler, *M A*, II, 523; *Relaciones geográficos de Michoacán*, II, 70; Romero, 228.

11. *C D I España*, C, 468; Grijalva, 243; *Tesoros documentales*, 355.

12. Cuevas, *Documentos*, 262.

13. Ponce, I, 221.

14. *Fuentes de trabajo*, III, 43, 102; Kubler, *M A*, II, 451; Vera, 5.

15. Palacio, *Huexotzinco*, 28 n118; Ponce, II, 46; Tello, II, 309; IV, 29.

16. Beaumont, II, 84; Ponce, I, 223; Powell, "Presidios," 186, 193; Romero, 238.

17. Grijalva, 274; Powell, "Presidios," 195.

18. Burgoa, *G D*, II, 234.

19. Casarrubias, 54.

20. Gay, I/2, 556.

21. La Mota Padilla, I, 134.

22. Kubler, *M A*, II, 502–03; Ponce, II, 115–16; *Relaciones geográficas de Michoacán*, II, 93, 94; Tello, IV, 24.

23. García Granados and MacGregor, 151; Palacio, *Huexotzinco*, 78–79.

24. *C D I Indias*, XLI, 33; Torquemada, III, 325.

25. Cuevas, *Historia*, II, appendix, 489; López de Cogolludo, I, 297.

26. Beaumont, II, 50; *C D I España*, LIII, 21; Rivera Cambas, III, 548.

27. Vetancurt, *Chrónica*, 73; *Catálogo de Hidalgo*, I, 461; Burgoa, *G D*, I, 392; Gay, II/1, 27–28.

28. Burgoa, *G D*, I, 290, 292; II, 5.

29. Azcoitia, 12.

30. *C D H Oaxaca*, 16–17; *Epistolario*, II, 92–93; Gay I/2, 532; *Instrucciones*, 239–40; Ternaux-Compans, XVI, 296.

31. Alamán, II, 390; Calderón Quijano, xxix; *C D I Indias*, XXIII, 436, 443; *C D I Ibero-América*, I, 85ff; Cuevas, *Documentos*, 111–12; *Epistolario*, IV, 53, 101; Fernández, Gómez de Orozco, and Toussaint, 12; Puga, f23r; Sigüenza y Góngora, *Piedad heroyca*, 12; *Sumario*, I and II, *passim* in most of the answers to Question XVI.

32. Ancona, in *Antología de Yucatán*, 143; Motolinía, *Carta*, 76–77.

33. Cortés, *Letters*, II, 202.

34. *Epistolario*, X, 192.

35. Cervantes de Salazar, *Dialogues*, 39.

36. Nuttall, "Ordinances," 253, 254, 750.

37. Alcedo, V, 84; *Papeles de N E*, V, 23; Peñafiel, 60–61; *Rugendas en México*, fig 34.

38. Torquemada, I, 640.

39. Nuttall, "Ordinances," 744; Zorita, I, 175.

40. Alamán, IV, 110–12; Blom, 23; *C D I Indias*, II, 199; Cortés, *Escritos sueltos*, 28; Lizana, II, ch. 19, f190; López de Villaseñor, 63; MacNutt, in Cortés, *Letters*, II, 274 n1; Motolinía, *Memoriales*, 209; Puga, ff109v–110r; Suárez de Peralta, 101, 210 n35.

41. *Anales de Tarécuato*, 17; Bravo

Ugarte, II, 85; Díaz del Castillo, *Historia,*
II, 363; *Fuentes de trabajo,* II, 274; IV,
254, 269; Gibson, 184; Konetzke, I, 191;
la Mota y Escobar, 134; Motolinía, *Carta,*
76; *Ordenanzas del trabajo,* 47; Powell,
"Warfare," 598; Puga, ff23v, 42; Zavala,
intro. to *Ordenanzas del trabajo,* xiv, xxiii.
  42. La Cruz y Moya, I, 285.

43. Torquemada, I, 605.
44. La Cruz y Moya, II, chs. x–xiv;
Juarros, II, 91–93.
45. Moreno, 141.
46. *Epistolario,* XII, 185.
47. *D I H México,* XV, 228.
48. Grijalva, 294, 599.

VIII. POSAS

1. Motolinía, *History,* 152.
2. Cervantes de Salazar, *Dialogues,*
51, 54.
3. Burgoa, *G D,* II, 7; Escobar, 154.
4. Information kindly supplied by María Luisa Cabrera de Block and Daniel
Rubín de la Borbolla.
5. La Rosa y Figueroa, in Ocaranza,
Capítulos, I, 192.
6. Escobar, 153–54.
7. Basalenque, I, 121–22; Escobar,
153–54, 661–62.
8. Burgoa, *G D,* II, 4.
9. The last two in Chiapas discovered
by Jorge Olvera; the last two in Guatemala discovered by Sidney Markman.
10. Burgoa, *G D,* II, 7, 101.
11. Escobar, 661–62; Marco Dorta,
"Atrios y capillas," 173–76 and "Iglesias
en Bolivia," 239–40; Ponce, I, 203;
Wethey, "Bolivia," 49–51.
12. Kubler, "Two Modes of Franciscan
Architecture," 48; la Maza, in *Anales del
I I E,* XXXI (1962), 153; talk by Mario
Buschiazzo at 1961 International Congress of the History of Art, in New York.
13. Arroyo, 46; Soria, "Notes on Murals," 239.
14. Motolinía, *Memoriales,* 184; Mendieta, III, 61; Torquemada, III, 212.
15. "Relación de Zempoala," pl v.
16. *Catálogo de Hidalgo,* I, 7.
17. Torquemada, I, 438.
18. *Epistolario,* XI, 189; Kubler, *M A,*
II, 480; Vetancurt, *Chrónica,* 26.
19. *Catálogo de Hidalgo,* I, 319ff;
Epistolario, VII, 15ff, 56; Grijalva, 237;
Relación de los obispados, 133.
20. García Preciat, in *Enciclopedia
Yucatense,* IV, 480.
21. Burgoa, *G D,* I, 363–64; Cervantes de Salazar, *Crónica,* 319; Escobar,
154; Ponce, II, 398, 421, 450, 463, 464,
472; Tello, III, 60; IV, 144.

22. *Códice Ramírez,* 95; Nuttall, "Gardens," 459–60; Rees, 33.
23. Mendieta, III, 84.
24. Burgoa, *G D,* II, 7; Dávila Padilla,
II, 636.
25. Sartorius, 160–61.
26. Acosta, *History,* II, 383.
27. Ponce, I, 163.
28. Domínguez, 15.
29. Barlow, "Azcatítlan," 131–33, pl
xviii; Kubler, I, 164 (inc. n127); Pomar
and Zurita, 242.
30. Lampérez y Romea, *Arquitectura
cristiana,* II, 95–96.
31. Díaz del Castillo, *Historia,* II,
310–12; Florencia, 309; Hughes, 13, 15,
36; Pereyra, *Cortés,* 274.
32. Torquemada, II, 141.
33. Flores Guerrero, *Posas,* 78, disagrees about date; Rivero Carvallo, 61–
63; Vera, 57.
34. La Maza, in *Cuadernos americanos,* VIII, 235.
35. Ceán Bermúdez, in Llaguno y
Amírola, III, 56–57.
36. Harth-Terré, "Becerra," *passim;*
Kubler, *M A,* I, 123; Marco Dorta, *Fuentes,* 65ff; Rivero Carvallo, 59; Toussaint,
"Arquitecto de Cuzco," 59–62; *Puebla,*
57, 64–65; Wethey, *Peru,* 40–44, 247–
49.
37. Pineda, 43; information on Tumbalá kindly supplied by Jorge Olvera.
38. Cervantes de Salazar, *Crónica,*
539; Chauvet, in Mendieta, Oroz, and
Suárez, 167 n184; Flores Guerrero, *Posas,*
53–54, in part disagrees; Kubler, *M A,*
II, 458.
39. Toussaint, in *Arquitectura XVI,*
23–24.
40. La Maza, *San José Chiapa,* 27–28.
41. Palm, *Española,* II, 81, 101.
42. Martínez Cosío, 71, 111.
43. Arfe y Villafañe, bk 4, ch. v; Neu-

meyer, 110 n35 (citing Kubler); Palacio, *Huexotzinco,* '60.

44. Sagredo ffL–Lii (32–36); similarly in Arfe y Villafañe, 252–53.

45. Vetancurt, *Chrónica,* 58, 190.

46. Flores Guerrero, *Posas,* 32, 33; García Granados, "Calpan," 370ff.

47. García Granados, "Calpan," 373.

48. Bandelier, 88; Fernández Echeverría y Veytia, 11ff; Kubler, *M A,* II, 297; Leicht, 141; López de Villaseñor, 154–60, 169, 296; Motolinía, *History,* 320; *Memoriales,* 208; Toussaint, *Puebla,* 53; Ulloa Ortiz, 20.

49. Bandelier, 256.

50. Moreno Villa, *Lo mexicano,* 10–13; Weismann, 58–61, 198–99.

51. García Granados, "Calpan," 370, 374; García Granados and MacGregor, 86.

52. García Granados, "Calpan," 374; Ponce, II, 114.

53. Weismann, 61.

54. Kubler, *M A,* II, 392–93; *Libros y libreros, passim.*

55. Berlin, "Huejotzingo," 63ff; la Maza, *Retablos,* 22–24.

56. Fernández Echeverría y Veytia, 143–44; Icaza, *Pobladores,* I, 211; Orozco y Berra, in Dorantes de Carranza, 170–71, 307, 315.

57. Rojas Garcidueñas, "Alameda."

58. García Granados and MacGregor, 105–06; Kubler, *M A,* I, 117; Mendieta, IV, 104; Mendieta, Oroz, and Suárez, 160; Ocaranza, *Capítulos,* I, 24; *Sumario,* I, 407; Torquemada, I, 319; III, 478; Toussaint, in conversation (and in MacGregor, *Actopan,* 39) questioned whether Alameda really was an architect; Vetancurt, *Menologio,* 126; (Wethey) in *Hand-*

book Latin-American Studies XIV, 726, also questions Alameda an architect.

59. Santiago Cruz, *Gremios,* 24–27.

60. Altolaguirre y Duvale, 31; *Códice Mendieta,* II, 91–92; *C D I Indias,* XIII, 162–63; XL, 477, 523, 535; Cuevas, *Historia,* appendix, 490–91; *Epistolario,* I, 141; Kubler, *M A,* II, 459; Mendieta, IV, 104; Rojas Garcidueñas, "Alameda," 14ff; Ternaux-Compans, XVI, 93; Torquemada, I, 283, 321; Vetancurt, *Chrónica,* 58.

61. Chauvet, in Mendieta, Oroz, and Suárez, 166–67 n188; García Granados and MacGregor, 32, 69, 74–75.

62. *Cartas de Indias,* 62; Fernández Echeverría y Veytia, I, 145ff; Ulloa Ortiz, 21.

63. Chauvet, in Mendieta, Oroz, and Suárez, 166–67 n181.

64. García Icazbalceta, *Documentos,* II, 200.

65. Aguilar, 98; *Anales de Tecamachalco,* 25; Cook and Simpson, 67; Kubler, *M A,* II, 459–60; Ponce, I, 151.

66. *Catálogo de Hidalgo,* II, 449; Cuevas, *Historia,* II, 169; *D I H México,* XV, 128–29; Kubler, *M A,* II, 484; Mendieta, IV, 142; Mendieta, Oroz, and Suárez, 85; Payno, letter in *Museo mexicano,* III (1844), 395; Rivera Cambas, III, 184; Rojas Garcidueñas, "Alameda," 23ff; Vera, 79, 156; Vetancurt, *Menologio,* 60.

67. *Fuentes de trabajo,* I, 138–39.

68. (Enciso, etc.), *Edificios coloniales,* 204; García Granados and MacGregor, 106; Toussaint, in *Anales del I I E,* IV, 78, disagrees with attribution.

69. Angulo Iñiguez, *Historia,* I, 199, 202.

IX. THE OPEN CHAPEL

1. Motolinía, *History,* 141–42.

2. Kubler, *M A,* II, 326–27, disagrees.

3. *Descripción del Arzobispado,* 268–69; *Relación de los obispados,* 121.

4. Motolinía, *Memoriales,* 93.

5. Basalenque, I, 5, 63; Carrión, 30; Chauvet, in Mendieta, Oroz, and Suárez, 99 n103.

6. *Códice franciscano,* 9; "Contrato de Patamban," 93–94; Ponce, I, 108,

218; *Relación de los obispados,* 109; dated inscription on church at Tlalnepantla.

7. *Concilio III,* 305.

8. Kubler, "Colonial Extinction," 21, largely disagrees; Palm, "Capillas abiertas," disagrees.

9. Leicht, 60.

10. Mendieta, III, 70.

11. Arroyo, 5; Remesal, II, 562.

12. Motolinía, *Memoriales,* 144; Remesal, II, 562.

13. Motolinía, *Memoriales*, 208; Ponce, I, 10.

14. *Códice franciscano*, 24, 25, 26; Cook and Simpson, 68, 70, 72; López de Velasco, 223.

15. *Anales de Tecamachalco*, 60; *Fuentes de trabajo*, II, 323ff.

16. Gorbea Trueba, *Culhuacán*, 10, 41; *Papeles de Nueva España*, VI, 40; Rosell, in *Mapa*, I (1934), 31.

17. Cook and Simpson, 143; la Rea, 112, 113.

18. Fernández, *Uruapan*, 19; la Rea, I, ch. 25.

19. Mendieta, III, 85.

20. Vetancurt, *Chrónica*, 61.

21. Kubler, *M A*, II, 341; MacGregor, *Estudios*, 80 n1.

22. Ponce, I, 411; Remesal, II, 246, Vázquez, I, 245.

23. *Catálogo de Hidalgo*, I, 117–18; Moyssen, 45; information on Xocoltenango kindly supplied by Frans Blom and Jorge Olvera.

24. "Relación de Tancítaro," 213.

25. Torquemada, I, 653.

26. Escobar, 95, 660; González Dávila, I, 39; la Rea, 281.

27. Borah, *Depression, passim;* Cook and Simpson, *passim,* particularly 46; Gómez de Cervantes, 137.

28. La Cruz y Moya, II, 185; Cuevas, *Documentos*, 69; Dávila Padilla, I, 196; II, 618–19; Florencia, 331–35; Franco, 32; González Dávila, I, 54, 60; Grijalva, 465, 525; Mendieta, Oroz, and Suárez, 96–97; Moreno, 74; Ochoa, 52; Ponce, I, 173–74, 234; (Villerías), *Relación,* 45–46.

29. Díaz del Castillo, *History*, 120.

30. Díaz del Castillo, *History*, 310.

31. Burgoa, *G D*, I, 397; Martínez Gracida, 91 n1; Ocaranza, *Capítulos*, I, 94.

32. Remesal, I, 431.

33. Remesal, I, 362.

34. Ponce, I, 289; Remesal, I, 437.

35. *Códice franciscano*, 73; Focher, 46.

36. Stephens, *Central America*, II, 48–49; information kindly supplied by Manuel Toussaint and Jorge Olvera.

37. Ponce, I, 140.

38. Alcedo, V, 60; Cobo, in Vázquez de Espinosa, appendix, 203; *Papeles de N E, V*, 40; Vetancurt, *Chrónica*, 69, and *Sucessos naturales*, 23; Villaseñor y Sánchez, I, 322.

39. Ponce, I, 528; Torquemada, II, 558; III, 210.

40. Fernández de Oviedo, 89, 92.

41. Mendieta, III, 204; Remesal, II, 428.

42. Ponce, I, 115; II, 446.

43. Ponce, I, 165, 518, 525.

44. Mendieta, III, 223.

45. Cortés, *Letters*, II, 272.

46. *C D I Indias*, XLI, 84; Cuevas, *Historia*, I, appendix, 467; *Desconocido cedulario*, 63–64; Escalante Plancarte, appendix, xii; González Dávila, I, 42; Stevenson, 83.

47. Carrera Stampa, 50; *C D I Indias*, XLI, 168; Cervantes de Salazar, *Túmulo*, ff25r, 26r; Cuevas, *Documentos*, 99, 245; *D I H México*, XV, appendix, 240; Motolinía, *Memoriales*, 178; Santiago Cruz, *Gremios*, 41–43; information kindly supplied by Isabel Pope Conant.

48. Remesal, I, 229.

49. Bataillon, "Vera Paz," doubts las Casas' claims.

50. Herrera Carrillo, 616.

51. *Crónicas de la Conquista*, 208.

52. Motolinía, *Memoriales*, 29.

53. Carreño, *Betanzos*, 131.

54. *Cartas de Indias*, 52; *Códice franciscano*, 214; Mendoza, 38; Torquemada, III, 213.

55. *C D H México*, I, 210; García Icazbalceta, *Obras*, III, 175; Mendieta, II, 68; Stevenson, 23, 33; Torquemada, III, 213.

56. Las Casas, *Apologética historia*, 161; *Códice Mendieta*, II, 251, 252; *Códice Ramírez*, 91; Dávila Padilla, I, 97; Lorenzana, 140; Mendoza, 36–38; Motolinía, *History*, 296–97; Ricard, *Conquête*, 214–15, 256; Stevenson, 63–64, 83; Torquemada, I, 229; III, 213–14; Zorita, I, 284–85.

57. *Cartas de Indias*, 52; *Códice franciscano*, 206, 214; Fernández de Oviedo, 104; Motolinía, *History*, 296–97; Stevenson, 53.

58. Dávila Padilla, I, 97; Mendieta, III, 63–64; Ricard, *Conquête*, 214–15, 256; Torquemada, III, 213–14; Zorita, I, 284–85.

59. Castañeda, in *H A H R*, XX, 678;

Fuentes de trabajo, IV, 423; Stevenson, 69, 75.

60. *Códice franciscano,* 58; Zorita, I, 283–84.

61. *C D I Indias,* XIII, 287.

62. *Descripción del Arzobispado,* appendix, 442; *Epistolario,* VIII, 90; Santiago Cruz, *Gremios,* 100.

63. *Códice Sierra,* 20, 41; López Cogolludo, I, 230; Mendieta, III, 64; Torquemada, III, 214.

64. Lorenzana, 140.

65. *Códice Mendieta,* I, 22; *Códice Osuna,* 178; Cuevas, *Historia,* II, 182; Santiago Cruz, *Gremios,* 100; Spell, 304 n54; Stevenson, 63–64.

66. Aiton, 50; *D I H México,* XV, 141.

67. Calderón de la Barca, 365; Lumholtz, II, 388; Stevenson, 51, 94–95.

X. THE FIRST OPEN CHAPELS: I

1. García Icazbalceta, *Obras,* II, 408ff; Kubler, *M A,* II, 329–33, 466–68; Mendieta, III, ch. xx; Ramírez Aparicio, 346–50; Torquemada, I, 303; III, bk 17, ch. viii; Valle-Arizpe, *Ciudad de México,* 162ff; Vetancurt, *Chrónica,* 31, 40ff.

2. *Cartas de Indias,* 100; *Cartas de religiosos,* 180; *Códice franciscano,* 215; *Epistolario,* IX, 162; Mendieta, III, 76; Torquemada, III, 216, 228.

3. Valadés, 222.

4. Most of the material in this section has been drawn from Chávez, *Fray Pedro de Gante,* I, II; *Códice franciscano,* 203–16; García Icazbalceta, *Bibliografía,* 90–104; *Obras,* III, 5ff; Mendieta, IV, bk 5, ch. xviii; Nicolás Kuri, *Fray Pedro de Gante;* Torquemada, III, bk 20, chs. xix, xx; Vetancurt, *Chrónica,* 26, 31; *Menologio,* 67–68; and notices on three posthumous portraits in the collections of the Museo Nacional, Mexico.

The following additional secondary sources have not been used: Ceuleneer, *Pedro de Gante;* Kiekens, *Les anciens missionaires belges en Amérique; Fray Pedro de Gante;* Nuñez y Domínguez, *Le frère Pierre de Gand;* Valle, *Fray Pedro de Gante;* Verhelst, *Vijftig jaren bij de Indianen of levenschets von broeder Pieter de Mura van Gent.*

5. Pedro de Gante, in Cuevas, *Historia,* I, 160.

6. *Cartas de Indias,* 92ff; Mendieta, IV, 55; Vetancurt, *Menologio,* 67.

7. Chauvet, in Mendieta, Oroz, and Suárez, 97 n97; Kubler, *M A,* II, 329; Toussaint, *Arquitectura XVI,* 22.

8. Alamán, *Obras,* I, 354–56; Beaumont, II, 105, 115; Castillo, 105–06; *Cartas de Indias,* 52, 98–101; Chauvet, "San Francisco," 22, 23; *Códice franciscano,* 215; Conway, in Cortés, *Testamento,* 53 n1, 56 n5; Cuevas, *Historia,* I, 261; *C D I Indias,* XLI, 9, 12, 14, 24, 33; Díaz del Castillo, *Historia,* II, 275; Fernández Echeverría y Veytia, 45; Kubler, *M A,* II, 463–64; Mendieta, II, 65; IV, 54; Mendieta, Oroz, and Suárez, 46; Motolinía, *Memoriales,* 184; Orozco y Berra, I, 155; la Rosa y Figueroa, in Ocaranza, *Capítulos,* I, 355, dates San José incorrectly in 1523; *Sumario,* II, 26, 296, and *passim;* Torquemada, I, 303, 594; III, 428; Vetancurt, *Chrónica,* 50.

9. Beaumont, II, 105; Fernández Echeverría y Veytia, 45; Ocaranza, *Capítulos,* I, 356, 357; Vetancurt, *Chrónica,* 31.

10. *Anales uno pedernal,* 66; *Códice franciscano,* 264; Tello, II, 48–49.

11. Zumárraga, in *Códice franciscano,* 264.

12. *Codex Telleriano-Remensis,* f45r.

13. *Anales uno pedernal,* 66; *Codex Telleriano-Remensis,* ff43, 44, 45; Kubler, *M A,* II, 467.

14. *Anales uno pedernal,* 67–68; *Codex Telleriano-Remensis,* f44r; Kubler, *M A,* II, 467; Mengin, 476, 477, 479.

15. Motolinía, *History,* 226; Ricard, "Remarques bibliographiques," 151.

16. Steck, intro. to Motolinía, *History,* 4–5; Vetancurt, *Menologio,* 67–68.

17. *Cartas de Indias,* 99–100; Mengin, 478.

18. *Anales uno pedernal,* 73; *Cartas de Indias,* 98; Cervantes de Salazar, *Crónica,* 319; *Códice franciscano,* 207, 215; *Códice Osuna,* 126, 130; Kubler, *M A,* II, 330, 466, 467; Mengin, 479.

19. Cervantes de Salazar, *Túmulo,* f3v; *Códice Osuna,* 115, 131.

20. *Anales uno pedernal,* 81, 89, 92, 103; *Códice Osuna,* 135, 145; Kubler, *M A, II,* 467; Mengin, 480, 483.
21. García Icazbalceta, *Obras, II,* 408; Kubler, *M A, I,* 132; II, 467; Torquemada, III, 580–82; Vetancurt, *Menologio,* 76–77.
22. *Anales uno pedernal,* 106; *Anales 1589–96,* 12, 23, 28.
23. *Anales uno pedernal,* 94; *Anales 1589–96,* 28, 40–41; Chimalpahín, 313–14; Mendieta, III, 88; Ocaranza, *Capítulos, I,* 341, 357; Vetancurt, *Chrónica,* 39.
24. Cervantes de Salazar, *Dialogues,* 54.
25. Cervantes de Salazar, *Túmulo,* f2r.
26. Cervantes de Salazar, *Crónica,* 319.
27. Mendieta, III, 88; Torquemada, III, 227–28.
28. Vetancurt, *Chrónica,* 40, 41.
29. *Anales 1589–96,* 28; Motolinía, *History,* 262.
30. Cervantes de Salazar, *Túmulo,* ff2r, 15r and v.
31. Cervantes de Salazar, *Túmulo,* f1v.
32. Kubler, *M A, II,* 467.
33. Cervantes de Salazar, *Túmulo,* ff2r, 3v, 15r.
34. Alamán, *Obras, II,* 233; Cervantes de Salazar, *Túmulo,* ff15r, 23v.
35. Ocaranza, *Capítulos, I,* 200.
36. Carrillo y Gariel, 65, 66; Kubler, *M A, I,* 132; II, 467; la Maza, *Retablos,* 14; "Valadés," 19; Santiago Cruz, *Gremios,* 78; Torquemada, III, 580–82; Vetancurt, *Chrónica,* 41; *Menologio,* 76.
37. *Anales 1589–96,* 33; Carrillo y Gariel, 65; Couto, 133–34 n14; Focher, 163ff; Kubler, *M A, II,* 375; la Maza, *Guadalupanismo,* 13; *Retablos,* 13, 14; "Valadés," figs 8, 9; Torquemada, III, 193; Toussaint, *Arte colonial,* 32; *Pintura en México,* 13; Vera, 63; Vetancurt, *Chrónica,* 132.
38. Cervantes de Salazar, *Túmulo,* f I v; Kubler, *M A, II,* 332
39. Toussaint, *Mudéjar,* 3, 9, and *passim.*
40. Rosenthal, *Granada,* 7, 8, 11, 28; Torres Balbás, in *Al-Andalus, X* (1945), 411, 419; *Arte Almohade,* 141.
41. Cervantes de Salazar, *Dialogues,* 54.

42. Chueca Goitia, *Arquitectura del XVI,* 198.
43. Serlio (Toledo, 1563), bk 3, flii.
44. Mendieta, III, 88.
45. *Concilio III,* 136, 142–43, 465 n93; Dubois, 167, 193; Ghyvelde, 294, 331; Lorenzana, 67, 69; Seitz, 208–10.
46. Seitz, 210, 272–77.
47. Ocaranza, *Capítulos, I,* 19; Seitz, 208, 210, 230; Vetancurt, *Menologio,* 90.
48. *Códice franciscano,* 215.
49. Mendieta, IV, 159; Ocaranza, *Capítulos, I,* 193; Vetancurt, *Menologio,* 90.
50. Cárdenas Valencia, 52; Chimalpahín, 241, 245, 262–63; Gemelli Carreri, 158; López de Velasco, 43, 228, 443; Pérez, "Provincia de San José," 145ff; Seitz, 190; Vetancurt, *Tratado de Puebla,* 47; (Villerías), *Relación,* 46, 54.
51. Angeli, 199–200; Cornaro, 109; Malvasia (Bianconi), 434–35; information from the Venetian Archives kindly supplied by the director, Dr. Luigi Lanfranchi.
52. Santiago Cruz, *Gremios,* 55; Vetancurt, *Chrónica,* 39.
53. Rosenthal, *Granada,* 145; Torres Balbás, in *Al-Andalus, VI* (1951), 427–28.
54. La Rosa y Figueroa, in Ocaranza, *Capítulos, I,* 192; Vetancurt, *Chrónica,* 40.
55. "Alegato de Osorio," 286; Berlin, "Artífices," 33; Chauvet, "San Francisco," 28, 29; Chimalpahín, 311–12; Couto, 44; García Cubas, *Recuerdos,* 72–73; García Icazbalceta, *Obras, II,* 409; Kubler, *M A, II,* 333; Marroquí, II, 475, 478, 487–88; Millares Carlo, in García Icazbalceta, *Bibliografía,* 95 nl; Ocaranza, *Capítulos, I,* 199, 486; Ramírez Aparicio, 348–50; Rivera Cambas, I, 226–27; Santiago Cruz, *Gremios,* 55; la Rosa y Figueroa, in Ocaranza, *Capítulos, I,* 192; Smith, *Umbrella,* 106; Valle-Arizpe, *Ciudad de México,* 166–67; Veira, 53–54; Vetancurt, *Chrónica,* 40; Williams, 94.
56. La Maza, *Cholula,* 15, 38; "Relación de Cholula," 169; *Relación de los obispados,* 121.
57. Ponce, I, 162–63.
58. La Maza, *Cholula,* 75.
59. García Icazbalceta, *Documentos, II,* 200.

60. *C D I Indias,* XLI, 496; López de Villaseñor, 45, 46; Mendieta, II, 183; Zorita, 147.

61. Aguilar, 51; Cook and Simpson, 37; Cortés, *Letters,* I, 220; la Maza, *Cholula,* 17; "Relación de Cholula," 158, 163; Torquemada, I, 281.

62. Aguilar, 98; Cook and Simpson, 37, 67; Durán, II, 119; *Epistolario,* X, 22; López de Velasco, 210, 223; Mendieta, III, 75; Suárez de Peralta, 99; Torquemada, III, 215.

63. Chauvet, in Mendieta, Oroz, and Suárez, 166 n160; *Códice franciscano,* 22; Kubler, *M A,* II, 454–55; la Maza, *Cholula,* 61, 62, 141; Mendieta II, 183; Motolinía, *History,* 213; Toussaint, *Arquitectura XVI,* 23.

64. *Códice franciscano,* 22; "Relación de Cholula," 160.

65. Berlin, "Artífices," 22, 23; Castro Morales, 17ff; Marco Dorta, *Fuentes,* I, 82, 315; Toussaint, *Pintura en México,* 51.

66. Castro Morales, 26.

67. National Archives, *Ramo Indios,* Tomo VI/1 (1592–97), exps. 1010–13, 1057; petition, testimonials, note by Arciniega, in private collection, copy kindly supplied by Heinrich Berlin (cited in part also in la Maza, *Cholula,* 76–79, and Castro Morales, 30).

68. Bandelier, 111–12; Gemelli Carreri, 162, Kubler, *M A,* II, 445; la Maza, *Cholula,* 79–81; Peñafiel, 7.

69. Vetancurt, *Chrónica,* 55.

70. Cobo, in Vázquez de Espinosa, appendix, 204.

71. Bandelier, 112; Clavigero, in *Tesoros,* 330.

72. *Cartas de religiosos,* 180; Chauvet, "San Francisco," 23; *C D I Indias,* XLI, 188ff; Molíns Fábrega, 53; Zorita, I, 185.

73. La Maza, "Valadés," 22.

74. Chevalier, *Grands domaines,* 116 (inc. n2); *Epistolario,* XII, 18; Gibson, 182; López de Velasco, 197; Puga, f149v.

75. Ponce, I, 221.

76. Vetancurt, *Chrónica,* 64; Villaseñor y Sánchez, I, 137.

77. Tello, II, 224; Torres, 37–38.

78. Beaumont, II, 283; Espinosa, 215, 217, 500 n80; Ochoa, 28; Tello, II, 308; IV, 27–28, 116; Torquemada, III, 605; Torres, 40.

79. Beaumont, II, 362; Espinosa, 217ff, 222ff, 496–98 n66; Mendieta, IV, 192–95; Torquemada, III, 606ff.

80. *Cartas de Indias,* 104; *Códice franciscano,* 152; *D I H México,* II, 166ff; López, "Misiones y doctrinas," 349; Mendieta, IV, 195–97; Muñoz, 390; Tello, IV, 116.

81. Tello, II, 308, 309; IV, 29.

82. Tello, IV, 116.

83. Tello, IV, 29–30.

84. Espinosa, 228ff, 245; Mendieta, IV, 76; Muñoz, 409–10; "Relación histórica," in Ocaranza, *Capítulos,* II, 22; Tello, III, 30; Vetancurt, *Menologio,* 49; Zaldívar, 8–10.

85. Chauvet, in Mendieta, Oroz, and Suárez, 144 n153; Chevalier, *Grands domaines,* 105, 115, 124; *Códice Mendieta,* I, 72; Ponce, I, 31; Rivera Cambas, III, 38; Rivera Cambas, in Colín, *Toluca,* 156; Salinas, *Toluca,* 58, 70 (inc. n11), 73 illus.; Smith, *Umbrella,* 157; Vetancurt, *Chrónica,* 61–62, 71; *Menologio,* 125–26.

XI. THE FIRST OPEN CHAPELS: II

1. Motolinía, *History,* 156.

2. Chauvet, *Tlaxcala,* 4, disagrees; Mazihcatzín, 70.

3. Motolinía, *History,* 156.

4. Except by Chauvet, *Tlaxcala,* 17.

5. *Epistolario,* II, 224; Fernández Echeverría y Veytia, 141; Gage, 49; García Icazbalceta, *Documentos,* II, 200; López de Villaseñor, 197, 199, 201; Motolinía, *Memoriales,* 189–90; Ocaranza, *Capítulos,* I, 24; Suárez Peredo, in Quíroz y Gutiérrez, 11; summaries in Chauvet, *Tlaxcala,* 9–10, 27, 36; Gibson, 43–46; Kubler, *M A,* II, 481–82.

6. Motolinía, *History,* 240; Mendieta, IV, 43.

7. Mendieta, IV, 43; Mendieta, Oroz, and Suárez, 126.

8. Chauvet, intro. to Mendieta, Oroz, and Suárez, 11; *Tlaxcala,* 37; Ponce, I, 116–17.

9. *Códice franciscano,* 207; Gibson, 124; Ricard, 196, believes set on a teocalli; Torquemada, I, 257; Toussaint,

Arte colonial, 81; Vázquez Santa Ana, 27–28.

10. *Códice franciscano,* 214; Cortés, *Letters,* I, 209–10; Torquemada, III, 20.

11. Cervantes de Salazar, *Crónica,* 242; Gibson, 46.

12. Las Casas, *Historia,* 165.

13. Mendieta, III, 86.

14. Cervantes de Salazar, *Crónica,* 242; *Epistolario,* IV, 139; González Dávila, I, 113, 129; Salazar Monroy, *Tlaxcala,* 7; Vetancurt, *Chrónica,* 54; *Menologio,* 28.

15. Motolinía, *Memoriales,* 184; Mendieta, III, 61.

16. Chauvet, *Tlaxcala,* 56–57; Gibson, 46, 47; Kubler, *M A,* II, 332, 452, questions date; Motolinía, *History,* 307; Ramírez, *Motolinía,* 43.

17. Chauvet, *Tlaxcala,* 54; Kubler, *M A,* II, 452.

18. Chauvet, *Tlaxcala,* 44; Gibson, 46; Motolinía, *History,* 318; *Memoriales,* 190; Ponce, I, 131; Romero de Terreros, "Topoyanco," 303.

19. Vetancurt, *Chrónica,* 54.

20. Mendieta, III, 84.

21. Chauvet, *Tlaxcala,* 14, doubts sixteenth-century date.

22. Vetancurt, *Chrónica,* 54.

23. *Epistolario,* IV, 139; González Dávila, I, 113, 129.

24. Vetancurt, *Chrónica,* 54.

25. Chauvet, *Tlaxcala,* 18; Kubler, *M A,* I, 163; II, 331; Moedano Koer, 141; Torquemada, I, 275; Toussaint, *Paseos,* 131ff.

26. Aldana, 33; Gibson, 31, 43; González Dávila, I, 112, 114; Ixtlilxóchitl, *Obras,* II, 369, 403–04; Mazihcatzín, 69, 71; Mendieta, II, 160; Motolinía, *History,* III, ch. xlix; Remesal, I, 433; Torquemada, III, 71–72, 200–02; Vetancurt, *Chrónica,* 53.

27. González Dávila, I, 114.

28. Torquemada, III, 71.

29. Cook and Simpson, 36, disagree; Gibson, 10.

30. Gage, 46; López de Gómara, 143; Motolinía, *History,* 315; *Memoriales,* 190; Zorita, I, 270.

31. Chimalpahín, 270; *Descripción del Arzobispado,* 68, 71; *Papeles de Nueva España,* I, 17; Torquemada, I, 82.

32. Chauvet, in *The Americas,* I, 122; Cortés, *Testamento,* 65 n2; Gómez de Orozco, *Cuernavaca,* 8–9, 16, 55 n16; Mendieta, II, 142; Plancarte y Navarrete, 42.

33. Chauvet, in *The Americas,* I, 122; *Códice de Cuernavaca,* 27–28; Gómez de Orozco, *Cuernavaca,* 14–18; de Pol, 4; Salinas, "Doña Juana," 197.

34. *Códice de Cuernavaca,* 28.

35. *D I* Cortés, 408; Domínguez Assayn, 8–10; (Enciso, Martínez Cosío, and Rosell), *Edificios,* 171; López González, 14–15; Toussaint, "Supervivencias," 60, dates 1536; Vetancurt, *Chrónica,* 59; information kindly supplied by George R. G. Conway and Pedro Rendón of Cuernavaca, Federico Gómez de Orozco, and Manuel Toussaint of Mexico City.

36. Alamán, II, 55; Angulo Iñiguez, *Planos,* atlas I, 136; cat. I, 57; *C D I Indias,* XLI, 58, 66, 85; Cortés, *Testamento,* 65 n2; Díaz del Castillo, *Historia,* II, 303; López González, 14–15; Salinas, "Doña Juana," 190; *Sumario,* I, answers to question XVI; II, answers to question XXXIX; Toussaint, "Criterio de Cortés," 68.

37. Carreño, "La marquesa," 47, 50, 52; *Epistolario,* III, 2.

38. Angulo Iñiguez, *Historia,* I, 101, 459–60; *Planos,* atlas I, pl. 36; *C D I Indias,* XLI, 58; Palm, *Española,* I, 87, 104; II, 104, 107; Ternaux-Compans, XVI, 156–57, 162–63; Wagner, *Cortés* 455–56; Wethey, in *Art Bulletin,* XL (1958), 80.

39. Calderón de la Barca, 300; *D I* Cortés, 409, 412, 415; Kubler, *M A,* I, 200–01 doubts survival of much work before 1550; García Granados, *Filias,* 184; López González, 11, 20; Toussaint, in conversation, disagreed with Kubler.

40. López González, 12.

41. Kubler, *M A,* I, 208.

42. *C D I Indias,* XLI, 69; Fernández, Gómez de Orozco, and Toussaint, 30; Kubler, *M A,* I, 77, 149.

43. *Códice de Cuernavaca,* 44, 47.

44. Angulo Iñiguez, *Historia,* I, 101, 459–60; Smith, in *The Americas,* II (1945), 363.

45. Cortés, *Cartas y relaciones,* 519; Cuevas, *Documentos,* 76, 98; Díaz del Castillo, *Historia,* II, 314; *Epistolario,* III,

2; Suárez de Peralta, 81; *Sumario*, II, 505, 506.

46. Cortés, *Cartas y relaciones*, 511; *D I Cortés*, 231–34, 241; Molíns Fábrega, 43, 48; Simpson, *Encomienda*, 106–07; Wagner, *Cortés*, 455.

47. Beaumont, II, 105; Mendieta, II, 65; Ocaranza, *Capítulos*, I, 340.

48. *D I Cortés*, 351–52; Martínez Cosío, 71; *Sumario*, II, 296.

49. Alamán, *Obras*, II, 45, 55, 74, 78–79; III, 299; *D I Cortés*, 239, 356–57, 366–68; López González, pl 90; Gómez de Orozco, "Monasterios de San Agustín," 46; MacNutt, intro. to Cortés, *Letters*, I, 58.

50. García Granados, *Filias*, 183; Gómez de Orozco, *Cuernavaca*, 29.

51. Vetancurt, *Chrónica*, 59.

52. Rivera Cambas, III, 233; Weismann, 20–21; Vetancurt, *Chrónica*, 59.

53. Kubler, *M A*, II, 328; Plancarte y Navarrete, appendix I, 3; Vetancurt, *Chrónica*, 59.

54. Chauvet, in Mendieta, Oroz, and Suárez, 147 n159.

55. Mendieta, IV, 149.

56. Motolinía, *Memoriales*, 335; Zorita, I, 125.

57. Kubler, *M A*, II, 346–49.

58. La Cruz y Moya, I, 163; *Procesos de indios*, 37.

59. Cervantes de Salazar, *Crónica*, 243; *Documento del siglo XVI*, 40; *Epistolario*, VII, 117; Zorita, I, 296.

60. Kubler, *M A*, II, 348.

61. Ponce, I, 200.

62. Kubler, *M A*, II, 521.

63. Kubler, *M A*, I, 62.

XII. SINGLE–CELL CHAPELS

1. Flores Guerrero, *Posas*, 19, citing Kubler, *M A*, II, 315 n99, citing McAndrew, unpublished ms.

2. Espinosa, 93, 173, 343; Kubler, *M A*, II, 492; Palacio, in Tello, IV, 227; Ponce, I, 530; la Rea, 159; *Relación de los Obispados*, 41; Romero Flores, *Michoacán*, 28.

3. *Catálogo de Hidalgo*, II, 269ff; León, intro. to *Códice Mariano Jiménez*, 4; la Maza, "Valadés," 22.

4. See Ch. IV n5; also, Ricard, "Un document inédit," 32–33.

5. Lees-Milne, 18.

6. Rohde, 5ff; Toussaint, "Angahua," 24ff; *Arte colonial*, 49; *Mudéjar*, 28–29.

7. Kubler, *M A*, II, 297, disagrees; information about Sacán kindly supplied by Elisa Vargas Lugo.

8. Basalenque, I, 244; Grijalva, 497; López de Velasco, 244; *Relación de los Obispados*, 37; Romero, 96; Villaseñor y Sánchez, II, 23; information kindly supplied by Doctor Isabel Kelly.

9. López de Cogolludo, I, 237; Ponce, II, 413–17.

10. Acosta, *History*, 84; la Cruz y Moya, II, 133; *Descripción del Arzobispado*, appendix, 438; Franco, 129–30; Jiménez Moreno, intro. to Alvarado, 14, 23; Kubler, *M A*, I, 137; Ojea, 55; *Papeles de N E*, I, 124; *Procesos de indios*, 185ff.

11. *Catálogo de Yucatán*, II, 299ff; García Preciat, in *Enciclopedia Yucatense*, IV, 492, 494; Lizana, II, ff89r and v; López de Cogolludo, I, 235.

12. Cárdenas Valencia, 108; Ponce, II, 469–72; Stephens, *Yucatan*, I, 273.

13. First noticed by Angulo Iñiguez, *Historia*, I, 272; Serlio (Toledo, 1563), bk III, xiii.

14. Grijalva, 245, 441.

15. Alcedo, III, 463; Borah, *Silk Raising*, 21; *Catálogo de Hidalgo*, I, 461ff; *C D I Indias*, IV, 532; *Epistolario*, VII, 127; López de Velasco, 196; *Relación de Metztitlán* (typescript in Museo Nacional, Mexico).

16. *C D I Indias*, IV, 531; *Fuentes de trabajo*, III, 42; Ramírez, *Carta*, 12; Scholes, *Ramírez Visita*, 69ff; Simpson, *Encomienda*, 196 n5.

17. Kubler, in *The Americas*, III, 125.

18. Philips, in Hackluyt, 78.

19. *Catálogo de Hidalgo*, I, 463.

20. Toussaint, *Paseos*, 91ff.

21. Aguirre, intro. to Marroquin, 10, 27; Borah, *Silk Raising*, 26; 135 n87; *Códice Ramírez*, 129; Jiménez Moreno, intro. to *Códice de Yanhuitlán*, 10; Molíns Fábrega, 43, 45, 46, 50, 52; Simpson, *Encomienda*, 170; Torquemada, III, 41.

22. Alcedo, I, 717; Belmar, 54; Borah, *Silk Raising*, 99–100; Leicht, 23; López de Velasco, 235; information kindly supplied by the *presidente municipal* of Coixtlahuaca.

23. Dávila Padilla, 802; *Fuentes de trabajo*, I, 67, 92.

24. Cuevas, *Historia*, II, 168; Franco, 174, 517; Jiménez Moreno, intro. to Alvarado, 14, 16.

25. Gorbea Trueba, *Yanhuitlán*; Toussaint, *Paseos*, 61ff, 100.

26. Burgoa, *G D* I, 290–91; Gillow, 64; Gorbea Trueba, *Yanhuitlán*, 8.

27. Dávila Padilla, 238–44; Franco, 120, 518; Gillow, 64; Jiménez Moreno, intro. to Alvarado, 24; Kubler, *M A*, I, 63; II, 535; Toussaint, *Paseos*, 100.

28. Burgoa, *G D*, I, 286ff; Cobo, in Vázquez de Espinosa, appendix, 202; Gorbea Trueba, *Yanhuitlán*, 39, disagrees; Jiménez Moreno, intro. to *Códice de Yanhuitlán*, 14, 15, 30.

29. Burgoa, *G D*, I, 290.

30. *Relaciones de Yucatán*, 102.

31. Palm, "Capillas abiertas," 53–54, disagrees.

32. Burgoa, *G D*, II, 4; Dávila Padilla, II, 636; Gay, II/1, 9.

33. *Anales del I I E*, III, frontispiece, and note by Toussaint; MacGregor, *Estudios*, 88; (Toussaint), *Acolman*, 6.

34. *Anales de Tecamachalco*, 13–14, 30; Escobar, 113–14, 292; Kubler, *M A*, II, 472; Toussaint, *Paseos* (new ed.), 117; Vetancurt, *Chrónica*, 65.

35. Basalenque, I, 171; *C D I España*, C, 466; Escobar, 113–14, 292; Rivera Cambas, III, 524–26; Romero, 140.

36. See Ch. VIII n58.

37. *Relaciones de Yucatán*, II, 146–47.

38. *D I México*, XV, 126; Ponce, I, 200; Vetancurt, *Chrónica*, 26.

39. *C D I Indias*, XIII, 239; Toussaint, *Arquitectura XVI*, 32; Toussaint, in conversation.

40. Angulo Iñiguez, *Historia*, I, 198ff.

41. Mendieta, IV, 104; Sotomayor, *passim*; Toussaint, "Huaquechula"; see also Ch. VIII n58.

42. Ponce, II, 445–46.

43. *Códice de Calkiní*, 111, 113, and inner flap of jacket; Cuevas, *Historia*, I, 413; García Preciat, in *Enciclopedia Yu-*catense, IV, 487ff; López de Cogolludo, I, 290, 308.

44. *Anales de Tecamachalco, passim*; Camón Aznar, I, 132; Chueca Goitia, *Arquitectura XVI*, 254; *Vandelvira*, 16–17; Lorenzana, 352; López de Cogolludo, I, 488–89; Mendieta, IV, 157; Molina Hipólito, *Baeza*, item #14; Romero de Terreros, *Arte colonial*, III, 27–28; Torquemada, III, 537–38; Vetancurt, *Menologio*, 42.

45. *Catálogo de Hidalgo*, II, 419; Vargas Lugo, 104; Vetancurt, *Chrónica*, 64; Weismann, 53.

46. *Códice franciscano*, 16.

47. García Granados, "Capillas de Indios," 13.

48. Juarros, I, 53; Ternaux-Compans, X, 425; Vázquez, I, 87.

49. Angulo Iñiguez, *Historia*, I, 285, and García Granados, *Capillas abiertas*, 46, both mistakenly see a chapel elsewhere; Toussaint, *Paseos* (new ed.), 84, believed no chapel there.

50. *Catálogo de Yucatán*, II, 798ff; García Preciat, in *Enciclopedia Yucatense*, IV, 483ff; Lizana, II, 89vff; López de Cogolludo, I, 224; *Relaciones de Yucatán*, 20, 39–40; inscription over main doorway of church.

51. García Preciat, in *Enciclopedia Yucatense*, IV, 486–87; Ponce, II, 400.

52. Bravo Ugarte, II, 48; Cárdenas Valencia, 86; *Cátalogo de Yucatán*, II, 803; López de Cogolludo, cited in Toussaint, *Arquitectura XVI*, 30; Stephens, *Yucatan*, II, 326.

53. Romero, 80; Toussaint, *Pátzcuaro*, 207, has 1621, misprint for 1612. Date given on inscription in chapel.

54. Cook and Simpson, 143; Simpson "22 Towns," 249.

55. Espinosa, 332; Jiménez Moreno, "Guanajuato," 14; León, "Gilberti," 133; la Rea, 82, 241–42; Torquemada, III, 375; Toussaint, *Pátzcuaro*, 210, considers church seventeenth-century.

56. *Catálogo de Hidalgo*, I, 145.

57. *Catálogo de Hidalgo*, I, 319ff; *Epistolario*, VII, 15, 22; Grijalva, 237–39; *Papeles de N E*, VI, 183.

58. Aguilar, 98; Cook and Simpson, 67; García Icazbalceta, *Documentos*, II, 200; Ponce, I, 151; *Tesoros documentales*, 330, 384; Torquemada, I, 384.

5off; Molíns Fábrega, 30; Pomar and Zurita, 4, 63; Ponce, I, 109–11; *Relaciones geográficas de Indias,* 104; Rivera Cambas, II, 496ff; Torquemada, I, 304; Vetancurt, *Chrónica,* 3, 51.

11. Kubler, *M A,* II, 477–78; Torquemada, III, 37; Toussaint, *Arquitectura XVI,* 23.

12. Chauvet, in Mendieta, Oroz, and Suárez, 131–32 n128bis; Cuevas, *Historia,* I, appendix 457 n2; Ixtlilxóchitl, *Décima tercia relación,* 70; Motolinía, *Memoriales,* 89; Mendieta, II, 109; Vera, 152.

13. See Ch. XI n46.

14. *Fuentes de trabajo,* I, 108; Ponce, I, 110.

15. García Icazbalceta, *Bibliografía,* 93 n25; Mendieta, IV, 53, 72; Vetancurt, *Menologio,* 75.

16. Mendieta, III, 175–76.

17. Angulo Iñiguez, *Historia,* I, 133; *Catálogo de Hidalgo,* I, 461ff.

18. Basalenque, I, 250ff; *C D I España,* C, 467; Escobar, ch. xlv; García Icazbalceta, *Documentos,* II, 251; Grijalva, 243; Kubler, *M A,* II, 508; López de Velasco, 246, unaccountably gives population of only 5000 in 1571; *Lo que proveyó el licenciado Lebrón,* 20; *Relaciones geográficas de Michoacán,* I, 47, 59; *Relaciones geográficas del siglo XVIII,* 144; Simpson, "Population Michoacán," 249; Toussaint, *Arte colonial,* 91.

19. Escobar, 662; Rivera Cambas, III, 488ff.

20. Alcedo, I, 650; Basalenque, I, 292, 383–87; Beaumont, III, 207; Grijalva, 388; López de Velasco, 246; *Relaciones geográficas de Michoacán,* I, 60; Rivera Cambas, III, 497; Rojas, "Copándaro," 115ff.

21. Basalenque, I, 177, 179, 387.

22. Angulo Iñiguez, *Historia,* I, 357–60; Basalenque, I, 117; Carrera Stampa,

38, 223, 226, 235; Escobar, 667; Gómez de Orozco, "Monasterios de San Agustín," 49; Romero de Terreros, *Arte colonial,* III, 32; Toussaint, "Cuitzeo"; inscription on facade at Acolman.

23. Arenas, in *Mapa,* LXXIV, 7; Kubler, *M A,* II, 325.

24. Basalenque, I, 215; Toussaint, *Paseos* (new ed.), 93.

25. Rojas, "Copándaro," 117.

26. Angulo Iñiguez, in *Archivo español de arte,* XVII, 186; *Historia,* I, 364.

27. Beaumont, III, 294, 379; Kubler, *M A,* II, 489; *Libros y libreros,* 27; López de Velasco, 246; *Lo que proveyó el licenciado Lebrón,* 24; Moreno, 89; Ponce, II, 6; Puga, f147r; Weismann, in *Magazine of Art* (1949), 74.

28. Ojea, 56–57, 70.

29. Beaumont, III, 289; *Quiroga, documentos,* 457ff; Vera, 79.

30. Escobar, 583; Kubler, *M A,* II, 523, believes portería is of seventeenth century; *Relaciones geográficas de Michoacán,* II, 67.

31. (Enciso, etc.), *Edificios coloniales,* 188; Ocaranza, *Capítulos,* II, 310; Ponce, I, 161.

32. Escobar, 660; Vetancurt, *Chrónica,* 57, 59.

33. Flores Guerrero, *Posas,* 38; García Granados, "Calpan," 373.

34. Rivera Cambas, III, 551; Romero, 65; Alcedo, I, 329.

35. Chimalpahín, 311–12; Lizana, II ch. v; López de Cogolludo, I, 356; López de Velasco, 251; Ponce, II, 450–51; Toussaint, *Arquitectura XVI,* 29.

36. Ponce, I, 113–15.

37. Chauvet, *Tlaxcala,* 73ff; *Relación de los obispados,* 11; Vera y Zuria, 296.

38. *Concilio* III, 305; Lorenzana, 80.

39. *Papeles de N E,* VII, frontispiece.

XV. A POSTSCRIPT: TWO UNUSUAL CHURCHES

1. Arenas, "Cuilapan"; Barlow, "Dos relaciones de Cuilapa," 18 n4a, 19; Burgoa, *G D,* I, 396ff, 401; *Palestra,* 95; *C D H Oaxaca,* 12; Gay, II/1, 27ff; López de Velasco, 239; *Relación de los obispados,* 70; Ternaux-Compans, XVI, 153; van de Velde, 54.

2. Burgoa, *Palestra,* 94–95; *Instrucciones,* 239; Jiménez Moreno, intro. to Alvarado, 15 particularly n11; Ricard, *Conquête,* 91 inc. n6.

3. Barlow, "Dos relaciones de Cuilapa," 19, 23, 25; Burgoa, *G D,* I, 399–400, 402; *Palestra,* 89, 94–95; Franco,

518; Gay, I/2, 490, 560, 564; Kubler, *M A*, II, 300, 526–27; Jiménez Moreno, *Códice de Yanhuitlán*, 69.

4. Cuevas, *Historia*, I, 341; Gay, I/2, 560; Kubler, *M A*, II, 298; Puga, 182ff.

5. *Descripción de Antequera*, 23; *Epistolario*, IV, 143; Serlio (Toledo 1563), bk IV, pl ixr, xvr.

6. Serlio (Toledo, 1563), bk III, pl xxxviii.

7. *Descripción de Antequera*, 35.

8. Burgoa, *G D*, I, 402.

9. Burgoa, *G D*, I, 402.

10. Burgoa, *G D*, I, 402.

11. Kubler, *M A*, I, 167.

12. Gay, II/1, 29, 30.

13. Arenas, "Cuilapan," 12.

14. Cook and Simpson, 89; *Relación de los obispados*, 64, 70.

15. Barlow, "Dos relaciones de Cuilapa," pl 1, opp. 36; Burgoa, *G D*, I, 402; photographs in files of Dirección de Monumentos Coloniales.

16. Alcedo, V, 97; Burgoa, *G D*, II, 313–14; "Descripción de Tehuantepec," 166–68; Ponce, I, 287; *Relación de los obispados*, 72.

17. Cobo, in Vázquez de Espinosa, appendix, 187; Cuevas, *Historia*, II, appendix, 486; Gay, I/2, 559, 619; Kubler, "Urbanism," 160–61; López de Velasco, 281; *Papeles de N E*, IV, 43; *Relación de los obispados*, 69, 71.

18. Alcedo, III, 319, 320; Burgoa, *G D*, II, 251; Cobo, in Vázquez de Espinosa, appendix, 198; Gage, 124.

19. Santiago Cruz, in *Abside*, XVIII, 125.

20. Cobo, in Vázquez de Espinosa, appendix, 197; Palm, "Capillas abiertas americanas," 49, 57.

21. Burgoa, *G D*, II, 5; Ponce, I, 272, 496.

22. Alcedo, III, 352; Burgoa, *G D*, I, 400, 403; Franco, 129; Gay, II/1, 27–28; Jiménez Moreno, intro. to Alvarado, 41; intro. to *Códice de Yanhuitlán*, 23, 74 n5; intro. to *Vocabulario*, 13; Kubler, *M A*, I, 130; Ojea, 41–43.

23. Burgoa, *G D*, I, 404; Franco, 211.

24. Burgoa, *G D*, I, 401; Franco, 209; Gay, II/1, 29.

25. Burgoa, *G D*, I, 404; Gay, II/1, 29.

26. Quoted in Zavala, *Ideario*, 23.

Most of the information about Vasco de Quiroga and his hospitals in the next sections has been drawn from: Aguayo Spencer, ed., *Don Vasco de Quiroga, documentos*; Beaumont, *Crónica*, II, bk 2, chs. i, vi; Cuevas, *Historia*, I, ch. xiii; Fernández and O'Gorman, *Santo Tomás More y la "Utopia"*; Grijalva, *Crónica*, ch. ix; León, *El ylmo Señor don Vasco de Quiroga*; León and Quintana, *D I referentes a Quiroga*; Muriel, *Hospitales de Antaño*; Zavala, *Ideario de Vasco de Quiroga*; "Sir Thomas More in New Spain"; "La Utopia de América en el siglo XVI"; *La "Utopia" de Tomás More en la Nueva España*.

27. Ternaux-Compans, XVI, 193.

28. Beaumont, III, 50; la Rea, 4.

29. Acosta, *History*, II, 352; Moreno, 139; Motolinía, *Memoriales*, 218; Toussaint, *Pátzcuaro*, 228.

30. Ponce, I, 532–33.

31. Carreño, *Nuevos documentos de Zumárraga*, 63, 78; *D I H México*, XV, 96–98; García Icazbalceta, *Obras*, III, 45; León and Quintana, intro., xi; López de Velasco, 241; Marco Dorta, *Fuentes*, I, 18, 153ff; not consulted: seventeenth-century *ms.* description of Pátzcuaro in Newberry Library, Chicago.

32. Marco Dorta, *Fuentes*, I, 18, 19.

33. Benítez, *Morelia*, viii–x; Espinosa, 116; García Icazbalceta, *Documentos*, II, 246; Méndez Plancarte, intro. to Ramírez, *Pedro Plancarte*, 28.

34. León and Quintana, 13.

35. León and Quintana, 10ff; Romero, 78ff.

36. Beaumont, III, 50; *Epistolario*, V, 207.

37. *Epistolario*, V, 206.

38. *Anales de Tarécuato*, 11; Aguayo Spencer, in *Quiroga documentos*, 215 n208; Díaz del Castillo, *Historia*, II, 370; López de Velasco, 241; Moreno, 74ff; Romero Flores, 47.

39. Cuevas, *Historia*, II, 321–22; Fernández and O'Gorman, 15; Florencia, 67–68; García Icazbalceta, *Documentos*, II, 244; Moreno, 84ff.

40. Angulo Iñiguez, in *Archivo español*, XVI, 186; Marco Dorta. *Fuentes*, I, 20; Wethey, "Alcaraz," 165ff.

41. *Epistolario*, VIII, 33; Icaza, *Pobladores*, II, 140; *Instrucciones*, 230; Ku-

bler, in *H A H R,* XXIII, 113, disagrees; Toussaint, in *Novedades,* April 23, 1943, refuting Kubler.

42. Beaumont, III, 296; *D I H México,* XV, 105; Marco Dorta, *Fuentes,* I, 20; Moreno, 50, 72–73; Puga, ff146v–148r.

43. Beaumont, II, 368; III, map 5 opp. 410, 436; García Icazbalceta, *Documentos,* II, 244; León and Quintana, 27; López de Velasco, 241; Moreno, 52, 87–88; Toussaint, *Pátzcuaro,* 120–21.

44. Benítez, *Morelia,* xxxvi; García Icazbalceta, *Documentos,* II, 88; Méndez Plancarte, intro. to Ramírez, *Pedro Plancarte,* 30–31; Romero Flores, 45ff; Toussaint, *Pátzcuaro,* 228; Vallejos, 2.

45. Alcedo, IV, 109; Beaumont, II, 268; III, 296–97; Marco Dorta, *Fuentes,* I, 28; Moreno, 81ff; Steck, intro. to Motolinía, *History,* 50–51; Toussaint, *Pátzcuaro,* 119–20.

46. Bevan, 151; Kubler, *M A,* II, 309–14, largely disagrees; Rosenthal, *Granada,* 127 n86, 131; "Renaissance 'Copy,'" 2–4.

47. *Lo que proveyó el licenciado Lebrón,* 15, 37; Simpson, "Population, Michoacán," 248.

48. Basalenque, I, 449; García Icazbalceta, *Documentos,* II, 244; Marco Dorta, *Fuentes,* I, 21, 24 n21.

49. Marco Dorta, *Fuentes,* I, 21.

50. Beaumont, *Memoriales,* quoted in Aguayo Spencer, *Quiroga, documentos,* 210 n154; Marco Dorta, *Fuentes,* I, 26; *Relaciones geográficas de Michoacán,* II, 115; Toussaint, *Pátzcuaro,* 234.

51. See Ch. XIV n27.

52. Beaumont, III, 406; *Cartas de Indias,* 132; Puga, f190r.

53. Aguayo Spencer, in *Quiroga, documentos,* 215 n204; Beaumont, III, 379.

54. Aguayo Spencer, in *Quiroga, documentos,* 210 n157; Angulo Iñiguez, *Catedrales,* 180–81; Basalenque, I, ch. xx, 449; Beaumont, II, 156–57; Marco Dorta, *Fuentes,* I, 21.

55. Berlin, in *H A H R,* XXVIII, 555, questioning Kubler and Cuevas; Castro Morales, 17, 18; Cuevas, *Historia,* III, 66–67; Kubler, *M A,* I, 105, 121; Marco Dorta, *Fuentes,* I, 21–22.

56. Marco Dorta, *Fuentes,* I, 21–22; *Relaciones geográficas de Michoacán,* II, 112.

57. Toussaint, *Puebla,* 55.

58. *Epistolario,* IX, 119–21.

59. Beaumont, II, 380, 383; *Epistolario,* IX, 188; Marco Dorta, *Fuentes,* I, 25.

60. *Libros y libreros,* 25–26; Ricard, *Conquête,* 294.

61. Cuevas, *Documentos,* 262; *Historia,* II, 191; *Epistolario,* XIV, 22; López de Velasco, 241; *Relación de los obispados,* 32; Toussaint, *Pátzcuaro,* 230–31.

62. León, "Reyes tarascos," 174–75; *Relaciones geográficas de Michoacán,* I, 105; II, 109; *Relación de los obispados,* 32.

63. Aguayo Spencer, in *Quiroga, documentos,* 223 n307; "Auto de posesión de Zintzuntzan," 183; Florencia, 231–32; Jarnés, 311; Moreno, 125–26; *Relación de los obispados,* 32.

64. Angulo Iñiguez, *Historia,* I, 361–64; Espinosa, 328.

65. *C D I España,* C, 464; *Fuentes de trabajo,* III, 53, 89; López de Velasco, 242, 244; *Relaciones geográficas de Michoacán,* II, 109; Toussaint, *Pátzcuaro,* 238.

66. Ponce, I, 533.

67. Vázquez de Espinosa, 139.

68. La Rea, 109, 183, 187.

69. Escobar, 356; González Dávila, I, 168, 171.

70. Basalenque, I, 448–49.

71. Villaseñor y Sánchez, II, 13.

72. Moreno, 49–50.

73. Beaumont, II, 388–89; III, 434.

74. Quoted by Aguayo Spencer, in *Quiroga, documentos,* 210, n154.

75. Beaumont, illus. opp. III, 462.

76. Angulo Iñiguez, *Historia,* I, 454, disagrees; Kubler, *M A,* II, 308, disagrees; Marco Dorta, *Fuentes,* I, 29–30, disagrees.

77. Angulo Iñiguez, in *Archivo español,* XVI, 186; *Historia,* I, 454.

78. Alcedo, IV, 108–09.

79. Rivera Cambas, III, 504; Romero, 72 n1, 73; inscription on nineteenth-century painting of Cathedral in Morelia Museum.

80. Corona Núñez, in *Universidad Michoacana* #25 (March 1959); Florencia, 216.

81. Calderón de la Barca, 484; Moreno, *passim; Tesoros documentales,* 342.

82. Eliot, "Lune de Miel," in *Collected Poems* (New York, 1934), 56.

INDEX

Inasmuch as this book deals mainly with architecture, its index is made of entries dealing mainly with architecture: buildings, materials, techniques, styles, and elements of related arts. It does not itemize the historical material in the first two chapters and occasional parts of later ones, nor historical figures or chroniclers except as they had dealings with building. Hence there are no kings, viceroys, or bishops, and no friars who were not builders or possible builders. Cortés will not be found, but Cortés' palaces will. Quotations and citations of Father Motolinía will not be found, but his equivocal building activity will. Some subjects of such major interest as the open chapel will not be found here since their discussion is clearly measured out in the Contents.

All the Mexican sites named in the text are listed, with the standard abbreviated form for their States (Pue., Hgo.) and a reference to the maps which follow this index (M I, M II). Towns joining an Indian place name with the name of a saint are under the Indian name unless the saint's name is much more commonly used. This cannot be entirely consistent, since usage varies so much, even in the same town when the men favor the Indian name and the women the name of the saint to whom their church is dedicated. When there might be difficulty in finding the proper half, both are given with a cross reference. Friars who relinquished their family names are under their Christian names: Fray Pedro de Gante will be found under P, but Fray Diego de Chávez is under C. Proper names, personal or place, which begin with an article or combined article and preposition are alphabetized by the main name: El Teul is among the T's.

An asterisk following a page number indicates an illustration on that page. Augustinian, Dominican, and Franciscan monasteries are abbreviated to Ag., Dom., and Fr. mons., and preconquest and postconquest to preconq. and postconq.

INDEX

INDEX

INDEX

INDEX

INDEX

MAPS

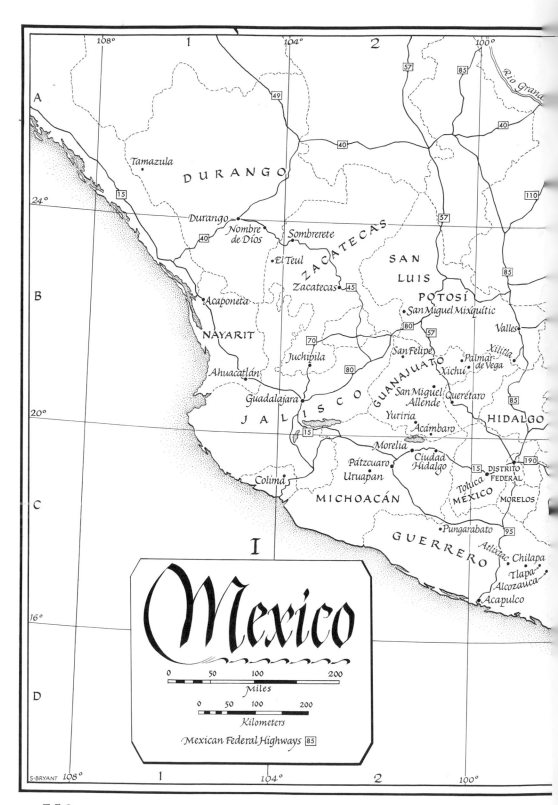

Mexico

Mexican Federal Highways 85

0 50 100 200
Miles

0 50 100 200
Kilometers

S·BRYANT

750

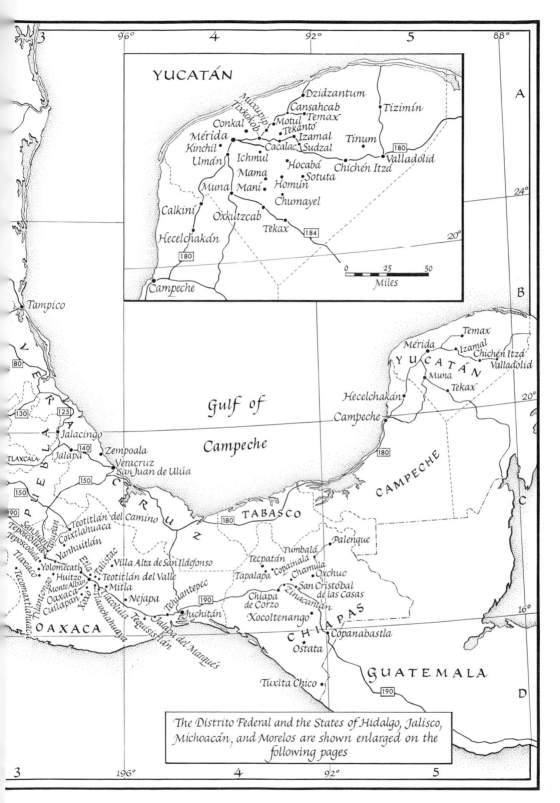

YUCATÁN

Dzidzantum
Cansahcab
Muxupip
Tixkokob
Motul
Temax
Conkal
Tekanto
Tizimín
Mérida
Izamal
Kinchil
Cacalac
Sudzal
Tinum
Umán
Ichmul
Tinum
Mama
Hocabá
Chichén Itzá
Valladolid
Muna
Maní
Sotuta
Homún
Calkiní
Chumayel
Oxkutzcab
Hecelchakán
Tekax

180

184

180

0   25   50
Miles

Tampico

VERACRUZ

80

130

125

Jalacingo

140

Jalapa

TLAXCALA

Zempoala

Veracruz

San Juan de Ulúa

150

150

190

Gulf of
Campeche

San Juan
Teposcolula
Teotitlán del Camino
Coixtlahuaca
Yanhuitlán
Teposcolula
Tlaxiaco
Tamazulapa
Tlaxiaco
Tecomaxtlahuaca
Yolomecatl
Etla
Talistac
Villa Alta de San Ildefonso
Huitzo
Teotitlán del Valle
Tlantongo
Monte Albán
Mitla
Oaxaca
Cuilapan
Xoxo
Nejapa
Tlacochahuaya
Tlacolula
Tequisistlán
Juchitán
Tehuantepec
Jalapa del Marqués

OAXACA

180

TABASCO

CAMPECHE

Palenque
Tumbalá
Tecpatán
Copainalá
Tapalapa
Chamula
Oxchuc
San Cristóbal
de las Casas
Chiapa
de Corzo
Zinacantán
Xocoltenango

CHIAPAS

Copanabastla

Ostata

190

Tuxtla Chico

GUATEMALA

190

YUCATÁN

Mérida
Temax
Izamal
Chichén Itzá
Valladolid
Muna
Tekax

Hecelchakán
Campeche

CAMPECHE

180

20°

16°

A

B

C

D

The Distrito Federal and the States of Hidalgo, Jalisco,
Michoacán, and Morelos are shown enlarged on the
following pages

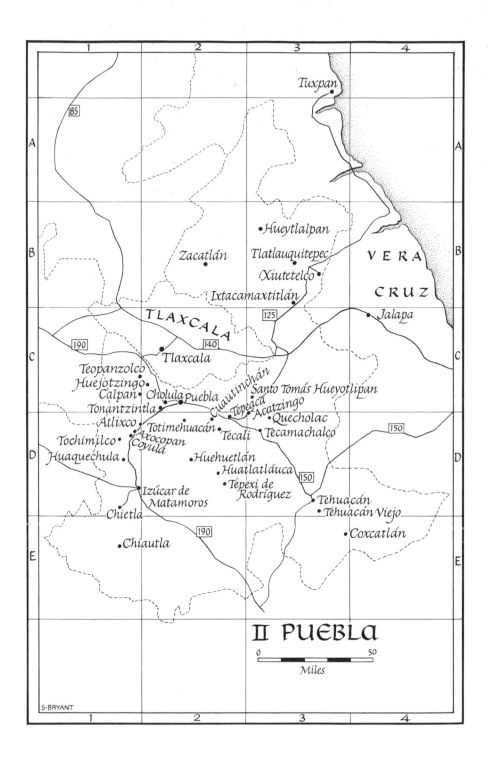

1   2   3   4

85

A   A
                                            •Tuxpan

                                    •Hueytlalpan

B   Zacatlán•   •Tlatlauquitepec   V E R A   B
                      •Xiutetelco•
                •Ixtacamaxtitlán   C R U Z
         T L A X C A L A   125   •Jalapa
190   140
C   •Tlaxcala   C
      Teopanzolco•
      Huejotzingo•
         Calpan• Cholula•Puebla •Cuautinchán
      Tonantzintla•   •Tepeaca •Santo Tomás Hueyotlipan
         Atlixco•   Tepeaca• •Acatzingo
                •Totimehuacán   •Quecholac
      Tochimilco• Atocopan• •Tecali •Tecamachalco
D   Huaquechula• Coyula   150   D
                •Huehuetlán
            •Huatlatláuca
         Izúcar de •Tepexi de   150
         Matamoros Rodríguez
      •Chietla   •Tehuacán
                •Tehuacán Viejo
            190   •Coxcatlán
E   •Chiautla   E

II PUEBLA

0   50
Miles

S·BRYANT

1   2   3   4

752

III HIDALGO AND TLAXCALA

0   25 Miles

Mexican
Federal 190
Highway

S·BRYANT

753

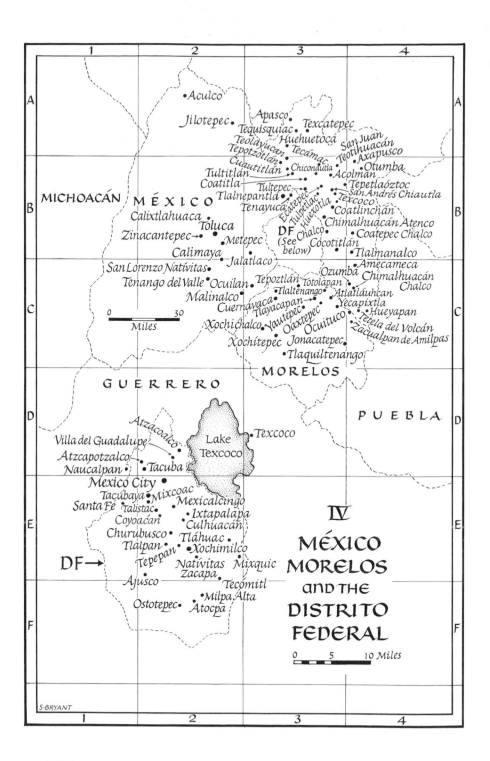

	1	2	3	4	
A		•Aculco	Apasco• •Texcatepec Jilotepec• Tequisquiac• Teolayucan• Huehuetoca• Tepotzotlán• Tecamac Cuautitlán• •Chiconautla	San Juan Teotihuacán• Axapusco• •Otumba	**A**

MICHOACÁN

M É X I C O

GUERRERO

PUEBLA

MORELOS

DF
(See
below)

0 ____ 30
Miles

•Aculco

Apasco•
Jilotepec•   •Texcatepec
Tequisquiac•
Teolayucan•   Huehuetoca•
Tepotzotlán•   Tecamac   San Juan
Cuautitlán•   •Chiconautla   Teotihuacán•
Tultitlán•   Acolman•   Axapusco•
Coatitla   Tultepec   •Otumba
Tlalnepantla•   Tepetlaóztoc•
Tenayuca•   Texcoco   San Andrés Chiautla
Ecatepec   Coatlinchán•
Calixtlahuaca•   Tulpetlac   Chimalhuacán Atenco
Toluca•   Chalco   •Coatepec Chalco
Zinacantepec→   Metepec•   Cocotitlán
Calimaya•   •Tlalmanalco
San Lorenzo Natívitas•   Jalatlaco   Ozumba   •Amecameca
Tenango del Valle•Ocuilan   Tepoztlán•   Totolapan   Chimalhuacán
Malinalco•   •Tlaltenango   Atlatláuhcan   Chalco
Cuernavaca•   •Yecapixtla   •Hueyapan
Xochichalco•   Nauhtepec   Oaxtepec   Ocuituco•   Tetela del Volcán
Xochítepec•   Jonacatepec•   Zacualpan de Amilpas
•Tlaquiltenango

Villa del Guadalupe•   Lake   •Texcoco
Atzacoalco•   Texcoco
Atzcapotzalco•   •Tacuba
Naucalpan•
México City•
Tacúbaya•   Mixcoac•   •Mexicalcingo
Santa Fé•   Talistac•   •Ixtapalapa
Coyoacán•   Culhuacán•
Churubusco•   Tláhuac•
Tlalpan•   •Xochimilco
DF→   Tepepan•   Natívitas   Mixquic
Zacapa
Ajusco•   •Tecómitl
•Milpa Alta
Ostotepec•   •Atocpa

IV

MÉXICO
MORELOS
and the
DISTRITO
FEDERAL

0 ___ 5 ___ 10 Miles

S·BRYANT

754

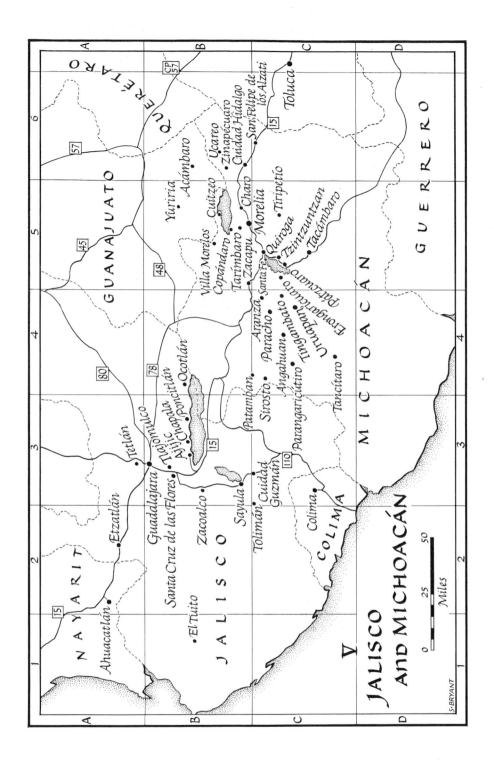

V

JALISCO AND MICHOACÁN

S-BRYANT

Miles

0   25   50

755